# Princeton Readings in Islamist Thought

PRINCETON STUDIES IN MUSLIM POLITICS
Dale F. Eickelman and Augustus Richard Norton, Editors

# Princeton Readings in Islamist Thought

## TEXTS AND CONTEXTS FROM AL-BANNA TO BIN LADEN

*Edited and Introduced by*
## Roxanne L. Euben
## and Muhammad Qasim Zaman

PRINCETON UNIVERSITY PRESS

PRINCETON AND OXFORD

*Library of Congress Cataloging-in-Publication Data*

Princeton readings in Islamist thought : texts and contexts
from al-Banna to Bin Laden / edited and with an introduction
by Roxanne L. Euben and Muhammad Qasim Zaman.
　p. cm.
　Includes bibliographical references and index.
　ISBN 978-0-691-13588-5 (pbk. : alk. paper)—
　ISBN 978-0-691-13587-8 (hbk. : alk. paper)
　1. Islam—20th century.　2. Islam—21st century.
3. Religion and politics—Islamic countries.　4. Islamic
fundamentalism.　5. Islamic modernism.　I. Euben,
Roxanne Leslie, 1966–　II. Zaman, Muhammad Qasim.
　BP163.P72 2009
　320.5′57—dc22　　2009006772

British Library Cataloging-in-Publication Data is available

This book has been composed in Sabon

Printed on acid-free paper. ∞
press.princeton.edu

Printed in the United States of America

10　9　8　7　6　5　4　3　2

*To our families*

---

# CONTENTS

# ACKNOWLEDGMENTS

WE HAVE drawn support and assistance from many quarters in the course of writing and assembling this volume. First and foremost, we wish to thank our families, whose love and patience made this scholarly challenge all the easier. We are indebted to Fred Appel of Princeton University Press, whose vision and encouragement first brought this collaborative project into being and has continually helped sustain it. We also wish to thank Deborah Tegarden for her supervision of the production process and Brian R. MacDonald for his excellent work in copyediting our manuscript. In addition, we are grateful to Terry Ball, Robert W. Hefner, Saba Mahmood, Hossein Modarressi, and Keith Topper for their willingness to lend their time and expertise to each of us as the many and varied parts of this volume took shape. The feedback provided by Dale F. Eickelman and by the anonymous readers of our manuscript has helped make this a better book, and we are most grateful to them. We further wish to thank Samia Adnan and Deborah Hayden for their assistance in producing our translations of al-Qaradawi and Nadia Yassine respectively, as well as our research assistant, Caitlin Hu, who cheerfully helped in the demanding labor of tracking down rare materials, obscure citations, and elusive copyright information. Finally, we are grateful for the research support for this project provided by the Committee on Faculty Awards at Wellesley College, and indebted to the library staff at Wellesley College, Brown University, and Princeton University for their assistance.

# PERMISSIONS

*The editors would like to thank the following authors and organizations for permission to reprint their material. In preparing the material for this volume, minor revisions have been made to some of these texts.*

*Hamid Algar,* for permission to reprint pp. 40–45, 48–64 from *Islam and Revolution: Writings and Declarations of Imam Khomeini* (Berkeley: Mizan Press, 1981). Translated by Hamid Algar.

*Dar El Shorouk,* for permission to print a translation of pp. 3–10 and 12–19 from Sayyid Qutb's *Ma'alim fi'l-Tariq* (Cairo: Dar El Shorouk, 1991). Translated by Roxanne L. Euben.

*Dar El Shorouk,* for permission to print a translation of pp. 130–46 from Yusuf al-Qaradawi's *Min fiqh al-dawla fi'l-Islam* (Cairo: Dar El Shorouk, 1997). Translated by Samia Adnan and Muhammad Qasim Zaman.

*Al Firdous,* for permission to reprint pp. 17–21 and 91–97 from 'Umar 'Abd al-Rahman's *The Present Rulers and Islam: Are they Muslim or Not?* Translated by Omar Johnstone (London: Al Firdous, 1990).

*Valerie Hoffman,* for permission to reprint "An Islamic Activist: Zaynab al-Ghazali," pp. 233–254 in *Women and the Family in the Middle East: New Voices of Change,* edited by Elizabeth W. Fernea (Austin: University of Texas Press, 1985). Translated by Valerie Hoffman.

*Johannes J. G. Jansen,* for permission to reprint sections 30–35, 47–71, and 76–94 from *The Neglected Duty: The Creed of Sadat's Assassins and Islamic Resurgence in the Middle East* (New York: Macmillan, 1986). Translated by Johannes J. G. Jansen.

*The Islamic Foundation,* for permission to reprint pp. 6–15 from vol. 7 from Sayyid Qutb's *In the Shade of the Qur'an* (London: Islamic Foundation, 2003). Translated by Adil Salahi.

*Hassan Mneimneh,* for permission to reprint "The Final Instructions," pp. 319–27, appendix to K. Makiya and H. Mneimneh's "Manual for a Raid," in *Striking Terror: America's New War,* edited by Robert B. Silvers and Barbara Epstein (New York: New York Review of Books, 2002). Translated by Hassan Mneimneh.

*The Muhammadi Trust of Great Britain,* for permission to reprint pp. 175–84, 192–203 from Muhammad Baqir al-Sadr's *Iqtisaduna* in *Alserat: Selected Articles (1975–1983)* (London: Muhammadi Trust of Great Britain, n.d.). Translated by I.K.A. Howard.

xiv PERMISSIONS

*Oxford University Press,* for permission to reprint Hassan al-Turabi's "The Islamic State," pp. 241–51 in *Voices of Resurgent Islam,* edited by John Esposito (New York: Oxford University Press, 1983).

*Signandsight.com,* for permission to reprint the English translation of "A New Layeha for the Mujahideen" and "The New Taliban Codex" (an interview with a Taliban commander, conducted by Sami Yousafzai and Urs Gehriger). Both texts were first published by Urs Gehriger in *Die Weltwoche,* November 16, 2006. Translated for signandsight.com (November 28–29, 2006) by Myron Gubitz.

*The University of California Press,* for permission to reprint Hasan al-Banna's "Towards the Light," pp. 103–32 in Charles Wendell's *Five Tracts of Hasan al-Banna (1906–1949)* (Berkeley and Los Angeles: University of California Press, 1978). Translated by Charles Wendell.

*The University of California Press,* for permission to reprint "Islamic Unity and Political Change: Interview with Shaykh Muhammad Hussayn Fadlallah," pp. 61–70 in *Journal of Palestine Studies* 25(1, Autumn 1995). The interview was conducted in Beirut by Dr. Mahmoud Soueid on May 16–17, 1995.

*The University of California Press,* for permission to reprint "11 September, Terrorism, Islam, and the Intifada: An Interview with Shaykh Muhammad Husayn Fadlallah," pp. 78–84 in *Journal of Palestine Studies* 31(2, Winter 2002). The interview was conducted by Ahmad Khalifah, Khalid 'Ayid, Saqr Abu Fakhr, and Samir Saras for *Majallat al-Dirasat al-Filastiniyya* (MDF). Translated for the *Journal of Palestine Studies* by Joseph Massad.

*The World Organization for Islamic Services,* for permission to reprint pp. 113–44 from Murtada Mutahhari's *The Rights of Women in Islam* (Tehran: World Organization for Islamic Services, 1998).

*Nadia Yassine,* for permission to print a translation of "Modernité, femme Musulmane et politique en Méditerranée," pp. 105–10 in *Quaderns de la Mediterrània* 7 (2007). Translated by D. A. Hayden and Roxanne L. Euben.

*The provenance of the other texts included in this volume is as follows:*

*The "Charter of the Islamic Resistance Movement (Hamas) of Palestine"* was translated by Muhammad Maqdisi for the Islamic Association for Palestine, Dallas, Texas, in 1990 and originally published in the *Journal of Palestine Studies* 22 (1993): 122–34.

*The translation of Usama bin Laden's "Declaration of War against the Americans Occupying the Land of the Two Holy Places"* (www.pbs.org/ newshour/terrorism/international/fatwa_1996.html) was taken by PBS from a U.S. Department of State translation and adapted by Roxanne L. Euben.

*Sayyid Abu'l-A'la Mawdudi's "The Islamic Law"* is being reprinted here from Sayyid Abul A'la Maududi, *The Islamic Law and Constitution*, translated and edited by Khurshid Ahmad, 2nd ed. (Lahore: Islamic Publications,1960), 39–71. Despite repeated attempts, the editors were not able to contact the publishers of this work.

*Selections from Sayyid Abu'l-Hasan 'Ali Nadwi, Islam and the World* are included here from the 2005 edition of this work (Leicester: UK Islamic Academy, 2005), 79–89, 92–95, 97–101, 153–54, 183–86. Translated by Muhammad Asif Kidwai. Despite repeated attempts, the editors were not able to contact either the Indian or the U.K. publishers of this work.

# A NOTE ON TRANSLITERATION, SPELLING, AND OTHER CONVENTIONS

THIS VOLUME includes texts originally published in a number of languages (Arabic, Persian, Urdu, French, German, and English). Although the translators of these texts often followed different conventions of transliteration and spelling, we have tried as far as possible to standardize these conventions. In the interest of some degree of consistency, we have kept our own transliteration of non-English terms to a minimum. With the exception of the ' to indicate the Arabic letter '*ayn* (as in shari'a) and ' to indicate the *hamza* (as in Qur'an), we have dispensed with diacritical marks in this volume. The hamza is, moreover, indicated only when it occurs within a word (as in Qur'an) but not when it comes at the end (thus 'ulama rather than 'ulama').

With some exceptions, we have usually indicated the plural form of Arabic terms with the addition of an *s* to the singular form, e.g., madrasas rather than madaris, fatwas rather than fatawa. The main exception is 'ulama (singular: 'alim), which we normally use in its Arabic plural form. For the term Shi'i, we interchangeably use Shi'a and Shi'is to indicate the plural.

Non-English words have normally been italicized only on their first occurrence or when defined, though certain words of a very common occurrence (e.g., shari'a, hadith, 'ulama) are not italicized. Many of these terms are listed in a glossary for reference. All dates are Common Era, unless otherwise indicated.

Quotations from the Qur'an usually follow M.A.S. Abdel Haleem, *The Qur'an: A New Translation* (Oxford: Oxford University Press, 2004). Many of the texts included in this volume use other translations of the Qur'an. In several instances, we have retained those translations with some modifications. In certain other instances (notably in chapters 18 and 19), we have substituted the original translations with Abdel Haleem's rendering.

# Princeton Readings in Islamist Thought

*Chapter 1*

# INTRODUCTION

THIS VOLUME is intended as a broad introduction to the evolution and scope of Islamist political thought from the early twentieth century to the present. Our sample is relatively small, and unavoidably so. Given the complexity of Islamist trends and how they relate to other religio-political orientations, even a much larger selection of texts could not capture the full range of arguments and commitments that constitute the Islamist movement. As a result, this reader aims not to be exhaustive or comprehensive but rather to be illustrative: we seek to map what is distinctive about Islamist discourses by attending to the regional breadth, gender dynamics, and political, theoretical, and theological complexity that currently travel under the rubric of Islamism. Our selections are drawn from the Arab Middle East, Africa, Iran, and South and Central Asia; include Sunni and Shiʻi activists and intellectuals; incorporate those trained as ʻulama as well as the "new religious intellectuals" (cf. Eickelman and Piscatori 1996, 13, 44); and attend to a range of positions on the relationship between jihad and violence as well as Islam and democracy. Many of the voices herein reflect the fact that most Islamist ideologues and activists are male, yet women have become an increasingly crucial part of the movement. Consequently, this volume illustrates not only how male Islamists conceive of the role of women but also how certain prominent women have articulated their own Islamist vision. Such perspectives further provide a window onto those unwritten gender norms that help establish the parameters and content of Islamist arguments about politics, virtue, action, and the family.

The focus on Islamist thought inevitably tends to privilege writing over speech, ideas over particular practices. Yet this reader ultimately challenges the very opposition between "theory" and "practice" by showing the interrelation of thought and action in the lives of individual Islamists as well as in Islamist ideas and the dynamics of their political appeal. Thus, while the following chapters do not delve into the recent rise of Islamist organizations in Indonesia and Bangladesh or the strategies of such "radical" groups as Egypt's Gamaʻa al-Islamiyya and the Islamic Salvation Front in Algeria, they do illuminate the contours and complexity of an interpretive framework many Islamists share. The language of "interpretive framework," in turn, signals both an approach to Islamism and an argument for understanding it as a lens on the world rather than a mere reflection of material conditions or conduit for socioeconomic grievances. Among other things, Islamist thought is a complex system of representation that articulates and defines a range of identities, categories, and norms; organizes human experience into narratives that assemble past, present, and future into a compelling interpretive frame; and specifies the range and meaning of acceptable and desirable practices.

Unlike other anthologies of Islamist writings, ours balances attention to broader political and theoretical frames with relatively substantial introductions to the life and work of each of the authors included here. The selected texts must speak for themselves, of course, but it is our hope that these individual introductions offer a more nuanced sense of the multifaceted contexts in which Islamist thought and activism have been articulated than is commonly found in the literature on contemporary Islamism. Within each chapter, we attend not only to the multiple and various ways Islamist thinkers reinterpret Islam but also to the specific historical, cultural and political contexts in which they are embedded, along with the particular problems, partisans, and audiences they seek to address. At the same time, we have organized the chapters thematically rather than chronologically to bring into view the web of concerns animating Islamists, as well as the polyvalent conversations across history and culture in which they participate.

Our approach and argument implicitly challenge the Manichaean worldview that currently pervades common perceptions and popular rhetoric about Islamism, one in which oppositions between good and evil or us and them are grafted onto a division between "the West" and "Islam."[1] Such a perspective is, paradoxically, endorsed and reinforced by those who share little else, from Islamists who see themselves as the forces of light against infidel darkness, to patriots who depict America as God's bulwark against encroaching heathendom, to proponents of the "clash of civilizations" thesis who posit a future riven into two clearly delineated and constitutively antagonistic cultural traditions (Mahbubani 1992; Huntington 1993, 1996). As this worldview congeals, it becomes increasingly difficult to recognize, let alone to make sense of, the wealth of information that challenges or disrupts it. In this way, the very opposition between Islam and the West becomes a self-fulfilling prophecy, presuming and sustaining a view of the world in which contradictory, multiple, and cross-pollinating histories and identities are pressed into the service of

---

[1] Binaries such as West–non-West or West-Islam carve up the world in ways that obscure critical points of engagement and commonality between them, as well as the complex differences subsumed within each term. Given that such terminology not only is invoked by peoples all over the world but evokes allegiances and enmities with quite real political consequences, however, it is not possible simply to dispense with it. This is particularly true in the case of Islamist discourse, in which the opposition between "the West" and "Islam" frequently functions as a structuring premise. Subsequent references appear without quotation marks, but should be understood as representations of the world rather than accurate historical, cultural, or territorial descriptions.

neat binaries that distort rather than illuminate the political landscape (R. Euben 2002a).

If this volume is an implicit corrective to such reductionist generalizations, it is also intended as an explicit guide through the haze of polemic, fear, and confusion swirling around the subject of Islamism in the early twenty-first century. Such confusion even characterizes what might seem to be simple matters of terminology. What we call Islamism here has been described in the media and policy circles in numerous other ways, from "Islamic extremism" to "political Islam" to "fundamentalism," still the most commonly used English term to refer to religio-political movements, Muslim or otherwise.[2] In the wake of the events of September 11, 2001, the array of names for the phenomenon has only proliferated, thereby adding to the terminological confusion. A case in point is "jihadism," a neologism derived from the Arabic *jihad* (to struggle, to strive) that is frequently used in the press to denote the most violent strands of Islamism, those associated with what are alternatively called "suicide bombings" or "martyrdom operations" in particular. Older words put to new uses have also gained currency in the years since 9/11: such is the case with "Salafism," which refers to contemporary Muslims who generally eschew the interpretive methods and norms of the medieval Islamic schools and take as a guide for proper behavior only the word of God, the teachings of the Prophet Muhammad, and the example set by the pious forbears.

But there is perhaps no other term with which Islamism has been more closely identified in recent years than "terrorism," so much so that the two terms and the phenomena they name are often depicted as synonymous (Desai 2007, 23; Richardson 2007, 61–69). Some of the most violent Islamists clearly do engage in what the U.S. State Department defines as terrorism: "premeditated, politically motivated violence perpetrated against non-combatant targets by sub-national groups or clandestine agents, usually intended to influence an audience" (Title 22 of the United States Code, Section 2656f(d)). Yet, inasmuch as many terrorists past and

---

[2] "Fundamentalism" was coined in 1920 specifically to describe Protestant evangelicals anxious to rescue American Christianity and culture from what they viewed as the moral degeneration inaugurated by modernism, rationalism, and materialism. Such warriors for God sought to "do battle royal for the Fundamentals" by (re)establishing the Bible as the authoritative moral compass for American life, infallible not only in regard to theological issues but also in matters of historical, geographical, and scientific fact (Laws 1920, 834; Massee 1920, 5, 8; Barr 1978, 1, 37, 40, 46–47, 52; Marsden 1980, 118–23, 159). It is revealing that there was no equivalent for "fundamentalism" in Arabic, the language of the Qur'an, until the need to approximate the English term called for one. *Usuliyya*, derived from *usul*, the word for fundamentals or roots, has emerged as an Arabic name for Islamism, but its currency is due to the way it approximates the English "fundamentalism" rather than any correspondence with aspects of the Islamic tradition. Within this tradition, *usuli* is associated with scholarship on the roots and principles of Islamic jurisprudence, and experts in this discipline are often referred to as *al-usuliyyun*.

present are neither religious nor Muslim (Bloom 2005; Gambetta 2005; Pape 2005), and Islamists themselves are divided about the legitimacy of terrorist tactics, the terminology of "Islamist terrorism" takes a part for the whole while implicitly collapsing diverse Islamist perspectives about retaliatory action into an argument for violence against noncombatants. While such equations and assumptions have recently gathered steam, they are structured by broader cultural discourses that predate the U.S.-led "War on Terror" by decades and even centuries. As Richard Jackson shows, the field of terrorism studies, Orientalist scholarship on the Middle East, and long-standing Euro-American suspicions about Islam now interact and reinforce one another to produce a discourse on Islamist terrorism that is "highly politicized, intellectually contestable, damaging to community relations and largely counter-productive in the struggle to control subaltern violence in the long run" (R. Jackson 2007, 395, 397–400).

In contrast to many of these designations and the assumptions animating them, we prefer "Islamism," perhaps the most widely used term among scholars of Muslim societies.[3] We take Islamism to refer to contemporary movements that attempt to return to the scriptural foundations of the Muslim community, excavating and reinterpreting them for application to the present-day social and political world. Such foundations consist of the Qur'an and the normative example of the Prophet Muhammad (*sunna*; *hadith*), which constitute the sources of God's guidance in matters pertaining to both worship and human relations. In general, Islamists aim at restoring the primacy of the norms derived from these foundational texts in collective life, regarding them not only as an expression of God's will but as an antidote to the moral bankruptcy inaugurated by Western cultural dominance from abroad, aided and abetted by corrupt Muslim rulers from within the *umma* (Islamic community).

In contrast to those Muslims who primarily seek to cultivate a mystical understanding of the divine (which is not itself devoid of political implications) or who strive to carry on their devotional practices and scholarly pursuits indifferent to their political surroundings, Islamists may be characterized as explicitly and intentionally political and as engaging in multifaceted critiques of all those people, institutions, practices, and orientations that do not meet their standards of this divinely mandated political engagement. Using Max Weber's terminology, Islamism is not defined by an "other-worldly" orientation in which salvation requires withdrawal from worldly affairs but rather is defined as a movement in which salvation is possible only through participation in the world or, more precisely, "within the institutions of the world, but in opposition to them" (Weber 1964, 166).

---

[3] "Islamism" is not, however, universally accepted and is frequently invoked with caution and caveats. An Algerian writer has argued, for example, that Islamism wrongly implies that those who claim the name have captured the essence of Islam, and thus its use is no more appropriate than calling David Koresh a Christianist (cited in Bennoune 1994, 37, n. 1).

In the following pages, we refine this preliminary definition further by delineating several aspects of Islamism that should be considered broad tendencies and "family resemblances" rather than fixed attributes, characteristics of Islamism that not every Islamist exhibits all of the time, yet which interweave to form a "complicated network of similarities overlapping and criss-crossing: sometimes overall similarities, sometimes similarities of detail" (Wittgenstein 1953, §66). We bring such tendencies and resemblances into sharp relief by way of contrast with several other Muslim orientations and groups crucial to modern and contemporary Islamic thought: modernists, *'ulama* (traditionally educated religious scholars), Salafis, and Sufis. This way of situating Islamism is both an argument and a heuristic device designed, first, to identify the commonalities among Islamist thinkers; second, to make visible the heterogeneity of Islamist arguments and ideas; and, third, to suggest that the relationship between Islamist and non-Islamist religio-political orientations past and present is marked as much by continuities, complex overlaps, and subtle differentiations as by radical breaks.

## Situating Islamism

### The Muslim Modernists and the 'Ulama

The onset of European colonial rule across Muslim societies inaugurated a great deal of soul searching on the nature and causes of Muslim political decline and what could be done to reverse it. Many Muslim reformers of the nineteenth century insisted that the political subjugation of Muslims to foreign, non-Muslim rulers was the result of a falling away from adherence to their authoritative religious norms. The best, indeed the only way Muslims could hope to remedy their circumstances was through a renewed adherence to God's commands. This would entitle them once again to God's favor, the argument went, not just beyond the grave but in this world. This perspective was not new. Long before the advent of European colonialism, reformers and *mujaddidun* (renewers) had periodically arisen to guide the community out of what they saw as its moral anarchy. Not infrequently, such reformers had made common cause with members of the political and military elite in efforts to set things right as they thought God had intended.

Yet, if neither the diagnosis nor the remedy was new, calls for a revived Islamic piety did come to carry a new burden in colonial societies. In South Asia, a decade or so after the formal establishment of British colonial rule in 1857, some Muslim religious scholars began calling for a reinvigorated adherence to Islam in light of the Qur'an, hadith, and the norms of the Hanafi school of law dominant in India, embarking on sustained efforts to educate members of the Muslim community in these norms.[4] This reformist effort centered on a *madrasa*—a school of advanced Islamic learning—founded at Deoband in northern India in 1867, which gradually became the nucleus of numerous madrasas sharing the same reformist orientation and spread throughout South Asia and eventually beyond the Indian subcontinent (Metcalf 1982; Zaman 2002). The conviction that guided these religious scholars, the 'ulama, was not just that the sorry state of their fellow Muslims reflected a laxity in adhering to God's commands but also that, in the absence of Muslim political rule, religious knowledge, anchored in the foundational and other religious texts, was the best guarantee for the preservation of a distinct Muslim identity.

Such 'ulama have had their analogues across modern Muslim societies (cf. Zeghal 1995; Zaman 2002, 144–80; Hefner and Zaman 2007). They have also had their opponents. Many of the opponents are what might be characterized as internal, that is, other 'ulama committed to a rival doctrinal orientation or to different beliefs about, say, how the memory of a saint or of the Prophet Muhammad ought to be venerated or what customary norms might be accommodated into legitimate ways of being Muslim. But other Muslim reformers—whom scholars have often referred to as the "modernists"—have had very different ideas about what had gone wrong with the Muslim world and how to remedy it.[5] To the modernists, the sort of institutions and practices represented by the 'ulama, and the remedies proposed by them, pointed not to a solution of the problems Muslims had come to face in the colonial context but to their perpetuation. Modernist reformers also professed firm commitment to Islamic norms but with some crucial differences. They argued that it was no longer enough for Muslims simply to hold firm to the teachings of their faith as conventionally understood. The times had changed drastically. Muslims needed to acquire modern, Western forms of knowledge and to accommodate themselves to European practices, technologies, and institutions if they were to improve their lot and, indeed, to survive at all as a community. The early modernists also insisted—as have their successors to this day—that Islam itself needed to be reinterpreted in order to

[4]Most Sunni Muslims have long belonged to one of four *madhhabs* (schools of law) whose beginnings are attributed to scholars who lived in the eighth and the ninth centuries. The Hanafi school of law is named after Abu Hanifa (d. 767), the Maliki school after Malik b. Anas (d. 795), the Shafi'i school after Muhammad b. Idris al-Shafi'i (d. 820), and the Hanbali school after Ahmad ibn Hanbal (d. 855). Among the Shi'a, there are several sectarian divisions. Of these, the largest community—the Imamis or the Ithna 'asharis ("Twelvers")—adhere to a legal system whose early articulation is attributed to the sixth Shi'i imam, Ja'far al-Sadiq (d. 765).

[5]The scholarly literature on Muslim modernism is substantial but uneven. Notable studies include Hourani 1983 (first published in 1962); Ahmad 1967; Troll 1978; Brown 1996; Khalid 1998; and Hefner 2000. The spectrum of modernist thought may usefully be seen in two anthologies edited by Kurzman, *Liberal Islam* (1998) and *Modernist Islam* (2002) and in Kamrava 2006.

meet the new challenges that confronted Muslims. It was not Islam that bore the responsibility for the political and intellectual weaknesses afflicting Muslim societies—as many a European observer of Islam suggested—but the failure of Muslims to properly interpret their foundational texts in accordance with changing needs.

While many among the 'ulama have long affirmed the authority of their *madhhabs* (schools of law) and the need for strict adherence (*taqlid*) to school doctrines in order to maintain the continuity and coherence of their scholarly and especially their juridical tradition, modernists have seldom seen anything redeeming in such conceptions of authority.[6] Taqlid, to them, is "blind imitation" of long dead masters and of their anachronistic views, which has stood in the way of people's ability to adapt themselves to new challenges. The modernists have also alleged that, in holding firm to their outmoded ways, the 'ulama were interested neither in the welfare of Islam nor in that of the community; they were only defending their own privileges as the guardians and authoritative interpreters of the religious tradition and the considerable social standing that often went with it. As the modernist reformers have understood it, there is nothing in Islam to stop people from interpreting its norms according to the needs of changing times. Indeed, the Qur'an invites people to reflect on it ("Will they not think about this Qur'an?" Q 4:82), which is the very opposite of the 'ulama's insistence on firm adherence to earlier authorities. As Muhammad Rashid Rida (d. 1935), the editor of the Egyptian journal *al-Manar* (1898–1935) and a disciple of the famous reformer Muhammad 'Abduh (d. 1905), wrote in his commentary on Qur'an 4:82:

> The only unavoidable requisite [to be able to reflect on the Qur'an] is knowledge of the language of the Qur'an, its words and its style, which [in any case] is the sort of thing required of anyone who becomes a Muslim. . . . Taqlid signifies preventing [people] from reflecting on the Qur'an. . . . Yet God himself has commanded us to reflect on His book and to reason with it; and no one from among His creatures can forbid what He has made obligatory. . . . By the rejection of taqlid, we do not mean that every Muslim can possibly become a Malik [d. 795] or a Shafi'i [d. 820] in deriving the juristic rules relating to the community, or that everyone ought to do so. We mean only that every Muslim is obligated to reflect on the Qur'an and to be guided by it in accordance with his abilities. It is never permissible for a Muslim to abandon [the Qur'an] and to turn away from it, or to prefer—over what he understands of its guidance—the words of anyone else, be it a *mujtahid* [a practitioner of *ijtihad*, i.e., of independent legal reasoning] or one committed to taqlid (*muqallid*). A Muslim's religion is lifeless without the Qur'an. There is no

---

[6] On the 'ulama's conception of tradition, see Zaman 2002, especially 3–16; 2007b, 63–70.

book, by a master mujtahid or by a muqallid, that can make up for
[direct] reflection on the Book of God. . . . If Muslims had stood firm
in reflecting on the Qur'an and in being guided by it in every age,
their morals and manners would not have been ruined, their rulers
would not have been unjust and despotic, their authority would not
have declined, and they would not have become dependent on others
for their livelihood. (Rida 1947–54, 5:296–97)[7]

As this passage illustrates, central to modernist discourses across Muslim societies is the idea of ijtihad (cf. Kurzman 2002, 9–14), by which
they have often meant not only the effort to formulate Islamic legal rulings on matters the foundational texts had left unregulated but *also* the
reinterpretation of matters on which the generality of earlier scholars and
even the foundational texts themselves had had a reasonably clear view.
Many among the 'ulama have insisted that their school doctrines provide
sufficient resources to meet all contingencies, and what remains to be
done is to find a particular norm or doctrine that matches the question or
problem at hand. Not all 'ulama of modern times have been averse to
particular forms of ijtihad; indeed, the continuing necessity of ijtihad in
at least some of its forms has come to be increasingly recognized by many
among them (cf. Zaman 2008, 16–17, 64, 126). Still, the idea that specific legal rulings enunciated in the foundational texts might themselves
be set aside in the name of *darura* (necessity) or subordinated to considerations of *maslaha* (common good) is, to them, tantamount to taking
liberties with God's eternal word (cf. Zaman 2004, 133–39).

Needless to say, modernist reformers have never thought of their initiatives as taking liberties with God's commands. They have often insisted,
however, that the literal word of God must always be understood in light
of the overall "spirit" of the divine injunctions, taken both in their entirety and in their original historical context.[8] Modernist discourses on

---

[7]This commentary, the *Tafsir al-Manar*, reflects the views of both Muhammad 'Abduh
and Rashid Rida, though it was largely written by Rida.

[8]Invocations of the "spirit" of the Qur'an, of the Prophet's example, or of Islam at large
are a common motif in modernist (and some Islamist) writings. Syed Ameer Ali (d. 1928),
a Shi'i modernist scholar and judge in colonial India, had characteristically titled his best-
known book *The Spirit of Islam*. For some other instances of the appeal to the spirit of
Islam and the Qur'an, and related formulations, cf. Iqbal 1934, 149, 156; Kurzman 2002,
60, 256; Ramadan 2007, xi. The medieval juridical idea of the overarching "purposes"
underlying the sacred law (*maqasid al-shari'a*), an understanding of which ought to guide
the jurist in all his endeavors, might be thought to have something in common with modernist appeals to the spirit of Islam. And it is no accident that the work of the medieval
Spanish jurist al-Shatibi (d. 1388), who is among those most closely associated with the
elaboration of this idea, has remained especially popular in modernist circles. Medieval jurists understood the idea of the maqasid al-shari'a to mean that the shari'a was concerned,
above all, with the preservation of life, religion, rationality, progeny, and property and that
no legal rulings should violate these fundamental concerns. In marked contrast, however, to
the careful exegetical and legal argumentation that went into demonstrating what the pur-

polygamy offer an illustration of their approach. The Qur'an allows polygamy: "If you fear that you will not deal fairly with orphan girls, you may marry whichever women seem good to you, two, three, or four. If you fear that you cannot be equitable [to them], then marry only one, or your slave(s): that is more likely to make you avoid bias" (Q 4:3). The Qur'an thus permits polygamy, but simultaneously insists on equity as the necessary condition for a polygamous household, a qualification supplemented by Qur'an 4:129: "You will never be able to treat your wives with equal fairness, however much you may desire to do so, but do not ignore one wife altogether, leaving her suspended. . . ." Modernist reformers have often seen the Qur'anic sanction for polygamy not just as being specific to extraordinary circumstances—as a way of providing for girls made orphan by war—but as effectively ruled out by the Qur'anic statement that men can never really be equitable toward more than one wife (cf. Rahman 1989, 47–48). To the 'ulama, this is specious reasoning, for if God had really wanted to prohibit polygamy He could simply have said so (cf. Shafi' 2005–7, 2:313–14, 592–93). That medieval jurists and exegetes are practically unanimous in allowing polygamy is, for their latter-day successors, further confirmation of the correctness of their own understanding of the Qur'an on this matter.

As this example suggests, at issue between modernists and the 'ulama is not only how particular norms are viewed but also how they are affirmed and defended. The 'ulama's scholarly tradition is constituted by a long and complex history of commentary, debate, agreements, and disagreements about the foundational texts and about all matters Islamic. As they see it, this tradition is not closed, frozen, or monolithic, yet it is with reference to the scholarly tradition that any given reading of the foundational or other texts finds meaning and legitimacy in their discourses. Modernist reformers, for their part, have usually seen this tradition precisely as closed and anachronistic, as occluding the true spirit of Islamic teachings, and therefore as unworthy of serious and sustained engagement.

### Modernists, Islamists, and the 'Ulama

The contestation between the modernists and the 'ulama provides a way of situating the Islamists within a broad spectrum of competing but also overlapping orientations in the Muslim public sphere. Like the modernists, who themselves hold varied positions on the relationship between Islam and politics, many among the Islamists are products of modern, Western institutions of learning. Sayyid Qutb (d. 1966) was not trained

---

poses of the law were, how one knew what they were, and how the law was to be interpreted with reference to them (cf. Hallaq 1997, esp. 162–206; Weiss 1998, 78–87, 145–71), modernist appeals to the spirit or essence of Islam are often extremely vague.

as a religious scholar. Nor was Hasan al-Banna (d. 1949), the founder of the Muslim Brotherhood of Egypt, the oldest and one of the most influential of Islamist organizations in the Sunni Muslim world. Both were educated at the Dar al-'Ulum in Cairo, an institution founded in the late nineteenth century to establish something of a middle ground between al-Azhar University in Cairo and modern, secular education, although it gradually veered toward the latter and in 1946 became part of Cairo University (cf. Reid 1990, 139–49). Abu'l-A'la Mawdudi (d. 1979) of Pakistan did receive an intermittent madrasa education, but it was the vocation of a journalist, not that of an 'alim (plural: 'ulama), that he adopted. Thanks in part to this broadly similar educational background, Islamists also share with modernists a supreme confidence in their own ability to discern the true meaning or spirit of Islam through a more or less direct encounter with the foundational texts. As Charles J. Adams (1966, 396) has observed in comparing Mawdudi with Muslim modernists, "Both have claimed the ability to disengage the spirit or essentials of God's guidance . . . to liberate themselves from the authority of the cumulative Muslim past and to undercut the position of the *ulama* who represent that authority." Much the same might be said of Sayyid Qutb, as well as of many contemporary Islamists.

Despite such commonalities, Islamists frequently position themselves in opposition to the modernists. As the Islamists see it, the modernists have made Islam itself subservient to the project of establishing its compatibility with Western norms and institutions, rejecting or explaining away anything that does not conform to these norms. Mawdudi put it this way in deriding modernist discomfort with the implementation of punishments mandated by Islamic law:

> I would like to put a straight question to these votaries of "modernity": "What are the values that you believe in? Do you believe in the Islamic values of life and standards of morality or those of the modern civilization?" If you have made your choice and accepted some other values and some different standard of right and wrong, of virtue and vice, of the permissible and the prohibited as against those envisaged by Islam, it is then a difference of a very fundamental nature. It means that you differ with and disbelieve in the Islamic ideology itself. In this case you should have the courage to declare that you reject Islam outright. Is it not foolish to allege faith in a God whose laws you consider as barbarous? Anyhow, nobody can remain inside the pale of Islam after holding such an opinion about the law of God. (Mawdudi [Maududi] 1960, 67)

Polemics of this sort not only suggest the Islamists' sense of what separates them from the modernists but also point to intermittent Islamist efforts to make common cause with the 'ulama. Such efforts are often predicated on both the rhetorical claim that all sincere Muslims fully concur in their conception of the *shari'a* (Islamic law) and the Islamists' astute recognition of the 'ulama's considerable standing in society. Unsurprisingly, some leading Islamists have sought to blur distinctions between themselves and the 'ulama to enhance their own authority. Usama bin Laden (b. 1957) styled his famous 1996 "Declaration of War against the Americans Occupying the Land of the Two Holy Places" as a *fatwa*, that is, a juridical opinion, thereby rhetorically obscuring the historical fact that fatwas have typically been the preserve of the 'ulama and, more specifically, of the *fuqaha* or *mufti*s (jurists) among them. Bin Laden, however, has no formal scholarly credentials in matters Islamic. Mawdudi was commonly styled as *mawlana*, a common honorific for the 'ulama in South Asia. A deliberate blurring of distinctions is likewise evident in the statement of the Sudanese Islamist Hasan al-Turabi (b. 1932): "Because all knowledge is divine and religious, a chemist, an engineer, an economist, or a jurist are all 'ulama" (Turabi 1983, 245; also chapter 8 in this volume).

Yet, there *are* leading Islamists—in this volume, Khomeini, Mutahhari, Baqir al-Sadr, Fadlallah, 'Ali Nadwi, 'Umar 'Abd al-Rahman, and Qaradawi—who were trained as 'ulama, which means that porous boundaries between Islamists and the 'ulama are not just a matter of self-serving rhetoric by autodidacts. Given this fact, the distinction between Islamists and 'ulama turns less on stark differences in educational background and more on the character and content of their political commitments. More than anything else, Islamists seek to implement Islamic law through the agency of the state. Not all are willing to resort to violent means in pursuit of this end. Many, such as Yusuf al-Qaradawi (b. 1926), a highly influential Islamist and one of the most prominent 'ulama of contemporary Islam (Skovgaard-Petersen 2004; Krämer 2006), profess democratic commitments. But whatever the stance toward either democracy or violence, the public implementation of the shari'a is at the heart of all Islamism, in both its Shi'i and Sunni forms. This suggests an important contrast with many among the 'ulama.

Since the first centuries of Islam, the 'ulama have often sought to maintain a careful distance from the ruling elite, jealously guarding their institutions and practices from governmental interference. The 'ulama generally recognized that the functioning of legal and other Islamic institutions presupposed the existence of a Muslim government, and they defined a legitimate government as one that oversaw the implementation of shari'a norms. But they have typically understood the government's commitment to the shari'a to mean that the ruler defended the borders of the polity, regulated public morality, suppressed heretics, and appointed those proficient in legal matters to implement the law (cf. Crone 2004, 286–314). They have *not* understood any of this to mean either that the ruler should be able to offer absolute interpretations of God's law or that the realm of politics and statecraft should become synonymous with Islam itself. Yet this is precisely how Islamists have often conceived of the relationship between Islam and politics and, more specifically, between Islam and the state: no calling is higher than striving toward the establishment of an Islamic state, and, once brought about, all will be in accordance with God's purposes. Mawdudi (1960, 177) claimed that "the struggle for obtaining control over the organs of the state, when motivated by the urge to establish the *din* [religion] and the Islamic Shari'ah and to enforce the Islamic injunctions, is not only permissible but positively desirable and as such obligatory."

To many 'ulama, this amounts to nothing less than making religious norms subservient to political goals. As Mufti Muhammad Taqi 'Uthmani, a leading Deobandi scholar of Pakistan, notes in his rejoinder to views such as Mawdudi's,

> In their zeal to refute secularism, some writers and thinkers of the present age have gone so far as to characterize politics and government as the true objective of Islam, the reason why the prophets were sent [by God to the people], indeed the very reason for the creation of the human being. And they have not only given other Islamic commandments—for instance, on matters of worship—a secondary position, they have even deemed them to be mere means for political ends, just a way of training people [toward political mobilization]. ('Uthmani 1998, 25–26; cf. Zaman 2008, 116–18)

Not all 'ulama share such misgivings about the subordination of Islam to politics, though it should be noted that they would see this in terms not of any such subordination but rather of the utter inseparability of the religious and the political. By far the most notable of these among the Shi'a is Ayatollah Khomeini (d. 1989) of Iran. Against a long-standing tradition of Shi'i political quietism in the absence of the hidden Shi'i *imam*, Khomeini argued that the Shi'i 'ulama ought to assume direct political leadership, and he then proceeded to spearhead the movement that culminated in the fall of the Iranian monarchy and the establishment of the Islamic Republic of Iran.[9] His doctrine of the *velayat-e faqih* (guardianship of the jurist) is a radical rethinking of Shi'i political theology, blurring any meaningful boundary between religious and political authority (see chapter 6). It is precisely Khomeini's commitment to establishing an Islamic state along these lines that warrants his classification as an Is-

---

[9]The Imami or Ithna 'ashari Shi'a believe that the twelfth and last of their imams went into *ghayba* (hiding) in 874 and that he will eventually return as the mahdi—a messianic figure who alone can restore proper order to the world, inaugurate an era of unalloyed justice, and reclaim for the Shi'a the rights of which they have been dispossessed by the Sunnis and by corrupt rulers for much of the history of Islam. Shi'i scholars have long debated the question of what sort of authority the leading religious scholars ought to have in officiating in the imam's absence. Khomeini's view, disputed by many other scholars, was that the leading scholar(s) ought to discharge the full range of the imam's functions, including the political headship of the community.

lamist, notwithstanding his well-recognized status as one of the leading Shi'i 'ulama of his generation.

The Azhar-educated Yusuf al-Qaradawi has, for his part, criticized many fellow Islamists on several issues but not on the fundamental question of their political orientation. Just as Khomeini had chastised the "propaganda institutions of imperialism . . . [for trying] to persuade us that . . . the religious leaders must not interfere in social matters and that the fuqaha [jurists] do not have the duty of overseeing the destiny of the Islamic nation" (Algar 1981, 141), Qaradawi insists that denying the political orientation of Islam amounts to its willful distortion:

> Among the interpretations with which the secularists ['almaniyyun] and the modernists [al-hadathiyyun] calumniate [Islam, properly understood, and those committed to it] is the notion of "political Islam," which, without doubt, is an idea alien to our Islamic society. By [political Islam] they mean an Islam that concerns itself with the internal and external affairs of the Muslim community. [They mean by it] actions aimed at freeing the community from the foreign power that directs [Muslim] affairs, physically and morally, as it pleases. [They also mean by it] actions seeking to cleanse the community of the cultural, social, and legal sediments of Western colonialism so that the community can return once again to submission to God's law in different areas of life. They use this characterization of "political Islam" in order to alienate people from its [aforementioned] content and to frighten them away from those calling to a comprehensive conception of Islam—one that is inclusive of belief and law, worship and social interaction, proselytism and the state. (Qaradawi 2007, 93)

Islamist political commitments are often intertwined with critiques of the scholarly tradition and its attendant institutions and practices, and this criticism provides us a crucial way of thinking further both about what distinguishes Islamists from the 'ulama and about how to view Islamism itself. What the 'ulama cannot but see as a cavalier attitude toward their scholarly tradition is, we suggest, better viewed as part of a larger Islamist critique, one that goes to the heart of how Islamism ought to be understood as a phenomenon. It is a critique of particular Muslim beliefs, practices, mores, and institutions that are deemed to have only a tenuous basis in "true" and "authentic" Islam; of the repeated wrong turns Muslims have taken throughout their long history; of the corrupting "foreign" influences—from Sufism to Greek philosophy, to the lure of modern Western cultures—by which Muslims have allowed themselves to be seduced; and of their unwillingness to do whatever it takes to establish the *hakimiyya* (sovereignty) of God on earth. That it is the sovereignty of God that Islamists seek ultimately to affirm in their individual and public lives reminds us that their critique of the past and the present is a political critique, anchored in and driven by aspirations to institute a new religio-political order. Whether this critique is articulated in concrete or vague terms, in a seemingly moderate or plainly militant language, there is no mistaking either its principal target—facets of the Islamic tradition—or its fundamentally political orientation.[10]

Islamists have often insisted that the word of God can and should be approached directly, without the mediation of present or past scholars, and without any need for the edifying tales, the philological debates, and the long-winded theological disquisitions so often found in medieval exegetical literature, a major facet of the Islamic scholarly tradition (cf. Carré 2003, 18). Shukri Mustafa, an Egyptian Islamist executed in 1977 for the murderous activities of his Society of Muslims (popularly known as the Society of Excommunication and Emigration), had famously asserted that all one needed to resolve uncertainties in one's understanding of the word of God was a dictionary (Kepel 1993, 79). Sayyid Qutb did not go quite that far. But he, too, affirmed that the fundamental teachings of Islam were entirely transparent: "What we are saying about Islam is no invention of ours, or any new interpretation of its essence. It is simply plain Islam as it was understood by its first adherent, Muhammad, and his sincere Companions and those close to its authentic source" (Qutb 1996, 9, with minor change).

The implication of Qutb's striking assertion is twofold. First, behind a rhetoric of humility in relation to divine knowledge, Qutb implicitly claims the full backing of God and His Prophet for the "plain Islam" he sets forth. More specifically, he essentially depicts his own understanding of Islam as synonymous with God's eternal intent, much as Khomeini's pronouncements as the *vali-ye faqih* (guardian jurist) presumed to articulate what Islam itself stood for or required on any given matter. Second, the statement implies not only that views other than his are mere interpretations but that they are the more reprehensible for being "novel"—a suggestion that evokes the notion of *bid‘a*, that is, of illicit, capricious in-

[10]That Islamism should be seen as a wide-ranging *critique* of the world and of the Islamic tradition is a reminder, of course, that critique is not an inherently secular phenomenon nor does it necessitate a secular framework. As Talal Asad (2008) has observed, given a wide variety of "possible instances of critique/criticism . . . what we have . . . is a family concept for which it is not possible to provide a single theory because the *practices* that constitute them differ radically" (also cf. Mahmood 2008; Taylor 2008). Nor should our viewing Islamism as a politically motivated critique suggest that other, competing orientations in modern Islam cannot also be seen as critiques of particular practices, particular forms of knowledge. What does distinguish an Islamist orientation from others is, once again, both the degree to which Islamist critiques break with their past and present *and* their aspiration to remake the world in accordance with their understanding of immutable divine commands. This is markedly different from how the ‘ulama might critique particular aspects of their scholarly tradition in the interest of a stronger sense of continuity with that tradition or in order to make it more receptive to what they see as the community's changing needs. It is also very different from how Muslim modernists often break with the scholarly tradition in order to *adapt* Muslim norms and institutions to the dominant political and cultural institutions of their contemporary world.

novation in matters of religion. Such a view of Islam jettisons much of what would normally count as its history and civilization. "The history of 'Islam,'" Qutb tells his readers, "is the history of the true application of Islam—in people's conceptions and their practices, in their lives and their social systems. Islam is the fixed axis, around which people's lives revolve in a fixed frame. When they go out of this frame, or when they categorically abandon this axis, what then do they have to do with Islam?" (Qutb 1967a, vol. 2, part 4, 169; quotation marks around "Islam" in original). It is for the fixed axis, the plain Islam—and in opposition to much of its history—that the Islamist professes to stand (cf. Grunebaum 1962, 251–52).

Qutb, however, is far from consistent in his attitude toward the scholarly tradition or in how he seeks to articulate his own authority in relation to it. His faith in the transparency, and the transformative immediacy, of God's words would appear to make *all* exegesis superfluous, yet he himself had proceeded to write a major commentary, *In the Shade of the Qur'an*, that would exceed four thousand pages in print. The justification he offers for it in the opening lines of the commentary is audacious, not apologetic:

> Life in the shade of the Qur'an is a blessing. It is a blessing unknown to anyone who hasn't tasted it. . . . All praise be to God! He has granted me the opportunity to live in the shade of the Qur'an for a period of time, during which I have tasted His blessings as I never had earlier in my life. . . . I have listened to God the exalted conversing with me through this Qur'an—with me, a small, little slave. . . . I have lived, in the shade of the Qur'an, looking from an elevation at the *jahiliyya* [pagan ignorance] raging in the land and the petty concerns of its people. [From this vantage], I have seen the pride the people of this jahiliyya take in their childish knowledge, their childish ideas, their childish preoccupations. [I have looked upon them] like an elder looks upon the frivolities of children, upon their efforts, and upon their lisps. (Qutb 1967a, 1:3)

These resounding words serve, inter alia, to explain why a new commentary should have been needed at all: the mind-numbing impact of the jahiliyya has made people incapable of responding to even the most direct of divine summons, and only someone who has lived "in the shade of the Qur'an" can understand their plight and remedy it. From the perspective Qutb adopts here, any appeal to the scholarly tradition, any effort to rest his authority on it, would appear altogether out of place. Yet Qutb's claims to authority do not derive exclusively from his conversing with God through the Qur'an. To some degree, they also depend on his being seen as having mastery over the very exegetical tradition of which he is otherwise frequently dismissive. Qutb cites a small number of earlier commentators and other authorities when it suits his purpose to do so,[11] just as he sidesteps the exegetical tradition when doing so offers a rhetorically more effective way of arriving at a conclusion. More traditional exegetes, past and present, also pick and choose, of course. But they have typically done so within an overall framework that is defined by a continuous engagement with the exegetical tradition as a whole (cf. Saleh 2004). By contrast, Qutb and other Islamist exegetes write *outside*, and often in conscious opposition to, any such framework. The conversation is not with the earlier exegetes but directly with God, though this might, on occasion, be aided by illustrations from the earlier exegetical tradition.

If there are unacknowledged ambiguities in Qutb's relationship with the Islamic tradition, as we have observed, a frequently acerbic stance does nonetheless remain characteristic of how he views it most of the time. Qutb is anything but unique in this respect. Yet if Islamists share, almost by definition, a critical stance toward facets of this tradition, there is much that also separates them from one another in precisely how this critique and its implications are articulated in different instances. Although the mere presence of disagreement among Islamist intellectuals and activists is hardly remarkable, the scope and implications of some of the disagreements, inasmuch as they relate to the scholarly tradition, are nonetheless worth examining here. For they suggest that, while Islamists share the conviction that particular institutions, practices, and norms need to be refashioned in light of immutable divine commands, this conviction often rests on quite different views of Islamic history and civilization, of contemporary Muslim societies, and, not least, of religious authority and its loci. Nowhere, perhaps, is this more evident than in some of the writings of Yusuf al-Qaradawi. Like Qutb, Qaradawi is among the most influential Islamist ideologues in the Sunni world. He is also one of Qutb's severest critics from within the Islamist camp (see especially Qaradawi 1994, 101–31).

That "Muslim" societies lacked a proper Islamic foundation made it futile, Qutb had argued, to debate specific questions of Islamic law and

[11]These include, inter alia, Muhammad ibn Ishaq (d. 767), the author of the *Sirat rasul Allah*, one of the earliest biographies of the Prophet Muhammad; al-Tabari (d. 923), the author of *Jami' al-bayan li-ta'wil ay al-Qur'an*, one of the most influential commentaries of the Qur'an ever produced; al-Baghawi (d. 1117), whose commentary is titled *Ma'alim al-tanzil*; al-Qurtubi (d. 1273), the author of a work, *al-Jami' li-ahkam al-Qur'an*, which is especially attentive to the legal content of the Qur'an; and Ibn Kathir (d. 1373), the author of a Qur'an commentary, *Tafsir al-Qur'an al-'azim*, which has been popular among many Muslims of a Salafi orientation. On occasion, Qutb also cites influential fellow Islamists. See, for example, Qutb, *Fi zilal al-Qur'an*, vol. 2, part 4, 132 (Mawdudi); vol. 2, part 5, 25 (Nadwi); vol. 2, part 6, 143 and 150–53 ('Abd al-Qadir 'Awda, an Egyptian Islamist and legal scholar executed under the Nasser regime in 1954). Occasionally, Qutb cites Rida's *Tafsir al-manar* as well, though, more often than not, to register his disagreements with Rida and with the latter's mentor, Muhammad 'Abduh. For a detailed comparison between the commentaries of Rida and Qutb, see Carré 2003.

how it dealt with particular social or economic issues. The ʿulama were pathetically deluded if they thought that the interests of Islam could be furthered through disquisitions on the shariʿa in such conditions of pervasive ungodliness (Qutb 1967b, 183–90). What people needed before anything else was a return to the basics of the faith. The task of righteous preachers was to instruct them in these matters and to help them recognize what the sovereignty of God demanded of them (Qutb 1991, 35; cf. Qaradawi 1994, 102–4). All other matters, including the niceties of juristic discussion, were best postponed until a properly Islamic society based on this foundation had been realized.

Qaradawi vehemently disagrees with Qutb, arguing that educated Muslims are not pagans but believers and, as such, do not need to be tutored in the fundamentals of their faith. What they often do not understand very well—and here Qaradawi concurs with other Islamists—is the nature of Islam as a *nizam* (social and political system). The problem of Muslims, in other words, is not godlessness but simply *ignorance* (which is what the term jahiliyya literally means) of the teachings of Islam in their comprehensive, all-encompassing dimensions. As Qaradawi sees it, many "captives of Western thought" have doubts not about the essentials of their faith but rather about Islam as a comprehensive system; and it is their unaddressed misunderstandings, their ignorance, on the latter score that sometimes opens the door to doubts about matters of belief itself (Qaradawi 1994, 113–14). To continue to expound on the social, political, and other teachings of Islam while the society is yet imperfect is not to endorse or strengthen the jahili order, as Qutb had alleged, but only to help ordinary people in their effort to lead virtuous lives even in iniquitous circumstances.

This view represents an appeal to what Qaradawi has repeatedly referred to as the moderate path or *al-madrasa al-wasatiyya* (the "centrist school"; cf. Qaradawi 2006, 137–217)—one that locates itself on a putative middle ground between a complete rejection of the world, including Muslim societies, and its total embrace. Qaradawi is equally concerned with rescuing Islamic history and civilization from outright dismissal at the hands of Islamists like Qutb.[12] The idea that jahili norms had begun to creep back into the Muslim community shortly after the death of the Prophet and that they have remained unchallenged for much of Islam's history ignores all those, Qaradawi says, who have continued to represent the path of righteousness throughout the history of Islam. Contrary to the conviction of the Sunnis that "the community will never agree on error"—as the Prophet is said to have promised—the notion of a perva-

[12] Among leading figures Qaradawi singles out for criticism in this regard are, besides Qutb, Mawdudi, and the Egyptian Islamist scholar Muhammad al-Ghazali (d. 1996). See Qaradawi 2005b, 46–64. It is worth noting that, despite these and other disagreements, Qaradawi has written respectfully of all three, devoting an entire book to his long association with Muhammad al-Ghazali (see Qaradawi 1995).

sive jahiliyya suggests, moreover, that the community did, indeed, agree on error.[13] Most grievously, perhaps, Islamist critiques tend to suggest that the shari'a has almost never been implemented in Muslim societies after the very first years of Islam. Ironically, says Qaradawi, such indiscriminate rejection of Islamic history inadvertently reinforces *secularist* arguments that the shari'a is unsuited to practical application (Qaradawi 2005b, 46). Qaradawi's critique of Qutb and other Islamists is, finally, an argument for the continuing centrality of the 'ulama to the task of providing authoritative guidance to the community. His understanding of who constitutes the 'ulama is far more expansive than that of most Deobandi 'ulama of South Asia. But, like them, he is in no doubt that serious religious scholars, as distinguished from amateurish autodidacts, are crucial to the task of providing authoritative religious and moral guidance to the community.

Although we have sought to illustrate certain facets of the Islamist critique of the scholarly tradition and of the world as some key Islamist thinkers have articulated it, we do not wish to suggest, of course, that Islamists are necessarily "intellectuals." Whatever Qutb, Khomeini, Mawdudi, and Qaradawi might think of other scholars and intellectuals, or of themselves in relation to them, the former obviously *are* religious intellectuals. The same is hardly true of many other Islamists. Yet even those with little or no intellectual pretensions are often recognizable *as Islamists* not only for their commitment to the public implementation of Islamic norms grounded in the foundational texts but also—and as a corollary of the former—for their often self-conscious critique of and disengagement from the norms and mores they see around them. In contemporary Lebanon, for instance, Shi'i Islamists have often seen their text-based religious commitments as marking a clear departure from earlier and existing religious practices. As anthropologist Lara Deeb (2006, 20) observes, "They viewed it as new and different—different from what they often referred to enigmatically as 'before' or 'how we were' and different from what they called *al-taqalid* (traditions). . . . In lieu of practices and beliefs cast as traditional, they espoused . . . [an] 'authenticated' Islam, expressed in public piety."[14] Many Islamists living in refugee camps in Gaza have had a similar view. To them, "Palestinians . . . had either become lost in foreign ideologies . . . or they had become 'Muslims by con-

---

[13]The conviction that the community at large is divinely protected from error is an important basis of the authority of "consensus" as a major source of juridical norms in Sunni Islam. For modern debates on consensus and some of the literature on this subject, see Zaman 2006.

[14]The "traditions" here primarily refer to customary norms and devotional practices, rather than to the centuries-old discursive tradition from which the 'ulama, both Shi'i and Sunni, derive their authority. Islamist critiques are often directed as much, however, at traditions in the sense of "inauthentic," culturally rooted religious practices as they are at the scholarly tradition of the 'ulama, which, to them, is equally inauthentic in having obscured the simple and fundamental teachings of the foundational texts.

vention' who went along with the fast or prayed now and then because this was 'custom and tradition' (*'ada wa taqlid*). This lack of conscious, zealous adherence to Islam had resulted in social weakness leading to defeat at the hands of Israel" (Lybarger 2007, 211). There is much that such analyses share with the writings and pronouncements of the leading Islamist intellectuals.

### Islamists and Salafis

Just as it is not always easy to differentiate 'ulama from Islamists or Islamists from modernists, it is sometimes difficult to clearly distinguish between Islamists and the Salafis. The latter derive this self-designation from claims of strict adherence to the normative practice of *al-salaf al-salih* (the pious forbears), usually understood as the Muslims of the first generations of Islam. The guiding Salafi assumption is that these first Muslims, in being contemporaries of the Prophet Muhammad and the immediate successors of those contemporaries, exemplify most perfectly what it means to be a virtuous Muslim and that later generations can do no better than emulate the example of these first generations. Some version of this view would find broad resonance among Islamists, but also ordinary believers, though the Shi'a of various doctrinal orientations have always had a far more restrictive view of precisely who is worth emulating. Again like the Islamists, the Salafis insist on deriving their norms directly from the Islamic foundational texts, the Qur'an, and the example of the Prophet Muhammad, unmediated by the medieval schools of law. This means doing away with the sort of historically articulated scholarly tradition from which the 'ulama have tended to draw much of their authority. The Salafis do have their own 'ulama—Qaradawi is a notable instance, as are members of the Saudi religious establishment—but even their authority is based far more on directly interpreting the foundational texts than it is on any systematic engagement with the Islamic scholarly tradition.

All this sounds a good deal not just like the Islamists but also like the modernists. This should not be surprising, for the Salafi orientation is an important part of the genealogy of both modernism and Islamism. The Salafi reformer Muhammad 'Abduh, though a traditionally educated scholar who served toward the end of his life as the grand mufti of Egypt, was a key influence in the development of Islamic modernism. But while some of 'Abduh's disciples developed his ideas in the direction of secular nationalism, others—notably the Salafi journalist and Qur'an commentator, Rashid Rida—eventually took them, despite his modernist proclivities, in a decidedly conservative direction (Hourani 1983; also cf. Dallal 2000). Hasan al-Banna, the founder of the Muslim Brotherhood, was close to many Egyptian Salafis: Muhibb al-din al-Khatib (d. 1969), a leading Salafi of the time and the owner of the Salafi Publishing House in

Cairo, was in charge of one of the Brotherhood's first journals (Mitchell 1993, 185); and after Rida's death in 1935, it was at Banna's initiative that Rida's influential journal, *al-Manar*, would continue to be published for some years (R. Mitchell 1993, 186).

For all their affinities, however, Salafis cannot simply be subsumed with the Islamists any more than they can with the modernists. Unlike the early Salafis and other modernists, Islamists have almost invariably sought to address themselves to a wide, popular audience rather than to the intellectual elite (cf. R. Mitchell 1993, 211). The Salafis have also been far more preoccupied with matters of correct belief, the nuances of doctrine, than have either the Islamists or the modernists (cf. Haykel 2009 [forthcoming]). By the same token, while many Islamists have had a somewhat ambivalent relationship with Sufism, Salafis have usually been unrelentingly hostile to devotional Sufi practices. But if it is useful to distinguish the Salafis from other competing orientations in modern Islam, it is important also to recognize that there is much on which Salafis themselves have disagreed, sometimes sharply. In question in these "internal" differences is not their overall orientation—toward the Islamic foundational texts and the pristine norms of Islam's first generations—but rather the precise implications of this orientation for belief and conduct in the present. A consideration of some of these differences should, in turn, further illustrate how the Salafis ought to be distinguished from other competing camps.

Where many Salafis see the schools of law as obstructing and, indeed, distorting the simple message of the foundational texts, others view the legal tradition as representing Islam's rich intellectual legacy from which Muslims ought to draw both inspiration and guidance. Qaradawi, for instance, has been critical not just of the Muslim modernists but also of fellow Salafis for their irreverence toward the riches of the legal tradition, their uneducated proclivity to set it aside all too callously. On this view, a rejection of the taqlid-bound 'ulama should not lead to the other extreme—exemplified by not a few Salafis—of jettisoning the scholarly tradition altogether.

Salafis also differ among themselves in their attitudes toward modern, Western institutions and practices. In the late nineteenth and early twentieth centuries, Salafi reformers like Muhammad 'Abduh and Rashid Rida in Egypt and Jamal al-din al-Qasimi (d. 1914) in Syria had called for a reorientation toward the foundational texts as a way of justifying, not resisting, changes in law and education as well as other facets of social reform (cf. Hourani 1983; Commins 1990). On this view, a direct recourse to the Qur'an and the sunna offered the best way of demonstrating the accord between their teachings and the reformist project.[15] In

---

[15]Symptomatic of other disagreements among the Salafis is the very question of precisely who the salaf are whose example ought to be emulated. The narrower views limit the salaf to the first three generations of Islam—the age of the Prophet Muhammad and his companions, their successors, and the latter's immediate successors—but even these narrow views

contemporary Europe, Tariq Ramadan, an influential Swiss Arab philosopher, has argued that Muslims living in Western societies ought to feel
at home in, and contribute toward, those societies while retaining and
cultivating their distinct Islamic identity. He, too, appears to see himself
in the genealogy of what he characterizes as "Salafi reformism" (on this
characterization, see Ramadan 2004, 26–27), and he has echoed Qaradawi in some of his views (cf. Ramadan 1999, 93–99).

Other Salafis have remained staunchly opposed to institutions and
practices of a Western provenance. An especially influential figure in the
genealogy of the latter position is the eighteenth-century puritanical reformer Muhammad ibn 'Abd al-Wahhab (d. 1792), whose alliance in
1744 with Muhammad ibn Sa'ud contributed to the establishment of
the first Saudi state in the late eighteenth century. Ibn 'Abd al-Wahhab
was hostile not only to Shi'ism and to Sufi devotionalism but also to anything he deemed not to be in strict conformity with the teachings of the
foundational texts. There was much that seemed to him to fail this standard, all of which he branded as one or another form of unbelief. The
Wahhabis—as the followers of Ibn 'Abd al-Wahhab are often known,
though they prefer to think of themselves simply as good Muslims or, at
best, as Salafis—often adhere to the legal norms of the Hanbali school of
law, though it is the teachings of the foundational texts, irrespective of
this or any other school doctrine, that they profess to follow. The most
stringent of the Saudi Salafis, as well as others elsewhere, are a very far
cry indeed from what Qaradawi would characterize as "centrist" Salafi
reformers, let alone from the early twentieth-century Salafi modernists.

The political views of the Wahhabis and, more broadly, of the Salafis
are likewise anything but uniform. In Saudi Arabia, Wahhabi religious
scholars have long affirmed a quietist political stance, which has meant
leaving matters of the state to the ruling family. For much of the history
of modern Saudi Arabia, the ruling elite, for its part, has imposed few
constraints on the Saudi 'ulama in matters of religious life, the regulation
of social norms, and judicial administration (cf. Vogel 2000). On several
occasions, however, this relationship has come under severe strain. In
1979 a group of Wahhabis who rejected the legitimacy of the Saudi state
yet had ties with some prominent religious scholars—including 'Abd al-

---

feel constrained to make room for such revered figures as Ahmad ibn Hanbal, the putative
founder of the Hanbali school of law, and the fourteenth-century Damascene scholar Ibn
Taymiyya (d. 1328). Other views are rather more expansive, not just in chronological but
also, and crucially, in intellectual terms. Thus, Muhammad 'Abduh thought the salaf to also
include such theologians as al-Ash'ari (d. 935), al-Baqillani (d. 1013), and al-Maturidi (d.
944). See Hourani 1983, 149. Such a view obviously opens the door for precisely the sort
of theological debates that other Salafis, as well as Islamists, often frown upon for taking
the believers very far from the simple and direct words of God. 'Abduh's disciple, Rida,
again took a narrower view of the salaf and, later in his career, became a strong defender of
the Wahhabis. Cf. Hourani 1983, 230–32.

'Aziz Bin Baz (d. 1999), later the grand mufti of Saudi Arabia—took over the sacred precincts of the Ka'ba in Mecca in a short-lived but extremely embarrassing challenge to Saudi royal authority (cf. Hegghammer and Lacroix 2007). In 1990 King Fahd's decision to invite American troops to defend the kingdom against the threat of an Iraqi invasion created widespread resentment among Saudis, the effects of which continue to this day. The stationing of non-Muslim military personnel in Islam's holiest land was deemed by the king's critics to be scandalous and even sacrilegious. A number of prominent Saudi Salafis publicly criticized the king's decision on this occasion, calling upon him, as well as on Bin Baz and others at the helm of the Saudi religious establishment, to reorient the Saudi polity toward its true religious foundations. Many of these dissidents—who were also joined by "secular" Saudi critics of the royal family—were, and have remained, restrained in their criticism even as they called for stricter conformity to Islamic norms as the panacea for all ills (cf. Fandy 1999). Others, however, have denounced the royal family and its Western allies in no uncertain terms. Bin Laden is only the most notorious of those who broke with the royal family in the wake of King Fahd's decision to invite Western troops in 1990, and who called for the overthrow of the royal family and for jihad against Western powers. Such strident calls have been continued by other Salafis, both before and after the terrorist attacks of September 11, 2001, as well as in the aftermath of the U.S.-led invasion of Iraq (al-Rasheed 2007).

It should be clear, in light of the foregoing, that any understanding of the differences between Islamists and the Salafis must rest on taking account of the diversity *among* the Salafis. Salafis who often reject much of the Islamic scholarly tradition in favor of a direct recourse to the foundational texts are not necessarily rendered "Islamist" simply by virtue of this stance. For, as noted, many of these Salafis continue to profess a resolutely quietist stance, which, in the case of the Saudi Salafis, means affirming allegiance to the Saudi royal family. This position is represented, for instance, by Bin Baz, the erstwhile grand mufti, as well as by other leading members of the Saudi religious establishment. A pro-regime stance or one indifferent to politics is no less "political," of course, than a position of strident hostility to the established order at home and abroad. For our purposes, however, it is only when the Salafis reject the existing dispensation and begin striving—though not necessarily through militant means—for a new religio-political order that they can be said to join the ranks of the Islamists.

It is worth noting, finally, that Salafi positions, among Saudis and elsewhere, are marked not only by diversity but also by considerable fluidity (al-Rasheed 2007). The same activist or intellectual might, at various times, move among a variety of seemingly incompatible positions—appearing to be more "moderate" on some issues than on others. For all his criticism of radical Islamists, Qaradawi, for instance, has himself written in justification of suicide bombings by Palestinians against Israelis (see chapter 9 on Qaradawi). And Saudi Salafis like Safar al-Hawali and Salman al-'Awda—who came to prominence in the early 1990s—have alternated between criticism of the Saudi policies and denunciations of radical Salafi calls to jihad against the Saudi regime (see al-Rasheed 2007, 59–101; on al-Hawali, also see Reichmuth 2006). Their shifting views reflect changes in their relations with the Saudi regime, but they also point to the broad spectrum of positions which Salafis have taken at different times, in different contexts, and before different audiences. Thus, even as al-Hawali and al-'Awda have condemned terrorist acts directed against Saudi Arabia and advised Saudis not to fight American troops in post–Saddam Hussein Iraq, they have called upon the Iraqis themselves to resist American troops and have characterized that effort as a "defensive jihad" (al-Rasheed 2007, 94–95).

## Sufis and Islamists

It seems much simpler, on the face of it, to distinguish between Islamists and Sufis. The characteristic Sufi conviction that there are levels of meaning in the Qur'an that go beyond the literal and the obvious and that a select few—the "friends of God"—are endowed with the unique ability to discern them is anathema to all those who insist that God intends His teachings to be equally intelligible to all. Despite their tendency to view themselves as bearers of true Islam, Islamists typically regard the Sufi idea that some people have a privileged relationship with God as suspect, the basis not only for sanctioning interpretations of Islam that lack warrant in the plain teachings of God and the Prophet but also for practically "worshiping" these friends of God. Islamists (and modernists) have frequently also been critical of the way Sufi devotionalism can yield a turning away from the world rather than an effort to change it, as well as a preoccupation with personal spiritual transformation at the expense of concerns for the welfare of the community at large.

Sufi practices and the teachings of the Sufi masters have varied enormously throughout the history of Islam, yet Islamist critiques of Sufism are seldom attentive to its nuances or to the complex ways it has related to other facets of Islam. Nor have Islamists taken much account of the fact that many leading figures of earlier times were, besides much else, Sufis as well. This is true even of Ibn Taymiyya (d. 1328), whose prestige in Islamist and Salafi circles is matched by few others, and who was, in his day, a member of the Qadiri Sufi order (Makdisi 1974). Even if one argues—as an Islamist might be inclined to—that "good" Sufism is nothing but proper Islam itself, the very fact that such figures had a Sufi identity at all necessarily complicates what is supposed to be the pristine simplicity of a faith shared equally by all believers.

Complicating things still further is the variety of ways in which some leading Islamists relate to Sufism. Ayatollah Khomeini was a lifelong student of Islamic mysticism, and the influence of the medieval Spanish

Sufi Ibn 'Arabi loomed especially large in his thought. To Khomeini, mysticism—often referred to as *'irfan* (gnosis), especially when intertwined with Islamic philosophy and theology (Knysh 1992, 632)—was crucial to a proper understanding of God's relationship with the world and with the human being. It was also essential for one's ethical formation, for a mastery over the self, and ultimately for realizing in oneself the attributes of what Ibn 'Arabi had called "the perfect man" (cf. Knysh 1992, 635; also Mottahedeh 1985, 180–85). Some of the austerity of Khomeini's personal life probably also derived from Sufi asceticism. And though he anchored his conception of Islamic government in an exposition of Shi'i juridical thought rather than in Islamic mysticism, the sort of religious authority he came to enjoy on the basis of his reformulation of Shi'i political theology seems to echo mystical ideas of the perfect man who embodies and upholds the moral order as the microcosm of the universe.

Unlike Khomeini, Qutb was not a Sufi, and he gives no indication of sharing any of Khomeini's enthusiasm for the great Sufi thinkers of earlier times. Even so, echoes of a mystic's direct encounter with the fountainhead of truth and knowledge are hard to miss in Qutb's writings, especially in his commentary on the Qur'an (cf. Carré 2003, 95–97). The very first sentence of his commentary—"life in the shade of the Qur'an is a blessing . . . unknown to anyone who hasn't *tasted* it"—evokes the familiar Sufi idea that incontrovertible knowledge of Reality is ultimately acquired only through direct personal experience (*dhawq*, that is, the "taste" of the Truth). The great medieval Sufi al-Ghazali (d. 1111) had authored a famous autobiographical account of how it was only through the immediacy of his personal mystical experience that he was able to overcome his debilitating epistemological doubts and reassure himself of the necessary truths (Watt 1998, 57). Qutb does not mention Ghazali in this context, but it is difficult not to be struck by the mystical resonance of some of his language. Here is one example, which occurs in his commentary on *sura* (chapter) 53 of the Qur'an:[16]

[16]The early verses in this sura of the Qur'an have been understood by Muslim exegetes as referring to the Prophet's revelatory experience as well as to his "night journey" and his ascension to heaven, or mi'raj: in the course of one night, he was transported first from Mecca to Jerusalem and then to the presence of God before being returned to Mecca.

Unrelated to the night journey but related to his revelatory experiences, the exegetical significance of this Qur'anic sura also lies in its connection with the so-called Satanic Verses. According to certain exegetical reports, Muhammad was in the course of receiving a revelation when Satan interpolated some verses into it—verses praising three goddesses revered by the polytheists of Mecca. It was not until sometime later that Muhammad realized his error, whereupon the verses interpolated by Satan were removed. The episode of the "Satanic Verses" has been a controversial one in Islamic history long before Salman Rushdie's novel of that name and Khomeini's juridical ruling (fatwa) calling for Rushdie's death. Most Muslim scholars have found it too shocking to believe that the Prophet could have made such a grievous error and have denied that any such incident ever took place. Yet some

I was chatting one evening with some companions when to our ears came the sound of someone reciting the Qur'an nearby, reciting the Sura of the Star [al-Najm], and we interrupted our conversation to listen to the Noble Qur'an. . . . Little by little my heart entered into what was being recited, into the heart of Muhammad as he journeyed to the Heavenly Host. I was with him as he saw Gabriel in the angelic form in which God had created him. . . . I was with him in his lofty and free-flying journey to the Lote Tree of the Boundary and the Garden of the Refuge. . . . I was with him to the extent that my imagination could form a vision of it and to the extent that my feelings could bear it. . . . Then came the final cry and my whole being shook at the fearful reproach: "Do you marvel at this discourse, and do you laugh and not weep, and make merry?" [Q 53:59–61]. When I heard "Bow down before God and serve Him" [Q 53:62], the trembling in my heart had become a physical and visible trembling throughout my body that I could not resist. My body kept shaking and I could not control it. Nor could I hold back the tears that were pouring forth, however much I tried. (Qutb, *Zilal*, vol. 7, part 27, 74–75; quoted from Carré 2003, 333–34, with minor changes)

The Qur'an's profound impact on the aesthetic sensibilities of its listeners is a familiar motif in discussions of its literary qualities (cf. Graham and Kermani 2006). As someone whose early writings were concerned with Arabic literary criticism and specifically with the literary excellence of the Islamic scripture (Qutb 1949b), Qutb was especially receptive to this aspect of the Qur'an. The sense of being transported back to the time of the Prophet and to witnessing the Prophet's ascension (*mi'raj*) to the presence of God—which is how the passage being commented on by Qutb here has commonly been interpreted by the exegetes—can likewise be seen as an illustration of the overpowering impact the words of the Qur'an can have on the believer. Qutb's account of conversing with God through the Qur'an (cited earlier) is, again, something he may have wanted to see all believers do. Yet all believers can scarcely do so, anymore than all aspirants even on the Sufi path can experience the transformative mystical "states" that God bestows on His special friends (*awliya*). Irrespective of whether he saw it in quite this way, Qutb's assertion that he is able to enter "into the heart of Muhammad" and to see Gabriel as *Muhammad* saw him surely gives him a perspective that others encountering the word of God do not have.

The point is not, of course, that Qutb was ever recognized by his followers as a Sufi master but that some of the hermeneutical authority he claims has a distinctive Sufi ring to it. More broadly, the sort of unques-

---

leading scholars of early and medieval Islam—including Ibn Taymiyya—accepted the historicity of this incident. See S. Ahmed 1998.

tioning religio-political authority Islamist leaders have often enjoyed over their followers is not unlike that of the Sufi master over his followers. Beginning with Hasan al-Banna, the founder of the Muslim Brotherhood and once himself a member of a Sufi order, the leader of this organization is formally referred to as the *murshid* (guide) or, more specifically, *al-murshid al-'am* (the general guide [R. Mitchell 1993, 165]), which is a familiar term for the master in Sufi contexts. For his part, Abdessalam Yassine, the founder and leader of 'Adl wa'l-Ihsan Party of Morocco (often referred to as the Justice and Spirituality Association, or JSA), has, like Khomeini, gone well beyond simply echoing Sufi conceptions of authority in his own discourses. He, too, was once a member of a Moroccan Sufi order, and he has continued to draw on Sufi themes in his writings. The very name of Yassine's political organization evokes a central Sufi idea, namely, *ihsan*. This is a Qur'anic term (cf. Q 7:56) that, translated literally, means "to do good," though Sufis have understood it to mean much more than that. Following a well-known statement attributed to the Prophet Muhammad, they have often interpreted ihsan to mean going beyond the externals of Islamic ritual practices to "worship God as if you see Him" (Schimmel 1975, 29), that is, cultivating a sense of personal communion and intimacy with God. Even as Yassine has sought to distance himself from what he deems to be the excesses of Sufism, there is little doubt that his political appeal owes much to carefully calibrated efforts to combine distinctive Sufi ideas with his own brand of Islamism (cf. Lauzière 2005; see also chapter 12 on Nadia Yassine in this volume).

Finally, Mawdudi's Jama'at-i Islami—one of the earliest Islamist organizations in the Sunni world—illustrates both the Islamists' complex relationship with Sufism and their pragmatic recognition of its appeal in many Muslim societies. Mawdudi had once been a harsh critic of Sufism, blaming it for many ills afflicting Muslim societies. Yet, the Jama'at-i Islami gradually came to soften its stance on Sufi practices considerably, no doubt in the interest of broadening some of its support base in Pakistan, where saints and Sufi shrines are an important part of the religious and political landscape. Already in Mawdudi's lifetime, Mian Tufayl Muhammad, his successor as the head of the Jama'at-i Islami, had taken the extraordinary initiative of translating an early Sufi classic, the *Kashf al-mahjub*, into Urdu. The author of this work, Shaykh 'Ali Hujwiri (d. 1072), is buried in Lahore in Pakistan, and his much-frequented shrine is home to precisely the sort of devotional practices that Islamists and modernist reformers, let alone Salafis, have often frowned upon (Nasr 1996, 124).

These diverse examples are not intended to obscure the real differences between the generality of Islamists and most Sufis. Their significance lies rather in illustrating the difficulty of distinguishing between Islamism and other religious, intellectual, and political trends in terms of neat characterizations, of grand, translocal generalizations. As the foregoing suggests, the same is true, and more so, when it comes to characterizing Islamists in relation to the 'ulama, the Muslim modernists, and the Salafis. Indeed, as Loren Lybarger has argued with reference to those usually character- ized as "secular nationalist" *or* "Islamist" Palestinians in the West Bank and Gaza, differences within the ranks of young secular nationalists and Islamists can sometimes *also* shade into significant similarities between these supposedly rival orientations (Lybarger 2007). Many Islamists have sought to distance themselves from what they see as the rigidity and au- thoritarianism of other Islamists and to argue not just for the implemen- tation of the shari'a but also for democracy and pluralism. Conversely, not a few of the younger secular nationalists have "adopted Islamist theodicies that explained the failure to overcome Israel as the result of falling away from piety; their conclusions mirrored Islamist ones, too: the road back from the brink had to trace its course through a renewed com- mitment to Islam, but not necessarily in the manner that the Islamist move- ments might have intended" (Lybarger 2007, 237–38; quotation at 238).

Yet if neat categories remain elusive, a combination of the Islamists' self-consciously political goals, their multifaceted if not always explicit political critiques of many past and present ways of understanding and living Islam, and an unshakeable confidence in their own ability to dis- cern God's will from the foundational texts do often provide enough grounds to broadly distinguish them from other activists, intellectuals, and orientations in the Muslim public sphere. What this combination amounts to varies from one social, political, religious, and cultural con- text to another, and so therefore do the ways in which Islamists relate to one another or compete and overlap with other groups and orientations.

## The Politics of Islamism

From Aeneas's mythical founding of Rome to the death and resurrection of Jesus Christ to Muhammad's migration to Medina, foundational nar- ratives are as common to collective life as the movements that periodi- cally arise to revive them and claimants to the mantle of legitimacy they confer. So understood, Islamists' political aspirations to restore founda- tions located in a mythical past are far from unique. Nor are Islamists alone in their conviction that scriptural authority is guaranteed by its di- vine author—for in that all Muslims agree. Rather, the chapters in this volume suggest that what makes Islamist politics distinctive (if not *sui generis*) is the claim to recuperate an "authentic Islam" comprised of self- evident truths purged of alien and corrupting influences, along with an insistence on remaking the foundations of the state in its image. Given the limits of human understanding relative to God's knowledge, Islamists simultaneously depict such fidelity to the unadulterated word of Allah as the ultimate expression of deference to divine omniscience and portray humility as a constitutive feature of the human condition. Aspirations to fully know and master the natural and social worlds thus entail not only a human hubris deaf to the Qur'anic admonition that "Allah knows, but/ and you do not know" (Q 3:66) but also a transgression against a divinely-ordained ontological order.

It is notable, however, that the Islamist emphasis on the limits of human knowledge requires humility only in relation to Allah; it rarely yields humility in regard to their own claims to speak in His name or toward other human beings who dissent from the premise of divine omnipotence and Islamist accounts of what it requires. This suggests that while Islamist challenges to state power are obviously political, the Islamist claim to authenticity is also political in the coercive power it routinely enacts and justifies, most notably by way of the silences it imposes and the debates it forecloses. Aziz al-Azmeh points out that "the notion of authenticity is not so much a determinate concept as it is a node of associations and interpellations, a trope by means of which the historical world is reduced to a particular order, and a token which marks off social and political groups and forges and reconstitutes historical identities" (al-Azmeh 1993, 41). Whether in the service of Arab nationalism, Christian fundamentalism, European romanticism, or Muslim modernism, the claim of authenticity is an act of power that functions not just to reflect the world but to construct it by determining who is included and excluded, who may and may not speak authoritatively, what is the proper realm of debate, and what is beyond contestation.

It is certainly the case that a single "Islam" captures and organizes the perspectives of millions who self-identify as Muslim (among other things), yet what travels under its rubric is inescapably diverse, multiethnic, and defined as much by disagreement as consensus. Just as the Torah and Bible lend themselves to at times radically divergent interpretations of what it means to be Jewish or Christian, the Qur'an and hadith are complex and susceptible to many different, and at times contradictory, enactments. So understood, Islam is less a fixed essence than a living tradition that captures what is imagined as continuous and unitary in dialectical relationship to those concrete articulations and practices by which it is transformed and adapted in different contexts for plural purposes. It is precisely this understanding of religion that is anathema to Islamists who seek to fix the parameters of Islamic authenticity once and for all and thereby arrogate for themselves the right to determine who qualifies as a good Muslim; to discredit those 'ulama unable or unwilling to purge Islam of purported impieties; to declare nominally Muslim rulers apostates unfit to govern; and to characterize all who disagree as corrupt, heretical, guilty of unbelief, or victims of false consciousness.

These general political tendencies, however, must be carefully situated within a dialectic of the global and the vernacular, understood to reflect the ways in which unifying macrohistorical dynamics inform and are in turn transformed by diverse, contingent, and fluid local circumstances. In a world stamped by Western dominance and the consolidation of postcolonial authoritarian regimes, Islamists confront a common set of constraints and challenges. Inasmuch as such constraints and challenges have made Islamist thinkers (often reluctant) participants in conversations across both culture and history, their efforts to remake the foundations of collective life reveal a shared interpretive framework and common religio-political grammar. At the same time, this frame and grammar are continually being reworked in relation to the distinct public spheres in which Islamists operate and to which they carefully calibrate their political commitments.

Attention to this complex dynamic suggests that the Islamist movement cannot simply be characterized as violent, antidemocratic, and oppressive of women, labels invoked so frequently in scholarly and popular literature on the subject that they have become virtually synonymous with Islamist politics. Such characterizations do capture crucial dimensions of Islamist politics, yet they also sidestep the paradoxes its variegated and often contradictory expressions present. Instead, we argue that Islamist politics can be productively read *in terms of* and *against the grain* of such broad categorizations as antidemocratic, antiwoman, or violent— that is, as commitments that, at different moments in various locales, both encourage and constrain broad-based political participation, disrupt and ratify hierarchical gender norms, resist and reproduce state-sanctioned brutality. The point of reading Islamist politics in this way is not to suggest that Islamists are secretly democratic, feminist, and opposed to violence. Rather, the point is to draw attention to the complexity and contradictions erased by easy generalizations, on the one hand, and the often unacknowledged fluidity and cultural adaptability of otherwise familiar political categories, on the other.

## Islamism and Democracy

Despite important differences among Islamist thinkers, they have in common a tendency to view human sovereignty as transgressive of divine law and share the aspiration to establish shari'a as the primary or sole source of authority. As is often noted, such premises and aspirations run afoul of assumptions about popular rule at the heart of democracy, namely, that human beings have the right to legislate rules for collective behavior and are capable of the wisdom required to devise just laws. In recent years, policy makers and commentators have evinced a particular preoccupation with the ways in which Islamist notions of divine authority throttle the spirit and practice of popular sovereignty. Some have even gone so far as to characterize Islamists as "Islamo-fascists," animated by hatred of the "democratic West," psychologically unable to contend with the fluidity and indeterminacy that mark popular rule, and eager to convert elections into a "one-man, one-vote, one-time" mechanism for establishing an Islamic state (Murdock 2002; M. Rubin 2005; Kramer 1993).

Such views are echoed by those Islamists keen to portray democracy not only as antithetical to the supremacy of divine law but as a Trojan horse for Western imperialism. For many Islamists, including several in this volume, democracy is just one symptom of a metastasizing moral and spiritual bankruptcy whereby moral transgressions are transfigured into natural urges, crass self-interest becomes the bedrock of collective life, and the divine plan for the universe and all things in it is reduced to a system of physical causality just waiting to be mastered by way of human ingenuity (R. Euben 2007). Qutb calls this diseased view of the world jahiliyya, and it signals not only human arrogance but a transgression against divine authority, the scope of which encompasses both public and private domains of human affairs as well as both visible and unseen dimensions of the universe. For many Islamists, such transgression is at the root of much of what passes for Muslim rule in the contemporary world—nationalist, democratic, and monarchical alike. Such arrogance is also said to be the pattern underlying a long history of unrelieved Western aggression against Islam in which the Christian Crusades, European colonialism, Israeli treatment of Palestinians, ethnic cleansing in Bosnia, German anti-Turkish violence, the American invasion of Iraq, and Dutch cartoons of Muhammad are but a few examples.

Yet there is a range of views among Islamists about both the substance of democracy and its compatibility with the religio-political renewal they advocate. According to Qaradawi, for example, "the essence of democracy . . . is that people choose who rules over them and manages their affairs; that no ruler or regime they dislike is forced upon them; that they have the right to call the ruler to account if he errs and to remove him from office in case of misconduct; and that people are not forced in economic, social, cultural or political directions that they neither recognize nor accept" (Qaradawi 1997, 132; also chapter 9 in this volume). To him, there is no heavier burden oppressing Muslims in the contemporary world than despotism; indeed, it is through despotic governments that Muslims have been forced to submit to other ills, including the neglect of the shari'a and the coercive imposition of secularism and westernization. Democracy then recommends itself to Qaradawi as the most effective available antidote to despotism and the afflictions of which it serves as a vehicle.

Where many among the Islamists and the 'ulama have seen considerable tension between Islam and democracy, Qaradawi professes to see none. As we suggested earlier, by far the most common of the Islamist reservations about a democratic system relates to the sovereignty of the people, which is taken to contravene the idea that God alone is sovereign. Qaradawi, however, is unperturbed by such concerns. The rule of the people ought to be seen, he argues, not in opposition to the rule of God, but rather in opposition to the rule of the despot. More fundamentally, Qaradawi's view of democracy does not necessarily require that the people should be able to overturn divinely instituted norms. Rather, his assumption is that people exercise their sovereignty within constitutional bounds, and Muslims living in a predominantly Muslim democratic polity would, likewise, not wish to transgress the parameters of legitimate human action laid down in the Islamic foundational texts (see Qaradawi, chapter 9 in this volume; and cf. Feldman 2007).

Nadia Yassine of Morocco's Justice and Spirituality Association is another case in point. While critical of the democratic gestures embraced by a monarchy that she depicts as allergic to genuinely popular sovereignty, Yassine insists that the model of Muslim rule adumbrated in the umma founded by the Prophet Muhammad and, in particular, the Constitution of Medina[17] is nothing short of democratic (N. Yassine 2005d; 2005e). Unlike the Muslim dynasties that arose to usurp it, Yassine contends, this community was participatory, egalitarian, committed to freedom, and expressive of God's mercy. Most important, it was governed always by the Qur'anic principle of *shura* (consultation), by which Yassine means a philosophy of power that places sovereignty in the community rather than in any individual, links virtue to deliberation rather than obedience, and exhorts believers to continually adapt Qur'anic principles through ijtihad rather than adhere reflexively to precedent (N. Yassine 2006a, 182–86; 2005d). Many scholars and journalists remain skeptical of the JSA's as yet untested commitment to procedural democracy and worry that Nadia and her father, Abdessalam, ultimately seek to establish an Islamic state inhospitable to tolerance, pluralism, and civil liberties (Maghraoui 2001; Brandon 2007; Whitlock 2006). Yet others argue that the JSA is a genuinely populist organization that represents the unrepresented, tends to the welfare of the dispossessed, and both expresses and contributes to an increasingly vibrant civil society in Morocco (Cavatorta 2006; Entelis 2002).

Qaradawi's and Yassine's arguments together suggest that democracy can and has served as either a cosmetic cover for despotism or an authentically Islamic check upon corrupt and arbitrary rule. At issue in Islamist arguments for and against democracy, then, are not only what counts as "authentic Islam" and the intentions of those who claim to know it but also the content and character of democracy itself. Paradoxically, both Islamists opposed to democracy and those who take Islamism as inherently antidemocratic regard this as a simple matter with an obvious answer: democracy is an expression of, and even synonymous with, liberalism, capitalism, and the West. Yet democracy is both more capacious and

[17]The Constitution of Medina was an agreement the Prophet had entered into with the local communities, including Jewish tribes, upon his emigration from Mecca to Medina.

more distinct than this presumption suggests. The word itself, of course, derives from the ancient Greek *demokratia*, which means rule (*kratos*) of the people (*demos*), and many derive the equation of democracy and the West from this association with classical Greece. Yet ancient Greek philosophers such as Plato saw in democracy the specter of mob rule particularly vulnerable to demagoguery and despotism (a suspicion notably echoed by American founder James Madison). Contrary to the democratic ideal of inclusiveness, moreover, citizenship in Greek democracy excluded a substantial part of the population, including women, slaves, and foreigners. Finally, the extent to which the ancient Greeks may even be called Western is a matter of great dispute, particularly as the "West" is a category of relatively recent provenance through which history and geography have been retroactively organized.[18] Despite depictions of the Hellenic world as Western, ancient Greeks did not, in fact, view themselves in these terms.[19]

The equation of democracy with the West also presupposes the existence of a coherent "Western civilization" with either culturally homogeneous roots or clearly delineated historical and contemporary boundaries, or both. Yet what is called the West is an amalgamation of multiple traditions, including the Greek, Roman, Judaic, Christian, and Islamic—traditions that are themselves polyvalent rather than homogeneous—and is today characterized by porous borders, hybrid subcultures, and myriad debts to diverse civilizations past and present.[20] As a geographic marker, it is virtually impossible to pinpoint exactly where the West begins and ends, and this is especially so now that peoples, information, and material goods crisscross cultural and national borders at will, creating all kinds of transnational, subnational, and multiple identities that shift and reconstitute themselves in unpredictable ways. Even those values identified as Western often appear elsewhere in other guises. Indeed, scholars suggest that a variety of the "standards exported by the West and its cultural industries themselves turn out to be of culturally mixed character if we examine their cultural lineages" (Pieterse 1995, 53).

Many also argue that democracy is not only distinct from but in tension with both the theory and practice of politics in "Western" societies,

---

[18]Michael Gillespie (1999, 7–10) argues that the rereading of history, geography, and culture through the prism of this sense of "the West" began no earlier than the nineteenth century. The idea of a timeless and bright line between West and East is also challenged by Jeremy Brotton's study (1998, 90, 96–97) of the diplomatic and intellectual exchanges between Europe and the Ottoman Empire in the early modern period. Brotton shows not only the extent and amity of such exchanges but a persistent uncertainty about where, precisely, Europe "ended" and Asia "began."

[19]Ancient Greeks understood themselves as geographically west of the barbarians but not Western in the contemporary sense, that is, as both a cultural and historical category.

[20]Steven Runciman's work (1954, 3:480) on the Crusades, for example, demonstrates a "long sequence of interaction and fusion between Orient and Occident out of which our civilization has grown."

many of which are more accurately classified as liberal and capitalist (Wood 1994; Wolin 2001; Ball and Dagger 1999). While it is now commonplace to speak of "liberal democracy" in a single breath, liberalism and democracy are concepts and practices with very different histories and presuppositions. Unlike democracy, for example, liberalism emerged from the crucible of Christian religious wars, and in tandem with the ascendance of a middle class that presaged the end of European feudalism. The liberal nation-state can thus be viewed as both an expression and a consolidation of capitalism, on the one hand, and the principle of a separation between church and state, on the other. By contrast, there is nothing about democracy either as a system of governance or a culture of participation that is inherently secular. Indeed, Alexis de Tocqueville famously insisted that American democracy cannot and should not be secular, as religion helps shift attention away from immediate material preoccupations to larger concerns of community, cooperation, and morality. In fact, many democratic theorists argue that genuinely inclusive popular sovereignty is antithetical to the sharp inequalities of wealth and political power that capitalism often produces and legitimates.

Such ongoing definitional and substantive debates suggest that there is much more at stake in democratic politics than procedures pertaining to government, authority, and order and point to a widespread, if elusive, understanding of democracy not just as a set of institutions but, as Tocqueville suggests, a way of life. Several political theorists have characterized this elusive understanding in terms of a "democratic ethos." By this they mean both an ideal and an argument for a culture of participation, active power sharing, mutual accountability, inclusiveness, and deliberation in which citizens may routinely and safely challenge not only specific policies and political institutions but also the values that govern collective life, principles of inclusion and exclusion, and the premises of authority itself (Connolly 1995; J. P. Euben 2003; Sadiki 2004). A democratic ethos is much more difficult to measure or quantify than, for example, Samuel Huntington's parsimonious definition of democracy as a polity in which there have been two consecutive, peaceful changes of government by way of free and fair elections (Huntington 1991).[21] Yet a democratic ethos makes it possible to both recognize and disaggregate the preconditions, aspirations, mechanisms, and institutions bundled into "democracy," thereby bringing into focus, for example, the frequently antidemocratic

---

[21] Many political scientists prefer to define democracy in terms of procedures designed to realize popular rule, including free, competitive, and fair elections, along with state protection of certain rights and liberties. Such a formal, minimalist definition has the advantage of detaching democracy from questions of origins and offering a standard to which all governments may be held regardless of culture and place. As Keith Topper (2005, 205–7) argues, however, it also tends to sidestep knotty questions about the substance of representation, power, responsiveness, and accountability that are arguably central to democratic politics.

cast to elections imposed by elites or foreign powers, the felt impotence of many citizens in established democracies, and those highly participatory civil societies that flourish even under monarchic or theocratic rule.

For our purposes in particular, a democratic ethos makes visible the paradox of an Islamist movement that seeks to mobilize ordinary Muslims against coercive power but in the name of a religio-political order largely immunized from challenge. Qutb is an apt illustration here, as his tendency to ground his own special authority and insight in the unsullied wisdom of ordinary believers makes it possible to read his work as either a brief against democracy (among other things) or an enactment of it. Inasmuch as democracy as a form of governance is identified with popular sovereignty, Qutb's basic premise that the foundation of legitimate authority must be divine rather than human suggests that he is unambiguously antidemocratic. Moreover, Qutb's efforts to pluralize religious and political authority express, not a confidence in common wisdom, but rather a desire to claim for himself the stature of a religious expert who, despite his lack of Islamic academic credentials, can clearly see what others cannot. Qutb characterizes the real Islam as self-evident, but he also assumes that only a small vanguard of believers besides himself will have the ability to recognize it and act decisively to remake the world in its image. So understood, the sign of "chosenness" is unyielding commitment to establishing a religio-political order that simultaneously presumes the supremacy of the few capable of true knowledge and promises a world in which dissent itself will become both unnecessary and illegitimate.

Yet, if democracy refers not only to a system of governance or set of procedures to realize popular sovereignty but also to practices that disrupt those forces which concentrate power and establish political exclusion, the characterization of Qutb's work as simply antidemocratic misses a crucial dimension of its significance and appeal. As the sacred texts contain the rules and regulations meant to govern both public and private affairs, Qutb's insistence that ordinary, untrained Muslims must engage them directly is, in many ways, a democratization of access to authority. Such access can disrupt deeply entrenched patterns of power and powerlessness, particularly when conjoined to Islamist arguments that arbitrary power is un-Islamic; that religious knowledge depends on commitment rather than training or expertise; that Muslims have the right and obligation to determine when rulers are illegitimate; and that those who prefer order to justice, security to freedom, and money to piety have forfeited any claim to authority.

This aspect of Islamism has frequently been compared to the Protestant Reformation and, more specifically, to Calvinists' attempts to transfer "religious authority away from officially sanctioned individuals who interpret texts to ordinary citizens" (E. Goldberg 1991, 3; also cf. Loimeier 2005). Such a parallel has sparked a great deal of scholarly speculation regarding a possible "Islamic Reformation"[22] and a range of arguments about whether and how Islamism might facilitate the democratization of Muslim societies, much as the Protestant Reformation is said to have heralded the emergence of European "liberal democracy." While such comparisons are evocative, a fuller understanding of Islamism requires first situating it in relation to a historical shift in the nature and locus of religious authority in Islam beginning in the nineteenth century. As scholars of Muslim societies have pointed out, the impact of mass education, new technologies for disseminating knowledge and information, and dramatically changed social, economic, and political contexts have made available to amateurs what had previously been the purview of religious experts. At the same time, it has inaugurated a fragmentation of authority within the very ranks of the 'ulama that continues to the present day.[23] In this context, the ascendance and influence of autodidacts such as Qutb, Hasan al-Banna, 'Abd al-Salam Faraj, and Bin Laden simultaneously express and accelerate an ongoing renegotiation of authority over who may speak for Islam and on what basis, the path of which is still unfolding and the outcome as yet uncertain.

## Islamism and Gender

One already apparent consequence of this ongoing renegotiation over who may speak for Islam and on what basis is the entry of women into the interpretive fray. This development is increasingly unsettling those unwritten gender norms arguably at the very heart of Islamist thought, disrupting the standards of masculinity and femininity that reflect how particular cultures organize human beings' social and reproductive activities into roles that are, in turn, thought to express the "nature" of men and women. Such norms are frequently considered tangential to the knotty problems of defining Islamism and adumbrating its central ideas, yet a range of scholarship on cultures past and present has shown that gender is consistently the terrain over which battles for political control and cultural identity are fought. More specifically, research in disciplines such as anthropology, history, classics, and postcolonial studies has demonstrated that cultures in which female bodies and behavior are regarded as indices of moral purity tend to symbolically transform women into conduits of cultural corruption in times of internal crisis and external threat (Papenek 1994; Chatterjee 1990; Tavakoli-Targhi 1991; Just 1989; Cohen 1991; Welter 1966; Bloch 1978). This is especially true of contem-

---

[22] For a late nineteenth-century assessment of the prospects for a "Muhammadan Reformation," see Blunt 1882, 132–73.

[23] Eickelman and Piscatori 1996, 37–39, 131–35; Zaman 2006. Such fragmentation has in many ways been accelerated by the explosion of digital cultures, which promote, among other things, a "form of empowered amateurism" (Mirzoeff 2002, 6).

porary religio-political movements, whose members tend to "idealize patriarchal structures of authority and morality," endorse gender dualism as god-given or natural, and condemn vigorously recent changes in gender relations as a symptom and symbol of secularist moral bankruptcy (Riesebrodt 1993; Moghadam 1992; Hawley 1994).

Several chapters in this volume illuminate Islamist gender norms by revealing the character and content of Islamist concerns about the place and purity of Muslim women—preoccupations Fatima Mernissi (1991, 99) has gone so far as to characterize as an obsession. Despite important differences among Islamists thinkers, many endorse gender norms in which the fairly conventional insistence that female nature is defined in and through reproduction undergirds an understanding of women as symbols of moral virtue and vessels of cultural purity. This view sustains the claim that men and women are equal in religious belief but perform fundamentally different and complementary functions in society. While men are naturally made to rule in both the public and private domain, a woman belongs in the domestic realm where her primary role is to be a wife and mother, as well as to insure the integrity of the family, the first school of moral education. As such functions are rooted in an inescapable human nature fashioned by God, a woman's inability or unwillingness to perform her duties signals a disobedience to the divine will and presages the corruption of the Muslim family from within. From this vantage point, the Western insistence on full equality between the sexes is doubly pernicious: it at once liberates women from basic moral constraints and enslaves them to mutually reinforcing sexual and capitalist exploitation. As Murtaza Mutahhari (1998, xxxi) argues, capitalism makes use of women to market its goods "by trading in honour and respect, through [their] power to entice," thereby "transform[ing] man into an involuntary agent of consumption." Inasmuch as women are responsible for producing the next generation of Muslim men destined to restore Islam to its former glory, it is not only the virtue of women or the integrity of the family that hangs in the balance but the future of Islamic civilization itself.

Zaynab al-Ghazali and Mutahhari make several of these arguments explicitly and in detail (see chapters 10 and 11), but in much of Islamist rhetoric, the nature and significance of women are established indirectly and symbolically, and through three recurrent images in particular. The first is of women as silent symbols of cultural, moral, and sexual vulnerability, voiceless figures in need of masculine protection or, when it is too late, defiled bodies that mutely demand vengeance. So, for example, 'Abdallah 'Azzam (one of Bin Laden's mentors; see chapter 18) graphically details the agonizing humiliation of young men unable to act when the Afghan woman is "crying out for help, her children are being slaughtered, her women are being raped, the innocent are killed and their corpses scattered" ('Azzam 1987a). In the second image, women function much like a chorus that speaks in permitted cadences to ratify masculine endeavors. Such is the case, for example, in Bin Laden's 1996 "Declaration of War against the Americans Occupying the Land of the Two Holy Places" (see chapter 18), where the women exhort men to jihad in the following way: "Prepare yourself like a struggler, the matter is bigger than words! Are you going to leave us . . . for the wolves of Kufr [unbelief] eating our wings?! . . . Where are the free men defending free women by arms?! Death is better than life in humiliation! Some scandals and shames will never be otherwise eradicated."[24] In the third image, women are creatures not of this world but of another, virginal rewards for the courageous martyr in the afterlife. This is evident in the final instructions for the 9/11 hijackers, for example, where Muslim "brothers" are urged to purify their carnal impulses, sharpen their knives for the *dhabh* (slaughter), and heed the call of the *hur 'ayn* (the black-eyed ones) awaiting them in Paradise (see chapter 19).

Such rhetoric primarily registers women as an extension, mirror, or measure of masculinity and, together with explicit Islamist arguments about human nature and the family, articulates Islamist gender norms in which men and women each have a proper location and purpose in a divinely ordained social hierarchy. Deviance from this gendered script thus signals disruption of a much broader religio-political order it both presumes and seeks to bring into existence. The disruption caused by foreign aggression in particular exacerbates the tendency to translate conflict into an assault on Muslim masculinity and to conceptualize women as potential vehicles for Western corruption in need of guiding and guarding. Women such as Zaynab al-Ghazali and Nadia Yassine who seek a prominent place and voice within the Islamist movement have had little choice but to contend with this gendered script. Doing so has entailed, among other things, navigating carefully between Islamist characterizations of women's visibility and agency as symptomatic of the new jahiliyya, on the one hand, and essentializing arguments that equate Islam with veiling, female genital mutilation, and honor killings, on the other.

As the chapters on Ghazali and Yassine suggest, Islamist women have negotiated between such constraints and pressures and their own ambitions in different ways. A pioneering *da'iya* (one who invites Muslims to greater piety), Ghazali's own life reveals a fierce resistance to conventional norms of domesticity, even as much of her (earlier) work appears to embrace an Islamist gender ideology that defines women as wives, mothers, and "builders of men" (al-Hashimi 1990, 118). By contrast, Yassine is a wife and mother who embraces an "Islamic feminism" that requires "reappropriating the instruments of classical theology" and en-

---

[24]The Islamist journal *Sawt al-Jihad* has gone so far as to feature "women's voices" in the form of role models named, for example, *umm al-shahid* (mother of the martyr), although it is unclear that these "voices" are actually women's (S. Usher 2004).

gaging the texts directly through ijtihad (N. Yassine 2003). In this respect, Yassine must be understood as part of a broader effort among Muslim women with different political commitments to simultaneously advocate and enact their right to recuperate the "original intent" of the Islamic texts. If women and men do, in fact, have distinct perspectives on the world, Yassine suggests, women have a special obligation to excavate what they see as the gender parity of the Qur'an buried beneath those "macho interpretations" of Islam upon which men have built their privilege and power (Khalaf 2006).[25]

Many Anglo-American and European feminists worry that Islamists seek only to secure or restore patriarchal power. Conversely, many Islamist women view feminism as a term and a movement inescapably Western in origin, freighted with the legacy of colonialism, and uneasily implicated in cultural imperialism. This applies even to Yassine, who is unwilling to adopt without qualification a label she associates with agendas opposed to her own: the West, the Moroccan state, Maghribi (Northwest African) elites. Yet feminism itself is a highly contested term *within* the so-called West: it is the bearer of multiple meanings, some of which are even opposed, and is characterized by deep disagreements about who women are, what women need, who is authorized to work on women's behalf and by what means. Inasmuch as these various feminisms may share only a stated concern for women's welfare, there is nothing incoherent in modifying "feminism" with "Islamic," "Muslim," or even "Islamist," unless one is committed to arguing that, first, Islam is an unchanging essence beyond history, politics, and culture; second, there is a neutral, objective vantage from which to identify this essence once and for all; and, finally, the Islamic essence so identified is fundamentally incompatible with efforts to improve the conditions and quality of women's lives. By the same token, Islamist women who reject the term feminism can be (although not always are) deeply committed to improving women's welfare, as well as actively resistant to efforts that reduce or transform them into silent accessories of male power.

Yassine and Ghazali differ about what women are and should be yet, broadly speaking, both may be considered part of a recent trend toward the feminization of *da'wa*. Da'wa literally means call, appeal, or summons, but the term has come to signify a variety of practices and arguments meant to exhort, invite, and guide Muslims to what is regarded as proper conduct and moral devotion. Women's participation in da'wa is

[25]Women's participation in the "production of official Islamic knowledge" has a long history, although they have often done so in relative obscurity and without the benefit of education in the Islamic sciences that has legitimated direct engagement with the sacred texts (Cooke 2001, xiv; Badran and Cooke 2004). Pioneering attempts to read gender equality in Islam are also not confined to writing by women, as evinced by Qasim Amin's *Tahrir al-mar'a* [The Liberation of Woman] (1899) and Mumtaz 'Ali's *Huquq-e niswan* [The Rights of Women] (1898).

not a brand new phenomenon, as is evident in Ghazali's work with the Egyptian Society of Muslim Ladies in the 1930s. Yet, from Egypt to Pakistan to Saudi Arabia to the United States, the number of female da'iyas has proliferated exponentially in recent years (Cooke 2001; Mahmood 2005; Hirschkind 2006). This reflects, in part, current doctrinal emphases on da'wa as incumbent upon both men and women, and dependent less upon technical knowledge than moral virtue and practical familiarity with the Islamic tradition (Mahmood 2005, 65–66). It is also a consequence of recent political and socioeconomic transformations in Muslim societies, including the expansion of mass education that has not only increased women's literacy and social mobility but also made Islamic texts more accessible; the proliferation of technologies—from the cassette tape to the Internet—that facilitate the circulation of religious knowledge even among those who cannot read or travel; the precedent set by the vigorous participation of Iranian women in postrevolution debates about Islam; and the model of legal activism evident in the Islamist movement's own challenge to the 'ulama's status as gatekeepers of religious knowledge (Singerman 2005; Mir-Hosseini 1999).

If Ghazali and Yassine exemplify the feminization of da'wa among elites, the mosque movement in Egypt illustrates the growing participation of women from diverse social backgrounds in religious classes devoted to studying and debating what Islam requires for a woman to be "morally upright" in the contemporary world (Mahmood 2005). Conceptualizing piety in terms of a deep and holistic commitment to self-transformation, participants in the mosque movement are concerned less with matters of sovereignty and politics conventionally understood and more with the "moral cultivation" of those daily practices seen as crucial to becoming closer to God (Mahmood 2005). Some Islamists have criticized this focus on practices of worship as apolitical and overly privatized, yet such criticism misses the force of Islamists' own insistence on din (religion) as a way of life in which the domains of public and private are inextricably linked.[26] As Saba Mahmood (2005, 193, 194) shows, these women's intense efforts at "retraining ethical sensibilities" have a "sociopolitical force" that extends well beyond matters of governance, facilitating no less than the emergence of a "new social and moral order." Evidence of its transformative power may be found not only in the sheer numbers and variety of women—wealthy and poor, literate and illiterate—participating in the mosque movement but also in the rhetorical and political efforts by the state and some Islamists to curtail, control, or discredit it (Mahmood 2005, 71, 194).

[26]Participants in the mosque movement, in turn, are often critical of what they see as the reduction of Islam to tokens of cultural authenticity, or of its instrumentalization by both nationalists and Islamists they characterize as more interested in political maneuvering than religious piety.

Understood to include both written and embodied practices, the feminization of da'wa illustrates the ways in which women from different perspectives and social classes are insisting on engaging the sacred texts directly for and with one another, without the mediating authority of men, who have traditionally held the monopoly on such activities. As Sudanese Islamist Lubabah al-Fadl argues, "As an *insan* [human being] who happens to be a woman, I have a right to reject the manipulative exegeses of our *shari'a* that threaten my existence in a way that is not consistent with the Godly way, and to apply my own *ijtihad* to rectify erroneous tendencies by some *shuyukh* [plural of shaykh]" (Sadiki 2004, 290). Despite the proliferation of voices intent on claiming for themselves the authority to demarcate what is authentically Islamic and un-Islamic once and for all, contestation over its scope and meaning proceeds apace, facilitated at least in part by women formerly excluded from the conversation. At the same time, Islamist women's agency and claims to authority are frequently still predicated on a willingness to follow fairly patriarchal rules about where, how, and with whom they may practice their vocation (Hirschkind 2003; Sadiki 2004, 283).

## Islamism and Violence

If gender is frequently an implicit preoccupation among Islamists, jihad is arguably Islamists' most consistently explicit concern. Jihad is derived from the Arabic verb that means to struggle or to strive, yet it is a particular kind of struggle that is of concern to many of the figures collected here: the often violent struggle against apostates and infidels both at home and abroad to which every individual Muslim must contribute. The claim that fighting unbelievers is the preeminent enactment of individual Muslim piety seems to justify characterizations of Islam in general and Islamism in particular as sanctioning, even encouraging, violence. Yet what Islamists represent as jihad *tout court* is a historically specific understanding derived from a highly selective use of texts and precedents, prominent among them a formerly obscure claim by the influential fourteenth-century jurist Ibn Taymiyya that Mongol rulers who had contravened Islamic law could be subject to forcible removal. Far from a definitive expression of Islam "properly understood," such Islamist arguments not only mark a significant departure from much of antecedent doctrine and practice but also diminish the importance of ongoing disagreements among Muslims about the form and purposes of jihad.

To begin with, Muslim scholars have tended to consider jihad against foreign enemies a *fard kifaya* (collective obligation), that is, a duty a group of people within the community may perform on behalf of the rest, and one that presupposes a legitimate Muslim leader to declare or lead the charge. Jurists have distinguished this from the *fard 'ayn* (individual duty) that must be fulfilled by every single Muslim in cases of defensive jihad, that is, when the umma is under attack. Many Islamists included here take a much less nuanced view of jihad. As a mode of political action, Qutb argues, jihad must be regarded as a "permanent condition, not an occasional concern," one that in current circumstances requires deeds rather than words, struggle rather than contemplation, revolution at home as well as resistance abroad (Qutb 1991, 67–68, 82). 'Abd al-Salam Faraj argues along similar lines that the nature of the attack on Islam makes political authorization by a caliph ("deputy," referring to a legitimate successor to the Prophet's leadership) unnecessary: after all, "leadership over the Muslims is (always) in their own hands if only they make this manifest. . . . If there is something lacking in the leadership, well, there is nothing that cannot be acquired" (Jansen 1986a, sec. 93).

Such arguments are a deliberate rejection of early Muslim modernists who had emphasized the largely defensive character of jihad and sought to show that relations between Muslims and non-Muslims were normally peaceful rather than antagonistic. Mahmud Shaltut (d. 1963), the rector of al-Azhar from 1958 to 1963, had argued, for example, that the Qur'anic verses on fighting "prohibit the provocation of hostility and this prohibition is reinforced by God's repugnance to aggression and by his dislike of those who provoke hostility" (Peters 1996, 74; on Shaltut, see Zebiri 1993). Conversion by force is anathema to Islam, Shaltut avers, and fighting is commanded only in defense, in response to aggression initiated by others. Even defensive jihad must aim at "the termination of the aggression and the establishment of religious liberty devoted to God and free from any pressure or force" (Peters 1996, 75).

Many Islamists explicitly dismiss such arguments as a symptom of false consciousness, one among many destructive effects of colonial domination. Mawdudi argues, for example, that while imperialists ravage the world to satisfy their greed, jihad alone "conjures up the vision of a marching band of religious fanatics with savage beards and fiery eyes brandishing drawn swords and attacking the infidels wherever they meet them." Having internalized this image, Muslims rush to apologize and renounce armed struggle. In this way, he laments, colonialists retain the exclusive right to "fight with arms and ammunition while we are contented with our pen and our tongue" (Mawdudi 1948, 1–3). Sayyid Qutb, for his part, agreed that Islam does not countenance spreading its message by force and coercion, yet he had little patience with those who sought to present jihad as legitimate only in self-defense:

> If we insist on calling Islamic jihad a defensive movement, then we must change the meaning of the word "defense" and mean by it "the defense of man" against all those forces that limit his freedom. . . . When we take this broad meaning of the word "defense," we understand the true character of Islam, in that it proclaims the universal freedom of every person and community from servitude to any other

individual or society, the end of man's arrogance and selfishness, the establishment of the sovereignty of Allah and His Lordship throughout the world, and the rule of the divine shari'a in human affairs. (Qutb 1990, 50)

Qutb does not name any names in castigating the "writers with defeatist and apologetic mentalities [who] write about 'jihad in Islam' and try to remove this 'blot' from Islam" (Qutb 1990, 46), but he could very well have had his distinguished fellow Egyptian Mahmud Shaltut in mind.

These arguments about jihad may be said to constitute a common grammar and framework of analysis for many Islamists, although several thinkers in this volume carefully calibrate such claims to suit various purposes and different public spheres. In his justification for the assassination of Egyptian president Anwar al-Sadat, for example, 'Abd al-Salam Faraj depicts the struggle to reclaim the moral foundations of the Egyptian state as a fight against jahiliyya from within, arguing that the jihad against a corrupt nationalist regime at home must take precedence over fighting enemies elsewhere. The Charter of Hamas (see chapter 15), however, insists that all Muslims recognize the primacy of the jihad for Jerusalem, welding Islamist rhetoric to that of nationalist resistance in an effort both to fight Israeli occupation and to compete for adherents with the Palestinian Liberation Organization (PLO). In contrast to both Faraj and Hamas, Bin Laden embraces a global jihad that essentially collapses distinctions between national and international, offensive and defensive fighting, enemies at home and those from afar.

Yet despite such differences, these arguments tend to presume that violent jihad is a necessary response to the pervasive power of those with demonstrated hostility to Muslim lives, lands, pieties, and sensibilities, a form of retaliation whose urgency and legitimacy derive from the violence—psychological and economic as well as physical—of the initial assault. This view of jihad subsumes individuals into archetypes of "infidels" and "believers" and, in so doing, vitiates more conventional distinctions between, for example, soldier and civilian, or collective and individual responsibility. It is far from inevitable that those who harbor such views will automatically act upon them, yet the carnage wrought by the attacks on the World Trade Center and the Pentagon in 2001, a Bali nightclub in 2002, Madrid commuter trains in 2004, and throughout Iraq on a daily basis suggest just how lethal such claims can be, given the right circumstances. The fact that such violence does not discriminate among victims only further fuels rhetoric characterizing Islamists as irrational fanatics "in love with death," terrorists animated by a religion characterized by a propensity for violence and authoritarianism.[27]

---

[27] Anxieties about the particular susceptibility of Muslims to irrationality, insularity, and fanaticism have a long and distinguished pedigree in Euro-American history and political thought. See, for example, Renan 1883, 3.

As in so many other matters, however, Islamists are hardly of one mind on the subject of jihad; indeed, there are Islamists who explicitly reject the reduction of struggle to violence. A case in point is Nadia Yassine (2003; 2005c), who insists that jihad is the dedicated struggle against *istikbar* (arrogance), particularly in its common form as the lust for power and domination. As jihad against istikbar is both a final goal and a prescription for action, Yassine suggests, it is antithetical to violent practices that aim at domination. The primary instruments of jihad are not bombs but words, particularly those deployed in the art of persuasion (Faramarzi 2005; N. Yassine 2006a). When Islamists such as 'Abd al-Salam Faraj and 'Umar 'Abd al-Rahman seek to legitimize violent revolution by recourse to Islamic texts, she argues, they contravene the true meaning of jihad to serve their own arrogant ends. By the same token, Bin Laden's decision to "fight evil with evil and barbarity with barbarity" not only violates specific Islamic prohibitions against harming civilians, women, and children but also betrays the ethical imperative to embody the message of a merciful God who cautions believers that (Q 88:22) "You have no power over them" (N. Yassine 2005c; *Daily Excelsior* 2002).

Such persistent disagreements among Muslims past and present suggest that Islam is no more inherently violent and bloody-minded than it—or Christianity or Judaism, for that matter—is inherently peaceful. Islamists often claim to speak for an unchanging authentic Islam that exists outside of time and space, yet the political purchase of their perspective derives from the ways it assembles disparate yet recognizable contemporary experiences of suffering, frustration, and loss into an explanation that resonates with Muslims who live in communities culturally, linguistically, and geographically distant from one another. The extent to which Islamist arguments resonate broadly across Muslim societies thus depends upon a set of experiences and phenomena that mark this particular moment in history, including the ways in which contemporary global inequalities compound a legacy of historical asymmetries to continually reproduce a sense of Muslim powerlessness—both real and imagined—relative to the West; continuing Euro-American political and financial support of corrupt autocrats, many of whom preside over nation-states brutally stitched together by Western fiat; the persistence of authoritarian regimes eager to control domestic unrest by catalyzing "Muslim rage" toward external targets; the sense of emasculation produced by decades of political repression and economic frustration; and the continual flow of images of bloodied Muslim bodies delivered by a burgeoning array of video, satellite, and electronic media.

It is notable that the understanding of jihad many Islamists proffer mirrors the very state-sanctioned violence against which they have struggled for almost a century. Along with thousands of Muslims caught in the machinery of twentieth-century state violence, prominent Islamists from Qutb to Ghazali to Ayman al-Zawahiri—al-Qa'ida's second in command—

are well known to have been radicalized by extended and often brutal terms of incarceration in Egypt, Syria, Iraq, Jordan, Israel, Algeria, and elsewhere (on al-Zawahiri and prison, cf. Kepel and Milelli 2008, 152–54). It is thus far from surprising that Islamists forged by interrogation torture in prison camps would conclude that the preeminent enactment of Muslim piety is violent struggle. "Prison," as Palestinian Khaled Abu Hilal has said, "is my university" (Erlanger 2007), an argument made in greater detail in a different time and place by Russian writer and revolutionary Maxim Gorky (1868–1936):

> A people brought up in a school that reminds one of the torments of hell on a small scale; a people accustomed to the clenched-fist, prison, and the whip, will not be blest with a tender heart. A people that the police agents have ridden over will be capable in their turn of walking over the bodies of others. In a country where unrest has reigned so long it is difficult for the people to realize from one day to the next the power of right. One cannot demand from a man who has never known justice that he should be just. (Gorky 1920)

In this context, as Timothy Mitchell (1990, 195–96, 199, 207–8) suggests, Islamist views of the world can be characterized as both a mode of resistance to state mechanisms of coercion and an expression of them. Such is the dynamic evident in Ghazali's memoirs, for example, when she describes how the "darkness of prisons, the blades of torture, and the vicious beatings only increase the endurance and resolve of the faithful" (Ghazali 1978, 6).

There is, no doubt, a great deal of pragmatism at work in Islamist arguments about violence. As Qutb (1991, 64, 47–48) dryly notes, the path to freedom must occasionally be hewn by way of the sword because tyrants are not reasoned out of power and "jahiliyya is not 'abstract theory' . . . [it] consciously or unconsciously strives to preserve its own existence, to defend its essence . . . to annihilate dangerous elements which threaten its very being." Yet it is also the case that, for many of these Islamists, jihad is both a means and an end, an effort to eradicate those obstacles to restoring a just community on earth that simultaneously brings human action into accord with God's plans and purposes (Haddad 1983, 21). While the Qur'an (2:256) states that "there is no compulsion in religion," Islamists contend that only in a state in which Islamic law reigns supreme are human beings free from enslavement to one another's rule and all are equal by virtue of their common submission to God. As Qutb (1991, 107–8) argues:

> When the highest authority in society is God alone—expressed in the rule of divine law—only then is humanity truly and completely liberated from slavery to men. Only this is "human civilization," because the essential foundation of human civilization is the true and com-

plete freedom of humanity and the absolute dignity of every individual in society. There is no true freedom and dignity for humanity or the individual in a society where some people are lords who legislate and others are slaves who obey.

From this perspective, the realization of justice, liberty, equality, and choice itself necessitates the forcible removal of the constraints imposed by jahiliyya, along with those who aid and abet it, *no matter the cost*. As Mawdudi (1954, 160–61) writes,

> [W]hy is it that in religion such importance is given to jihad that the Qur'an pronounces the judgment of hypocrisy upon those who shirk and evade it? Jihad is but another name for the attempt to erect the system of truth, and the Qur'an declares jihad to be a touchstone on the same footing with a man's faith. In other words, he who has faith in his heart will neither be content with the domination of the system of evil, nor will he grudge the expenditure of life and wealth in the struggle for erecting the system of truth. If one shows weakness in this matter, his faith itself is doubtful. What can anything else beside then profit him? . . . The man who professes faith in this religion cannot fulfill his duty only by trying as far as possible to pattern his life on Islam. The nature of his faith itself requires that he should concentrate all his effort upon wresting leadership from unbelieving and corrupt men to entrust it to the righteous, and upon erecting the system of truth that has been ordained for the conduct of the world according to the will of God. Because this end is unattainable without the highest degree of collective effort, there must exist a righteous community committed to the principle of truth and devoted to the sole purpose in the world of erecting, maintaining, and properly realizing the system of truth.

The fact that some Islamist thinkers sanctify violent struggle in such terms does not mean, of course, that all those who advocate or engage in jihad endorse violence.[28] Nor does it imply that those who claim to kill for Islam are entirely without ulterior motives, those manipulative purposes and psychological motivations that even the most rarified scriptural arguments can express or serve. What the preceding analysis does suggest, however, is that the reduction of this view of jihad to irrational blood lust, the self-interested grab for temporal power, or a door through which to pass into the hereafter misses a crucial dimension of its significance and appeal: for true believers, jihad is no less than an enactment of

---

[28]Even as he spoke of a new era of jahiliyya and of jihad, Mawdudi himself stopped well short of recommending or condoning the actual resort to violence in the manner many other Islamists did. As Nasr (1996, 70) observes, Mawdudi's organization, the Jama'at-i Islami, "has avoided violent social change and has instead viewed the path to the Islamic state as lying within the existing sociopolitical order." Also see the chapters 5 and 3 on Qutb and Mawdudi in this volume.

a divine imperative to remake the foundations of collective life. In this respect, Islamist views of jihad can be seen as part of a long-standing association between violence and political foundings upon which no particular culture or historical epoch has a monopoly. This association and the "legacy of violence" it bequeaths to future generations are no less apparent in those radical revolutions of renewal that move by way of the sword from the margins to the center than those political foundings that claim to create something out of nothing (Connolly 1995, 251). In either case, the toll of such brutality can be immeasurable, for in addition to the victims who suffer directly, the "practice of violence, like all action, changes the world, but the most probable change is to a more violent world" (Arendt 1972, 177).

# PART I

# Islamism

## *An Emergent Worldview*

*Chapter 2*

# HASAN AL-BANNA
## 1906–1949

HASAN AL-BANNA is frequently characterized as the father of contemporary Islamism, and with good reason. In 1928 Banna founded al-Ikhwan al-Muslimun, or the Egyptian Society of Muslim Brothers, an organization that has spawned branches throughout the Middle East, North Africa, South Asia, and beyond and has directly or indirectly inspired virtually every Sunni Islamist group now in existence. As Banna was assassinated in 1949, the tumultuous history of the Muslim Brotherhood and its offshoots extends far beyond the life of its founder by many decades. Yet, at the time of his death at forty-three, Banna had already built a formidable organization with deep roots in Egyptian society and a broad base of membership, ranging from civil servants to soldiers, urban laborers to rural peasants, village elders to university students. Although the appeal of the Brotherhood's message of Islamic "rearmament" had much to do with timing and specific political circumstances, it was also and crucially about Banna himself. A watchmaker by training and schoolteacher by profession, Banna exuded selfless religious devotion and unflagging energy and, by all accounts, was preternaturally gifted with remarkable personal charisma, rhetorical skill, and organizational acumen. More activist than theologian, Banna would largely leave the task of developing an Islamist theoretical framework to thinkers who came after him. Yet many of the positions and arguments associated with Islamists such as Qutb, Mawdudi, and Khomeini are a systematic articulation of a worldview already evident in the model of leadership and sociomoral reform Banna left behind.

Banna is so closely identified with the Brotherhood that its early history and his biography are almost indistinguishable. Banna was born in 1906 in Mahmudiyya, a village north of Cairo. His father was a shaykh, scholar, and imam for the local mosque as well as a watch repairer, and he conveyed his religious devotion, love of learning, and practical expertise to his son.[1] Throughout his life, Banna was drawn to a life of learning and study in addition to engagement and action—and precociously so. At thirteen, Banna was already deeply immersed in Hasafiyya, a Sufi mystical

---

[1] Banna's life has been amply documented in several excellent studies of the Muslim Brotherhood, and Banna himself also provides extensive (if occasionally self-serving) information about his early life and the founding of the Brotherhood in his memoirs. See R. Mitchell (1993), Banna (1974), and Harris (1964).

order, and active in the strikes and demonstrations of the 1919 Egyptian rebellion against British rule. From a very early age, he was also a fervent participant in several Muslim student associations devoted to self-discipline and moral reform, an agenda that included strident opposition to Christian missionary activity and any behavior deemed "un-Islamic."

When he was seventeen, Banna opted to study at the Dar al-'Ulum, a well-established state teachers' college in Cairo, rather than pursue an advanced religious education. Yet the understanding of education (*tarbiyya*) that he held throughout his life more closely resembled what Aristotle had called moral instruction than mastery of a particular set of skills or academic discipline. In Banna's view, the ultimate aim of all knowledge is neither personal advancement nor material success but rather inculcation of the Good Life as dictated by the truths of Islam, and this is equally true whether the subject of study is the Qur'an or economics. He similarly saw teaching as a vocation—in the sense of a religious calling—rather than just a profession: embracing the role of murshid (religious guide, teacher), Banna cast himself as a leader who, like his own teachers, instructs by argument and example; figures to his pupils much as a father does to his children; and commands the same kind of fierce loyalty, emotional attachment, and strict obedience from his followers as does a Sufi shaykh from his disciples (Harris 1964, 157; Commins 1994, 150; R. Mitchell 1993, 300–301).[2]

Banna graduated from the Dar al-'Ulum in 1927, and his first posting was as an Arabic instructor in a school in Isma'iliyya, a city in the Suez Canal Zone. There he honed his skills as an orator in mosques, clubs, and coffeehouses, adapting his rhetoric to suit different audiences in an effort to draw into his orbit elites and peasants, shaykhs and laborers, family elders and students alike. His lectures on the necessity of reviving the true Islam found a particularly receptive audience in Isma'iliyya, headquarters of the British-owned Suez Canal Company, site of several British military camps, and home to a substantial and conspicuously wealthy foreign population. Here, as in Cairo, Banna was repulsed by what he saw as the domination of materialism and secularism, the abandonment of Muslim virtue, widespread imitation of Western moral decadence, and the galling sight of native Egyptians laboring in their own country for the profit of foreign powers. In his memoirs, Banna characterizes Isma'iliyya as the stark embodiment of the evils besetting Egypt and all Muslim societies dominated by foreign capital and cultural influence (Banna 1974, 73).

Such was the setting of the birth of the Muslim Brotherhood in 1928. As Banna tells it, the Brotherhood was founded when several Egyptian laborers from the British camps beseeched him to deliver them from the

---

[2]Banna preferred to be called a *murshid* rather than *ra'is* (president) or *qa'id* (commander), although as the organization grew, he came to be known as *murshid al-'am*, literally "guide general" (R. Mitchell 1993, 299; Harris 1964, 154).

humiliation of foreign domination and guide them to the glory of Islam (Banna 1974, 74). From these modest beginnings, Banna worked relentlessly over the next two decades to build a broad base of membership for the Society of Muslim Brothers, along with a complex structure that facilitated tight discipline within the organization and mobilized members for continual outreach and indoctrination. This cadre would serve as the foot soldiers for a wide array of social welfare projects designed to improve the living conditions of ordinary Egyptians, such as establishing schools, providing sustenance for orphans as well as for the needy and sick, bringing electricity to villages, creating health clinics, and building mosques.[3] For Banna, such efforts were not only essential to sociomoral reconstruction but also critical for generating grass-roots support and recruiting new Brotherhood members.

The crises plaguing Egyptian politics at the time provided fertile soil for such efforts and strategies. A British protectorate since World War I, Egypt had been declared independent in 1922. Britain retained control over several domains of national politics, however, including security and foreign policy. Despite Egyptian independence then, actual power was split three ways between the often-conflicting interests of the Egyptian monarchy, the nationalist Wafd Party, and the British. The shifting alliances and animosities among these three poles of power frequently paralyzed the government, transforming what might have been an era of constitutional rule into a cauldron of intra-elite conflict and corruption (al-Sayyid Marsot 1977; 1985). The facade of Egyptian independence came under increasing strain during World War II, as nationalist agitation mounted and the British maneuvered aggressively to maintain control and facilitate Egyptian support for, or at least acquiescence to, the Allied cause.

While much of the Brotherhood's activities before 1936 were aimed at recruitment and social welfare programs, the years leading up to and during the Second World War marked Banna's ascendance as a powerful figure in Egyptian politics, as well as the expansion of Brotherhood activities to British Mandate Palestine in support of the Arab Rebellion (1937–39).[4] In 1941 Banna decided to run for elected office but agreed to withdraw when pressured by Wafdist officials. In exchange, Banna secured from the government a pledge to ease restrictions on the Brotherhood and curtail prostitution and alcohol consumption. In 1945 Banna again entered the field of electoral politics but was defeated along with

---

[3] The society also pursued several commercial and industrial projects (Harris 1964, 154–57).

[4] The Arab Rebellion was a coordinated effort among Palestinian Arabs to fight British colonial rule and prevent the transformation of Palestine into a Jewish state. It was critical to articulating the Arab claim to Palestine as well as to the emergence of a Palestinian national identity that transcended clan, class, and sectarian divisions.

other society candidates in what one scholar characterized as the most "obviously dishonest" election held in Egypt to date (R. Mitchell 1993, 33).

As the reins of the Egyptian government changed hands over the years, the Brotherhood continued to agitate from outside the formal institutions of government, pressing demands to liberate Egypt from British control, reverse the tide of secularism, and restore Islamic sovereignty over both public and private domains. As relations between the state and the Brotherhood grew progressively hostile, the Society would add to its structure a "secret apparatus" designed to defend Brothers against government harassment and pursue extralegal and at times violent jihad operations (R. Mitchell 1993, 32). The Brotherhood now "operated on the edge of, or beneath the surface of, Egyptian political life" and increasingly took on the characteristics of a resistance movement (Harris 1964, 158, 180, 182). It was in this climate that the prime minister of Egypt, Nuqrashi Pasha, issued a 1948 proclamation dissolving the Muslim Brotherhood, only to be assassinated shortly thereafter by one of its members. The next prime minister arranged to have Banna shot to death on February 12, 1949, thereby assuring the transformation of the Brotherhood leader into "the martyr of the nation."

Under Banna's leadership, the Muslim Brothers disseminated an array of publications and propaganda and even established its own press. The centerpiece of these efforts was Banna's "Epistles" (al-rasa'il). These tracts were largely written in response to specific events and ranged from letters to various Egyptian officials to pamphlets detailing the ideas, duties, and purposes of the Society for its expanding membership (R. Mitchell 1993, 13). Along with Banna's memoirs, these epistles presage many of the features of later radical Muslim thought both rhetorically and substantively. Several of these features have become well-known components of an Islamist lexicon. There is, for example, an analysis of the conditions of the Muslim umma in terms of infection, disease, diagnosis, and cure. There is a narrative of history in which Western ascendance is characterized as the triumph of and vehicle for materialism and moral bankruptcy. There is an insistence on Islam as a comprehensive way of life, a set of religio-political imperatives distorted by foreign domination and Western cultural corruption on the one hand, and Muslim impotence, sectarianism, and indifference on the other. There is a rejection of pacific forms of jihad in favor of the armed fight against unbelievers, preparations for which include physical training, moral self-discipline, and cultivating the "art of death" (R. Mitchell 1993, 207–8). And there is a sharp contrast between righteous Brothers and the array of hostile forces conspiring to persecute them and destroy the truths they aim to restore.

Banna's work also presages many less obvious features of contemporary Islamist thought. For instance, as in much of later Islamist rhetoric, Banna's writing tends to transform women's bodies and sexual behavior into symbols of moral purity or indices of cultural decay.[5] Like Qutb, Faraj, Bin Laden, and other Islamists without advanced religious training, moreover, Banna harbors bitter disappointment with members of the religious establishment, particularly those he claims place their own ambitions and interests above their vocation as custodians of Islam. In addition, Sufism is central to Banna's experience of Islam and his model of leadership, much as it would be to Qutb (although he would later disavow it) and Khomeini, whose own immersion in mysticism would undergird his claims for the special knowledge required for just Islamic rule (see chapter 1). Finally, by both argument and example, Banna insists that the multiple crises facing the Muslim umma require a commitment to action over words, deeds over slogans, practical over theoretical knowledge, unity over dissent. Untempered by Banna's love of learning, this emphasis on the primacy of action would devolve into the anti-intellectualist tendencies of Islamists such as Qutb and Faraj, those for whom the "life of the mind" is but a cowardly substitute for the "sweat and blood" of great deeds.

At the same time, there is a strain of pragmatism, compromise, and conciliation in Banna's thought and practice that differentiates him from many of the radical Islamists that followed, one that would serve as precedent and inspiration for such "moderate" Islamists as Nadia Yassine (see chapter 12). Here the contrast with Qutb in particular is instructive: in Qutb's later work, there is a pervasive sense of despair about a world enveloped by a new jahiliyya and a concomitant hardening of his thought around a stark polarity between good and evil, the solution to which is as radical as it is unspecific. By contrast, Banna's life and writing speak eloquently if didactically of his hope that individual and collective action in the service of concrete sociomoral programs might reform the world he was given. While profoundly critical of Egyptian politics, for example, Banna was not averse to playing by its rules, attempting to run for elected office not once, but twice. By the same token, much of the Brotherhood's early activities were geared toward gradualist transformation from the ground up rather than direct seizure of state power.

A man with astute political instincts, Banna insisted that the Brothers always calibrate action to circumstance. For much of his life, Banna sought with great effort to coax action out of acquiescence without acceding to the demands of (in his own words) "the overzealous and hasty," impatient to accomplish with force what could not be achieved through persuasion (Banna 1950, 22; Heyworth-Dunne 1950, 27–28). Hardly

---

[5] Consistent with this view, Banna established an "Institute for the Mothers of the Believers" in Isma'iliyya, a school meant to mobilize women in their role as mothers for the moral reform of the family. This eventually became the first chapter of the "Muslim Sisters." Banna asked Zaynab al-Ghazali (see chapter 11) to merge her own "Muslim Women's Association" into the organization and assume its leadership; she declined.

opposed to violent action on principle—although he took different positions depending upon his audience—Banna refused to be pushed into it
precipitously. He was quite explicit about the succession of phases integral to social transformation, insisting that "execution" may commence
only after the prior stages of "propaganda, education, and preaching" and
"selection, formation, and mobilization" (Banna 1950, 20, 21). Thus,
when confronted by the hadith, "He among you who sees an abomination must correct it with his hand; if he is unable, then with his tongue; if
he is unable, then with his heart. The last of these is the weakest of faith,"
Banna was known to respond with Qur'an 16:125: "Call unto the way
of thy Lord with wisdom and fair exhortation, and reason with them in
the better way. Lo! Thy Lord is best aware of him who strayeth from His
way and He is best aware of those who go aright."

These aspects of Banna's life and work situate him politically, intellectually, and historically between the radicalism of much of contemporary
Islamist thought and the reformism of such nineteenth-century Muslim
thinkers as Muhammad 'Abduh (d. 1905) and Jamal al-Din al-Afghani
[al-Asadabadi] (d.1897). Although quite critical of the reformists who
preceded him, Banna's agenda is in many ways continuous with their earlier efforts to excavate Islamic foundations to serve as a bulwark against
the encroachments of foreign power and the weakening of the umma
from within. Much as Afghani and 'Abduh sought to meet this double
challenge by recasting Islam and scientific truth as fundamentally harmonious, Banna insists that the neglect of science is a central cause of Muslim decline and repeatedly characterizes education in the natural and applied sciences as integral rather than antithetical to Islamic faith.

Indeed, despite the fact that the caliphate had been abolished in 1924,[6]
the geopolitical landscape in which Banna found himself posed a challenge that his predecessors would also have recognized, one in which allegiance to an Islamic umma defined not by territory but by faith required
increasing justification in the face of crosscutting national and ethnic loy-
alties. So understood, Banna's endeavors may be seen as confronting the

---

[6]The Caliphate is an institution of rule whose origins are located in questions about who
would lead the Muslim community in the wake of the Prophet Muhammad's death and
about the appropriate criterion for succession. Here, too, are the origins of what would become the sectarian division between Shi'a and Sunnis. Those who believed that the Prophet's son-in-law and cousin, 'Ali, had already been designated as successor became known as
the Shi'a (literally: "partisans" of 'Ali). Those who believed that the question of succession
was to be determined by the community were called Sunnis, or those who followed the
sunna (the normative example of the Prophet). The evolution of the Caliphate both as an
institution and a theory of political power over the centuries reflects various historical, political, economic, cultural, and regional transformations in different Muslim societies too
complex to encapsulate. By the eighteenth century, however, the multiethnic Ottoman Empire had claimed the mantle of the Caliphate, but that was to be undone in the early decades
of the twentieth century: the Ottoman Empire was dismembered at the end of World War I
and the Caliphate abolished in 1924 by the architect of the Turkish state, Mustafa Kemal.

very question that had so preoccupied earlier Muslim reformists: to what extent and in what form can the Islamic tradition and the umma built upon it survive and flourish in a modern landscape increasingly defined by the authority of scientific rationality, the sovereignty of the nation-state, and the dominance of the West? It is in part because of Banna's efforts and example that, for generations of Islamists to come, the answer would be clear and the question itself unnecessary.

# TOWARD THE LIGHT

In the Name of God, the Merciful, the Compassionate!

## PREFACE

In Rajab 1366 [May–June 1947], the imam and martyr Hasan al-Banna, Supreme Guide of the Muslim Brotherhood, sent this message to His Majesty Faruq I, King of Egypt and the Sudan, His Excellency Mustafa al-Nahhas Pasha, his then prime minister, and to the kings, princes, and rulers of the various countries of the Islamic world, as well as to a great number of civic and religious leaders in those countries. We are now publishing and distributing it once more. Many of the viewpoints and directives it contains still represent the dearest hope of every Arab and every Muslim. Let us pray God that it be fulfilled!

> In the Name of God, the Merciful, the Compassionate! Praise be unto God, and may God bless and save Our Master Muhammad, his House, and his Companions. "Our Lord, grant us Your mercy, and find us a good way out of our ordeal" [Q 18:10].

Cairo, Egypt, Rajab 1366

Your Excellency,

Peace be with you, and God's mercy and blessings! To proceed: all that impels us to submit this message to Your Excellency is a keen desire to guide the nation, whose leadership God has placed in your care and whose affairs He has delegated to you during its modern era, in a benevolent manner which will set it on the most excellent of paths, trace out for it the best of programs, protect it from shocks and disturbances, and spare it protracted and painful experiences.

Beyond this, we desire no more than to have done our duty and submitted our advice . . . for God's reward is better and more lasting.

## THE SHEPHERD'S RESPONSIBILITY

Your Excellency,

God has delegated rulership over this nation to you and has made its interests, its affairs, its present and its future your trust and your charge:

you are responsible for all of these before God (Blessed and Almighty is He!). If the present generation is your instrument, the coming generation is your product. How mighty is this trust, and how great this responsibility, that a man should be held answerable for a nation: [A hadith reads] "Each of you is a shepherd, and each is responsible for his flock." In ancient times, the Just Imam [the second caliph, 'Umar ibn al-Khattab, 634–44] said: "If a mule were to stumble in Iraq, I would hold myself responsible for her before God (Blessed and Almighty is He!), as to why I had not leveled the road for her." The imam 'Umar ibn al-Khattab depicted the immensity of his responsibility in a saying of his: "How I would like to come out of it evenly—owning nothing and owing nothing!"

## Introduction

### A. A Period of Transition

The most dangerous period in the life of nations, and the most deserving of critical study, is the period of transition from one state of affairs to another. It is then that plans for the new period are laid and its guiding principles and policies drawn up, according to which, it is expected, the nation will be formed and to which it will adhere. If these plans, principles, and policies are clear-cut, sound, and solid, the nation will rejoice in this triumph, and its guides, because of this well-being, will have a great reward, eternal fame, the just verdict of history, and fair renown.

### B. At the Crossroads

This important task poses two conditions: the first is the liberation of the nation from its political bonds so that it may obtain its freedom and regain its lost independence and sovereignty.

The second is its reconstruction, so that it may take its own way among the nations and compete with these others in its progress toward social perfection.

For the time being, the political struggle has come to a halt, and you have begun, along with the nation, to face a new period. Now you will see two ways before you, each one urging you to orient the nation in its direction and to proceed with it along its path. Each one has its particular characteristics, its advantages, its effects, its results, its propagandists, and its promoters. The first is the way of Islam, its fundamental assumptions, its principles, its culture, and its civilization; the second is the way of the West, the external features of its life, its organization, and its procedures. It is our belief that the first way, the way of Islam, its principles and its fundamental assumptions, is the only way that ought to be followed, and toward which the present and future nation should be oriented.

## C. Advantages of the Islamic Orientation

If we take the nation along this path, we shall be able to obtain many benefits—among them the fact that the Islamic way has been tried before and that history has testified as to its soundness. It has produced for the benefit of mankind an umma that is one of the strongest, most excellent, most merciful, most godly, and most blessed for all of humanity. It possesses a sanctity and stability in the minds of men that makes it easy for all to adopt it, to understand it, and to respond to it, as well as to adhere to it once they are properly oriented to it, to say nothing of pride in nationalism and the extolment of sincere patriotism. For then we will construct our lives on our own principles and fundamental assumptions, taking nothing from others. Herein lie the highest ideals of social and existential independence, after political independence.

To take this course means to strengthen Arab unity, in the first place; and in the second, to strengthen Islamic unity. The Islamic world in its entirety will support us through its spirit, its sensibility, its sympathy, and its endorsement and will see in us brethren whom it will stand behind as they stand behind it, and whom it will support as they support it. And herein lies a great moral advantage that no intelligent person will spurn.

This course is complete and all-encompassing, guaranteeing the establishment of the most excellent institutions for public life in the nation, both practically and spiritually. This is the advantage that distinguishes Islam, for it places the institutions of the life of nations on two important bases: adherence to the good, and avoidance of the harmful.

If we pursue this path, we shall be able to avoid the vital problems that beset the other nations, which have neither known of this way nor followed it. Indeed, we shall be able to solve many complicated problems that present institutions are unable to, and here we cite the words of Bernard Shaw: "How much the world in the modern age needs a man like Muhammad to solve its stubborn, complicated problems over a cup of coffee."

After all this, if we follow this path, God's support will stand behind us, fortifying us at moments of weakness, sustaining us in difficulties, easing our toil for us, and urging us forward: "Do not falter in pursuing the people; if you suffer, they suffer as do you, and you hope from God that which they do not. God is Knowing, Wise" (Q 4:104).

## D. Western Civilization Today

In concluding this discussion, we assert that the civilization of the West, which was brilliant by virtue of its scientific perfection for a long time, and which subjugated the whole world with the products of this science to its states and nations, is now bankrupt and in decline. Its foundations are crumbling, and its institutions and guiding principles are falling apart. Its political foundations are being destroyed by dictatorships, and its economic foundations are being swept away by crises. The millions of its wretched unemployed and hungry offer their testimony against it, while its social foundations are being undermined by deviant ideologies and revolutions that are breaking out everywhere. Its people are at a loss as to the proper measures to be taken and are wandering far astray. Their congresses are failures, their treaties are broken, and their covenants torn to pieces: their League of Nations is a phantasm, possessing neither spirit nor influence, while their strong men, along with other things, are overthrowing its covenant of peace and security.

This is one side of the matter. Meanwhile, on the other side too, they are being dealt violent blows, so that the world, thanks to these tyrannical and self-seeking policies, has become like a ship in the midst of the sea, with its captain distraught while blustering gales assault it on all sides. All of humanity is tormented, wretched, worried, and confused, having been scorched by the fires of greed and materialism. They are in dire need of some sweet portion of the waters of True Islam to wash from them the filth of misery and lead them to happiness.

The leadership of the world was at one time in the hands of the East entirely; then it fell to the West after the rise of the Greeks and Romans. After that, the Mosaic, Christian, and Muhammadan dispensations brought it back to the East for a second time, but then the East fell into its long sleep, and the West enjoyed a new rebirth. It was God's *sunna* (the normative example of the Prophet) that may not be gainsaid, and the West inherited world leadership. But lo and behold! It was tyrannical and unjust, insolent, misguided, and stumbling blindly, and it only remained for a strong Eastern power to exert itself under the shadow of God's banner, with the standard of the Qur'an fluttering at its head, and backed up by the powerful, unyielding soldiery of the faith. And there was the world turned Muslim and at peace, and the universe singing out: "Praise be unto God who guided us to this, for truly we had not been guided if God had not guided us" (Q 7:43).

This is not in the least a product of the imagination: this is no other than the true verdict of history. And if it is not fulfilled through us, "Then God will bring a people whom He loves and who love Him, humble toward believers and powerful against unbelievers, striving in the way of God, and fearing not the reproach of any reproacher. That is the bounty of God, which He brings to whom He will" (Q 5:54).

## ISLAM IS GUARANTEED TO SUPPLY THE RENASCENT NATION WITH ITS NEEDS

No regime in this world will supply the renascent nation with what it requires in the way of institutions, principles, objectives, and sensibilities to the same extent that Islam supplies every one of its renascent nations. The Noble Qur'an is full of passages descriptive of this particular aspect, and contains numerous exemplary parables concerning it—in general or in detail—while it deals with these aspects clearly and precisely. No nation adheres to it without succeeding in its aspirations.

## A. Islam and Hope

A renascent nation needs a broad, all-encompassing hope, and the Qur'an has supplied its nations with this consciousness in a manner that creates out of a dead nation one that is all life, ambition, hope, and determination. It is enough that it labels despair the road to unbelief, and hopelessness a manifestation of error.

In fact, if only the weakest nation heard these words of the Almighty: "And We desired to show favor to those who had been rendered weak on the earth, and to make them leaders, and to make them inheritors, and to make them strong on the earth" (Q 28:5–6).

And in the words of the Almighty: "Falter not, nor grieve, for you will be paramount if you are believers. If a wound touches you, a wound like it has already touched the people. These are the days which We apportion to mankind in turn" (Q 3:139–40).

And in the words of the Almighty: "He it is who expelled those of the People of the Book [Christians and Jews] who disbelieved from their abodes at the first gathering. You did not think that they would go forth, and you thought that their fortresses would render them impregnable to God. But God came to them from whence they had not reckoned, and He cast terror into their hearts, while they made ruins of their homes by their own hands and the hands of the believers. Consider then, O you who have eyes!" (Q 59:2).

And in the words of the Almighty: "Do you suppose that you will enter the Garden without first having suffered like those before you? They were afflicted by misfortune and hardship, and they were so shaken that even [their] messenger and the believers with him cried, 'When will God's help arrive?' Truly, God's help is near" (Q 2:214).

Truly the weakest of nations, if it heard these good tidings and read the real stories pertinent to them, would absolutely emerge thereafter as the strongest of nations in faith and spirit. It would unquestionably see in this hope encouragement to plunge into difficulties, however severe they might be, and to confront events, however overwhelming, until it won the perfection to which it aspired.

## B. Islam and National Greatness

The renascent nations need to glory in their nationalism as a superior and splendid nation with its own merits and its own history, so that its image will be imprinted on the minds of its sons, and they will offer up their blood and their lives on behalf of this splendor and nobility, and work for the welfare of this fatherland and for its aggrandizement and prosperity. We will not see this ideal clearly in any regime to be as just, excellent, and merciful as it is in True Islam. For if the nation knows that its nobility and honor have been sanctified by God in His fore-knowledge, and that He has registered it in His unswerving Book—for as He, the Blessed and Almighty, says: "You are the best nation which has been brought forth for mankind" (Q 3:110); and in the words of the Almighty: "We have made you [believers] into a just community, so that you may bear witness [to the truth] before others and so that the Messenger may bear witness [to it] before you" (Q 2:143); "Greatness belongs to God, and to His Apostle, and to the believers" (Q 63:8)—then it is the nation most worthy of sacrificing the world and all it contains for its God-given greatness.

The modern nations have labored to foster this ideal firmly in the minds of their youth, men, and boys alike; thus we hear: "Germany above all!" and "Italy above all!" and "Rule, Britannia!" But the difference between the sentiments that the Islamic ideology fosters and the sentiments fostered by these slogans and ideologies is that the sentiments of the Muslim seek to rise to communion with God, whereas the sentiments of the non-Muslim do not go beyond the literal import of the words. Furthermore, in creating these sentiments, Islam defined its goal, made it a stringent duty to keep to it, and proclaimed that it was not a matter of chauvinism or false pride, but of leading the world to its welfare. Concerning this, He, the Blessed and Almighty, says: "You command the good and forbid the evil, and believe in God" (Q 3:110).

This implies the support of virtue and the combating of vice, and reverence for the ideal as well as bearing it in mind while performing any act. Therefore, these sentiments, by virtue of their hold upon the early Muslims, produced the maximal justice and mercy reported historically of any of the nations. On the other hand, the ideology of domination in the minds of the Western nations did not define its goal without involving a fallacious chauvinism, and therefore it brought about internecine warfare and aggression against weak nations. In this respect, the Islamic ideology adopted the best course and sought to instill it in its sons and to turn them away from anything characterized by wickedness and oppression. Islam has extended the domain of the Islamic fatherland and has ordained toil for its welfare and self-sacrifice for the sake of its freedom and greatness. According to the Islamic understanding, the fatherland comprises: (1) the particular country first of all; (2) then it extends to the other Islamic countries, for all of them are a fatherland and an abode for the Muslim; (3) then it proceeds to the first Islamic Empire which the Pious Ancestors erected with their dear and precious blood, and over which they raised God's banner. Their monuments within it still extol their superiority and grandeur; and for all these regions, the Muslim will be asked before God (Blessed and Almighty is He!) why he did not labor to restore it. (4) Then the fatherland of the Muslim expands to encompass the entire world. Do you not hear the words of God (Blessed and Almighty is He!): "Fight them until there is no more persecution, and worship is devoted to God" (Q 2:193)?

Thus did Islam reconcile the sentiments of local nationalism with that of a common nationalism, with all the benefits thereof for all of humanity: "O mankind, We created you male and female, and We created you peoples and tribes, that you might know one another" (Q 49:13).

## C. Islam and the Armed Forces

Similarly, renascent nations require strength, and need to implant the military spirit in their sons, especially in these times when peace can be guaranteed only by preparedness for war, and when the slogan of all their sons is: "Strength is the surest way to guarantee the enforcement of justice."

Islam did not overlook this factor but, as a matter of fact, made it a stringent duty and did not differentiate in any way between it and prayer or fasting. In the entire world, no regime has concerned itself with this factor, neither in antiquity nor in modern times, to the extent that Islam has in the Qur'an, and in the Traditions and life of the Apostle of God (may God bless and save him!). You can see this presented in clear and exemplary fashion in the words of the Almighty: "And prepare against them such force and troops of horses as you can, by which to frighten the enemies of God and your enemies" (Q 8:60). And in the words of the Almighty: "Fighting is prescribed for you, though it be detestable to you. But it may be that you detest something which is good for you, and it may be that you love something which is bad for you" (Q 2:216).

And have you ever seen a military proclamation in a sacred book read aloud in prayer, *dhikr* (invocation, remembrance of Allah), public worship and private communion with God, like the proclamation that begins with an abrupt command in the words of the Almighty: "Let those of you who are willing to trade the life of this world for the life to come, fight in God's way" (Q 4:74). Then He specifies the reward immediately afterward: "To anyone who fights in God's way, whether killed or victorious, We shall give a great reward" (Q 4:74).

Then follows an exhortation to arouse the noblest sentiments in men's hearts, namely, the deliverance of the people and the fatherland, as He says: "What ails you that you do not fight in the way of God and for those rendered weak—men, women, and children— who say: 'Our Lord, bring us forth from this city whose people are unjust, and appoint for us from Thyself a guardian, and appoint for us from Thyself a Protector!'" (Q 4:75).

Then He shows them the nobility of their goal and the baseness of their enemies' goal, demonstrating clearly that they are sacrificing something of great value—their lives—for a precious commodity that deserves it and exceeds it in value—God's approval—while non-Muslims are fighting with no goal before them. Therefore, they are weaker in spirit and more confused in their hearts. He, the Almighty, says: "Those who believe fight in the way of God, and those who disbelieve fight in the way of idolatry, so fight the auxiliaries of Satan! Truly the wiles of Satan are weak" (Q 4:76).

Then He upbraids those who shirked doing their duty, taking the easy way out and abandoning the difficult demands of heroism, and shows them their mistake in adopting this attitude. He shows them that boldness would not harm them one bit and that they would reap the great reward, whereas abstention profits them nothing, because death lies before them in any event. Directly following the preceding verses, He says: "[Prophet], do you not see those who were told, 'Restrain yourselves from fighting, perform the prayer, and pay the prescribed alms?' When fighting was ordained for them, some of them feared men as much as, or even more than, they feared God, saying 'Lord, why have You ordained fighting for us? If only You would give us just a little more time.' Say to them, 'Little is the enjoyment in this world, the Hereafter is far better for those who are mindful of God; you will not be wronged by as much as the fiber in a date stone. Death will overtake you no matter where you may be, even inside high towers'" (Q 4:77–78).

By your Lord, what military proclamation is there possessing such force and clarity as this, which will awaken within the soldier's breast all the zeal, pride, and faith the commander desires?

And if the mainstay of military life according to their practice consisted of two things—discipline and obedience—God has conjoined them in two verses from His Book, when He, the Blessed and Almighty, says: "Truly God loves those who fight in His way, in ranks, as if they were a solidly constructed building" (Q 61:4). And as He, the Almighty, says: "And more fitting for them are obedience and civil speech" (Q 47:20–21).

And if you read what Islam prescribes concerning the preparation of equipment, the provisioning of the armed forces, the teaching of archery, the sheltering of horses, the virtue of the *shahada* (martyrdom), the wage of jihad, the reward for expenditures made on its behalf, the consideration due those who campaign in it, the comprehension of its varieties—you will see all these treated exhaustively, whether in noble Qur'anic verses, the honored Traditions, the pure prophetic biography, or the true Islamic jurisprudence: "Our Lord encompasses all things in knowledge" (Q 7:89).

The modern nations have paid close attention to this and have been founded on these principles: we see that Mussolini's Fascism, Hitler's Nazism, and Stalin's Communism are based on pure militarism. But there is a vast difference between all of these and the militarism of Islam, for the Islam that has sanctified force to such an extent has also preferred peace. Directly after the verses extolling force, the Blessed and Almighty says: "And if they incline to peace, then incline thou to it, and trust in God" (Q 8:61).

And it is He who defined the price of victory and its manifestations when He said: "God will surely aid one who aids Him. God is Mighty, Glorious! Those, who if We make them powerful on the earth, perform the prayer and pay the alms, and command the good and forbid the evil. For unto God belongs the consequence of affairs" (Q 22:40–4l).

And it is He who set down the basis of international military law, when He, the Almighty, said: "And if thou fearest treachery from any people, repudiate them likewise. Truly God does not love the treacherous" (Q 8:58).

For one particular ordinance, the counsel of the Apostle (may God bless and save him!) and his successors to the commanders of their armies stands out as the most remarkable manifestation of mercy and kindliness: "Commit no treachery, do not exceed the bounds, do not mutilate, do not kill women, children, and the aged, do not cut down fruit-bearing trees, and do not finish off the wounded. You will come across people who lead lives of devotion in hermitages: leave them and that to which they devote themselves, in peace."

This was the military force of Islam—comprising the police of justice and the security forces of law and order. As for the present military force of Europe, everyone knows that it comprises the army of injustice and the soldiery of greed. Which of the two sides is of loftier stature and greater magnanimity?

### D. Islam and Public Health

Because renascent nations need a superior military force, and the mainstay of such a force is physical health and strength, the Qur'an has made allusion to this concept while narrating the story of a struggling nation that took on the task of bearing the burden of fighting for the sake of its freedom, independence, and self-formation. For God chose for it a leader who was equally strong in mind and body and made physical strength one of his chief supports in bearing his burden. This is what the Noble Qur'an relates concerning the Children of Israel and the confirmation of their leader, Saul: "Indeed God has chosen him above you and has increased him signally in knowledge and robustness" (Q 2:247).

The Apostle (may God bless and save him!) has commented on this idea in many of his Traditions and urged the believers to preserve their bodily strength, just as he urged them regarding their spiritual strength. The veracious Traditions say: "The strong believer is better than the weak believer." And: "Truly your body has a right over you." The Apostle of God (may God bless and save him!) often expounded the principles of public health to the umma, especially concerning preventive medicine, the more excellent of the two aspects of medicine. He (may God bless and save him!) said: "We are a people who do not eat unless we are hungry, and when we eat, it is not to satiety." And as to his seeking (may God bless and save him!) for water to drink, the Traditions say: "He (may God bless and save him!) used to look for sweet water." And he forbade urinating and defecating in stagnant water and declared a quarantine against plague-ridden countries and their populations so that they should not leave them nor any outsider enter them. And finally, he (may God bless and save him!) paid much attention to physical culture, such as archery, swimming, horsemanship, and running, and urged his umma to practice them and show interest in them. There is even a Tradition that states: "He who once knew archery and then forgot it, is not one of mine." And he (may God bless and save him!) stringently forbade celibacy, monasticism, and the tormenting and weakening of the body in order to draw near to God (blessed and almighty is He!). In all these matters he guided the umma in the direction of moderation. All of this testifies to Islam's deep concern for the health of the umma at large, to the strenuous efforts it made in order to safeguard it, and to its receptivity to anything that might conduce to its welfare and happiness in this important respect.

## E. Islam and Science

Just as nations need power, so do they need the science that will buttress this power and direct it in the best possible manner, providing them with all their requirements in the way of inventions and discoveries. Islam does not reject science; indeed, it makes it as obligatory as the acquisition of power and gives it its support. It suffices to say that the very first verse of the Book of God to be revealed says: "Recite, in the Name of thy Lord who created; created man from a clot of blood. Recite, for thy Lord is the Most Generous, who taught man with the pen; taught man what he did not know" (Q 96:1–5).

The Apostle of God (May God bless and save him!) stipulated as part of the ransom for the polytheist captured at Badr[7] that one of these prisoners teach ten Muslim children reading and writing, in the endeavor to wipe out illiteracy from the umma. God did not make the learned and the ignorant equal. He, the Blessed, the Almighty, says: "Are those who know and those who do not know equal? Only those who possess understanding are mindful" (Q 39:11). Islam has given the

[7]The Battle of Badr (624) was the first major military encounter between the Muslims, who had emigrated from Mecca to Medina in 622, and the polytheists of Muhammad's hometown, Mecca.

same weight to the ink of scholars as to the blood of martyrs. The
Qur'an links science and power together in two noble verses: "For why
should not a few from every group of them march out as a party, so that
they may gain knowledge of religion and warn their people when they
return to them? Perhaps they will beware. O ye who believe, fight those
unbelievers who are close to you, and let them encounter harshness in
you, and know ye that God is with the godfearing" (Q 9:122–23).

The Qur'an does not distinguish between secular and religious science
but advocates both, summing up the natural sciences in one verse,
expostulating on their behalf and making knowledge of them a means
of reverencing Him and a path toward knowing Him. This is what the
Almighty says: "Have you [Prophet] not considered how God sends
water down from the sky?" (Q 35:27). Here there is an allusion to
astronomy and the celestial sphere and to the connection between
heaven and earth. Then the Almighty says: "We produce with it fruits
of varied colors" (Q 35:27). Here there is an allusion to the science of
botany and its marvels and wonders and to its chemistry.

"[T]here are in the mountains layers of white and red of various
hues, and jet black" (Q 35:27). Here there is an allusion to the science
of geology, the strata of the Earth and their modes and types. "[T]here
are various colors among human beings, wild animals, and livestock
too" (Q 35:28). Here there is an allusion to the science of biology and
animals in their divisions of mankind and smaller and larger beasts. Do
you think that this verse has left out any of the natural sciences? To all
of this the Almighty appends: "The learned among His worshipers
alone fear God" (Q 35:28).

Have you not seen in this remarkable concatenation of verses that
God commands mankind to study nature and that He prompts them to
it, rendering the learned among them, by virtue of His arcana and His
secrets, the people who truly revere and know Him? O God, enlighten
the Muslims in their religion!

### F. Islam and Morality

The renascent nation, above all else, needs a code of morality . . . a
strong, unbending, and superior morality, together with a magnanimous
spirit fired by lofty aspirations. For it will have to face some demands of
the new age that cannot be answered except through the possession of a
strong and sincere morality founded on deep faith, unwavering con-
stancy, great self-sacrifice, and considerable tolerance. Islam alone can
create such a perfect soul, for it has made rectitude of the soul and its
purification the foundation of success. The Almighty says: "He who has
purified it will succeed: he who has corrupted it will fail" (Q 91: 9–10).

And it has made change in the affairs of nations contingent on change
within their moral character and the rectitude of their souls. He, the

Almighty, says: "Surely God will not change the circumstances of a people until they change what is in themselves" (Q 13:11).

You will hear penetrating verses dealing with individual aspects of higher morality, and you will see that they represent an insuperable force for correcting the soul, fortifying it, purifying it, and cleansing it, as He, the Almighty, says: "Of the believers are men who were sincere in their covenant with God, and of them are those who fulfilled their vow, and of them are those who are waiting, not having changed at all, for God to reward the sincere for their sincerity" (Q 33:23–24).

And concerning generosity, self-sacrifice, patience, tolerance, and surmounting obstacles: "And that is because neither thirst nor hardship nor hunger assails them in God's way, nor do they take a step that angers the unbelievers, nor do they gain anything from the enemy, but that a good deed is recorded on their behalf. Truly God does not lose the wage of the doers of good, nor do they spend little or much, nor do they cross a valley, but it is recorded for them, so that God may reward them for the best of what they were doing" (Q 9:120–21).

There is no agent like Islam to awaken the conscience, vivify the finer sentiments, and station a warder over the soul—the best of all warders—for apart from it, there is no organized body of law that will penetrate the depths of the heart or affairs kept hidden.

## G. Islam and Economics

The renascent nation needs above all to regulate its economic affairs, the most important question during these recent eras. Islam has not neglected this aspect, but rather has set down all its fundamental principles without exception. You may hear God (blessed and almighty is He!) speaking of the safeguarding of property, explaining its value and the necessity to be concerned with it: "Do not give the foolish your property of which God has appointed you the manager" (Q 4:5).

And He says, concerning the balancing out of expenditures and income: "Do not let thy hand be manacled to thy neck, or open it to its fullest extent" (Q 17:29).

And the Apostle of God (may God bless and save him!) says: "He who economizes will not be in need." What is true for the individual is just as true for the nation, as he (may God bless and save him!) says: "How excellent is righteous wealth for a righteous man!" Any good economic system is welcomed by Islam, which urges the nation to promote it and puts no obstacles in its path. Islamic jurisprudence is filled with rules for financial transactions, and it has given them in such minute detail as to obviate further elaboration.

Finally, when the nation possesses all these reinforcements—hope, patriotism, science, power, health, and a sound economy—it will, without a doubt, be the strongest of all nations, and the future will belong to it. This is especially true if to all these is added the fact that it has been purified of selfishness, aggressiveness, egotism, and arrogance and has come to desire the welfare of the whole world. Indeed, Islam has guaranteed this. . .

### H. The Public Institutions of Islam

This is one aspect of the perfection to be found in certain Islamic institutions, namely those concerned with the resurgence of nations, always remembering that we are facing a period of resurgence. As for reviewing all aspects of the perfection of all Islamic institutions, it would require bulky volumes and vast and far-flung investigations. Suffice it to discuss this perfection in a few concise words: the institutions of Islam with respect to the individual, the nation, and the family, in terms of both government and people, or the relations between nations—in all these respects, the institutions of Islam have combined both great breadth and precision and have chosen the common good as well as given it clear exposition. They are the most perfect and most beneficial institutions known to mankind and confirmed by painstaking research in every aspect of national life.

This judgment, which was once limited to particular persons, has now become general, and is attested to by every fair-minded individual. Whenever investigators delve into their researches, they uncover aspects of the perfection of these eternal institutions not previously discerned by their predecessors. God said in truth: "We shall show them Our signs on the horizons and in their souls until it is apparent to them that it is the truth. Is it not sufficient that thy Lord is a witness over all things?" (Q 41:53).

### ISLAM PROTECTS MINORITIES AND SAFEGUARDS THE RIGHTS OF FOREIGNERS

Excellency,
People imagine that adherence to Islam and making it the basis for regulating life are incompatible with the existence of non-Muslim minorities within the Islamic umma and with the unity of the various elements comprising the umma, which is one of the strongest supports of national revival during the present era. But the truth is precisely the contrary. Islam, which was originated by the Wise and Knowing One who knows the past, present, and future of the nations, took full cognizance of this problem, and solved it before it ever came up. Its holy and wise institutions had hardly been revealed when it already contained a clear and unambiguous text concerning the protection of minorities. Does mankind require anything more self-evident than this

text: "God does not forbid you to deal with those who have not fought against you in religion and have not driven you from your homes with benevolence, or to show them justice. Surely God loves those who are just" (Q 60:8).

This text does not merely include protection, but it also counsels benevolence and the doing of good on their behalf. Islam sanctified the unity of humanity as a whole, in the Almighty's saying: "O mankind, We have created you male and female and have made you nations and tribes that you may know one another" (Q 49:13).

In the same way, it sanctified universal religious unity, put an end to fanaticism, and ordained that its sons have faith in all the revealed religions. As the Almighty says: "Say [Prophet], 'No, [ours is] the religion of Abraham, the upright, who did not worship any god besides God.' So [you believers], say, 'We believe in God and in what was sent down to us and what was sent down to Abraham, Ishmael, Isaac, Jacob, and the Tribes, and what was given to Moses, Jesus, and all the prophets by their Lord. We make no distinction between any of them, and we devote ourselves to Him. So if they believe like you do, they will be rightly guided. But if they turn their backs, then they will be entrenched in opposition. God will protect you from them: He is the All Hearing, the All Knowing. And say [believers], '[Our life] takes its color from God, and who gives a better color than God?'" (Q 2:136–38).

Then it sanctified denominational religious unity without arrogance or aggressiveness. The Blessed and Almighty said: "The believers are no other than brothers. Therefore, make peace between your brothers and fear God; perhaps you will find mercy'" (Q 49:10).

This Islam, which was founded according to such a pattern of moderation and deep-rooted equity, could not possibly be the cause of its followers' disrupting a long continuing unity. On the contrary, it has endowed this unity with a character of religious holiness, though formerly it drew its strength solely from civil authority.

And Islam has defined very precisely those whom we ought to oppose and boycott, and with whom we should cut off all relations. Following the verse cited earlier (Q 60:8), the Almighty says: "God forbids you to befriend only those who fought you in religion, and drove you from your homes, or aided in driving you forth. Whosoever befriends them— they are wrongdoers" (Q 60:9).

No fair-minded person in the world would compel any nation to rest content with an internal enemy of this type, or any great discord among its sons, or any impairment of its internal organization.

This is Islam's position with respect to the non-Muslim minorities— clear, unambiguous, and free from injustice. Its position with respect to foreigners is one of peacefulness and sympathy, so long as they behave with rectitude and sincerity. But if their consciences grow corrupt and their crimes increase, the Qur'an has already defined the position we should take regarding them: "O you who believe! Do not take for confidants those who are not of you; they will not fail to hinder you; they are pleased by what troubles you. Hatred has been revealed out of their mouths; what their hearts conceal is yet greater. We have made the signs clear to you, if you would but understand. Behold, you love them, but they do not love you!" (Q 3:118–19).

And with this, Islam has dealt with all of these aspects as precisely, benevolently, and sincerely as possible.

## ISLAM IS NOT A DISTURBING INFLUENCE ON RELATIONS WITH THE WEST

Similarly, people may imagine that Islamic institutions in our modern life create estrangement between us and the Western nations and that they will muddy the clarity of our political relations with them just when these were on the point of being settled. This too is a notion rooted in pure fantasy. For those nations which are suspicious of us will like us no better whether we follow Islam or anything else. If they are truly our friends, and mutual trust exists between us, their own spokesmen and leaders have already declared that every nation is free to adopt whatever organization it wishes within its own borders, provided it does not infringe on the rights of others. It is up to all the leaders of these nations to understand that the honor of international Islam is the most sacred honor known to history and that the principles set down by international Islam to guard this honor and to preserve it are the most firmly fixed and solidly confirmed of principles.

It is Islam that spoke out for the safeguarding of treaties and fulfillment of obligations: "And keep the covenant, for of the covenant question will be made" (Q 17:34); "Except for those of the polytheists with whom you have a treaty, and who since then have not diminished you in any way and have not helped anyone against you—fulfill your covenant with them up to its stated term. Truly God loves the godfearing" (Q 9:4). And He said: "So long as they behave with rectitude toward you, behave with rectitude toward them" (Q 9:7). And He said, regarding the generous reception of refugees and the good neighborliness of those who receive them: "And if any one of the polytheists seeks refuge with thee, give him refuge so that he may hear God's discourses, then take him to a place of security" (Q 9:6).

If this is the treatment accorded polytheists, how do you suppose the People of the Book would be treated?

The Islam that prescribes these principles and takes its adherents along this path must surely be regarded by Westerners as guaranteeing still another type of security, namely, for themselves. We maintain that it would be to Europe's benefit if these sound concepts governed its own internal relations—this would be better for them and more enduring!

## The Fundamental Sources of the Renaissance in the East Are Not Those of the West

Excellency,

Among the causes which have impelled some of the Eastern nations to deviate from Islam, and to choose to imitate the West, was the study of the Western Renaissance made by their leaders, and their conviction that it was accomplished only by overthrowing religion, destroying churches, freeing themselves from papal authority, controlling the clergy and prelates, putting an end to all manifestations of religious authority in the nation, and definitively separating religion from the general policy of the state. If this is true in the case of the Western nations, it is absolutely untrue for the Islamic nations, because the nature of Islamic doctrines is quite unlike that of any other religion. The jurisdiction of the religious authorities in Islam is circumscribed and limited, powerless to alter its statutes or subvert its institutions, with the result that the fundamental principles of Islam, across the centuries, have kept pace with the changing eras and have advocated progress, supported learning, and defended scholars. What happened there is inappropriate for conditions here. There are extensive studies concerning this that take up many volumes: our purpose in this essay is to survey the subject briefly in order to bear it in mind and dispel all ambiguities. We are sure that every fair-minded person will agree with us on this basic principle; accordingly, it is simply not possible that this sentiment should be our guiding precept in our modern renaissance, which must first of all be sustained by the strong pillars of a high morality, a flourishing science, and far-reaching power, which is what Islam enjoins.

## The Clerics Are Not Religion Itself

One of the excuses adopted by some of those who followed the path of the Westerners was that they had begun to be aware of the course taken by the Muslim religious authorities, in view of their hostile attitude toward nationalist revival, their base activities against the nationalists and their alliance with the exploiters, and their choice of selfish interests and worldly ambitions over the welfare of the country and the nation. If true, this was a flaw within the religious establishment itself, not in the faith as such. Does the faith command such things? Or are they enjoined by the lives of the most virtuous and illustrious ‘ulama of the Islamic umma, who used to burst in upon kings and princes, past their gates and walls, censuring them, forbidding them, rejecting their gifts, declaring what the truth was before them, and bringing them the demands of the nation? Nay, they even took up arms in the face of tyranny and injustice! History has not yet forgotten the phalanx of legists in the ranks of Ibn al-Ash'ath[8] in the eastern region of the Islamic Empire, or the rebellion of the *qadi* (Muslim judge) Yahya b. Yahya al-Laythi al-Maliki[9] in its western region.

Such are the teachings of the faith, and such is the past history of the legists of Islam. Is there any trace in these of what they assert? Or is there any justice in compelling the faith to tolerate the followers of those who have deviated from it?

Nevertheless, even if these allegations hold true for some people, they do not hold for the totality. And if they can be substantiated for some particular circumstance, they are not so for all circumstances. This is the history of the modern renaissance in the East, so redolent of the attitudes of the Muslim religious authorities in every single nation. The position taken by al-Azhar [the preeminent Muslim mosque and university] in Egypt; by the [Arab] Higher Committee[10] in South Syria or Palestine, and North Syria or Lebanon; by Mawlana Abu'l-Kalam [Azad][11] and his brethren among the most illustrious of the Indian 'ulama; and by the Muslim leaders in Indonesia, is not forgotten nor is it alien. Therefore, these assertions must not be used as a pretext for diverting any nation from its religion simply in the name of nationalism; for is it not the most productive solution for a nation to reform its religious authorities and to be reconciled with them, rather than to adopt an annihilatory attitude toward them? Even if these expressions that have crept into our language by way of imitation, like "religious

---

[8]'Abd al-Rahman b. Muhammad b. al-Ash'ath (d. 704) was the commander of a military campaign sent by the Umayyad viceroy of Iraq, Hajjaj b. al-Yusuf, against a local ruler based in what is now Afghanistan. On the way, Ibn al-Ash'ath and his troops rebelled against Hajjaj, marching back to Iraq and posing a grave threat to the viceroy's authority. The revolt is remembered in Islamic history for, inter alia, the participation of a large number of religious scholars in it.

[9]Yahya b. Yahya al-Laythi (d. 848) was a Berber religious scholar credited with having played a key role in establishing the Maliki school of law in Muslim Spain. He is known to have participated in a revolt against al-Hakam I, the Umayyad ruler of Spain, which is the incident to which Banna refers here. He later emerged as the most influential religious scholar at the court of the Umayyad ruler 'Abd al-Rahman II.

[10][Editors' note: endnotes 10–12 are reproduced from the Wendell translation, with some changes]. The Arab Higher Committee was formed in 1936 in Palestine under the presidency of the grand mufti of Jerusalem, al-Hajj Amin al-Husayni. It succeeded a number of Arab nationalist committees and associations that had come into existence from 1920 on, to protest and counter Zionist aspirations in the mandated territory. It was recognized as the official representative for the Arab point of view by the British administration, but it was subsequently outlawed in 1937 because of excesses committed during the Arab Rebellion of 1936–39, and because of the collaboration of the Mufti and other Arab leaders with the governments of the Fascist states of Italy and Germany.

[11]Abu'l-Kalam Azad (1888–1958), a noted Indian theologian, editor of the influential Muslim newspaper *Al-Hilal* in Calcutta from 1912 to 1914. He was a prolific writer in Urdu and one of the outstanding Muslim political and intellectual leaders of the twentieth century. During his last years, he was minister of education in the government of India.

authorities," do not accord with our own usage—because this one is peculiar to the West, in the sense of "clergy"—it includes every Muslim, according to the Islamic usage, for all Muslims from the least to the most outstanding of them, are "religious authorities."

## A BOLD STEP BUT A SUCCESSFUL ONE

Excellency,

After all the foregoing, it would be inexcusable for us to turn aside from the path of truth—the path of Islam—and to follow the path of fleshly desires and vanities—the path of Europe. Along the path of Europe are to be found outer show and cheap tinsel, pleasures and luxuries, laxity and license, and comforts that captivate the soul, for all of these things are loved by the soul, as the Almighty says: "Made beautiful for mankind is the love of fleshly desires for women, and children, and heaped-up mounds of gold and silver, and branded horses, and cattle, and tilled land. That is the comfort of this world" (Q 3:14).

But the path of Islam is glory, impregnability, truth, strength, blessedness, rectitude, stability, virtue, and nobility. Follow it along with the umma, may God grant you success! "[Prophet] say, 'Would you like me to tell you of things that are better than all of these? Their Lord will give those who are mindful of God gardens graced with flowing streams, where they will stay with pure spouses and God's good pleasure—God is fully aware of His servants'" (Q 3:15).

Luxuries only annihilate nations, and its comforts and coveted possessions have only convulsed Europe: "When We wish to destroy a town, We command those corrupted by wealth [to reform], but they [persist in their] disobedience; Our sentence is passed, and We destroy them utterly" (Q 17:16).

God (blessed and almighty is He!) sent His Apostle as a mercy to the world until the Day of Resurrection, and sent His Book with him as a light and guidance until the Day of Resurrection. The leadership of the Apostle (May God bless and save him!) survives in his sunna, and the authority of the Qur'an is secure through his proof. Humanity is marching inevitably toward them both, with the might of the mighty and the humility of the humble, from near and from afar, so that God's Word should be realized—"to show that it is above all [other] religions" (Q 9:33).

Be the first to come forward in the name of God's Apostle (may God bless and save him!) bearing the vial of Qur'anic healing, to save the tormented, sick world! It is a bold step, but one crowned with success, God willing (Blessed and Almighty is He!), for God is victorious in His affairs: "Then the believers will rejoice in God's succor. He succors whom He will, for He is the Mighty, the Merciful" (Q 30:4–5).

## SOME STEPS TOWARD PRACTICAL REFORM

Excellency,

Having given a clear presentation of the spiritual mood that should prevail within the nation in its modern renaissance, we would like to point out, by way of conclusion, some of the practical manifestations and results which this mood should dictate. We are going to mention here only the broadest topics, because we are well aware that each one of these questions demands extensive and intensive study, taxing the energies and capacities of specialists. We know too that we have not yet plumbed all the puzzling problems and demands of the nation or all the manifestations of the renaissance. We do not believe that the fulfillment of these demands is a mere trifle that can be accomplished overnight, and we know that before many of them there are manifold obstacles that will require vast patience, great wisdom, and keen determination. We know all this and can take it in our stride. And besides this, we know that, where there is genuine resolve, the way will be made plain, and that if a strong-willed nation chooses the path of goodness, it shall, by God Almighty's will, attain what it desires. Stride forward, and God will be with you! Following are the principal goals of reform grounded on the spirit of genuine Islam:

First: Political, judicial, and administrative:
1. An end to party rivalry, and a channeling of the political forces of the nation into a common front and a single phalanx
2. A reform of the law, so that it will conform to Islamic legislation in every branch
3. A strengthening of the armed forces, and an increase in the number of youth groups—the inspiration of the latter with zeal on the bases of Islamic jihad
4. A strengthening of the bonds between all Islamic countries, especially the Arab countries, to pave the way for practical and serious consideration of the matter of the departed caliphate
5. The diffusion of the Islamic spirit throughout all departments of the government, so that all its employees will feel responsible for adhering to Islamic teachings
6. The surveillance of the personal conduct of all its employees and an end to the dichotomy between the private and professional spheres
7. Setting the hours of work in summer and winter ahead, so that it will be easy to fulfill religious duties, and so that keeping late hours will come to an end

8. An end to bribery and favoritism, with consideration given only to capability and legitimate reasons [for advancement]
9. Weighing all acts of the government in the scales of Islamic wisdom and doctrine; the organization of all celebrations, receptions, official conferences, prisons, and hospitals so as not to be incompatible with Islamic teaching; the arranging of work schedules so that they will not conflict with hours of prayer
10. The employment of graduates of al-Azhar in military and administrative positions, and their training

Second: Social and educational:
1. Conditioning the people to respect public morality and the issuance of directives fortified by the aegis of the law on this subject; the imposition of severe penalties for moral offenses
2. Treatment of the problem of women in a way that combines the progressive and the protective, in accordance with Islamic teaching, so that this problem—one of the most important social problems—will not be abandoned to the biased pens and deviant notions of those who err in the directions of deficiency or excess
3. An end to prostitution, both clandestine and overt: the recognition of fornication, whatever the circumstances, as a detestable crime whose perpetrator must be flogged
4. An end to gambling in all its forms—games, lotteries, racing, and gambling-clubs
5. A campaign against drinking, as there is one against drugs: its prohibition, and the salvation of the nation from its effects
6. A campaign against ostentation in dress and loose behavior; the instruction of women in what is proper, with particular strictness as regards female instructors, pupils, physicians, and students, and all those in similar categories
7. A review of the curricula offered to girls and the necessity of making them distinct from the boys' curricula in many of the stages of education
8. Segregation of male and female students; private meetings between men and women, unless within the permitted degrees [of relationship],[12] to be counted as a crime for which both will be censured

[12] The "permitted degrees" are defined in Q 24:31: "And say to the believing women that they lower their eyes and guard their private parts, and display not their adornments except for that which is external; and let them throw their veils over their bosoms, and let them not display their adornments except to their husbands, or their fathers, or their fathers-in-law, or their sons, or their husbands' sons, or their brothers, or their brothers' sons, or their

9. The encouragement of marriage and procreation, by all possible means; promulgation of legislation to protect and give moral support to the family, and to solve the problems of marriage

10. The closure of morally undesirable ballrooms and dance halls, and the prohibition of dancing and other such pastimes

11. The surveillance of theaters and cinemas and a rigorous selection of plays and films

12. The expurgation of songs and a rigorous selection and censorship of them

13. The careful selection of lectures, songs, and subjects to be broadcast to the nation; the use of radio broadcasting for the education of the nation in a virtuous and moral way

14. The confiscation of provocative stories and books that implant the seeds of skepticism in an insidious manner and of newspapers that strive to disseminate immorality and capitalize indecently on lustful desires

15. The supervision of summer vacation areas so as to do away with the wholesale confusion and license that nullify the basic aims of vacationing

16. The regulation of business hours for cafés; surveillance of the activities of their regular clients; instructing these as to what is in their best interest; withdrawal of permission from cafés to keep such long hours

17. The utilization of these cafés for teaching illiterates reading and writing; toward this end, the assistance of the rising generation of elementary schoolteachers and students

18. A campaign against harmful customs, whether economic, moral, or anything else; turning the masses away from these and orienting them in the direction of ways beneficial to them, or educating them in a way consonant with their best interests. These involve such customs as those having to do with weddings, funerals, births, the zar,[13] civil and religious holidays, etc. Let the government set a good example in this respect.

---

sisters, or their sisters' sons, or their women, or what their right hands possess, or such men as attend them having no desire, or small children having no knowledge of women's private parts; and let them not stamp their feet so that what they conceal of their adornments becomes known. And turn to God, all of you, O believers, and perhaps you will prosper." The phrase "what their right hands possess" refers to slaves, but whether only to female slaves, or also male slaves and eunuchs is disputed by the jurists. The phrase "such men as attend them having no desire" is generally taken to mean eunuchs, very aged men of good character, or even simpletons without sexual appetites or experience.

[13]Zar is a non-Arabic word denoting a spirit, a master who communes with them, or a ritual exorcism of spirits; it is considered by Banna a heterodox practice of non-Islamic origins.

19. Due consideration for the claims of moral censorship, and punishment of all who are proved to have infringed upon any Islamic doctrine or attacked it, such as breaking the fast of Ramadan, willful neglect of prayers, insulting the faith, or any such act

20. The annexation of the elementary village schools to the mosques, and a thoroughgoing reform of both, as regards employees, cleanliness, and overall custodial care, so that the young may be trained in prayer and the older students in learning

21. The designation of religious instruction as a subject in all schools, in each according to its type, as in the universities

22. Active instigation to memorize the Qur'an in all the free elementary schools; making this memorization mandatory for obtaining diplomas in the areas of religion and [Arabic] language; the stipulation that a portion of it be memorized in every school

23. The promulgation of a firm educational policy which will advance and raise the level of education, and will supply it, in all its varieties, with common goals and purposes, which will bring the different cultures represented in the nation closer together and will make the first stage of its process one dedicated to inculcating a virtuous, patriotic spirit and an unwavering moral code

24. The cultivation of Arabic language instruction; the use of Arabic alone, as opposed foreign language, in the primary stages

25. The cultivation of Islamic history, and of the national history and national culture, and the history of Islamic civilization

26. Consideration of ways to arrive gradually at a uniform mode of dress for the nation

27. An end to the foreign spirit in our homes with regard to language, manners, dress, governesses, nurses, etc., with all these to be Egyptianized, especially in upper-class homes

28. To give journalism a proper orientation and to encourage authors and writers to undertake Islamic, Eastern subjects

29. Attention to be given to matters of public health by disseminating health information through all media; increasing the number of hospitals, physicians, and mobile clinics; facilitating the means of obtaining medical treatment

30. Attention to be given to village problems as regards their organization, their cleanliness, the purification of their water supply, and the means to provide them with culture, recreation, and training

Third: The economic:

1. The organization of *zakat* (Islamic alms tax) in terms of income and expenditure, according to the teachings of the magnanimous Sacred Law; invoking its assistance in carrying out necessary benevolent projects, such as homes for the aged, the poor, and orphans, and strengthening the armed forces

2. The prohibition of usury, and the organization of banks with this end in view. Let the government provide a good example in this domain by relinquishing all interest due on its own particular undertakings, for instance in the loan-granting banks, industrial loans, etc.

3. The encouragement of economic projects and an increase in their number; giving work to unemployed citizens in them; the transfer of such of these as are in the hands of foreigners to the purely national sector

4. The protection of the masses from the oppression of monopolistic companies; keeping these within strict limits, and obtaining every possible benefit for the masses

5. An improvement of the lot of junior civil servants by raising their salaries, granting them steady increases and compensations, and lowering the salaries of senior civil servants

6. A reduction in the number of government posts, retaining only the indispensable ones; an equitable and scrupulous distribution of the work among civil servants

7. The encouragement of agricultural and industrial counseling; attention to be paid to raising the production level of the peasant and industrial worker

8. A concern for the technical and social problems of the worker; raising his standard of living in numerous respects

9. The exploitation of natural resources, such as uncultivated land, neglected mines, etc.

10. Priority over luxury items to be given to necessary projects in terms of organization and execution

This is the message of the Muslim Brotherhood. We submit it, and place ourselves, our talents, and all we possess in the hands of any committee or government desirous of taking a step forward, hand in hand with an Islamic nation, toward progress and advancement. We will answer the call, and we are prepared to sacrifice ourselves. We hope that by so doing we will have fulfilled our trust and said our piece, for religion means sincerity toward God, His Apostle, His Book, the imams of the Muslims, and their community at large. God is our sufficiency; He is enough; and peace to His chosen worshipers!

## Chapter 3

# SAYYID ABU'L-A'LA MAWDUDI
# 1903–1979

ISLAMISM IS often associated in the public imagination with the Arab
Middle East and, since the revolution of 1979, with Iran. It is in the Indian subcontinent, however, that Sunni Islamist thought found one of its
earliest and most sustained articulations. The person responsible for this
was Sayyid Abu'l-A'la Mawdudi, one of the most prolific Islamist writers
of the twentieth century. Over a career extending from the 1920s to the
late 1970s, Mawdudi both formulated and popularized key themes in Islamist discourse. Although it is only in translation that his writings in
Urdu reached an international Muslim readership, no figure has influenced the political vocabulary of Sunni Islamism more than Mawdudi.
Yet, like Islamists everywhere, Mawdudi's thought was shaped not only
by his understanding of the Islamic foundational texts but also by his
particular intellectual and political context. This perspective has sometimes made for important differences of emphasis between him and those
appropriating facets of his thought in other contexts.

Sayyid Abu'l-A'la Mawdudi was born in Awrangabad, in southern
India, in 1903. His birthplace was a city in Hyderabad, one of the many
"princely states" whose formal autonomy the British had recognized
when they had brought much of the rest of the Indian subcontinent under
direct colonial rule. Although Mawdudi's formative years were spent in
Hyderabad, it was the north Indian Muslim culture with which his family
identified most closely. His father, Ahmad Hasan, had briefly studied at
the Muhammadan Anglo-Oriental College (later Aligarh University), the
premier institution of Western education that Sayyid Ahmad Khan (d.
1898) had established in 1875 in order to help Muslims cope better with
the challenges of British colonial rule. Ahmad Hasan subsequently trained
as a lawyer, though he was far more committed to Sufi piety than he was
to his legal practice (Nasr 1996, 10–11). It was under his guidance that
Mawdudi completed the earliest stages of his education.

Mawdudi received a largely traditional education, of the sort common
for young men training to become 'ulama.[1] Unlike many of his contemporaries among the Indian 'ulama, however, this education did not take
place at a single institution, with which he could have identified but

---

[1]For a discussion of Mawdudi's education, on which we draw here, see Nasr 1996,
11–19.

rather at a number of disparate madrasas in Hyderabad, Bhopal, and Delhi. At a time when the 'ulama of British India had come to have distinct doctrinal orientations, each associated with its own network of madrasas, Mawdudi's lack of identification with a particular madrasa meant that he would not be fully recognized by other 'ulama as a properly credentialed religious scholar. From Mawdudi's perspective, this was not an altogether undesirable outcome, for it allowed him considerably greater independence in his view of the Islamic scholarly tradition than is typically found among the 'ulama. The madrasas Mawdudi did study at were known for considerable experimentation: the Hyderabad madrasa was then headed by Hamid al-din Farahi (d. 1930), a noted Qur'an commentator who was viewed with considerable suspicion by other 'ulama on account of a modernist orientation centering on efforts to reinterpret the Qur'an in light of what he took to be the concerns and needs of contemporary Muslims. And the madrasa in Delhi was located on the same premises as a Qur'anic school founded by 'Ubayd Allah Sindhi (d. 1944), a controversial religious scholar who was among the most vociferous critics of the 'ulama in colonial India (on Sindhi, cf. Zaman 2006). Mawdudi was to interact with the 'ulama throughout his life, although his relations with them were never easy.

Mawdudi began his career as a journalist. In the mid-1920s, he was the editor of *al-Jami'at*, the principal organ of the Jam'iyyat al-'Ulama-yi Hind, a religio-political organization of 'ulama belonging to the Deobandi doctrinal orientation in British India. One of Mawdudi's earliest works, *On Jihad in Islam*, was first serialized in this journal (Nasr 1996, 23). From 1932, he became the publisher and editor of *Tarjuman al-Qur'an* (The Interpreter of the Qur'an), a magazine that would serve as Mawdudi's mouthpiece for the rest of his life.

Leaders of the Jam'iyyat al-'Ulama, of whom Husayn Ahmad Madani (d. 1957) was the most notable, attributed much of the social and economic backwardness of the Muslims of British India to the onset of colonial rule and therefore saw the end of that rule as the panacea for these ills. On this analysis, Muslims could do no better than join hands with the Hindus—and especially with the avowedly secular Indian National Congress—in order to rid India of the British. The Congress, however, was overwhelmingly dominated by the Hindus, and the rhetoric of its leaders, especially but not only of M. K. Gandhi (d. 1948), was suffused with a Hindu idiom (Gould 2004). Where Madani and the "nationalist" 'ulama confidently envisaged a harmonious Muslim coexistence with the Hindus in a united, postcolonial India, Mawdudi had deep misgivings about the future of the Muslim community and its religious and cultural institutions in a Hindu-dominated India. And he castigated Madani for failing to understand that a "united nationhood" would mean the destruction of the Muslim community in India (Zaman 2002, 34–35).

Mawdudi shared these fears with leaders of the Muslim League, who, from 1940, had begun calling for the establishment of a separate Muslim homeland as the best way of protecting the interests of the Indian Muslims. Yet, in the years leading up to the partition of the Indian subcontinent and the establishment of Pakistan in 1947, Mawdudi was a bitter critic of the Muslim League leadership. He argued that nationalism had no place in Islam and that clothing nationalism in a religious garb, as the Muslim League leaders had sought to do, did not make it any more legitimate. Mawdudi believed that an Islamic state ought to be established in South Asia, but he argued that it required a concerted *prior* effort at training people in the proper Islamic norms. The thoroughly westernized leadership of the Muslim League seemed to him uniquely ill suited for the establishment of the Islamic state. Nonetheless, it was in Pakistan rather than in postcolonial India that Mawdudi chose to live, focusing his energies on calls for the implementation of Islamic law, on educating people in the norms of what he saw as true Islam, and in mobilizing religio-political groups for the establishment of an Islamic state.

Mawdudi's conception of the Islamic state rests on the conviction that affirming the oneness of God—*tawhid*, a cardinal Islamic belief—is not merely a theological tenet but also an eminently political imperative. It entails recognizing the full legal and political implications of the "sovereignty of God": God alone is the source of the law, all people must submit to this law, and the sole mandate of the Islamic state is to implement this law. Islamic norms exist not merely to be followed by Muslims on their personal initiative and in their individual lives but to be put into effect through the coercive power of the state (Mawdudi 1960, 165–213). Mawdudi was highly critical of the 'ulama for their absorption in "ordinary external observances," by which he meant Islamic ritual practices and other markers of an Islamic identity, at the expense of "the real spirit of the religion" (Mawdudi 1976, 49–56; quotations at p. 49). The Sufis appeared to him to be especially egregious in violating "true" Islam. Indeed, Mawdudi went so far as to range Sufi asceticism alongside atheism and polytheism in speaking of the "conflict between Islam and un-Islam" (Mawdudi 1963, 5–33). This is remarkable not only for the uncompromising harshness of its appraisal but also because Mawdudi's family claimed descent from an early figure in the genealogy of the Chishti Sufis— one of the most important of South Asia's Sufi orders—and his own father had been a practicing Sufi (Nasr 1996, 9–10).[2] Mawdudi, however, had little patience with "mere" piety, whether of the Sufis or the 'ulama, for "without the power to enforce, it is meaningless merely to believe in or present a doctrine or a way of life" (Mawdudi 1963, 22–23).

[2]The exigencies of Pakistani politics would later force Mawdudi's organization, the Jama'at-i Islami, to make some overtures toward Sufi devotionalism. See the section on "Sufis and Islamists" in chapter 1.

Everything depended, in Mawdudi's view of the world, on the right sort of leadership:

> If . . . leaders and rulers be pious and devoted to God, the entire so-ciety will certainly follow the course of righteousness and devotion to the Almighty. Even the wicked will be constrained to do good. . . . But if the reins of [the] state are in the hands of agnostics and evil men, the entire fabric will be permeated by the spirit of disobedience to God, tyranny and immorality. . . . God's earth will be inundated by tyranny and oppression. (Mawdudi 1976, 3–4)

Given this pivotal role he assigned to the ruler, the *amir*, it is remarkable that Mawdudi showed little interest in the institutions and mechanisms through which the ruler's power might be kept in check. But then, to Mawdudi, there was no real danger that the ruler would misuse the au-thority and power vested in him, for his virtue and piety—to which he owed his position in the first place—would keep him perennially mindful of his accountability to God. Nothing could be more effective in prevent-ing him from becoming corrupted by power than this moral restraint. In its implications, this view is not very different from Ayatollah Khomeini's doctrine of velayat-e faqih, which, too, gives virtually unconstrained au-thority to the "guardian jurist" in overseeing the affairs of the state (see chapter 6). It is, however, a short step to despotism in the name of reli-gion, as some of Mawdudi's younger Islamist contemporaries have not failed to notice (Qaradawi 1997, 149–50).

If an Islamic state is to exist, it is not only the ruler but also its citizens who must be fashioned in an Islamic mold. As Mawdudi saw it, igno-rance of true Islam was rampant among Muslims, and especially among those educated in westernized institutions of learning. This was undesir-able in itself, of course, but it also led them to oppose the idea of an Is-lamic state. Many among them tended to view the shari'a in the darkest colors, as medieval and barbaric, and they therefore opposed its imple-mentation. Mawdudi argued that Muslims did not really have the free-dom to decide whether or not to submit to the shari'a. Yet he also insisted that Islamic law was anything but barbaric, that it was misunderstood precisely because of ignorance about what it stood for. It was through education in Islamic norms that the leadership of the Islamic state would be groomed; but the people at large had to imbibe Islamic teachings as well if they were to facilitate rather than obstruct the establishment and functioning of the Islamic state. Such socialization was, to him, far more important than "ordinary external observances." It was to lead people on this path to the cultivation of Islamic virtues that Mawdudi had founded his Jama'at-i Islami in 1941; and it was with a similar purpose that he had embarked, in 1942, on an ambitious commentary on the Qur'an, which he would complete in six large volumes some thirty years later (for an English translation, see Mawdudi [Maududi] 1988—).

A critical tension was already apparent in Mawdudi's discourses in the years leading to the partition of the Indian subcontinent, and it continued to characterize his thought and his politics in Pakistan. Even as he continued to write extensively throughout his life to educate the people, Mawdudi's active involvement in Pakistani politics clearly suggested that he was unwilling to wait for the people to acquire proper Islamic norms *before* trying to bring about the Islamic state. Many among the 'ulama have had serious reservations about Mawdudi's single-minded insistence on the Islamic state as the only effective means of living according to Islamic norms, of making all Islamic practices and institutions subservient to this overarching political goal (see chapter 1). But several even among those who had supported Mawdudi in the early years of the Jama'at-i Islami felt alienated when Mawdudi decided that political mobilization and electoral politics offered better hopes of establishing an Islamic state than did the previously envisaged project of fostering a new generation of rightly guided Muslims as a *prelude* to any such state (cf. Nasr 1994). Participation in active politics has entailed much compromise in the Jama'at's utopian ideals, not least in the form of alliances with unsavory groups and accommodations to institutions and practices that fall well short of anything the kingdom of God might have promised. Yet such compromises also gave to Mawdudi ample opportunities to mold the religious and political discourses in Pakistan in accordance with some of his aspirations.

The Islamic provisions of the 1956 constitution of Pakistan bear many signs of Mawdudi's influence. That constitution, as well as the two subsequent ones (promulgated in 1961 and in 1973), has continued to underline the state's commitment to the implementation of Islamic norms and to promise that existing or new legislation would not contradict the teachings of the Islamic foundational texts. Mawdudi was hardly the only one to make these demands but, in his prolific writings and speeches, was by far the most articulate of those who did so. In uneasy alliance with the 'ulama, Mawdudi was also among the most influential of those reminding successive Pakistani governments of what the constitutions— in part under his own influence—had laid down regarding the public implementation of Islamic norms, relentlessly pressing the ruling elites to translate their own rhetoric about the state's Islamic commitments into public policy.

Much of the Jama'at-i Islami's standing, in Pakistan and in Islamist circles elsewhere, has had to do with Mawdudi's abilities as a highly effective writer, reaching an audience well beyond those committed specifically to his teachings or to necessarily supporting his Islamist organization. Mawdudi, a gifted polemicist, was especially concerned to address people schooled in modern, westernized institutions of learning. Unlike most 'ulama of his generation, Mawdudi was able to read works in the English language (Nasr 1996, 15), and he drew on his uneven but not insubstantial acquaintance with Western thinkers, sociologists, and journalists to present stark contrasts between Islamic ideals and what he saw as the moral depravity of contemporary Western societies, illustrated through the writings of contemporary Western observers (for an example of this well-worn polemical style, see Mawdudi 1983). It was not only a matter of demonstrating the moral superiority of Islam over the West, however. Like many other Islamists, Mawdudi also wanted to speak in an idiom that the English-educated would find intelligible and appealing. As Maryam Jameelah, an American Jewish convert to Islam who was deeply influenced by Mawdudi but gradually distanced herself from some of his views, put it, Mawdudi "did not hesitate to apply Western terminology . . . in defining his conception of Islam. To him, Islam was a 'revolutionary ideology' and a 'dynamic movement,' the Jama'at-e-Islami was a 'party,' the Shari'ah a complete 'code' in Islam's 'total scheme of life.' His enthusiasm was infectious among those who admired him, encouraging them to implement in Pakistan all his 'manifestos,' 'programmes' and 'schemes' to usher in a true Islamic 'renaissance'" (Jameelah 1987, 127).

Those he was able to reach through his writings included students, members of the intelligentsia, and not a few military officers. General Muhammad Zia al-Haqq (d. 1988), who came to power through a military coup in 1977 and governed Pakistan for the next eleven years, was among those influenced by Mawdudi's writings. Although Mawdudi died early in Zia al-Haqq's reign, and the Jama'at-i Islami's relationship with the military regime was seldom free of tension, Zia al-Haqq's halfhearted but much publicized program of "Islamizing" all aspects of Pakistani society and economy had unmistakable echoes of Mawdudi's thought.

Mawdudi also had an international audience. The political implications of "the sovereignty of God," the concomitant imperative upon Muslims to establish an Islamic state as the expression of God's will, the contours of an Islamic constitution, and questions relating to how the state ought to implement the shari'a were spelled out by Mawdudi in greater detail and with more consistency than practically any other Islamist had before him. These ideas have had considerable impact far beyond South Asia. Mawdudi has also been credited with first formulating the idea that a new age of jahiliyya had come to engulf much of the world—an idea that Sayyid Qutb of Egypt would later make the cornerstone of his thought (see chapters 1, 4, and 5).

Saudi patronage also helped reinforce Mawdudi's international standing. Like Abu'l-Hasan 'Ali Nadwi, Mawdudi shared the Saudi ruling elite's misgivings about secular nationalism and the desire to counter it with a reinvigorated pan-Islamism. Again rather like Nadwi, Mawdudi had cordial relations with the Wahhabi religious establishment. Although he had no particular attachment to the teachings of Muhammad ibn 'Abd al-Wahhab, his effort to anchor his understanding of Islam directly in the foundational texts rather than in the cumulative teachings and methodological principles associated with medieval schools of law was in broad accord with how the Saudi religious scholars approached the foundational texts. He was among those advising the Saudi government on the establishment of the Islamic University of Medina (founded in 1963), the first of several such universities in Saudi Arabia and, subsequently, in Pakistan and Malaysia (cf. Zaman 2007a, 254–56). Mawdudi was an honored guest in Saudi Arabia, and the first recipient of the King Faysal Award, instituted by the Saudi government to recognize service to Islam.

Mawdudi was not a profound thinker. But he was a prolific author, and the highly organized publication and propaganda machinery of the Jama'at-i Islami, in and outside Pakistan, and the affinities of his party with Islamist organizations elsewhere have all contributed to a broad dissemination of his ideas. The fact, moreover, that Mawdudi and his organization were able to remain part of the political process in Pakistan allowed him to be considerably less extreme and more pragmatic in his politics, to adjust his thinking in light of changing circumstances, and to shape the religio-political discourse in the country in ways not possible for most Arab Islamists of his age (cf. Nasr 1994).[3] Yet his influence can scarcely be reduced to fortuitous political circumstances any more than it can to the formidable propaganda machinery of the Jama'at-i Islami. As noted earlier, it has also had much to do with the clarity and force of some of the ideas to which he gave expression, as well as with his efforts over a long and prolific career to demonstrate how these ideas were anchored in the foundational texts *and* how they could be articulated in the language of modern constitutionalism. Yet even as he sought to appeal to those educated in modern, Western institutions of learning, Mawdudi was able to draw on a traditional religious education in ways that few of his contemporaries among the Sunni Islamists could match. This did not ease his relations with the leading 'ulama, anymore than his "modern" idiom convinced everyone even among his admirers. But it did contribute toward making him one of the most influential and widely quoted thinkers in contemporary Islamism.

[3] Thus, while Qutb came to speak of the need to destroy jahili societies and those associated with them, Mawdudi—for all the ambiguities of his language—desisted from drawing such militant implications from his own understanding of the jahiliyya. Also cf. Nasr 1996, 69–79.

# THE ISLAMIC LAW

IT IS AN IRONY of fate that, nowadays, the demand for the enforcement
of Islamic law has come to be surrounded by such a thick mist of
misgivings that a mere reference to it, *even in a Muslim country* like
Pakistan, raises a storm of criticism. Thus, for instance, the questions
are asked: Can a centuries-old legal system be adequate to fulfill the
requirements of our modern state and society? Is it not absurd to think
that the laws, which had been framed under certain particular circumstances in bygone days, can hold good in every age and every clime?
Do you seriously propose to start chopping off the hands of thieves
and flogging human beings in this modern, enlightened age? Will our
markets again abound in slaves and deal in the sale and purchase of
human beings as chattels and playthings? Which particular sect's legal
system is going to be introduced here? What about the non-Muslim
minorities who will never tolerate the dominance of the Muslim religious law and will resist it with all the force at their command? One
has to face a volley of such questions while discussing the problem, and,
strangely enough, not from non-Muslims but from the Muslim educated
elite!

To be sure, these questions are not the outcome of any antagonism
toward Islam but mostly of sheer ignorance, which must quite naturally
breed suspicion. And, to our utter misfortune, ignorance abounds in
our ranks. We have people who are otherwise educated but who know
practically nothing about their great ideology and their glorious heritage. No wonder, then, that they labor under strong prejudices.

This state of degradation, however, has not come as a bolt from the
blue; it is, rather, the culmination of a gradual process of decay spread
over many centuries. Commencing with stagnation in the domains of
knowledge and learning, research and discovery, and thought and
culture, it finally culminated in our political breakdown, making many
a Muslim country the slave of non-Muslim imperialist powers. Political
slavery gave birth to an inferiority complex, and the resultant intellectual serfdom eventually swept the entire Muslim world off its feet, so
much so that even those Muslim countries that were able to retain their
political freedom could not escape its evil influences. The ultimate
consequence of this evil situation was that when Muslims woke up
again to the call of progress, they were incapable of looking at things

except through the colored glasses of Western thought. Nothing that was not Western could inspire confidence in them. Indeed, the adoption of Western culture and civilization and aping the West even in the most personal things became their craze. Eventually, they succumbed totally to the slavery of the West.

This trend toward westernism was also the result of the disappointment that came to the nation from the side of the Muslim religious leaders. Being themselves the victims of the widespread degeneration that had engulfed the entire Muslim world, they were incapable of initiating any constructive movement or taking any revolutionary step that could combat the evils afflicting the Muslim society. Quite naturally, this disappointment turned the discontented Muslims toward that system of life that had the glamor of being successful in the modern world. Thus, they succumbed to the onslaughts of modern thought, adopted the new culture of the West, and began to ape blindly Western modes and manners. Slowly but surely, the religious leaders were pushed into the background and were replaced, as regards power and control over the people, by men bereft of all knowledge of their religion and imbued only with the spirit of modern thought and Western ideals. That is why we find that many a Muslim country has, in the recent past, either completely abrogated the Islamic law or confined its operation to the domain of purely personal matters only—that is, a position conferred on the non-Muslims in a truly Islamic state.

In all those Muslim countries, which suffered from foreign domination, the leadership of political and cultural movements fell into the hands of those who were shorn of all Islamic background. They adopted the creed of nationalism, directed their efforts toward the cause of *national* independence and prosperity along secular lines, and tried to copy, step by step, the advanced nations of this age. So, if these gentlemen feel vexed with the demand for an Islamic constitution and Islamic laws, it is quite natural for them. It is also natural for them to sidetrack or suppress the issue, as they are ignorant of even the ABCs of the Islamic shari'a. Their education and intellectual development has alienated them so completely from the spirit and the structure of Islamic ideology that it is, at least for the moment, very difficult for them to understand such demands.

As regards the Muslim religious leadership, it has in no way fared better, because our religious institutions are tied to the intellectual atmosphere of the fifth century AH, as a consequence of which they have not been able to produce such leaders of Islamic thought and action as could be capable of administering the affairs of a modern state in the light of Islamic principles. This is the situation prevailing throughout the Muslim world and is, indeed, a very real obstacle facing the Islamic countries in their march toward the goal of Islamic renaissance.

Notwithstanding certain similarities of situation, the case of Pakistan is not, however, the same as that of other Muslim countries. This is so because it has been achieved exclusively with the object of becoming the homeland of Islam. For the past ten years, we have been ceaselessly fighting for the recognition of the fact that we are a separate nation by virtue of our adherence to Islam.[4] We have been proclaiming from housetops that we have a distinct culture of our own, and that we possess a worldview, an outlook on life, and a code of living fundamentally different from those of non-Muslims. We have all along been demanding a separate homeland for the purpose of translating into practice the ideals envisaged by Islam, and, at last, after a long and arduous struggle, in which we sustained a heavy loss of life and property and suffered deep humiliation in respect of the honor and chastity of a large number of our womenfolk, we have succeeded in attaining our cherished goal—this country of Pakistan. If, now, after all these precious sacrifices, we fail to achieve the real and ultimate objective of making Islam a practical, social, political, and constitutional reality—a live force to fashion all facets of our life—our entire struggle and all our sacrifices become futile and meaningless.

Indeed, if instead of an Islamic one a secular and godless constitution was to be introduced, and if instead of the Islamic shari'a the British Civil and Criminal Procedure Codes had to be enforced, what was the sense in all this struggle for a separate Muslim homeland? We could have had them without that. Similarly, if we simply intended to implement any socialistic program, we could have done so in collaboration with the Communist and the Socialist parties of India without plunging the nation into this great bloodbath and mighty ordeal.

The fact is that we are already committed before God, Man, and History for the promulgation of Islamic constitution and the introduction of Islamic way of life in this country, and no going back on our words is possible. Whatever the hurdles and howsoever great they may be, we have to continue our march toward our goal of a full-fledged Islamic state in Pakistan.

No doubt there do exist many hardships and difficulties in the way of achieving this goal. But what great goal can be or has ever been achieved without bracing difficulties boldly and intelligently! And I must emphatically say that the difficulties that impede our way are in no way insurmountable. Indeed, none of them is *real* except the difficulty that many among those who hold the reins of power are devoid of faith in the efficacy of the Islamic ideology, which, in its turn, is not

---

[4]Mawdudi gave this lecture in January 1948, shortly after the establishment of Pakistan. He is referring here to the struggle for the establishment of a separate Muslim homeland in South Asia, while obscuring the fact that he had been among those opposing rather than supporting this movement.

because of any defect in Islam but is purely a product of their own gross ignorance of the Islamic teachings.

The first task, therefore, is to explain to our educated people the meaning and the implications of Islamic law—its objectives, its spirit, its structure, and its categorical and unchangeable injunctions along with the reasons for their permanence. They should also be informed of the dynamic element of Islamic law and how it guarantees the fulfillment of the ever-increasing needs of the progressive human society in every age. Then, they should be enlightened in regard to the rational foundations of the shari'a. Finally, it is also needed to expose the hollowness of the vituperative criticisms against Islam and to remove thereby the fog of misunderstandings that shroud the issue. If once we succeed in accomplishing this task and consequently gaining the support of Muslim intelligentsia, we will pave the way for the establishment of an Islamic state and the creation of an Islamic society in Pakistan. It is with this intention that I am making this speech before the students of the Law College.

## II. LAW AND LIFE

The term "law" bears reference to the query: What should be the conduct of man in his individual and collective life? This query presents itself to us in connection with innumerable matters. Hence, its reply covers a very wide range of topics, wider than what the term law technically signifies. It includes our system of education and training in the light of which we strive to mold the character of individuals; it comprehends our social system, which regulates our social relationships; it encompasses our economic order according to which we formulate the principles of production, distribution, and exchange of wealth. Thus, we get a vast system of rules that determine our conduct in various walks of life. Technically speaking, all these sets of rules are not "law."

The term law is technically applied only to such of the rules as are enforceable by the coercive power of the state. But, obviously, no one who wants to understand them can afford to confine his attention to them alone. He will have to take into consideration the entire scheme of moral and social guidance prescribed by a particular ideology, because it is only then that he will be able to appreciate the spirit and objectives of the law and to form a critical opinion about its merits and demerits.

It should not be difficult to understand that the principles we recommend relating to a particular system of life are basically derived from and are deeply influenced by our conceptions about the ends of human life and by our notions of right and wrong, good and evil, and justice and injustice. Consequently, the nature of a legal system depends entirely upon the source or sources from which it is derived. Thus, the differences discernible in the legal and social systems of different societies are mainly a result of the differences of their sources of guidance and inspiration.

This means that unless we are prepared to take into consideration the origins and the background of the whole system of life and of the society that it brings into existence and to appreciate the complete process of the development of that system and the evolution of that society, we will not be able to understand, much less to criticize on any rational basis, the mandatory legal provisions of the system—especially when our knowledge of those provisions consists, in the main, of hearsay and conjecture.

I do feel that a comparative critical study of the Islamic and the Western systems of life would be the best way to explain and elucidate my viewpoint. If the differences between the original sources and the basic postulates of both systems are kept in mind, the radically different schemes of life that both envisage can be easily understood. But the paucity of time at my disposal does not permit such a digression, and, consequently, I shall confine myself, at present, to the exposition of the Islamic shari'a only.

## Sources of the Islamic System of Life

The first source of the Islamic system of life is a book, or, to be more exact, "The Book." The world received several editions of it under the titles of the Old Testament, the New Testament, the Psalms, and so forth, the last and the final edition being the one presented to mankind under the name of the Qur'an.

The second source of this system are the persons to whom the different editions of the Book were revealed and who, by their preachings and their conduct, interpreted them to the people. As different personalities, they bore the names of Noah, Abraham, Moses, Jesus, and Muhammad (peace be on them all), but as the bearers and upholders of the same mission of life, they all stand under the general title of "The Messenger."

## The Islamic Concept of Life

The view of life that Islam has presented is that this universe of ours, which follows a set course of law and functions according to an intelligent and well-laid-out plan, is in reality the Kingdom of the One God—*Allah*. It is He Who created it. It is He Who owns it. It is He Who governs it. The earth on which we live is just a small part—a province—of this huge universe, and like all other parts thereof, it also functions completely under the control of God. And as regards ourselves—that is, we human beings—we are nothing more than His "born subjects." It is He Who created us, sustains us, and causes us to live. Hence, every notion of our *absolute independence* is nothing but a sheer deception and misjudgment. God controls every fiber of our being, and none can escape his grip.

Every thinking mind is aware of the fact that a very large sector of our life is governed and directly controlled by a Higher Power and with such absoluteness that we are practically helpless in respect of it. From the time we are conceived in the wombs of our mothers till the moment we breathe our last, we are subject to God's inexorable laws of nature to such an extent that we cannot claim to be free from their control even for a single moment.

Of course, there is another sphere of our life in which we possess a certain amount of freedom. This is the moral and social sphere of our life in which we are bestowed with a free will and independence of choice in respect of individual as well as collective affairs and behavior. But this independence can hardly justify our getting away from the guidance of our Creator and His laws. It is only to give us a choice of either leading our lives as the obedient subjects of God—an attitude consistent with the real order of things—or being disregardful of His commandments and thus rebelling against Him and our own true nature.

Obviously, to faithfully follow the guidance and law of God is the truest and most consistent attitude for mankind. It sets the standard for the orderly behavior of man both individually and collectively and in respect of the biggest as well as the smallest task he may have to face. Having once accepted the philosophy of life enunciated by "The Book" and "The Messenger" as the embodiment of reality, one has no justification for not obeying God's revealed guidance in the sphere of one's choice also. Indeed, it is but rational that we should admit God's sovereignty in this sphere as well, just as we are perforce doing in the domain of our physical life. And this for several reasons: First, the powers and the organs through which our free will functions are gifts from God and not the result of our own efforts. Second, the independence of choice itself has been delegated to us by God and not won by us through our personal endeavor. Third all those things in which our free will operates are not only the property but also the creation of God. Fourth, the territory in which we exercise our independence and freedom is also the territory of God. Fifth, the harmonization of human life with the universe dictates the necessity of there being one Sovereign and a common source of law for both spheres of human activity—the voluntary and the involuntary or, in other words, the moral and the physical. The separation of these two spheres into watertight compartments leads to the creation of an irreconcilable conflict, which finally lands not only the individuals but even biggest nations in endless trouble and disaster.

The Final Book of God and the Final Messenger stand today as the repositories of this truth, and they invite the whole of humanity to accept it freely and without compulsion. God Almighty has endowed man with free will in the moral domain, and it is to this free will that this acceptance bears reference. Consequently, it is always an act of volition and not of compulsion. Whosoever agrees that the concept of reality stated by the Holy Prophet and the Holy Book is true, it is for him to step forward and surrender his will to the will of God. It is this submission that is called *Islam,* and those who do so, that is, those who of their own free will, accept God as their Sovereign and surrender to His divine will and undertake to regulate their lives in accordance with His commandments, are called *Muslims.*

All those persons who thus surrender themselves to the will of God are welded into a community and that is how the "Muslim society" comes into being. Thus, this is an ideological society—a society radically different from those which spring up from accidents of races, color, or country. This society is the result of a deliberate choice and effort; it is the outcome of a "contract" that takes place between human beings and their Creator. Those who enter into this contract undertake to recognize God as their sovereign, His guidance as supreme, and His injunctions as absolute law. They also undertake to accept, without question or doubt, His classification of good and evil, right and wrong, the permissible and prohibited. In short, the Islamic society agrees to limit its volition to the extent prescribed by the All-Knowing God. In other words, *it is God and not man whose will is the source of law in a Muslim Society.*

When such a society comes into existence, the Book and the Messenger prescribe for it a code of life called the shari'a, and this society is bound to conform to it by virtue of the contract it has entered into. It is therefore inconceivable that any Muslim Society worth the name can deliberately adopt a system of life other than the shari'a. If it does so, its contract is automatically broken and the whole society becomes "un-Islamic."

But we must clearly distinguish between the everyday sins of the individuals and a deliberate revolt against the shari'a. The former may not imply breaking up of the contract, while the latter would mean nothing less than that. The point that should be clearly understood here is that if an Islamic society consciously resolves not to accept the shari'a, and decides to enact its own constitution and laws or borrow them from any other source in disregard of the shari'a, such a society breaks its contract with God and forfeits its right to be called Islamic.

### III. The Objectives and Characteristics of the Shari'a

Let us now proceed to understand the scheme of life envisaged by the shari'a. To understand that, it is essential that we should start with a clear conception of the objectives and the fundamentals of shari'a.

The main objective of the shari'a is to construct human life on the basis of *ma'rufat* (virtues) and to cleanse it of the *munkarat* (vices). The term ma'rufat, denotes all the virtues and good qualities that have always been accepted as "good" by the human conscience. Conversely, munkarat denotes all the sins and evils that have always been condemned by human nature as evil. In short, the ma'rufat are in harmony with human nature and its requirements in general and the munkarat are just the opposite. The shari'a gives a clear view of these ma'rufat and munkarat and states them as the norms to which the individual and social behavior should conform.

The shari'a does not, however, limit its function to providing us with an inventory of virtues and vices; it lays down the entire scheme of life in such a manner that virtues may flourish and vices may not poison human life.

To achieve this end, the shari'a has embraced in its scheme all the factors that encourage the growth of good and has recommended steps for the removal of impediments that might prevent its growth and development. This process gives rise to a subsidiary series of ma'rufat consisting of the causes and means initiating and nurturing the good and, further, of ma'rufat consisting of prohibitions of preventives to good. Similarly there is a subsidiary list of munkarat that might initiate or allow growth of evil.

The shari'a shapes the Islamic society in a way that is conducive to the unfettered growth of good, virtue, and truth in every sphere of human activity and gives full play to the forces of good in all directions. And at the same time it removes all impediments in the path of virtue. Along with this, it attempts to eradicate evils from its social scheme by prohibiting vice, by obviating the causes of its appearance and growth, by closing the inlets through which it creeps into society, and by adopting deterrent measures to check its occurrence.

## Ma'rufat

The shari'a classifies ma'rufat into three categories: *fard* and *wajib* (the mandatory), *matlub* (the recommendatory), and *mubah* (the permissible).

The observance of the mandatory ma'rufat is obligatory on a Muslim society, and the shari'a has given clear and binding directions about them. The recommendatory ma'rufat are those which the shari'a wants that a Muslim society should observe and practice. Some of them have been very clearly demanded of us, while others have been recommended by implication and deduction from the sayings of the Holy Prophet (peace be upon him). Besides this, special arrangements have been made for the growth and encouragement of some of them in the scheme of life enunciated by the shari'a. Others still have simply been recommended by the shari'a, leaving it to the society or to its more virtuous elements to look to their promotion.

This leaves us with the permissible ma'rufat. Strictly speaking, according to the shari'a everything that has not been expressly prohibited by it is a permissible ma'ruf. It is not at all necessary that an express permission should exist about it or that it should have been expressly left to our choice. Consequently, the sphere of permissible ma'rufat is very wide, so much so that except for a few things specifically prohibited by the shari'a, everything under the sun is permissible for a Muslim. And this is exactly the sphere where we have been given freedom and where we can legislate according to our discretion, to suit the requirements of our age and conditions.

## Munkarat

The munkarat (or the things prohibited in Islam) have been grouped into two categories: *haram* (those things which have been prohibited absolutely) and *makruh* (those things which have been simply disliked). It has been enjoined on Muslims by clear and mandatory injunctions to refrain totally from everything that has been declared haram. As for the makruhat, the shari'a signifies its dislike in some way or the other, either expressly or by implication, giving an indication also as to the degree of such dislike. For example, there are some makruhat bordering on haram, while others bear affinity with the acts that are permissible. Of course, their number is very large, ranging between the two extremes of prohibitory and permissible actions. Moreover, in some cases explicit measures have been prescribed by the shari'a for the prevention of makruhat, while in others such arrangements have been left to the discretion of the society or to the individual.

## The Characteristics of the Shari'a

The shari'a thus prescribes directives for the regulation of our individual as well as collective life. These directives touch such varied subjects as religious rituals, personal character, morals, habits, family relationships, social and economic affairs, administration, rights and duties of citizens, judicial system, laws of war and peace, and international relations. In short, it embraces all the various departments of human life. These directives reveal what is good and bad; what is beneficial and useful and what is injurious and harmful; what are the virtues that we have to cultivate and encourage and what are the evils which we have to suppress and guard against; what is the sphere of our voluntary, untrammeled, personal and social action and what are its limits; and, finally, what ways and means we can adopt in establishing such a dynamic order of society and what methods we should spurn. The shari'a is a complete scheme of life and an all-embracing social order—nothing superfluous, nothing lacking.

Another remarkable fact about the shariʻa is that it is an organic whole. The entire scheme of life propounded by Islam is animated by the same spirit and hence any arbitrary division of the scheme is bound to harm the spirit as well as the structure of the shariʻa. In this respect, it might be compared to the human body which is an organic whole. A leg pulled out of the body cannot be called one-eighth or one-sixth man, because, after its separation from the living human body, the leg can no more perform its human function. Nor can it be placed in the body of some other animal with any hope of making it human to the extent of that limb. Likewise, we cannot form a correct opinion about the utility, efficiency, and beauty of the hand, the eye, or the nose of a human being separately, without judging its place and function within a living body.

The same can be said in regard to the scheme of life envisaged by the shariʻa. Islam signifies the entire scheme of life and not any isolated part or parts thereof. Consequently, neither can it be appropriate to view the different parts of the shariʻa in isolation from one another and without regard to the whole, nor will it be of any use to take any particular part and bracket it with any other "ism." The shariʻa can function smoothly and can demonstrate its efficacy only if the entire system of life is practiced in accordance with it and not otherwise.

Many of the present-day misunderstandings about the shariʻa owe themselves to this faulty attitude in judging its worth, namely, forming opinions about its different aspects separately. Some injunctions of it are isolated from the main body of Islamic laws and then they are considered in the perspective of modern civilization, or they are viewed as if they were something completely self-contained. Thus, people take just one injunction of the shariʻa at random, which becomes maimed after its removal from the context, and then view it in the context of some modern legal system and criticize it on the score of its incongruity with present-day conceptions. But they fail to realize that it was never meant to be isolated like that for it forms an organic part of a distinct and self-contained system of life.

There are some people who take a few provisions of the Islamic penal code out of their context and jeer at them. But they do not realize that those provisions are to be viewed with the background of the whole Islamic system of life covering the economic, social, political, and educational spheres of activity. If all these departments are not working, then those isolated provisions of our penal code can certainly work no miracles.

For example, we all know that Islam imposes the penalty of amputating the hand for the commitment of theft. But this injunction is meant to be promulgated in a full-fledged Islamic society wherein the wealthy pay zakat to the state, and the state provides for the basic necessities of the needy and the destitute; wherein every township is enjoined to play host to visitors at its own expense for a minimum period of three days;

wherein all citizens are provided with equal privileges and opportunities to seek economic livelihood; wherein monopolistic tendencies are discouraged; wherein people are God-fearing and seek His pleasure with devotion; wherein the virtues of generosity, helping the poor, treating the sick, and providing the needy are in the air to the extent that even a small boy is made to realize that he is not a true Muslim if he allows his neighbor to sleep hungry while he has taken his meal. In other words, it is not meant for the present-day society where you cannot get a single penny without having to pay interest; where in place of *baitul mal* there are implacable moneylenders and banks that, instead of providing relief and succor to the poor and the needy, treat them with callous disregard, heartless refusal, and brutal contempt; where the guiding motto is: "Everybody for himself and devil takes the hindmost"; where there are great privileges for the privileged ones, while others are deprived even of their legitimate rights; where the economic system, propelled by greed and piloted by exploitation, leads only to the enrichment of the few at the cost of crushing poverty and intolerable misery of the many; and where the political system serves only to prop up injustice, class privileges, and distressing economic disparities. Under such conditions, it is doubtful if theft should be penalized at all, not to speak of cutting off the thief's hands! Because to do so would, as a matter of fact, amount to protecting the ill-gotten wealth of a few bloodsuckers rather than awarding adequate punishment to the guilty.[5]

On the other hand, Islam aims at creating a society in which none is compelled by the force of circumstances to steal. For, in the Islamic social order, apart from the voluntary help provided by individuals, the state guarantees the basic *necessities of life to all. But, after providing all that,* Islam enjoins a severe and exemplary punishment for those who commit theft, as their action shows that they are unfit to live in such a just, generous, and healthy society and would cause greater harm to it, if left unchecked.

Similar is the case of the punishment for adultery and fornication. Islam prescribes a hundred stripes for the unmarried and stoning to death for the married partners in the crime. But, of course, it applies to a society wherein every trace of suggestiveness has been destroyed; where mixed gatherings of men and women have been prohibited; where public appearance of painted and pampered women is completely

---

[5]Here it must not be misunderstood that I am defending theft or any other form of lawlessness. Not the least! My intention is only to show the vast and radical differences that reign between the context in which the punishment *was* and *is* applicable and the state of affairs we are today enveloped in. The only logical conclusion that follows is the need for a change in the entire system of life. When the entire structure of society is changed and a new way of life is established, the incongruity between the injunction and the present context of affairs would be obliterated and the avenues for its application would be opened. [This is Mawdudi's own note, which we have retained. –Editors]

nonexistent; where marriage has been made easy; where virtue, piety, and charity are current coins; and where the remembrance of God and the hereafter is kept ever fresh in men's minds and hearts. These punishments are not meant for that filthy society wherein sexual excitement is rampant; wherein nude pictures, obscene books, and vulgar songs have become common recreations; wherein sexual perversions have taken hold of the cinema and all other places of amusement; wherein mixed, seminude parties are considered the acme of social progress; and wherein economic conditions and social customs have made marriage extremely difficult.

## IV. Legal Aspects of the Shari'a

From this discussion, I think, it has become fairly clear that what we, at present, technically call Islamic law is only a part of a complete scheme of life and does not have any independent existence in isolation from that scheme. It can be neither understood nor enforced separately. To enforce it separately would, in fact, be against the intention of the Lawgiver. What is required of us is to translate into practice the entire Islamic program of life and not merely a fragment of it. Then and then alone can the legal aspects be properly implemented.

This scheme of the shari'a is, however, divided into many parts. Aspects of it do not need any external force for their enforcement; they are and can be enforced only by the ever-awake conscience kindled by his faith in a Muslim. Other parts are enforced by Islam's program of education, training of man's character, and the purification of his heart and his morals. To enforce certain other parts, Islam resorts to the use of the force of public opinion: the general will and pressure of the society. Still other parts have been sanctified by the traditions and the conventions of Muslim society. A very large part of the Islamic system of law, however, needs for its enforcement, in all its details, the coercive power and authority of the state. Political power is essential for protecting the Islamic system of life from deterioration and perversion, for the eradication of vice and the establishment of virtue, and for the enforcement of all those laws that require the sanction of the state and the judiciary for their operation.

Speaking from a purely juridical viewpoint, it is to this last part, out of the whole Islamic scheme of life, that the term law can be appropriately applied. For only those injunctions and regulations that are backed by political authority are, in modern parlance, termed as law. But as far as the Islamic conception is concerned, the entire shari'a stands as synonymous with law, because the entire code of life has been decreed by the All-Powerful Sovereign of the universe. To avoid confusion, however, we shall apply the term Islamic law only to those portions of the shari'a that demand the sanction of the state power for their enforcement.

## Major Branches of Islamic Law

The establishment of a political authority that may enforce Islamic Law requires a *constitutional law,* and the shari'a has clearly laid down its fundamentals. The shari'a has provided answers to the basic questions of constitutional law and has solved its fundamental problems, namely: What is the basic theory of the state? What is the source of the authority of its legislation? What are the guiding principles of state policy? What are the qualifications of the rulers of an Islamic state? What are the objectives of an Islamic state? In whom does sovereignty reside, and what are the different organs of the state? What is the mode of the distribution of power between the different organs of the state—the legislature, the executive, and the judiciary? What are the conditions for citizenship? What are the rights and duties of Muslim citizens? What are the rights of non-Muslim citizens (*zimmis*)? The guidance that the shari'a has provided in respect to these questions constitutes the constitutional law of Islam.

Besides laying down the fundamentals of constitutional law, the shari'a has also enunciated the basic principles of *administrative law.* Besides that, there are *precedents* in administrative practice established by the Holy Prophet himself (peace be on him) and the first four rightly guided caliphs of Islam. For instance, the shari'a enumerates the sources of income permissible for an Islamic state and those which are prohibited. It also prescribes the avenues of expenditure. It lays down rules of conduct for the police, the judiciary, and the administrative machinery. It defines the responsibilities of the rulers regarding the moral and material well-being of the citizens, laying particular emphasis on their obligations as regards the suppression of vice and the establishment of virtue. It also specifically states as to what extent the state can interfere with the affairs of the citizens. In this connection, we find not only directive principles but also many categorical injunctions. The shari'a has given us the broad framework of administrative law—exactly in the same way as it has given the fundamentals of constitutional law—and has left it to the discretion of the Muslims to build up the details in accordance with the demands of the age or the country in which they live—subject, of course, to the limits prescribed by the shari'a.

Proceeding further, we find the shari'a guiding us in connection with *public* as well as *personal law*—both are essential for the administration of justice. This guidance covers such an extensive field that we can never feel the need of going beyond the shari'a for meeting our legislative requirements. Its detailed injunctions are such that they can always fulfill the needs of human society in every age and in every country— provided, of course, that the entire Islamic scheme of life is in operation. They are so comprehensive that we can frame detailed laws for every emergency and every fresh problem on their basis, for which the legislature has been given the right of legislation. All the laws thus framed are to be considered an integral part of the Islamic law. That is why the laws framed by our jurists in the early days of Islam for the sake of "public good" form a part and parcel of the Islamic law.

Last, we have that part of the law that deals with the relations of the Islamic state with other states, the *international law*. In this connection, too, the shari'a gives us comprehensive regulations relating to war and peace, neutrality and alliance, and related topics. Where, however, no specific injunctions are to be found, the laws can be framed in the light of the general directives as laid down in that behalf.

### Permanence and Change in Islamic Law

This brief classification and elucidation shows that the guidance of the shari'a extends to all the branches of law which have been evolved by the ingenuity and need of the human mind so far. This is a standing testimony to the independence of the Islamic law and its inherent potentialities. Anybody who takes the trouble of making a detailed study of the subject will be able to distinguish between that part of the shari'a which has a permanent and unalterable character and is, as such, extremely beneficial for mankind and that part which is flexible and has thus the potentialities of meeting the ever-increasing requirements of every time and age.

The unalterable elements of Islamic law may be classified under the following heads:
  (1) Those laws that have been laid down in explicit and unambiguous terms in the Qur'an or the authentic Traditions of the Prophet, like the prohibition of alcoholic drinks, interest, and gambling, or the punishments prescribed for adultery and theft and the rules for inheritance
  (2) The directive principles laid down in the Holy Qur'an and authentic Traditions, for example, prohibition of the use of intoxicants in general, or the nullification of all exchange transactions that are not the outcome of the free will of both the parties, or the principle that men are protectors and in charge of women
  (3) The limitations imposed on human activity by the Qur'an and the Traditions of the Prophet, which can never be transgressed, for example, the limitation in connection with the plurality of wives where the maximum number has been fixed at four, or the limitation that the number of divorces to a wife cannot exceed three, or the limitation imposed on will, the amount of which cannot exceed one-third of the total inheritance

These unalterable mandatory provisions of the Islamic law give a permanent complexion to the Islamic social order and the characteristic features to its culture. In fact, one cannot find a single culture in the entire history of mankind that can retain its separate entity and its distinct character without possessing an unalterable and permanent element.

If there are no permanent elements in a culture and every part of it is subject to change, amendment, and modification, it is not an independent culture at all. It is just like a fluid, something which can take any and every shape and can always suffer transfiguration and metamorphosis.

Moreover, a thorough study of these directives and injunctions and limitations will lead every reasonable man to the conclusion that they have been given to us by the shari'a only for those matters where the human mind is likely to commit errors and go astray. On all such occasions, the shari'a has, so to speak, set the signposts by issuing directives or making categorical prohibitions so that we may proceed along the right path. And these signposts, far from impeding the march of human progress, are meant to keep us along the road and to save us from skidding away. In this connection, it might not be out of place here to refer to the laws of the shari'a governing marriage, divorce, and inheritance, which were the target of very bitter criticism in the recent past. It is these very laws, however, to which the world is now turning for guidance, though after innumerable bitter experiences!

The second part of Islamic law is that which is subject to modification according to the needs and requirements of the changing times, and this part of the Islamic law endows it with wide possibilities of growth and advancement and makes it fully capable of fulfilling all the needs of an expanding human society in every age.

This part consists of the following

(a) *Ta'wil* (interpretation) consists in probing into the meanings of the injunctions found in the Qur'an and the sunna. As such, it has always occupied and still occupies a place of immense importance in Islamic jurisprudence. When those endowed with penetrating insight and legal acumen ponder over the injunctions of the Qur'an and the sunna, they find that many of them are open to different fruitful and valid interpretations. Consequently, every one of them accepts some particular interpretation *according to his lights* on the merits of the case. In this way, the doors of difference of opinions have always been open in the past, are open even today, and will continue to remain so in the future.

(b) *Qiyas* (deduction by analogy) consists in applying to a matter with respect to which there is no clear guidance, a rule or injunction present for some similar matter.

(c) *Ijtihad* (disciplined judgment of jurists) consists in legislating on matters for which neither any explicit injunctions nor even precedents exist, subject, of course, to the general principles and precepts of the shari'a.

(d) *Istihsan* (juristic preference) means framing rules, if necessary, in nonprohibited matters in conformity with the spirit of the Islamic legal system.

Anyone who considers the possibilities inherent in the previously mentioned four ways of legislation can never reasonably entertain any misgivings as to the dynamism, adaptability, progressive nature, and power of evolutionary growth of the legal system of Islam. But it should be remembered that every Tom, Dick, and Harry is not entitled to exercise the right of ta'wil, qiyas, ijtihad, or istihsan. Nobody has ever recognized the right of every passerby to give verdicts on problems of national importance. Undoubtedly, it requires profound legal knowledge and a trained mind to enable one to speak with authority on any legal matter.

Similar is the case with the Islamic law. Obviously, to achieve the status of a jurist one should be fully conversant with Arabic language and literature. He should also have a complete grasp of the real historical background of the injunctions of Islam. He should have special insight into the Qur'anic style of expression. He should have a thorough knowledge of the vast literature on the Traditions of the Holy Prophet as well as of the Traditions themselves.

In the special field of analogous deduction a Muslim jurist is required to possess a keen sense of legal judgment and the requisite capacity for interpretation of facts on the basis of analogy; otherwise it would not be possible for him to save himself from falling into errors. As regards ijtihad, or original legislation, it requires the jurist to have not only a deep knowledge of Islamic law but also a developed sense of interpreting matters in the true Islamic spirit. Similarly, as regards istihsan or the consideration of public good and legislation for that purpose, it calls for a complete understanding of the entire Islamic scheme of life as also a complete grasp of the spirit of Islam so that he may adopt only those things which can be appropriately assimilated in the Islamic scheme and which do not amount to driving square pegs in round holes.

And, over and above all these intellectual accomplishments, another thing is vitally essential, and that is unstinted devotion and loyalty to Islam and a deep sense of accountability before God. As regards those who care little for God and the Final Accountability, whose watchword in life is sheer expediency, and who prefer the non-Islamic values of culture and civilization to those given by Islam, they must be regarded as the last persons to whom the work of Islamic legislation can be entrusted. For, in their hands, the Islamic law will only suffer perversion and corruption. It will not grow, evolve, and prosper.

## V. An Examination of Objections on Islamic Law

We shall now try to examine briefly some of the objections usually
raised against the demand for the introduction and enforcement of
Islamic law in Pakistan. These objections are many but it would be an
unnecessary waste of time to mention all of them here. Therefore, I
propose to confine to the examination of only those objections which
are of a fundamental nature.

### Islamic Laws Are Antiquated

The first objection that is raised is that, because the Islamic laws were
framed thirteen centuries ago in the light of the requirements of a pri-
mitive society, they cannot be of any use for a modern state of our age.

I doubt very much whether people who take this stand are conversant
even with the rudiments of the Islamic law and possess even an elementary knowledge of it. Perhaps, they have heard from somewhere that the
fundamentals of the Islamic law were enunciated more than thirteen
hundred years ago, and they have assumed that this law has remained
static since then and has failed to respond to the requirements of
changing conditions of human life. On this misconception they have
further assumed that the Islamic law will be unsuited to the needs of the
present-day society and will clog the wheels of progress. These critics
fail to realize, however, that the laws propounded thirteen and a half
centuries ago, did not remain in a vacuum; they formed part and parcel
of the life of Muslim society and brought into being a *state* that was run
in the light of these laws. This naturally provided an opportunity of
evolution to Islamic law from the earliest days, as it had to be applied
to day-to-day matters through the process of ta'wil, qiyas, ijtihad, and
istihsan.

Very soon after its inception, Islam began to hold sway over nearly
half the civilized world stretching from the Pacific to the Atlantic and,
during the following twelve hundred years, the Islamic law continued to
be the law of the land in all Muslim states. This process of the evolution
of Islamic law, therefore, did not stop for a moment up to the beginning
of the nineteenth century, because it had to meet the challenge of the
ever-changing circumstances and face countless problems confronting
different countries in different stages of history. Even in our Indo-
Pakistan subcontinent, the Islamic civil and penal codes were in vogue
up to the beginning of the nineteenth century.

Thus, it is only for the past one hundred years that the Islamic Law
remained inoperative and suffered stagnation. But, first, this period does
not form a big gap, and we can easily make up for the loss with some
amount of strenuous effort; second, we possess full records of the

development of our jurisprudence century by century, and there can be absolutely no ground for frustration or despondency. Our path of legal progress is, thus, fully illuminated.

Once we have grasped the fundamental principles and the basic facts concerning the evolution of the Islamic system of law, we cannot remain in doubt that this law shall be as responsive to the urges of a progressive society in the present and the future as it has been in the past. Only those who suffer from ignorance can fall a prey to such nonsense, while those who have a grasp of Islam and the Islamic law are aware of its potentialities of progress, and those who possess even a cursory knowledge of the history of its development can never suspect it of being an antiquated or stagnant system of law, incapable of keeping pace with the march of history.

## Islamic Laws Are Relics of Barbarism

The second most common objection—an objection put forward publicly only in a roundabout manner but which is presented with much vehemence and venom in private talks—is that Islam is just a relic of the dark ages! And those who say so also argue, with an air of haughtiness and arrogance, that the "progressive, cultured, and humane" outlook of the modern, enlightened age can never tolerate such "cruel" penalties as the cutting of the hands, or flogging, or stoning to death—penalties imposed by Islam for certain crimes.

This objection and this allegation, coming as it does from the supporters of modern Western civilization, makes one gasp with wonder. It is, indeed, amazing to hear that the normal values of the present age are "advanced" and "progressive." The heartlessness shown by the "enlightened" man of today to his fellow beings hardly finds a parallel in the darkest ages of history. He does not punish by stoning to death, but he can kill people indiscriminately with the atom bomb. He does not merely cut off the hands of the people, but he also tears their bodies into shreds. He is not content with flogging; he would like to burn alive the people en masse and manufacture soap out of the fat extracted from their dead bodies. Leaving aside these demonstrations of heartlessness during the period of war wherein everything is considered fair nowadays, the modern man brutally chastises—and does it unsparingly—the political "criminals": the *alleged* "traitors" to the national cause and the rivals in the economic and political fields. The highly objectionable and inhuman modern methods of investigation and extortion of confession employed *even before proving the charges* are an open secret. In view of these facts, it is nonsensical to say that the modern man cannot tolerate the punishments prescribed by Islam for *proven* and *established* criminals because he possesses a more refined outlook; and it does not lie in the mouth of those who can tolerate bloody "purges" after concocted confessions and phony trials, and who uphold political inquisitions and concentration camps, to pour out venom against the Islamic penal code.

The truth is that it is not the severity of the punishments in Islam that the upholders of modern civilization abhor, for they resort to even more tortuous punishments themselves. The reason for their hysteric outbursts against this alleged "barbarism" lies actually in the perversion of moral values—that is, in the fact that they do not think that crimes like drunkenness and adultery deserve even a word of reproach, let alone painful punishments. Had they been opposed to these punishments on humanitarian considerations, they would have likewise condemned the brutal punishments given to people on flimsy political and economic grounds. They complain in respect of Islam only because they do not at all deem as a sin or crime many a thing condemned by it.

I would like to put a straight question to these votaries of "modernity": "What are the values that you believe in? Do you believe in the Islamic values of life and standards of morality or those of the modern civilization?" If you have made your choice and accepted some other values and some different standard of right and wrong, of virtue and vice, of the permissible and the prohibited as against those envisaged by Islam, it is then a difference of a very fundamental nature. It means that you differ with and disbelieve in the Islamic ideology itself. In this case you should have the courage to declare that you reject Islam outright. Is it not foolish to allege faith in a God whose laws you consider as barbarous? Anyhow, nobody can remain inside the pale of Islam after holding such an opinion about the law of God.

### The Bogey of Sectarian Differences

We have dealt with two objections so far. The third objection is that there being many schools of Islamic jurisprudence, it is not possible to evolve an agreed code of law that might be acceptable to all the schools of Muslim thought. On this objection rests the last hope of the opponents of the Islamic law, and they seem to feel confident that on this count they will be able to score a point by driving a wedge among the Muslims. Moreover, this problem also baffles many sincere people who are loyal to Islam and who, not being fully conversant with its teachings, fail to understand how this "complication" can be removed. The fact is that this complication is merely a figment of fertile imagination, for, the existence of different schools of law can never become an obstacle in the way of the enforcement of Islamic law.

The first point to be understood in this connection is that the broad outlines of Islamic law, consisting of mandatory and unalterable commandments and fundamental principles and limitations, have always been accepted unanimously by all the Muslim schools of thought.

Neither was there ever, nor is there now, any conflict of opinion regarding this portion of our laws. Whatever differences had ever arisen were always in connection with the details that were to be framed through interpretation, deduction, and ijtihad—all, of course, within the limits prescribed by Islam.

The nature of these differences can also be understood by the fact that rules derived by jurists through interpretation, deduction, ijtihad, or istihsan could never acquire the force of law without either being accepted unanimously (*ijma'*) or having the approval of the majority (*jumhur*). This explains why the phrases like *'alayhi al-ijma'* (unanimous agreement), *'alayhi al-jumhur* (majority agreement), and *'alayhi al-fatwa* (adopted judgment) are appended to the expression of final opinions by our jurists in discussing legal matters, and it signifies that their opinion had finally to obtain legal sanction in order to become a law for Muslims.

These unanimous or majority decisions can be of two kinds: those which have always been accepted by the entire Muslim world or by the majority of Muslims, and those based on the unanimous agreement of the Muslims of a particular country at a particular period or of their majority.

Decisions coming under the first category, if based on unanimous agreement, are not subject to review and should always be accepted as part and parcel of Muslim law.

Decisions made by majority agreement can be accepted as law only if the majority of the Muslims of the country wherein they have to be promulgated also accepts them as such. If the majority of that country accepts them, they will become a law for this country, otherwise not.

So much about the past. As for the future, the laws that are accepted unanimously by majority of the Muslims of this country will be enacted here. In the past, too, this has been the practice, and no law used to operate without either the unanimous approval or the approval of the majority of the Muslims. This method is practicable even today. I do not think that any other procedure can be prescribed from the democratic point of view either.

A question may be asked as to what would be the position of those Muslims who might not agree with the majority. They are entitled to demand the enforcement of their own code in their personal matters, and this demand of theirs must be accepted. But, of course, the "law of the land" shall be the one which has the sanction of the majority.

I am sure that no Muslim of any sect would ever adopt the foolish position of preferring the continuance of un-Islamic laws in Pakistan on the ground that he is not in agreement with the views of the majority of Muslims on certain points of Islamic law. Obviously we cannot discard the Islamic way of life simply because we are not unanimous on all details of its law. Has there ever been or can there ever be any law or system of life on all details of which all its followers were, are, or can ever be unanimous? What do you say about the legal system that is in force in the country at present or anywhere else?

### The Problem of Non-Muslim Minorities

The last important objection in this respect is that there is a substantial non-Muslim minority living in Pakistan who cannot tolerate being governed by the religious laws of the Muslims.

This objection is based on a very superficial observation and shows a lack of proper analysis of the problem. For even a little amount of cool thinking can dissipate the fog of this misunderstanding.

The law with which we have been and are concerned here is the *law of the land* and not the personal law of any community. In personal matters, every community is welcome to adopt its own personal law. Indeed, only Islam guarantees this right in the most liberal manner to all the minorities living in an Islamic state. Islam has taught to the modern world the real difference between the law of the land and the personal law and enunciated the principle that in a multinational state the personal affairs of a man should be settled according to his own personal law. Therefore, no members of a minority group should feel afraid that we would thrust our own religious laws on them in their personal matters and thus violate an injunction unambiguously laid down by Islam itself.

The question that now remains to be dealt with is, What should be our "law of the land"? I think it is the demand of justice and fairness that the law that commands the approval of the majority alone has the right to become the law of the land.

Minorities are entitled to demand safeguards for their legitimate rights and interests, and we are bound to concede this demand as Islam itself enjoins us to do so. But it is not fair for the minorities to ask us to throw our ideology overboard and introduce laws that are against our convictions merely for the sake of appeasing them. When we were helpless because of foreign domination, we tolerated the supremacy of un-Islamic laws. But now when we are masters of our destiny, we cannot replace Islamic laws by those of any other type without conscious apostasy and betrayal of Islam. Are the minorities really entitled to ask the majority to give up its religion and its way of life? Have they the right to demand that the majority should give up the principles that it considers right and adopt others that are against its convictions? Or, is it reasonable that in a multireligious country all the communities should become irreligious? If the answers to all these questions are in the negative, I find no reason why Islamic law should not become the law of the land in a country where Muslims are in a predominant majority.

# Chapter 4

# SAYYID ABU'L-HASAN 'ALI NADWI
# 1914–1999

No ISLAMIST intellectual of the twentieth century better illustrates the ties between South Asia and the Arab Middle East than the Indian religious scholar Abu'l-Hasan 'Ali Nadwi. Over the course of a long and prolific career, Nadwi became one of the most visible South Asian scholars in the Arab Middle East and, indeed, in the greater Muslim world. Nadwi was an influential contributor to Islamist discourses from the early 1950s onward. He was also an early conduit for transmitting the ideas of Sayyid Abu'l-A'la Mawdudi to Arab Islamists. Nadwi is one of several prominent religious intellectuals—some of them discussed elsewhere in this volume—whose thought blurs the boundaries between Islamists and the 'ulama. Yet it also reveals considerable ambivalence toward other Islamists.

Abu'l-Hasan 'Ali Nadwi received much of his advanced education at the Dar al-'Ulum of the Nadwat al-'Ulama in Lucknow, in northern India. This institution had been founded in the early years of the twentieth century in efforts to reform the curriculum of traditional institutions of Islamic learning, the madrasas, to find a common ground between Muslim religious scholars of varied sectarian orientations and, perhaps most ambitiously, to bridge some of the differences between products of westernized institutions of learning and the madrasas. These goals have proved elusive during the more than hundred years of the Nadwa's existence. Those associated with the Nadwa have tended to be much closer to the madrasa at Deoband (on this institution, see chapter 1) than they have to English institutions of learning. The Nadwa, however, has been far more oriented toward the contemporary Arab Middle East than most other institutions of Islamic learning in South Asia. This orientation, which Nadwi himself did much to foster during his long tenure as the rector of the Nadwat al-'Ulama, has enabled graduates of this institution not only to be more thoroughly attuned to intellectual trends in the Arab Middle East but also to often write in the Arabic language and to contribute to debates in the larger Muslim world.

Nadwi wrote both in his native Urdu, the literary language of the Muslims of northern India and Pakistan, and in Arabic, and his books have been translated into English and a number of other languages. His first book in Arabic is also his most influential: *Madha khasira'l-'alam bi'l-inhitat al-muslimin?* (What Did the World Lose with the Decline of Islam?), later

translated into English as *Islam and the World*, was first published in
Cairo in 1950. It was in its fifteenth edition by the mid-1990s, and the
Urdu and Arabic translations have continued to be reprinted. This work,
from which selections are included here, is a broad-ranging albeit tenden-
tious review of the moral and social ills afflicting human societies before
the advent of Islam, followed by illustrations of ethical virtue, good governance, piety, and rectitude that the world witnessed with the advent of
Islam. Next comes a catalog of the moral depravation and the materialism of modern Western societies, and the book concludes by appealing to
the Muslims in general, and to the Arabs in particular, to return to an uncompromising devotion to their religious norms and thereby to once
again assume the leadership of the world.

Nadwi's term of choice for servitude to false gods and for the moral
depravity and chaos that necessarily results from it is jahiliyya. Muslim
historians and theologians have used this term since the first centuries of
Islam to designate pre-Islamic, pagan Arabia. Nadwi applies this term
much more broadly in referring to pre-Islamic cultures and civilizations
in general. He also uses it for modern, Western cultures, which he sees as
pervaded by materialism, godless ideologies, and sexual promiscuity.
More strikingly, he deems the latter-day Muslims to have themselves re-
lapsed into a new jahiliyya, which is reprehensible not only for the moral
chaos it entails but also because it signifies a virtual renunciation of Islam
itself—an act of apostasy (cf. Nadwi 1983–94, 1: 452–53). This view of
a new jahiliyya engulfing non-Muslims and Muslims alike was indebted
in some measure to Sayyid Abu'l-A'la Mawdudi, though its origins in
modern Muslim discourse are more complex. In any case, Nadwi developed it further and, with historical interests that were much stronger
than Mawdudi's, applied it to his reading of world history as well as the
history of Muslim societies.

It was through Nadwi's hands that this dark notion of a new jahiliyya
made its way into Arab Islamist thought. A laudatory foreword to the
second edition of *Islam and the World* was written by the Egyptian Islamist Sayyid Qutb, in which Qutb held out Nadwi's work as an example
of how Muslims ought to write their history (Qutb's foreword to Nadwi
1970, 20–21). Qutb also commended Nadwi for his use of the term jahiliyya to describe not a specific age in history (as earlier Muslim historians
and theologians usually did),[1] but "a particular spiritual and intellectual
character that comes to the fore solely to dislodge the fundamental values
that God has ordained for human life and to replace them with fabricated

---

[1] That jahiliyya was not exclusively a pre-Islamic phenomenon was recognized by some
medieval commentators as well. Qur'an 33:33 speaks of the "first jahiliyya" in instructing
the wives of the Prophet to "stay at home and not to flaunt your attractions as in the first
jahiliyya" (translation modified from Abdel Haleem 2004). On this, the tenth-century exegete al-Tabari (d. 923) comments that "there is a jahiliyya after Islam [too]. And the morals
of some Muslim men and women are the morals of the jahiliyya" (Tabari 1997, 6:199).

values that rest on fleeting whims." To Qutb, as for Nadwi, jahiliyya is an apt description as much of an earlier age of barbarism as it is of the present age of material advancement (Qutb's foreword to Nadwi 1970, 20). Qutb came to adopt this term in all the expansive connotations Mawdudi and Nadwi had given it, but he took the implications of the idea much further. The new jahiliyya afflicting Muslims needed a radical response, he argued in his last work, *Signposts*, and this included over-throwing rulers who claimed to be Muslim but were, in fact, among the greatest impediments to the implementation of a true Islamic order.

The political milieu in which Nadwi spent much of his life was very different from those of Qutb and Mawdudi. Unlike Mawdudi's Pakistan, there was no prospect for the public implementation of Islamic norms in India, with its overwhelming Hindu majority and its secular constitution. And unlike Egypt, as well as Pakistan for a substantial part of its history, the state was not authoritarian but democratic. The secular Indian state has always promised and often provided important protections to the Muslim community and culture and, like most other Indian Muslim lead-ers in postcolonial India, Nadwi had little doubt that it was in this secu-lar, democratic framework that Muslim interests were best served. Yet he saw secular nationalism *elsewhere* in the Muslim world as a major threat to the long-cherished Muslim sense of belonging to an umma, the com-munity of Muslims worldwide. During the heyday of Arab nationalism in the 1950s and the 1960s, Nadwi was tireless in denouncing it as a form of modern idolatry, a prime manifestation of jahiliyya, which threatened to cut Muslims off from one another and thus to collectively rob them of any prospects of regaining their political vigor. Any endorsement of secu-lar nationalism by Muslims elsewhere also meant, of course, that the Hindu-dominated Indian secular state would be further emboldened in its efforts to make the Muslims of India submit to the "man-made laws" that their coreligionists elsewhere had already accepted.

Nadwi's deep misgivings about secular nationalism coincided well with Saudi efforts to promote an Islamic universalism of a distinctly Wahhabi orientation. This was meant to counter Nasserism, an ideology that takes it name from the "Arab socialism" and pan-Arabism of the Egyptian leader Gamal 'Abd al-Nasser (d. 1970), whose appeal was felt through-out the Arab Middle East in the 1960s; and, in the 1980s, it was to be an antidote to Iranian efforts to "export" the 1979 revolution to the Arab states. If some of the success of *Islam and the World* had to do with the timeliness of its message, as Nadwi liked to think, some of it also owed to Saudi patronage: of a 1982 print run of 100,000 copies, the Saudi Min-istry of Education immediately bought 80,000 (Zaman 1998, 72, n. 68). Nadwi was also the recipient of much other Saudi patronage. He was the president of the Rabitat al-Adab al-Islami (League of Islamic Literature), which was founded in 1984 as an affiliate of the Saudi-sponsored Rabitat al-'Alam al-Islami (Muslim World League); and he was closely associated with several other Saudi-supported organizations. Like Mawdudi, he was also an early recipient of the King Faysal Prize, Saudi Arabia's highest honor for service to Islam and Islamic scholarship.

Yet for all the concord with Saudi interests (which did not, however, preclude Nadwi's tensions with some members of Saudi Arabia's Wahhabi religious establishment [cf. Hartung 2006]), the Indian context remains crucial to an understanding of Nadwi's thought and even of his Islamic universalism. This is evident in at least two ways. First, apart from his other ties and affiliations, Nadwi remained closely associated throughout his life with the Tablighi Jama'at, a proselytizing movement founded in India in the early twentieth century and now with a presence in many other countries (on the Tablighi Jama'at, see Masud 2000). The Tablighi Jama'at has primarily been concerned with preaching to the converted, so to speak: in the first instance, it has sought to heighten a commitment to Islamic norms among those who already profess to be Muslims rather than to win new converts, without, however, foreclosing opportunities to also seek such converts. Nadwi's association with the Tablighi Jama'at, as well as with other Muslim groups and organizations, frequently brought him to Europe, giving him a sort of direct, personal access to Muslims in the West that neither Qutb nor Mawdudi had ever enjoyed, and highlighting his role as a Muslim preacher that is matched, and superseded, only by Yusuf al-Qaradawi (see chapter 9).

Second, throughout his career, Nadwi devoted considerable energy to documenting what he took to be the contributions of the Muslims of India to Islamic civilization. This had much to do with demonstrating to fellow Indian Muslims what a "genuine" Islamic culture and Muslim identity lay in: it consisted in fostering ties with the greater Muslim world and in remaining true to the unalloyed beliefs and practices anchored in the Islamic foundational texts, not in cultivating specifically "Indian" ways of being Muslim or of compromising on Islamic norms in the interest of a more harmonious life with other inhabitants of the Indian subcontinent. This effort also had something to do, however, with demonstrating to the Arabs and to Muslims elsewhere—especially those he perceived as wavering in their commitment to Islam if not as latter-day apostates—that if a Muslim minority in India had been able to persevere in its devotion to Islam, those living in predominantly Muslim societies could do at least as much.

Nadwi wrote much in commemorating particular Muslim reformers of India, and he often argued that the major Muslim reformers of late medieval Islam had practically all been from the Indian subcontinent. Irrespective of its historical merit, this view—already set forth in *Islam and the World*—points to a significant tension in how the jahiliyya that Nadwi often spoke about is to be visualized. The jahiliyya, it turns out, is not quite as all-pervasive as might have been imagined: a long series of Muslim reformers did, of course, need to combat it, yet the continuous emergence of such reformers meant that the effects of the jahiliyya had usually been held at bay. The influence of Islam on the life of Muslims was such, moreover, that, even in conditions of decline, the Muslim community was still morally superior to any other people. Qutb, for his part, had a much more pessimistic view of an unrelenting latter-day jahiliyya; and he drew far more radical conclusions about how to combat it.

Nadwi's view points to differences among Islamists not only on how Islamic history is to be viewed but also, and specifically, on the place of the 'ulama in that history. As noted in chapter 1, many Islamists have been bitterly opposed to the 'ulama. Yet Islamist intellectuals like Nadwi were also part of the 'ulama. He was critical of facets of the 'ulama's scholarly culture, inter alia, for its becoming entangled in what he saw as sterile academic debates at the expense of direct guidance from the Islamic foundational texts. But, unlike many other Islamists, he also identified with this culture and its representatives, and the reformers whom he saw as leading the charge against Muslim decline were predominantly 'ulama. There is a strong affinity between Nadwi and Yusuf al-Qaradawi in this respect, and considerable distance between them, on the one hand, and Qutb and Mawdudi, on the other (for Qaradawi's laudatory view of Nadwi, see Qaradawi 2001b; also cf. Hartung 2006, 151–52).

There were other disagreements between Nadwi and leading Islamist intellectuals as well. He had initially been associated with Mawdudi's Jama'at-i Islami, but soon parted ways with it. And though Qutb's foreword has remained part of *Islam and the World* since the publication of its second edition in 1951, Nadwi was severely critical of what he characterized as "the political interpretation of Islam" that Qutb and Mawdudi had put forth. Islam was much more than politics, he insisted; and a single-minded pursuit of an Islamic state threatened to make Islamic norms and institutions subservient to political goals (Nadwi 1991). Nadwi believed, moreover, that the best means of promoting the interests of Islam was by inculcating devotion to Islamic norms among the people; this would entail political dividends, too, but their pursuit ought never to be an end in itself (cf. Qaradawi's account of Nadwi's position in Qaradawi 2001b, 121–26). Yet even Nadwi left little doubt that political power was critical to the defense of Islam at particular times in its history, that the leadership of the world he wanted Muslims to reassert was also a political leadership and that jihad might be an important means in restoring God's law to its proper position, "the object then being to crush the forces of evil that pull in the direction of unbelief and involve people in the highly hazardous spiritual tussle of having to choose between Truth and Untruth" (Nadwi 1978, 93).

# MUSLIM DECADENCE AND REVIVAL

## THE BEGINNINGS

A certain writer has remarked that there are two happenings in human life, the exact time of which one can never tell. One is related to the individual, the other to collective existence; one is the coming of sleep, the other is the decline or fall of a nation. No one can tell exactly when a person passes from wakefulness to sleep, or at what point a nation begins to decline. With the Islamic Empire, however, it was different. If we have to draw a line between its ascent and decline, we can do it easily: the time between the *Khilafa Rashida* and the emergence of Arab imperialism.

The caliphate was primarily a religious institution, and its political character was subsidiary. The caliphate retained its spiritual orientation during the regime of the first four caliphs because the men who then guided its destiny were what may be described as the living miracles of the Prophet Muhammad. They were the true specimens of the comprehensiveness of faith. They were ascetics, imams, preachers, judges, lawgivers, chancellors of the exchequer, generals, administrators, and statesmen. On this account all power in the empire—spiritual and temporal—was vested in one man, the caliph, who surrounded himself with a body of advisers, molded and modeled by the same master-craftsman who had trained the caliph. The caliph acted in consultation with his advisers, and the spirit of these ideal pupils of the Prophet pervaded the entire life of the *milla* (religious community), leaving no room for a clash between the spiritual and the temporal spheres of its activity.

## JIHAD AND IJTIHAD

There being no separate realms of "God" and "Caesar" in Islam, the Muslim caliphate or *imama* calls for a large variety of human qualities. A caliph or imam should, in addition to possessing a high degree of personal virtue, be keenly alive to the needs of jihad and ijtihad. Jihad, in Islamic terminology, means to strive to one's utmost for what is the most noble object on earth. There can be nothing more noble for a

Muslim than the earning of God's pleasure through complete submission to His will. For this, a long and sustained inner struggle is required against the false deities that may lay claim to his spiritual allegiance, as well as against all those whims and desires that may try to lure him away from the fold of goodness and piety. When this has been attained, it becomes his moral responsibility to exert himself for the improvement of his fellow beings and the establishment of Divine sovereignty over the world around him. It is a privilege as well as a necessity, for it often becomes impossible to remain true to God even in one's individual capacity in an ungodly environment. This latter circumstance has been described in the Qur'an as *fitna,* meaning calamity, sedition, treachery, sin, temptation and seduction.

It is true that everything that exists in the world—animals, plants, or minerals—bows to the sovereignty of God and is subservient to His Will. Says the Holy Qur'an:

> While all creatures in the heavens and on earth have, willingly or unwillingly, bowed to His will, (accepted Islam), and to Him shall they return. (Al 'Imran 3:83)

> Seest thou not that to God bow and worship all things that are in the heavens and on earth—the sun, the moon, the stars, the hills, the trees, the animals; and a great number among mankind? But a great number are (also) such as are fit for punishment. (al-Hajj 22:18)

But this has nothing to do with human endeavor. All created things are subject to the unfailing laws of nature. They, in due course, pass through the different phases of birth, growth, and decay that have been ordained for them. The law for the enforcement of which the Muslims are required to strive is the one that was brought into the world by the prophets. Opposition to this law will not cease as long as the world endures. There will always be some force or other to resist and to reject it. Jihad is, therefore, an eternal phase of human life. It may take various forms, one of which is war, which may sometimes be the highest form to take, the object of which is to crush the forces of evil which pull in the direction of unbelief and involve people in the highly hazardous spiritual tussle of having to choose between Truth and Untruth. Says the Holy Qur'an:

> And fight them on until there is no more tumult or oppression, and there prevail justice and faith in God. (al-Baqarah 2:193)

It is essential for those who take part in jihad to be well versed not only in the teachings and practices of Islam but also in the philosophy and ways of unbelief, so that they may be able to recognize unbelief in whatever disguise it may manifest itself. It was said by 'Umar, may Allah be pleased with him, "I am afraid, he who has been brought up in

Islam and has no knowledge of jahiliyya [un-Islamic culture and philosophy], may become an instrument disintegrating Islam unknowingly." It is, however, not possible for every Muslim to acquire an intimate understanding of the ways of jahiliyya ; however, he who directs and controls the affairs of the Islamic state should be better informed in this respect. The Muslim leaders also should build up their strength to the best of their capacity and to hold themselves constantly in readiness to meet the challenge of their enemies and of the enemies of faith. It is a command of God, as the Holy Qur'an says:

> Against them make ready your strength to the utmost of your power, including steeds of war, to strike terror into (the hearts of) the enemies of God and your enemies and others besides them, whom ye may not know, but whom God doth know. Whatever ye shall spend in the cause of God shall be repaid unto you, and ye shall not be treated unjustly. (al-Anfal 8:60)

Ijtihad means the ability to cope with the ever-changing pattern of life's requirements. It calls for a deep insight into the soul of Islam, and a thorough knowledge of the basic principles of Islamic jurisprudence. It also includes the ability to use the treasures of nature in the service of Islam instead of letting them fall into the hands of the unbelieving materialists who use them for spreading arrogance and mischief in the world.

## THE UMAYYADS AND THE 'ABBASIDS

Unfortunately, those who succeeded to the caliphate after the first four caliphs were greatly lacking in these qualities. They did not have the moral or spiritual caliber one would expect of Muslim leadership. They were not able to wear down the pagan attitudes and habits of their race. None of the Umayyad and the 'Abbasid caliphs, with the solitary exception of 'Umar ibn 'Abdul Aziz (d. AH 101), came fully up to the standard of Islam.

## THE EVILS OF MONARCHY

As a result, there soon occurred a rift between the church and state in the religio-political order of Islam. The caliphs, not being proficient or interested enough in religion, addressed themselves solely to political and administrative matters and disregarded their religious duties. When a religious need arose, they turned to the 'ulama for advice but accepted only that which suited their purpose. Thus, secular activity became independent of religion. The 'ulama, except those few who succumbed to the worldly advantage gained by joining the Imperial Court, arrayed themselves against it and initiated revolts within the empire from time to time, or they quietly withdrew into religious establishments and devoted their energies to individual improvement and reform.

As the hold of religion weakened, the standards in morality also deteriorated rapidly among Muslims. The perverse influence of the demoralized attitude of the caliphs, who were far from being models of Islamic morality (some were positively the reverse), was inevitably to adversely affect the moral structure of society as a whole. The Qur'anic injunction regarding "the enjoining of right and the forbidding of wrong" ceased to have any meaning in practice, because it did not enjoy the backing of the state and, the vigilance of religion having ended, the un-Islamic tendencies began to affect the followers of Islam, ruining the rugged simplicity of their faith. The Muslims settled down to a life of ease and pleasure. They became lazy and self-indulgent. In such circumstances it was futile to expect that they would discharge their duties as true followers of the Prophet and carry forward the message he had bequeathed to them.

The fine impression that Islam had made on non-Muslims during the earlier days was nullified owing to the moral degeneration of its followers. The non-Muslims naturally attributed the failings of the Muslims to their faith. They lost confidence in Islam. A European writer remarked— and correctly—that the decline of Islam began when people started to lose faith in the sincerity of its representatives.

### Philosophical Mind Games

From the natural sciences, Muslim thinkers drifted toward metaphysics and the theology of the Greeks, which was, in fact, merely a revised version of their mythology. The Greeks had ingeniously imparted a scholastic look to their mythology by dressing it up in philosophical garb. Their philosophy was purely speculative. The spirit of the Qur'an, on the other hand, is anticlassical. The Muslims, in fact, had no need to enter into theoretical disputes regarding the being and the attributes of God after the concrete knowledge the Qur'an had placed in their hands. But they did not appreciate its worth and, instead of concentrating on solid spiritual and material welfare which would have paved the way for the universal expansion of Islam, they wasted their energies in profitless metaphysical discussion.

### Religious Innovations

Thus, pagan beliefs and practices infiltrated into Muslim society. The superiority the Muslims had over others flowed solely from their religion and the secret of the greatness of their religion lies in it being the revealed law. This law is the creation of God and, says the Holy Qur'an: "(Such is) the artistry of God who disposes of all things in perfect order" (al-Naml 27:88).

If this Divine Law becomes polluted with human intervention, it will cease to be what it should be—a guarantee of success in this world and the next. Neither the human intellect will submit to it nor will the mind of man be won over.

## REVIVAL AND RESTORATION

So far, however, the basic values of religion remained intact and free from distortion. They remained absolutely free from all kinds of innovation, interpolation, misconstruction, and suppression. Islam did not close its eyes to the lapses of its followers. It was always on the alert, correcting, mending, admonishing. The Qur'an and the sunna were continually there—intact and unpolluted—to guide and to judge on occasions of doubt and dispute. They kept alive the spirit of defiance against the libertinism of the ruling classes and against other un-Islamic influences. The whole course of Islamic history is alight with the crusading endeavors of conscientious, determined, brave-hearted men who, like the true successors of the Prophets, faced the challenges of the time and restored, revived, and kept on moving the millah by resorting to jihad and ijtihad. These two principles, which embody the dynamism of Islam, never caused a vacuum in its structure. They remained always active in the body of Islam as living factors, holding aloft the torch of religious endeavor in the midst of the severest tempests. Thus, it was that darkness was never allowed to spread over the whole world of Islam.

Similarly, at every critical turn of its history, some mighty man of action, some inspired defender of the faith invariably burst upon the scene to beat off whatever threatened the existence of the millah. Two of the many such outstanding personalities produced by the undying spirit of Islam to defend itself were Nuruddin Zangi and Salahuddin Ayyubi.

## THE CRUSADES AND THE ZANGI DYNASTY

Europe had been harboring evil designs against the followers of Islam ever since they annexed the eastern wing of the Roman Empire, including all the Christian holy places. But, as the Muslims were then strong enough to defy all incursions, the Christian nations of Europe could not bring themselves to challenge them. Toward the end of the eleventh century, however, the situation underwent a change, and great armies of Crusaders were organized all over the European continent to attack the Muslim countries of Palestine and Syria. The Crusaders regained possession of Jerusalem in 1099 (AH 492) and took over the greater part of Palestine. Describing their invasion, Stanley Lane-Poole says: "The Crusaders penetrated like a wedge between the old wood and the new, and for a while seemed to cleave the trunk of Muhammedan Empire into splinters."

Of the unspeakable cruelties perpetrated on the helpless Muslims by the Christians on their entry into Jerusalem, one Christian historian writes: "So terrible, it is said, was the carnage which followed that the horses of the Crusaders who rode up to the mosque of Omar were knee-deep in the stream of blood. Infants were seized by their feet and dashed against the walls or whirled over the battlements, while the Jews were all burnt alive in their synagogue."

The conquest of Jerusalem by the Christians was a momentous event. It exposed the rot that had started in the lands of Islam. Besides that, it announced the awakening of Europe after the Dark Ages, which had followed the decline of Rome. It threw the entire Muslim world into jeopardy. The spirits of the Christians rose so high after it that Reginald, the master of Krak, began to dream of laying his hands on the holy cities of Mecca and Medina.

The most calamitous hour in the history of Islam since the Tragedy of Apostasy was at hand. However, at that moment there arose, from an unexpected quarter, a new star on the horizon of Islam. This was the Zangi dynasty of Mosul, two members of which, 'Imaduddin Zangi and Nuruddin Zangi, repeatedly defeated the Crusaders and drove them out of almost every town in Palestine except Jerusalem. Nuruddin holds a high place in the history of Islam for his administrative merit, piety, humility, justice, and zest for jihad. A contemporary chronicler, Ibn Athir al-Jazari, while speaking of Nuruddin, observes, "I have studied the lives of all the former sultans. I can say that but for the first four rightly guided caliphs and 'Umar ibn 'Abdul 'Aziz, none among them was more religious, just and clement than he."

When Nuruddin died, Salahuddin became the spearhead of Muslim resistance. Fighting battle after battle, he inflicted a crushing defeat on the Crusaders at Hittin, Palestine, on July 4, 1187 (Rabi' II 14, AH 583). The hopes of the Christians were dashed to the ground and their armies were so totally demoralized that "a single Saracen was seen dragging some thirty Christians he had taken prisoners and tied together with ropes. The dead lay in heaps, like stones upon stones, among broken crosses, severed hands and feet, whilst mutilated heads strewed the ground like a plentiful crop of melons."

Salahuddin then proceeded to retake Jerusalem. The fire that had been blazing in the breasts of the Muslims since that city had fallen into the hands of the Christians was at last quenched. Qadi Ibn Shaddad, an intimate friend and counsellor of the Sultan, described the stirring spectacle of the victory of Jerusalem in these words:

On all sides prayers were being offered; from all sides the cries of "Allah-u-Akbar" could be heard. After ninety years the Jumu'ah prayers were offered in Jerusalem. The cross, which the Christian soldiers had mounted on the Dome of the Rock, was pulled down. It was a wonderful spectacle. The grace of the Almighty and the triumph of Islam were visible everywhere.

The generosity, the magnanimity, and the high sense of Islamic morality, which Salahuddin displayed in that hour of his triumph, have been universally applauded by historians. Says Stanley Lane-Poole: "If the taking of Jerusalem were the only fact known about Saladin, it were enough to prove him the most chivalrous and great-hearted conqueror of his own and perhaps of any age."

Europe was furious at these reverses. In desperation, Crusaders from every European country converged on Syria and another series of bitter battles was fought between the Christians and the Muslims. Once again Salahuddin stood gallantly against the storm of concentrated Christian fury. After five years of relentless fighting, a truce was signed at Ramla in 1192. The Muslims retained Jerusalem and all the other towns and fortresses they had captured, while the Christians reigned over only the small state of Acre. Thus, at last, the task that Salahuddin had set himself, or rather, the mission God had charged him with, was accomplished. Lane-Poole observes:

> The Holy War was over; the five years' contest ended. Before the great victory at Hittin in July 1187, not an inch of Palestine west of the Jordan was in the Muslims' hands. After the Peace of Ramla in September 1192, the whole land was theirs except a narrow strip of coast from Tyre to Jaffa. Saladin had no cause to be ashamed of the treaty.

Salahuddin was a man of extraordinary ability and energy. His capacity for organization and leadership was astounding. After hundreds of years he had succeeded in uniting the various nations and tribes among Muslims under the banner of jihad, by making them forget their feuds and jealousies for the sake of Islam:

> All the strength of Christendom concentrated in the Third Crusade had not shaken Saladin's power. His soldiers may have murmured at their long months of hard and perilous service year after year, but they never refused to come to his summons and lay down their lives in his cause. . . .
> Kurds, Turkmans, Arabs and Egyptians, they were all Moslems and his servants when he called. In spite of their differences of race, their national jealousies and tribal pride, he had kept them together as one host—not without difficulty and, twice or thrice, a critical waver.

## The Death of Salahuddin

Salahuddin, the faithful son of Islam passed away on March 4, 1193 (Safar 27, AH 598). His selfless, crusading spirit had made the Muslim world safe from the tyranny of the West for a long time to come. But the Christians had derived immense benefit from these wars, and they busied themselves at once in preparing for a new assault. Their turn came in the nineteenth century. The Muslims, however, wavered again and allowed the ground to slip from under their feet. They began to fight among themselves. Unfortunately, they were no longer blessed with a leader possessing the iron purpose, glowing enthusiasm, and unflinching sincerity of Salahuddin.

## Muslims Still an Obstacle in the Path of Ignorance

Even with all their failings, the Muslims were nearer to the path of the prophets than any other people. For this reason, whatever of their former power and prestige was left continued to serve as a deterrent to ignorance. They were still a force in the world, commanding respect from near and far. But, internally, they were steadily declining. This fact could not be concealed for very long from the outside world. The facade of their strength was finally broken toward the middle of the thirteenth century, when they were attacked by wave after wave of savage nations and hostile powers, and Islamic lands fell into the hands of their enemies.

## The Impact of the Tartar Invasion on the Muslim World

The Muslim World suffered a grave setback as a result of the Tartar invasion. Its intellectual progress was arrested and a general feeling of pessimism was created among the Muslims about the future of Islam. Overwhelmed by it, the 'ulama and Muslim intellectuals closed the door of ijtihad. Stagnation crept over them, and they believed that the safety of Islam lay in rigidly containing everything in its existing state.

It was exceedingly unfortunate for the stewardship of the world to have passed into the hands of a people who had just stepped out of a barbaric condition. Although the conversion of the Tartars had made it possible for Muslims to live in peace and had reinstated Islam as the religion of the empire, the Tartars were greatly lacking in the qualities of the Islamic imama (leadership). It would have taken those qualities a long time to develop in them, and the Islamic world, in such circumstances, could ill afford to wait. What the Muslims urgently needed was an ardent and energetic nation that could instill new life into them and discharge the function of their leadership with the dedication of an inspired people.

## THE ADVENT OF THE OTTOMAN TURKS

Within a short time, in the fifteenth century (ninth century AH), the Ottoman Turks made their debut on the stage of history. They shot to the notice of the world in 1455 (AH 853) [sic] when their twenty-four-year-old sultan, Muhammad the Conqueror, took Constantinople, the hitherto impregnable capital of the Eastern Roman Empire. This victory, which had eluded the Muslims for eight hundred years, in spite of repeated attempts, thrilled the entire Muslim world and revived its spirits. The Muslims felt they could pin their hopes on the Ottoman Turks as the potential leaders of a Muslim revival; they could be trusted with the leadership of the Islamic world. They had sufficient endurance, foresight, and strength and had given ample proof of their ability in the pursuit of their ideals. Baron Carra de Vaux rightly observed:

> The victory of Muhammad the Conqueror was not a gift of fortune or the result of the Eastern Empire having grown weak. The Sultan had been preparing for it for a long time. He had taken advantage of all the existing scientific knowledge. The cannon had just been invented and he decided to equip himself with the biggest cannon in the world and for this he acquired the services of a Hungarian engineer, who constructed a cannon that could fire a ball weighing 300 kilograms to a distance of one mile. It is said that this cannon was pulled by 700 men and took two hours to be loaded. Muhammad marched upon Constantinople with 300,000 soldiers and a strong artillery. His fleet, which besieged the city from the sea, consisted of 120 warships. By great ingenuity the Sultan resolved to send a part of his fleet by land. He launched seventy ships into the sea from the direction of Qasim Pasha by carrying them over wooden boards upon which fat had been applied (to make them slippery).

The Sultan had struck so much fear into the heart of Europe that, when he died, the pope ordered continuous thanksgiving for three days throughout Christendom.

## ADVANTAGES ENJOYED BY THE OTTOMANS

The Ottomans enjoyed a number of distinct advantages which destined them for the leadership of the Muslim world:

1. They were a vigorous, big-hearted, and enterprising race, charged with a crusading zeal. Used to a nomadic existence,

they were free from the lazy and voluptuous habits that had been the ruin of the Eastern Muslims.

2. They possessed great military strength and could be relied upon to safeguard the spiritual and temporal interests of Islam and defend the Muslim world against its enemies. Their rule extended over three continents—Europe, Asia, and Africa. The Muslim world from Iran to Morocco was in their possession. Asia Minor they had subjugated, and in Europe they had advanced as far as the walls of Vienna. They were masters of the Mediterranean Sea. A trusted friend of Peter the Great wrote to him from Constantinople, saying that the Ottoman sultans regarded the Black Sea as their private lake in which they allowed no foreigners. The Turkish navy was so powerful that the combined maritime strength of Europe could not compete. In 1547 (AH 945), the combined fleets of Rome, Venice, Spain, Portugal, and Malta were badly beaten. During the reign of Sulaiman the Great, the Ottoman Empire stretched over an area of 400,000 square miles—from the river Sava in the north to the mouth of the Nile in the south and from the Caucasus in the east to Mount Atlas in the west. Every important city of the ancient world, with the exception of Rome, was included. The Ottoman fleet consisted of 3,000 ships. Many Christian monarchs sought the favors of the Ottoman sultans and even church bells would be silenced as a mark of respect.

3. The Ottomans occupied a place of vital strategic importance on the world map. Their capital, Istanbul (Constantinople), was unrivaled in its geographic and strategic situation. It stood at the meeting-point of Europe and Asia, from where the Ottomans could control all three continents of the Old World. It was said by Napoleon at a later date that if a world government was ever established, Constantinople would be the ideal capital.

The Ottomans were established in Europe, which was to acquire great importance in the near future and was already beginning to throb with a new life. They had a glorious opportunity of stealing a march on Christian Europe in heralding the New Age and guiding the world along the path of enlightened progress that Islam had chalked out for it before Europe emerged to lead it to its doom.

## THE DECLINE OF THE OTTOMAN TURKS

But, to their misfortune, and to the misfortune of the entire Islamic world, the Turks surrendered to the temptations of ease and luxury; their morals deteriorated, and their rulers became tyrannical. Internal feuds and dissensions began, and provincial governors and army generals became corrupt and disloyal.

The greatest error the Ottomans made was that they allowed their minds to become static. In the sphere of warfare and military organization, they utterly ignored the divine injunction, reproduced earlier, enjoining them to preserve their strength to the utmost in order to strike terror into the hearts of their enemies. Slowly they allowed their magnificent fighting machine to rust and decay.

Again, the advice of the Prophet, "Wisdom is the lost property of a Muslim—wherever he finds it, it is his," failed to influence them. Placed as they were in the midst of the hostile nations of Europe, it was expected that they would permanently keep before them the wise advice 'Amr ibn al-'As had given to the Egyptians: "Don't forget that you are eternally in danger. You are standing at an outpost of vital importance. Therefore, be always vigilant and ready with your arms. You are surrounded by enemies whose covetous eyes are on you and your country." But the Ottomans became complacent. While the European nations were making rapid progress, the Turks remained at a standstill.

As the well-known Turkish scholar, Halide Edib, said in her book, *Conflict of East and West in Turkey:* "As long as the world remained scholastic, [the] Moslem Religious Body did its duty admirably, and the Sulemanieh and the Fatih Medressehs were the centers of learning and of whatever science there was at that time. But when the West broke the chains of scholasticism and created a new learning and science, the effects of which were to change the face of the world, the Moslem Religious Body failed very badly in its educational function. The 'ulama took it for granted that human knowledge had not grown beyond what it was in the thirteenth century, and this attitude of mind persisted in their educational system down to the middle of the last century."

Intellectual sterility and the inefficiency of the educational system were not peculiar to Turkish life but were common to the entire Muslim world. Muslims, universally, had grown inert both mentally and spiritually. If we do not, for the sake of caution, trace this stupor back to the fourteenth century, the fifteenth century was definitely the last to reveal any real intellectual life among the followers of Islam. It was during this century that Ibn Khaldun wrote his *Prolegomena*. In the sixteenth-century indolence of mind, slavish pedantry, and blind imitation became complete. One does not find even one in a hundred among the 'ulama of the last four centuries who may, with justice, be called a genius or who may have produced anything to set beside the bold and noble intellectual activities of the earlier centuries. Only a few were above the low intellectual level of their age and, incidentally, they all came from India. One of these eminent personalities was Shaikh Ahmad Sirhindi Mujaddid Alf Thani (seventeenth century) who left a lasting impression on the whole Muslim world. His *Letters* made a valuable contribution to Islamic religious thought.

Another prominent figure was Shah Waliyyullah Dehlawi (eighteenth century). His *Hujjatullah-i'l-Balighah, Izalat-ul-Khifa', al-Fauz-ul-Kabir,* and *al-Insaf* were unique works in their particular fields. The third prominent person was his son, Shah Rafi'uddin Dehlawi, who, in the nineteenth century, wrote *Takmil-ul-Adhhan* and *Asrar-ul-Mahabbat.* Also outstanding was Shah Isma'il Shahid, whose *Mansab-i-Imamat* and *'Abaqat* remain to this day works of great merit. Similarly, the 'ulama of Farangi Mahal and of some of the educational centers of the eastern areas, who were worthy of note for their high degree of learning and scholarship, did much to improve the educational standards of their time. But their talents were confined largely to scholastics, the only exception being Shah Waliyyullah who wrote on ethics, politics, economics, mysticism, history, and sociology.

Excessive conservatism and servility to tradition also robbed poetry and literature of its freshness. Language became heavy with embellishments. Even personal letters, official notes, memoranda, and royal edicts were not free from this defect. The madrasas and other institutions of learning were afflicted with an inferiority complex, which degraded literature and thought. Classics were gradually expelled from the syllabi, and their place taken by the compilations of latter-day writers who lacked originality of thought and were merely blind imitators or interpreters of the old masters. Classical texts written by early scholars were replaced by annotations and commentaries, in the compilation of which the authors practiced extreme economy and reduced them to mere notes.

## EASTERN CONTEMPORARIES OF THE TURKS

Along with the Ottoman Empire were two important Muslim empires in the East, one of which was the Moghul Empire of India. Founded in 1526 by Babur, it had the rare good fortune to be ruled, one after the other, by a number of wise and powerful emperors, the last of whom was Aurangzeb, who will always be remembered in the history of Islam in India for the purity of his personal character, religious ardor, and wide conquests. He ruled for about half a century. After his death in the first half of the eighteenth century, the Moghul Empire declined and his successors proved weak, inefficient, and utterly unworthy. Simultaneously, this was the time of Europe's resurgence. Not to speak of protecting the world of Islam against the hostile intentions of the West, the Moghals could not save their own empire from falling prey to the onslaught of the West and became, on account of their weakness and incapability, the stepping-stone for England's boundless prosperity and the enslavement of the Muslim world.

The other was the Safavid Empire of Iran. In its earlier days, it was a very enlightened and progressive state, but exaggerated Shi'ism and senseless quarreling with Turkey sapped its energy and rendered it ineffective.

Both these empires isolated themselves completely from the outside world. They lost touch with time and shut their eyes to the numerous changes that were taking place around them. Europe was a far cry, and even the developments in adjoining Muslim countries did not excite any interest.

## INDIVIDUAL EFFORTS

The ability of Islam to sustain itself when everything appears to have conspired against it runs through the whole course of its history. In various Muslim lands, there arose men of strength and vision who tried to reverse the process of history. In India, the lionhearted Tipu Sultan made a heroic attempt to win back his country from the foreigners. A little later, Sayyid Ahmad Shahid dreamed of founding a state extending up to Bukhara on the lines of the *Khilafa Rashida*. He encouraged thousands of earnest and noble-minded preachers and fighters who, through their religious enthusiasm, sincerity, and selflessness, revived the memories of the first centuries of Islam. But collective degeneration had become so extensive that individual exertions could not arrest the march of decay.

## EUROPE'S SCIENTIFIC AND INDUSTRIAL PROGRESS

Europe, meanwhile, was making colossal scientific and industrial progress. Europeans were conquering hidden forces of matter, unveiling new secrets of nature and discovering "unknown" lands. During the sixteenth and seventeenth centuries, Europe produced a large number of outstanding men in all fields of creative activity. Scientists such as Copernicus, Bruno, Galileo, Kepler, and Newton revolutionized the world of physics, while Columbus, Vasco da Gama, and Magellan discovered the New World and many other lands and sea routes.

The destiny of mankind was being recast in the West and the world was changing at a breathtaking pace. He who lost a moment in idleness lost a great deal. The Muslims, alas, neglected not minutes but centuries, whereas the European nations realized the value of time and covered the distance of centuries in years.

The Turks lagged so far behind in the field of industry that shipbuilding was not started until the sixteenth century. The printing press, health services, and the defense academies were introduced in Turkey only in the seventeenth century. Toward the end of the eighteenth century, when a balloon was seen flying over Constantinople, the Turks thought it was a magic trick.

With imperial Turkey lagging so far behind, what could have been the plight of those Muslim countries that were under its suzerainty? They did not possess even minor industries. A French traveler, Volney, who travelled in Egypt in the eighteenth century and stayed for four years in Syria, wrote that "this country (Syria) is so backward in the matter of industry that if your watch goes wrong here, you will have to go to a foreigner to get it mended."

In their heyday, the Turks were unmatched in the world for military proficiency. But now, even in this area, the Europeans had surpassed them. In 1774 the Ottoman Empire suffered a crushing defeat at the hands of Europe. The shock of this defeat helped somewhat to open the eyes of the Turks to the ugly realities of their situation and some efforts were made by them to improve things. Military reorganization was taken in hand with the help of foreign experts. The real work of national reconstruction was, however, undertaken by Sultan Salim III who had, incidentally, been brought up outside the palace. He opened new-fashioned schools including an engineering college in which he himself taught. He also laid the nucleus of a modern army called the "New Order" and introduced political reforms. But stagnation had become so firmly entrenched in Turkey that before any substantial headway could be made, the old army rebelled against the Sultan and he was slain. After him, Mahmud II and his successor, 'Abdul Majid I, devoted themselves to the task of nation building, and the country took some steps forward during their reigns.

But these few attempts at reconstruction were nothing compared to the mighty strides of Europe. The fate that befell the Muslims in Morocco, Algiers, Egypt, India, Turkestan, and elsewhere in the eighteenth and the nineteenth centuries could easily have been predicted in the sixteenth and seventeenth centuries.

## MANKIND'S REAL LOSS UNDER WESTERN DOMINATION

We will not speak now of the grievous material losses the Eastern countries have suffered since the rise of the West. We will speak only of the real—the moral and spiritual—losses of mankind as a whole. In this regrettable development of history, the greatest losers have been the followers of Islam. Their philosophy of life was radically opposed to Western ideas and way of life. With the domination of the new barbarism, therefore, it was but natural that they should suffer the greatest loss.

## Absence of a Spiritual Sense

The Oriental character has always tended toward the spiritual.[2] Since time began, thousands of questions have entered the mind of the Easterner. What is the end of this world? Is there life after death? Where should one look for guidance regarding the afterlife? What is the secret of eternal happiness? The Easterner never failed to take note of these questions, not even on occasions of his deepest absorption in secular needs and interests. He gave them an unqualified priority in the manifold occupations of his life. During the whole course of his intellectual and cultural endeavors he kept himself steadily engaged in finding satisfactory solutions to them. His asceticism, his philosophy, his metaphysics, his mysticism were all directed toward it. Sometimes this quest took him along wrong paths. Sometimes he erred and stumbled. But he never shut his ears to the voice of his soul.

Questions relating to spiritual truths arose in Europe before the Renaissance, but as the innate character of its civilization gradually unfolded and the West got lost in the adoration of its material achievements, they were disregarded. If one still hears of them, it is only as problems of metaphysics. They do not occupy any place in practical life. The anxiety, the solicitude, the uneasiness which for thousands of years these questions evoked in the East is not at all felt in the West. And this is so, not because the soul of the West has become illumined with divine truth or that peace has dawned upon it. The surroundings that the West has succeeded in creating for itself are not related to the eternal and the infinite; they have imprisoned man in the world of matter and the West has made him forgetful of his true self.

The only thing that can cure the world of its present ills is that its leadership should pass from the hands of those who worship materialism to the hands of those who worship the One God.

## Renaissance of Faith

To attain this objective the world of Islam will have to rediscover its spiritual roots. It will have to rededicate itself to Islam. There is absolutely no need for a new religion, a new canonical law or a new set of

[2]The sharp contrast Nadwi draws between a "spiritual" East and a "materialist" West has much in common with nineteenth-century Orientalist constructions of a degenerate Eastern spirituality as contrasted with the practical rationality characteristic of Western societies. Nadwi's formulation reassigns moral superiority to this Eastern spirituality while branding its putative rivals as sheer materialism, but the starkness of the contrast remains unmitigated (cf. Zaman 1998, 70). Incidentally, Nadwi's quotations from the English Orientalist Stanley Lane Poole (d. 1931) also illustrate the complex relationship between Islamism and Orientalism, with the latter serving not just as the object of Islamist critique but also, as in the instances here, as corroboration—even from supposedly hostile witnesses—for the truth of particular assertions.

moral teachings. Like the sun, Islam was, is, and will be timeless. The mission of Prophet Muhammad is endowed with the quality of timelessness. No other messenger of God is to be raised now. His religion is everlasting, his teachings are immortal. But the Muslims do require a renaissance of faith. One cannot face new hazards and meet new challenges with a weak faith and unauthorized practice. A decaying building cannot withstand a flood. One must have a living, glowing, and firm faith in the cause one seeks to uphold. If the Islamic world aspires to inject new life into humanity, to give it the courage to resist and reverse the torrents of materialism and religious disbelief, it will first have to produce that enthusiasm and life in itself.

The Muslims will have to regenerate themselves internally. They cannot brave the onslaught of the ungodly West by imitating its empty cultural forms, customs, and social concepts, for these have no place in the growth and rise of nations. All cultural imitations are bound to make a people small. The Muslims can exert themselves only by means of that inner force, regarding which the West is becoming increasingly worried.

The secret of a Muslim's strength lies in his faith in the divine recompense and reward in the afterlife. If the Muslim world, too, establishes the same worldly ideals and gets caught in the same web of material desires as the West, the latter, with its larger fund of material knowledge and power, has a prior claim to superiority.

History speaks of times when Muslims grew indifferent to the value of the inner force and the wells of spiritual vigor within them dried up owing to disuse. Then, occasions arose calling for great feats of faith, and the Muslims tried to draw upon that force, but to their dismay they learned that it had deserted them long ago. It then dawned upon them that they had done themselves a great injury by neglecting it, and they made frantic efforts to induce it artificially, but this proved futile.

During such times there also occurred events in the course of which the honor of Islam seemed to be at stake, and it was hoped that the entire Muslim world would be set ablaze with fury and Muslims would rush forth from every quarter to defend their sacred rights, but nothing happened beyond a ripple here and a wave there. Under the surface, everything remained motionless and dead.

The major task before the Muslim leaders and thinkers today is to rekindle the flame of faith in the hearts of Muslims. They should do all that the early preachers of Islam did, and at the same time avail themselves fully of all the opportunities the modern age has put into their hands.

The Qur'an and the sunna can still revitalize the withered arteries of the Islamic world. Their study and influence still fire one with the desire to smash the citadel of ignorance. They have a rousing quality about them that can spur a slumbering people into new life. Under their inspiration mighty struggles can once again ensue between belief and unbelief, faith and treachery, heart and intellect. The world can once again be made to rouse itself to the battle between the tranquillity of the mind and ease of the body—a battle that all the prophets had to wage, and without which no vital change in the moral makeup of men can be brought about. There will then be born in every Muslim home good men who will fully correspond to the description contained in the following verses of the Holy Qur'an:

> They were youths who believed in their Lord, and We advanced them in guidance. We gave strength to their hearts; behold, they stood up and said: "Our Lord is the Lord of the heavens and of the earth; never shall we call upon any god other than Him; if we did, we should indeed have uttered an enormity." (al-Kahf 18:13–14)

The world will then again see living specimens of the religious earnestness and sacrificial spirit of Bilal and 'Ammar, Khabbab and Khubaib, Suhaib and Mus'ab ibn 'Umair and 'Uthman ibn Maz'un and Anas ibn an-Nadr; the gentle breeze of faith will once again kiss the face of the earth and a new world quite different from the one we know will come into existence.

Today, Muslim society is a victim of complacency and compromise with prevailing circumstances. The perils which are so relentlessly closing in from all sides leave it unmoved. It is drifting and it does not know to what end. Its heart is without the warmth of desire.

There is a dire need to disturb the complacency of this community of the faithful; it must be persuaded to care for human welfare more than its own interests.

# Chapter 5

# SAYYID QUTB
## 1906–1966

SAYYID QUTB is one of the most influential architects of contemporary Sunni Islamist political thought, a stature that has prompted one journalist to dub him "The Philosopher of Islamic Terror" (Berman 2003a). Yet Qutb's work and legacy are far more complex, polyvalent, and susceptible to multiple readings than such labels suggest. While some of the most brutal Islamists call themselves his acolytes, there are many others for whom Qutb has inspired nonviolent mobilization and gradualist political reform. In place of such sensationalist characterizations, then, it is more accurate to say that Qutb has provided several generations of Sunni Islamists with a moral map of history and politics in which Muslim experiences of impotence and suffering are simultaneously explained and offered redress.

In wide-ranging articles, books, letters, and an extensive *tafsir* (Qur'anic commentary) composed between 1948 and his execution in 1966, Qutb weds an increasingly strident indictment of Western culture, Euro-American power, and the corruption of Middle Eastern regimes to an ambitious project of social transformation, one aimed at bringing into existence a cadre of righteous Muslims dedicated to remaking the foundations of collective life through sustained political action. Both critical and revolutionary dimensions of Qutb's thought have proved remarkably flexible and mobile, traveling well beyond the specific context of mid-twentieth-century Egypt to inflect the practice and discourse of twenty-first-century Islamists from Syria to Pakistan, Sudan to the United States, Algeria to France. Qutb's influence does not derive solely from the substance of his arguments, however; his appeal is bound up with the ways in which the events of his later life and the circumstances of his death have become an extension and symbol of his life's work, investing his writing with an unusual power and political purchase.

Born in 1906 in a village in Upper Egypt, Qutb began his career in the 1930s as an elementary school teacher, and went on to serve as an inspector of public schools for the Egyptian Ministry of Education. A frequent participant in the literary debates among Egypt's leading intellectuals, Qutb's contributions at this time were often less than original, and his politics tended toward the "liberal" nationalism of his early mentors.[1]

---

[1] The quotation marks here signal the fact that what is called "liberalism" in this context is not an uncomplicated embrace of the ideas and processes associated with Anglo-American liberalism, but rather reflects a complex and eclectic amalgamation of liberal political theory and reinterpreted Islamic traditions.

His religious and political commitments would undergo a radical transformation in the years that followed, precipitated by a series of personal crises as well as growing dismay with the Egyptian constitutional experiment; British manipulation of domestic politics; the impoverishment of a growing number of his compatriots; and the opening of Palestine to Jewish immigration following World War II.

By 1948 the Ministry of Education found it prudent to ship the forty-two-year-old off to the United States to study the American system of education. The assignment was largely a pretext; the trip was designed to quell the increasingly strident moralism of Qutb's writing by exposing him to the attractions of a world he hated but had never directly experienced. The effort backfired. Qutb viewed his almost two-year stay in America through the lens of a stark division between an embattled Islam and a West he characterized as anti-Muslim, racist, sexually promiscuous, reflexively pro-Israeli, and morally and spiritually impoverished despite its material prosperity. To Qutb, even Americans' propensity to attend church in droves was not what it seemed. Americans do not seek spiritual reflection in their religion, Qutb wrote in one of a series of articles later published under the title *Amrika min al-dakhil bi minzar Sayyid Qutb* (America from Within as Seen by Sayyid Qutb), but rather social intercourse of the basest kind. In one instance, a church social was nothing more than an excuse for men and women to dance closely, their bodies undulating to the tune of "Baby It's Cold Outside" under lights dimmed by the Pastor himself (Qutb 1986).

Soon after his return home, Qutb joined al-Ikhwan al-Muslimun (the Muslim Brotherhood), the organization Hasan al-Banna had founded in Egypt in 1928. Deeply opposed to British power in Egypt, Qutb and many other members of the Brotherhood initially supported the 1952 coup that brought Gamal 'Abd al-Nasser to power and abolished the official vestiges of colonial control. Yet Nasser had no intention of acceding to the demands and concerns of the Brotherhood, and the brief period of comity ended in a break that rapidly turned rancorous. Many of the Brothers were subsequently imprisoned and brutalized. Qutb himself was arrested several times and reportedly endured torture so severe that he suffered three heart attacks while incarcerated. After the publication of his final book, *Ma'alim fi'l-tariq* (Signposts along the Road) in 1964, Qutb was arrested for the third and final time, accused of participating in a conspiracy against the Nasser regime; the book was used as evidence against him.[2] After a quick trial in 1966, the ailing sixty-year-old was

[2]Historians, leftists, and Brotherhood members disagree about the existence and significance of the alleged 1965 conspiracy to overthrow the Egyptian regime. Some have speculated that what has been called a "plot" was only unrealized and unattainable aspirations. Others have argued that the supposed conspiracy was the pretext Nasser sought to renew his flagging popularity. Still others are convinced that the plot was an invention of a "Zionist conspiracy" (Kepel 1985, 31–35).

hanged on the gallows, martyr to a movement that would radically reshape Muslim politics in the decades that followed.

The conceptual framework articulated in Qutb's most influential work
is organized around a systematic indictment of the visible political and
social world as well as its underlying logic and epistemological premises.[3]
Much as some Western thinkers claim that modernity augurs not the triumph of human achievement but the decay of institutions and certainties
that had previously given meaning to political life, Qutb argues that the
contemporary world is plagued by jahiliyya (age of pagan ignorance). Jahiliyya, a term taken directly from the Qur'an, originally referred to the
period of time in Arabia before divine truth had been revealed by the
Prophet. As used by Qutb, jahiliyya becomes an epithet rather than a historical condition, a way to simultaneously characterize and condemn
what he viewed as the pervasive moral bankruptcy produced by human
usurpation of God's authority (R. Euben 1999). According to Qutb, a society is jahili when it has repudiated Allah's hakimiyya (sovereignty) in
favor of a philosophy and epistemology that claims for human beings the
right to legislate rules for collective behavior and the authority to define
how life is to be lived. By this definition, all regimes that explicitly ratify
human sovereignty are jahili, whether they call themselves communist,
liberal, democratic, socialist, or nationalist. Beneath any surface differences, he avers, such regimes "all share one common truth: their way of
life is not established on complete submission to Allah alone. In this respect, they share the same characteristic of other societies, the characteristic of jahiliyya" (Qutb 1991, 93).

For Qutb, the West bears a particular responsibility for unleashing this
pathology on the world. The legacies of Greek philosophy, Judaism,
Christianity, the scientific revolution, and the European Enlightenment
have produced and sustained a worldview that is simultaneously unable
to apprehend the broad scope of divine authority and hostile to all those
who can (Qutb 1962; 1991). Yet crucial to Qutb's continuing influence
among contemporary Islamists is his insistence that what began as a foreign pathology has ceased to be so exclusively. No less than the "unbelieving" West, Qutb argues, Arab nationalists and socialists, Muslim
monarchs and theocrats are all jahili. By claiming for themselves the legislative authority that belongs only to Allah, such so-called Muslims represent a metastasizing cancer within the umma, inaugurating an internal
crisis of unprecedented scope and scale.

Given such a diagnosis, the antidote is clear and its implementation urgent: divine sovereignty must be acknowledged throughout the earth by
establishing Islamic law as the sole source of legislation. Yet, as jahiliyya

---

[3] *Ma'alim fi'l-tariq*, the book that sealed Qutb's fate, is perhaps best known among Europeans and Americans, but several chapters of it are taken from Qutb's even more influential
Qur'anic commentary, *Fi zilal al-Qur'an* [*In the Shade of the Qur'an*], which he had begun
years before. Selections from both are reproduced below.

has penetrated deeply into society, poisoning the very fount of human perception and imagination, it cannot simply be reasoned into remission; rather, it must be cut out with surgical precision to preserve the health of the body politic. This requires human action, for while shariʿa is an expression of divine will, it is realized on earth only by *jihad fi sabil Allah*, struggle in the path of God (Qutb 1967a; 1991). Actualization of God's sovereignty thus necessitates a vanguard of Muslims, believers who, like Qutb himself, have penetrated the miasma of jahiliyya and its false gods of materialism, science, and rationalism. Overcoming the alienation intrinsic to jahiliyya requires, however, that an individual first fight "the greater battle [*al-jihad al-akbar*] within himself against Satan, against his appetites, desires, and ambitions, against the interests of his family and of his nation—against anything that is not from Islam" (Qutb 1991, 75–76). Those who emerge victorious—the chosen few who can clearly see the "signposts along the road"—are thus capable not only of recognizing the scope of Islam as a way of life but also of cultivating the discipline, faith, and courage to reshape the world in its image (Qutb 1962; 1991).

Unlike several nineteenth-century Muslim reformists, Qutb repudiates the liberal shibboleth that in a world where diverse visions of the good compete, religion must be a private affair, and the state must remain neutral on matters of religious truth. On the contrary, he rejects the claim that there is a meaningful political distinction between practices of *ʿibadat* (worship) and those pertaining to *muʿamalat* (social relations). All facets of life express a unity (tawhid) subject to the authority of Islamic law, from prayer to rules of inheritance to ritual washing to criminal punishments. Acknowledging the Qur'anic admonition that "there is no compulsion in religion" (Q 2:256), Qutb contends that "*after* [people] are liberated from the lordship of men and the sole authority of Allah is established, *then* there is no compulsion to adopt the faith" (Qutb 1991, 74; emphasis added).

Qutb's arguments here are animated by the conviction that there is but one authentic, unified Islam constituted by self-evident imperatives that require immediate enactment in all domains of life rather than endless debate, analysis, and study. In an echo of the Marxist understanding of praxis as both a "tool for changing the course of history and a criterion for historical evaluation" (Avineri 1968, 138), Qutb argues that Islam is beyond intellectualism, beyond the theory and practice divide:

> Islam is intended to penetrate into the veins and arteries of a society and to form a concrete organized movement designed to transform it into a vibrant dynamic community. We should be aware therefore that any attempt to change the living faith of Islam into purely theoretical teachings and academic discussions is an attempt to show the superiority of the "Islamic theory" over the valueless and useless theories formulated by man. Such an attempt would be not only erroneous but also dangerous. (Qutb 1990, 32)

This emphasis on praxis enables Qutb to eschew, as a matter of principle, any attempt to detail the institutions of a legitimate Islamic state as inappropriately theoretical and speculative. For Qutb, a system of rules and regulations becomes necessary—indeed, even possible—only under specific historical conditions: Islam "does not posit hypothetical problems in order to prescribe solutions to them; rather it considers the reality at the time when an existent Muslim society has submitted to God's law" (Qutb 1991, 34). Such historicism, in turn, allows him to sidestep the interpretive challenges of specifying how, why, and under what circumstances particular provisions of Islamic law must be applied.

Qutb's claim that there is an authentic Islam, the essence of which is praxis rather than theory, also provides the terms in which he discredits religious scholars and secular intellectuals as jahili pawns who traffic in abstractions and technicalities that blind them to what really matters in the world. Such arguments take aim at what Qutb sees as the epistemological hubris at the heart of the modern philosophical enterprise: the transgression of divine authority evinced equally in Enlightenment rationalism and European colonialism, Marxism and positivism, materialism and Darwinism, Zionism and Arab socialism. At the same time, Qutb's antipathy to "scholars and intellectuals" is part and parcel of a particular strain of anticlericalism that recurs throughout his later work, much as it does in the writing of several other Egyptian Islamists. Just as Hasan al-Banna and 'Abd al-Salam Faraj accuse religious scholars of selling their integrity to ungodly regimes, Qutb characterizes "establishment" 'ulama as "opportunists" who transform religion into a profession, manipulate religious texts to serve their own material interests, and, in so doing, paralyze and deceive Muslims "in the name of religion" (Qutb 1975, 106; 1999–2004, 2:128).[4]

While Sunni Islam has never had a central clerical hierarchy akin to that of the Roman Catholic Church, it is nevertheless the case that the 'ulama have historically served as custodians of the Islamic tradition. Qutb takes direct aim at this legacy: he suggests that religious scholars have a greater stake in stability than truth and then sets out to demonstrate by example and argument that Muslims without specialized training have the right and obligation to engage the sacred texts without the mediation of the religious elite. As Qutb writes in the opening reflections to his multivolume tafsir, *In the Shade of the Qur'an*:

> I have listened to God the exalted conversing with me through this Qur'an—with me, a small little slave. What a sublime and heavenly honor this is for the human being! To what a high rank one is raised by this revelation! What a noble station the human being is granted by his generous Creator! I have lived, in the shade of the Qur'an,

---

[4]For an analysis of the complex relationship between 'ulama and Islamists, see discussion in chapter 1.

looking from an elevation at the pagan ignorance [jahiliyya] raging
in the land and the petty concerns of its people. [From this vantage
point], I have seen the pride the people of this jahiliyya take in their
childish knowledge, their childish ideas, their childish preoccupations. [I have looked upon them] like an elder looks upon the frivoli-
ties of children, upon their efforts, and upon their lisps. And I have
wondered: what's wrong with these people! Why is it that they are
stuck in this infested mire, and why can they not hear the sublime
and heavenly call—the call that elevates life and blesses and purifies
it? (Qutb 1967a, 1: 3; for another translation of this passage, cf.
Qutb 1999–2004, 1: xxii).

Here and elsewhere, Qutb deftly conflates his own claim to the special
knowledge usually reserved for the 'ulama with a championing of the
common wisdom of ordinary believers. Islam speaks to all mortals, Qutb
avers, but it speaks particularly clearly to true believers of humble origin; they are the "only ones who understand the Qur'an" in part because,
unlike scholars and intellectuals, they do not waste time and effort on
codifying abstract principles of Islamic jurisprudence (Qutb 1999–2004,
9:334, 10: 96). The truest believers are thus those for whom Islam is
praxis rather than theory, Muslims who "face up to jahiliyya with the
message of Islam, and who endeavor to return erring humanity to the
faith based on submission to God alone, and who strive against tyranny
in order to liberate mankind from servitude to others" (Qutb 1999–2004,
9: 334; also 1: 316–17). As we argued in chapter 1, Qutb's tendency to
ground his own special authority and insight in the "unsullied" wisdom
of ordinary believers makes it possible to read his work as either a brief
against democracy or as an enactment of it. While his insistence that the
foundation of legitimate authority must be divine rather than human suggests that he is clearly and unambiguously opposed to popular sovereignty, his challenge to religious and political authority in the name of
ordinary Muslims can also be seen as an attempt to "democratize" access
to the sacred texts and the authority such access confers.

In these respects and in many others, Qutb owes much to other twentieth-century Islamist thinkers. Crucial components of his analysis, particularly his formulation of hakimiyya and jahiliyya, were purloined from
the work of Sayyid Abu'l-A'la Mawdudi as well as from Abu'l-Hasan
'Ali Nadwi, who was largely responsible for introducing Qutb to Mawdudi's thought. In addition, Qutb stepped into a political arena that had
already been significantly reshaped by Banna. When Qutb was still a bureaucrat at the Egyptian Ministry of Education, Banna was advancing a
regimen of Islamic activism and renewed Qur'anic commitment as an antidote to British domination and Egyptian political paralysis. After Banna
was assassinated in 1949, Qutb helped forge his legacy into a system of
ideas that simultaneously proffered an indictment of Egyptian politics
and transcended its particulars.

While Qutb's particular worldview is in many ways defined in opposition to the modern corruption it excoriates, his work is also embedded in a long and complex tradition of religious reform, revivalism, and even insurrectionism in the history of Muslim societies. For instance, Qutb's attempt to explain and transfigure the problems plaguing the umma by selectively excavating Islamic sources and precedents simultaneously builds on and challenges similar efforts by such nineteenth-century Muslim thinkers as Jamal al-Din al-Afghani, Muhammad 'Abduh, and Rashid Rida. In addition, Qutb may be understood as recuperating the specific "exaltation of action as a criterion of faith" and the "uncompromising attachment to the Qur'an" (Enayat 1982, 6–7) characteristic of the seventh-century Khariji rebels (a comparison Qutb rejects). Still others argue he owes a debt to Ibn Taymiyya's fourteenth-century formulation of a right to revolt against rulers who violated the terms of Islamic law, an argument that would prove crucial not only for those who assassinated Anwar al-Sadat but also for Islamists now living thousands of miles from Cairo (Sivan 1983; 1985, 94–96).

Qutb's work must be understood in relation to these diverse intellectual figures and historical transformations, but the continuing political purchase of his worldview cannot be entirely reduced to them. Forged in the crucible of one man's life, the perspective he articulates is a prism that both reflects and reinforces the grievances of all those who would see themselves as engaging in a permanent jihad on behalf of Islam and against a corrosive human arrogance inaugurated by Western power that is abetted a corrupt Muslim leaders who no longer know what Islam really is. Like Qutb's life, the appeal of his worldview is also tied to its pathos, to its sense of loss and suffering, and to its conviction that a world defined by overwhelming confidence in human knowledge and laws has lost the capacity to answer the most profound questions of the human condition: why we are born, how we ought to live, and why we all die. For Qutb, only a return to Islam enables a human being to realize that

> his existence on earth is neither unplanned nor transitory; rather, it is foreordained and destined, his path planned, his existence designed with purpose. He has come into being in this world in order to act and work for his own sake and for the sake of others around him . . . and he cannot show his gratitude to God for the blessing of his existence and his true faith, nor can he hope for redemption from God's appraisal and punishment, unless he fulfills his positive role as God's vice-regent on earth. (Qutb 1962, 188–89)

# SIGNPOSTS ALONG THE ROAD

HUMANITY today is standing at the brink of an abyss, not because of the threat of annihilation hanging over its head—for this is just a symptom of the disease and not the disease itself—but because humanity is bankrupt in the realm of "values," those values which foster true human progress and development. This is abundantly clear to the Western world, which realizes that it cannot provide values for humanity and cannot even persuade itself of the justification for its own existence. "Democracy" in the Western world has resulted in bankruptcy, to the point where it must obviously borrow—incrementally—from the systems of the Eastern bloc, particularly from its economic methods under the name of socialism.

The condition of the Eastern bloc is much the same. Its primary social theory is Marxism, and at first Marxism appealed to a large number of people in the East—and in the West as well—as an ideology that bears the imprint of faith. But now it is so diminished in the realm of "thought" that it would not be far from the truth to say that there is no country left that follows its system. It is, in general, antithetical to the nature of human instincts and its needs; it thrives only in a destructive environment or in an environment long habituated to a dictatorial system. Even under these conditions, the failure of its economic system—although this is just a part of the foundation upon which it is built—has become abundantly clear. Russia, which is at the forefront of the communist systems, is being destroyed by rising prices. Russia used to have a surplus in the era of the tsars, but now it must import wheat and foodstuffs and is in a situation where it must sell its gold to procure food. The reason for this is the failure of collective farming, and ultimately the failure of any system that is antithetical to human nature.

Humanity must have new leadership!

The leadership of humanity by Western man is close to an end, not because Western civilization is materially impoverished or because its economic and military power has diminished. Rather, the epoch of the West is ending because it no longer has any of the "values" that make such leadership possible.

Such new leadership must possess and continually cultivate the material fruits of civilization associated with European ingenuity and unique material achievements. But it must also enrich humanity with new values entirely—those unlike anything humanity has ever known—by way of an original method that is practical and realistic at the same time.

Islam alone possesses such values and this approach.

The era dominated by scientific progress—an epoch that first arose at the time of the Renaissance in the sixteenth-century and reached its heyday in the eighteenth and nineteenth-centuries—has also come to an end, as it does not possess this spirit of renewal. Moreover, the "patriotism" and "nationalism" that appeared at this time have withered, as have the territorial movements associated with them. There are no other ideologies capable of providing this spirit of renewal. Both individualist and collective theories have ended in failure; neither these nor any others have this revivalist spirit.

At this critical moment of confusion and disorder, the time of "Islam" and the "umma" has arrived. Islam does not stand in the way of material innovation; on the contrary, Islam has regarded such creativity to be man's duty from the very start, when Allah gave the *khilafa* (vice-regency) over the earth to man, and deems it—under appropriate conditions—worship of God and fulfillment of the purpose of human existence. "[Prophet], when your Lord told the angels, 'I am putting a successor [*khalifa*] on earth'" (Q 2:30); "I created jinn [invisible spirits] and mankind only to worship me" (Q 51:56). The Muslim community has come to fulfill what God's will has enjoined upon humankind: "[Believers], you are the best community singled out for people: you order what is right, forbid what is wrong, and believe in God" (Q 3:110); "We have made you [believers] into a just community, so that you may bear witness [to the truth] before others and so that the Messenger may bear witness [to it] before you" (Q 2:143).

Islam is unable to perform this role, however, unless it is actualized in society or in a community. Humankind does not listen—especially at this time—to abstract theory that never materializes in real life. The Muslim community has not existed for many centuries, for it is not a "land" in which Islam has been located, nor is it a "people" whose forebears lived under an Islamic system at one time in history. Rather "the Muslim community" is a group of human beings whose customs, ideas, practices, laws, statutes, values, and guidelines all emanate from the *manhaj* (Islamic way). The community with these characteristics ceased to exist the moment that rule of God's law vanished from the earth entirely.

This umma must be restored to its original form so that Islam can once again perform its appointed role as leader of humankind. It is essential to excavate this umma buried beneath the rubble accumulated from generations of ideas, practices, and systems entirely unrelated to Islam and the Islamic way. This is so despite the fact that the "umma" of today claims for itself the name of "the Islamic World"!

I know that there is a vast distance between attempting such "revival" and assuming this leadership, for the real Muslim community vanished from existence and awareness long ago, and the leadership of humankind has long since passed to other ideas, other communities, other concepts and customs. This was the point at which European ingenuity had created a remarkable and vast fund of achievements in science, culture, organization, and material production and, in this respect, brought human progress to its zenith. It is not easy to disregard such achievements and blame those who invented them, especially as the so-called Islamic world is almost devoid of such accomplishments.

Yet in spite of all these considerations, it is still essential to "revive" Islam. Whatever vast distance there may be between the attempt at revival and the attainment of leadership, the effort at Islamic revival is the necessary first step.

So that we do not make any mistakes in our first attempt at Islamic revival, we must clearly understand—in exact terms—this umma's qualifications for the leadership of humankind. The Muslim community now is not capable—nor required—to present evidence of extraordinary material achievements in order for humankind to bow before its supremacy and appoint it to world leadership. In this domain, European genius has already overtaken it; there is no contesting its material supremacy, at least for the next few centuries.

We must thus posses another quality, one that this civilization does not have. This does not mean that we should neglect material creativity. On the contrary, it is incumbent upon us to pursue it as much as is possible, not because such creativity is required to assume the leadership of humankind at this stage but, rather, because it is a characteristic essential to our very existence. Moreover, the "Islamic conception"—which entrusts to humankind vice-regency on earth and deems such material creativity to be, under appropriate conditions, tantamount to the worship of God and a fulfillment of man's purpose—has made it obligatory.

To assume the leadership of humankind, then, it is essential to have a quality other than material creativity. This is none other than the "faith" and "way of life," which both enable humanity to preserve the fruits of material progress and fulfill the needs of human nature. This faith and program must then be actualized in a human collectivity— that is, a Muslim society.

When considering the sources from which the values of human life and its structure currently emanate, it is clear that the entire world today exists in a state of "jahiliyya." Tremendous material success and extraordinary material creativity do not diminish this jahiliyya in the slightest. The foundation upon which this jahiliyya rests is transgression of God's authority on earth and of the most specific of divine attributes, namely, sovereignty. It ascribes to men Allah's hakimiyya (sovereignty) and makes some men masters of others. It does not do so in the original, simple form of the first jahiliyya but rather by way of arrogating to humankind the right to establish ideas and values, laws and statutes, systems and conventions that are entirely detached from and heedless of the way of life prescribed by God. From this transgression against Allah's authority ensues the abuse of His creatures. The humiliation of the "common man" in collectivist systems, and the oppression of "the individual" and peoples dominated by capitalism and its colonialist ventures, are among the symptoms of this transgression against God's authority and disavowal of the dignity with which He has endowed humankind.

In this respect, Islam's way of life is unique. Where some people worship others in one form or another in all systems that are not Islamic, the Islamic way of life alone liberates all humans from the servitude of some to others, freeing them to worship God alone, be guided by God alone, and obey God alone. Here is the parting of the ways—the new worldview that we can offer to humanity. This worldview and way of life attend to the deepest dimensions of human practical life. This is the resource humankind does not now possess, because it is not among the "products" of Western civilization and European ingenuity, Eastern or Western.

Without a doubt, we have something new that is absolutely perfect, something that humanity does not recognize and is unable to "produce." But this renewal must—as we've said—be actualized in the real world. It is thus essential that a community live in accordance with it. This requires a process of revival in some segment of Islamic land. Sooner or later, this revival will succeed in assuming the leadership of humanity.

How should the process of reviving Islam begin?

There must be a vanguard committed to this undertaking, a vanguard resolved to stay the course and navigate a vast sea of jahiliyya that has taken root in every region on earth. As it proceeds, this vanguard must, on the one hand, remain detached from the surrounding jahiliyya and, on the other hand, keep in contact with it. The vanguard committed to such an undertaking must recognize the "signposts along the road" to know the nature of its role, the essence of its task, the purpose of its commitment, and the point of its departure on this long journey. It must also recognize its position in relation to the jahiliyya that is firmly entrenched throughout the globe.

When should this vanguard join forces with other people, and when should it remain apart? What are the attributes of this vanguard, and what are the characteristics of the jahiliyya surrounding it? How can it communicate with the followers of this jahiliyya in the language of Islam, and what should be discussed? From where and how can guidance for all this be obtained? Such signposts must be derived from the primary source of this faith—the Qur'an—from its basic prescriptions, from the worldview it created in the souls of the chosen best [the first generations], those whom Allah created to do His will on earth, those who once changed the contours and course of history in the direction willed by Allah. . . .

The primary spring from which the first generation [of Muslims] drank was the Qur'an and the Qur'an alone, for the hadith of the Messenger of Allah—peace be upon him—was just one of the fruits of this spring. When 'Aisha [Muhammad's wife] was asked about the character of the Prophet—peace be upon him—she said: "His character is the Qur'an."

Thus, the Qur'an was the only spring from which this generation drank, the only source that shaped, molded, and educated it. This was not due to a lack of human civilization, culture, knowledge, books, and schools at the time. On the contrary, there was Roman civilization and its culture, books, and laws, which still live on in or alongside European culture. Then there were the legacies of Greek civilization, its logic, its philosophy, its art, which remain a source of Western thought to this day. There was Persian civilization, its art, its poetry, its myths, its beliefs as well as its system of government. There were other civilizations, both near and far: Indian civilization, the civilization of China, and so forth. Roman and Persian cultures had settled to the north and south of the Arabian Peninsula, while the Jews and Christians were living in the heart of it. Hence, it was not for lack of cosmopolitan civilizations and cultures that this generation was restricted solely to the Book of God at that formative time; rather, it was a "decision," planned and pursued deliberately.

This intent was evident in the anger of the Prophet—peace be upon him—when he saw in the hand of 'Umar ibn al-Khattab[5]—may God be pleased with him—pages of the Torah. He said: "By God, even if Moses had been alive among you today, he would have no recourse but to follow me." The intent of the Messenger of God here was to restrict the sources that would shape this generation —in this period of initial development—solely to the Book of God, so that their souls and lives would develop in accordance with its method alone. This is why he was angered at seeing 'Umar ibn al-Khattab—may God be pleased with him—drawing from another source. The Messenger of God—peace be upon him—wanted to build a generation that was pure of heart and mind, pure in imagination and consciousness. Their training was to be free of any influence other than God's way, which is comprised of the holy Qur'an.

This generation drew solely from this source and attained something unparalleled in history. However, it subsequently came to pass that

[5] The Prophet's son-in-law and the second caliph (r. 634–44).

other influences intermingled with this source. Successive generations thus drew from sources such as Greek philosophy and logic, Persian myths and their ideas, the Jewish scriptures and Christian theology, along with the residue of other civilizations and cultures. All of this came to be mixed with Qur'anic commentaries, Islamic theology, and principles of jurisprudence. As a result, subsequent generations were educated by a corrupted source, and so a generation like the first has never again appeared.

There is thus no doubt that the dilution of this primary source was the principal determinant of the clear difference between these later generations and the unique and distinctive first generation.

The nature of this source was not the only crucial difference, however; another critical factor was the method by which the members of this unique first generation were trained. They did not study the Qur'an for the purpose of obtaining information or refinement, or for taste or pleasure. Not one of them studied the Qur'an to increase knowledge for its own sake or to address outstanding scientific or legal issues. Instead, he studied the Qur'an to learn what God commands, particularly in regard to the community in which he lived and the life he lived in his community. He studied it to immediately put such instruction into practice, much as a soldier studies "The Daily Command" to act immediately upon what he learns in the battlefield. Consequently, he did not try to read very much of the Qur'an in a single sitting; he recognized that doing so would put too heavy a burden of duties and obligations upon his shoulders. He was content with reading ten verses at a time, memorizing them, and then putting them into practice, as is reported in the hadith of 'Abd Allah ibn Mas'ud.

This understanding—that knowledge is for action—opened vistas of delight and perception that would not have been available to them if they had approached the Qur'an for the sake of debate, academic study, and information. This way of understanding the Qur'an facilitated action and lifted the burden entailed in the fulfillment of obligations. The Qur'an merged with their very souls, transforming their personalities and lives into concrete embodiments of the [Islamic] way of life, converting instruction usually confined within minds and books into a movement that changed the components, events, and course of life.

Indeed, the Qur'an does not open its treasures to any but those who have accepted this spirit—the spirit that comes from awareness that knowledge is for action. The Qur'an was not revealed to be a book of intellectual enjoyment, or a book of literature or art, fables or history, although it contains all of these elements. Rather, it was revealed to be a way of life, a pure mode of being from Allah. God Almighty disclosed this path to them incrementally, to be read little by little: "[It] is a recitation that We have revealed in parts, so that you can recite it to people at intervals; We have sent it down little by little" (Q 17:106).

The Qur'an was not revealed as a totality; instead, it was revealed in stages according to evolving needs, the constant development of ideas and concepts, the growth of society and human life, and the practical problems facing the Muslim community in real life. One verse or several verses would be revealed for a particular situation or a specific event, addressing what was in the people's minds, showing them the truth of a matter, prescribing for them an appropriate action, correcting errors in understanding and conduct. All of this would bring them closer to the Lord God and illuminate a universe suffused with His attributes. They would thus realize that they lived every moment with the heavenly host (al-mala al-aʻla [cf. Q 38:69]) under the eye of Allah, subject to the guidance of His boundless power. As a result, their lives actually came to be molded according to the way of life ordained by God Himself.

Learning for the sake of taking action was the method of this first generation [of Muslims], whereas instruction for the sake of study and pleasure was the method of education of successive generations. There is no doubt that this is the second critical factor distinguishing all of these generations from this remarkable and unique first generation.

There is a third cause that deserves careful attention. When a man embraced Islam at that time, he would immediately sever all contact with jahiliyya. He was aware that the moment he committed to Islam, he began anew, separate from everything in his life that had existed in jahiliyya. He came to view all that was jahili in his past with suspicion, doubt, wariness, and fear, realizing that these were corrupt and impermissible in Islam. Whenever he lost control, whenever old habits tempted him anew, whenever he felt too weak to fulfill the Islamic obligations, he immediately became aware of his sinfulness and of the need to cleanse his soul of what he had fallen into, renewing the effort to transform himself in accordance with guidance from the Qur'an.

Thus, there was a completely conscious break between a Muslim's jahili past and his Islamic present, followed by a complete separation from the jahili society surrounding him, a radical detachment from the jahili environment and his social ties to it. When he finally withdrew from the jahili environment, he decisively joined the Islamic one, even if the world of trade and daily interaction involved some exchange with the polytheists. Conscious detachment is one thing, daily commerce is another.

This repudiation of the jahili environment, its customs and ideas, practices and ties, is the result of replacing polytheism with belief in tawhid, that is, replacing the jahili worldview with the worldview of Islam. As a result, [Muslims] could join the new Islamic community under new leadership and pledge to this community and leadership all their loyalty, allegiance, obedience, and deference.

This was the crossroads, the beginning of a journey on a new road, a journey free from the burden of all the pressures to imitate jahili

society, from the concepts and values prevailing in it. A Muslim endured nothing there but abuse and strife, but in his soul he had already
resolved that the demands of the jahili worldview, and the pressure to
imitate jahili society, would not deflect him from this path.

We are today immersed in jahiliyya, a jahiliyya like that of early Islam
or darker (*azlam*). Everything around us is jahiliyya: people's ideas,
their beliefs, their habits, their traditions, the sources of their culture,
their art, their literature, rules, and laws. Even all that we have come to
consider Islamic culture, Islamic sources, philosophy, and thought—
these are all products of jahiliyya. This is why the values of Islam have
not taken root in our souls, why the Islamic worldview (*tasawwur*)
remains obscured in our minds, why no generation has arisen from
among the people equal to the caliber of the first Islamic generation.

In the course of the Islamic movement—and in the period of initial
training and preparation in particular—we must divest ourselves of all
the jahili influences in which we live and from which we draw. We must
return to the beginning, to the unadulterated source from which these
men [of the first generations] derived guidance, the content of which
was unalloyed and free of defect. We must return to it to derive our
conception of the nature of the universe, the nature of human existence,
and all the connections between these two dimensions of existence and
the Perfect, true Being, God Almighty. From this we derive our concepts
of life, our values, our ethics, our approach to government, politics,
economics, and all the other components of life.

When we return, we must do so with the recognition that instruction
is for the sake of action rather than for study or pleasure. We must
return to it to find out what it wants us to be and then become it. Along
the way, we will find what academics and acolytes of pleasure generally
find in the Qur'an—artistic beauty, marvelous tales, scenes of the Day
of Judgment, intuitive logic. We will find all of this in the Qur'an but
this is not our primary purpose. Our primary aim is to discover: What
does the Qur'an want us to do? What is the comprehensive worldview
that it intends us to have? How does the Qur'an develop our understanding of God? What are the ethics, principles, and systems we must
actualize in life?

Then we must rid ourselves of the oppression of jahili society, jahili
ideas, jahili traditions, and jahili leadership. Our mission is not to
accommodate the fact of jahili society and not to profess allegiance to
it; because of the characteristics of jahiliyya, it is not possible to negotiate with it. Therefore our task is first to change ourselves so that we
may change this society and then to transform the reality of this society
by changing the very foundations of jahiliyya.

There is a fundamental clash between jahiliyya and the Islamic way
of life and the Islamic worldview; indeed, jahili coercion and oppression prohibit us from living in the way ordained by God. Therefore, our

first step along the road must be to rise above this jahili society and its values and ideas. We must not change our own values and ideas in the least, nor should we meet it halfway. Oh no! We and it [jahiliyya] are on different paths and if we happen to accompany it for one step, we will lose our way entirely and miss this path!

We will encounter pain and hardship along this road, and enormous sacrifices will be required of us. But we cannot be masters of our own wills if we wish to follow the path of the first generations [of Muslims] through whom God established His way by helping it triumph over jahiliyya. To emerge from jahiliyya as the distinguished and unique first generation did, then, it is best that we be alert at all times to the nature of our path and the road we must follow.

# IN THE SHADE OF THE QUR'AN

THE DIFFERENT stages of the development of jihad, or striving for God's cause [reveal] a number of profound features of the Islamic approach that merit discussion; but we can only present them here very briefly.

The first of these features is the serious realism of the Islamic approach. Islam is a movement confronting a human situation with appropriate means. What it confronts is a state of ignorance, or jahiliyya, that prevails over ideas and beliefs, giving rise to practical systems that are supported by political and material authority. Thus, the Islamic approach is to confront all this with vigorous means and suitable resources. It presents its arguments and proofs to correct concepts and beliefs; and it strives with power to remove the systems and authorities that prevent people from adopting the right beliefs, forcing them to follow their errant ways and worship deities other than God Almighty. The Islamic approach does not resort to the use of verbal argument when confronting material power. Nor does it ever resort to compulsion and coercion in order to force its beliefs on people. Both are equally alien to the Islamic approach, as it seeks to liberate people from subjugation so that they may serve God alone.

Second, Islam is a practical movement that progresses from one stage to the next, utilizing for each stage practically effective and competent means, while preparing the ground for the next stage. It does not confront practical realities with abstract theories, nor does it use the same old means to face changing realities. Some people ignore this essential feature of the Islamic approach and overlook the nature of the different stages of development of this approach. They cite Qur'anic statements stating that they represent the Islamic approach, without relating these statements to the stages they addressed. When they do so, they betray their utter confusion and give the Islamic approach a deceptive appearance. They assign to Qur'anic verses insupportable rules and principles, treating each verse or statement as outlining final Islamic rules. Themselves a product of the sorry and desperate state of contemporary generations who have nothing of Islam other than its label, and defeated both rationally and spiritually, they claim that Islamic jihad is always defensive. They imagine that they are doing Islam a service when they cast away its objective of removing all tyrannical powers from the face of the earth, so that people are freed from serving anyone other than God. Islam does not force people to accept its beliefs; rather, it aims to provide an environment where people enjoy full freedom of belief. It abolishes oppressive political systems depriving people of this freedom, or forces them into submission so that they allow their peoples complete freedom to choose to believe in Islam if they so wish. Third, such continuous movement and progressive ways and means do not divert Islam from its definitive principles and well-defined objectives. Right from the very first day, when it made its initial address to the Prophet's immediate clan, then to the Quraysh, and then to the Arabs, and finally putting its message to all mankind, its basic theme remained the same, making the same requirement. It wants people to achieve the same objective of worshiping God alone, submitting themselves to none other than Him. There can be no compromise over this essential rule. It then moves toward this single goal according to a well-thought-out plan, with progressive stages and fitting means.

Finally, we have a clear legal framework governing relations between the Muslim community and other societies, as is evident in the excellent summary quoted from *Zad al-Ma'ad* [by Ibn Qayyim al-Jawziyya; see note 6]. This legal framework is based on the main principle that submission to God alone is a universal message which all mankind must either accept or be at peace with. It must not place any impediment to this message, in the form of a political system or material power. Every individual must remain free to make his or her absolutely free choice to accept or reject it, feeling no pressure or opposition. Anyone who puts such impediments in the face of the message of complete submission to God must be resisted and fought by Islam.

Writers with a defeatist and apologetic mentality who try to defend Islamic jihad often confuse two clearly different principles. The first is that Islam comes out clearly against forcing people to accept any particular belief, while the second is its approach that seeks to remove political and material forces that try to prevent it from addressing people, so that they may not submit themselves to God. These are clearly distinct principles that should never be confused. Yet it is because of their defeatism that such writers try to limit jihad to what is called today "a defensive war." But Islamic jihad is a totally different matter that has nothing to do with the wars people fight today or their motives and presentation. The motives of Islamic jihad can be found within the nature of Islam, its role in human life, the objectives God has set for it and for the achievement of which He has sent His final Messenger with His perfect message.

We may describe the Islamic faith as a declaration of the liberation of mankind from servitude to creatures, including man's own desires. It also declares that all Godhead and Lordship throughout the universe belong to God alone. This represents a challenge to all systems that assign sovereignty to human beings in any shape or form. It is, in effect, a revolt against any human situation where sovereignty, or indeed Godhead, is given to human beings. A situation that gives ultimate authority to human beings actually elevates those humans to the status of deities, usurping God's own authority. As a declaration of human liberation, Islam means returning God's authority to Him, rejecting the usurpers who rule over human communities according to man-made laws. In this way, no human being is placed in a position of Lordship over other people. To proclaim God's authority and sovereignty means the elimination of all human kingships and to establish the rule of God, the Lord of the universe. In the words of the Qur'an: "He alone is God in the heavens and God on earth" (Q 43:84); "All judgment rests with God alone. He has ordered that you should worship none but Him. That is the true faith, but most people do not know it" (Q 12:40); "Say: 'People of earlier revelations! Let us come to an agreement which is equitable between you and us: that we shall worship none but God, that we shall associate no partners with Him, and that we shall not take one another for lords beside God.' And if they turn away, then say: 'Bear witness that we have surrendered ourselves to God'" (Q 3:64).

Establishing the rule of God on earth does not mean that sovereignty is assigned to a particular group of people, as was the case when the church wielded power in Christian Europe, or that certain men become spokesmen for the gods, as was the case under theocratic rule. God's rule is established when His law is enforced and all matters are judged according to His revealed law.

Nothing of all this is achieved through verbal advocacy of Islam. The problem is that the people in power who have usurped God's authority on earth will not relinquish their power at the mere explanation and advocacy of the true faith. Otherwise, it would have been very simple for God's messengers to establish the divine faith. History, however, tells us that the reverse was true throughout human life.

This universal declaration of the liberation of man on earth from every authority other than that of God and the declaration that all sovereignty belongs to God alone as does Lordship over the universe are not theoretical, philosophical, and passive proclamations. They constitute a positive, practical, and dynamic message that seeks to bring about the implementation of God's law in human life, freeing people from servitude to anyone other than God alone. This cannot be achieved unless advocacy is complemented with a movement that confronts the existing human situation with adequate and competent means.

In actual life, Islam is always confronted with a host of obstacles placed in its way: some belong to the realm of beliefs and concepts; others are physical, in addition to political, social, economic, and racial obstacles. Deviant beliefs and superstitions add further obstacles trying to impede Islam. All these interact to form a very complex mixture working against Islam and the liberation of man.

Verbal argument and advocacy face up to beliefs and ideas, while the
movement confronts material obstacles, particularly political authority
that rests on complex yet interrelated ideological, racial, class, social,
and economic systems. Thus, employing both verbal advocacy and its
practical movement, Islam confronts the existing human situation in its
totality with appropriate, effective methods. Both are necessary for the
achievement of the liberation of all mankind throughout the world.
This very important point merits strong emphasis.

This religion of Islam is not a declaration for the liberation of the
Arabs, nor is its message addressed to the Arabs in particular. It addresses
itself to all humanity, considering the entire earth its field of work. God is
not the Lord of the Arabs alone, nor is His Lordship limited to Muslims
only. God is the Lord of all worlds. Hence, Islam wants to bring all
mankind back to their true Lord, liberating them from servitude to
anyone else. From the Islamic point of view, true servitude or worship
takes the form of people's submission to laws enacted by other human
beings. It is such submission, or servitude, that is due to God alone, as
Islam emphasizes. Anyone that serves anyone other than God in this
sense takes himself out of Islam, no matter how strongly he declares
himself to be a Muslim. The Prophet clearly states that such adherence to
laws and authorities was the type of worship that classified the Jews and
Christians as unbelievers, disobeying God's orders to worship Him alone.

Al-Tirmidhi relates on the authority of 'Adi ibn Hatim that when the
Prophet's message reached him, he fled to Syria. [He had earlier accepted Christianity.] However, his sister and a number of people from
his tribe were taken prisoner by the Muslims. The Prophet [peace be
upon him] treated his sister kindly and gave her gifts. She went back
to her brother and encouraged him to adopt Islam and to visit the
Prophet. People were speaking about his expected arrival. When he
came into the Prophet's presence, he was wearing a silver cross. As
he entered, the Prophet was reciting the verse which says: "They [i.e.,
the people of earlier revelations] have taken their rabbis and their
monks, as well as the Christ, son of Mary, for their lords beside God"
(Q 9:31). 'Adi reports: "I said, 'They did not worship their priests.'
God's Messenger replied, 'Yes they did. Their priests and rabbis forbade
them what is lawful, and declared permissible what is unlawful, and
they accepted that. This is how they worshiped them.'"

The explanation given by the Prophet is a clear statement that
obedience to man-made laws and judgments constitutes worship that
takes people out of Islam. It is indeed how some people take others for
their lords. This is the very situation Islam aims to eradicate in order to
ensure man's liberation.

When the realities of human life run contrary to the declaration of
general human liberation, it becomes incumbent on Islam to take
appropriate action, on both the advocacy and the movement fronts. It
strikes hard against political regimes that rule over people according to

laws other than that of God, or in other words, that force people to serve beings other than God, and prevent them from listening to the message of Islam and accepting it freely if they so desire. Islam will also remove existing powers, whether they take a purely political or racial form or operate as class distinctions within the same race. It then moves to establish a social, economic, and political system that allows the liberation of man and man's unhindered movement.

It is never the intention of Islam to force its beliefs on people, but Islam is not merely a set of beliefs. Islam aims to make mankind free from servitude to other people. Hence, it strives to abolish all systems and regimes that are based on the servitude of one person to another. When Islam has thus freed people from all political pressure and enlightened their minds with its message, it gives them complete freedom to choose the faith they wish. However, this freedom does not mean that they can make their desires their gods, or that they can choose to remain in servitude to people like them, or that some of them are elevated to the status of lordship over the rest. The system to be established in the world should be based on complete servitude to God alone, deriving all its laws from Him only. Within this system, every person is free to adopt whatever beliefs he or she wants. This is the practical meaning of the principle that "all religion must be to God alone." Religion means submission, obedience, servitude, and worship, and all these must be to God. According to Islam, the term "religion" is much wider in scope than belief. Religion is actually a way of life, and in Islam this is based on belief. But in an Islamic system, it is possible that different groups live under it even though they may choose not to adopt Islamic beliefs. They will, however, abide by its laws on the basis of the central principle of submission to God alone.

When we understand the nature of Islam, as it has already been explained, we realize the inevitability of jihad, or striving for God's cause, taking a military form in addition to its advocacy form. We will further recognize that jihad was never defensive, in the narrow sense that the term "defensive war" generally denotes today. This narrow sense is emphasized by the defeatists who succumb to the pressure of the present circumstances and to the Orientalists' wily attacks. Indeed, the concept of striving, or jihad, for God's cause represents a positive movement that aims to liberate man throughout the world, employing appropriate means to face every situation at every stage.

If we must describe Islamic jihad as defensive, then we need to amend the meaning of the term "defense" so that it means defending mankind against all factors that hinder their liberation and restrict their freedom. These may take the form of concepts and beliefs, as well as of political regimes that create economic, class, and racial distinctions. When Islam first came into existence, this world was full of such hindrances, some forms of which persist in present-day jahiliyya. When we give the term defense such a broader meaning, we can appreciate the motives for

Islamic jihad all over the world, and we can understand the nature of Islam. Otherwise, any attempt to find defensive justification for jihad, within the contemporary narrow sense of defense, betrays a lack of understanding of the nature of Islam and its role in this world. Such attempts try to find any evidence to prove that early Muslims went on jihad to repel aggression by their neighbors against Muslim land, which to some people is confined to the Arabian Peninsula. All this betrays a stark defeatism.

Had Abu Bakr, 'Umar, and 'Uthman, the first-three caliphs, felt secure against any attack on Arabia by the Byzantine or the Persian empires, would they have refrained from carrying the message of Islam to the rest of the world? How could they present Islam to the world when they had all types of material obstacles to contend with: political regimes, social, racial, and class systems, as well as economic systems based on such social discrimination, all of which are guaranteed protection by the state?

Jihad is essential for the Islamic message if it is to be taken seriously as a declaration of the liberation of man, because it cannot confine itself to theoretical and philosophical arguments. It must confront existing situations with effective means, whether the land of Islam is secure or under threat from neighboring powers. As Islam works for peace, it is not satisfied with a cheap peace that applies only to the area where people of the Muslim faith happen to live. Islam aims to achieve the sort of peace that ensures that all submission is made to God alone. This means that all people submit themselves to God, and none of them take others for their lord. We must form our view on the basis of the ultimate stage of the jihad movement, not on the early or middle stages of the Prophet's mission. All these stages led to the situation described by Imam Ibn Qayyim[6] as follows:

> Thus, after the revelation of Sura 9 [Repentance], the unbelievers were in three different categories with regard to the Prophet's relations with them: combatants, or bound by a specified-term treaty, or loyal. The second category embraced Islam shortly thereafter, leaving the other two groups: combatants who feared him, and those who were loyal. Thus, all mankind was divided into three classes: Muslims who believed in the Prophet's message; those at peace with him who enjoyed security; and those who were hostile and feared him.

Such is the attitude that is consistent with the nature of Islam and its objectives. When Islam was still confined to Mecca, and in the early period of the Prophet's settlement in Medina, God restrained the

---

[6]Ibn Qayyim al-Jawziyya (d. 1350) was a Muslim scholar, adherent of the Hanbali school of Islamic law, and one of the best-known pupils of Ibn Taymiyya.

Muslims from fighting. They were told: "Hold back your hands [from fighting], and attend regularly to prayer, and pay your zakat" (Q 4:77). They were later permitted to fight, when they were told: "Those who have been attacked are permitted to take up arms because they have been wronged—God has the power to help them—those who have been driven unjustly from their homes for saying, 'Our Lord is God.' If God did not repel some people by means of others, many monasteries, churches, synagogues, and mosques, where God's name is much invoked, would have been destroyed. God is sure to help those who help His cause—God is strong and mighty—those who, when We establish them in the land, keep up the prayer, pay the prescribed alms, command what is right, and forbid what is wrong: God controls the outcome of all events" (Q 22:39–41). They were then required to fight those who fight them but not other people: "Fight for the cause of God those who wage war against you, but do not commit aggression" (Q 2:190). But then they were ordered to fight against all idolaters: "Fight against the idolaters all together as they fight against you all together" (Q 9:36). They were also told: "Fight against those among the people of the scriptures who do not believe in God or the Last Day, and do not forbid what God and His Messenger have forbidden, and do not follow the religion of truth until they pay the submission tax with a willing hand and are utterly subdued" (Q 9:29)This means, as Ibn Qayyim puts it, that "fighting was first forbidden, then permitted, then ordered against those who fight Muslims, and finally against all unbelievers who associate partners with God."

The seriousness that is characteristic of the Qur'anic texts and the Prophetic Traditions on jihad, and the positive approach that is very dear in all events of jihad in the early Islamic periods and over many centuries, make it impossible to accept the explanation concocted by defeatist writers. They have come up with such an explanation under pressure from the present weakness of the Muslim community and the unsavory attacks on the concept of jihad by Orientalists.

When we listen to God's words and the Prophetic Traditions on jihad and follow the events of early Islamic jihad, we cannot imagine how anyone can consider it a temporary measure, subject to circumstances that may or may not come into play, or having the limited objective of securing national borders.

In the very first Qur'anic verse that gives Muslims permission to fight for His cause, God makes it clear to believers that the normal situation in this present life is that one group of people is checked by another so as to prevent the spread of corruption on earth: "Those who have been attacked are permitted to take up arms because they have been wronged—God has the power to help them—those who have been driven unjustly from their homes for saying, 'Our Lord is God.' If God did not repel some people by means of others, many monasteries,

churches, synagogues, and mosques, where God's name is much invoked, would have been destroyed" (Q 22:39–40). We thus see that it
is the permanent state of affairs for truth to be unable to coexist with
falsehood on earth. Hence, when Islam makes its declaration for the
liberation of mankind on earth, so that they may serve only God alone,
those who usurp God's authority try to silence it. They will never tolerate it or leave it in peace. Islam will not sit idle, either. It will move to
deprive them of their power so that people can be freed of their shackles. This is the permanent state of affairs that necessitates the continuity
of jihad until all submission is made to God alone.

[Thus,] holding back from fighting in Mecca, by divine order, was
only a stage in a long-term strategy. The same was the case in the early
days after the Prophet's migration to Medina. However, what made
the Muslim community in Medina take its stance was not merely the
need to defend Medina and make it secure against attack. This was
certainly a primary objective, but it was by no means the ultimate one.
Achieving this objective provided the means and the secure base from
which to remove the obstacles that fettered man and deprived him of
his freedom.

PART II

# Remaking the Islamic State

# Chapter 6

## AYATOLLAH RUHOLLAH KHOMEINI
## 1902–1989

WITH THE EXCEPTION of Usama bin Laden, no figure epitomizes Islamism more vividly for Western observers than Ayatollah Ruhollah Khomeini of Iran. Khomeini was by far the most important leader of the movement that culminated in the Iranian revolution of 1979. This event marked much more than the overthrow of the Iranian monarchy, headed by Muhammad Reza Shah Pahlavi and widely considered at the time as among the most stable of Muslim governments in the Middle East. The revolution also signified one of the rare occasions when Islamists have been able to make the transition from challenging the constituted political authority to actually taking it over. But if this has been rare in the Muslim world at large, it was practically unheard of in the context of Shi'i Islam, whose scholars had long maintained a resolutely quietist political stance toward the government.

Ruhollah Khomeini was born in a town named Khomein, in southwestern Iran, in 1902. He was a student of the noted scholar 'Abd al-Karim Ha'iri (d. 1936), with whom he studied in Arak, a city not far from Khomein. When Ha'iri moved to Qom, Khomeini joined him there, completing his education in that town and then embarking on his own teaching career there. The history of Qom extends back to early Islamic times, and it has long been revered by the Shi'a as the burial place of a sister of the eighth Shi'i imam, 'Ali al-Rida. Until Ha'iri's arrival in the mid-1920s, however, Qom did not seriously compete with Najaf, in Iraq, then the most prestigious center of teaching and scholarship in the Shi'i world. Part of the reason Ha'iri had been invited to come to Qom was to help invigorate its scholarly culture and, with his own considerable reputation, to draw other scholars and students to the town (Algar 1988, 267–68).

Khomeini's studies in Qom focused on Islamic law, which lay at the heart of the academic concerns of al-Hawza al-'ilmiyya, as the town's many madrasas are collectively known. Only when an advanced student had demonstrated his mastery of the intricacies of Islamic law and legal theory was he recognized as a mujtahid, one capable of arriving at independent judgments (ijtihad) in legal matters. Walking in the footsteps of his distinguished teacher, Khomeini gradually rose to be a leading jurist (*faqih*; plural: *fuqaha*) and a mujtahid in the Shi'i religious establishment. Unlike his teacher, Khomeini was never averse to political involvements, and these would shape the last thirty or so years of his career. His stature as a legal scholar, with well-established credentials to provide religious guidance to the people and, indeed, to speak authoritatively for Islam, was crucial to the political challenges he took upon himself. Yet Islamic law was not the only thing that occupied him. Not long after his arrival in Qom, Khomeini had become part of small study circles in which texts and topics relating to Islamic philosophy and mysticism were discussed. And it was in teaching some of these texts, including the writings of the noted philosopher Mulla Sadra (d. 1640), that Khomeini began his own career (Algar 1988, 268–69).[1]

Khomeini was a young man when, in 1925, Riza Khan became the king, founding the Pahlavi dynasty that would rule Iran until 1979. Like many others, Khomeini watched with consternation as the new king— now Riza *Shah*—launched Iran on a course of relentless westernization with the full might of an authoritarian state. The religious scholars were not necessarily averse to change, but they approved of neither its pace nor its direction under Riza Shah's leadership. The king, for his part, viewed the 'ulama as a major rival to his own authority, acting in ways that the 'ulama saw as hostile not only to their own interests but—in a typical conflation—to Islam itself. Under Riza Shah's son, Muhammad Riza Shah, Iran would continue on the path to rapid westernization, with increasingly close ties with the United States. Yet the Hawza itself was dominated during this time by religious scholars with a largely quietist political orientation (Algar 1988, 267–68, 277–78). Not until the death of Ayatollah Muhammad Husayn Borujerdi (d. 1961), the most influential scholar (*marja' al-taqlid*) of his time, was the regime challenged with any vigor from within the Hawza.

---

[1]Islamic philosophy and mysticism have often been viewed with some suspicion in the Hawza. It was not only that many jurists saw both as peripheral to the real work of a scholar, teacher, and preacher, all of which was assumed to be best concerned with Islamic law and legal scholarship. It was also that the jurists had never had an altogether comfortable relationship with the Sufis, and even less so with the Muslim philosophers. At issue were competing conceptions of how to arrive at the ultimate truth, and the implications of this quest for what the jurists regarded as the most important of all obligations—living according to God's law. There is no dearth of Muslim mystics and philosophers who have had only a tenuous relationship with Islamic norms as the jurists have prescribed and upheld them. Khomeini had little doubt about their fundamental concordance, however. And mysticism and philosophy were to remain his lifelong companions. Not long after his return to Iran following the 1979 revolution, Khomeini gave televised lectures on al-Fatiha, the first chapter of the Qur'an, in a distinctly Sufi idiom (Algar 1988, 271; for the text of these lectures, see Algar 1981, 363–425). And in a public letter he wrote to Mikhail Gorbachev in early 1989, a few months before his death, Khomeini invited Gorbachev to begin looking beyond Marxist materialism to more effectively deal with the problems then facing the Soviet Union, urging him to have Soviet scholars study the writings of medieval Muslim philosophers like al-Farabi (d. 950), Ibn Sina (Avicenna [d. 1037]), and al-Suhrawardi (d. 1191), and of Sufis like Ibn 'Arabi ([d. 1240]; see Khomeini 1994, esp. 18; Knysh 1992, 652). See also chapter 1 of the present volume.

The opportunity arose less than two years after Borujerdi's death, when the government gave women the right to vote in local council elections. Though women would later actively participate in bringing about the 1979 revolution, and they did so with Khomeini's unambiguous endorsement, he was still among the most vocal opponents of the measure in the early 1960s, leading an opposition that was strong enough to force the government to temporarily withdraw the measure (cf. Martin 2000, 60–62). In 1963 Khomeini led the charge against government initiatives toward, inter alia, limiting the size of private landholdings. The government now responded with a heavy hand. Students were attacked outside the Fayziyyeh, the madrasa at which Khomeini taught in Qom. Khomeini himself was subsequently arrested, and several hundred people were killed in the ensuing riots. Khomeini was released from prison in 1964, but it was not long before he confronted the government once again, this time on the question of the diplomatic immunity the parliament had granted to American military personnel and their families in Iran. As Khomeini put it on this occasion,

If some American's servant, some American's cook, assassinates your marja [leading religious scholar, viewed as the "object of emulation" by lay Shi'a] in the middle of the bazaar, or runs over him, the Iranian police do not have the right to apprehend him. . . . [The members of the Iranian parliament] have reduced the Iranian people to a level lower than that of an American dog. If someone runs over a dog belonging to an American, he will be prosecuted. . . . But if an American cook runs over the Shah, the head of the state, no one will have the right to interfere with him. Why? Because they wanted a loan and America demanded this in return. . . . The government has sold our independence, reduced us to the level of a colony, and made the Muslim nation of Iran appear more backward than savages in the eyes of the world. . . . If the religious scholars have influence, they will not permit this nation to be the slaves of Britain one day, and America the next. (Algar 1981, 181–83)

Needless to say, it is not the shah's authority that Khomeini was defending here. To Khomeini, the shah was a mere pawn of Western powers, and especially of the United States, and it was not so much his own dignity as that of the Iranian nation that he had compromised. A dexterous conflation of Islam and Iranian nationalism, an implacable hostility toward the United States, and a view of the 'ulama as not only the guardians of Islam but also the leaders of national resistance against foreign encroachments are all themes that Khomeini would develop with consummate skill in the following years. The immediate outcome of his challenge to the shah was, however, his exile from Iran. He first went to Turkey and then to Najaf, in Iraq, where he lived until shortly before his return to Iran in February 1979.

In hindsight, by far the most important event of Khomeini's long Najaf years was the lectures on Islamic law he delivered before advanced madrasa students in 1970. It is in these lectures, selections from which are included here, that he offered a sustained elucidation of his vision of an Islamic government. For centuries, Shi'i scholars had concurred in deferring the establishment of a just and properly Islamic government to the time when the twelfth imam, who is believed to have gone into hiding in the late ninth century, would make himself visible once again. Until then, the best they could do was to offer religious guidance to the Shi'i community, oversee the ritual and other religious practices of the believers, and act as deputies of the hidden imam in collecting and disbursing the taxes (notably the *khums*, "the fifth" of one's annual income) due to him. Existing governments were barely, if at all, legitimate in the absence of the imam. And though they were to be tolerated, it was only with the reappearance of the hidden imam that a truly desirable state of affairs would be inaugurated. This political theology had characterized the quietist views of Ha'iri and Borujerdi; in Iraq, they have continued to guide the views of leading Shi'i scholars like Abu'l-Qasim al-Khu'i (d. 1992) and 'Ali al-Sistani (b. 1930).

Khomeini's 1970 lectures represented a radical break with this dominant view. As he saw it, the 'ulama's deputyship of the hidden imam extends to *all* facets of his functions, including the political. God intends his law to be implemented, not simply expounded or such implementation to be deferred to some indeterminate moment in the future. If it is to be implemented, however, then it is those most knowledgeable in it, the jurists, who ought to take the lead in doing so. The public implementation of the sacred law falls within the scope of "the [pre-eminent] jurist's authority" (*velayat-e faqih*), and it is obligatory on the 'ulama to mobilize and lead the people in establishing a state in which this law would be implemented.

Throughout the 1970s, Khomeini strove to deepen his following within the Hawza in Iran and to bring together varied groups on a platform of shared opposition to the shah. By the time he had been exiled from Iran, Khomeini already had a vast network of students (cf. Algar 1988, 280–82), and these, alongside new converts to his cause, were instrumental in mobilizing support for him in Iran and in forging ties among the college- and university-educated Iranians, Iranians studying and living abroad, and the bazaar merchants, on whose financial support the 'ulama had long depended. By 1978 the movement had coalesced around Khomeini, who returned to Iran in February 1979. The shah had left Iran in the face of massive popular demonstrations two weeks earlier. The monarchy was now abolished, Iran declared itself to be an Islamic Republic, and Khomeini's vision of the Islamic state guided by the *vali-ye faqih* (guardian jurist) defined the new constitution.

In analyzing Islamist movements and the pronouncements of their leaders, scholars and observers have often speculated on the sort of society that would come about should the Islamists succeed in their political aspirations. The case of Iran is of signal importance not only because the Islamist movement here was led by the 'ulama rather than those educated in westernized colleges and universities—as has usually been the case in other Muslim societies—or because this movement had direct implications for long-established trends in Shi'i political theology. Its importance lies also in the fact that this movement actually succeeded in its professed objective of overthrowing the regime of the shah and replacing it with a radically different government. There was not much consensus on the movement's objectives beyond that, however. For all the reverence in which Khomeini was held as the galvanizing force behind the movement, not everyone expected that he would emerge as, let alone remain, the ultimate arbiter in all matters of public policy, or that the 'ulama would gradually come to consolidate their control over key political positions in the state, or that the consequences of being on the wrong side of the paths the state came to chart for itself would be quite so dire. And it was only after the revolution that Iranian women found themselves decidedly disadvantaged in relation to men in matters of marriage, divorce, and inheritance, as well as in the opportunities available to them in the public and political sphere.

Khomeini, of course, had pronounced on what he took an Islamic government to be long before the revolution, though it was in a highly specialized context that he had done so; and he would not have warmed up to having the implications of his arguments in those lectures elucidated to the rank and file of the revolutionary movement. Yet it is important to note that Khomeini's 1970 lectures themselves reveal a crucial ambiguity on the relationship between Islamic law and the Islamic state—an ambiguity that extends well beyond Khomeini's political thought to encompass Islamist discourses in other contexts as well. As Khomeini had put it in those lectures, God's law is there to be implemented, and it is the mandate, and the obligation, of the jurist to see that this is done with exactitude:

> If a faqih wishes to punish an adulterer, he must give him one hundred lashes in the presence of the people, in the exact manner that has been specified. He does not have the right to inflict one additional lash, to curse the offender, to slap him, or to imprison him for a single day. . . . If a faqih acts in contradiction to the criteria of Islam (God forbid!), then he will automatically be dismissed from his post, since he will have forfeited his quality of trustee. (Algar 1981, 79)

Yet Khomeini had also argued that "Islam regards law as a tool, not as an end in itself. Law is a tool and an instrument for the establishment of justice in society, a means for man's intellectual and moral reform and his purification" (Algar 1981, 80). The latter statement obviously suggests a much more malleable view of the sacred law than does the former; and it is this latter view that Khomeini would affirm shortly before his death. In early 1988, Khomeini was asked to intervene in a constitutional crisis that centered on the division of powers in the Iranian state. In a letter to 'Ali Khamene'i, then the president of Iran (and soon to be Khomeini's successor as the guardian jurist), Khomeini publicly rebuked him for taking too narrow a view of the powers of the government in relation to Islamic law. The scope of governmental authority, Khomeini now argued, is *not* constrained by stipulations of Islamic law:

> I should state that the government, which is a part of the absolute vice-regency of the Prophet of God . . . is one of the primary injunctions of Islam and has priority over all other secondary injunctions, even prayers, fasting and *hajj*. . . . The government is empowered to unilaterally revoke any shari'ah agreements which it has concluded with the people when those agreements are contrary to the interests of the country or of Islam. It can also prevent any devotional or non-devotional affair if it is opposed to the interests of Islam and for so long as it is so. (quoted in Eickelman and Piscatori 1996, 50)

On this view, the state, as guided by the guardian jurist, was the arbiter of where the interests of Islam lay and how they were best served. Far from merely *upholding* the law, the edicts of the state became its most authoritative expression. This explicit collapsing of any clear distinction between Islam and Islamic law, on the one hand, and the will of the state, on the other, has to do with Khomeini's view of the extraordinary authority the supreme jurist enjoyed by virtue of his scholarly standing. It probably also has to do with Khomeini's lifelong immersion in Islamic philosophy and mysticism, which seems to have rendered God's purposes more transparent to him than the 'ulama have usually professed them to be.

The doctrine of the preeminent jurist's overarching authority has proved contentious among the Shi'i 'ulama. Muhammad Baqir al-Sadr of Iraq did, indeed, have a view similar to Khomeini's, and Sadr's writings had some influence on constitutional deliberations following the revolution in Iran (Mallat 1993). But other leading religious scholars in Iraq have remained notably cool to Khomeini's doctrinal innovations. In Iran, there were few explicit challenges to the velayat-e faqih while Khomeini was alive: the coercive powers of the revolutionary state were scarcely conducive to open debate on a doctrine that bore the imprimatur of the founding father. That there *were* some challenges at all is therefore especially significant, as is the fact that they came from some highly regarded scholars. Khomeini was under no illusions about the depths of opposition to his views within the Hawza. Already in his 1970 lectures, he had issued what amounted to an ominous warning to those who, unlike him, were committed to politically quietist views. They were "pseudo-saints" allied to "imperialists and . . . oppressive governments," he had said on that occasion (Algar 1981, 141). "Our youths must strip them of their turbans," by which he meant that people should neither recognize them as accredited religious scholars nor permit them to perform their functions as such. "They don't need to be beaten much; just take off their turbans, and do not permit them to appear in public wearing turbans" (Algar 1981, 145). In 1982 Ayatollah Kazem Shari'atmadari (d. 1986), one of the highest-ranking religious scholars in the Qom establishment and a critic of Khomeini's doctrine of velayat-e faqih as well as of many of his policies, would essentially meet that fate after being accused of supporting a plot to overthrow the revolutionary regime.[2]

Doubts about Khomeini's doctrine were exacerbated by the question of his succession. Khomeini had anointed Husayn 'Ali Montazeri, one of his students and a respected scholar, as the guardian jurist after him. But shortly before Khomeini's death, Montazeri fell from favor on account of his criticism of some government policies, and it was 'Ali Khamene'i, not Montazeri, who came to succeed Khomeini. A key assumption underlying Khomeini's doctrine had been, of course, that the most learned jurist would occupy this position *and* that the stature of this scholar would be recognized not only in Iran—where it was anchored in the new constitution—but also by the Shi'a everywhere. Yet Khamene'i who, until Khomeini's death, was the president of Iran, was anything but preeminent as a religious scholar, which means that he has seldom been recognized as a religious authority outside Iran; and Iranians themselves have often looked to religious scholars elsewhere for their most revered authorities (see chapter 16 on Fadlallah). Even so, and as mandated by the Iranian constitution, the guardian jurist has continued to enjoy overarching religious and, by extension, political authority in Iran, not infrequently overruling the popularly elected Iranian president himself.

Since his death, Khomeini's doctrine has been vigorously debated in Iran (cf. Akhavi 1996; Arjomand 2002). The significance of this debate lies not only in that it concerns a major institution in contemporary Shi'ism or that participants have sometimes risked imprisonment and intimidation for engaging in it. Its significance consists also in the fact that, in its scope and implications, this debate has come to encompass questions well-beyond the velayat-e faqih: the debate is now also about the relationship between religious and political authority in general, about whether intellectual, social, political, and economic practices and institutions ought to be governed by religious norms at all, and about how foundational religious texts are to be interpreted (cf. Soroush 2000; Mir-Hosseini 1999; Kamrava 2008). If Khomeini's doctrine of velayat-e faqih had marked a major departure in the history of Shi'i Islam and had

---

[2]Khomeini's preoccupation with the threat posed by fellow scholars skeptical of his political theology is also in ample evidence in his *Last Will and Testament*. For the text of this document, see Khomeini n.d.

helped provide the theoretical justification for the Iranian revolution, it has also produced a rich, varied, and altogether unintended legacy of contestation in the contemporary Iranian public sphere—part of a varied phenomenon that some observers have characterized as "post-Islamism" (cf. Bayat 2007).

# ISLAMIC GOVERNMENT

A BODY OF LAWS alone is not sufficient for a society to be reformed. In order for law to ensure the reform and happiness of man, there must be an executive power and an executor. For this reason, God Almighty, in addition to revealing a body of law (e.g., the ordinances of the shari'a), has laid down a particular form of government together with executive and administrative institutions.

The Most Noble Messenger (peace and blessings be upon him) headed the executive and administrative institutions of Muslim society. In addition to conveying the revelation and expounding and interpreting the articles of faith and the ordinances and institutions of Islam, he undertook the implementation of law and the establishment of the ordinances of Islam, thereby bringing into being the Islamic state. He did not content himself with the promulgation of law; rather, he implemented it at the same time, cutting off hands and administering lashings and stonings. After the Most Noble Messenger, his successor had the same duty and function. When the Prophet appointed a successor, it was not for the purpose of expounding articles of faith and law; it was for the implementation of law and the execution of God's ordinances. It was this function—the execution of law and the establishment of Islamic institutions—that made the appointment of a successor such an important matter that the Prophet would have failed to fulfill his mission if he had neglected it. For after the Prophet, the Muslims still needed someone to execute laws and establish the institutions of Islam in society, so that they might attain happiness in this world and the hereafter.

By their very nature, in fact, law and social institutions require the existence of an executor. It has always and everywhere been the case that legislation alone has little benefit: legislation by itself cannot assure the well-being of man. After the establishment of legislation, an executive power must come into being, a power that implements the laws and the verdicts given by the courts, thus allowing people to benefit from the laws and the just sentences the courts deliver. Islam has therefore established an executive power in the same way that it has brought laws into being. The person who holds this executive power is known as the *vali amr*.

The sunna and path of the Prophet constitute a proof of the necessity for establishing government. First, he himself established a government, as history testifies. He engaged in the implementation of laws, the establishment of the ordinances of Islam, and the administration of society. He sent out governors to different regions; both sat in judgment himself and appointed judges; dispatched emissaries to foreign states, tribal chieftains, and kings; concluded treaties and pacts; and took command in battle. In short, he fulfilled all the functions of government. Second, he designated a ruler to succeed him, in accordance with divine command. If God Almighty, through the Prophet, designated a man who was to rule over Muslim society after him, this is in itself an indication that government remains a necessity after the departure of the Prophet from this world. Again, because the Most Noble Messenger promulgated the divine command through his act of appointing a successor, he also implicitly stated the necessity for establishing a government.

It is self-evident that the necessity for enactment of the law, which necessitated the formation of a government by the Prophet (upon whom be peace), was not confined or restricted to his time, but continues after his departure from this world. According to one of the noble verses of the Qur'an, the ordinances of Islam are not limited with respect to time or place; they are permanent and must be enacted until the end of time. They were not revealed merely for the time of the Prophet, only to be abandoned thereafter, with retribution and the penal code of Islam no longer to be enacted, or the taxes prescribed by Islam no longer collected, and the defense of the lands and people of Islam suspended. The claim that the laws of Islam may remain in abeyance or are restricted to a particular time or place is contrary to the essential creedal bases of Islam. Because the enactment of laws, then, is necessary after the departure of the Prophet from this world and, indeed, will remain so until the end of time, the formation of a government and the establishment of executive and administrative organs are also necessary. Without the formation of a government and the establishment of such organs to ensure that, through enactment of the law, all activities of the individual take place in the framework of a just system, chaos and anarchy will prevail and social, intellectual, and moral corruption will arise. The only way to prevent the emergence of anarchy and disorder and to protect society from corruption is to form a government and thus impart order to all the affairs of the country.

Both reason and divine law, then, demonstrate the necessity in our time for what was necessary during the lifetime of the Prophet and the age of the Commander of the Faithful, 'Ali ibn Abi Talib (peace be upon them)—namely, the formation of a government and the establishment of executive and administrative organs.[3]

---

[3]'Ali ibn Abi Talib was the cousin and son-in-law of the Prophet Muhammad. He ruled as a caliph from 656 to 661. The Shi'a consider him as the first of their divinely guided imams and consider all other caliphs to have been illegitimate. The Sunnis regard him as the

In order to clarify the matter further, let us pose the following questions: From the time of the Lesser Occultation[4] down to the present (a period of more than twelve centuries that may continue for hundreds of millennia if it is not appropriate for the Occulted Imam to manifest himself), is it proper that the laws of Islam be cast aside and remain unexecuted, so that everyone acts as he pleases and anarchy prevails? Were the laws that the Prophet of Islam labored so hard for twenty-three years to set forth, promulgate, and execute valid only for a limited period of time? Did God limit the validity of His laws to two hundred years? Was everything pertaining to Islam meant to be abandoned after the Lesser Occultation? Anyone who believes so, or voices such a belief, is worse situated than the person who believes and proclaims that Islam has been superseded or abrogated by another supposed revelation.

No one can say it is no longer necessary to defend the frontiers and the territorial integrity of the Islamic homeland; that taxes such as the *jizya, kharaj, khums,* and *zakat*[5] should no longer be collected; that the penal code of Islam, with its provisions for the payment of blood money and the exacting of requital, should be suspended. Any person who claims that the formation of an Islamic government is not necessary implicitly denies the necessity for the implementation of Islamic law, the universality and comprehensiveness of that law, and the eternal validity of the faith itself.

After the death of the Most Noble Messenger (peace and blessings be upon him), none of the Muslims doubted the necessity for government. No one said: "We no longer need a government." No one was heard to say anything of the kind. There was unanimous agreement concerning the necessity for government. There was disagreement only as to which person should assume responsibility for government and head the state. Government, therefore, was established after the Prophet (upon whom be peace and blessings), both in the time of the caliphs and in that of

---

fourth of their four "rightly guided caliphs" (see note 9). When Khomeini speaks of the Commander of the Faithful—a designation used by the Sunnis for their caliphs in general—it is only ʿAli to whom he refers.

[4]The Twelver Shiʿa believe that their twelfth imam, Muhammad al-Mahdi, disappeared in 874 and remains in hiding, whence he will reappear as a messianic figure, the *mahdi*, at some indeterminate time before the Day of Resurrection. The hidden imam is believed to have remained in sustained contact with four successive representatives during about seventy years following his disappearance. This period is known to the Shiʿa as the Lesser Occultation. The period following the death of his fourth representative in 940 inaugurated the Greater Occultation, during which no one can legitimately claim to be in regular contact with the hidden imam.

[5]These are the designations of taxes mandated by Islamic law. Jizya is the tax imposed in early and medieval Islam on non-Muslim residents of Muslim lands. Kharaj was an early Islamic tax on agricultural lands; initially imposed only on lands held by non-Muslims, it later came to be extended to agricultural holdings in general. Zakat is an annual tax that all Muslims of means are required to pay on their accumulated wealth or their agricultural produce. And khums, according to Twelver Shiʿism, is an annual tax that Shiʿis of means pay to their leading religious scholars.

the Commander of the Faithful (peace be upon him); and apparatus
of government came into existence with administrative and executive
organs.

The nature and character of Islamic law and the divine ordinances
of the shariʻa furnish additional proof of the necessity for establishing
government, for they indicate that the laws were laid down for the
purpose of creating a state and administering the political, economic,
and cultural affairs of society.

First, the laws of the shariʻa embrace a diverse body of laws and
regulations, which amounts to a complete social system. In this system
of laws, all the needs of man have been met: his dealings with his
neighbors, fellow citizens, and clan, as well as children and relatives;
the concerns of private and marital life; regulations concerning war and
peace and intercourse with other nations; penal and commercial law;
and regulations pertaining to trade and agriculture. Islamic law contains
provisions relating to the preliminaries of marriage and the form in
which it should be contracted, and others relating to the development
of the embryo in the womb and what food the parents should eat at the
time of conception. It further stipulates the duties that are incumbent
upon them while the infant is being suckled and specifies how the child
should be reared and how the husband and the wife should relate to
each other and to their children. Islam provides laws and instructions
for all of these matters, aiming, as it does, to produce integrated and
virtuous human beings who are walking embodiments of the law, or to
put it differently, the law's voluntary and instinctive executors. It is
obvious, then, how much care Islam devotes to government and the
political and economic relations of society, with the goal of creating
conditions conducive to the production of morally upright and virtuous
human beings.

The Glorious Qur'an and the sunna contain all the laws and ordinances man needs in order to attain happiness and the perfection of his
state. The book al-Kafi[6] has a chapter entitled, "All the Needs of Men
Are Set Out in the Book and the Sunna," the "Book" meaning the
Qur'an, which is, in its own words, "an exposition of all things."
According to certain traditions, the imam also swears that the Book
and the sunna contain without a doubt all that men need.

Second, if we examine closely the nature and character of the provisions of the law, we realize that their execution and implementation
depend upon the formation of a government, and that it is impossible
to fulfill the duty of executing God's commands without there being

---

[6]The Shiʻa and the Sunnis regard different collections of hadith as authoritative. In case
of the Shiʻa, such collections include not only the words of the Prophet Muhammad but
also those of their imams. Al-Kafi, compiled by Muhammad b. Yaʻqub al-Kulayni (d. 941),
is one of the most authoritative collections of Twelver Shiʻi hadith.

established properly comprehensive administrative and executive organs. Let us now mention certain types of provision in order to illustrate this point; the others you can examine yourselves.

The taxes Islam levies and the form of budget it has established are not merely for the sake of providing subsistence to the poor or feeding the indigent among the descendants of the Prophet (peace and blessings be upon him); they are also intended to make possible the establishment of a great government and to assure its essential expenditures.

For example, khums is a huge source of income that accrues to the treasury and represents one item in the budget. According to our Shi'i school of thought, khums is to be levied in an equitable manner on all agricultural and commercial profits and all natural resources whether above or below the ground—in short, on all forms of wealth and income. It applies equally to the green grocer with his stall outside this mosque and to the shipping or mining magnate. They must all pay one-fifth of their surplus income, after customary expenses are deducted, to the Islamic ruler so that it enters the treasury. It is obvious that such a huge income serves the purpose of administering the Islamic state and meeting all its financial needs. If we were to calculate one-fifth of the surplus income of the Muslim countries (or of the whole world, should it enter the fold of Islam), it would become fully apparent that the purpose for the imposition of such a tax is not merely the upkeep of the *sayyids* or the religious scholars, but on the contrary, something far more significant—namely, meeting the financial needs of the great organs and institutions of government. If an Islamic government is achieved, it will have to be administered on the basis of the taxes that Islam has established—khums, zakat (this, of course, would not represent an appreciable sum), jizya, and kharaj. . . .

Both law and reason require that we not permit governments to retain this non-Islamic or anti-Islamic character. The proofs are clear. First, the existence of a non-Islamic political order necessarily results in the nonimplementation of the Islamic political order. Then, all non-Islamic systems of government are the systems of *kufr,* because the ruler in each case is an instance of *taghut,*[7] and it is our duty to remove from the life of Muslim society all traces of kufr and destroy them. It is also our duty to create a favorable social environment for the education of believing and virtuous individuals, an environment that is in total contradiction with that produced by the rule of taghut and illegitimate power. The

---

[7]Kufr, which literally means "ungratefulness," is the standard Qur'anic term for unbelief. Taghut is also a Qur'anic term, meaning an "idol" and, more broadly, any symbol of ungodliness. In the course of the Iranian revolution of 1978–79, *taghuti* was a common way of referring to those viewed as opposed to the revolution. *Shirk*, a term Khomeini uses further below in this paragraph, is the standard Islamic term for any implicit or explicit contravening of tawhid, the oneness of God.

social environment created by taghut and *shirk* invariably brings about
corruption such as you can now observe in Iran, the corruption termed
"corruption on earth." This corruption must be swept away, and its
instigators punished for their deeds. It is the same corruption that the
Pharaoh generated in Egypt with his policies, so that the Qur'an says of
him, "Truly he was among the corruptors" (28:4). A believing, pious,
just individual cannot possibly exist in a sociopolitical environment of
this nature and still maintain his faith and righteous conduct. He is
faced with two choices: either he commits acts that amount to kufr and
contradict righteousness or, in order not to commit such acts and not to
submit to the orders and commands of the taghut, the just individual
opposes him and struggles against him in order to destroy the environment of corruption. We have in reality, then, no choice but to destroy
those systems of government that are corrupt in themselves and also
entail the corruption of others, and to overthrow all treacherous,
corrupt, oppressive, and criminal regimes.

This is a duty that all Muslims must fulfill, in every one of the Muslim countries, in order to achieve the triumphant political revolution of
Islam.

We see, too, that, together, the imperialists and the tyrannical self-
seeking rulers have divided the Islamic homeland. They have separated
the various segments of the Islamic umma from each other and artificially created separate nations. There once existed the great Ottoman
state, and that, too, the imperialists divided. Russia, Britain, Austria,
and other imperialist powers united, and through wars against the
Ottomans, each came to occupy or absorb into its sphere of influence
part of the Ottoman realm. It is true that most of the Ottoman rulers
were incompetent, that some of them were corrupt, and that they
followed a monarchical system. Nonetheless, the existence of the
Ottoman state represented a threat to the imperialists. It was always
possible that righteous individuals might rise up among the people and,
with their assistance, seize control of the state, thus putting an end to
imperialism by mobilizing the unified resources of the nation. Therefore, after numerous prior wars, the imperialists at the end of World
War I divided the Ottoman state, creating in its territories about ten or
fifteen petty states. Then each of these was entrusted to one of their
servants or a group of their servants, although certain countries were
later able to escape the grasp of the agents of imperialism.

In order to assure the unity of the Islamic umma and to liberate the
Islamic homeland from occupation and penetration by the imperialists
and their puppet governments, it is imperative that we establish a
government. In order to attain the unity and freedom of the Muslim
peoples, we must overthrow the oppressive governments installed by
the imperialists and bring into existence an Islamic government of
justice that will be in the service of the people. The formation of such a

government will serve to preserve the disciplined unity of the Muslims; just as Fatima az-Zahra (upon whom be peace) said in her address: "The Imamate exists for the sake of preserving order among the Muslims and replacing their disunity with unity."

Through the political agents they have placed in power over the people, the imperialists have also imposed on us an unjust economic order, and thereby divided our people into two groups: oppressors and oppressed. Hundreds of millions of Muslims are hungry and deprived of all form of health care and education, while minorities comprised of the wealthy and powerful live a life of indulgence, licentiousness, and corruption. The hungry and deprived have constantly struggled to free themselves from the oppression of their plundering overlords, and their struggle continues to this day. But their way is blocked by the ruling minorities and the oppressive governmental structures they head. It is our duty to save the oppressed and deprived. It is our duty to be a helper to the oppressed and an enemy to the oppressor. This is nothing other than the duty that the Commander of the Faithful (upon whom be peace) entrusted to his two great offspring in his celebrated testament: "Be an enemy to the oppressor and a helper to the oppressed."

The scholars of Islam have a duty to struggle against all attempts by the oppressors to establish a monopoly over the sources of wealth or to make illicit use of them. They must not allow the masses to remain hungry and deprived while plundering oppressors usurp the sources of wealth and live in opulence. The Commander of the Faithful (upon whom be peace) says: "I have accepted the task of government because God, Exalted and Almighty, has exacted from the scholars of Islam a pledge not to sit silent and idle in the face of the gluttony and plundering of the oppressors, on the one hand, and the hunger and deprivation of the oppressed, on the other." Here is the full text of the passage we refer to:

> I swear by Him Who causes the seed to open and creates the souls of all living things that were it not for the presence of those who have come to swear allegiance to me, were it not for the obligation of rulership now imposed upon me by the availability of aid and support, and were it not for the pledge that God has taken from the scholars of Islam not to remain silent in the face of the gluttony and plundering of the oppressors, on the one hand, and the harrowing hunger and deprivation of the oppressed, on the other hand— were it not for all of this, then I would abandon the reins of government and in no way seek it. You would see that this world of yours, with all of its position and rank, is less in my eyes than the moisture that comes from the sneeze of a goat.

How can we stay silent and idle today when we see that a band of traitors and usurpers, the agents of foreign powers, have appropriated the

wealth and the fruits of labor of hundreds of millions of Muslims—
thanks to the support of their masters and through the power of the
bayonet—granting the Muslims not the least right to prosperity? It is
the duty of Islamic scholars and all Muslims to put an end to this
system of oppression and, for the sake of the well-being of hundreds
of millions of human beings, to overthrow these oppressive governments and form an Islamic government.

Reason, the law of Islam, the practice of the Prophet (upon whom be
peace and blessings) and that of the Commander of the Faithful (upon
whom be peace), the purport of various Qur'anic verses and Prophetic
Traditions—all indicate the necessity of forming a government. As an
example of the Traditions of the imams, I now quote the following
Tradition of Imam Riza[8] (upon whom be peace):

> 'Abd al-Wahid ibn Muhammad ibn 'Abdus an-Nisaburi al-'Attar
> said, "I was told by Abu'l-Hasan 'Ali ibn Muhammad ibn Qutayba
> al-Naysaburi that he was told by Abu Muhammad al-Fadl ibn
> Shadhan al-Naysaburi this Tradition. If someone asks, 'Why has
> God, the All-Wise, appointed the holders of authority and com-
> manded us to obey them?' then we answer, 'For numerous reasons.
> One reason is this: Men are commanded to observe certain limits
> and not to transgress them in order to avoid the corruption that
> would result. This cannot be attained or established without there
> being appointed over them a trustee who will ensure that they
> remain within the limits of the licit and prevent them from casting
> themselves into the danger of transgression. Were it not for such a
> trustee, no one would abandon his own pleasure and benefit
> because of the corruption it might entail for another. Another
> reason is that we find no group or nation of men that ever existed
> without a ruler and leader, because it is required by both religion
> and worldly interest. It would not be compatible with divine
> wisdom to leave mankind to its own devices, for He, the All-Wise,
> knows that men need a ruler for their survival. It is through the
> leadership he provides that men make war against their enemies,
> divide among themselves the spoils of war, and preserve their
> communal solidarity, preventing the oppression of the oppressed
> by the oppressor.

> A further reason is this: were God not to appoint over men a
> solicitous, trustworthy, protecting, reliable leader, the community
> would decline, religion would depart, and the norms and ordi-
> nances that have been revealed would undergo change. Innovators
> would increase and deniers would erode religion, including doubt
> in the Muslims. For we see that men are needy and defective,

---

[8]'Ali al-Riza (Arabic: Rida; d. 818) is the eighth imam of the Twelver Shi'a.

judging by their differences of opinion and inclination and their
diversity of state. Were a trustee, then, not appointed to preserve
what has been revealed through the Prophet, corruption would
ensue in the manner we have described. Revealed laws, norms,
ordinances, and faith would be altogether changed, and therein
would lie the corruption of all mankind.

We have omitted the first part of the hadith, which pertains to prophethood, a topic not germane to our present discussion. What interests us
at present is the second half, which I will now paraphrase for you.

If someone should ask you, "Why has God, the All-Wise, appointed
holders of authority and commanded you to obey them?" you should
answer him as follows: He has done so for various causes and reasons.
One is that men have been set upon a certain well-defined path and
commanded not to stray from it, nor to transgress against the established limits and norms, for if they were to stray, they would fall prey
to corruption. Now men would not be able to keep to their ordained
path and to enact God's laws unless a trustworthy and protective
individual (or power) were appointed over them with responsibility for
this matter, to prevent them from stepping outside the sphere of the licit
and transgressing against the rights of others. If no such restraining
individual or power were appointed, nobody would voluntarily abandon any pleasure or interest of his own that might result in harm or
corruption to others; everybody would engage in oppressing and
harming others for the sake of their own pleasures and interests.

Another reason and cause is this: we do not see a single group, nation,
or religious community that has ever been able to exist without an
individual entrusted with the maintenance of its laws and institutions—
in short, a head or a leader; for such a person is essential for fulfilling
the affairs of religion and the world. It is not permissible, therefore,
according to divine wisdom, that God should leave men, His creatures,
without a leader and guide, for He knows well that they depend on the
existence of such a person for their own survival and perpetuation. It
is under his leadership that they fight against their enemies, divide the
public income among themselves, perform Friday and congregational
prayer, and foreshorten the arms of the transgressors who would
encroach on the rights of the oppressed.

Another proof and cause is this: were God not to appoint an imam
over men to maintain law and order, to serve the people faithfully as a
vigilant trustee, religion would fall victim to obsolescence and decay. Its
rites and institutions would vanish; the customs and ordinances of Islam
would be transformed or even deformed. Heretical innovators would
add things to religion and atheists and unbelievers would subtract things
from it, presenting it to the Muslims in an inaccurate manner. For we see
that men are prey to defects; they are not perfect and must strive after

perfection. Moreover, they disagree with each other, having varying inclinations and discordant states. If God, therefore, had not appointed over men one who would maintain order and law and protect the revelation brought by the Prophet, in the manner we have described, men would fall prey to corruption; the institutions, laws, customs, and ordinances of Islam would be transformed; and faith and its content would be completely changed, resulting in the corruption of all humanity.

As you can deduce from the words of the imam (upon whom be peace), there are numerous proofs and causes that necessitate formation of a government and establishment of an authority. These proofs, causes, and arguments are not temporary in their validity or limited to a particular time, and the necessity for the formation of a government, therefore, is perpetual. For example, it will always happen that men overstep the limits laid down by Islam and transgress against the rights of others for the sake of their personal pleasure and benefit. It cannot be asserted that such was the case only in the time of the Commander of the Faithful (upon whom be peace) and that afterward, men became angels. The wisdom of the Creator has decreed that men should live in accordance with justice and act within the limits set by divine law. This wisdom is eternal and immutable, and constitutes one of the norms of God Almighty. Today and always, therefore, the existence of a holder of authority, a ruler who acts as trustee and maintains the institutions and laws of Islam, is a necessity—a ruler who prevents cruelty, oppression, and violation of the rights of others; who is a trustworthy and vigilant guardian of God's creatures; who guides men to the teachings, doctrines, laws, and institutions of Islam; and who prevents the undesirable changes that atheists and the enemies of religion wish to introduce in the laws and institutions of Islam. Did not the caliphate of the Commander of the Faithful serve this purpose? The same factors of necessity that led him to become the imam still exist; the only difference is that no single individual has been designated for the task. The principle of the necessity of government has been made a general one, so that it will always remain in effect.

If the ordinances of Islam are to remain in effect, then, if encroachment by oppressive ruling classes on the rights of the weak is to be prevented, if ruling minorities are not to be permitted to plunder and corrupt the people for the sake of pleasure and material interest, if the Islamic order is to be preserved and all individuals are to pursue the just path of Islam without any deviation, if innovation and the approval of anti-Islamic laws by sham parliaments are to be prevented, if the influence of foreign powers in the Islamic lands is to be destroyed— government is necessary. None of these aims can be achieved without government and the organs of the state. It is a righteous government, of course, that is needed, one presided over by a ruler who will be a trustworthy and righteous trustee. Those who presently govern us are of no use at all for they are tyrannical, corrupt, and highly incompetent.

In the past, we did not act in concert and unanimity in order to establish proper government and overthrow treacherous and corrupt rulers. Some people were apathetic and reluctant even to discuss the theory of Islamic government, and some went so far as to praise oppressive rulers. It is for this reason that we find ourselves in the present state. The influence and sovereignty of Islam in society have declined; the nation of Islam has fallen victim to division and weakness; the laws of Islam have remained in abeyance and been subjected to change and modification; and the imperialists have propagated foreign laws and alien culture among the Muslims through their agents for the sake of their evil purposes, causing people to be infatuated with the West. It was our lack of a leader, a guardian, and our lack of institutions of leadership that made all this possible. We need righteous and proper organs of government; that much is self-evident. . . .

Islamic government does not correspond to any of the existing forms of government. For example, it is not a tyranny, where the head of state can deal arbitrarily with the property and lives of the people, making use of them as he wills, putting to death anyone he wishes, and enriching anyone he wishes by granting landed estates and distributing the property and holdings of the people. The Most Noble Messenger (peace be upon him), the Commander of the Faithful (peace be upon him), and the other caliphs did not have such powers. Islamic government is neither tyrannical nor absolute, but constitutional. It is not constitutional in the current sense of the word, that is, based on the approval of laws in accordance with the opinion of the majority. It is constitutional in the sense that the rulers are subject to a certain set of conditions in governing and administering the country, conditions that are set forth in the Noble Qur'an and the sunna of the Most Noble Messenger. It is the laws and ordinances of Islam comprising this set of conditions that must be observed and practiced. Islamic government may therefore be defined as the rule of divine law over men.

The fundamental difference between Islamic government, on the one hand, and constitutional monarchies and republics, on the other, is this: whereas the representatives of the people or the monarch in such regimes engage in legislation, in Islam the legislative power and competence to establish laws belongs exclusively to God Almighty. The Sacred Legislator of Islam is the sole legislative power. No one has the right to legislate, and no law may be executed except the law of the Divine Legislator. It is for this reason that in an Islamic government, a simple planning body takes the place of the legislative assembly that is one of the three branches of government. This body draws up programs for the different ministries in the light of the ordinances of Islam and thereby determines how public services are to be provided across the country.

The body of Islamic laws that exist in the Qur'an and the sunna has been accepted by the Muslims and recognized by them as worthy of obedience. This consent and acceptance facilitate the task of government and make it truly belong to the people. In contrast, in a republic or a constitutional monarchy, most of those claiming to be representatives of the majority of the people will approve anything they wish as law and then impose it on the entire population.

Islamic government is a government of law. In this form of government, sovereignty belongs to God alone, and law is His decree and command. The law of Islam, divine command, has absolute authority over all individuals and the Islamic government. Everyone, including the Most Noble Messenger (peace be upon him) and his successors, is subject to law and will remain so for all eternity—the law that has been revealed by God, Almighty and Exalted, and expounded by the tongue of the Qur'an and the Most Noble Messenger. If the Prophet assumed the task of divine vice-regency upon earth, it was in accordance with divine command. God, Almighty and Exalted, appointed him as His vice regent, "the vice regent of God upon earth"; he did not establish a government on his own initiative in order to be leader of the Muslims. Similarly, when it became apparent that disagreements would probably arise among the Muslims because their acquaintance with the faith was recent and limited, God Almighty charged the Prophet, by way of revelation, to clarify the question of succession immediately, there in the middle of the desert. Then the Most Noble Messenger (upon whom be peace) nominated the Commander of the Faithful (upon whom be peace) as his successor, in conformity and obedience to the law, not because he was his own son-in-law or had performed certain services, but because he was acting in obedience to God's law, as its executor.

In Islam, then, government has the sense of adherence to law; it is law alone that rules over society. Even the limited powers given to the Most Noble Messenger (upon whom be peace) and those exercising rule after him have been conferred upon them by God. Whenever the Prophet expounded a certain matter or promulgated a certain injunction, he did so in obedience to divine law, a law that everyone without exception must obey and adhere to. Divine law obtains for both the leader and the led; the sole law that is valid and imperative to apply is the law of God. Obedience to the Prophet also takes place in accordance with divine decree, for God says: "And obey the Messenger" (Q 4:59). Obedience to those entrusted with authority is also on the basis of divine decree: "And obey the holders of authority from among you" (Q 4:59). Individual opinion, even if it be that of the Prophet himself, cannot intervene in matters of government or divine law; here, all are subject to the will of God.

Islamic government is not a form of monarchy, especially not an imperial system. In that type of government, the rulers are empowered over the property and persons of those they rule and may dispose of them entirely as they wish. Islam has not the slightest connection with this form and method of government. For this reason, we find that in Islamic government, unlike monarchical and imperial regimes, there is not the slightest trace of vast palaces, opulent buildings, servants and retainers, private equerries, adjutants to the heir apparent, and all the other appurtenances of monarchy that consume as much as half of the national budget. You all know how the Prophet lived, the Prophet who was the head of the Islamic state and its ruler. The same mode of life was preserved by his successors until the beginning of the Umayyad period. The first two successors to the Prophet adhered to his example in the outer conduct of their personal lives, even though in other affairs they committed errors, which led to the grave deviations that appeared in the time of 'Uthman,[9] the same deviations that have inflicted on us these misfortunes of the present day. In the time of the Commander of the Faithful (peace be upon him), the system of government was corrected and a proper form and method of rule were followed. Even though that excellent man ruled over a vast realm that included Iran, Egypt, Hijaz, and the Yemen among its provinces, he lived more frugally than the most impoverished of our students. According to tradition, he once bought two tunics, and finding one of them better than the other, he gave the better one to his servant Qanbar. The other he kept for himself, and because its sleeves were too long for him, he tore off the extra portion. In this torn garment the ruler of a great, populous, and prosperous realm clothed himself.

If this mode of conduct had been preserved, and government had retained its Islamic form, there would have been no monarchy and no empire, no usurpation of the lives and property of the people, no oppression and plunder, no encroachment on the public treasury, no vice and abomination. Most forms of corruption originate with the ruling class, the tyrannical ruling family, and the libertines that associate with them. It is these rulers who establish centers of vice and corruption, who build centers of vice and wine drinking, and spend the income of the religious endowments constructing cinemas.

If it were not for these profligate royal ceremonies, this reckless spending, this constant embezzlement, there would never be any deficit in the national budget forcing us to bow in submission before America and Britain and request aid for a loan from them. Our country has become needy on account of this reckless spending, this endless

---

[9]'Uthman b. 'Affan (r. 644–56) was the third caliph to succeed the Prophet Muhammad. Together with Abu Bakr, 'Umar, and 'Ali, the Sunnis count him among the "rightly guided caliphs," while the Shi'a consider only 'Ali to have been a legitimate caliph. The murder of 'Uthman in 656 precipitated the First Civil War (fitna) in Islamic history, which ended with the death of 'Ali in 661 and the emergence of the Umayyad dynasty (661–750). Though the Shi'a have usually been highly critical of all three of 'Ali's predecessors, Khomeini here adopts a notably milder tone toward Abu Bakr and 'Umar—referred to here as the "first two successors of the Prophet"—than he does towards 'Uthman (cf. Algar 1985, 155). The latter has had a mixed reputation even among the Sunnis, and not just in early Islam but also in some modern Islamist circles. Mawdudi, for instance, was much criticized by many 'ulama for his criticism of 'Uthman on grounds of his political ineptitude. For one instance of such criticism, cf. Qaradawi 2005b, 47–49.

embezzlement, for are we lacking in oil? Do we have no minerals, no natural resources? We have everything, but this parasitism, this embezzlement, this profligacy—all at the expense of the people and the public treasury—have reduced us to a wretched state. Otherwise he [the shah] would not need to go all the way to America and bow down before that ruffian's desk, begging for help.

In addition, superfluous bureaucracies and the system of file keeping and paper shuffling that is enforced in them, all of which are totally alien to Islam, impose further expenditures on our national budget not less in quantity than the illicit expenditures of the first category. This administrative system has nothing to do with Islam. These superfluous formalities, which cause our people nothing but expense, trouble, and delay, have no place in Islam. For example, the method established by Islam for enforcing people's rights, adjudicating disputes, and executing judgments is at once simple, practical, and swift. When the juridical methods of Islam were applied, the shari'a judge in each town, assisted only by two bailiffs and with only a pen and an inkpot at his disposal, would swiftly resolve disputes among people and send them about their business. But now the bureaucratic organization of the Ministry of Justice has attained unimaginable proportions and is, in addition, quite incapable of producing results.

It is things like these that make our country needy and produce nothing but expense and delay.

The qualifications essential for the ruler derive directly from the nature and form of Islamic government. In addition to general qualifications like intelligence and administrative ability, there are two other essential qualifications: knowledge of the law and justice.

After the death of the Prophet (upon whom be peace), differences arose concerning the identity of the person who was to succeed him, but all the Muslims were in agreement that his successor should be someone knowledgeable and accomplished; there was disagreement only as to his identity.

Because Islamic government is a government of law, knowledge of the law is necessary for the ruler, as has been laid down in tradition. Indeed, such knowledge is necessary not only for the ruler but also for anyone holding a post or exercising some government function. The ruler, however, must surpass all others in knowledge. In laying claim to the imamate, our imams also argued that the ruler must be more learned than everyone else. The objections raised by the Shi'i 'ulama are also to the same effect. A certain person asked the caliph a point of law, and he was unable to answer; he was therefore unfit for the position of leader and successor to the Prophet. Or, again, a certain act he performed was contrary to the laws of Islam; hence, he was unworthy of his high post.

Knowledge of the law and justice, then, constitute fundamental qualifications in the view of the Muslims. Other matters have no importance or relevance in this connection. Knowledge of the nature of the angels, for example, or of the attributes of the Creator, Exalted and Almighty, is of no relevance to the question of leadership. In the same vein, one who knows all the natural sciences, uncovers all the secrets of nature, or has a good knowledge of music does not thereby qualify for leadership or acquire any priority in the matter of exercising government over those who know the laws of Islam and are just. The sole matters relevant to rule, those that were mentioned and discussed in the time of the Most Noble Messenger (upon whom be peace) and our imams (upon whom be peace) and were, in addition, unanimously accepted by the Muslims, are: (1) the knowledgeability of the ruler or caliph, that is, his knowledge of the provisions and ordinances of Islam; and (2) his justice, that is, his excellence in belief and morals.

Reason also dictates the necessity for these qualities, because Islamic government is a government of law, not the arbitrary rule of an individual over the people or the domination of a group of individuals over the whole people. If the ruler is unacquainted with the contents of the law, he is not fit to rule; for if he follows the legal pronouncements of others, his power to govern will be impaired, but if, on the other hand, he does not follow such guidance, he will be unable to rule correctly and implement the laws of Islam. It is an established principle that "the faqih [jurist; plural: *fuqaha*] has authority over the ruler." If the ruler adheres to Islam, he must necessarily submit to the faqih, asking him about the laws and ordinances of Islam in order to implement them. This being the case, the true rulers are the fuqaha themselves, and rulership ought officially to be theirs, to apply to them, not to those who are obliged to follow the guidance of the fuqaha on account of their own ignorance of the law.

Of course, it is not necessary for all officials, provincial governors, and administrators to know all the laws of Islam and be fuqaha; it is enough that they should know the laws pertaining to their functions and duties. Such was the case in the time of the Prophet and the Commander of the Faithful (peace be upon them). The highest authority must possess the two qualities mentioned—comprehensive knowledge and justice—but his assistants, officials, and those sent to the provinces need know only the laws relevant to their own tasks; on other matters they must consult the ruler.

The ruler must also possess excellence in morals and belief; he must be just and untainted by major sin. Anyone who wishes to enact the penalties provided by Islam (i.e., to implement the penal code), to supervise the public treasury and the income and expenditures of the state, and to have God assign to him the power to administer the affairs of His creatures must not be a sinner. God says in the Qur'an: "My covenant does not embrace the wrongdoer" (2:124); therefore, He will not assign such functions to an oppressor or sinner.

If the ruler is not just in granting the Muslims their rights, he will not conduct himself equitably in levying taxes and spending them correctly and in implementing the penal code. It becomes possible then for his assistants, helpers, and confidants to impose their will on society, diverting the public treasury to personal and frivolous use.

Thus, the view of the Shi'a concerning government and the nature of the persons who should assume rule was clear from the time following the death of the Prophet (upon whom be peace and blessings) down to the beginning of the Occultation. It specified that the ruler should be foremost in knowledge of the laws and ordinances of Islam and just in their implementation. Now that we are in the time of Occultation of the Imam (upon whom be peace), it is still necessary that the ordinances of Islam relating to government be preserved and maintained and that anarchy be prevented. Therefore, the establishment of government is still a necessity.

Reason also dictates that we establish a government in order to be able to ward off aggression and to defend the honor of the Muslims in case of attack. The shari'a, for its part, instructs us to be constantly ready to defend ourselves against those who wish to attack us. Government, with its judicial and executive organs, is also necessary to prevent individuals from encroaching on each other's rights. None of these purposes can be fulfilled by themselves; it is necessary for a government to be established. Because the establishment of a government and the administration of society necessitate, in turn, a budget and taxation, the Sacred Legislator has specified the nature of the budget and the taxes that are to be levied, such as kharaj, khums, zakat, and so forth.

Now that no particular individual has been appointed by God, Exalted and Almighty, to assume the function of government in the time of Occultation, what must be done? Are we to abandon Islam? Do we no longer need it? Was Islam valid for only two hundred years? Or is it that Islam has clarified our duties in other respects but not with respect to government?

Not to have an Islamic government means leaving our boundaries unguarded. Can we afford to sit nonchalantly on our hands while our enemies do whatever they want? Even if we do not put our signatures to what they do as an endorsement, still we are failing to make an effective response. Is that the way it should be? Or is it rather that government is necessary, and that the function of government that existed from the beginning of Islam down to the time of the Twelfth Imam (upon whom be peace) is still enjoined upon us by God after the Occultation, even though He has appointed no particular individual to that function?

The two qualities of knowledge of the law and justice are present in countless fuqaha of the present age. If they would come together, they could establish a government of universal justice in the world.

If a worthy individual possessing these two qualities arises and establishes a government, he will possess the same authority as the Most
Noble Messenger (upon whom be peace and blessings) in the administration of society, and it will be the duty of all people to obey him.

The idea that the governmental powers of the Most Noble Messenger (peace and blessings be upon him) were greater than those of the
Commander of the Faithful (upon whom be peace), or that those of the
Commander of the Faithful were greater than those of the faqih, is false
and erroneous. Naturally, the virtues of the Most Noble Messenger
were greater than those of the rest of mankind, and after him, the
Commander of the Faithful was the most virtuous person in the world.
But superiority with respect to spiritual virtues does not confer increased governmental powers. God has conferred upon government in
the present age the same powers and authority that were held by the
Most Noble Messenger and the imams (peace be upon them) with
respect to equipping and mobilizing armies, appointing governors and
officials, and levying taxes and expending them for the welfare of the
Muslims. Now, however, it is no longer a question of a particular
person; government devolves instead upon one who possesses the
qualities of knowledge and justice.

When we say that after the Occultation, the just faqih has the same
authority that the Most Noble Messenger and the imams had, do not
imagine that the status of the faqih is identical to that of the imams
and the Prophet. For here we are not speaking of status but rather of
function. By "authority" we mean government, the administration of
the country, and the implementation of the sacred laws of the shari'a.
These constitute a serious, difficult duty but do not earn anyone extraordinary status or raise him above the level of common humanity. In
other words, authority here has the meaning of government, administration, and execution of law; contrary to what many people believe, it
is not a privilege but a grave responsibility. The governance of the faqih
is a rational and extrinsic matter; it exists only as a type of appointment, like the appointment of a guardian for a minor. With respect to
duty and position, there is indeed no difference between the guardian
of a nation and the guardian of a minor. It is as if the Imam were to
appoint someone to the guardianship of a minor, to the governorship
of a province, or to some other post. In cases like these, it is not reasonable that there would be a difference between the Prophet and the
imams, on the one hand, and the just faqih, on the other.

For example, one of the concerns that the faqih must attend to is the
application of the penal provisions of Islam. Can there be any distinction in this respect between the Most Noble Messenger, the imam, and
the faqih? Will the faqih inflict fewer lashes because his rank is lower?
Now the penalty for the fornicator is one hundred lashes. If the Prophet

applies the penalty, is he to inflict one hundred, and the faqih fifty? The ruler supervises the executive power and has the duty of implementing God's laws; it makes no difference if he is the Most Noble Messenger, the Commander of the Faithful, or the representative or judge he appointed to Basra or Kufa, or a faqih in the present age.

Another of the concerns of the Most Noble Messenger and the Commander of the Faithful was the levying of taxes—khums, zakat, jizya, and kharaj on taxable lands. Now when the Prophet levied zakat, how much did he levy? One-tenth in one place and one-twentieth elsewhere? And how did the Commander of the Faithful proceed when he became ruler? And what now, if one of us becomes the foremost faqih of the age and is able to enforce his authority? In these matters, can there be any difference in the authority of the Most Noble Messenger, that of 'Ali, and that of the faqih? God Almighty appointed the Prophet in authority over all the Muslims; as long as he was alive, his authority extended over even 'Ali. Afterward, the imam had authority over all the Muslims, even his own successor as imam; his commands relating to government were valid for everyone, and he could appoint and dismiss judges and governors.

The authority that the Prophet and the imam had in establishing a government, executing laws, and administering affairs exists also for the faqih. But the fuqaha do not have absolute authority in the sense of having authority over all other fuqaha of their own time, being able to appoint or dismiss them. There is no hierarchy ranking one faqih higher than another or endowing one with more authority than another.

Now that this much has been demonstrated, it is necessary that the fuqaha proceed, collectively or individually, to establish a government in order to implement the laws of Islam and protect its territory. If this task falls within the capabilities of a single person, he has personally incumbent upon him the duty to fulfill it; otherwise, it is a duty that devolves upon the fuqaha as a whole. Even if it is impossible to fulfill the task, the authority vested in the fuqaha is not voided, because it has been vested in them by God. If they can, they must collect taxes, such as zakat, khums, and kharaj, spend them for the welfare of the Muslims, and also enact the penalties of the law. The fact that we are presently unable to establish a complete and comprehensive form of government does not mean that we should sit idle. Instead, we should perform, to whatever extent we can, the tasks that are needed by the Muslims and that pertain to the functions an Islamic government must assume.

# Chapter 7

# MUHAMMAD BAQIR AL-SADR
# 1934–1980

MUHAMMAD BAQIR AL-SADR was among the most prominent symbols of Shi'i resistance to the Saddam Hussein regime, at whose hands he was executed in 1980. He was a major proponent of the view that Islam has a coherent body of teachings governing all aspects of economic life, that these teachings are distinct from other economic systems, and that putting them into effect is among the crucial markers of an Islamic state. Like his contemporary Ayatollah Khomeini, but unlike many other Shi'i religious scholars of his time, Sadr also argued that the Shi'i 'ulama ought to provide active political leadership to the community in facing the challenges confronting it and, indeed, that an Islamic state was best led by none other than the most learned of the jurists.

Sadr was born in Kazimiyya, in Iraq, in 1934. His was a family of religious scholars and, like them, he received all his education in Najaf. With its many madrasas, collectively known, like those of Qom in Iran, as al-Hawza al-'ilmiyya (the enclave of learning), Najaf is a major center of advanced Shi'i religious learning. It is also the burial place of 'Ali ibn Abi Talib (d. 661), the cousin and son-in-law of the Prophet Muhammad, whom the Shi'a consider to be the first of their divinely guided imams. The study of Islamic law has long been at the center of madrasa learning in both Shi'i and Sunni Islam, and it is in terms of a scholar's legal acumen, his ability to arrive at legal rulings in his own right (ijtihad), that one's standing is typically determined in the Shi'i scholarly hierarchy. The twentieth century witnessed several efforts, in both Iraq and Iran, to reform educational practices in the Hawza (cf. Zaman 2007a, 242–52). Sadr was educated at an institution representing such efforts toward introducing its students to modern, Western sciences alongside the traditionally Islamic ones. During much of his career, Sadr, too, sought to make Shi'i learning responsive to what he took to be the demands of his contemporary age. Despite considerable misgivings about his critique of the Hawza and his political involvements, his scholarly standing came to be well recognized within the Hawza establishment; and by the time of his death, he was among the most authoritative of the Shi'i religious scholars.

In Najaf in the 1950s and the 1960s, no challenge seemed more grave than that represented by the appeal of Marxism to young Muslims, in Iraq and elsewhere and, indeed, in the Hawza itself. In two early works— *Falsafatuna* (Our Philosophy [first published in 1959]) and *Iqtisaduna*

(Our Economy [first published in 1961])—but also in his other writings, Sadr gave extensive attention to socialism and Marxism. Islam, Sadr insisted, was incompatible with such ideologies, as, indeed, it was with capitalism. It had its own, specific norms in matters of economic life, and these were not only deducible from the foundational texts but were also intertwined with Muslim history and culture. Yet it was not simply a matter of implementing Islamic norms: they needed to be rethought in modern circumstances, in some cases quite drastically. Against the generality of Muslim jurists, Sunni as well as Shiʻi, Sadr argued, for instance, that the right to private property was not inviolable and that the government could impose limits on private property in pursuit of the common good.

The question of private property was, to Sadr, part of the larger problem of how human freedom was to be visualized. Here, again, he saw a vivid contrast not only between socialism and capitalism but also between them, on the one hand, and Islam, on the other. Where liberal capitalism intemperately valued individual freedom above all else, socialist economies imposed inordinate limits on it. But if people manifestly lacked freedom in a socialist polity, the sort of freedom capitalist societies guaranteed to their members was itself a mirage. Bondage to material needs, to the basest of one's desires and whims, was nowhere more strikingly apparent than in such societies; and though the success of a capitalist economy depended on fostering such desires, and subjugating other countries in the ceaseless effort to find new markets for their goods, people who found themselves helpless in the face of such materialistic dependence could hardly be deemed free. Islam, with its insistence that God alone be worshiped, stripped people of all other attachments; as such, it was radically liberating (cf. Sadr 1980a, 157–64).

Islam did impose its own limits on the scope of human freedom, but these, Sadr argued, were good limits to have. It is a measure of their engagement with modern, Western societies—and of their concern to win over Muslims educated in modern institutions of learning—that Islamists seldom affirm the views they espouse simply as the will of God. Howsoever speciously, they have often sought to *argue* that their positions make sense in "rational" terms; that an objective observer would see the merit of their reasoning; and, indeed, that it is in their properly Islamic rather than rival, Western formulations that the genuine intent or scope of particular values is best realized. It is in this spirit that Sadr was keenly attentive to how Islam promoted rather than curtailed human freedom. As he saw it, true fulfillment consisted not in mere gratification of desire but rather in harmonizing individual interest and the common good. He recognized that impulses toward the fulfillment of individual needs and desires were deeply ingrained in human nature, but so too, he insisted, were mechanisms to check these impulses. No mechanism was stronger than that represented by religion, and no religion was more effective in mediating the inherent conflict between individual and collective interest and in thereby helping realize the potentialities that inhered in human beings than Islam. Viewed thus, Islam was anything but antithetical to the sort of human freedom that really mattered (cf. Sadr 2004, 284, 311–12).

The limitations on the scope of human freedom can also come from the state, of course. But as long as the state was a properly Islamic one, Sadr fully endorsed these. As he put it in one of his last writings, completed in the wake of the Iranian revolution of 1979, the relationship between an Islamic state and its Muslim citizens is a reciprocal one, and the constraints imposed by the state do not imperil the scope of genuine freedom. For inasmuch as the state is guided by Islamic norms, the limits it imposes on its citizens are not only anchored in considerations of the common good but also speak to the norms and inclinations people come to acquire in the course of their upbringing in Muslim societies. (A delineation of the contours of an Islamic society was presumably to have been provided in "Our Society," a work Sadr had intended as a sequel to "Our Philosophy" and "Our Economy." But that work was never written. Cf. Mallat 1993, 16.) In a view he shared with many other Islamists, notably Sayyid Qutb of Egypt, whom he is said to have held in high esteem (cf. Mottahedeh 2003, 32), Sadr believed that the Islamic state did not need to coerce people on the path to righteous living but only to remove the impediments that stood in the way to doing so (cf. Qutb 1990], 48–51). Even if ordinary Muslims were reluctant to sacrifice much in pursuit of *establishing* such a state, once it has been established, the purposes of the state and the aspirations of the people would be in complete concord (Sadr 1980b, 216–17).

In being anchored in values that came from the historical experience of the Muslims rather than as imports from Western societies, an Islamic state also conformed best to people's sense of authenticity. In this respect, too, it could be expected to enhance their freedom and to minimize needless contradictions and conflicts. Much the same argument underlies Sadr's advocacy of "Islamic economics." An Islamic economic system offers the best prospects for social justice; but it is also desirable because it is independent of Western models. However attenuated under the onslaught of colonialism, Muslims have managed to retain their religious commitments, so that an economic system guided by Islamic norms can be certain of their support in a way that no other economic system can (Sadr, "Preface to the Second Edition," in Sadr 2004, 30–34; cf. Tripp 2006, 109–10, 121–23).

Despite his widely recognized stature as one of the most authoritative Shi'i jurists of his time, Sadr's statist views were at odds with those of the more conservative scholars of the Hawza. In both Iraq and Iran, many have remained unconvinced, for instance, that restrictions on private property can be justified in Islamic terms. Members of the Hawza establishment in Najaf also had serious misgivings about Sadr's political activism. He was closely associated with al-Da'wa al-Islamiyya (The Islamic Call), an Islamist organization committed, since the late 1950s, to making Iraq into an Islamic state. After the pan-Arabist, Sunni, and secular Ba'th (Resurrection) Party came to power in Iraq in 1968, those associated with the Da'wa bore the major brunt of the new regime's repression. The Ba'thist regime (1968–2003) saw the Shi'i religious establishment as the source of the gravest challenge to its authority and sought, systematically, to suppress or weaken it. A quietist political stance by 'ulama at the apex of the Shi'i hierarchy—Muhsin al-Hakim in the 1960s, al-Khu'i (d. 1992) in the 1970s and 1980s—helped avert many a clash between the Shi'a and the regime. Baqir al-Sadr was critical of this quietism, though he did not break with the Hawza or openly challenge the Ba'thist regime.

Matters came to a head, however, with the Iranian revolution of 1979. Ayatollah Khomeini, the leader of the Iranian revolution, had spent much of the time between his exile from Iran in 1964 and his triumphant return to Iran in 1979 in Najaf; and it was there, in 1970, that he had delivered his lectures to advanced Hawza students in which he had argued for the necessity of the Shi'i 'ulama assuming the mantle of political leadership. Not much is known about the personal relations between Khomeini and Sadr, but they were clearly in agreement in their dissatisfaction with the political quietism that had long dominated the circles of the Shi'i 'ulama. Sadr enthusiastically welcomed the Iranian revolution of 1979; and when he spoke of the ideal Muslim ruler who does not seek to personally enrich himself but rather gives voice to the oppressed and whose austere life-style evokes that of 'Ali, the first Shi'i imam, it was Khomeini to whom he specifically referred (Sadr 1980b, 210). Shortly after the revolution, Sadr wrote a short tract outlining his vision for the new Iranian constitution and, in particular, articulating the sort of authority the preeminent Shi'i jurist ought to have in it. This vision exercised considerable influence on the framers of the new Iranian constitution (Mallat 1993).

Sadr's unequivocal endorsement of the Iranian revolution, and the mere fact that a revolution led by Shi'i religious scholars had taken place in neighboring Iran, greatly alarmed the Ba'athist regime of Saddam Hussein, which presided over a large Shi'i majority as well as some of their most revered shrines and centers of learning. Khomeini had made no secret of his desire to see the Shi'a of Iraq rise in rebellion or of his hope that Sadr would lead the charge. This contributed its share to precipitating the Iraqi government's massive suppression of all efforts at Shi'i political mobilization. Sadr was executed, along with his sister Bint al-Huda, herself an Islamist activist, in April 1980.

Baqir al-Sadr's oppositional stance has been continued by his successors. Many of his close associates had fled to Iran in the face of severe Ba'thist persecution, returning only with the fall of the Saddam Hussein regime in 2003. In Iraq, during this time, his cousin and former student,

Muhammad Sadiq al-Sadr (d. 1999) guardedly led the Shi'i opposition with an especially strong base among the Shi'i tribesmen of southern Iraq as well as among the two million or so Shi'a living in the slums of Baghdad, the so-called Sadr City (Cole 2003, 550–54). Like Baqir al-Sadr before him, Sadiq al-Sadr also continued to represent internal dissent within the Hawza against what he saw as the excessive quietism of its leading scholars. In the aftermath of the fall of the Saddam Hussein regime, that role has fallen to Sadiq al-Sadr's son, Muqtada al-Sadr (Cockburn 2008). The Da'wa Party with which Baqir al-Sadr was closely associated has, for its part, emerged as one of the major Shi'i political organizations in post-Ba'athist Iraq. Baqir al-Sadr's legacy extends well beyond the intricacies of Shi'i politics in contemporary Iraq, however. His influence looms large over Shi'i conceptions of an Islamic state and visions of "Islamic economics" and, more broadly, over ways of refashioning the shari'a on the path to its implementation in modern Muslim societies.

# THE GENERAL FRAMEWORK
# OF THE ISLAMIC ECONOMY

THE ISLAMIC economy is composed of three basic components, according to which its theoretical content is defined. Thus, it is distinguished from other economic theories in terms of the broad lines of these components, which are:

1. The principle of multifaceted ownership
2. The principle of economic freedom within a defined limit
3. The principle of social justice

We first describe and explain these basic components so that we may form a general view of the Islamic economy. Thus, the scope of the study with regard to its general form will be available to us in examining its theoretical details and characteristics.

## 1. THE PRINCIPLE OF MULTIFACETED OWNERSHIP

Islam differs essentially from capitalism and socialism in the nature of the ownership that it acknowledges.

Capitalist society believes in the private individual form of ownership, that is, private ownership. It allows individuals private ownership of different kinds of wealth in the country according to their activities and circumstances. It recognizes public ownership only when required by social necessity and when experience demonstrates the need for the nationalization of this or that utility. This necessity is an exceptional circumstance, by which a capitalist society is compelled to go outside the principle of private ownership—it is an exception with regard to a utility or form of utility, whose area is clearly defined.

Socialist society is completely contrary to that. In it, common ownership is the general principle, which is applied to every kind of wealth in the land. In its view, private ownership of any of the wealth is an anomaly and an exception, which it may sometimes admit as a result of a prevailing social need.

On the basis of these two contradictory theories, capitalism and socialism, the term "capitalist society" is applied to every society that believes in private ownership as its exclusive principle and regards nationalization an exception and as a means of treating a social necessity. Similarly, the term "socialist society" is applied to every society that regards common ownership as a principle and which recognizes private ownership only in exceptional circumstances.

However, the basic characteristic of both the societies is not applicable to Islamic society because Islamic society does not agree with capitalism in the doctrine that private ownership is the principle or with socialism in its view that common ownership is a general principle. Rather, it acknowledges different forms of ownership at the same time. Thus, it lays down the principle of multifaceted ownership—that is, ownership in a variety of forms—instead of the principle of only one kind of ownership, which capitalism and socialism have adopted. It believes in private ownership, public ownership, and state ownership. It designates to each of these kinds of ownership a special area in which to operate, and it does not regard any of them as anomalous and exceptional, or as a temporary treatment required by circumstances.

For this reason, it would be a mistake to call Islamic society a capitalist society, even though it allows private ownership of a number of kinds of property and means of production, because in its view private ownership is not the basic rule. In the same way it would be a mistake to use the term socialist society for Islamic society, even though it has adopted public ownership and state ownership for some kinds of wealth and property, because in its view the socialist form of ownership is not the general rule. Similarly, it would be a mistake to consider it a mixture constructed from this and that, because the variety of the principal forms of ownership in Islamic society does not mean that Islam has blended together the two theories—capitalist and socialist—and adopted a feature from each of them. It gives expression to that variety in the forms of ownership only through a pure theoretical design, which is dependent upon clearly defined intellectual bases and rules, and which is put forward within a special framework of values and concepts. These are in contradistinction to the bases, rules, values, and concepts on which liberal capitalism and Marxist socialism depend.

There is no greater evidence for the correctness of the Islamic view of ownership than the reality of the capitalist and socialist experiences. Both these experiments necessitate the recognition of another kind of ownership that is not compatible with the general rule involved in each of them because the reality is proof of the mistake of the ideology that upholds the doctrine of there being only one kind of ownership. A long time ago, capitalist society began to adopt the concept of nationalization and to exclude some utilities from the framework of private ownership. This movement toward nationalization is nothing but an implicit recognition by capitalist societies of the unsuitability of the capitalist principle with regard to ownership, and an attempt to treat the weaknesses and contradictions that derive from that principle.

On the other hand socialist society finds itself—despite its recentness—compelled to recognize private ownership, sometimes legally and sometimes in a form that is outside the law. An example of the legal recognition of that is the seventh article of the Soviet constitution which stipulates that every family of a collective farm has the right—in addition to its basic income, which comes from the joint provision of the collective farm—to a piece of land exclusively for itself and attached to the place of residence. Thus it has an additional income in the land, a house for habitation, productive livestock, fowl, and simple agricultural tools as private ownership. In the same way the ninth article allows individual peasants and craftsmen to own small economic enterprises and for these small kinds of ownership to exist alongside the prevailing socialist system.

## 2. The Principle of Economic Freedom within a Defined Limit

The second of the components of the Islamic economy is to allow individuals, at the economic level, a limited freedom, within the bounds of the spiritual and moral values in which Islam believes.

In this component, we also find an outstanding difference between the Islamic economy and the two economies of capitalism and socialism. While individuals practice unrestrained freedom under the protection of the capitalist economy, and while the socialist economy seizes the liberties of all, Islam adopts an attitude that conforms with its general nature. Therefore, it permits individuals to practice their freedom within the limit of values and ideals that will train and burnish that freedom and make it into a better tool for the whole of mankind.

The Islamic limitation on social freedom in the economic field has two parts: personal limitation, which springs from the roots of the person and which extends its power and balance from the spiritual and intellectual recesses to the Islamic personality; and the objective limitation, which gives expression to an external power, limiting and restraining social behavior.

As for the personal limitation, it is formed naturally under the guidance of the special education, according to which Islam rears the individual in the society over which Islam holds sway in every facet of its life—the Islamic society. The intellectual and spiritual frameworks, within which Islam forms the Islamic personality when it gives the opportunity of direct contact with the reality of life and with the work of history, which is at its basis—these frameworks have extraordinary ideational power and great influence in the personal and natural definition of the freedom that has been given to the individual members of Islamic society. They direct them in a righteous restrained direction without the individuals feeling robbed of any of their liberty. Because the definition springs from their spiritual and intellectual reality, they do not find any limit to their liberties in it. Therefore, the personal limitation is not really a limitation of freedom. It is only the process of training the innermost heart of the free man truly spiritually so that under its care freedom performs its true mission.

This personal limitation has had its profound results and its great influence on the formation of the nature of Islamic society and its general disposition. Despite the fact that the complete Islamic experiment was short in duration, it has brought results and thrown light, in the soul of mankind, on their ideal potentialities. It has bestowed on mankind a spiritual stock overflowing with feelings of justice, goodness, and charity. If it had been possible for that experiment to continue and to extend into the life of mankind for a longer period than it did extend in a short historical phase, it would have been able to prove man's competence to take up custodianship of the earth. It would have made a new world overflowing with feelings of justice and mercy. It would have rooted out from the soul of man most of the elements of evil and tendencies for oppression and corruption, which could be rooted out.

It is sufficient to mention from among the results of personal limitation that it remains the only basic guarantor for works of piety and good in the society of the Muslim, because Islam lost its own actual experiment in life and was deprived of its political and social leadership. Despite the fact that the Muslims have been set apart from the spirit of that experiment and leadership through a temporal separation that stretches many centuries and a spiritual separation that can be measured by the decrease of their intellectual and psychological standards, and despite the fact that they have become accustomed to different kinds of social and political life, despite all this, personal limitation, whose essence Islam laid down in its complete experiment for life, had a positive and active role in guaranteeing works of piety and good. These are represented in millions of Muslims paying zakat, performing other duties to God, and participating in the realization of the concepts of Islam concerning social justice, doing all this with a freedom that was crystallized within the framework of that personal limitation. What do you think would be the result, in the light of this reality, if those Muslims were living the complete Islamic experience and if their society was a complete embodiment of Islam in its ideas, values, and policy and if their society was a practical expression of its concepts and ideals?

As for the objective limitation of freedom, we mean by it the limitation that is imposed on the individual in Islamic society from outside by the force of revealed law. This objective limitation of freedom in Islam is based on the principle that says that there is no freedom for the person in what the sacred law stipulates concerning the types of activity that contradict the ideals and aims in whose necessity Islam believes.

The execution of this principle in Islam was performed in the following way.

1. The sacred law, in its general sources, provided the textual stipulation to forbid a group of social and economic activities, which hinder, in the view of Islam, the realization of the ideals and values adopted by Islam, such as usury, monopoly, and the like.

2. The sacred law laid down the principle of the supervision of the ruler over general activities and the intervention of the state to protect and safeguard public interest (*al-masalih al-'amma*) through the limitation of the freedom of individuals in the actions they perform. It was necessary for Islam to lay down this principle in order to guarantee the realization of its ideals and concepts concerning social justice in the course of time. The requirements of the social justice that Islam propagates differ according to the economic circumstances of the society and the material situations that surround it. The performance of an action may be harmful to society and its necessary form at one particular time while it is not at another. Thus, it is not possible to detail that in fixed constitutional forms. The only way is to provide the ruler with the opportunity to carry out his duty as an authority, which controls, directs, and limits the freedoms of the individuals with regard to the permissible actions in revealed law that they may do or not do, in accordance with the Islamic ideal for society.

The legal source for the principle of supervision and intervention is the Holy Qur'an where it says: "Obey God and obey the Messenger and those who have authority among you." This text indicates clearly the necessity of obeying those who have authority. There is no dispute among Muslims that "those who have authority" are those who hold legal authority in Islamic society, even though they disagree about how they are appointed and the definition of their conditions and qualities. Then, the high Islamic authority has the right to be obeyed and the right to intervene to protect the society and to realize the Islamic equilibrium in it. However, this intervention should be within the context of the sacred law. Thus, it is not possible for the state or the ruler to allow usury, to permit cheating, not to apply the law of inheritance, to annul ownership already established on an Islamic basis in society. Yet the ruler is allowed in Islam to intervene in actions and activities, permitted by the sacred law. He can forbid them or order them to be done according to the Islamic ideal of the society. Thus, revival of the land, extraction of minerals and making canals and other such activities, and trading are permissible actions that the sacred law has permitted in a general way. It has laid down for each action the legal consequences that are entailed by it. If the ruler considers that he should forbid or order some kind of activity within the limits of his authority, he has the right to do so according to the previously mentioned principle.

The Messenger of God—may God bless him and his family—applied this principle of intervention when there was a need or situation that required some kind of intervention and direction. An example of this is reported in the authentic Tradition on the authority of the Prophet, may God bless him and his family: "He gave a judgment to the Medinans concerning the irrigation channels between palm trees that the benefit of good may not be prevented. He also gave a judgment to the people of the desert that an excess of water may not be prevented [from flowing] in order that pasture may be prevented [from growing]. And he said: There should be no harm or attempt to cause harm." It is clear according to the jurists that the prevention of the benefit of a thing or the prevention of an excess of water is not forbidden in general in the sacred law. In this light, we know that the Prophet did not forbid the people of Medina from preventing the benefit of a thing nor did he forbid the prevention of the excess of water as a Messenger bringing general revealed laws. He only forbade that as a ruler responsible for the organization of the economic life of the society and for directing it in such a way that does not conflict with public interests as he estimates them. It may be for this reason that the Tradition expresses the prohibition of the Prophet as a judgment and not as an absolute religious prohibition because judgment is a kind of nonrevealed legal decision.

We treat this principle (the principle of supervision and intervention) in a more detailed and elaborate later discussion.

### 3. The Principle of Social Justice

The third component in the Islamic economy is the principle of social justice. This is embodied in Islam by the elements and guarantees that Islam provided for the system of the distribution of wealth in Islamic society. These enable the distribution to achieve the realization of Islamic justice and to be in harmony with the values with which it is concerned. When Islam put social justice within the basic principles from which its economic theory is composed, it did not adopt social justice in its general abstract conception, nor did it call for a form capable of every kind of explanation, nor did it entrust the matter to human societies that differ in their view of social justice according to their cultural ideas and concepts about life. Rather, Islam defined and crystallized this concept within a specific social plan. After that, it was able to embody this determination in a living social reality, all of whose veins and arteries throbbed with the Islamic concept of justice.

It is not sufficient to know only Islam's calls for social justice; we should also know its detailed concepts of justice and the special Islamic evidence for them.

The Islamic image of social justice contains two general principles, each one of which has its own lines and particularities. The first of them is the principle of general mutual responsibility; the other is the principle of social balance. Just social values are realized within the Islamic conception of mutual responsibility and balance, and it is in them that the Islamic ideal of social justice is found, as we shall see in the following section. The steps that Islam took in the course of creating the most excellent human society during its glorious historical experiment were plain and clear with regard to its concern for its principal component of its economy.

This concern was clearly reflected in the first speech that the Prophet delivered and the first political action he took in his new state.

The great Messenger inaugurated his guiding statement—as it is reported—with this speech:

> People, make preparation for yourselves. By God, each of you should know that he will die and he will leave his sheep without a shepherd. Then his Lord will say to him: Did not my Messenger come to you and tell you? And I gave you wealth and showed preference to you. What have you prepared for yourself. Then each of you will look to the left and the right and will see nothing. You will look in front and see only Hell. Whoever is able to protect his face from the Fire—even with half of a date—let him do it. Whoever does not find that, let him use a good word. For one good action will be rewarded ten times to seven hundred times. Peace be on you and the mercy and blessings of God.

His political activity began with the making of a brotherhood between the emigrants from Mecca and the supporters from Medina, and the application of mutual responsibility between them, for the sake of the realization of the social justice that Islam aimed at.

These are the basic elements in the Islamic economy:

1. Ownership of varied kinds, in the light of which distribution is determined
2. A freedom, limited by Islamic values, in the fields of production, exchange, and consumption
3. A social justice, which will guarantee happiness to society, and whose foundation is mutual responsibility and balance

The economic theory is Islam has two main qualities, which radiate through its lines and particularities: realism and morality. Therefore, the Islamic economy is both a realistic and a moral economy in the goals that it sets out to realize and in the method which it adopts for that.

It is a realistic economy in its goals because in its systems and laws it aims at goals that are in harmony with the nature, tendencies, and general characteristics of human reality; it always tries not to ask more than is humanly possible in its legal reckoning; and it does not take humanity soaring into high imaginary skies beyond its powers and abilities. It always determines its economic plan on the basis of a real view of man. It sets out real aims that agree with that view. An imaginary economy, like for example communism, may be content to adopt an unreal aim and set forth to attain a new humanity, purified from all tendencies of egotism and capable of distributing works and wealth among men without any need for an instrument of government to direct the distribution, a humanity secure from all kinds of disputes and strife. . . . However, this does not conform with the nature of Islamic legislation or with the realism that it is characterized by in its goals and aims.

In addition to this, it is also real in its method. Just as it aims at real goals, which are capable of being realized, similarly it gives a real material guarantee for the realization of these goals. It is not satisfied with the guarantees of advice and guidance, which preachers and teachers give because it means going beyond such aims to the sphere of execution. Therefore it is not content to entrust them to the providence of chance and guesses. For example, when it aims at the creation of general mutual responsibility, it does not seek for this only by methods of direction and the arousal of emotion; rather, it supports it with a legal guarantee that makes its realization essential in every circumstance.

The second quality of the Islamic economy, the moral quality, means in terms of goal that Islam does not derive the goals, which it strives to realize in the economic life of society, from material circumstances and natural conditions that are independent of man himself, in the same way that Marxism derives its goals from the position and circumstance of productive forces. Rather, it views those goals in terms of them being an expression of practical values that must be realized from the moral angle. For example, when it prescribes the guarantee of life for the worker, it does not believe that this social guarantee, which it has laid down, is something that has arisen out of the material circumstances of production. Rather, it considers it as a representative of a practical value that has to be realized. We study that in a detailed manner in the course of the discussions in this section.

The moral quality, in terms of method, means that Islam is concerned with the psychological factor throughout the method that it has laid down to achieve its aims and goals. In that method, it is not only. concerned with the objective aspect—namely, that those goals be achieved. Indeed, in a special way it attends to the blending of the psychological and personal factor with the method that realizes those goals. For example, money may be taken from the rich to provide sufficient funds for the poor, and in that it is feasible that the poor may satisfy their needs. Thus, the objective goal, which the Islamic economy aims at in terms of the principle of mutual responsibility, would come into existence. However, in the reckoning of Islam, this is not the problem. Rather, there is the method by which general mutual responsibility is reached. For this method may mean simply the use of force to take tax revenues from the rich in order to support the poor. Even though this would be sufficient to realize the objective aspect of the problem—namely, providing sufficient funds for the poor—Islam would not accept that as long as the method of attaining mutual responsibility was without a moral motive and factor of goodness in the hearts of the rich. For this reason, Islam has intervened and made legally required acts of religion out of financial duties, by which the creation of mutual responsibility is sought. It is necessary that they spring from a shining psychological motive that impels man to participate in realizing the goals of the Islamic economy in a consciously intended manner out of a desire to please God, the Exalted, and to draw close to Him.

No wonder that Islam has this concern for the psychological factor and this care for its spiritual and intellectual formation in accordance with its goals and concepts. The nature of the personal factor, which constitutes a struggle in the soul of man, has a great influence on the formation of the personality of man and defines his spiritual content. In the same way, the personal factor, together with its problems and solutions, has a great influence on social life. It has become clear to everyone today that the psychological factor plays a major role in the economic field. It has an influence on the occurrence of the periodic crises, from whose misfortunes the European economy clamors. Also, it affects the curve of supply and demand and the productive capacity of work, in addition to other elements of the economy.

Islam, then, is not limited, in its theory and doctrines, to the organization of the external aspect of society. It penetrates to its spiritual and intellectual depths to bring about a reconciliation between the internal content and the economic and social plan on which it draws. It is not satisfied in its method to adopt any way that guarantees the realization of its aims. Rather, it blends this way with the psychological factor and the personal motive that are in harmony with these aims and conceptions. . . .

Economic theory in Islam is distinguished from the other economic theories that we have studied by virtue of its general religious framework. In Islam, religion is the framework that encompasses every organization of life. Thus, when Islam treats any aspect of life, it mingles it with religion, and it molds it with a framework of man's religious connection with his Creator and with his next life.

It is this religious framework that makes the Islamic system capable of attaining ultimate success and brings about the guarantee of the realization of man's general social benefits. For the realization of these social benefits can be guaranteed only by means of religion.

In order to classify that, we must study the benefits of man in his daily life and consider what is the possible extent of their provision and the guarantee for their realization. In this way, we will be able to go from here to the reality that has been mentioned before—namely, that the social benefits of man can be provided and their realization can be guaranteed only by means of a framework that utilizes a sound religious system.

When we study the benefits of man in his daily life, it is possible for us to divide them into two groups. The first is the benefits of man that nature provides him as a special being, like medicaments. It is to the benefit of man to acquire them from nature. This benefit has no connection with his social relationship with others. Rather, man, as a being exposed to harmful germs, is in need of these medicaments, whether he lives alone or within an integrated society.

The second group is the benefits of man that the social system provides for him as a social being who is bound by relationships with others. An example of this is the benefit that man gains from the social system when it allows him to exchange his produce for the produce of others, or when it provides for him the security for his daily livelihood in circumstances of want and unemployment.

We refer to the first group as natural benefits and the second group as social benefits.

In order that man can be provided with his natural and social benefits, he must be provided with the ability to understand these benefits and the means of acquiring them and the motive that will impel him to strive for them. Thus, for example, the medicaments that provide treatment for tuberculosis will only be found by man when he understands that there is a medicine for tuberculosis and discovers the way to acquire it. Similarly, the security for daily livelihood in circumstances of want—as a social benefit—depends on man's understanding of the advantage of this security and the means of making it law and on the motive that will impel him to produce and execute this legislation.

There are, then, two basic conditions, without which it would be impossible for mankind to acquire a complete life in which his natural and social benefits would be provided. The first is that he understands those benefits and how they are attained. The second is that he possesses a motive that will impel him to attain them after he has understood what they are.

When we observe the natural benefits of man—like the acquisition of medicaments for the treatment of tuberculosis—we find that humanity has been provided with the abilities to obtain these benefits. Man possesses an intellectual power by which the phenomena of nature and the benefits hidden there can be comprehended. Even though this power only grows slowly in the course of time, nonetheless it carries on in a continuously improving way in the light of experience and new experiments. As this ability grows, so man is more capable of attaining his benefits and of understanding the advantages that he can gain from nature.

Alongside this intellectual ability, humanity possesses a personal motivation that guarantees its spontaneous drive toward its natural benefits. The acquisition of medicaments is not, for example, a benefit for one individual apart from any other individual, or an advantage for one group apart from others. Human society is constantly being propelled along the path toward the provision of natural benefits through the power of personal motivation in individuals. All of these agree in the concern for those benefits and their necessity, insofar as they have personal advantage for all individuals.

Thus, we know that man is composed of a special combination of mind and intellect that makes him capable of providing himself with natural benefits and of perfecting this aspect over his life through his experience of life and nature.

The social benefits, in their turn, are also dependent—as we know—on man attaining the social organization that is appropriate to him and on the psychological motivation toward the creation and implementation of that social organization. What is man's part with regard to those two conditions (knowledge of the benefits and the motive to attain them) in relation to social benefits? Has man been equipped with the intellectual ability to realize his social benefits, and with the motive that will impel him to attain them, in the same way as he has been equipped with that as far as his natural benefits were concerned?

Let us take the first condition. It is a widespread view that man cannot attain the social organization that would provide all his social benefits for him and which would be in harmony with his nature and his general makeup, because he is completely incapable of attaining a social attitude in all its aspects and because of all that is included in human nature. The holders of this view come to the following conclusion: the social system must be laid down for humanity, and it is not possible to leave humanity to lay down the system for itself, as long as its understanding is limited and its intellectual circumstances are incapable of discovering the solution to the whole social problem.

On this basis, they put forward evidence for the necessity of religion in the life of man and for the need of humanity for messengers and prophets, inasmuch as they are able, by means of inspiration, to define the true benefits for man in his social life and reveal them to people.

However, in our view, the problem will appear in a clearer form when we study the second condition.

The basic point in the problem is not how man attains social benefits. Rather, the basic problem is how man is impelled to realize them and to organize society in a way that will guarantee them. The cause of the problem is that social benefit does not on most occasions concur with personal motivation, because of its conflict with interests peculiar to individuals. Thus, the personal motivation, which assures that man is propelled toward the natural benefits for mankind, does not assume the same attitude toward mankind's social benefits. So although personal motivation has been making man attempt to find a medicine for tuberculosis, because finding this medicine will be a benefit to all individuals, we find that this same personal motivation obstructs the realization of many social benefits. It prevents the creation or implementation of the organization that would provide those benefits. Security of daily livelihood for the worker who is unemployed is in conflict with the interests of the rich, who will have to provide payment for the expenses of this security. The nationalization of land conflicts with the interests of those who are capable of monopolizing the land for themselves. Thus, every social benefit gives rise to opposition from the personal motivations of individuals, whose interest differs from the general social benefit.

In this light, we understand the basic difference between natural and social benefits. The personal motives of individuals do not clash with the natural interests of humanity. In fact, they urge individuals to find them and to take advantage of the reflective mind to this effect. In that way mankind has gained control over the abilities that will provide natural benefits for it, doing this in a gradual way in accordance with the development of ability through experience. Social benefits are contrary to that. Personal motives, which spring from man's love of himself and impel him to put his own interests before the interests of others, obstruct man from using his mind practically and sincerely to provide social advantages, to create the social organization that will provide those benefits and to cause that organization to be put into effect.

Thus, it is clear that the social problem, which comes between humanity and its social integration, is the contradiction that exists between social benefits and personal motives. As long as humanity is not equipped with the abilities to bring harmony between social benefits and the basic motives that dominate individuals, it will not be possible for human society to attain its social perfection. What, then, are those abilities?

Humanity is in need of a motive that is in harmony with the general social benefits in the same way that natural benefits found personal motives to be its ally.

Is It Possible for Science to Solve the Problem?

It is frequently repeated on some lips that science, which has developed in an astonishing way, is a guarantor of the solution for the social problem, because man is this obstinate giant who has been able to take gigantic strides in the fields of thought, life, and nature. He has been able to penetrate into its deepest secrets and to solve its most astonishing riddles such that he was successful in exploding the atom and releasing its fearful power. He has been able to discover planets, to send his projectiles to them, and to travel in rockets. He has been able to utilize the forces of nature so that he can transport what happens at a distance of hundreds of thousands of miles in terms of sounds that can be heard and pictures that can be seen. This man, who has recorded all these scientific conquests in a short history and has been victorious in all his battles with nature, is capable, through the science and vision that he has been given, of building a happy cohesive society, of laying down the social organization that will provide the social benefits for mankind. Thus, man is no longer in need of any source from which to seek inspiration for his social attitude other than science, which will lead him from victory to victory in every field.

This claim, in fact, only means ignorance of the function of science in the life of humanity. Science, whatever it may have caused to grow and develop, is only a tool to discover the objective truths in different fields and to explain reality in a neutral manner that will reflect it with the greatest possible degree of exactitude and profundity. It informs us, in the social field, for example, that capitalism leads to the iron law of wages and keeping them as low as the necessary minimum level of livelihood, just as it informs us, in the natural field, that the use of a certain chemical substance will lead to an ailment threatening a person's life. When science shows us this or that truth, it will have carried out its function and provided man with a new understanding. However, the specter of this serious disease and of that fearful law (the iron law of wages) does not disappear because of the mere fact that science has discovered the relationship between that specific substance and the disease or between capitalism and the iron law. Rather, man will be free of the disease by avoiding things that lead to it, and he will be free of the iron law of wages by eradicating the capitalist framework of society. Here we may ask: What is it that will guarantee that man may avoid that disease? Or that framework? The answer with regard to the disease is completely clear. The personal motivation, which man has, is sufficient by itself to keep him away from the special substance, whose serious effects science has revealed, because it contradicts the specific benefit of the individual. With regard to what is connected with the iron law of wages and the removal of the capitalist framework, scientific truth, which has demonstrated the connection between this framework and this law, is not a motivating force for action and changing the framework. Action needs a motivation, and the personal motives of individuals do not always coincide but can differ according to the difference of their special interests.

Thus, it is necessary to distinguish between the discovery of scientific truth and action, in the light of it, to make society happy. Science only reveals truth somewhat gradually. It does not develop it.

## HISTORICAL MATERIALISM AND THE PROBLEM

In this regard, Marxism puts forward—on the basis of historical materialism—a claim with regard to the same problem, that the laws of history will guarantee its solution one day. Yet, is not the problem that personal motives are unable to guarantee the benefits and happiness of society because they follow special interests that, on most occasions, differ with general social benefits? This (it answers) is not a problem. It is only the real nature of human societies since the dawn of history. Everything has been progressing in accordance with personal motives that are reflected in society by a class structure. Thus, strife will arise between the personal motivations of different classes, and victory will always be the lot for the personal motivation of the class that controls the means of production. In this way, personal motivation will always prevail in an inevitable way so that the laws of history will provide their radical solution to the problem by the formation of a classless society, in which personal motives will be removed and, instead of them, communal motives will be formed in accordance with communal ownership.

We have realized in our study of historical materialism that the prophecies that historical materialism makes do not rest on a scientific basis and it is impossible to expect a decisive answer to the problem from them.

In this way, the problem remains as it was, a problem of society in which personal motivation prevails. As long as the most important words for personal motivation, which it dictates to every individual, are "his own special interest," there will be domination by the interest that has possession of executive power. Amid the crush of conflicting egotisms, who can guarantee that the law will be fashioned in accordance with the social benefits for humanity, rather than being an expression of the power prevailing in society?

Nor can we expect a social apparatus, like the governmental apparatus, to solve the problem through force and to stop these personal motives at their borders, for this apparatus arises out of the same society. The problem for it is the problem for the whole society because personal motivation is what prevails in it.

We can deduce from this that personal motivation is the cause of the social problem and that this impulse is basic to man because it springs from his love of himself.

Has it been ordained that humanity should always live with this social problem, which arises out of its personal motivation and its natural disposition, and it should always be miserable because of this natural disposition?

Has humanity been excluded from the system of existence, which provides every being in it with the potentialities for attaining complete fulfillment and in which has been placed the natural disposition that will lead to its own particular perfection, as scientific experiments, in addition to philosophical proof, have indicated?

At this point, there enters the role of religion insofar as it is the unique solution for the problem. Religion is the unique framework within which it is possible for the social problem to find its correct solution. That is, the solution depends on the creation of harmony between personal motivations and the general social benefits. This harmony is something that religion can offer to humanity. For religion is the spiritual power that can compensate man for the temporary delights that he abandons in his earthly life out of hope for eternal happiness. It can impel him to sacrifice his existence through a belief that the limited existence that he sacrifices is nothing but a preparation for a perpetual existence and an eternal life. It can create in his thinking a new attitude toward his personal benefits, a concept of profit and loss that is higher than the material experimental conceptions of them. In this way, concern for others becomes the means of attaining delight, and loss for the advantage of society becomes a way of attaining profit. The defense of the benefits of others means implicitly the defense of the benefits of the individual in a more exalted and higher life. Thus, general social benefits are inextricably linked with personal motives insofar as the former are the benefits of the individual in terms of his religious reckoning.

In the noble Qur'an, we find magnificent assurances of this meaning scattered everywhere. They all aim to form that new idea in the individual about his benefit and profits. Thus, the Qur'an says:

> Whoever, male or female, does a righteous action, is a believer. They shall enter Heaven where they will be provided for without any account (40:40). Whoever does a righteous action, it will be credited to him, and whoever does wrong, it will be used against him (41:46). On a day the people will come forth in groups to see their deeds. Whoever has done an atom's weight of good will see it and whoever has done an atom's weight of evil will see it (99:6–8). Do not consider those who have been killed on the path of God as dead but rather as living with the Lord and being provided for (3:169). It was not (proper) for the people of Medina and the bedouin around them to hold back from the Apostle of God and prefer themselves to him. (They did) that because (they wanted) neither thirst, nor tiredness, nor hardship to afflict them on the path of God. They could not take a step that would vex the unbelievers, nor take anything from an enemy unless a righteous action had been ordained for them for it. Indeed, God does not cause the reward for those who do good to be lost. They could spend neither a small amount nor a large one; they could not cross a valley, unless the best actions that they performed had been ordained for them to reward them (9:120–21).

These are glorious pictures that religion presents in the texts of the Qur'an in order to make the link between personal motives and good actions in life and to bring about a development out of the benefit of the individual, which will cause him to believe that his own special benefits and the true general interests of mankind, as defined by Islam, are inextricably linked together.

Religion then, has the basic role in the solution of the social problem in terms of mobilizing personal motivation to the side of the general benefit.

In this way, we understand that religion is a natural need for humanity. For as long as natural disposition is the basis of personal motives, out of which the problem arises, it is inevitable that they should be provided with the capacities to solve this problem so that man should not be an exception to the rest of beings, all of whose natural dispositions have been provided with the capacities that lead every creature to its own particular perfection. These capacities that human nature possesses to solve the problem are nothing but the instinct to profess religion and the natural inclination to link life to religion and to mold life in the general framework of religion.

The natural disposition of humanity has, then, two elements. From one aspect, it dictates to man his personal motivations, out of which springs the great social problem in the life of man (the problem of the conflict between those motives and the true general interests of human society). From another aspect, it provides man with the potentiality of solving the problem by means of his natural inclination toward the profession of religion, and the fact that religion gives judgment over life in a way that harmonizes general benefits and personal motives. In this way, the natural disposition fulfills its function by guiding man to his perfection. If the problem continued to arise, and human nature was not provided with its solution, this would mean that human beings would remain chained down by the problem, incapable of solving it and led by the decision of their natural dispositions into manifold evils. This is what Islam has propounded very clearly in the words of God, the Exalted: "Set your face toward religion as a *hanif* (a person of pure faith) with the natural disposition from God, with which he has naturally endowed men. There is no change in the creation of God. That is the guarding religion, but most people do not know" (30:30).[1]

---

[1] *Hanif*, a Qur'anic term, is usually understood to mean a person of pure faith and a generic monotheist, that is, one who is neither Jewish nor Christian (cf. Q 2:135). Qur'an 30:30 seems to tend toward the idea of natural law, though medieval Muslim theologians generally rejected that idea and argued instead that moral and religious obligations were knowable *only* through the shari'a. Many Islamists as well as Muslim modernists have been rather more open to the idea of natural law, though not in the sense of an independent source of norms but rather as a way of asserting that Islam is the most perfect means of optimally balancing the competing demands of human nature. Also cf. Griffel 2007.

This blessed verse lays down:

1. Religion is one of the concerns of the natural human disposition, with which God has endowed all men, and there can be no change in the creation of God.

2. This religion, which mankind has been endowed with, is nothing but the hanif religion—namely, the religion of the undivided unity of God because the religion of the unity of God is alone capable of carrying out the greatest function of religion and of unifying mankind in a practical way and in a social organization in which his social benefits will be preserved. The religions of polytheism or of different lords, according to the Qur'anic definition are, in reality, a result of the problem. They have not been able to treat this problem because, as Joseph described to his two companions in prison: "What you worship apart from God are nothing but names given by you and your fathers. God has given them no authority" (12:40). By that he means that they are the product of personal motivations that dictate men to set up a religion of polytheism in accordance with their different personal interests, so that their natural inclination toward the hanif religion can be completely diverted and the true response to their basic religious inclination can be impeded.

3. The hanif religion, with which man has been endowed, is characterized by being a guarding religion for life, capable of controlling life and fashioning it within the religion's general framework. As for the religion that does not assume the leadership and direction of life, it is not able to respond fully to the needs of the natural disposition in man for religion, and thus it is not capable of dealing with the basic problem in the life of man.

From that, we arrive at several concepts of Islam about religion and life. The basic problem in the life of man arises out of his natural disposition because it is a problem of personal motives in terms of their conflicts and contradictions with general benefits. Yet, at the same time, the natural disposition of mankind provides it with the means of dealing with the problem. This means is nothing but "guarding hanif religion," because it alone is capable of reconciling personal motives and uniting their interests and practical judgments. Thus, guarding hanif religion is essential for social life. Social organization in the different branches of life must be put in the framework of that religion which is capable of being in harmony with the natural disposition and of dealing with the basic problem in the life of man.

In light of this, we realize that the Islamic economy, insofar as it is part of a comprehensive social organization for life, must be included within the general framework of that organization, and that is religion. Thus, religion is the general framework for our theoretical economy.

The function of religion, as a framework for the social and economic organization in Islam, is to bring harmony between personal motives and special benefits on the one hand and the true general interests for human society, from the Islamic viewpoint, on the other.

Each of the theories of the economy, which we have described, is a part of a comprehensive theory dealing with different branches and aspects of life. Thus, the Islamic economy is part of the comprehensive Islamic theory for the various branches of life. The capitalist economy is part of capitalist democracy, which, in its organizational view, encompasses the whole of society. Similarly, the Marxist economy is also part of the Marxist theory, which crystallizes the whole of social life with its special framework.

These theories differ in the basic intellectual seeds and the principal roots, from which their spirit and their entity derive. Accordingly, they differ in their special character.

The Marxist economy bears, in the view of Marxism, a scientific character because, according to the belief of its adherents, it is considered as a final outcome of the natural dispositions that control and administer the course of history. Contrary to that, the supporters of the capitalist economy, as we mentioned in a previous study, do not make it a necessary result of the nature and laws of history. Rather, they designate it by the social form that agrees with the practical values and ideals that they embrace.

The Islamic economy does not claim for itself a scientific character like the Marxist economy. Similarly, it is not divested of a specific creedal basis and a fundamental attitude toward life and existence like capitalism.

When we say that the Islamic economy is not a science, we mean that Islam is a religion that undertakes to call for the organization of economic life just as it deals with the other aspects of life, and therefore it is not a science in the manner of the science of political economy. In another sense, it is a revolution to overturn a corrupt existing situation and transform it into a sound situation. It is not an objective explanation of the existing situation. When, for example, it puts forward the principle of multifaceted ownership, it does not claim by that to explain the historical reality of a specific stage in the life of mankind or that it reflects the results of the natural laws of history, as Marxism claims when it preaches the principle of common ownership as the ultimate condition of a specific stage of history and as the only explanation for it.

In this aspect, the Islamic economy is like the theoretical capitalist economy insofar as it is an attempt to change the situation, not explain it. The theoretical function, facing the Islamic economy, is to reveal the comprehensive form of economic life in accordance with Islamic legislation and to study the general ideas and concepts that radiate from that form, such as the idea of the separation of the mode of distribution from the nature of production and other similar ideas.

The role of the scientific function facing the Islamic economy will come after that in order to reveal the actual course of life and the laws for it within an Islamic society in which the theory of Islam is completely applied. The scientific researcher will take the theoretical economy in Islam as an established basis for the society, which he attempts to explain and in which events are linked one with another. In this, it is similar to the political economy of the capitalist theorists of economy, who have completed formulating their theoretical lines and then have begun to explain the existing situation within those lines and to study the nature of the laws that prevail in a society in which they are applied. The outcome of this study of theirs is the science of political economy.

Thus, it is possible that a science may be formed for the Islamic economy after a comprehensive theoretical study has been made by means of studying the situation within this framework. The question is, When and how will it be possible to formulate the science of the Islamic economy in the same way as the capitalists have formulated the science of political economy or, in other words, the science of the economy that explains events in capitalist society?

The answer to this question is that the scientific explanation of the events of economic life are concentrated in one of two approaches:

1. To gather evidence for the economic events from the actual experience of life and to organize them scientifically to reveal the laws by which they are controlled within the field of that life and the special circumstances of that life
2. To begin by studying specific postulated facts and in the light of these to infer the economic direction and the course of events

The scientific explanation according to the first approach depends on the embodiment of the theory in an actual existing entity so that the researcher is given the opportunity to record the events of this situation and to infer their general outward forms and laws. This is what capitalist economists have accomplished when they live in a society that believes in capitalism and applies it. They have been given the opportunity to formulate their views on the basis of the experience of an actual social situation in which they have lived. However, nothing like this will be given to Islamic economists as long as the Islamic economy remains far from the living stage. Therefore, they do not have in their daily lives the experiences of the Islamic economy being applied in order to comprehend, in the light of such experiences, the nature of the laws that prevail in a life that is based on Islam.

The scientific explanation according to the second approach could be used as a means of elucidating some of the realities with which economic life is distinguished in Islamic society. This could be done by starting with specific theoretical points and by deducing their effects in the field of a postulated application and then by formulating general views about the economic aspect in Islamic society in the light of those theoretical points.

For example, it is possible for the Islamic researcher to maintain that the interest of commerce in Islamic society is in agreement with the interest of financiers and bankers because banking, in Islamic society, is based on *mudaraba* (partnership), not on usury. Thus, the banker conducts commercial activities with the wealth of his customers and divides the profits between them and himself according to a fixed percentage of the profit. In the last analysis, his financial progress depends upon the size of the financial profit that he acquires, not on interest that he takes from debts. This phenomenon—the phenomenon of the agreement between the interests of banks and the interests of commerce—is in its very nature an objective phenomenon, which the researchers may begin to deduce from one point, which is the abolition of the interest-taking system of banks in Islamic society.

The researchers can also, beginning from another point like this, lay down another objective phenomenon. This is the attitude of Islamic society to the principal factor for the crises that beset economic life in capitalist society. For the great part of the people's wealth, which is stored away out of a desire for usurious interest, obstructs the roles of production and consumption in a society based on usury and is, thus, withdrawn from areas of production and consumption. This is something that leads to the stagnation of a great proportion of social production of capitalist commodities and consumer products. However, when society is based on the Islamic economy, in which usury is completely forbidden and where there is also a prohibition against hoarding or else what is hoarded is taxed, this will result in people all spending their wealth.

In these explanations, we postulate a social and economic situation dependent on specific principles, and we then make the explanation of this postulated situation and the deduction of its general characteristic in the light of those principles.

However, these explanations do not form for us, with any exactness, a comprehensive scientific conception of economic life in Islamic society, as long as the substance of the scientific study has not been gathered from the experience of a tangible situation. Frequently, differences may occur between the actual life of a system and the explanations that are offered for this life on the basis of hypothesis. Similarly, it occurs that capitalistic economists, who have built many of their analytic theories on a hypothetical basis, arrive at results that contradict the situation in which they are living, because of the uncovering of a number of factors in the actual field of life that did not come within the compass of the hypothesis.

In addition, the spiritual and intellectual element or, in other words, the general psychological disposition of Islamic society possesses a great influence over the course of economic life. This disposition does not have a defined stage or a specific form that can be postulated before it, and on which different ideas can be based. Therefore, the science of the Islamic economy can be truly born only when this economy is embodied in the existence of society, in its roots, its outlines, and its details. Then the events and economic experiences through which its passes can be studied in a systematic way.

# Chapter 8

# HASAN AL-TURABI
## 1932–

MUSLIM MODERNISTS have frequently allied themselves with authoritarian regimes in order to have their reformist ideas implemented by the state. Unlike populist politicians, modernist reformers have seldom had any clear constituency or support base in their local societies. Schooled in educational systems bequeathed by colonial rule and often more at home in European languages than in their native tongue, many modernists have had little choice but to try to shape their societies from the top down. The association with the governing elite has necessitated many compromises for the modernists, but it has not necessarily been a difficult alliance to forge. This has had much to do with the fact that modernist intellectuals and the modernizing governing elite have typically had a broadly shared view of how to reform and reorient their societies, what institutions to patronize, which "traditional" sectors to marginalize. It is not just the Muslim modernists who have forged such unsavory alliances, however. So, too, have some Islamists. For all their critique of a medieval despotism and a servile religious establishment enabling it in all its un-Islamic excesses, Islamists, too, have made common cause with the "right" sort of authoritarian rulers. Few are better known for this than the influential Sudanese Islamist Hasan al-Turabi.

Turabi was born in eastern Sudan in 1932. His father was a judge trained in Islamic law, and it is from him that Turabi acquired much of his early education in the Islamic sciences. Turabi's formal education was in Western institutions of learning, both in Sudan and abroad. He graduated from the Gordon Memorial College in Khartoum (later called the University of Khartoum) and subsequently studied at the University of London and the Sorbonne, receiving his Ph.D. in law from the latter in 1964. He returned to Sudan in the mid-1960s to teach at the University of Khartoum and soon also began to take active part in national politics.

The Sudan of the 1960s had four principal political organizations. The Communist Party was the largest in the Arab world at the time, with a strong appeal among university students, including young, educated women. Two other organizations were self-consciously anchored in traditional ways of practicing Islam in Sudan. One of these was the Umma Party, long headed by Sadiq al-Mahdi, a great-grandson of Muhammad Ahmad al-Mahdi, who had led a messianic, anticolonial movement in the late nineteenth century. The other traditionalist Islamic organization was the Democratic Unionist Party, whose influence derived principally from its roots in the Khatmiyya, one of the largest of Sudan's Sufi orders. The Islamic identity of both of these parties was, and continues to be, anchored in popular forms of devotional piety. This clearly sets them apart from the Muslim Brotherhood, the fourth of Sudan's main political groups in the 1960s. While the Islamist trend has continued to be strong in Sudan, the parties serving as its principal embodiment have adopted new names and identities over the course of the past half century. These have included the Islamic Charter Front in the late 1960s; the National Islamic Front from the 1970s through the 1990s; and the National Congress Party and its splinter group, the Popular Congress Party, since the late 1990s. Each of these is best viewed as a new iteration of the Muslim Brotherhood; and Turabi has been associated with every one of them.

The public implementation of Islamic law has always been at the forefront of the Islamists' agenda. Sudan's traditionalist Islamic parties have also remained vaguely supportive of an Islamic state, though, unlike them, the Islamists have meant something quite specific by this. The Sudanese Islamists have demanded that the shari'a be implemented in all facets of life, irrespective of how Islam and its legal norms have been understood in local contexts. By the same token, they have sought to distance themselves from the Sufi, customary, and local practices often inextricably tied to other ways of being Muslim, as represented by rival Islamic organizations. As Sadiq al-Mahdi, the leader of Umma Party had put it in 1980 with reference to the Muslim Brothers, "They are a branch of a movement which originated and developed outside Sudan. We have developed *in Sudan* and would give it a leading role in the revival of Islam" (quoted in Warburg 2003, 175; emphasis added). Yet, as in Pakistan, where Mawdudi's Jama'at-i Islami had to soften its initial hostility toward Sufi devotional practices in the interest of political expediency (see chapters 1 and 3), Sudan's Muslim Brothers, too, have struggled with the question of whether to forge political alliances with these other organizations. Against an older generation of Islamist purists, Turabi was an early advocate of such alliances, both in order to combat the Communists and to better confront the military regime that governed Sudan in the early 1960s. In various guises, this pragmatism would remain a characteristic feature of Turabi's politics (cf. El-Affendi 1991; Miller 1997; Warburg 2003).

Turabi's evolving relations with Ja'far al-Numayri (often spelled as Jaafar Nimeiri), who came to power through a military coup in 1969, represent another facet of his pragmatic politics. Numayri had begun his reign as a secular Arab nationalist in the mold of the Egyptian Free Officers, though he was noticeably lacking in Nasser's charisma. Over the years, both to bolster his legitimacy and to ward off leftist challenges to his rule, Numayri moved toward an increasingly close alliance with the Islamists. As in the case of the Jama'at-i Islami's uneasy alliance with

General Muhammad Zia al-Haqq of Pakistan, Numayri's rediscovery of Islam offered opportunities for state-sponsored Islamization the Sudanese Islamists had never had before. Turabi became the attorney general of Sudan in 1979, and he later served as an adviser to the president on law and foreign policy (El-Affendi 1991, 126). It was during these years that Islamic laws were implemented with much fanfare in the Sudan, including the so-called *hudud* punishments (Layish and Warburg 2002).

The Qur'an prescribes severe punishments for certain infractions. For example, the punishment for theft is cutting off the hand (Q 5:38); for banditry, the amputation of a hand and a foot (Q 5:33); for drinking, eighty lashes; for adultery, one hundred lashes (Q 24:2, though the classical legal doctrine prescribed stoning to death as the punishment for adultery); and for false accusation of adultery, eighty lashes (Q 24:4). Medieval jurists referred to these punishments as the hudud (literally "limits"; singular: *hadd*) and, because they are set forth in the Qur'an itself, invested them with the highest authority. Unlike other punishments, devised by and implemented according to the discretion of the ruler or subject to negotiation by the victim's kin, the hudud were "fixed" punishments. Yet many jurists were keenly conscious of the harshness of these punishments, and this often led them to efforts to circumscribe their scope and to substantially limit the possibilities of their actual implementation (cf. Weiss 1998, 101–10).

Yet, in Numayri's Sudan, as indeed in Saudi Arabia and in the Taliban's Afghanistan, many of the constraints that the medieval juristic tradition had painstakingly put on the hudud were notably absent. As Rudolph Peters has observed, the penal code implemented in Sudan in 1983 was concerned with both "broadening the definitions, by applying fixed punishments to offences other than the traditional hadd crimes, and . . . relaxing the rules of evidence" (Peters 2005, 165). The hudud penalties came to be both a marker of the government's religious commitment and a blunt means of asserting governmental authority at a time when it had become increasingly fragile (cf. Kepel 2002, 181).[1] Even the implementation of the hudud did little to bolster the regime's prospects for survival, however. Instead, it led to an international outcry as well as new problems within the country.

While the writ of Islamic law has usually been limited to those who profess to be Muslims, some of Sudan's Islamic laws were extended to the Christian and animist population of the country's south as well. This created widespread resentment and contributed to rekindling the civil war between the north and the south. Ironically, Numayri, in his early years,

[1] "In 1984," according to Rudolph Peters (2005, 167), "at least sixty-five judicial amputations took place, among which there were twenty cross-amputations (i.e., amputation of the right hand and the left foot). The total number of amputations carried out in the period from September 1983 to April 1985, when the Numayri regime was overthrown, varied according to different reports between 96 and 120."

had negotiated an end to the very conflict that his Islamization policies now helped exacerbate (cf. Layish and Warburg 2002, 60). But the Islamization program also led to conflicts within the ruling elite. Islamists had begun using the newly established Islamic courts not just to further the cause of Islamization but also to settle scores with other members of the government. This brought them into increasing conflict with Numayri. Turabi fell out with Numayri and was briefly imprisoned, though it was not long before Numayri himself was ousted from power, in 1985.

While the Islamists were still allied with the Numayri regime, they had been able not only to improve their economic circumstances but also to penetrate the military (Warburg 2003, 189–93). This helped pave the way for another Islamizing regime, which came to power in 1989 with a military coup led by General 'Umar Hasan al-Bashir. Turabi was widely regarded as Bashir's mentor. He was to enjoy unprecedented influence over the policies of the Sudanese government over the next decade, as well as a new prominence on the global scene. Though the only position he held during this time was as Speaker of the Sudanese parliament, Turabi remained closely involved with efforts to implement Islamic law. As he would put it in 1993, "Islam is ruling in Sudan; Islamic values prevail in society and Islamic injunctions are being implemented in all fields" (quoted in Warburg 2003, 209).

Turabi's very visible identification with the making of an Islamic state in Sudan also enhanced his status in many Islamist circles worldwide. In part, this international stature was expressed, and enhanced, through his writings and interviews, in which Turabi has often sought to position himself as something of a theoretician of contemporary Islamism (for some of his writings, see Turabi 1980, 1999, 2004; for interviews, Hamdi 1988). In the 1990s, it also came to be expressed in efforts to distance himself from Saudi Arabia—long a patron of Islamist trends, and not just in Sudan (Kepel 2002, 180–81). During the First Gulf War, precipitated by Saddam Hussein's attack on Kuwait and his threatened attack on Saudi Arabia, Turabi decided to side not with Saudi Arabia but with Iraq. A similar stance was adopted by many Islamists elsewhere (cf. O. Roy 1994, 121). Significantly, this was not just a volte-face in relation to the Saudis but also a public affront to Turabi's protégé and chief ally, General Bashir, who had already expressed his support for Kuwait and Saudi Arabia before Turabi did his for Iraq (de Waal 2007, 14). Between 1991 and 1995, a series of international conferences was organized in Sudan with prominent Islamists from across the world in attendance (Kepel 2002, 184). This, too, was meant to signal Islamism's independence of Saudi patronage; it also helped underline Sudan's, and Turabi's own, global stature. If any doubts remained about Sudan's ascendance on the Islamist horizon, they would have been put to rest with the arrival, in 1991, of Usama bin Laden himself. He would live in the country, under official protection, until intense U.S. pressure forced Sudan to expel him in 1996.

For all his influence over the direction of government policies in Sudan and his efforts to project a global image for himself, Turabi did not have anything like the stature Ayatollah Khomeini had had in Iran. Turabi's power owed itself to pragmatic alliances with military rulers, not to a popular revolution. And it had no doctrinal or constitutional underpinnings, as it did in the case of Khomeini's velayat-e faqih. While Khomeini could rebuke the head of the state with impunity (see chapter 6), Turabi gradually discovered that there were serious limits on his ability to attempt anything similar. His affront to Bashir during the First Gulf War already suggested tensions within the Sudanese governing elite. Over the course of the following years, relations between Turabi and General Bashir began to deteriorate, a major split taking place in 1999, which was followed by nearly five years of imprisonment for Turabi (Wallis 2006).

The conflict between Turabi and the government of General Bashir has manifested itself in, inter alia, the ongoing insurgency in the Darfur region of western Sudan. This insurgency, which flared up in 2003, has often been portrayed in the Western media as a conflict between the "Arabs" of the north (including the Sudanese army and the mercenaries working with it) and the "Africans" of western Sudan. Yet the conflict, which has exacted an extremely heavy toll on the people of Darfur in terms of the destruction of life and property as well as the dislocation of vast numbers, is perhaps better viewed as expressing the political grievances of a people long marginalized and excluded from the centers of power and denied their share of state resources by the northern governing elite (cf. Mamdani 2007; Kamal El-Din 2007, 93). In this sense, the conflict in Darfur has some similarities with the long history of conflict between southern and northern Sudan, with which the Darfur insurgency has sometimes been intertwined. One difference between the two is, however, that the inhabitants of western Sudan, though ethnically and linguistically distinct from the northern ruling elite, are nonetheless Muslim. Islamists, too, have had a significant presence in Darfur; indeed, one of the leading figures in Turabi's Popular Congress Party—'Ali al-Haj Muhammad—comes from Darfur (de Waal 2007, 26).

While he was the Speaker of the Sudanese parliament, Turabi had supported a constitutional amendment for greater decentralization of the state. According to this initiative, the provincial governors were to be elected within their provinces rather than appointed by the federal government. General Bashir had opposed this initiative, not only because of his preference to retain a strong federal control over the state but apparently also because of his misgivings about Turabi's influence in the outlying provinces, which this decentralization would have strengthened. The constitutional amendment proved abortive, but not before the legislative assembly had been dissolved and the Islamist party had itself split between the government faction—the National Congress Party—and Turabi's new group, the People's Congress Party (on all this, see Kamal El-Din 2007, 105–6; on Turabi's involvement in the Darfur conflict, also see Prunier 2007, 81–88). Yet even those northern Islamists who, like Turabi, have been critical of the Sudanese government's brutal handling of Darfur are often less than clear on how far they would go in sharing power with these traditionally marginalized people of the outlying provinces. As one critic has put it, the people of Darfur are "too black for the Islamist movement" (quoted in Kamal El-Din 2007, 105; cf. de Waal 2007, 26–27). What this suggests is not only some ambiguity within the ranks of Sudanese Islamists on the degree to which they envisage, or agree on, a genuine leveling of ethnic and regional differences in the name of their Islamist principles; it also raises questions about whether Turabi's entanglement in the Darfur conflict, as part of his own conflict with the Sudanese government, may only have exacerbated the misery of that devastated region.

At several points in his career, Turabi has had greater opportunities than most Islamists elsewhere to make the state "Islamic." His vision of an Islamic state is briefly laid out in the text that follows. This is an altogether idealistic vision, at considerable remove from anything that has existed in Islamic history. It is also at odds with Sudan's own experience while Turabi was one of its most powerful men. Turabi envisages a system of "representative democracy," with a government that relies on "consultation" with the people and has very limited powers. None of this seems to accord much with Turabi's Sudan. Turabi would probably point to the proposed constitutional amendment for a decentralization of the state as an example of his continuing commitment to limited (federal) government. He might also argue that, inasmuch as a seemingly authoritarian regime upholds the shari'a, it accords, for practical purposes, with the will of the people. He says as much in the text included in this volume: "An Islamic republic is not, strictly speaking, a direct government of and by the people; it is a government of the shari'a. But, in a substantial sense, it is a popular government because the shari'a represents the convictions of the people and, therefore, their direct will." This suggests that, despite some of his rhetoric and for all the upheavals in his own relations with military dictators, Turabi would not necessarily see much disjunction between his idealistic vision of an Islamic state and the authoritarian regimes claiming to pursue it.

# THE ISLAMIC STATE

ALTHOUGH I am directly involved in a political process that seeks to establish an Islamic state, I am not going to describe the forms that an Islamic government might take in any particular country. Rather, I will try to describe the universal characteristics of an Islamic state. These derive from the teachings of the Qur'an as embodied in the political practice of the Prophet Muhammad and constitute an eternal model that Muslims are bound to adopt as a perfect standard for all time. However, the diversity of historical circumstances in which they try to apply that ideal introduces a necessary element of relativity and imperfection in the practice of Islam.

An Islamic state cannot be isolated from society because Islam is a comprehensive, integrated way of life. The division between private and public, the state and society, that is familiar in Western culture, has not been known in Islam. The state is only the political expression of an Islamic society. You cannot have an Islamic state except insofar as you have an Islamic society. Any attempt at establishing a political order for the establishment of a genuine Islamic society would be the superimposition of laws over a reluctant society. This is not in the nature of religion; religion is based on sincere conviction and voluntary compliance. Therefore, an Islamic state evolves from an Islamic society. In certain areas, progress toward an Islamic society may be frustrated by political suppression. Whenever religious energy is thus suppressed, it builds up and ultimately erupts in either isolated acts of struggle or resistance that are called terrorist by those in power or a revolution. In circumstances where Islam is allowed free expression, social change takes place peacefully and gradually, and the Islamic movement develops programs of Islamization before it takes over the destiny of the state because Islamic thought—like all thought— flourishes only in a social environment of freedom and public consultation (shura).

The ideological foundation of an Islamic state lies in the doctrine of tawhid—the unity of God and of human life—as a comprehensive and exclusive program of worship. This fundamental principle of belief has many consequences for an Islamic state: first, it is not secular. All public life in Islam is religious, being permeated by the experience of the divine. Its function is to pursue the service of God as expressed in a

concrete way in the shari'a, the religious law. The Christian West has
been through an important historical experience of secularization. There
have also been certain elements of secularization in the political conduct
of Muslims. But the difference between Christianity and Islam is that
Muslims are never fully resigned to such practices because the preserved
sources of religious guidance (the Qur'an and the example of the
Prophet) constantly remind them of any gap that develops between
their ideal and their practice and inspire a process of revitalization that
would completely integrate politics with religion. If one compares
Christian secularism in France with Muslim secularism in Turkey the
process would seem strikingly similar. All religious life is subject to
these historical challenges to their identity. But once the Muslims
experience the tension of a historical fall and become conscious of the
fact that public life has moved away from the moral values and norms
of religion, they rise to reform their political attitudes and institutions.

Second, an Islamic state is not a nationalistic state because ultimate
allegiance is owed to God and thereby to the community of all believers—
the *umma*. One can never stop at any national frontier and say the
nation is absolute, an ultimate end in itself. Islam does allow for limited
allegiances, either social, ethnic, or territorial. The state of Medina itself
was, for some time, a regional state; the Muslims of Mecca were not
citizens, and the duty to extend protection to them against any persecution was subject to the treaty obligations of the state. So there is an
Islamic concept of a territorial state that is not coextensive with the
whole umma. But that state is not nationalistic. In modern times
Muslims have adopted Arab-Turkish or other nationalities as a framework for development, but they were never enthusiastic about it and
always yearned for an open umma. However, this does not mean that
every Muslim all over the world should necessarily have immediate
access to an Islamic state; it does mean though that the state would
be much more open and less discriminatory in its domestic laws and
foreign policies. It would develop institutionalized international links
with other Muslim states and would work toward the eventual unity of
the umma and beyond. Ultimately there is nothing final even about the
so-called Muslim world or Muslim nation, because Islam is open to
humanity, is universal.

Third, an Islamic state is not an absolute or sovereign entity. It is
subject to the higher norms of the shari'a that represent the will of God.
Politically this rules out all forms of absolutism. Legally it paves the
way for the development of constitutional law, a set of norms limiting
state powers. In fact, the Islamic tradition of rules limiting the power of
the sovereign is much older than the concept of constitutional law in
the secular West. Because the Islamic state is not absolute, Muslims
have also known from the beginning the rules of international law that

derive from the supreme shari'a and bind the state in its relations to other states and peoples.

Fourth, an Islamic state is not primordial; the primary institution in Islam is the umma. The phrase "Islamic state" itself is a misnomer. The state is only the political dimension of the collective endeavor of Muslims. The norms of Islam are only partly legal depending on the sanctions of state power. For most of it, the implementation of the shari'a is left to the free conscience of believers or to informal means of social control.

States come and go; Islamic society can and has existed without the structures of a state for centuries. Of course society, if able to live religion in its integral, comprehensive manner, would have its political dimension in a government that seeks to fulfill some of the purposes of religious life.

The form of an Islamic government is determined by the foregoing principles of tawhid, entailing the freedom, equality, and unity of believers. One can call an Islamic state a republic because the shari'a rules out usurpation and succession as grounds of political legitimacy. In early Islam, the system of government, called a caliphate (al-khilafa), which emphasized succession to the Prophet and thereby subordination of all power to his sunna or way. But whereas the Prophet was appointed by God, the caliph was freely elected by the people, who thereby have precedence over him as a legal authority. Although the Prophet used to consult his companions systematically and normally would follow their consensus, he had the divine right to an overriding authority. The caliph, however, or any similar holder of political power, is subject both to the shari'a and to the will of his electors. As reflected in Islamic jurisprudence, this implies that, save for the express provision of the shari'a, the consensus (ijma') of the community is paramount. A process of consultation that leads ultimately to ijma' is mandatory for the resolution of all important public issues.

The caliphate began as an elected consultative institution. Later it degenerated into a hereditary, or usurpatory, authoritarian government. This pseudocaliphate was universally condemned by jurists, though many excused its acts on the grounds of necessity or tolerated them in the interest of stability. The question arises whether the proper Islamic form of government—elective and consultative—amounts to a liberal representative democracy?

In a large Islamic state consultation would have to be indirect, undertaken by representatives of the people. This was practiced in early Islam and recognized by jurists in their reference to *ahl al-hall wa'l-'aqd* or *ahl al-shura* (those who resolve public affairs). In a parallel development ijma', which is the conclusion of a process of consultation, came to mean the consensus of the 'ulama. This was a practical adaptation of the original popular concept of ijma' as the consensus of the community that had resulted from the Muslim expansion. In effect, Muslims were then to be found all over the world, and there was no practical way of consulting everyone in the general umma in those days. So the 'ulama posed as representatives of the people and maintained that their consensus was a form of indirect representation, of indirect, binding ijma'. In different circumstances other formal delegates can lawfully represent the umma in the process of consultation.

It follows that an Islamic order of government is essentially a form of representative democracy. But this statement requires the following qualification. First, an Islamic republic is not, strictly speaking, a direct government of and by the people; it is a government of the shari'a. But, in a substantial sense, it is a popular government because the shari'a represents the convictions of the people and, therefore, their direct will. This limitation on what a representative body can do is a guarantee of the supremacy of the religious will of the community. The consultative system of government in Islam is related to and reinforced by similar features of Muslim society because politics is an integral part of all religious life and not simply a separate secular vocation. The fair distribution of political power through shura, whether direct or indirect, is supported by an equally just distribution of economic wealth. So an Islamic democracy may never degenerate to a formal system where, because of the concentration of wealth, the rich alone exercise their political rights and determine what is to be decided. Also, ideally there is no clerical or 'ulama class, which prevents an elitist or theocratic government. Whether termed a religious, a theocratic, or even a secular theocracy, an Islamic state is not a government of the 'ulama. Knowledge, like power, is distributed in a way that inhibits the development of a distinct, religious hierarchy. Nor is an Islamic democracy government by the male members of society. Women played a considerable role in public life during the life of the Prophet; and they contributed to the election of the third caliph. Only afterward were women denied their rightful place in public life, but this was history departing from the ideal, just like the development of classes based on property, knowledge ('ilm), or other status. In principle, all believers, rich or poor, noble or humble, learned or ignorant, men or women, are equal before God, and they are his vicegerents on earth and the holders of his trust.

An Islamic government should be a stable system of government because the people consider it an expression of their religion and, therefore, contribute positively to the political process. In their mutual consultations, they work toward a consensus that unites them. The majority-minority pattern in politics is not an ideal one in Islam. That is not to say that decisions have to await a unanimous vote, because this could paralyze a government. But people can deliberate openly and argue and consult to ultimately reach a consensus and not simply assert or submit to a majority opinion. This raises the question of the party system. Can an Islamic government have a multiparty system or a single-party system? There is no legal bar to the development of different parties or to the freedom of opinion and debate. Such was the case in the constitutional practice of the caliph. However, a well-developed Islamic society would probably not be conducive to the growth of rigid parties wherein one stands by one's party whether it is wrong or right. This is a form of factionalism that can be very oppressive of individual freedom and divisive of the community, and it is therefore, antithetical to a Muslim's ultimate responsibility to God and to umma. While there may be a multiparty system, an Islamic government should function more as a consensus-oriented rather than a minority-majority system with political parties rigidly confronting each other over decisions. Parties should approach the decision-making process with an open mind and, after a consensus, adopt a mutually agreeable policy.

Finally, decisions should not be arrived at lightly. Parliament does not simply deliberate and come to a conclusion. Any agreement must be an enlightened decision with conscious reference to the guiding principles of the shari'a. Because of this, the 'ulama should have a role in the procedure, not as the ultimate authority determining what the law is but as advisers in the shura to enlighten the Muslims as to the options that are open to them. What do I mean by 'ulama? The word historically has come to mean those versed in the legacy of religious (revealed) knowledge, 'ilm. However, 'ilm does not mean that alone. It means anyone who knows anything well enough to relate it to God. Because all knowledge is divine and religious, a chemist, an engineer, an economist, or a jurist is each an 'alim. So the 'ulama in this broad sense, whether they are social or natural scientists, public opinion leaders, or philosophers, should enlighten society. There should be an intensive procedure of hearings, research, and deliberations and thus a wider consultation than that which sometimes takes place now in modern parliaments where bills can be rushed through and policies resolved on arbitrary passion and prejudice.

What are the functions and frontiers of an Islamic government? The functions that fulfill the aims of Islamic life pertain primarily to society. Because Islam is comprehensive, one might conclude that an Islamic government, acting for society, is a totalitarian one. However, in many ways, an Islamic government is a very limited government. First, not every aspect of Islam is entrusted to government to enforce. It is in the nature of a unitarian religious order of society that the individual should enjoy a wide degree of autonomy. Moreover, not everything is practically capable of enforcement through government law. Classical jurists have developed the distinction between religious obligations and juridical obligation, the latter being enforceable only through formal, objective sanctions. Most aspects of Islamic life are subjective or private

and outside the domain of law as applied by governments. Second, and
this is a question that depends on history, where society can manage,
government has no business interfering. This is similar to a liberal,
minimal theory of government. In the past a Muslim government had
a very limited function simply because the Muslims were spread over
such a wide territory and the government could not reach them. Today,
because of the revolution in communications, a government can easily
take over functions that an Islamic government did not oversee so many
centuries ago. But there are certain historical considerations that I
would want to underline very strongly. The Islamic government historically has been, for the most part, illegitimate as far as the election of
the head of a state is concerned. That explains why it was so severely
limited. The jurists, realizing that the state was not a legitimate, consultative government, deliberately restricted its domain in favor of private
social action. The jurists totally eliminated governmental authority as a
source of law in their development of *usul al-fiqh* (the sources of law).
A very important arm of government, the legislative power, was actually
assumed by the jurists themselves. They determined what the law was
and the judges, who were appointed by the government, looked to the
jurists to apply the law.

Another area where government was severely limited was in its power
to tax. There is nothing in Islam that inhibits or forbids the government
from imposing, from time to time, taxes other than zakat for the general
welfare of the community. The power to tax is one of the most oppressive weapons in the hands of any government. Many constitutional
conflicts in the West revolve around the slogan, "No taxation without
representation." Although Muslim jurists have effectively deprived
government of many means of exploitation, in a modern Islamic state
the representative legislature would probably assume all political
functions. A modern Islamic government could, subject to the shari'a,
establish and enforce further norms of law and policy derived from
the shari'a. It can establish complete legal codes. Such codes, as were
known to Muslims in the past, did not emanate from the state but from
the great jurists like Malik, Abu Hanifa, and Shafi'i. There were mainly
seven such operative legal codes throughout the Muslim world. It was
the absence of an official organ of government charged with the unification of the legal system that led to the closing of the door of ijtihad
(judicial research) for fear of the proliferation of laws and ensuing
threat to order and legal security. Subject to the shari'a and ijma' it is
up to a Muslim government today to determine its system of public law
and economics.

An Islamic government is bound to exercise all powers necessary for
providing a minimum of the basic conditions of Muslim life. The actual
scope of government depends on society. Where society on its own
manages to realize social justice, for example, then the government does

not need to interfere. In Muslim history, governments were mostly illegitimate and did not or were not allowed to develop a macroeconomic polity. Therefore, Muslims addressed questions of social justice within their private dealings. This was done especially through a wide, mutually supportive family system, through extensive charities and endowments, and through a system of private mutual insurance still operative in many parts of Muslim society today. Where this failed for any reason, the government was bound to step in and try to rectify the situation. This holds for other welfare services as well. Society can manage, for example, its own system of private education like that of Muslim Spain, which was so widespread that it almost eliminated illiteracy through free education for all. Otherwise, the government is bound and entitled to promote education, health services, and what have you.

What are the frontiers of government vis-à-vis society and the individual? This question has not been posed very acutely in the past. Why? Simply because the Islamic government was not a totally alien institution superimposed upon society. To the extent that it was alien— in the sense that it was not legitimate—the jurists saw to it that it should be relatively powerless. But, on the whole, the aims and means of government correspond to that of society, being related to religion and based on the shari'a. Furthermore, the individual was largely free because the law making and financial powers were so limited; so there was not any intolerable oppression. Even though the particular caliph might be a usurper, he was not a totalitarian, absolute dictator. Certainly, where his security was threatened, he would impinge on freedom, but otherwise people were left alone.

It was only recently, when secularized governments were introduced and established in Muslim lands and the protective shield of the shari'a withdrawn and the forms of government regulation expanded, that Muslims really felt the bitter oppression of totalitarian government, and that the issue of fundamental rights and liberties was raised.

The freedom of the individual ultimately emanates from the doctrine of tawhid, which requires a self-liberation of man from any worldly authority in order to serve God exclusively. Society (and particularly those in power) is inspired by the same principle, and the collective endeavor is not one of hampering the liberty of an individual but of cooperation toward the maximum achievement of this ideal. To promote this cooperation, the freedom of one individual is related to that of the general group. The ultimate common aim of religious life unites the private and the social spheres; and the shari'a provides an arbiter between social order and individual freedom.

I do not have to go into the various rights of man vis-à-vis the state or society in Islam. The individual has the right to his physical existence, general social well-being, reputation, peace, privacy, to education and a decent life. These are rights that the state ought to provide and guarantee for a better fulfillment of the religious ideals of life. Freedom of religion and of expression should also be guaranteed and encouraged. Thus, while a Muslim would not oppose the shari'a because he believes in it, if he does not agree to a particular interpretation of the law, he is entitled to his view. Actually, these are not pure rights that the individual is free to exercise. He owes it to God and to his fellow Muslims to observe these as a social obligation as well. He should contribute to the political solidarity and well-being of the state. If government becomes so alien as to transcend the shari'a, he has the right and obligation to revolt. This is the revolutionary element in Islam. A Muslim's ultimate obedience is to God alone.

What about representative institutions in an Islamic government? This depends on the particular historical circumstances. In the period of the Prophet all the functions of the state were exercised by him as teacher and sovereign. He wisely but informally consulted with his companions. Later this consultative process was almost developed into an indirect representative institution called *ahl al-shura* or *majlis-i-shura* (consultative council). The breakdown of the early legitimate political order did not allow the procedures and institutions of shura to crystallize. Today this could very well be formulated through a parliament, a council, or a majlis-i-shura. People may directly, through referendum, exercise their ijma' consensus or otherwise delegate power to their deputies. There would, however, be certain rules regulating the qualifications of candidates and election campaigns for the choice of deputies or other officers of the state. In Islam, for example, no one is entitled to conduct a campaign for themselves directly or indirectly in the manner of Western electoral campaigns. The presentation of candidates would be entrusted to a neutral institution that would explain to the people the options offered in policies and personalities. Factors of relative wealth or access to the communications media are also not allowed to falsify the representative character of deputies. The prevailing criteria of political merit for the purposes of candidature for any political office revolves on moral integrity as well as other relevant considerations. All this would, no doubt, influence the form and spirit of accession to positions of power.

The other central institution in an Islamic government is that which provides both leadership and effective execution of the general will: caliph, commander of the believers, president of the republic, or prime minister. As noted earlier, the word "caliph" was not originally chosen for any specific reason except to denote succession and compliance with the prophetic example of leadership. Most modern and contemporary constitutional theory tends to vest political leadership in one individual and not in a collegiate body—a presidency rather than a council of ministers. But neither a president nor a prime minister can be very powerful and representative of the unity of political purpose so essential to an Islamic polity. Whatever form the executive may take, a leader is always subject both to the shari'a and to the ijma' formulated under it. He enjoys no special immunities and can, therefore, be prosecuted or sued for anything he does in his private or public life. This is a fundamental principle of Islamic constitutional law, ensuing from the supremacy of the shari'a. No rigid theory of separation of government functions can develop in a comprehensive, coherent system like the Islamic political order, except to provide some necessary checks and balances to safeguard liberty or justice. Besides those powers delegated by the majlis-i-shura or consultative council and subject to its control, the executive may derive powers directly from both the shari'a and ijma'.

The judiciary, although appointed as part of the administration, plays an extremely important role in an Islamic state because of the special legalistic nature of the political order that is organized in accordance with a strict hierarchy of norms. The shari'a is the highest revealed law followed by popular laws based on ijma' and by executive orders and regulations. Because of this, judges, as the guardians of the shari'a, adjudicate in all matters of law. Early Muslims were very keen to provide judges with a generous income to protect them against temptation and to allow them a very large degree of autonomy with broad powers to administer justice. However, the legal systems of Islam did not know a lawyer's profession. The modern capitalist institution that requires the participation of solicitors and barristers in the administration of justice ultimately works in favor of the rich, who can afford the expenses and the delays of justice in a system administered in this way. I realize, as a lawyer myself, that adjudication in a contemporary society is a very complicated, time-consuming process. Judges cannot listen to all the complaints and determine the issues. But such a difficulty was resolved in early Islam by the office of a counsellor to the judge: an assistant who first heard the parties, ascertained the matters in issue, marshaled all the relevant evidence, and researched the law in preparation for a decision by the judge. In an Islamic state there would be a tendency to do away with or to minimize the role of the legal profession by establishing an extended system of legal counsel and assistance, especially for the poor.

As far as public law for the administration of an Islamic state or government is concerned, one can draw upon early Islamic history and tradition regarding service for forms of achieving the political ideals of Islam. But because of the transformation of public life in contemporary societies, the Muslim would also draw heavily on comparative constitutional history and practice. This has a legal basis in Islamic jurisprudence. Any form or procedures for the organization of public life that can be ultimately related to God and put to his service in furtherance of the aims of Islamic government can be adopted unless expressly excluded by the shari'a. Once so received, it is an integral part of Islam whatever its source may be. Through this process of Islamization, the Muslims were always very open to expansion and change. Thus, Muslims can incorporate any experience whatsoever if not contrary to their ideals. Muslims took most of their bureaucratic forms from Roman and Persian models. Now, much can be borrowed from contemporary sources, critically appreciated in the light of the shari'a values and norms and integrated into the Islamic framework of government.

Finally, I come to the interstate and interfaith relations of the Muslim state. I have remained quiet about the status of non-Muslims because I did not want to complicate issues. The historical record of Muslims' treatment of Christians and Jews is quite good especially compared with the history of relations between different religions and religious denominations in the West. The first Islamic state established in Medina was not simply a state of Muslims; it had many Jews, and many non-Muslim Arabs. Therefore, the problem of non-Muslim minorities within a Muslim state is nothing new. Muslims do not like the term "minorities." They call them the People of the Book (*ahl al-kitab*), the *dhimmi*, or protected people. These non-Muslims have a guaranteed right to their religious conviction, to profess and defend their own convictions, and even to criticize Islam and engage in a dialogue with Muslims. Non-Muslims also have the right to regulate their private life, education, and family life by adopting their own family laws. If there is any rule in the shari'a that they think religiously incompatible, they can be absolved from it. There can be a very large degree of legal and political decentralization under an Islamic government. The more important thing is that, morally, Muslims are bound to relate to non-Muslim minorities positively. It is more than a matter of tolerance and legal immunity. Muslims have a moral obligation to be fair and friendly in their person-to-person conduct toward non-Muslim citizens and will be answerable to God for that. They must treat them with trust, beneficence, and equity. There may be a certain feeling of alienation because the public law generally will be Islamic law. However, the public law of Islam is one related rationally to justice and to the general good, and even a non-Muslim may appreciate its wisdom and fairness. Christians in particular, who now, at least, do not seem to have a public law, should not mind the application of Islamic law as long as it does not interfere with their religion. It is a moral based on values that are common and more akin to Christian values than any secular law—Caesar's law.

As to the interstate or international relations of a Muslim state, we have noted earlier the limitations on state sovereignty imposed by the shari'a in favor of nationals of other states. The sanctity of treaty obligations and the vocation to world peace, except in situations of aggression, provide a basis for the development of extensive international relations. The international practice of Muslim states in history is well known. What is not as well known is its contribution to the development of modern international law.

In conclusion, it is important to note that an awareness of the general nature and features of the Islamic state is necessary for an understanding of modern Islam as a resurgent force seeking to make up for a failure to realize Islam fully. Muslims are presently focusing more on general ideals—ideals as standards for guiding their different attempts to implement Islam. Whatever diverse forms their practice assumes as these universal ideals come to be expressed in the light of differing circumstances of particular Muslim states, the clarity of the universal model is necessary, on the one hand, to guide Muslims toward a greater unity and, on the other hand, to enable them to grasp both the general and the particular in Muslim life. Otherwise, they run the risk of discerning nothing beyond the confusion of a multiplicity of Islams, determined purely by historical factors.

# Chapter 9

# YUSUF AL-QARADAWI
## 1926–

YUSUF AL-QARADAWI, by far the most prominent scholar and preacher in Sunni Islam at the beginning of the twenty-first century, is the founder of Islam Online, a major Web site that professes to provide authoritative guidance to Muslims on all matters of faith and practice. He is also the president of the European Council of Fatwa and Research, an organization concerned with addressing the problems faced by Muslims living in Western Europe, as well as the founding chairman of the International Union of Muslim Scholars, established in 2004 to foster ties among Muslim religious intellectuals throughout the world. Qaradawi has been a regular presence on the Qatar-based Arab satellite television station al-Jazeera, which, with an estimated audience of up to forty million, has given him a visibility in the Arab world unmatched by any other scholar. Over the course of a long and highly prolific career, Qaradawi has helped shape contemporary Islamism even as he has embodied some of the many tensions and ambiguities within it.

Qaradawi was born in 1926 in a village near Tanta in Lower Egypt. He studied in Tanta, at an institute of Islamic education affiliated to al-Azhar, the millennium-old seat of Islamic learning in Cairo, and later at al-Azhar itself. In 1973 he went on to receive a Ph.D. from this institution. Qaradawi had developed close ties with the Muslim Brotherhood while a student in Tanta. This brought him under the suspicion of the Egyptian state, and he was briefly incarcerated on several occasions in his youth. He would retain informal ties with the Muslim Brotherhood as well as a lifelong devotion to the teachings of the organization's founder, Hasan al-Banna, some of whose precepts have been the subject of elaborate published commentaries by Qaradawi (see Qaradawi 1991; n.d. [1992]; 2000b; 2001; 2005a).[1] In the early 1960s, Qaradawi left Egypt for Qatar

---

[1]This extraordinary series of books purports to be a systematic commentary on Banna's "Twenty Principles," a short tract in which the founder of the Muslim Brotherhood had laid out some key guidelines for his followers. The commentaries are meant, as Qaradawi puts it, to "treat diverse intellectual issues—of law and legal theory, faith and practice—where the [true] path might have become obscured" (Qaradawi 2001, 5). In its focus not on the Islamic foundational texts but rather on the work of an Islamist founding father, there are no parallels to this work in Islamist literature. It not only reveals something about the evolving genre of the commentary in contemporary Islam or Qaradawi's obvious admiration for Banna. It also provides a remarkable view of how an Azhar 'alim has sought to

to teach at a religious institute, and he has lived ever since in this oil-rich state on the Persian Gulf. Here, unlike Egypt, he has also enjoyed the patronage of the ruling elite.

Despite his long residence outside Egypt, Qaradawi's career has remained closely intertwined with the Azhar and reflects trends in the modern history of this institution. Since the nineteenth century, successive Egyptian governments have sought to reform the Azhar, with the most far reaching of these efforts taking place under President Nasser in 1961. The 1961 reforms established several new faculties specifically for the teaching of modern, secular sciences. The three existing faculties devoted to the Islamic religious sciences were themselves thoroughly restructured in the process. These reforms had sought to modernize the Azhar, to integrate it into the educational mainstream, and to bridge some of the distance between those educated in the religious sciences and the secular disciplines. In light of its stature in Egypt and abroad, an unstated goal in all this was to bring those associated with the Azhar under more effective regulation and thereby to shape the Egyptian religious sphere in accordance with the prescriptions of the governing elite. Over the course of the following decades, graduates of al-Azhar did indeed come to be better integrated into the educational mainstream but, as political scientist Malika Zeghal has argued, with consequences quite different from what the government had envisaged. By the 1980s, a sustained exposure to modern, secular education had given to the graduates of the Azhar a new ability to interact with those educated in other westernized Egyptian colleges and universities. Far from making the Azhar 'ulama more amenable to government regulation, this helped foster new alliances between them and the Islamists even as it substantially increased the Azhar's own influence in the Egyptian public sphere (Zeghal 1995; 1999). Qaradawi's religious training as an 'alim was largely complete before the 1961 reforms. But he received his Ph.D.—with a dissertation on the laws relating to zakat, one of the five "pillars of the faith" in Islam—a decade or so after these reforms had come into effect. Though he has no formal exposure to the Western sciences and he does not speak any Western languages, he has remained receptive to, and largely supportive of, the Azhar's expansion in the direction of the modern sciences. And none among the graduates of the Azhar has been more adept at forging ties with college- and university-educated Islamists, in Egypt and elsewhere, than Qaradawi.

A major theme in Qaradawi's discourses is what he characterizes as moderation or, more precisely, "centrism"—the teachings of "the centrist school" (*al-madrasa al-wasatiyya*) (Qaradawi 2000b, 243–307; 2006, 137–217; cf. Zaman 2004, 136, 144–46).[2] In matters of education, a

---

bridge some of the perceived distance between Islamists and the 'ulama by incorporating a key Islamist figure into the 'ulama's discursive tradition.

[2] "Moderation" is one of the characteristics of Qaradawi's centrism. The centrist school, he says, "views matters of religion and of life in a balanced and moderate way [*nazra mu-*

self-conscious path of moderation signifies the willingness of Muslims to be schooled in modern forms of knowledge even as they remain firmly anchored in the teachings of the Islamic foundational texts. (One of Qaradawi's daughters is a nuclear physicist: Bunting 2005.) So far as the Islamic intellectual heritage and especially the legal tradition is concerned, the path of moderation requires that people neither reject this tradition out of hand nor hold on to it in "blind imitation" of earlier authorities. The need for moderation, Qaradawi insists, ought to extend to politics as well. He has been severely critical of militant Islamist groups in Egypt and elsewhere, characterizing them as latter-day Kharijis in a reference to a sectarian orientation in early Islam, many of whose adherents branded other Muslims as unbelievers and resorted to indiscriminate violence against them. Like Muhammad Husayn Fadlallah of Lebanon, Qaradawi was among the most prominent of Muslim scholars condemning the terrorist attacks of September 11, 2001 (cf. Bunting 2005; also see chapter 16 on Fadlallah).

Qaradawi has also charted a self-consciously moderate path in rejecting Islamist contentions that democracy as a system of government is antithetical to Islam. Qaradawi has insisted, furthermore, that there is considerable scope for human legislation *within* the larger parameters laid down by God (cf. Qaradawi 1997, 64–65). People do not have the right to tamper with matters of ritual or render permissible things forbidden by God or vice versa. But in the broad arena where the foundational texts provide no explicit or detailed rules, it is for Muslims to devise specific laws. The broad "purposes of the shari'a" (*maqasid al-shari'a*) are discernible from the foundational texts, and these ought to guide Muslim conduct in all matters. But to put them into effect in particular situations again requires legislation, and this is the work not of God but of human beings (cf. Qaradawi 1997, 64–65). Though Qaradawi does not name either Mawdudi or Qutb in the context of his discussion of legislation by human beings, the contrast with their views is unmistakable. Neither

---

*tawazina mu'tadila*], without excess or deficiency. . . . It is at the center in its view of religion, of the universe ... and of the individual and the community" (Qaradawi 2006, 149–50). Qaradawi has also been one of the key intellectual influences on Egypt's Wasat (Center) Party (founded in 1996). Though an offshoot of the Muslim Brotherhood, those associated with the Wasat have insisted on their intellectual independence. They have professed strong commitment to women's rights, to democracy, and to pluralism (the founding members included not just Muslims but also some Coptic Christians); and they have been critical of the Muslim Brotherhood leadership and of many of what they see as their outmoded policies. These self-proclaimed "centrists" have faced considerable hostility from the leaders of the Muslim Brotherhood, but also from the Egyptian government, which has suspected it of simply being a new face of the outlawed Muslim Brotherhood (on the Wasat Party, see Norton 2006; Hatina 2007). Quite apart from such suspicions, there seems to be some uncertainty on the precise implications of the Wasat's centrism; and ambiguities in the discourse of centrist Islamists like Qaradawi have not helped clarify these implications (cf. Hatina 2007, 166–67).

Qutb nor Mawdudi envisaged much role for a legislative assembly. The proper role of a parliament in an Islamic state is, according to Mawdudi, not law making but only "finding" the law that God has already enunciated in the form of the shari'a. Beyond that, the parliament is meant only to be a consultative assembly, whose counsel the head of the Islamic state might choose to accept or reject. Qaradawi, for his part, not only sees the parliament as the legitimate arena for legislation; he also views it as a potentially effective check on the despotic tendencies of the rulers. Unlike many a fellow Islamist, he remains unconvinced that the Islamic commitment of the governing elites make them immune to the temptations of despotism, and this, to him, makes it necessary that the head of the state not merely "consult" the parliament but also be bound by its advice (cf. Qaradawi 2000b, 105).

A dexterous employment of modern technologies—print, satellite television, the Internet—has done much to enhance Qaradawi's visibility and influence in the contemporary Muslim world. It is not only the medium, however, but also the content of Qaradawi's discourses and the language in which they are articulated that underlie their broad resonance. A rhetoric of moderation and an insistence that varied Muslim groups and orientations share much more among themselves than they usually recognize, which accordingly ought to be the basis of an overarching unity against shared challenges, have also enabled Qaradawi to self-consciously speak to different audiences, including the 'ulama, the Islamists, and still others with a modern, Western education. In doing so, he has relied heavily on his credentials as one of the 'ulama to speak with authority on all matters Islamic. But in thinly veiled allusions to his own example, he has also insisted that the 'ulama's own authority depends not only on their grounding in the Islamic scholarly tradition but also on their ability to speak to people "in the language of the age."

There are significant ambiguities in Qaradawi's discourses, however. Nowhere are they more palpable than when it comes to the question of resorting to violence in pursuit of particular ends. For instance, even as he has continued to insist on moderation, in politics as in other areas of life, Qaradawi has endorsed Palestinian suicide bombings or, as he characterizes them, "martyrdom operations" (Qaradawi 2002). These are the new weapons of "those deemed weak" (al-mustad'afun)[3] against the haughty and the tyrannical, he says, and they constitute martyrdom rather than suicide, which Islamic law forbids. Indeed, they are the highest form of jihad (Qaradawi 2002, 6–7). Qaradawi quotes some medieval exegetes in suggesting that the Qur'anic injunction "not to contribute to your destruction with your own hands" (Q 2:195) need not be understood as an admonition against what might amount to suicidal attempts

---

[3]On this Qur'anic expression, see *Encyclopedia of the Qur'an*, s.v. "Oppressed on Earth."

to confront an enemy far superior to oneself. Laying down one's life would be abhorrent only if no benefit whatsoever is to come out of it. But if some harm can thereby be inflicted on the enemy forces, if they can be intimidated, or if other Muslims might be encouraged by one's own example to also challenge the enemy, then even the certain loss of one's life in the face of impossible odds is not a waste (cf. Qaradawi 2002, 11–13, citing, inter alia, the Hanafi exegete al-Jassas [d. 982]; see al-Jassas 1971, 1:262–63). That Palestinian suicide bombers kill Israeli civilians is justified, Qaradawi says, because Israel is "a military society whose men and women are soldiers in the army; they can be summoned at any moment" (Qaradawi 2002, 8). What distinguishes Palestinian suicide bombings from the terrorist attacks of September 11, 2001, is that the latter, according to Qaradawi, were not in self-defense. Further, the 9/11 hijackers "didn't just use their own bodies but those of all the others in the planes"; and their attacks killed numerous noncombatants, including many Muslims (Bunting 2005).

Other ambiguities lead to less strident pronouncements but are no less significant. Qaradawi's seemingly resounding endorsement of the compatibility between Islam and democracy is predicated, for instance, on the assumption that the citizens of the state are, in fact, predominantly Muslim and that, as such, they would not wish to legislate in ways that contravene God's commands. But if this is meant to reassure Islamist critics of democracy, it seems to suggest that Qaradawi would share some of their misgivings in cases where Muslims are a minority in a democratic polity. Yet so far as Muslims living as a minority in Europe are concerned, Qaradawi has urged them to participate in the political process in order to protect and promote their interests. There is no alternative to political mobilization for, as he puts it, "even if we leave politics alone, politics doesn't leave us alone" (Qaradawi 2007, 234). Western Muslims, he says, ought to preserve their distinct communal identity, as a society within the larger, non-Muslim society. At the same time, they ought to employ whatever political means might be available—for example, forming their own political organizations, joining parties attentive to their interests, or otherwise exerting their political influence—to ensure that their voice is heard and their demands heeded (ibid., 231–39). How his endorsement of Muslim political participation in Western democracies is to be reconciled with his suspicion of democratic polities in which non-Muslims outnumber Muslims remains unclear.

Qaradawi has also argued that Islam, properly understood, does not prevent women from participating in public and political affairs. Yet, he does not believe that a woman ought to serve as the head of the government, and this on grounds that Islam reserves supreme political authority for men. It is at this point that his exchange with his (unnamed) Islamist interlocutors is telling. As he reports it, those opposed to women's political participation argue that, if women are allowed entry into a legislative assembly, they would exert authority over men inasmuch as the legislative assembly represents a check on the executive branch of the government; restricting the highest political offices to men does not offer enough reassurance that men rather than women would ultimately be in charge. Qaradawi counters this objection by noting that the authority to check the conduct of the executive belongs not to any particular member of the legislative assembly but to the assembly as a whole, and most members of the assembly would, he assumes, continue to be men (Qaradawi 1997, 165, 168). This sort of reasoning again suggests that Qaradawi would share his critics' misgivings if women were, in fact, to outnumber men in a legislative assembly. It is in terms of the same logic that he favors, against other Islamists, the participation of non-Muslims in the electoral process and their membership in the legislative assemblies: such participation and membership is unproblematic as long as the Muslim majority continues to have a decisive voice (Qaradawi 1997, 193–98, esp. 194–95).

Qaradawi's commitment to democracy turns out to be less robust and more ambivalent than his rhetoric would suggest. His endorsement of its compatibility with Islam is nonetheless stronger than that of many fellow Islamists, and he is eager to put this difference on display. Even as he has sought to bridge the distance between Islamists and the 'ulama, as well as those within the ranks of each, it is in his public *disagreements* with them that he has sought to articulate his own authority in the transnational Muslim public sphere. Unlike many among them, a self-conscious commitment to centrism and moderation and a much vaunted ability to "speak the language of the age" have enabled him to reach audiences not only schooled in modern institutions of learning but also wary of secular *and* religious authoritarianism. Yet there are other audiences to keep and cultivate as well. The very stringency of some of his positions not only serves, paradoxically, to underscore his moderation in other areas but also helps enhance his appeal for those who might otherwise be insufficiently receptive to him precisely for what they deem to be an excessive moderation.

# ISLAM AND DEMOCRACY

QUESTION: You are aware of my astonishment, Your Excellency, on hearing certain religious zealots—some of whom are associated with Islamic groups—assert that democracy is incompatible with Islam. One of them even invoked some religious scholars as claiming that democracy is unbelief. His argument was that democracy signifies the rule of the people by the people, whereas in Islam it is not the populace but God who is the ruler: "Judgment [al-hukm] is for God alone" (Q 6:57). This is similar to what the Kharijis had said, to which 'Ali ibn Abi Talib [the fourth caliph, r. 656–61] had responded, "A truthful statement, albeit one through which falsehood is sought." People of liberal leanings (al-liberaliyyin) and advocates of freedom have come to believe that the Islamists (al-Islamiyyin) are the opponents of democracy and supporters of dictatorship and despotism. Is it true, then, that Islam is opposed to democracy and that democracy is a form of unbelief or something reprehensible, as some claim? Or is this rather a false accusation of which Islam is innocent?

This is an issue in need of a decisive clarification from scholars of the centrist school, those inclining neither toward extremism nor toward permissiveness, so that the matter is settled and Islam is not saddled with false interpretations. Even if it is religious scholars who have expressed these [incorrect views about democracy], they are only human and, as such, prone as much to being wrong as to being right. We pray that God helps you clarify the truth with textual evidence, so that you can demonstrate what is correct in this matter, answer doubts concerning it, provide decisive proof, and be rewarded [by God]. From "M.S.," a Muslim admirer from Algeria.

ANSWER: I am very sad that matters have all become so confused, with falsehood being mistaken for truth by pious people in general, and by some of those who speak for religion, in particular. The extent to which this has happened is indicated by the question of this inquiring brother: people easily accuse others of unbelief and sinfulness, as though this in itself is not a grave sin in Islamic law. Indeed, such accusations [of unbelief] rebound to the one who directs them at others, as is suggested by an authentic hadith report.

The question that has been put forward is not new to me. I have been asked this many times by brothers from Algeria, and very bluntly: "Is democracy unbelief?" I was in Sidon, in Lebanon, to give a lecture some weeks ago. Afterward, I was asked about whether it was legitimate for Turkey's Islamic party, Refah, to be part of a secular, democratic government.[4] To the questioner, I had said: "The judgment in this matter ought to be based on a 'jurisprudence of comparing [pros and cons].' If the interests of Islam and Muslims require such participation, it becomes permissible." To this the questioner retorted: "How can participation in a democratic government be permissible when democracy is unbelief!" He had also given me a tract on this topic.[5]

1

It is strange that some people condemn democracy as obviously sinful, even as unbelief, without any sophisticated knowledge or understanding of it, other than [an acquaintance with] its name and appearance. Yet, it is a well-established principle of our earlier scholars that the judgment on something flows from its concept: the judgment is erroneous if one is ignorant of what one is judging, even if one happens to arrive at the cor-rect decision. For that would be like shooting in the dark. Thus, as es-tablished by a hadith report, a judge who judges in ignorance will go to hell, as would one who knows the truth but does not judge according to it.

People around the world call for democracy. Countless multitudes have struggled for it in the East and the West. Some have attained it only after bitter struggle against tyrants, in which much blood has been spilled, and thousands—nay millions—have laid down their lives, as in Eastern Europe and elsewhere. Many among the Islamists see in democracy the preferred means for restraining the sort of individual, arbitrary rule and political despotism that afflicts our Arab and Muslim peoples. Is this democracy reprehensible, a matter of unbelief, as some rash and shallow people repeatedly assert?

---

[4]The Refah Party, a political organization founded in 1983 with conspicuous Islamic leanings, came to power as part of a coalition in 1996. But the government, headed by Necmettin Erbakan, did not survive for more than a year, falling in the face of opposition from the Turkish secular establishment, which feared that the Islamist Refah was seeking to undermine the fundamental norms of the Turkish Republic. The party was outlawed by the Turkish Constitutional Court in early 1998.

[5]The subheadings in the original Arabic text have been removed in this translation and replaced with consecutively numbered sections. Some of the paragraphs in the original have also been consolidated in the interest of clarity and coherence. The overall organization of the chapter remains faithful to the Arabic original, however.

2

The essence of democracy—regardless of academic definitions and terminology—is that people choose who rules over them and manages their affairs; that no ruler or regime they dislike is forced upon them; that they have the right to call the ruler to account if he errs and to remove him from office in case of misconduct; and that people are not forced in economic, social, cultural, or political directions that they neither recognize nor accept, such that if someone were to protest or oppose this, he would be punished or frightened off, tortured, even killed. This is the essence of real democracy, for which humanity has found such forms and practical approaches as elections and referenda, majority rule, multiparty systems, the right of the minority to express its opposition, the freedom of the press, and the independence of the judiciary. Does such democracy contradict Islam? Where does the contradiction come from? And what evidence from the Qur'an and the *sunna* supports claims regarding any such contradiction?

3

In fact, whoever contemplates the essence of democracy finds that it accords with the essence of Islam. Islam rejects the idea that people be led in prayer by someone they do not accept and, indeed, despise. As a hadith report says, "The prayer of three sorts of people does not rise even the span of one hand above their heads . . . ," the first of whom is "an imam who leads people in prayer even though they despise him." If this is the case with ritual prayers, it is all the more so in matters of life and politics. As another hadith report puts it: "The best of your imams—that is, rulers—are those who love you and whom you love, those who pray for you and you for them. The worst of your rulers are those you hate and who hate you, those you curse and who curse you."

4

The Qur'an launches an intense attack on "divine" rulers on earth, those who take the slaves of God as their own slaves. An example of these is Nimrod, who is mentioned in the Qur'an with reference to his stance toward Abraham and Abraham's stance toward him: "[Prophet], have you not thought about the man who disputed with Abraham about his Lord, because God had given him power to rule? When Abraham said, 'It is my Lord who gives life and death,' he said, 'I too give life and death.' So Abraham said, 'God brings the sun from the east; so bring it from the west.' The disbeliever was dumbfounded: God does not guide those who do evil" (Q 2:258). This tyrant claimed that he gave life and caused death—just like the Lord of Abraham, the Lord of all the worlds—so that people should submit to him just as they did to the Lord of Abraham! His insolence was such that he picked two passers-by, condemned them both to death for no crime, executed one of them and pardoned the other. "Here," he said, ". . . don't I give life and death?" Nimrod was like the Pharaoh, who declared to his people: "'I am your supreme lord'" (Q 79:24), and bragged: "Counsellors, you have no other god that I know of except me" (Q 28:38).

The Qur'an draws attention to an unholy alliance among three evil parties: first, the divine ruler oppressing God's lands, as represented by the Pharaoh; second, the upstart politician, who puts his intelligence and experience at the service of the tyrant to strengthen his rule and to make people submit to him (this [party] is typified by Haman); finally, the capitalist or the feudal lord who benefits from the regime of the tyrant and supports it with some of his wealth in order to extract more money from the sweat and blood of the people (this is represented by Korah). The Qur'an mentions this triad as allied in its evil and aggression and as standing in opposition to the prophethood of Moses, until God seized them with His power: "We sent Moses with Our signs and clear authority to Pharaoh, Haman, and Korah, and they said, 'Sorcerer! Liar!'" (Q 40: 23). "[Remember] Korah and Pharaoh and Haman: Moses brought them clear signs, but they behaved arrogantly on earth. They could not escape Us" (Q 29:39). Remarkably, Korah belonged to the people of Moses rather than to those of the Pharaoh. Yet he rebelled against his own people to join hands with their enemy, the Pharaoh, who accepted him. This shows that, for all the differences of lineage and race, it was material interests that united them.

5

One of the marvels of the Qur'an is the link it suggests between tyranny and the spread of corruption, which, in turn, is the reason behind the ruin and destruction of nations. As God says: "Have you [Prophet] considered how your Lord dealt with the people of 'Ad, of Iram, the city of lofty pillars, whose like has never been built in any land, and the Thamud, who hewed into the rocks in the valley, and the mighty and powerful Pharaoh? All of them committed excesses in their lands, and spread corruption there: your Lord let a scourge of punishment loose on them. Your Lord is always watchful" (Q 89:6–14). The Qur'an seems to refer to tyranny with the term 'uluww (grandeur) in the sense of arrogance and domination over God's creatures through their humiliation and oppression. It is in this vein that God says of Pharaoh: "he was a tyrant ['aliyan] who exceeded all bounds" (Q 44:31); "Pharaoh made himself high and mighty ['ala] in the land and divided the people into different groups: one group he oppressed, slaughtering their sons and sparing their women—he was one of those who spread corruption" (Q 28:4). We see, then, that tyranny and corruption go hand in hand.

6

The Qur'an does not limit its attack to "divine" tyrants alone. It extends [its criticism] to the people and nations that follow them, obey their commands, and submit to them; and it holds them responsible alongside [the rulers]. As God says concerning the people of Noah: "Noah said, 'My Lord, they have disobeyed me and followed those whose riches and children only increase their losses" (Q 71:21). Regarding 'Ad, the people of Hud, God says: "These were the 'Ad: they rejected the Lord's signs, disobeyed His messengers, and followed the command of every obstinate tyrant" (Q 11:59). And as regards the people of the Pharaoh, God says: "In this way he persuaded his people and they obeyed him—they were perverse people" (Q 43:54); ". . . they followed Pharaoh's orders, and Pharaoh's orders were misguided. He will be at the forefront of his people on the Day of Resurrection, leading them down towards the Fire. What a foul drinking place to be led to!" (Q 11:97–98). God holds the people wholly or partly responsible, for they are the ones who "make" the Pharaohs and tyrants. This is what is meant by the following saying: "The Pharaoh was asked, 'What made you the Pharaoh?' He responded: 'I found no one trying to resist me.'"

7

Those who are most culpable for the tyrants' misconduct are, however, the "instruments of his power." The Qur'an refers to these as "the armies," that is, as military prowess: these are the teeth and claws of political power, the whip that burns the backs of the people if they rebel, or even think of rebelling. The Qur'an says: "Pharaoh, Haman, and their armies were wrongdoers" (Q 28:8); "So We seized him and his armies and threw them into the sea. See what became of the wrong-doers!" (Q 28:40).

8

The teachings of the Prophet likewise condemn the unjust and oppressive rulers who lead the people by force, allowing no one to contradict or question them. These rulers will plunge into hellfire like moths. The Prophet, too, condemns those who associate with and assist these unjust rulers. He criticizes the people who become so fearful that no one among them can call an unjust ruler "unjust." According to a hadith report narrated by Abu Musa, the Prophet said, "There is a valley in hell with a well named Habhab. God will surely lodge every obstinate tyrant in it." According to a hadith report narrated by Mu'awiya, the Prophet said, "After me, there will be rulers who are never contradicted. They [that is, such rulers, and those submitting to them?] will plunge into hell like monkeys." According to a hadith reported by Jabir, the Prophet said to Ka'b ibn 'Ujra: "May God save you from the rule of the foolish, O Ka'b." Ka'b asked: "What does the 'rule of the foolish' mean?" The Prophet answered: "There will be rulers after me who do not guide others according to my guidance and who do not follow my example. Those who affirm their lies and assist them in their injustice will have nothing to do with me, nor I with them. They will not alight at my river [in Paradise]. As for those who do not affirm their lies and do not assist them in their injustice, they belong to me and I to them, and they will alight at my river [in Paradise]." According to a hadith report narrated by Mu'awiya, "God does not sanctify a people among whom matters are not judged rightfully and among whom the weak cannot secure his rights against the strong without difficulty." And a hadith report narrated by 'Abdallah ibn 'Amr says, "When you see my community too afraid to call an unjust [ruler] 'unjust,' bid farewell to them."

9

Islam has established the principle of consultation as one of the basic principles of an Islamic [way of] life. It has obligated the ruler to consult others and obligated the community to offer advice, making [the rendering of] advice [equivalent to following] the religion itself. The advice is for the imams of the Muslims, that is, for their notables and their rulers. Islam has likewise made "commanding right and forbidding wrong" an obligation. Indeed, it deems speaking the truth to the oppressive ruler to be the most meritorious form of jihad. This means that Islam considers resistance against domestic tyranny and corruption to have priority over resisting foreign aggression, for the former is frequently the cause of the latter.

10

The ruler, as viewed by Islam, is the representative of the community and thus its employee. It is a basic right [of the community] to hold its representative accountable or to divest him of this position whenever it wishes and especially if the representative fails in his obligations. In Islam, the ruler is not an infallible authority. He is, rather, a human being whose actions might be right or wrong, who might be just or unjust. Among the rights of the Muslims is to show him the right way when he errs, to set him straight when he deviates. This is what the greatest of Muslim rulers after the Prophet have declared, namely, the Rightly Guided caliphs whose example the Prophet has ordered us to assiduously follow inasmuch as it is an extension of the normative example of the First Teacher, Muhammad himself. In his first address, Abu Bakr, the first caliph [r. 632–34], said: "O people! I have been appointed over you though I am not the best of you. If you see me in the right, assist me. If you see me in error, guide me to the right way. . . . Obey me as long as I obey God in your matters. If I disobey Him, you have no obligation to obey me." The second caliph, 'Umar [r. 634–44], said: "May God have mercy on the person who points me to my faults." And he said, "O people, whosoever sees any crookedness in me ought to set me straight." Someone from among the people responded: "By God, O son of al-Khattab, if we see any crookedness in you, we will set it straight with the sharp edge of our swords!" A woman once contradicted him while he was speaking at the pulpit. He took no offense at this, but rather said: "The woman is right and 'Umar is wrong!" 'Ali ibn Abi Talib [likewise] said to a man remonstrating with him about something, "You are right, and I am wrong. 'Above everyone who has knowledge there is the One who is all knowing'" (Q 12:76).

## 11

Islam antedates democracy in establishing the basic principles on which the essence of democracy rests, but it has left the details to be worked out by Muslims through their independent reasoning (ijtihad) and in accordance with the principles of their religion, their worldly interests, the evolving circumstances of their lives in terms of time and place, and changing human conditions.

## 12

The virtue of democracy is that it has found—in the course of its long struggle against unjust and oppressive rulers—forms and means that still comprise the best guarantees for protecting people from tyrants. It is not free of faults, but the same is true of all human activities. There is nothing to stop people—and their thinkers and leaders—from seeking other forms and procedures that might be better. Until such procedures are found, however, it is necessary to adopt those of democracy, for they are indispensable to the application of justice, for consultation, respect for human rights, and resistance against exalted rulers on earth.

It is a well-established principle of the shari'a that anything that serves as an indispensable means toward fulfilling an obligation is itself to be deemed obligatory. When the desired goals of the shari'a (*al-maqasid al-shar'iyya*) can be attained only through particular means, such means have the same legal effect as the goals themselves. There is no Islamic legal impediment to acquiring an idea or a practical solution from non-Muslims. At the time of the Battle of the Joint Forces, the Prophet dug a trench [around his town, Medina], which was a tactic he took from the Persians. He had also benefited from polytheists taken prisoner at the Battle of Badr who could read and write, as he had them teach writing to Muslim children even though they were unbelievers.[6] Wisdom, after all, is the lost property of the believer; he has the most rightful claim to it, wherever he finds it.

In some of my books, I have noted that we have the right to borrow from others whatever ideas, methods, and systems might be beneficial to us as long as they do not contradict the clear dictates of the foundational texts or the established principles of the shari'a. We should be able, however, to modify what we borrow, to add to it, and to wrap it in our spirit so that it becomes a part of us and loses its original character. Thus, we ought to adopt the procedures of democracy, its mechanisms and its guarantees as they suit us, retaining the right to make alterations and modifications. But we are not to adopt its [underlying] philosophy, which can turn the forbidden (*al-haram*) into the permissible (*al-halal*) and vice versa, or invalidate things made obligatory by religion.

13

If we look at a system like that of elections or voting, we find that, from an Islamic point of view, voting is [the equivalent of] legal testimony for a candidate's abilities. Consequently, it is necessary for a voter to have the qualifications of a legal witness, namely, probity and good character. As God says, "Call two just witnesses from your people" (Q 65:2), "of those you approve as witnesses" (Q 2:282). It is possible to ease the proviso of probity and its conditions in a way that suits the situation, so that most of the citizens can "bear witness" and only those convicted for a dishonorable crime are excluded. If someone testifies that a bad person is actually good, he commits a grave sin, namely,

---

[6]The Battle of the Joint Forces, also known as the Battle of the Trench (627), was fought between the Muslims of Medina and the Meccan polytheists, the latter accompanied by a substantial number of their allies; hence its designation as the Battle of the Joint Forces. Chapter 33 of the Qur'an refers to this battle and takes its name from it. The Battle of Badr, fought between Muslims and the Meccan polytheists in 624, was the first major military encounter between them, following Muslim emigration (*hijra*) from Mecca to Medina in 622.

bearing false witness, which the Qur'an links to associating partners with God: "Shun the filth of idolatrous beliefs and practices and shun false utterances" (Q 22:30). If someone testifies to a candidate's qualifications merely on the ground that the candidate is a relative of his or is from the same town, or in hopes of some personal gain, he disobeys God's command to "establish witness for the sake of God" (Q 65:2). If someone avoids his electoral obligation, with the result that the competent and trustworthy candidate loses and the undeserving candidate— one not "strong and trustworthy" (Q 28:26)—wins a majority, he has thereby disobeyed God's command to bear witness when called to it, and he has concealed the sort of testimony of which the community is most in need. As God says, "Let the witnesses not refuse when they are summoned" (Q 28:26) and "Do not conceal evidence: anyone who does so has a sinful heart" (Q 2:283). The same is true, indeed all the more so, of the qualifications of the candidate. With the addition of such rules and guidelines to the electoral system, we can make it an Islamic system even though it is originally borrowed from others.

14

What I want to focus on here is what I alluded to at the beginning, namely, the essence of democracy. This is, most definitely, in agreement with the essence of Islam, provided we go back to the original sources— the Qur'an, the sunna, and the actions of the Rightly Guided caliphs— and derive it from them rather than from the history of unjust leaders and evil kings; from the fatwas of damned scholars of the throne; or from those who are sincere but hasty [in judgment] and lack any firm foundation in knowledge.

The assertion that democracy signifies the rule of the people by the people, and that this entails a rejection of the principle that sovereignty belongs to God, is not an acceptable view. For the principle of popular rule, which is the foundation of democracy, stands in opposition not to God's rule—the basis of Islamic law—but rather to the rule of the individual, which is the basis of dictatorship. A call for democracy does not necessitate a rejection of God's sovereignty over human beings. Indeed, this does not even occur to most people calling for democracy. What they do seek [in calling for democracy] is rather the rejection of dictatorship, a refusal to accept oppressive and tyrannical rulers—the sort characterized in hadith reports as "the lethal ruler" and "coercive government." Indeed, all they mean by democracy is that the people elect their rulers as they please, that they hold them accountable for their actions, that they refuse their orders when these violate the nation's constitution—that is, in Islamic terms, when the rulers command that which is sinful—and that the people have the right to remove

the rulers when they deviate and act unjustly and when they don't listen
to advice or warning.

15

I would like to emphasize here that the principle of God's sovereignty
(al-hakimiyya li'llah) is a genuine Islamic principle, affirmed by all
jurists in their discourses on Islamic government and on the [position
of] the ruler. They are agreed that the ruler is [ultimately] God Himself,
with the Prophet being our source of information about Him, and that
it is God who decrees and proscribes, who makes things permissible and
forbidden, who lays down the law and who judges.

The Khariji statement, "Judgment belongs to God alone," is true
and correct in itself, but what they were criticized for was their placing
it in the wrong context and arguing from it to deny human arbitration
in situations of conflict. Such a conclusion contradicts the Qur'an,
which recognizes arbitration on more than one occasion, most famously
in case of spouses should there be discord between them. It is for this
reason that 'Ali had responded to the Kharijis by saying, "[Theirs is]
a truthful statement, albeit one through which falsehood is sought."
He did acknowledge the truth of their words, but criticized them for
misunderstanding it. It could not but be a true statement, after all, for it
was derived from the clear words of the Qur'an: "All command belongs
to God alone" (Q 12:40; Q 6:57).

The sovereignty of God over all creatures is indisputable, then. This
sovereignty is of two kinds. The first is "universal" and "determinative"
(hakimiyya kawniyya qadariyya), in the sense that God governs all
existence, directing it with His commands and His unchanging practices, some of which we know and others remain unknown. This
[kind of sovereignty] is referred to in God's statement: "Do they not
see how We come to [their] land and shrink its borders? God decides
[yahkum]—no one can reverse His decision [hukmihi]—and He is swift
in reckoning" (Q 13:41). God's rule here evidently means a determinative sovereignty over the cosmos rather than a legislative sovereignty.

The second kind of sovereignty relates to legislation and commands
(hakimiyya tashri'iyya amriyya), that is, the authority to impose legal
obligations, to command and to forbid, to make things binding or a
matter of choice. This sort of sovereignty manifests itself in what God has
sent with the Messengers and in the Books He has revealed, whereby He
has set forth the law, instituted legal obligations, and made things permissible and forbidden. No Muslim who accepts God as his Lord, Islam
as his religion, and Muhammad as a messenger and prophet denies this.

The Muslim who calls for democracy seeks it as a form of governance
that embodies the political principles of Islam regarding the choice of

the ruler, consultation and advice, commanding right and forbidding wrong, resisting oppression and rejecting sinfulness, especially when the latter reaches the point of "open unbelief" (a matter on which God has provided clear proof). This is [to be] confirmed by the constitution's stipulation, even as it upholds democracy, that Islam is the religion of the state and that the shari'a is the source of law. This would affirm the sovereignty of God, that is, the sovereignty of His law and the fact that that law is supreme. By way of further emphasis, unambiguous articles could be added to the constitution to the effect that any law or system that violates the absolutely certain norms of the shari'a will be null and void. The call for democracy does not, then, entail the rule by the people as a *substitute* for God's rule, for there is no contradiction between the two. Even if this [substitution] was inherent in democracy, the correct view, according to Muslim scholars, is that what is unavoidable (*lazim*) as part of a legal doctrine (madhhab) is not to be reckoned as the standard doctrine [of a school of law], and that people should not be deemed infidels or sinners simply because, in adhering to the standard doctrines, they might also abide by their unavoidable corollaries. For it may well be that they do not really adhere to such corollaries and do not even think about them.


16


Among the arguments advanced by Islamists (*al-Islamiyyun*) who view democracy as an imported ideology with no relation to Islam is that democracy rests on majority opinion. This majority is always correct, be it in the appointment of the rulers, in the management of affairs, or in resolving disagreements. The vote is the source of all judgment and authority: whichever opinion wins an absolute or even a relative majority is implemented, even if it happens to be wrong. Islam, in the view of such critics, does not accept this procedure. It does not privilege one opinion over others simply because of the majority principle. Rather, Islam weighs the opinion in question to determine whether it is, in fact, correct or incorrect. If it is correct, it is implemented even if it has a single voice in support, indeed, even if no one supports it. And if the opinion in question is wrong, it is rejected even if it has the support of ninety-nine percent [of the voters].

[According to this view], Qur'anic passages themselves show that the majority is always with falsehood and on the side of the "idol" (taghut). God says, for instance: "If you obeyed most of those on earth, they would lead you away from the path of God" (Q 6:116); and "However eagerly you may want them to, most men will not believe" (Q 12:103). Qur'anic verses often end with phrases such as: ". . . though most people do not realize it" (Q 7:187); ". . . truly, most of them do not use their reason" (Q 29:63); ". . . though most people do not believe so" (Q 11:17); ". . . but most of them are ungrateful" (Q 2:243). The Qur'an likewise suggests that good people are few in number. As God says: ". . . few of my servants are truly thankful" (Q 34:13); and ". . . those who sincerely believe and do good deeds do not do this, but these are very few" (Q 38:24).

Such views, however, only undermine those who hold them, because they are based on error and confusion. For our discussion of democracy assumes a *Muslim* society, most of whose members "do realize," "do use their reason," "do believe," and "are grateful." We are not talking about a society comprising those who renounce the truth and go astray from the path of God.

## 17

There are things that do not belong to the realm of voting, for they are firmly established matters not subject to any change—except if the very nature of society changes in a way that it can no longer be considered a Muslim society. Thus, there is no scope for voting concerning the absolute certainties (*qat'iyyat*) of the shari'a, the fundamentals of the faith, and in matters of "necessary" religious knowledge. There can be voting only on matters of human judgment (*al-umur al-ijtihadiyya*), which are open to more than one opinion and about which people normally differ. These might include the choice of one among many candidates for a particular office, including that of the head of the state; traffic regulations; the organization of commercial and industrial complexes and hospitals; things referred to by the jurists as matters of the common good; the declaration of war and its cessation; the imposition or removal of taxes; the question of whether to declare a state of emergency; limiting or renewing the president's term of office; and so forth. If opinions differ on such matters, are they to be left unresolved? Should an opinion be preferred without any basis at all? Or should there be some grounds for doing so?

## 18

Reason, the sacred law, and the [demands of the] real world all affirm that some criterion is necessary to tip the balance in circumstances of disagreement. This criterion is the principle of numerical majority: the opinion of two is more likely to be correct than the view of a single person. As a hadith report puts it: "The devil accompanies the single person, but he is farther from two." The Prophet is also reported to have said to Abu Bakr and 'Umar: "If you had both agreed on a matter, I would not have opposed you." This means that two voices have preference over a single one even if the latter is that of the Prophet himself—as long as this does not concern the sacred law or the delivering of God's message [in which no one else has any say]. We likewise see the Prophet following the majority opinion on the occasion of the Battle of Uhud [624] and going out of Medina to confront the polytheists rather than staying within the town to fight in its streets, as had been his own opinion and that of his leading companions.

An even clearer proof [of the majority principle] comes from 'Umar's stance as regards the six members of the consultative council he had nominated [on his deathbed] for the caliphal office: they were to choose one of them by majority vote and all others were to obey the one chosen. If the council was evenly split, they were to take a tie-breaker from outside their ranks, namely, 'Abdallah ibn 'Umar. If they did not accept even his verdict, then they were to follow the decision of the three members that included 'Abd al-Rahman ibn 'Awf among them.

There is clear praise in hadith reports for "the great multitude" and the obligation to follow it. The "great multitude" means the generality of the people, their preponderant number. This is a hadith report that has been narrated through various chains of transmission, some of which are highly reliable. The idea of this hadith is supported by the scholars' reliance on the views of "the generality" in matters of disagreement and by their seeing in this—other things being equal—the basis for preferring [one opinion over another]. In some of his writings, Abu Hamid al-Ghazali [d. 1111] has also affirmed the principle of deciding by the majority in case the viewpoints [between which a decision is being made] are otherwise equivalent.

The statement that preference should be given to what is correct even if it has no support, and that what is wrong should be rejected even though ninety-nine percent of the voters support it, holds only for matters definitively settled by the sacred law, so that there is no scope for disputation or disagreement in them. But such matters are very few. They are the sort of things about which it is said: "The 'community' is that which agrees with the truth, even if it is a community of one." As for matters pertaining to considered human judgment, which are not regulated by the foundational texts, or the textual indications concerning them that are open to more than one interpretation, or such indications that are contradicted by others of equal or greater weight, there is no alternative to a means through which the disagreement is resolved. Voting is such a means. People are familiar with it; the wise, including Muslims, accept it; and there is no impediment to it in the shari'a—indeed, there are textual and historical indications to support it.

19

The first thing to afflict the Muslim community in its history was the neglect of the principle of consultation and the transformation of the Rightly Guided caliphate into a "grasping kingdom," referred to by some companions of the Prophet as the kingdom of the Caesar or of the Persian kings. The contagion of despotism came to be transferred to Muslims from the lands God had given them. They ought to have learned from the example [of the conquered people] and to have avoided the sins and vices that had become the cause of the decline of those kingdoms. But alas, the Muslims transferred the worst of what they found in the political life of the earlier kingdoms—namely, despotism and arrogance—to their own state, a state that ought to have been led by people who did not seek grandeur on earth and who were not corrupt.

Whatever has come to afflict Islam and Muslims in the present age has come from despotism, imposed on people with the carrot and the stick. It is only through coercion and tyranny, the resort to fire and sword, that the shari'a has been suspended, secularism imposed, and people forced to westernize. It is only through the power of despotism—sometimes brazen, at other times concealed in spurious democratic claims; sometimes openly controlled by anti-Islamic forces, at other times from behind the scenes—that the call to Islam and the Islamic movement have been suppressed and those associated with it tortured and banished.

20

The resurgence of Islam owes itself to whatever little freedom has been available to it. It is through this freedom that Islam has been able to raise its voice and spread its message, to demonstrate its harmony with the innate human dispositions awaiting it, so that eager ears can hear its message and starved intellects can be satiated with it. The very first battle confronting the call to Islam, the Islamic awakening, and the Islamic movement is the battle for freedom. It is therefore imperative on all those with an Islamic zeal to stand together in calling for this freedom and in defending it, for there is no alternative to it.

I am not fond of using foreign terms, such as democracy, to express Islamic ideas. I prefer to use Islamic terms to express Islamic values and concepts, for this is more appropriate in expressing our distinct identity. Yet, if a particular term becomes widespread in popular usage, we can hardly shut our ears to it. Rather, we ought to understand how it is used so we don't misunderstand it, or take it to mean something other than what those using it mean by that term. In doing so, our view of the term in question would be sound, irrespective of its foreign origins. After all, one's judgment must depend not on a thing's names and titles but rather on its contents. Many writers and preachers have, moreover, used the term "democracy" in their writings without finding anything wrong with it. For instance, the late Professor 'Abbas al-'Aqqad wrote a book titled "Islamic Democracy." And Khalid Muhammad Khalid has gone so far as to characterize democracy as Islam itself! (I have commented on the latter in my *Islamic Revival and the Concerns of the Arabs and the Muslims.*) Numerous Islamists have also called for democracy as a form of government, as a safeguard for freedom, and as a protection against the tyranny of the ruler, on the understanding that real democracy represents the interests of the people, not those of the ruler and his entourage. Yet simply raising the flag of democracy is hardly enough when its spirit is being eviscerated with prisons and flogging; when military tribunals mete out prison sentences, take away livelihoods, and execute people; and when emergency laws hound anyone who might have an independent opinion, anyone who dares to say "why," let alone "no," to the ruler.

I am one of those who call for democracy [not simply as a slogan but] because it is a feasible and disciplined means to an honorable life, one in which we can call others to God and to Islam according to our beliefs and without being thrown into dungeons or executed. This democracy would also be the means to a free and honorable life for our people, in which they enjoy the right to choose their rulers, to hold them accountable, and to change them if they go astray without having to resort to revolutions or assassinations.

21

It remains for me to comment on the assertion of some scholars that consultation is only for informational purposes rather than something binding, that the ruler ought to consult but that he is not bound to follow the advice of those he consults, [traditionally called] the People who Loosen and Bind. I have refuted this claim elsewhere, making it clear that consultation has no meaning if the ruler consults but then does as he and his retinue please. How can those referred to in our tradition as the People who Loosen and Bind be characterized as such when, in fact, they do not "loosen" or "bind" anything?

In his exegesis of the Qur'an, Ibn Kathir [d. 1373] quotes Ibn Mardawayh as reporting that 'Ali was asked about the meaning of "deciding [on a course of action]" in God's statement: "Consult with them about matters, then, when you have decided on a course of action, put your trust in God" (Q 3:159). 'Ali said that it meant consulting with people of considered opinion and then following them.

Even if there are two [different] opinions on this matter, the view that affirms the [ruler's] *obligation* to follow advice should be preferred in view of the history of despotism in our community. Whatever disagreement there might be on this matter, once the community—or a group in it—decides to opt for the view that consultation ought to be binding, then all disagreement ends and adherence to what has been agreed upon becomes religiously binding. Muslims are bound by their stipulations. Consequently, if the ruler is elected in accordance with *this* stipulation [regarding the binding character of the results of consultation], he cannot violate it in favor of anything else. Muslims—as I have said, and as a hadith report affirms—are bound by their stipulations; and fulfilling the contract is obligatory. "Fulfill any pledge you make in God's name and do not break oaths after you have sworn them, for you have made God your surety" (Q 16: 91).

When 'Abd al-Rahman ibn 'Awf offered to 'Ali that people would pledge allegiance to him on the stipulation that he adhere to the Book of God, the normative example of the Prophet, and the practice of his two predecessors, Abu Bakr and 'Umar, he refused the last stipulation, that is, adherence to the practice of his predecessors. For to accept it would have meant that he would be bound by it. He rejected this because he was a religious leader (*imam*) in his own right, with his own considered judgment independent of those of his predecessors; the times and circumstances, too, had changed. 'Uthman, for his part, did accept this stipulation and, accordingly, he was rendered the oath of allegiance on its basis. This testifies to the fact that the ruler must, as far as possible, adhere to the stipulations according to which people have pledged allegiance to him. This is how the Islamic principle of consultation is close to the spirit of democracy or, rather, how the essence of democracy comes to accord with the spirit of Islamic consultation. All praise belongs to God, the Lord of all worlds.

# PART III

# Islamism and Gender

*Chapter 10*

# MURTAZA MUTAHHARI
## 1920–1979

MURTAZA MUTAHHARI, a student of Ayatollah Khomeini, is widely recognized as one of the most important intellectuals associated with the movement culminating in the Iranian revolution of 1979. Mutahhari was never a revolutionary firebrand or, unlike Khomeini, a major contributor to conceptions of the Islamic state. His significance lies, rather, in efforts toward demonstrating that the teachings of Islam amount to a coherent system that encompasses all facets of life, that they can be put forth in an idiom intelligible and persuasive to the products of modern, Western institutions of learning, and that religious scholars and members of the intelligentsia ought to join hands in defense of Islamic norms. Yet he also insisted that it was the traditionally educated religious scholars, not religious intellectuals lacking Islamic scholarly credentials, who were the proper guardians and authoritative exponents of these norms. These themes helped shape the intellectual and religious milieu in which the revolution took place, and they have continued to echo in its aftermath. So, too, has Mutahhari's work on the "system of women's rights in Islam," selections from which are included here.

Born in 1920 near Mashhad in Iran, Mutahhari studied first at madrasas in Mashhad and then in the Hawza al-'ilmiyya of Qom, as the many formal and informal sites and institutions of Shi'i learning in that city are collectively known. Philosophy was among Mutahhari's major interests already before arriving in Qom, and it remained a life-long preoccupation. Among his teachers was Muhammad Husayn Tabataba'i (d. 1981), who is best known as the author of *al-Mizan fi tafsir al-Qur'an*, a twenty-one volume Arabic commentary on the Qur'an unparalleled in modern Islamic exegetical literature for its systematic attention to Islamic and Western philosophy. Part of Tabataba'i's concerns in this work was to address the "doubts" many Muslims, including not a few among the 'ulama and their students, had come to have about various Islamic beliefs. Like Muhammad Baqir al-Sadr of Iraq, Tabataba'i was especially concerned with the appeal of Marxism to young Muslims and sought an antidote to it in his commentary. Mutahhari was deeply influenced by Tabataba'i's work, and critiques of Marxism, as well as of Marxist interpretations of Islam, were to remain prominent among his own intellectual concerns.

Another teacher of Mutahhari in Qom was Ayatollah Khomeini. Mutahhari attended Khomeini's lectures on ethics, philosophy, and law (cf.
Algar 1985, 10–11); and he remained close to Khomeini after leaving
Qom for Tehran in the early 1950s. After Khomeini was exiled from Iran
in 1964, Mutahhari served as his principal representative in Iran, receiving, on Khomeini's behalf, the religious taxes individual Shi'is paid to
leading religious scholars. While in Qom, Mutahhari had also maintained
ties with the Feda'iyyan-i Islam (The Devotees of Islam), a militant group
seeking the implementation of Islamic law in Iran. Its members were involved in a series of assassinations, including that of the secular intellectual Ahmad Kasravi (d. 1946) and, in 1951, of the Iranian prime minister
'Ali Razmara (Davari 2005, 20–23). Though he did not endorse its violence, Mutahhari's informal ties with this organization did not endear
him to Ayatollah Borujerdi, the preeminent religious authority (marja'
al-taqlid) of his time and a pillar of the largely quietist religious establishment in Qom. As a consequence, Mutahhari moved to Tehran in 1952
and, two years later, began teaching at Tehran University's Faculty of
Theology.

While he was already acquainted with the work of several major modern Western thinkers, teaching at a university brought Mutahhari into
sustained contact with students and scholars very different from those he
had encountered at the Hawza in Qom. Mutahhari was among the founding figures of the Husayniyya-i Irshad, established in Tehran in 1965 specifically to articulate matters relating to Islam in a new idiom and with a
view to addressing those educated in westernized institutions of learning.
Among those who came to lecture there was 'Ali Shari'ati (d. 1977), a
Sorbonne-educated religious intellectual who sought a thoroughgoing reorientation of Islamic and specifically Shi'i thought in a politically activist, subversive, and, indeed, revolutionary direction. Like Mutahhari,
Shari'ati would emerge as a major influence on many of those who later
contributed to bringing about the Iranian revolution. The relationship between the intellectual orientations represented by the two men was complex and often tense, and it deserves a brief comment here (also cf. Dabashi 2006, 108, 157, 198–201; Behdad 1994, 780–83).

In his lectures, Shari'ati's target was not only the regime of the shah of
Iran but the Shi'i religious establishment itself, which he excoriated for
its political quietism and for what he saw as the utter anachronism of
its intellectual concerns. Mutahhari was critical of the Hawza establishment as well, and this had contributed to his departure from Qom, as
noted earlier. Though much more cautious than Shari'ati, let alone the
Feda'iyyan-i Islam, Mutahhari, too, sought a new, politically activist role
for the 'ulama. He was an active member, for instance, of the Association
of Combatant Scholars (Jam'iyyat-i ruhaniyyat-i mubariz), an organization established in the wake of Khomeini's exile from Iran to foster ties

among like-minded religious scholars (cf. Algar 1985, 18; also cf. Martin 2000, 71, 77). Against the politically quiescent 'ulama, Mutahhari argued that a true Islamic calling consisted not only in personal piety and religious scholarship but also in the implementation of Islamic norms in society. As he would put it in a later work:

> 'Ali [the first imam of the Shi'a] did not content himself with inward reform and spiritual liberation, just as he did not consider social reforms enough. He worked for reform in both directions. This is the program of Islam. Thus, Islam bore in one hand a logic, a summons, and a program for the individual and collective unity of people, directed at worship of God, and in the other a sword to sever unjust human relations, to overthrow social classes, and to destroy the *taghut*s [literally "idols" but, in revolutionary rhetoric, everything that stands between believers and their complete devotion to God]. (Mutahhari 1985, 94)

In some of his views on social and economic matters, Mutahhari went farther than most of his contemporaries in the Hawza. Like Muhammad Baqir al-Sadr of Iraq but unlike Khomeini, Mutahhari's efforts to refute Marxist doctrines were accompanied by a considerably greater openness to possibilities of reformulating Islamic norms on matters of economic life than other 'ulama were comfortable with. Indeed, while Mutahhari remains a much revered figure in the official discourse of postrevolution Iran, some of the writings in which he had argued for state-imposed restrictions on means of production have been suppressed in Iran (Behdad 1994, 802–3).

Yet it was not only in his politics that Mutahhari was more cautious than Shari'ati. At issue between them also were very different conceptions of Islam itself, which had eventually led Mutahhari to leave the Husayniyya-i Irshad. These differences are perhaps best expressed in Mutahhari's distinction between "Islamic revolution" and "revolutionary Islam. "Islamic revolution means a way," Mutahhari said. "Its aim is Islam and Islamic values. Revolution and fighting are merely for the establishment of Islamic values." Conversely, in an allusion to Shari'ati but also to the "Islamic Marxists," whose interpretations of the Qur'an Mutahhari had bitterly condemned and some of whom would assassinate him in May 1979, Mutahhari took them to hold that "revolution and struggle are the goal, and Islam is the means. They say that the part of Islam that leads us in the direction of combat is acceptable to us and that the one keeping us away from its course should be rejected" (Mutahhari n.d., 47–48). As Mutahhari saw it, however, theological doctrine, law, and ritual practice were as much a part of "Islam and Islamic values" as was the quest for social and economic justice. For all his other disagreements with the Hawza (cf. Mutahhari 2001), his view of many of these

Islamic values was fundamentally conservative. There is no more illuminating statement of this than his "System of Women's Rights in Islam," which "became the official discourse of the Islamic Republic on gender" (Mir-Hosseini 1999, 24).

This book, translated into English as *The Rights of Women in Islam*, had originated as a series of articles published in 1966–67 in *Zan-e ruz*, a prominent women's magazine. The Pahlavi regime was preparing to put into effect a major reform of the laws of personal status (i.e., laws governing marriage and divorce), which had hitherto been largely regulated according to shari'a norms. Before this new initiative took the form of the Family Protection Law, promulgated in 1967, a judge named Ibrahim Mahdavi Zanjani had proceeded to offer his own proposals on how the laws relating to marriage and divorce ought to be reformulated. These proposals, broadly similar to what the regime was already contemplating, were published in *Zan-e ruz*, provoking Mutahhari to enter into a debate with Zanjani. *Zan-e ruz* agreed to publish both Zanjani's commentary on his code and Mutahhari's critique in the form of an enunciation of what he regarded as authoritative Islamic norms relating to the status of women. Zanjani died soon afterward, but Mutahhari continued to publish his own articles, later to be collected as "The System of Women's Rights in Islam" (Mutahhari 1998, xxxvii–xxxix; Mutahhari 1974).

Central to Islamist discourses on gender is the insistence that God has intended different functions for men and women, that these are based on fundamental differences in their nature, that to deny these differences is unjust rather than just, and that no religious or social order determines the rights and obligations of men and women in light of these differences better than Islam. The obvious targets of attack in such arguments are, of course, the position of women in contemporary Western societies *and* a strong sensitivity to what Western observers—colonial officials, journalists, travelers, feminists, and scholars—have often said about the plight of Muslim women. On the Islamist view, to which Mutahhari gave a highly influential formulation, it is women in Western societies, not Muslim women, who are the ones truly exploited. The idea that men and women are equal in all respects and that women, too, ought to be part of the labor force is closely tied, Mutahhari says, with the needs of a capitalist economy for cheap labor (Mutahhari 1998, xxix–xx). A capitalist economy likewise needs women to market its goods "by trading in honour and respect, through [their] power to entice," thereby "transform[ing] man into an involuntary agent of consumption" (Mutahhari 1998, xxxi).

Islamist views of women—which admit of considerable variety—are not a mere reiteration of *traditional* Muslim discourses on women and gender, however. Where medieval scholars typically took the inequality of men and women for granted, Mutahhari, for all his impeccable credentials as a traditionally educated religious scholar, denies that women are inferior to men. A central argument of *The Rights of Women in Islam* is the need to distinguish between equality (*tasavi*), which Islam affirms for both men and women, and "identicalness" (*tashaboh*), which it rejects (cf. Mir-Hosseini 1999, 116). It is the confusion between the two that, according to Mutahhari, underlies not only the unfair critiques of the position of women in Islam but also the exploitation of women in other societies.

Although Mutahhari does not examine the implications of his view for the participation of women in politics, the conviction that women and men have different capabilities does obviously tend toward severely limiting their position in the public sphere. Yet Iranian women were an extremely significant part of the movement that overthrew the shah and—though Khomeini had once bitterly opposed women's right to vote (cf. Martin 2000, 60–61)—the legitimacy of their participation in this revolutionary movement was never questioned by the religious scholars. Mutahhari would not have seen cynical manipulation here nor acknowledged a paradox. Muslim jurists have long argued that "necessity" justifies actions that might otherwise be forbidden, and Mutahhari himself had written extensively on the need to take account of changing needs. (A two-volume book he had published in the early 1970s is titled "Islam and the Needs of the Time" [Mutahhari 1991].) In particular instances, the demands of the age, or of the moment, might justify new legal rulings or require excavating old ones—rulings that might be in some tension with conventional views and even with some of the positions a scholar himself held. For instance, where many insisted that a woman ought to cover herself from head to toe, and to also cover her face and hands, Mutahhari had argued in a work completed in the mid-1960s that earlier scholars were in fact agreed in *not* requiring the covering of the face, and that it was dishonest to pretend otherwise (Mutahhari 1989, 59–71; cf. Mir-Hosseini 1999, 232).

Rhetoric aside, these were small disagreements, however. On more substantive issues concerning the position of women and the laws relating to them, neither Khomeini nor Mutahhari was willing to countenance thoroughgoing change. Even as Khomeini lauded the sacrifices women had made on the path to, and in sustaining, the Iranian revolution (cf. Khomeini n.d., 14), he had little doubt that male religious scholars were the final arbiters of how, to what purpose, and under what conditions women ought to appear in the public sphere and when they should return to the oversight of their households, for which religion and nature had intended them all along. In this, Mutahhari was at one not only with Khomeini but also with the generality of Islamist thinkers. What Mutahhari also shared with many other Islamists was his broader analysis of the incompatibility between Western and Islamic norms, an analysis that is inextricably tied to his view of the position and rights of women in Islam.

# THE HUMAN STATUS OF WOMAN IN THE QUR'AN

As WHAT KIND of entity does Islam envisage woman? Does it consider her the equal of man in terms of dignity and the respect accorded to her, or is she thought of as belonging to an inferior species? This is the question we now wish to answer.

## THE PARTICULAR PHILOSOPHY OF ISLAM CONCERNING FAMILY RIGHTS

Islam has a particular philosophy concerning the family rights of men and women that is contrary to what has been going on in the past fourteen centuries and with what is actually happening now. Islam does not believe in one kind of right, one kind of duty, and one kind of punishment for both men and women in every instance. It considers one set of rights and duties and punishments more appropriate for men, and one set more appropriate for women. As a result, Islam has taken on some occasions a similar position as regards both women and men and on other occasions different positions.

Why is that so, and what is its basis? Is it because Islam, also, like many other religions, has derogatory views concerning women and has considered woman to be of an inferior species, or does it have some other reasons and another philosophy?

You may have heard repeatedly in the speeches, lectures, and writings of the followers of Western ideas that they consider Islamic laws concerning dowry, maintenance, divorce, and polygyny, and other laws like them, as being contemptuous of, and insulting to, the female sex. In this way, they try to create the impression that those provisions only prove that man alone has been favored.

They say that all the rules and laws in the world before the twentieth century were based on the notion that man, because of his sex, is a nobler being than woman and that woman was created simply for the benefit and use of man. Islamic rights also revolve in this same orbit of man's interest and benefit.

They say that Islam is a religion for men, that it has not acknowledged woman to be a complete human being, and that it has not ordained laws for her that are necessary for a human being. Had Islam gauged woman to be a complete human being, it would not have provided for polygyny, it would not have given the right of divorce to man, it would not have made the witnessing of two women equivalent to that of one man, it would not have given leadership of the family to the husband, it would not have made a woman's inheritance one-half of the inheritance of a man, it would not have countenanced that a woman be "priced" in the name of a dowry, it would not have provided for her economic and social independence, and it would not have made her a "pensioner" of man who is obliged to "keep" her. From the aforesaid things, they say, it is inferred that Islam has humiliating views about woman and has taken her to be just a means to procreating more people, and a necessary prerequisite for that. They add that, although Islam is a religion of equality and has maintained real equality in other situations, in the case of woman and man it did not observe it.

They say that Islam has provided discriminative and preferential rights for men. If it did not have in view discriminative and preferential rights for men, it would not have ordained the preceding laws.

If we resolve the argument of these gentlemen into an Aristotelian logical pattern, it would have the following form:

> If Islam had considered woman a complete human being, it would have ordained equal and similar rights for her, but it has not ordained equal and similar rights for her. Therefore, it does not consider a woman a complete human being.

### EQUALITY OR IDENTICALNESS?

The basic point that is used in these arguments is that the necessary result of men's and women's sharing in human dignity and honor is that their rights should be the same—identical. Now, the thing on which, philosophically speaking, we should put our finger is to determine exactly what is the necessary result of man's and woman's sharing in human dignity. Is the necessary conclusion that each of them should have rights equivalent to the other, so that there should be no privilege or preference in favor of either of them, or is it necessary that the rights of man and woman, besides having equivalence and parity, should also be exactly the same, and that there should be no division whatsoever of work and duty. No doubt the sharing of man and woman in human dignity and their equality as human beings demands their having equal human rights, but how can there be identicalness of rights?

If we can begin to put aside the imitation and blind following of western philosophy, and allow ourselves to think and ponder over the philosophical ideas and opinions that have come to us from them, we must see firstly whether identicalness of rights is or is not necessary for equality of rights. Equality is different from identicalness. Equality means parity and equitableness, and identicalness means that they are exactly the same. A father may distribute his wealth equally and equitably among his sons, but he may not distribute it identically. For example, it is possible that a father has different kinds of wealth: he may own a commercial firm, some agricultural land, and also some real estate; but, having examined his sons and found different talents among them, for example, he may have found that one of them had a gift for commercial affairs, and that the second had ability in agriculture, and the third had the capability to manage real estate. When he comes to distribute his wealth among his sons in his lifetime, bearing in mind that he must give equally to his sons in terms of the value of the property and that there should be no preference nor discrimination, he bequeaths his wealth according to the talents he has found in them.

Quantity is different from quality. Equality is different from being exactly the same. What is certain is that Islam has not considered there to be identicalness or exact similarity of rights between men and women, but it has never believed in preference and discrimination in favor of men as opposed to women. Islam has also observed the principle of equality between men and women. Islam is not against the equality of men and women, but it does not agree with the identicalness of their rights.

The words "equality" and "égalité" have earned a kind of sanctity because they embrace the meaning of equivalence and absence of discrimination. These words are attractive and draw respect from listeners, especially when these words are joined to the word "rights."

"Equality of rights"—how beautiful and sacred is this combination of words! Can there be anyone with a conscience and an innate moral sense who does not revere these two words?

But why is it that we who were once the standard-bearers of knowledge, philosophy, and logic have come to such a position that others want to impose their opinions on us concerning the identicalness of the rights of men and women in the sacred name of equality of rights.

It is exactly like someone who wants to sell boiled beetroots and calls them pears.

What is certain is that Islam has not granted the same rights to men and women in everything, in the same way as it has not imposed the same duties and punishment on both of them on all occasions. However, is the sum total of all the rights that have been established for women less in value than the rights that have been granted to men? Certainly not, as we shall prove.

Here a second question arises. Why has Islam granted dissimilar rights to men and women in certain instances? Why did it not allow the same rights for both of them? Would it not have been better for the rights of men and women to have been both equal and identical, or is it preferable that the rights should be only equal but not the same? To study this point thoroughly, it is necessary that we should discuss it in three parts:

1. What is the view of Islam concerning the human status of woman from the point of view of creation?

2. What is the reason for the differences that exist in the creation of man and woman? Are these differences the cause of there being dissimilarities in their natural rights?

3. What is the basic philosophy behind the differences that exist in Islamic law for men and women, which, in certain respects, place them in different positions? Are these philosophical reasons still justifiable and do they still hold good, or not?

## The Status of Woman in the Worldview of Islam

As for the first part, the holy Qur'an is not only a collection of laws. It does not contain merely a series of dry commands and laws without comment. It contains both laws and history, both exhortation and the interpretation of creation, and countless other subjects. Just as the Qur'an lays down rules of action in the form of law on some occasions, so it also comments upon existence and being. It explains the secrets of the creation of the earth and the sky; plants, animals, and mankind; and the secret of life and death, greatness and suffering, growth and decline, wealth and poverty.

The Qur'an is not a treatise on philosophy, but it has explicitly expressed its views concerning the three basic topics of philosophy: the universe, mankind, and society. Not only does the Qur'an teach its believers laws, and not only does it give exhortation and advice, but it also endows its followers with a special way of thinking, a particular worldview, by its interpretation of creation. The foundation of all Islamic commandments concerning social matters, for example, ownership, government, family rights, and so forth, is this same explanation that the Qur'an gives of creation and the things of the world.

One of the matters that have been commented on in the holy Qur'an is the subject of the creation of women and men. The Qur'an was not silent on this matter and did not provide an opportunity for those who talk nonsense to put forth their own philosophies for laws concerning men and women and then to accuse Islam of having a derogatory attitude towards women on the strength of their own theories. Islam has already laid down its views regarding women.

If we want to see what the view of the Qur'an is regarding the creation of woman and man, it is necessary to have a look at the question of their creation as it is treated in the books of other religions. The Qur'an also did not remain silent on this subject. We should see whether the Qur'an considers woman and man to be of one essence or two—in other words, whether woman and man have one nature and essence or two. The Qur'an most explicitly lays down in several verses that God created women from the same genus and essence as that of men. Concerning the first human, the Qur'an says that God created all of you from a single father and created his mate from his genus (Q 4:1). With regard to all men, the Qur'an says that God created your mate from your own kind (Qur'an, chs. 4, 3, 30).

There is no trace in the Qur'an of what is found in some sacred books: that woman was created out of an inferior stock to that of man, that they gave woman the status of a parasite and of an inferior, or that the mate of the first human was created from one of the left-side parts of his body. Besides that, in Islam there is no derogatory view about woman as regards her nature and innate constitution.

Another of the contemptuous views that existed in the past and have left their undesirable effects in world literature is that woman is the origin of sin and that her existence is the source of sin and temptation. Woman is a small devil. They say in every sin or crime committed by man, woman had her hand. According to them, man in himself is innocent of any sin: it is woman who drags him toward sin. They say Satan cannot find his way to man's being directly: it is only through woman that he can deceive man. Satan tempts woman, and woman tempts man. They say the first human, who was deceived by Satan and turned out of the Paradise of happiness, was deceived through woman. Satan tempted Eve, and Eve tempted Adam.

The Qur'an relates the story of the Paradise of Adam, but never says that Satan or a snake tempted Eve and she tempted Adam. The Qur'an neither describes Eve as the main person responsible, nor does it exonerate her from the sin. The Qur'an says: "O Adam, inherit, thou and thy wife, the Garden, and eat of where you will" (7:19). Wherever the Qur'an describes the matter of Satan's tempting, it uses the pronouns in the form of the dual (i.e., referring to two persons). It says: "Satan tempted both of them" (7:20); "So he led them both on by delusion" (7:22); "And he swore to both of them, 'Truly, I am for you both a sincere adviser'" (7:21).

In this way the Qur'an strongly refutes the misconception that was prevalent at that time and is still found in certain quarters and among certain people of this world, and it exonerates the female sex from the accusation that woman is the source of temptation and sin and is half a devil.

Another contemptuous view that exists concerning woman is in the field of her spiritual ability. They say: "A woman cannot go to Heaven. A woman cannot traverse the spiritual and divine stages of enlightenment. A woman cannot attain proximity to God as can a man." The Qur'an, on the other hand, has made it explicitly clear in a large number of verses that reward in the life after death and nearness to God do not depend upon sex, but upon faith and deeds, whether they be of a woman or a man. For every great and pious man, the Qur'an mentions a great and pious woman alongside him. The wives of Adam and Ibrahim (Abraham) and the mothers of Musa (Moses) and 'Isa (Jesus) are mentioned with great esteem. Although the Qur'an refers to the wives of Nuh (Noah) and Lut (Lot) as being unworthy of their husbands, it does not ignore the wife of Fir'awn (Pharaoh) as a woman of distinction under the control of a detestable man. It can be said that the Qur'an purposely seeks to keep a balance in its histories, and the leading role in them is not confined to men.

About the mother of Musa, the Qur'an says: "So we revealed to Moses' mother, 'Suckle him, then, when thou fearest for him, cast him into the water, and do not fear, neither sorrow, for We shall return him to thee'" (28:7).

About Maryam (Mary), the mother of 'Isa, the Qur'an says that she had attained such an elevated spiritual degree that the angels used to visit her in her prayer niche and converse with her. Sustenance was supplied to her from an invisible source. She had attained so high a position of divine favor that it completely astounded the prophet of that time and exceeded his own degree. Zakariyya (the prophet) was dumbfounded when he looked upon her.

In the history of Islam itself, there are many pious and distinguished women. There can be few men who are able to reach the high status of Khadijah, and no man except the Holy Prophet himself and 'Ali could attain the status of al-Zahra.[1] Al-Zahra excelled her sons, the imams, and all the prophets as well, excepting the Seal of the Prophet Muhammad. Islam does not make any difference between man and woman in the journey from this world toward al-Haqq (the Truth, i.e., toward God). The only difference that Islam makes is in the journey from al-Haqq to this world, in returning to mankind and bearing the prophetic message, and here it recognizes man as being more suitable.

Another derogatory view that was held was in connection with sexual abstinence and the sacredness of being single and celibate. As we know, in some religions, sexual intercourse is in its essence unclean. According to the followers of these religions, only those who live all their life in celibacy can attain the stations of the spirit. One of the world's well-known religious leaders said: "Root out the tree of marriage with the spade of virginity." The same religious leaders allow marriage only as one evil to ward off a greater evil. In other words they maintain that, as the majority of people are unable to endure the hardship of remaining

---

[1]Khadija (d. 619) was the first wife of the Prophet Muhammad. Al-Zahra is an honorific commonly used for Fatima (d. 633), a daughter of Muhammad and Khadija and the wife of 'Ali ibn Abi Talib, the first Shi'i imam.

celibate and may lose self-control and thus become victims of perversion, indulging in sexual contact with numerous women, it is better that they should marry and not have sexual relations with more than one woman. The root cause of sexual abstention and celibacy is a feeling of aversion against the female sex. These people consider love of women to be one of the great moral depravities.

Islam has combated fiercely against this superstition. It considers marriage to be sacred and celibacy to be impure. Islam considers love of women to be a part of prophetic morality, and says: "Love of women is of the morality of the prophets." The last Prophet used to say: "Three things are dear to me: perfume, women, and prayer."

Bertrand Russell says: "In all codes of moral conduct there appears a kind of aversion to sexual relations except in Islam. Islam has ordained regulations and limitations with regard to this relationship for social reasons, but it has never considered it an abominable and unclean matter."[2]

Another derogatory opinion held regarding women was that she is only a means for bringing man into existence and that she was created for man.

These ideas can never be found in Islam. Islam most explicitly explains the basis of the final cause; it says quite clearly that the earth and the sky, the clouds and the winds, plants and animals have all been created for man. But it never says that woman was created for man. Islam says that man and woman were each created for the other: "They are a vestment for you (man) and you are a vestment for them" (Q 2:187). If the Qur'an considered woman to be a means of making men and something created for them, it would certainly have kept this fact in view in its laws. As Islam, in its explanation of creation, does not have this opinion and does not consider woman to be a parasite on man's existence, there is no trace or reflection of this idea in its special precepts regarding man and woman.

Another of the derogatory views held in the past was that women were considered an unavoidable and necessary evil. Many men, in spite of all the gains and advantages they had derived from women, regarded them contemptuously and considered them to be a source of misfortune and misery. The holy Qur'an makes a special mention of the fact that woman is a blessing for man and is a source of solace and comfort for his heart.

---

[2]Mutahhari did not read any European languages but, like many other Islamists, he was an avid reader of Western works available to him in Persian or Arabic. In Islamist literature, as well as in the works of many modernists and 'ulama, selective quotations from Western writers can serve a variety of purposes: to corroborate particular Islamic viewpoints by showing that even otherwise hostile Western observers acknowledge their truth (see chapter 4 on Nadwi); to refute particular Western criticisms of Islam; to condemn particular "Western" practices in the words of Western writers themselves; and, not least, to demonstrate one's own acquaintance with Western thought as a way of more effectively appealing to a westernized Muslim audience.

Yet another derogatory view was that woman played a very insignificant part in bringing offspring into the world. Arabs of the pre-Islamic age, and certain other peoples, considered women to be only a repository for the sperm of the man, which, according to them, was the real seed of the child, and they said that her part was to keep that seed safe and to nourish it. The Qur'an says in several verses that: "You were created from man and woman." In other verses, which are analyzed in the commentaries, the final answer has been given in a similar way.

From what has been said, it is clear that both from a philosophical point of view and from its explanation of the nature of creation, Islam does not hold any derogatory ideas concerning women; rather, it has seen to it that all the previously mentioned derogatory views are discarded. Now it is appropriate to examine why there is an absence of identicalness in the rights of men and women.

## EQUALITY, BUT NOT UNIFORMITY

We said that Islam has a special philosophy concerning the relations and rights of men and women within the family that differs from that which was current fourteen centuries ago and does not conform either with what is accepted in the world of today.

We have already explained that according to the Islamic view it is never a matter of dispute as to whether a man and a woman are equal as human beings or not, and as to whether their family rights should or should not be equal in value with each other. According to Islam, a woman and a man are both human beings, and both are apportioned equal rights.

That which has been kept in view in Islam is that woman and man, on the basis of the very fact that one is a woman and the other is a man, are not identical with each other in many respects. The world is not exactly alike for both of them, and their natures and dispositions were not intended to be the same. Eventually this requires that in very many rights, duties, and punishments they should not have an identical placing. The Western world is now attempting to create uniformity and identicalness in laws, regulations, rights, and functions between women and men, while ignoring the innate and natural differences. It is here that the difference between the outlook of Islam and that of Western systems is to be found. Thus, the dispute between, on the one hand, those sections of the people who support Islamic rights and, on the other hand, those who support Western systems is about the identicalness and exact similarity of the rights of women and men, and not about equality of rights. "Equality of rights" is a counterfeit label that the followers of the West have stuck on as a souvenir of the West.

In my writings, conferences, and lectures, I always avoid the use of this counterfeit label, and the use of this phrase, which comes to mean nothing but uniformity and identicalness of rights for women and men, in place of genuine equality of rights.

I am not saying that nowhere in the world did or does the claim for equality of rights for women and men have any meaning, nor am I saying that every past and present law in the world concerning the rights of men and women was passed on the basis of equality of worth and estimation and that it is just identicalness that was eliminated.

No, I have no such claim. Europe, before the twentieth century is the best evidence. In Europe before the twentieth century, woman legally as well as practically lacked all human rights. She had rights neither equal to those of man nor the same as his. In the sudden development of the movement that sprang up in less than one century in the name of woman and for woman, she acquired rights almost the same as those of man. However, considering her natural build and her physical and spiritual needs, she never acquired rights equal to those of man. For if woman wishes to acquire rights equal to the rights of man and happiness equal to the happiness of man, the only way to get that end is for her to forget about an identicalness of rights with man and have faith in rights suitable for herself. Only in this way can unity and real sincerity between man and woman be achieved, and only then will woman obtain happiness equal to or better than man's. Man then, out of sincerity and without any derogatory thoughts, will be ready to concede to her equal and at times better rights than his own.

Similarly, I am not at all claiming that the rights that have in practice been the lot of women in our seemingly Islamic society are equal in value to the rights that men have had. I have many times said that it is essential to hold a thorough inquiry into the plight of women, and that many rights that have been given to women by Islam and have in practice been ignored should be restored to them; but not that we should blindly follow and imitate the ways of the West, which have brought thousands of misfortunes for them and give a pretty name to an erroneous principle and thus encumber women who already have misfortunes of the Eastern type with misfortunes of the Western type as well. Our point of view is that dissimilarity in the rights of man and woman should be observed to whatever extent nature has differently molded and created them. This is in better accord with justice and with natural rights; and will both secure goodwill in the family and result in the better development of society.

It must be completely understood that we claim that justice and the natural and human rights of man and woman call for dissimilarity in certain rights. Thus, our discussion has a completely philosophical orientation: it is linked to the philosophy of rights and linked with a principle that is called the principle of justice, which is one of the vital pillars of Islamic theology and jurisprudence. The principle of justice is the same fundamental principle that brought into existence the rule of the harmony of reason and religious law in Islam. It means that according to Islamic jurisprudence—or at least Shi'ite jurisprudence—if it can be established that justice demands that a particular precept should be such-and-such and not something else, then if it is something else it will be an iniquity and against justice; thus, we are obliged to say that the ruling of religious law is what reason and justice tell us it should be. For Islamic religious law, according to the fundamental principle that it has itself taught, can never leave the axis of justice and intrinsic, natural rights.

By expounding and elucidating the underlying meaning of justice, Islamic scholars have laid upon it the foundation of the philosophy of rights. As a result of the occurrence of regrettable historical events, they could not continue the work they had started. At any rate, preoccupation with the idea of human rights and the principle of justice as being something essential, in accordance with the order of things and beyond conventional law, was first of all propounded and put forward by the Muslims. They laid the foundation of the rights that are both natural and required by intellectual considerations.

However, it turned out that Islamic scholars could not carry on that work, and, after a gap of about eight centuries, European thinkers and philosophers continued it, and took upon themselves the credit for that task. On the one hand, they worked out social, political, and economic philosophies and, on the other hand, they informed individuals, societies, and nations and explained to them the value of life and their rights as human beings. They started movements, instigated revolutions, and changed the face of the world.

In my opinion, besides historical reasons, psychological and geographic reasons also played their part in creating this situation whereby the Islamic East did not follow up these rights that are intellectually indispensible and whose foundations they had laid. This is one of the differences in mentality between the East and the West, that the East has a tendency toward ethical thinking, whereas the West is inclined toward the idea of rights. The East is under the spell of morality, and the West is in love with rights. The easterner by virtue of his Eastern nature conceives of his humanity as consisting of behaving with kindness and toleration, in being friendly toward his fellow men, and in conducting himself with generosity toward them. On the other hand, a westerner takes pride in the realization of his rights, and in safeguarding them, and will not allow anybody to intrude upon the sacred territory of his rights.

Humanity needs ethics as well as rights. It is linked to rights as well as to morals, and neither of the two, rights or morals, is in itself the criterion of humanity.

The sacred religion of Islam has the great privilege of having approved both rights and ethics. In Islam, as was mentioned before, sincerity and right action in the moral sense is considered a virtue; and knowledge of rights and defending them is also considered a virtue and to be human. This matter has details that cannot be gone into here.

However, the particular mentality of the East set to work. In spite of the fact that in the beginning the concept of rights and the insistence on morality had both been acquired from Islam, the East gradually let go of rights and focused its attention on morals.

Our point is that the problem with which we are at present confronted is a problem of rights, a philosophical and intellectual problem, a problem based on arguments and reasoning. It is closely connected with reality of justice and the nature of rights. Justice and rights were in existence before any laws were passed in the world, so the enacting of a law cannot change the reality of justice and the human rights of mankind.

Montesquieu said: "Before man created laws there seem to have been relations founded on law and upon justice between creatures. The existence of these relations itself was the cause of the creation of laws. If we say that apart from the actual first laws, consisting of orders and prohibitions, nothing else just or unjust exists, it is as if we say that before man drew a circle, the radii of that circle were not all equal."

Herbert Spencer said: "Justice is associated, not with the sentiments, but with something else which is the natural rights of individuals. For justice to have external reality it is necessary to have regard for rights and innate differences."

The European philosophers who upheld, and still do hold this view, are numerous. The manifestos and proclamations that were drawn up, and the material that was incorporated under the heading of Human Rights, have as their source this very theory of natural rights. In other words, it was the theory of natural and innate rights that reappeared in the form of the Proclamation of Human Rights.

Once again, what Montesquieu, Spencer, and others have said concerning justice is, as we know, the very same thing that Islamic theologians have said concerning the inborn intellectual capacity to determine "right" and "wrong" and the real meanings of justice. Among Islamic scholars, there were some individuals who refused to accept the idea of instinctive rights and considered justice as something conventional. Among Europeans also, such a belief existed. The Englishman Hobbes refused to accept justice as having real existence.

## THE DECLARATION OF HUMAN RIGHTS
### IS PHILOSOPHY AND NOT LAW

The absurd thing is that they say that the text of the Declaration of Human Rights has been approved by the two Houses (of the Iranian Parliament), and, as the equality of rights for men and women is included in the text of the declaration, so, under the law approved by the two Houses, men and women should have equal rights—as if the text of the Declaration of Human Rights is something that is within the competence of the two Houses to approve of or reject. The contents of the Declaration of Human Rights is not the kind of thing that can be put up for the legislative assemblies of countries to approve of or reject.

The Declaration of Human Rights deals with the innate undeniable and unrelinquishable rights of mankind. It refers to rights that, as the declaration claimed, are prerequisites of man's humanity, and that the hand of the Almighty Creator established for them. In other words, the Source and Power that provided men with intellect, volition, and human dignity also bestowed upon man, as the declaration claims, human rights.

Human beings cannot make the contents of the Declaration of Human Rights law for themselves or cancel or depart from those rights on their own. Then what is the sense in saying that it had been approved by the two Houses and the legislative power?

The Declaration of Human Rights is philosophy and not law. It should be presented to the philosophers for their approbation and not for the approval of members of parliaments. The two legislative Houses cannot determine philosophy and logic for people by taking a vote. If legislative work is to proceed like this, then they should take Einstein's theory of relativity to Parliament and present it to the members to have it approved by them. The hypothesis that there is life on other planets should also be sent for their approval. The laws of nature cannot be approved or rejected just like conventional laws. It is as if we were to say that both the Houses of Parliament have passed an act saying that if we graft a pear onto an apple, the graft will be successful; but that if it is grafted onto a mulberry it will not.

If such a declaration is issued on behalf of a group of persons who are themselves thinkers and philosophers, the nations should entrust it to the hands of their philosophers and campaigners for rights. If in the opinion of the philosophers and thinkers of that particular community the matter can be confirmed, then it is the duty of all the members of that community to consider what they say as a truth above law. It is binding upon the legislative power also not to enact any law against what they say.

As for the other nations, they are not obliged to accept any declaration until it has been established and discovered in their eyes that such rights exist in the same state in nature. Besides this, these questions are not experimental matters that require equipment, laboratories, and so forth that Europeans have but others do not. It is not a question of breaking the atom, the secret of which and the necessary equipment for which are with a limited number of persons; it is philosophy and logic, and for this the tools are the brain, the intellect, and the power of reasoning.

Even if other nations are obliged to follow others in questions of philosophy and logic, because they do not consider themselves competent in philosophical thinking, we Iranians should not think like that. In the past, we reached a high standard of ability and showed our worth in philosophic and logical investigations. Why should we follow others in their solutions to philosophic problems?

It is strange that Islamic thinkers gave so much importance to the question of justice and the essential rights of man when it arose that, without any hesitation, in accordance with the law of the harmony between reason and Islamic law, they used to say that the law of Islam was indeed this. That is to say they did not see the necessity of ancillary corroboration by an Islamic law. Today we have been reduced to the level where we seek confirmation for these matters in approval by members of Parliament.

## Philosophy Cannot Be Proved by Questionnaires

More ludicrous than this is that when we want to make a study regarding the human rights of women, we refer the matter to young boys and girls, print questionnaires, and try to find out by the way in which they are filled in what human rights are and whether the human rights of women and men are the same or different.

Anyhow, we are seeking to make a study in a scientific and philosophic manner about the human rights of women on the basis of intrinsic human rights, and we want to see whether those same principles which require that human beings, as a general rule, have a series of natural and God-given rights also affirm that women and men should have the same kind of rights or not. So, I request the scholars, thinkers, and jurists of this country, who are the only persons who really matter and should set forth their opinions in such matters as this, to look into our arguments critically. I would be highly obliged if they gave their opinions together with their reasons for or against what I have written.

In order to study this point, it is necessary that we should firstly look at the basis and the roots of human rights, and then consider specifically the rights of men and women.

It would not be out of place to briefly refer in the first place to the movements in the present age to do with rights that culminated in the call for equality of rights for men and women.

## A Glance at the History of Women's Rights in Europe

In Europe, from the seventeenth century onward, voices began to be raised in the name of human rights. Writers and thinkers of the seventeenth and eighteenth centuries propagated their thoughts in respect of the natural, inherent, and undeniable rights of man with wonderful perseverance. Jean-Jacques Rousseau, Voltaire, and Montesquieu belong to this group of thinkers and writers. The first practical result of the propagation of the ideas of the supporters of natural human rights occurred when in England a protracted struggle took place between the rulers and the ruled. In 1688 the people succeeded in arguing for some of their social and political rights according to a manifesto of rights, and had them restored.

Another practical result of the propagation of these ideas was manifested in the War of Independence of America against England. Thirteen British colonies in North America, because of the strains and difficulties imposed upon them, rose in disobedience and rebellion and at last gained their independence.

In the year 1776 a Congress was formed in Philadelphia that declared its complete independence and published a document to that effect. In the introduction to that document they wrote, "that all men are created equal, that they are endowed by their Creator with certain unalienable Rights, that among these are Life, Liberty and the pursuit of Happiness. That to secure these rights, Governments are instituted among Men, deriving their just powers from the consent of the governed."

However, what is well known in the world under the name of the Declaration of Human Rights is that document which was issued after the Great French Revolution. This declaration consists of a series of general principles that are prefixed to the French Constitution, and it is considered an inseparable part of it. This proclamation consists of an introduction and seventeen clauses. The first section states that "Men are born, and always continue, free and equal in respect of their rights."

In the nineteenth century new changes and new thoughts occurred in the field of economics, sociology, and politics that culminated in the advent of socialism and the resultant requirement of the allocation of a share of profits to the working class, and the transfer of government from the hands of the capitalists to the workers.

Till the early part of the twentieth century, all the controversies concerning human rights were connected entirely with the rights of the people before their governments, or with rights of the proletariat and the working class before the employers.

It was in the twentieth century for the first time that the question of the rights of woman before man came to the fore. Britain, which is considered to be the oldest democratic country, acknowledged equal rights for men and women only in the beginning of the twentieth century. The United States of America, in spite of its generally admitting the rights of all human beings in the eighteenth century in its Declaration of Independence, passed the act giving equal political rights to men and women in the year 1920 and France also approved this matter in the twentieth century.

Anyhow, in the twentieth century, many groups all over the world favored a profound change in the relations of men and women concerning their rights and duties. According to these people, the change and transformation in the relations of peoples with their governments, and in the relations of the labor class and the proletariat with the employers and the capitalists did not suffice for social justice, so long as the relations of rights of men and women were not reformed.

Accordingly, a Universal Declaration of Human Rights was issued for the first time after the Second World War in 1948 on behalf of the United Nations Organization. In its introduction it was stipulated:

> Whereas the people of the United Nations have once again proclaimed their belief in human rights and the status and worth of an individual human being and equality of the rights of men and women. . . .

The crisis of changes due to mechanization in the nineteenth and the twentieth century and the eventual unfortunate condition of craftsmen, especially women, exaggerated the situation all the more, demanding that the matter of the rights of women should be especially attended to. In his *Nouvelle histoire universelle* (vol. 4, p. 387), Albert Malet writes: "Because the State no longer interfered in any way between the employers and the workers, except to forbid the latter to group together and strike, the employers were able to enforce a real 'economic despotism.' . . . In France, in 1840, in the Ronen region, cotton mill workers labored up to 16–17 hours a day. . . . The exploitation for work of women and children was particularly obnoxious . . . mortality in the working districts was horrifying."

This is a short and cursory history of the human rights movement in Europe. As we know, all the matters contained in the Declarations of Human Rights, which have novelty for the Europeans, were anticipated fourteen centuries ago in Islam. Some Arab and Iranian scholars have compared (the position of) Islam with these declarations in their books. Of course, there are differences in some parts between what the declarations say and what Islam has said, and this is itself an absorbing and interesting matter. One of these differences is the problem of the rights of men and women, in which Islam approves of equality, but does not agree with identicalness, uniformity, and exact similarity.

## THE DIGNITY AND THE RIGHTS OF HUMAN BEINGS

Whereas recognition of the inherent dignity and of the equal and inalienable rights of all members of the human family is the foundation of freedom, justice and peace in the world,

Whereas disregard and contempt for human rights have resulted in barbarous acts which have outraged the conscience of mankind, and the advent of a world in which human beings shall enjoy freedom of speech and belief and freedom from fear and want has been proclaimed as the highest aspiration of the common people,

Whereas it is essential, if man is not to be compelled to have recourse, as a last resort, to rebellion against tyranny and oppression, that human rights should be protected by the rule of law,

Whereas it is essential to promote the development of friendly relations between nations,

Whereas the people of the United Nations have in the Charter reaffirmed their faith in fundamental human rights, in the dignity and worth of the human person and in the equal rights of men and women and have determined to promote social progress and better standards of life in larger freedom,

Now, therefore, the General Assembly proclaims:

This universal Declaration of Human Rights as a common standard of achievement for all peoples and all nations, to the end that every individual and every organ of society, keeping this Declaration constantly in mind, shall strive by teaching and education to promote respect for these rights and freedoms and by progressive measures, national and international, to secure their universal and effective recognition and observance, both among the peoples of Member States themselves and among the peoples of territories under their jurisdiction.

The splendid sentences above form the preamble to the Universal Declaration of Human Rights. This is the preamble to the charter of which it has been said that it is "the greatest blessing ever to come to the lot of the world of humanity in support of human rights unto this day."

Every sentence and every part of it is numbered and, as I pointed out in the preceding article, is derived from the ideas of several centuries of world philosophers who sought freedom and recognized human rights.

### Important Points in the Preamble to the Declaration of Human Rights

This declaration was drawn up in thirty sections. We shall ignore the fact that some matters are repeated in some of the articles or at least that the mention of certain matter in one section makes another section redundant, and that some of the articles of the declaration could have been divided up into several smaller articles.

The important points of the preamble that should be noted are:

1. All human beings benefit from a single kind of dignity, honor, and inherent, inalienable rights.

2. Dignity, honor, and inherent human rights are universal and include all human individuals with no discrimination or distinction, white and black, tall and short, woman and man—all alike share in this benefit. Just as in a family, an individual member cannot claim to be of a nobler and higher origin than the other members of the family, so, in the same way, all human individuals are the members of a large family and organs of one body and are the same in their dignity. No one can consider himself to be of nobler birth than any other individual.

3. The basis of freedom, peace, and justice is that all individuals, . from the depth of their conscience, have belief and faith in the reality of the equal dignity and inherent honor of all human beings.

This Declaration wants to claim that it has discovered that the source of all the troubles that individual human beings create for each other, and the basic cause of the breaking out of wars, of the atrocities, transgressions, and acts of savagery that individuals and nations inflict on one another, is the nonrecognition of the dignity and inherent honor of human beings. This nonrecognition by one group compels the opposing group to explode, and it is thus that peace and security is endangered.

4. The highest aspiration that everyone must strive to attain is the advent of a world where freedom of conviction, security, and material prosperity are perfectly attained. Suppression of beliefs, fear, and poverty should be uprooted. The thirty articles of the declaration were drawn up to attain this ideal.

5. Belief in the inherent dignity of human beings, and regard for their undeniable and inalienable rights should be gradually created by teaching and education in all individuals.


### The Dignity and Respect of Man

Because the Declaration of Human Rights is based on the honor, freedom, and equality of human beings and was created in order to restore human rights, it should be met with due honor and respect by every conscientious person. We people of the East have been pleading in favor of the worth, position, and honor of the human being for a long time; as I mentioned in the preceding article, human beings as such, together with their rights, freedom, and equality are given the utmost attention, respect, and importance. Those who wrote and drew up this declaration, and likewise the philosophers from whom the writers of this declaration derived, in fact, their inspiration, deserve our tribute and regards. Nevertheless, because this declaration is a philosophical matter and is drawn up by human beings and not by angels, and because it is the conclusion of a group of human individuals, every thinker has the right to scrutinize it critically and, if he should find certain weak points in it, to point them out.

This declaration is not free from weak points; however, we shall not refer here to the weak points, preferring as we do, to refer to the strong points only.

The basis of this declaration is the "inherent dignity" of the human being. According to this declaration, a human being derives his claim to a series of rights and freedoms on the basis of a general dignity and honor that is special to him. Other animals do not have and enjoy these rights and freedoms, because they lack that dignity and honor. This is the strong point of this declaration.

## THE DECLINE AND FALL OF THE HUMAN BEING IN WESTERN PHILOSOPHY

Here, once again, we come across an old problem in philosophy: the value and worth of the human being, the position and dignity of the human being in comparison with all other creatures. What, we should ask, is that innate, inherent dignity of the human being that distinguishes him from a horse, a cow, a sheep, or a pigeon?

Here it is that a clear contradiction is observed between the basis of the Declaration of Human Rights, on the one hand, and the value and worth of humanity in Western philosophy, on the other.

In Western philosophy, mankind has for long been without worth and value. The previous observations that were made concerning human beings and their distinguished position had their source and origin entirely in the East. Today, in most Western philosophical systems, these observations are belittled and ridiculed.

A human being, in the eyes of the West, has been degraded to the level of a machine. His spirit and nobility is denied. Belief in a final cause and a plan or design for nature is considered a reactionary idea.

In the West, the belief in mankind being the noblest of creatures could not last for long, for the Western belief was based on the belief that all other creatures were dependent on and under the domination of human beings, and this derived from the ancient Ptolemaic theory of the earth and the heavens that the earth was the center and all the heavenly bodies revolved around it. Thus, when this belief was abandoned, there were no grounds left for considering mankind as the noblest of creatures. In the eyes of the West, all such thoughts were mere self-aggrandizements to which human beings were the victims in the past. A human being today is courteous, obliging, and modest and considers himself to be like other objects, nothing more than a handful of dust. From dust he comes and to dust he shall return, and it is here that he will finally come to an end.

A Westerner, in his humility, does not consider the soul to be an independent form of human existence and does not consider it to have the capacity of actual and real existence. He does not believe in there being any difference between himself and a plant or an animal in this respect. A westerner does not consider there to be any difference between the thought and actions of the soul and the heat generated from coal, as far as its entity and essence are concerned. He considers all of them to be manifestations of matter and energy. In the eyes of the West, the field of life for all living beings, including mankind, is the bloody battlefield that gave birth to them. The actual, ultimate controller of the life of living beings, including mankind, is the basic struggle for survival. Man always struggles to save himself in this battle. Justice, virtue, cooperation, benevolence, and all other moral and human values are all products of this fundamental struggle for existence. Man has constructed these concepts in order to make his own position secure.

According to some influential Western philosophers, a human being is a machine, under the fundamental control of nothing but financial interests. Religion, morals, philosophy, science, literature, and all the arts are all built on the foundation of the manner of production, sharing, and distribution of wealth. All these things are manifestations of the economic aspects of man's life.

But no, this is all too glorified for man. The real motivating and stimulating factors in all human actions are innate sexual drives. Morals, philosophy, science, religion, and art, all manifestations of humanity, are melted down and reshaped as the action of the sexuality of man's being.

What is difficult to understand is that if we decide that we should deny the purposefulness of creation and believe that nature quite blindly proceeds on its own course; if the only law that guarantees the life of the various species of living creatures is the struggle for survival, the selection of the fittest, and nothing but chance; if the survival and existence of a human being is the product of accidental change, devoid of any purpose, merely a chain of unnatural acts over a few million years, which his forefathers permitted with other species, and which resulted in him having the form he has today; if it is decided to believe that man is an example of the machines that he now manufactures himself with his own hand; if it is decided that belief in the spirit, its fundamentality and its permanence is, as it is considered to be, a sort of egotism or self-conceit, or an exaggeration by man about himself; if the real activating and stimulating factors in all human actions are economic or sexual drives or the desire for superiority; if ideas of right or wrong are wholly relative; and if reference to natural, inward inspiration is nonsense; if a human being is a species that is slave to his sensualities and passions and never lowers his head except by force; if . . . and so on, then how can it be possible for us to talk about the dignity and honor of man, his inalienable rights, and his noble individuality and make that the basis of all our activities?

## THE WEST IS INVOLVED IN A BASIC CONTRADICTION ABOUT MAN

In Western philosophy, the personal dignity of mankind had been destroyed as far as possible, and his position totally debased. Concerning the creation of man and the causes that gave him existence, concerning the purpose of Creation for him and the structure and warp and woof of his existence and being, and concerning the motivation and stimulation for his activity, his conscience and moral sense, the Western world has lowered him to the degree we have already pointed out. With this background, the West issues a great declaration about the worthiness and dignity of mankind, his inherent honor and nobility, his sacred and inalienable rights and invites all human individuals to believe in that lofty declaration.

For those in the West, they should firstly have revised the explanations and expositions they made concerning man, and then they could have issued a declaration for the sacred and inherent rights of human beings.

I admit that not all Western philosophers have presented man in the previously mentioned way. A large number of them have presented man almost in the same way as the East has done. My viewpoint concerns the way of thinking that exists among the majority of people in the West and is now influencing people all over the world.

The Declaration of Human Rights ought to have been issued by those who consider human beings of a higher rank than a material, mechanical compound. It would have been worthy of someone who did not consider the drives and motivations of the activities of human beings to depend exclusively upon animal and selfish motives: someone who believed in human nature. The Declaration of Human Rights should have been issued by the East, which believes that "I am setting on the earth a vicegerent" (Q 2:30) and perceives in man a sign of the manifestation of Divinity. He who goes after human rights should be someone who believes that man is built with the intention of traveling toward a destination of: "O Man! Thou art striving unto thy Lord with a striving, and thou shalt encounter Him" (Q 84:6).

The Declaration of Human Rights befits those systems of philosophy which agree with the Qur'anic verse: "By the soul, that which shaped it and inspired it to lewdness and god-fearing!" (Q 91:7–8) and believe that a human being is naturally disposed toward virtue.

The Declaration of Human Rights should have been issued by those who are optimistic about the nature of man according to: "We indeed created man in the fairest stature" (Q 95:4) and consider man to have the most harmonious and the most perfect structure.

If we look at the West's way of thinking in its explanations and presentations of man, the Declaration of Human Rights does not befit the West, because it is this way that the West uses in practice to deal with human beings—that is to say, doing away with all human sentiments, making fun of all human distinctions, maintaining the priority of capital for man, the primacy of money, worshiping the machine, deeming wealth supreme, exploiting man, and giving capital unlimited power. If, by chance, a certain millionaire should happen to bequeath his wealth to his dear dog, that dog would be regarded as being more honorable than man. Human beings would attend on the wealthy dog like butlers, clerks, and office hands and stand before it respectfully with folded hands.

## The West Has Forgotten Both Itself and Its God

The important problem of human society today is that man has forgotten what the Qur'an calls his "self" and also his God. The important thing is that he has debased himself. He has totally neglected to look inside himself, to listen to his inner self and conscience, and he has entirely focused his attention on material and solid things. He considers the aim of life to be nothing but to enjoy material things, and he knows nothing except that. He considers creation as if it were without purpose. He denies his own self and has forsaken his soul. Most of the misfortunes of human beings result from these misconceptions, and it may be feared that the day is not far off when this way of thought will be universal and will suddenly destroy humanity. This angle of viewing human beings is the cause of the fact that, as civilization spreads and develops, the civilized person slowly degenerates. This way of thinking about human beings has turned out to be the cause of the fact that man in his true meaning is to be found only in the past. The great machine of civilization has the capacity to manufacture every grand and first-class thing except man.

# Chapter 11

# ZAYNAB AL-GHAZALI
## 1917–2005

IF HASAN AL-BANNA is the father of the contemporary Islamist movement, Zaynab al-Ghazali is perhaps best characterized as its largely unsung mother.[1] Ghazali's life and work have received far less scholarly and popular attention than such influential Egyptian Muslim Brothers as Hasan al-Banna and Sayyid Qutb, yet she outlasted both by many decades to become a pioneering da'iya dedicated to bringing Muslims to Islam through education, exhortation, and example.[2] The legacy Ghazali bequeaths to her "daughters" is, however, far more complex and equivocal than the path of charismatic leadership Banna charted for the men who came after him. On the one hand, her own career bespeaks a fierce resistance to conventional norms of domesticity. On the other hand, many of her interviews, books, articles, and letters embrace a gender ideology that largely defines women as wives, mothers, and "builders of men" ("Ya Sayyidati" in al-Hashimi 1990, 118), and symbolically transforms them from individual agents into vessels of Islamic virtue or conduits for moral corruption. In this way, Ghazali's life and work at once subvert and ratify Islamist constraints on Muslim women's visibility and political participation, enabling her to step through a door that other Muslim women would later throw wide open.

Ghazali was born in 1917 in a village in the Nile Delta to a respected family that claimed descent from the second Muslim caliph, 'Umar ibn al-Khattab. By her own account, Ghazali's father, a cotton merchant, shaykh,

Unlike the other chapters in this volume, we have retained the endnotes written by Valerie Hoffman, the author and translator of this text selection, reproduced here as notes 8–27.

[1]Ghazali repeatedly refers to the Ikhwan (the Brothers) and to their female relations as her sons and daughters. In her memoirs, she has them all refer to her as "mother" (Ghazali 1978), and an admiring obituary of Ghazali calls her "the mother of men" (Altayeb 2005).

[2]In contrast to the voluminous literature on Banna and Qutb, for example, there are few biographies of Ghazali in Arabic and no complete history of her organization in English, French, or Arabic (Mahmood 2005). With the exception of Ghazali's memoirs, moreover, much of her writing is still only available in Arabic, whereas most of Qutb's work, including his multivolume tafsir (Qur'anic commentary), is now translated into many different languages. As Mahmood (2005, 67, 70–71, n. 75) notes, even women active in the contemporary Egyptian da'wa movement tend not to invoke her when interviewed. Her influence may be indirect, however: as Cooke (2001, 104) argues, "women in Islamist groups everywhere are now using her language of accommodation and resistance with no sense of contradiction."

and graduate of al-Azhar, encouraged his daughter to model her ambitions on the virtuous female companions of the Prophet, particularly those who were warriors in the cause of Islam (Hoffman 1985). Despite her ambitions, Ghazali's formal education in Islam ended in secondary school, where she studied hadith, preaching, and Qur'anic exegesis. Like Banna and Qutb, then, she was largely an autodidact in the religious tradition to which she devoted her life: her knowledge of the Islamic sciences came from her father, occasional lectures at the University of al-Azhar (women would not be permitted to formally enroll until the 1960s) and, most importantly, the informal study groups and seminars she conducted throughout her long life.

At sixteen, Ghazali joined Huda Sha'arawi's Egyptian Feminist Union, but left within a year. She would later characterize the EFU's approach to women's liberation as a deeply misguided failure to recognize that, as all rights derive from Islam, there is no "woman question" distinct from the emancipation of humanity, which is possible only through the restoration of Islamic law as sole sovereign.[3] While Ghazali rejected the EFU's politics, she took with her the commitment to women's activism and associational life it exemplified. At the age of eighteen, Ghazali founded Jama'at al-Sayyidat al-Muslimat (the Muslim Women's Association, or MWA), one of a "flurry of charitable organizations" to appear in Egypt from the late nineteenth to early twentieth century (Baron 1994, 169).

From its inception, the MWA was devoted to calling women to Islam, educating them in the Islamic tradition, and training them in the practice of da'wa; it would also publish its own magazine, run an orphanage, and organize a variety of social welfare activities such as aiding orphans and the poor. The activities of the MWA quickly drew the attention of Banna, who had founded the Egyptian Society of Muslim Brothers in 1928 and built it into a complex and highly disciplined Islamist organization within two decades. An astute political organizer, Banna envisioned chapters of "Muslim Sisters" throughout Egypt that would draw on a largely untapped resource for the Brotherhood. In Ghazali, Banna found a like-minded activist with cadres of women already at her disposal; he promptly asked her to incorporate the MWA into the Brotherhood and assume leadership of the Muslim Sisters. Ghazali was anxious to retain the independence of her new organization, however, and declined (Ghazali 1978; Cooke 1994, 2; Shehadeh 2003, 122). Well known for a style of leadership that brooked little dissent, Banna did not take her refusal well.

---

[3]Neither the EFU nor most of the other Egyptian women's organizations that proliferated in the late nineteenth and early twentieth centuries understood women's liberation as opposed to religion or Islamic belief. When it came to discussions of "the rights of women" (*huquq al-mar-a*), both Egyptian modernists and Islamists "argued within the context of Islam, with the intention of revitalizing and strengthening religion, and both condemned certain Western influences and excesses" (Baron 1994, 111).

Ghazali would later revisit this decision, but it was a radical change in the political climate, rather than Banna's displeasure, that prompted her to reverse course. Relations between the Egyptian state and the Brotherhood had become progressively antagonistic and finally violent by the late 1940s, culminating in a wave of arrests and the 1948 proclamation banning the Brotherhood entirely. Ghazali's organization fared only slightly better: the government issued a decree dissolving the MWA, although Ghazali challenged the decree in court and ultimately won (Sullivan and Abed-Kotob 1999, 105). It was in this context that Ghazali had finally agreed to affiliate the MWA with the Brotherhood, declaring herself Banna's humble "slave" (Ghazali 1978) shortly before his assassination in 1949.

The Egyptian Revolution of 1952 ushered in a brief period of comity between Islamists and the new regime, but such cooperation came to an abrupt halt in 1954, when a Muslim Brother allegedly attempted to assassinate President Gamal 'Abd al-Nasser. Relations between the regime and the Brotherhood rapidly deteriorated, culminating in the formal dissolution of the organization and the incarceration or execution of virtually all of its organizational and ideological leadership. Already involved in providing food, medical care, and other support to the Brothers and their families, Ghazali stepped in to help reconstitute the organization, serving as liaison among dispersed members and sympathizers, and conducting seminars on Islam with activists in her home (Kepel 1985, 29–30).

Despite her increasing prominence in the movement, Ghazali's memoirs make no mention of the Brotherhood's often violent "secret apparatus" (R. Mitchell 1993), and she has portrayed her activities at the time as pacific in nature, educational in purpose, and restrained in tone. Indeed, in her memoirs, she insists that Islam repudiates torture and violence and, in a 1981 interview with a Muslim Brother, explicitly argues that weapons are the instruments of Islam's enemies, while the tools of the coming Islamic revolution are exhortation and education.[4] Nasser evidently thought otherwise. In 1964 Ghazali survived an assassination attempt; in the same year, the Muslim Ladies Association was banned; and in 1965 she was accused of complicity in a Brotherhood conspiracy to overthrow the regime. Ghazali was sentenced to twenty-five years' hard labor and imprisoned for six brutal years, first in Liman Tura jail, then in Qanatir, a women's prison. She was ultimately released in 1971 under an amnesty granted by President Anwar al-Sadat, and continued her work as a da'iya until her death in 2005 at the age of 88.

An active Islamist for more than seven decades, Ghazali published innumerable articles, granted many interviews, corresponded extensively with young Muslims seeking guidance (Ghazali 1996a, 1996b), and pro-

---

[4]Ghazali 1978, 144, 185; Abdul Mohsen 1981. At the same time, however, Ghazali endorses Qutb's prediction that Islam will destroy the superpowers.

duced both a memoir (Ghazali 1978) and a Qur'anic commentary (Ghazali 1994). She greatly admired the work of Sayyid Qutb—incarcerated in the same prison in the 1960s—whom she describes as a "mujahid in the path of Allah . . . leader, reformer, and Islamic writer, indeed, among the greatest Islamic writers in the heritage of the Prophet Muhammad" (Ghazali 1978, 90). Her commitment to social welfare and preaching, however, along with her program of gradual reform through education, bear the unmistakable imprint of Banna's reformist vision for the sociomoral reconstruction of Egypt. And just as Banna saw himself in relation to his followers as father, political leader, murshid (religious teacher), and shaykh all at once, Ghazali envisioned herself as a murshida who, like a Sufi saint, rears children that are "spiritual protégés" rather than biological offspring (Cooke 1994, 18).

Yet, unlike both Qutb and Banna, Ghazali's self-conceptualization, political commitments, and strategic choices articulate a profound tension between her own aspirations and prevailing norms regarding a Muslim woman's proper behavior and role. Banna, for example, viewed social welfare projects as integral to Brotherhood recruitment and mobilization (Banna 1950, 20, 21). For Ghazali's organization, by contrast, the emphasis on education and charity helped legitimize their very political visibility by portraying such work as an extension of women's primary duties as wives, mothers, and "builders of men" (Baron 1994, 171–75; al-Hashimi 1990, 118). In this, Ghazali and the MWA were far from alone. Nationalist rhetoric in early twentieth-century Egypt was suffused with "kinship idioms" designed to transcend various ethnic and regional divisions. For Egyptian women, such idioms performed a particular legitimizing function: as "Mothers of the Nation," for example, nationalist women could claim the moral and "maternal authority to engage more openly in society and politics" (Baron 2005, 36).

Given this context, it is unsurprising that Ghazali couches her aspirations in the language of domesticity and casts her life in the image of a selfless, giving mother. By her own account, her yearning to write her memoirs is realized only by way of encouragement from her "sons and brothers" whose suffering she seeks to memorialize.[5] She later described even her ascent to the leadership of the Brotherhood as prompted by the "cries of the orphans who lost their fathers to torture, and the tears of the women who were widowed and whose husbands were behind prison bars, and the old fathers and mothers who lost their heart's delight."

---

[5]Ghazali 1978. Sayyida Salme, a nineteenth-century Arabian princess, similarly justifies her own memoirs as just some "sketches of my life" produced only "at the urgent request of many," and penned for the sake of "the dear children" (Salme 1993, 144). Such gestures are evocative of what Sandra Gilbert and Susan Gubar have called an anxiety of authorship among women, "an anxiety built from complex and often only barely conscious fears of that authority which seems to the female artist to be by definition inappropriate to her sex" (Gilbert and Gubar 1979, 51).

Such rhetoric points to a conceptualization of women's nature and purpose that Ghazali spells out with great vehemence in an array of articles, interviews, and polemics published in a variety of outlets, including the journal of the MWA, the Brotherhood's *al-Da'wa*, and the Islamist magazine *Liwa al-Islam*. Ghazali's starting premise is that Muslim men and women are equal in belief but perform fundamentally different and complementary functions in society. While men are naturally made to rule in both the public and private domain, a woman's "first, holy, and most important mission in life [is] . . . to be a mother and a wife," as "marriage is a sure sunna in Islam . . . instituted to reproduce children and to establish the family." As such functions are rooted in an inescapable human nature expressive of divine will, a woman's inability or unwillingness to perform her duties signals a disobedience to God and man requiring correction and chastening. Indeed, Ghazali's commentary on Qur'an 4:34 affirms the authority of men over women—although she defines this relation as one of "responsibility" rather than control—and goes on to anatomize the kinds of punishments a husband may impose upon his recalcitrant wife, calibrated to the severity of her *nushuz* (ill behavior).[6] "The woman seeking a divorce from her husband commits an offense deserving of punishment," Ghazali writes elsewhere, "for is there anything more repulsive than a woman destroying her marriage and her motherhood?" (Ghazali 1989a, 48).

For Ghazali, then, the Western insistence on complete equality between genders liberates women only from moral constraint, while enslaving them to capitalist exploitation and animalistic sexual desire, either their own or that of men. Importantly, it is not only the fate of particular women but the future of a civilization that hangs in the balance, for the family is both the first school of moral education and the incubator of sons destined to build the Islamic nation. The impotence and moral bankruptcy currently plaguing Islamic civilization thus demonstrate how effectively Western conceptions of ersatz gender equality have lured Muslim women into betraying their domestic vocation (Ghazali in al-Hashimi 1990, 105–12). In an article for *al-Da'wa* titled "To You: My Lady!" for example, Ghazali places the blame squarely on women's shoulders:

> Yes, my lady, you are responsible for our subjection to non-Muslims who are instigators of unbelief, licentiousness, and savagery . . . you have taken to showy adornment and rebellion against our religion and all of our inheritances. Yes, my lady, you are responsible for the decline of Islamic civilization, its supremacy and what it gives to life,

[6] Ghazali 1994, 1:297–98. Qur'an 4:34: "Husbands should take good care of their wives, with [the bounties] God has given to some more than others and with what they spend out of their own money. Righteous wives are devout and guard what God would have them guard in their husbands' absence. If you fear high-handedness from your wives, remind them [of the teachings of God], then ignore them when you go to bed, then hit them. If they obey you, you have no right to act against them: God is most high and great."

the gift that Allah—praise Him—bestowed upon the Islamic community. (Ghazali in al-Hashimi 1990, 115)

Ghazali's own domestic arrangements, however, appear to challenge such gender norms and the sexual division of labor they largely presuppose and reinforce. She has, for instance, described the fact that she had no biological children as a "great blessing" (Hoffman 1995, 216); divorced her first husband when he disapproved of her Islamist activities; stipulated to her second husband that she would leave him if married life interfered with her commitment to da'wa; and forbade him to ask any questions about her work while requiring him to assist her in it. Some have characterized the relationship between Ghazali's arguments and practices as at best inconsistent, a classic instance of Gramscian contradictory consciousness (Cooke 1994, 18; L. Ahmed 1992, 199–200; Gramsci 1971). Others suggest that Ghazali's life and arguments fit together, if not seamlessly, at least coherently, given a moral framework in which women's responsibilities to family are second only to work *fi sabil Allah*—in the path of God (Mahmood 2005, 180–82). Both assessments are complicated by the ways in which Ghazali's views, like those of many other lifelong activists, subtly shifted over time. Correspondences after her release from prison in particular evince nuances and ambivalences often absent from her earlier, more polemical publications, revealing moments in which, for example, she emphasizes a woman's agency in determining the precise balance between the duties of wife and mother and participation in jihad, or suggests that a woman has a measure of choice in determining whether she wishes to marry or to work (Ghazali, quoted in Karam 1998, 215; Helmore 1985).

Ghazali's tangled negotiations among Islamist political commitments, prevailing gender norms and her own ambitions are particularly clear in her memoirs, *Ayyam min hayati* (*Days of My Life*, first published in 1972). More reflexive hagiography than autobiography, *Days of My Life* is an act of self-creation designed to introduce readers to a *murshida* (female guide or teacher—the only title Banna used) and *mujahida* (fem.—one who struggles) whose wisdom, endurance, and suffering are unparalleled. This is accomplished by assembling her experiences into a narrative of uncompromising courage punctuated by several features and themes characteristic of the biographies of prominent Islamist men. There is, for example, the precocious dedication to Islam and fearless activism in the face of overwhelming evil that mark Banna's biography (she even refers to her jailors as *zabaniya*, identified in Qur'an 74:31 as the wardens of hell). There is also the detailed account of her harrowing experience in prison at the heart of the memoir; relentless cycles of interrogation torture at once establish her endurance and evoke the martyrdom of her fellow inmate, Qutb, who survived several heart-attacks in prison only to meet his death on the gallows in 1966.

Several scholars have argued that the experience of incarceration and interrogation torture has become a constitutive feature of the contemporary Islamist movement. Many of the most influential Islamists have been imprisoned, appalling physical suffering has continuously radicalized inmates, and prisons have been and continue to be fertile Islamist recruiting ground from Pakistan to America (Cooke 1995, 148; Hanafi 1982, 60–61). In fact, Islamist worldviews can in many ways be understood both as a mode of resistance to such state mechanisms of coercion and as an expression of them (T. Mitchell 1990, 195–96, 199, 207–8; see also chapter 1 in this volume). The shared endurance of incarceration, state-sanctioned torture, and accompanying experiences of impotence and humiliation have helped forge Islamist norms of masculinity in particular, norms that implicitly link the renewal of Islamic power to the reimposition of patriarchal gender relations.[7]

Ghazali locates her memoirs in an established genre of Islamist prison testimonials by deliberately appropriating features of this heretofore exclusively masculine rite of passage. Opening her memoirs with an avowal that the darkness of prisons, the blades of torture, and the vicious beatings will only increase the endurance and resolve of the faithful who practice da'wa and theorize its principles, Ghazali then unspools a narrative that establishes her insight, endurance, authority, and stature as unique among women and superior even to that of men (Ghazali 1978, 6; Cooke 2001, 95–98). She portrays herself as able to withstand greater interrogation torture than other (male) Islamist inmates. Her physical suffering inaugurates a series of mystical visions that position her as the chosen of the Prophet, peer of Muhammad's wife 'Aisha, and partner to Hasan al-Hudaybi, leader of the Muslim Brotherhood. Despite the hell she endures, moreover, she is still able to redeem one of her captors and bring him to the truth of Islam (Ghazali 1978, 87, 114–15, 52, 172–74, 169–70). When she is transferred to Qanatir, her fellow inmates again serve to bring her own stature into sharp relief, only in this instance the prisoners are women whose degradation she represents as a microcosm of the moral bankruptcy to which females have brought Muslim societies everywhere (Booth 1987, 39): "Here we were in the presence of a herd straying from the world of humanity, lost in the caverns of jahiliyya; this herd of miserable women who claim to be liberated but have instead become enslaved to their own appetites and desires" (Ghazali 1978, 193).

Here, as elsewhere, Ghazali's arguments tend to ratify a gender hierarchy embraced not only by Islamists such as Qutb and Murtaza Mutah-

[7]In her study of masculinity and interrogation violence in the Palestinian intifada, for example, Julie Peteet (2000, 120) points out that "young wives and sisters complained that their husbands and brothers returned from [Israeli] interrogation and detention with a new authoritarianism expressed in attempts to assert control over their mobility. . . . women were pressured to wear head scarves, [and] domestic violence, wives and social workers claimed, was on the rise."

hari but also by an array of Christian and Jewish religio-political thinkers intent on salvaging traditional values from what they see as the moral decadence of contemporary life (see, e.g., Riesebrodt 1990). So understood, it is perhaps unsurprising that assessments of Ghazali's political legacy have been mixed. For some, she is a feminist whose perspective "affirms women and women's subjectivity" (L. Ahmed 1992, 196–97). For others, she is an Islamist "womanist," a Muslim activist who seeks to "achieve a measure of freedom in the public domain, but always within the religious framework of a well understood and interpreted Islam" (Cooke 1995, 149). For still others, her tendency to "essentialize gender in terms of prescribed social duties" disqualifies her as an exemplar of female empowerment (Booth 2002). Such depictions may not, however, be as mutually exclusive as they initially appear; indeed, it may be precisely *because* Ghazali appeared to endorse such conventional social duties that she was able to publicly and powerfully argue for women's education in Islam, participation in jihad, and engagement in da'wa as a necessary expression of, rather than threat to, Muslim tradition. As Ghazali writes in response to a letter in *Liwa al-Islam*, while only "fools equate [women's] education with the education of men," it is still the case that "we need specialized programs that prepare the virtuous wife to create a loving motherhood, and to build happy families" (Ghazali 1989b, 50). On the day that an authentic Muslim state is raised on the ashes of Islam's enemies, then, women will ascend to "their natural kingdom, educating men of the umma" (Ghazali 1978, 144).

# AN ISLAMIST ACTIVIST

THE FOLLOWING are excerpts from the 1981 interview with Hagga Zaynab.

QUESTION: How did your contact with the Muslim Brotherhood begin?

ANSWER: The Muslim Brotherhood is the association of all Muslims in the world, so it is natural and imperative for every Muslim to be in contact with it. If I did not have contact with the Muslim Brotherhood, that would be strange and incomprehensible according to sound Islamic understanding, but the fact that I have had contact with it is natural. My contact with it began at the beginning of 1939. It was a direct contact with the martyred imam and renewer of the faith,[8] Hasan al-Banna.

Q: How did you come to know him?

A: I came to know him because he is an *imam* and a renewer of the faith, calling people to God. At that time I was actively propagating Islam, calling people to God. . . . I was working in the general head-quarters of the Muslim Women's Association, which I founded in AH 1356 (1936).

Q: How did you come to assume this role?

A: At the time I was eighteen years old. I was working with Mrs. Huda al-Sha'rawi in the women's movement, which calls for the liberation of women.[9] But I, with my Islamic upbringing, found that this was

[8]The imam, from the beginning of the Islamic community, is the one who leads the prayer in the mosque. Originally it was the Prophet himself, and after him his successors, the four caliphs, who filled this office; thus, imam came to be a title for the ruler of the Muslim community and in theory claims to the title should not be multiple. In the passage from her book translated here, the title imam is applied to Hasan al-Banna, Hasan al-Hudaybi, Banna's successor, and Sayyid Qutb, who became the intellectual leader of the Muslim Brotherhood. "Martyr" (*shahid*) is also used as an honorific title, appropriate for a society that claims that "death in the service of God is the loftiest of our wishes," for by martyrdom the Muslim attains the highest rank of piety. Hagga Zaynab refers to Hasan al-Banna as *al-imam al-shahid*, "the martyred imam." 'Abd al-Qadir 'Awda and Sayyid Qutb are also rarely referred to without the title of martyr. "Renewer of the faith" (*al-mujaddid*) is a title of even rarer honor. It refers to a tradition that God would send a renewer of the faith to the Islamic community in every century; Hagga Zaynab seems to believe Banna was the mujaddid for his century.

[9]Huda al-Sha'rawi was the famous leader of the women's liberation movement in Egypt in the 1920s. After attending the International Women's Union conference in Rome in 1922, she shed her face veil and founded the Egyptian Feminist Union in 1923.

not the right way for Muslim women. Women had to be called to Islam, so I founded the Muslim Women's Association after I resigned from the Feminist Union.

Q: At first you were with Mrs. Huda al-Sha'rawi, and then you discovered—

A: That this was a mistake.

Q: Why? How did you discover that this was wrong?

A: Islam has provided everything for both men and women. It gave women everything—freedom, economic rights, political rights, social rights, public and private rights. Islam gave women rights in the family granted by no other society. Women may talk of liberation in Christian society, Jewish society, or pagan society, but in Islamic society it is a grave error to speak of the liberation of women. The Muslim woman must study Islam so she will know that it is Islam that has given her all her rights. . . .

Q: But why were you convinced at first of the validity of Huda al-Sha'rawi's movement, but later changed your mind? What brought about this change of mind?

A: Studying, reading, and attending lectures and Islamic meetings.

Q: So you established the Muslim Women's Association when you were eighteen, by yourself.

A: Yes. I called women together for Islam.

Q: Was it successful?

A: Very.

Q: What were its activities?

A: Our goal was to acquaint the Muslim woman with her religion so she would be convinced by means of study that the women's liberation movement is a deviant innovation that occurred because of the Muslims' backwardness. We consider the Muslims to be backward; they must remove this backwardness from their shoulders and rise up as their religion commands, as it should be in Islamic lands.

Q: So there were lessons for women?

A: There were lessons for the women. The association also maintained an orphanage, offered assistance to poor families, and helped reconcile families. It attempted to give useful work to young Muslim men and women who were unemployed; that is, they helped in religious activities. The association also has a political opinion, that Egypt must be ruled by the Qur'an, not positivistic constitutions.

Q: You say that your contact with the Muslim Brotherhood was natural. Do you think that the Muslim who is not in the Brotherhood is not a true Muslim?

A: He is a deficient Muslim, and the remedy for this deficiency is for him to join the Muslim Brotherhood.

Q: What is the goal of the Brotherhood?

A: The return of the Islamic state, which rules by the Qur'an and sunna.[10]

Q: Would there be states other than the Islamic state?

A: The Islamic nation possesses one-third of the world. Geographically, we are richer than the rest of the world, in oil we are richer than the rest of the world. So why are we backward? Because we are not following our religion, we are not living in accordance with our constitution and laws. If we return to our Qur'an and to the sunna of our Prophet, we will live Islam in reality, and we will control the whole world.

Q: Do you think it is wrong for there to be something called Egypt, Saudi Arabia, or Pakistan?

A: They remain. But there would be a federation, like the United States.

Q: What methods does the Brotherhood use to attain its goal?

A: Very simple methods. We teach the child his religion, and that he should be governed by nothing but the Qur'an and should govern by nothing but the Qur'an. That is all. The day is coming when we will see the whole nation upholding the Qur'an. When all the people say, "Our religion is Islam," no ruler will be able to say, "I don't want Islam."

Q: Have you seen changes in the Brotherhood in the many years you have been with it?

A: Of course. Whenever one goes deeper, one becomes more refined, stronger. Of course, the Muslim Brotherhood passed through martyrdoms, imprisonments. Brothers were taken to prison, exiled from their country. All these trials gave them power, experience, wisdom, and an ability to patiently endure, so they will not be content unless they are following this path.

Q: Do you think the Brotherhood is stronger now than it was before?

A: Much stronger. Because it learned from the experience of persecution from such people as Gamal 'Abd al-Nasser. It has become wiser, more knowledgeable, in better contact with God, knowing more about human nature.

Q: What is the role of women in the Muslim Brotherhood? Are there many women like you?

A: The Brotherhood considers women a fundamental part of the Islamic call. They are the ones who are most active because men have to work. They are the ones who build the kind of men that we need to fill the ranks of the Islamic call. So women must be well educated,

[10]The sunna is the exemplary behavior of Muhammad, the Prophet of Islam, as depicted in the hadith literature. Although the hadith is not a revelation from God, it is considered, along with the Qur'an, as one of the foundations of Islamic law. Later Hagga Zaynab refers to marriage as a "sure sunna"; that is, marriage is the approved practice and the hadith does not contradict or cast doubt on this.

cultured, knowing the precepts of the Qur'an and sunna, knowing
world politics, why we are backward, why we don't have technology.
The Muslim woman must study all these things, and then raise her son
in the conviction that he must possess the scientific tools of the age, and
at the same time he must understand Islam, politics, geography, and
current events. He must rebuild the Islamic nation. We Muslims carry
arms only to spread peace. We want to purify the world of unbelief,
atheism, oppression, and persecution. . . . Islam does not forbid women
to actively participate in public life. It does not prevent her from
working, entering into politics, and expressing her opinion, or from
being anything, as long as that does not interfere with her first duty as a
mother, the one who first trains her children in the Islamic call. So her
first, holy, and most important mission is to be a mother and wife. She
cannot ignore this priority. If she then finds she has free time, she may
participate in public activities. Islam does not forbid her.

Q: Must all women marry in Islamic society? Is there no place for the
single woman?

A: Marriage is a sure sunna in Islam. There is no monasticism in
Islam. Men must marry unless they have an excuse, that is, an illness.
Women are also excused if they have an illness. But marriage was
instituted to reproduce children and to establish the family, which is
the fundamental unit in building the Islamic state. Marriage is a mission
and a trust in Islam. Sexual life in Islam is a necessity for both men and
women, but it is not the first and last goal of marriage. It is to preserve
the human race, establish the family, build the man and the woman, to
build the ruler, to bring about righteous government. . . . Any sexual
relations outside marriage are totally prohibited. When a man has
relations with his wife, it is sunna that they both wash themselves.
And it is sunna that before he approaches her he says, "In the name of
God, the Compassionate, the Merciful. God, protect us from Satan."
He begins in this way, because it is a human duty, a duty imposed by
God, a divine duty.

Q: You were married?

A: I married twice. I found that [my first] marriage took up all my
time and kept me from my mission, and my husband did not agree with
my work. I had made a condition that if we had any major disagreements we would separate, and the Islamic cause was essential. My
second husband knew that I left my first husband because of the cause.
He gave me written agreements that he would not come between me
and my mission, but that he would help me and be my assistant. And,
in fact, we had an enjoyable married life in which there was cooperation, love, faithfulness to God, and purity of soul and conscience. We
separated only when I was sent to prison, and he died twenty-one days
after I was sentenced. After that, because I had done my duty in marriage, I was free to give all my time to the cause.

Q: You said it was your father who had the greatest influence on you in your Islamic upbringing. Who was he, and how did he influence you?

A: He was Shaykh al-Ghazali al-Jabili, a scholar who completed his education in al-Azhar.[11] He refused to accept a government job, but he was a big cotton merchant. When it was not the cotton season, he devoted himself to preaching Islam. He went around the country, exhorting the people, preaching in the mosques on Fridays, teaching the Islamic call and religion. He always used to say to me that, God willing, I would be an Islamic leader. That's what he used to say to me. He would say, "Huda al-Sha'rawi does this, and Malak Hifni Nasif does that, but among the Companions of the Prophet Muhammad, may God bless him and grant him peace, there was a woman named Nusayba, the daughter of Ka'b al-Mazini.[12] He would tell me of how she struggled in the path of Islam, and then he would ask me, "Whom do you choose? Do you choose Huda al-Sha'rawi, or will you become Nusayba, daughter of Ka'b al-Mazini?" And I would say to him, "I will be Nusayba, daughter of Ka'b al-Mazini." So I decided to be a Muslim woman.

[11] Al-Azhar University, founded in 972, emerged after the thirteenth century as a major center of learning. Much of its prestige has faded with the establishment of a modem, secular educational system in Egypt, but it continues to be the center of Islamic religious learning for Egyptian and many foreign students. In Egypt it draws most of its students from the countryside and is known for its conservatism.

[12] Malak Hifni Nasif (b. 1886), also known by her nickname, "Bahithat al-Badiya" (seeker of the desert), was a prominent writer and lecturer on feminist and social issues. She was one of the first Egyptian women to graduate with a teaching diploma in 1903, and she publicly campaigned for women's education. Although there was a companion of the Prophet named Ka'b ibn 'Iyad al-Mazini (listed in al-Dhahabi 1970, 2:33, no. 352), there is no listing of a Nusayba bint Ka'b al-Maziniyya. It is probable that Hagga Zaynab was referring to Nusayba bint Ka'b ibn 'Amr al-Ansariyya, who was also of Mazin and was known as Umm 'Ammara (308, no. 3714). This Nusayba was famous for her distinction as a warrior in the battle of Uhud. She is mentioned in the works of Ibn Sa'd, Ibn Hisham, al-Baladhuri, al-Muqaddisi, and Ibn Hajr, among others. A summary of their accounts may be found in Kahhalah 1977, 171–75.

# FROM *DAYS OF MY LIFE,* CHAPTER 2

MY CONNECTIONS with the Muslim Brotherhood were not new, as the foolish would have people believe, for its history goes back to the year AH 1357 (1937).

On that blessed day, long ago, in about AH 1358 (1939), approximately six months after the founding of the Muslim Women's Association, I first met the martyred imam, Hasan al-Banna. This was after a lecture I gave to the Muslim sisters in the Brotherhood headquarters, which at that time was in 'Ataba Square.

The guiding imam was preparing to create a division for the Muslim Sisters. After first stressing that the ranks of all Muslims must be unified and there must be no differences of opinion, he asked me to head the Muslim Sisters' division. That would mean incorporating the newborn of which I was so proud, the Muslim Women's Association, and considering it a part of the Muslim Brotherhood movement. I no more than discussed the matter with the general assembly of the Muslim Women's Association, which rejected the proposal, though it approved of a first cooperation between the two organizations.

We continued to meet together, though each of us held to his own opinion. The Muslim Sisters' division was founded without changing our Islamic relationship at all. I tried, in our last meeting in the headquarters of the Muslim Women's Association, to appease his [Banna's] anger by promising to take it upon myself that the Muslim Women's Association be one of the supports of the Muslim Brotherhood on condition that it retain its name and independence, which would be more beneficial to the cause. But this too did not please him as a substitute for incorporation. Then events happened quickly, and the incidents of 1948 occurred.[13] A resolution was issued dissolving the Brotherhood and confiscating its possessions, locking up its people and

[13]In 1948 the government believed the Muslim Brotherhood was planning imminent revolution: a cache of arms was found in the Muqattam hills in January and another in Isma'iliyya in October, the Brothers were believed to be involved in the coup d'etat in Yemen, a respected judge was assassinated by a Brother, the confiscation of Society papers brought to light the existence of the Brotherhood's Secret Apparatus, and the Brothers were accused of inciting riots at the university in which the Cairo police chief was killed. The Society was dissolved by government order on December 6. For details, see R. Mitchell 1969, 58–67.

throwing thousands into prison camps. The Muslim Sisters did things for which they received much gratitude. One of them was Mrs. Tahiya al-Jabili, my brother's wife and my cousin; from her I learned many of the details, and for the first time I found myself longing to reconsider all of Banna's opinions and his insistence on complete incorporation. On the morning following the dissolution of the Muslim Brotherhood I was in my office in the headquarters of the Muslim Women's Association, in the same room in which I had had my last meeting with the guiding imam. I found myself sitting at my desk with my head in my hands, weeping bitterly. I felt that Hasan al-Banna was right, and that he was the leader to whom allegiance is due from all Muslims, to strive in the path of God to restore the Muslims to their responsibilities and their true and rightful existence, the apex of the world, which they will lead as God wills, and which they will judge by what God has revealed. I felt that Hasan al-Banna was stronger than I, and more sincere in unambiguously spreading and proclaiming the truth.

Such courage and boldness are the clothing that should be worn by every Muslim. Banna had worn it and called us to it.

Then I found myself calling my secretary and telling her to get me in touch with Brother 'Abd al-Hafiz al-Sayfi, whom I commissioned to carry a verbal message to Imam Banna, reminding him of my promise in our last meeting. When he returned to me with his greeting and appeal, I summoned my brother, Muhammad al-Ghazali al-Jabili, and asked him to deliver a slip of paper either by himself or via his wife to the guiding imam. On the paper was written:

My LORD, Imam Hasan al-Banna:

Zaynab al-Ghazali al-Jabili approaches you today as a slave who has nothing but her worship of God and her total devotion to the service of God's call. You are the only one today who can sell this slave at the price he wishes for the cause of God the Exalted.

Waiting for your orders and instructions, my lord the imam.

My brother returned to arrange a hasty meeting in the headquarters of the YMMA.[14] It was to happen as if it were a coincidence. I had no lack of justification for being there, for I was on my way to the YMMA hall to give a lecture. I met Mr. Banna and said to him as we went up the stairs, "By God I pledge allegiance to you, to work to establish the state of Islam. The least I can offer you to achieve it is my blood, and the Muslim Women's Association with its name." He said, "I accept your pledge of allegiance. The Muslim Women's Association may

[14]The Association of Muslim Youth (Jam'iyyat shubban al-Muslimin), commonly called the YMMA and thought of as the Muslim answer to the YMCA, was founded in 1927. It was actually more militant in its orientation than its constitution professed, according to Heyworth-Dunne (1950, 11–14), and both interacted and competed with the Muslim Brotherhood but never achieved anything like the latter's organization and strength.

remain as it is." We separated on the agreement that we would be in touch by means of my brother's family. The first charge I received from the martyred imam was a commission to mediate between al-Nahhas and the Brotherhood. At that time Mustafa Pasha al-Nahhas was outside the government; the late Nahhas appointed Amin Khalil to try to bring an end to the misunderstanding, and the martyred imam was pleased with this choice; I was the contact.[15] One night in February 1949 Amin Khalil came to me and told me, "Immediate steps must be taken for Banna to leave Cairo. The criminals are conspiring to kill him." I found no way to contact him directly, because my brother had been imprisoned. I tried to contact the martyred imam in person. While I was on my way to get in touch with him, I got word of the assassination attempt and that he was taken to the hospital. Then the news of his bad condition quickly got worse. He departed as a martyr to his Lord, with the prophets, the truthful, the martyrs, and the upright, and they are the best companions.

My grief was intense and my desire for revenge against the criminals was bitter; I made no attempt to hide it. The government of the coalition of parties came into power and issued an order dissolving the Muslim Women's Association. I opposed the order in court, which ordered us to resume our activities during the government of Husayn Sirri Pasha in 1950. The lawyer was Mr. 'Abd al-Fattah Hasan "Pasha." Then came the Wafd government, and the Brotherhood resumed its activities. At that time its allegiance was to the guiding imam, Hasan al-Hudaybi. On the first day of the opening of the general headquarters of the Muslim Brotherhood, I wanted to announce my faithfulness to the cause in an indirect way, and may God ordain whatever He wills in the matter. So I contributed the most expensive and precious piece of furniture in my house, an arabesque parlor set inlaid with mother of pearl, to furnish the office of the General Guide.

All was calm and peaceful. The martyr 'Abd al-Qadir 'Awda[16] visited me and thanked me for the donation, and said, "I am happy

---

[15]Mustafa al-Nahhas was leader of the Wafd Party, which rivaled the Muslim Brotherhood as champion of the anti-British nationalist movement prior to the revolution of 1952. The Wafd came into power a number of times prior to 1952, with Nahhas as prime minister. Relations between the Wafd and the Brotherhood were usually antagonistic, with periods of cooperation and mutual support when their interests coincided. As Hagga Zaynab explains later, she had a personal friendship with Nahhas but did not agree with the Wafd platform.

[16]'Awda was a lawyer and al-Hudaybi's deputy, but he quickly became part of the leadership clique antagonistic to al-Hudaybi (R. Mitchell 1969, 108). 'Awda favored cooperation with the Revolutionary Command Council government until the February 27, 1954, demonstrations in support of General Neguib against the RCC. 'Awda played a prominent part in the demonstration and distributed pamphlets hostile to the regime; R. Mitchell (1969, 129–30) calls his behavior a miscalculation of the situation that "proved to be a fatal error." In the aftermath of a Brother's attempt on the life of Nasser, 'Awda was among the six Brothers who were publicly executed (160–61).

that Zaynab al-Ghazali al-Jabili has become a member of the Muslim Brotherhood." I said, "May it be so, with God's permission." He said, "It is so, praise be to God."

Events passed in a calm and friendly atmosphere between me and many members of the Brotherhood. Then the revolutionary military government came under the leadership of Major General Muhammad Neguib, who had visited me only a few days before the revolution accompanied by Prince 'Abdallah al-Faisal, Yas Sirag al-Din, Shaykh al-Baquri,[17] and my brother 'Ali al-Ghazali on the occasion of Prince 'Abdallah al-Faisal's visit to Egypt. The Brotherhood was sympathetic to the revolution, and so was the Muslim Women's Association, for a while. Then I began to feel that things were not going as we had hoped, and this was not the revolution we had anticipated, a crowning of previous efforts at the hands of those who were working to save this country. I began to express my opinion to other members of the Brotherhood. When ministerial positions were offered to some Brotherhood members, I expressed my opinion in the magazine of the Muslim Women's Association that none of the Brotherhood should pledge loyalty to a government that does not rule by what God has revealed, and whoever does so must separate from the Brotherhood, and that the Brotherhood must define its position, now that the government's intentions had become clear.

The martyr 'Abd al-Qadir 'Awda visited me, asking me to postpone writing on this subject. So I withdrew two issues of the magazine. Then I resumed writing until the martyr 'Abd al-Qadir 'Awda visited me for the second time, this time bearing a command from the General Guide ordering me not to write on this subject. I recalled my pledge to Banna, may God have mercy on him, and I believed that loyalty was transferred to Hudaybi, so I obeyed the order.

From that time on my pledge of allegiance governed by behavior, even in such matters as the peace conference in Vienna. I did not travel until I had obtained permission from the guiding imam, Hudaybi.

Time passed, and then came the events of 1954 with its infamies and calamities, which revealed Gamal 'Abd al-Nasser for what he really is: an enemy of Islam, fighting it in the persons of its propagators and the leadership of its movement.[18] Heinous death sentences were passed on the top Islamic leaders: the martyr and councilor 'Abd al-Qadir 'Awda, a man of virtue, a scholar of al-Azhar, a pious man, for whom the British leadership in the canal zone in 1951 offered a reward of 10,000

[17]Shaykh Hasan al-Baquri was a member of the Muslim Brotherhood's Guidance Council. Later he became minister of Awqaf under the revolutionary government, for which he was expelled from the Brotherhood.

[18]See R. Mitchell 1969, 125–62, for the details of the growing enmity between Nasser and the Brotherhood that culminated in the dissolution of the Brotherhood, an attempt on Nasser's life, and the imprisonment and torture of some Brothers.

pounds to whomever brought him in dead or alive; Shaykh Muhammad Farghali, who was given to the imperialists dead without any loss to the British treasury; and the other noble martyrs.

Even the great struggler for God, Imam Hasan al-Hudaybi, was sentenced to death, though the sentence was not carried out because he was suddenly struck with a severe angina in the heart and was taken to the hospital. The doctors said he had only a few hours to live, so at that point Nasser issued a pardon for him, expecting to read his obituary in the papers the next morning. But God's power foiled his stratagem. The imam lived. Every life term is fixed by God. Yes, he lived, to again render services—and what services!—to the Muslims and to lead the Islamic call in its darkest hour. He demonstrated an ability to steadfastly cling to the truth while he was ill with a number of diseases. This baffled his torturers and caused them to take him to the war prison once more and torture him in the most hideous manner. But he continued to cling to the truth, taking the road of those who follow the call until he came to see the end of Nasser and his clique, while he survived, raising the banner of truth and the unity of God in which he believed, involved with every kernel of his being. He was steadfast, and allowed himself no weakness or languishing in the religion of God. He refused to be lenient with himself and remain in his home, disapproving only in his heart, as some religious scholars allow and practice.[19]

Indeed, I remember how brave and noble he was when some of those who felt things had gone on too long and who suffered from some weakness wanted him to be lenient and write to the tyrant expressing support for him and asking his pardon. They asked Imam Hasan al-Hudaybi for permission to do that. At this he uttered his famous words: "I will not force anyone to be determined and stand with us, but I tell you, the Islamic call never stood a single day with those who were soft."

He said that when he was an old man of eighty years. He remained in the Mazra'at Tarra prison until the last group of prisoners was released after the death of Nasser.

We return again to the details of the events of 1965.

In 1955 I found myself drafted into the service of the Islamic call without an invitation from anyone. It was the cries of the orphans who lost their fathers to torture, and the tears of the women who were widowed and whose husbands were behind prison bars, and the old fathers and mothers who lost their heart's delight. These cries and tears penetrated my innermost being. I found myself feeling as if I were one

---

[19]Hagga Zaynab's unambiguous praise for Hudaybi's resolve and leadership was not unanimously felt, as R. Mitchell's (1969, 111–26, 139, 142–50) account of the history of the Brotherhood makes clear, and opposition even took the form of one attempted "coup," though Hudaybi apparently had the support of the rank and file. Hudaybi's distaste for violence, emotionalism, and the separate leadership of the Secret Apparatus brought him into conflict with the leaders of the latter group.

of those responsible for the loss of the starving and the wounds of the tortured. I began to offer a little help.

But the numbers of the starving increased day by day, as well as the number of those who were naked, and the news of the martyrs who died under the whips of the debauched apostates, the cruel infidels. Schools and universities needed money, supplies, and clothes, and landlords were demanding rent. The problem grew more difficult, the burden grew heavier, and the hole in the garment grew larger, especially after a year and a half. It was precisely the middle of the year in 1956 when some of those who had been in prison but not sentenced were released. Some were in direst need of someone to provide them with money, food, clothes, and shelter. All of this was happening while the Muslims were in the good country, in Egypt, which veered with those who led the revolution; no one was aware of his duty. On the contrary, we found many religious scholars and shaykhs who washed their hands of those who struggled in the cause of Islam.

All those who were released, even those who wept at the tragedy and were in pain, hid their pain and their tears out of fear, lest the tyrant accuse them of being Muslims. When my grief at what had happened became overwhelming and I found no way out of it, I went to visit my honorable teacher, Shaykh Muhammad al-Awdan. He was one of the very few men of al-Azhar who was sincerely pious, and I used to ask his advice on everything pertaining to the Islamic cause and the religious sciences. He believed, as I did, that the fact that the Muslim Women's Association had not merged with the Brotherhood could prove useful to the Brotherhood at a later time. He knew of my pledge of allegiance to Banna, and he blessed it and supported it. Likewise, he knew of my loyalty to the cause after Banna's martyrdom, and he accepted it.

I sat with him and told him of the tragedy of the families, and he listened to me in profound grief. I finished what I had to say by explaining what I thought of doing within the limits of my capabilities. I saw that it was not enough for us to grieve while people in the circles of those involved in the Islamic cause, those who were obedient, those who struggled in the path of God, cruelly suffered from hunger, whip lashes, and nakedness and women and children were homeless; our grief was not enough to make the word of God paramount. I saw that as president of the Muslim Women's Association, God willing, I could help the families of the Brotherhood as God enabled me.

The shaykh kissed my head and wept, saying to me, "Don't hesitate to offer any assistance. God is the one who blesses our plans." I again explained to him my position in the association and my complete confidence in the women who were its members. The shaykh said to me, "It has become your irrevocable duty to not hold back any effort in this path and the work you are doing. Place it between you and God the Blessed and Exalted." Then he added, "The only salvation for Islam by

God's commandment is these tortured Muslim Brothers. We hope only in God and in their devotion and efforts in the path of the call. Do all you can, Zaynab." So I did in fact all I could. I spent my efforts to offer something, though no one knew that I was doing anything. I gave one or two individuals what I could, saying these things were sent to me and I was charged only with seeing that they were delivered to them.

Then I learned that the virtuous mother, the great struggler in the path of God, the wife of Mr. Hudaybi, also took great pains, along with some other noble and virtuous women in the Muslim Sisters, including Amal al-'Ashmawi, wife of the councilor Munir al-Dilla (she was head of the Muslim Sisters),[20] Khalida Hasan al-Hudaybi, Amina Qutb, Hamida Qutb, Fathiyya Bakr, Amina al-Jawhari, 'Aliya al-Hudaybi, and Tahiya Sulayman al-Jabili.

My contacts gradually widened. I contacted Khalida al-Hudaybi in extreme secret, then Hamida Qutb and Amina Qutb. All of this was for the sake of the tortured, the children, and the orphans.

My first meeting with 'Abd al-Fattah Isma'il[21] was in 1957 in the season of the pilgrimage. I was in the port of Suez at the head of a delegation from the Muslim Women's Association going on the pilgrimage. Among those bidding us farewell was my brother, Muhammad al-Ghazali al-Jabili. I saw him coming toward me, accompanied by a man whose face was clothed with light and reverence, averting his eyes. My brother introduced him to me, saying, "Brother 'Abd al-Fattah Isma'il, one of the young men who was best loved by the martyred imam, Hasan al-Banna. The honored Guide loved him and had absolute confidence in him. He asked me to introduce him to you in this way, so you would know him." The Brother greeted me and said, "God willing, I will be with you on the ship." I welcomed him, and he left.

We climbed up into the steamship and it moved far from the shore. I busied myself with the needs of the delegation of the Muslim Women's Association. When I went to my room to rest after lunch, I heard a knock on the door. I told the person to come in, but the knock came a second time, and the person who knocked had moved away from the door. When he heard my voice permitting him to enter for the third time, he came in. It was the Brother whom my brother had introduced to me at the pier. He said humbly with his head bowed, after greeting me, "I know, with praise to God, that there was a vow of allegiance between you and the martyred imam, Hasan al-Banna, after a long

[20]Munir al-Dilla was a member of the Guidance Council and adviser of Hudaybi. "It was in his home and at his inspiration that the name of Hasan Isma'il al-Hudaybi . . . was first mentioned as a candidate for the post of general guide" (R. Mitchell 1969, 85). He was sentenced to life imprisonment with hard labor after the attempt on Nasser's life.

[21]'Abd al-Fattah Isma'il, Hagga Zaynab's chief collaborator, was also arrested in 1965 and was executed along with Sayyid Qutb in 1966.

dispute." When I asked him how he knew this, he answered, "From the martyred imam himself, may God rest him in peace." I asked him what he wanted, and he answered, "That we meet in Mecca for the sake of God, to speak of what Banna wanted of you, God willing."

These words were simply expressed and well intentioned, soft in their simplicity, strong and truthful, with heavy responsibilities, carrying the implication of a command that leaves no room for thought.

I said, "God willing, in the house of the Muslim Women's Association delegation in Mecca or in Jidda." When he asked for the addresses, I told him of two Brothers in Jidda whom he said he knew, Shaykh al-'Ashmawi and Mustafa al-'Alim, either of whom could guide him to where I was staying in Mecca and Jidda.

The Brother bid farewell and left.

One night in the month of the pilgrimage I had an appointment after the evening prayer with the late shaykh, Imam Muhammad ibn Ibrahim, grand mufti of the Kingdom of Saudi Arabia at that time. We were studying a memorandum I had given to His Highness the King in which I explained the necessity of educating the girls in the kingdom. I asked him to hasten the implementation of this plan, explaining that this was in the kingdom's best interests. The memorandum was transferred to the mufti, who asked to see me.

I spent two hours studying the plan with him. When I left him, I went my way to the Gate of Peace, intending to go around the Ka'ba, when I was stopped by a voice calling my name and greeting me in the Islamic fashion. I turned, and there was 'Abd al-Fattah Isma'il. He asked me where I was going. When he heard I was going to go around the Ka'ba and then to the house where the delegation was staying, he accompanied me to the mosque, and we went around it together. After performing the prayer that accompanies the circumambulation, we sat facing the proper direction and he began to talk about what was on his mind.

He asked me my opinion of the resolution to dissolve the Brotherhood. I answered that it was a legally invalid resolution. He said, "That is the matter I wished to study with you." When I asked him to visit me in the house where the delegation was staying, he thought it an inappropriate place to discuss such matters for fear of Nasser's spy networks. We agreed to meet in the construction office of the sacred places of Mecca, the office of a righteous man, Shaykh Salih al-Qazzaz. We met there, but he whispered to me that it would be better for us to meet in the sacred place. So he left on agreement that we meet behind Abraham's abode.

After two prostrations of the circumambulation, we sat behind the Zamzam building near the place where Abraham stood, and he began to talk about the invalidity of the resolution to dissolve the Muslim Brotherhood and the necessity of organizing the ranks of the Brother-

hood and resuming its activities. We agreed to get in touch after returning from the holy land with Imam Hasan al-Hudaybi, the general guide,
to ask his permission to work.

When we turned to go, he said, "We must be linked here by a vow
with God to struggle in His path, and not to waver until we gather the
ranks of the Brotherhood and separate out those who do not want to
work, whatever their circumstances and status." We made a vow to
God to struggle even to the point of death in the path of His call.

And I returned to Egypt.

In the first months of 1958, my meetings with 'Abd al-Fattah Isma'il
became more frequent, both in my home and in the headquarters of the
Muslim Women's Association.

We studied the affairs of the Muslims, attempting with all our might
to do something for Islam, to restore to this nation its glory and its
creed, beginning with the life of the Prophet, blessing and peace be
upon him, and the pious ancestors, and those who came after them,
deriving our program from the Book of God and the sunna of His
Messenger, may God bless him and grant him peace.

Our plan of action aimed at bringing together everyone who wanted
to work for Islam to join with us. All this was only studies and setting
up rough outlines, so we would know the way to go. When we wanted
to start working, we had to ask permission from Mr. Hudaybi, as
general guide of the Brotherhood, because our legal studies on the
resolution to dissolve the society ended in the conclusion that it was
null and void, because Nasser has no claim to allegiance and cannot
command obedience from the Muslims, because he is fighting against
Islam and does not rule by the Book of God.

I met with Mr. Hudaybi to ask his permission in my name and in the
name of 'Abd al-Fattah Isma'il, and he granted us permission to work
after several meetings, in which I explained to him the purpose and
details of the studies 'Abd al-Fattah and I had done.

We decided to begin the work by having Brother 'Abd al-Fattah
'Abduh Isma'il conduct a survey throughout the length of Egypt at the
level of the province, the administrative center, and the village with the
aim of finding out which Muslims wanted to work and were suitable to
work with us. We would begin with the Muslim Brothers, to make them
the first nucleus of this coming together.

Brother 'Abd al-Fattah Isma'il began his tour, starting with those
Brothers who were released from the prisons and who had not been
sentenced, to test their mettle: did the persecution affect their determination, and did imprisonment make them withdraw from what might
expose them to imprisonment once again? Or were they still loyal to the
cause, ready to sacrifice everything, great and small, in the path of God
and the support of His religion?

The survey was necessary so we might begin to work on firm ground, so we might know who was really suitable. Together we studied the reports 'Abd al-Fattah Isma'il brought from each region, and I would visit the general guide and inform him of what we had agreed upon and the conclusions to which we had come. If we presented him with descriptions of the difficulties we would encounter, he would say, "Keep going, and do not look back. Do not be misled by the titles or reputations of men. You are building a new structure from its foundation."

Sometimes he would support what we presented to him, and sometimes he would give some instructions. One of his instructions was that we add to our sources of study the *Muhalla* of Ibn Hazm.[22]

In 1959 our studies ended, and we drew up a program of Islamic education. I call God as my witness that our program consisted of nothing but the education of the Muslim individual so he would know his duty toward his Lord, and the creation of the Muslim society, which will of necessity be separate from pagan society.[23]

Because the activities of the Society of the Muslim Brotherhood were halted as a result of the pagan resolution of dissolution of 1954, it was necessary for these activities to be secret.

My work in these activities did not prevent me from fulfilling the duties of my mission in the general headquarters of the Muslim Women's Association or cause me to neglect my family duties, though my noble husband, the late Muhammad Salim Salim, noticed the frequent visits of Brother 'Abd al-Fattah and some of the pure Muslim youth to our house. My husband asked me, "Are the Muslim Brothers having activities?" I said, "Yes." He asked me about the extent and type of these activities. I said, "They are to restore the organization of the Society of the Brotherhood." When he began to ask me probing questions, I said to him, "Do you remember, dear husband, what I said to you when we agreed to marry?"

He said, "Yes. You stipulated certain conditions. But now I'm afraid for you, that you will expose yourself to the tyrants."

Then he was silent, his head bowed. I said to him, "I remember well what I said to you. I told you that day, 'There is one thing about my life that you must know, because you will become my husband; if you still

---

[22]Abu Muhammad 'Ali ibn Hazm (994–1064) was a famous theologian and legist of Muslim Spain. He belonged to a school known for its rigorously literal interpretation of the Qur'an and hadith and is therefore called *al-Zahiriyya*, "those who adhere to the apparent meaning" (*al-zahir*). His *Kitab al-muhalla bil-athar fi sharh al-mujalla bil-iqtisar*, a commentary on the hadith, belongs to an earlier period when he was an ardent follower of the Shafi'i school (*Shorter Encyclopaedia of Islam* 1953, 148).

[23]Ghazali uses the term *jahili*, a reference to pre-Islamic times. She compares modern Egypt to the "times of ignorance" (*al-jahiliyya*) that existed in pre-Islamic Arabia. In the interview, when she speaks of women's liberation in a "pagan society," she uses the word *kafir*, "unbelieving" or "infidel." In that context it could just as well read "atheistic society."

agree to marry me, then I must tell you, on condition that you not ask me about it later. I will not go back on my conditions with regard to this matter. I am the president of the general headquarters of the Muslim Women's Association. This is true, but most people think I adhere to the political principles of the Wafd Party. That is not true. What I believe in is the mission of the Muslim Brotherhood. I am linked with Mustafa al-Nahhas by personal friendship; but I have given my oath of loyalty to Hasan al-Banna to die in the path of God, though I am not planning a single step toward entering the circle of that divine honor. But I believe I will take this step some day—in fact, I dream of it and hope for it. On that day, if your personal welfare and economic work conflict with my Islamic work, and I find that my married life interferes with the way of the call and the establishment of the Islamic state, then we will separate.'

"On that day you lowered your eyes to the ground. Then you lifted your head, and your eyes were filled with tears. You said, 'I asked you what material goods you wanted, and you asked for no dowry or wedding gifts. You stipulated that I not keep you from the path of God. I didn't know that you had any ties with Mr. Banna. What I knew was that you had a disagreement with him over his request that the Muslim Women's Association be incorporated into the Muslim Brotherhood.'

"I said, 'Praise be to God; we came to an agreement during the persecution of the Brothers in 1948, before Banna's martyrdom. I had decided to banish marriage from my life, and to devote myself entirely to the call. I cannot ask you today that you join me in this struggle, but it is my right to stipulate that you not interfere with my struggle in the path of God, and that the day that responsibility places me in the ranks of the struggles, that you not ask me what I am doing. Let the trust between us be complete, between [me and] a man who wants to marry a woman who gave herself to the struggle in the path of God to establish the Islamic state when she was eighteen years old. If there is a conflict of interests between marriage and the call to God, then the marriage will come to an end and the call will remain in my whole being.'"

Then I stopped speaking for a moment. I looked at him and said, "Do you remember?"

He said, "Yes."

I said, "Today I ask you to keep your promise. Don't ask with whom I am meeting. I ask God to give you a portion of the reward of my struggle as a grace from Him if He accepts my work. I know that you have the right to give me orders, and it is my duty to obey you. But God is greater in our souls than ourselves, and His call is dearer to us than our own selves. We are in an important phase in the life of the cause."

He said, "Forgive me. Do your work, with God's blessing. May I live to see the day that the Brothers achieve their goal and the Islamic state is established."

The work and activities increased, and the young men crowded into my house night and day. My believing husband would hear the knocks on the door in the middle of the night and get up to open the door. He would escort the visitors to the office, then he would go to the maid's room and wake her, asking her to prepare some food and tea for the visitors. Then he would come to me and wake me gently, saying, "Some of your sons are in the office. They look like they have been traveling or working hard." I would dress and go to them, while he went back to sleep, saying to me, "Wake me if you pray the morning prayer together so I can pray with you, if that's no bother." I would say, "God willing."

And if we prayed the morning prayer together, I would wake him so he could pray with us. Then he would leave, greeting those who were present in a fatherly way, full of warmth, love, and compassion. .

In 1962 I met with the two sisters of the martyred imam, the legist and great struggler in the path of God, Sayyid Qutb, with the agreement of Brother 'Abd al-Fattah 'Abduh Isma'il and permission from Mr. Hasan al-Hudaybi, the general guide of the Muslim Brotherhood. The purpose of this meeting was to contact Imam Sayyid Qutb in prison to solicit his opinion on some of our studies and to ask for his guidance.

I asked Hamida Qutb[24] to convey our greetings to Brother Sayyid Qutb and to inform him of the assembled society's desire to study an Islamic course under the guidance of his views. I gave her a list of references that we were studying. This included the *Tafsir* of Ibn Kathir, the *Muhalla* of Ibn Hazm, *al-Umm* by al-Shafi'i, books on the unitarian religion by Ibn 'Abd al-Wahhab, and *In the Shadow of the Qur'an* by Sayyid Qutb.[25] After a short time Hamida returned to me with instructions to study the introduction to *Surat al-an'am*, second edition. She gave me a section of a book, saying, "Sayyid is preparing it for publication. It is called *Ma'alim fi'l-tariq* (Signposts along the Road)."[26] Sayyid

[24]Hamida Qutb and Zaynab al-Ghazali were the only women brought to trial in 1966 along with the Brothers, including Sayyid Qutb. They spent five years together as cellmates. At the end of her book, Hagga Zaynab describes her grief at being released while her "daughter" remained in jail.

[25]Isma'il ibn 'Umar 'Imad al-Din ibn Kathir (1301–73), an Arab historian of Damascus and pupil of Ibn Taymiyya, wrote a classic Qur'an commentary (tafsir). Abu 'Abd Allah Muhammad ibn Idris al-Shafi'i (767–820), founder of one of the four schools of law, grew up in Mecca but lived the latter part of his life in Egypt, where his tomb in Cairo is a major shrine. *Kitab al-umm* (the mother book) is a seven-volume collection of his writings and lectures. Muhammad ibn 'Abd al-Wahhab (1703–87) was founder of the Wahhabiyya community, the spiritual force behind the Saudi dynasty in Arabia. The Wahhabiyya call themselves *muwahhidun*, "unitarians." They derived their doctrine from the school of Ibn Hanbal as interpreted by Ibn Taymiyya, who attacked the cult of the saints in many of his writings. Portions of Ibn Taymiyya's works are published in pamphlet form in Cairo bookstalls today; he continues to inspire Islamic "fundamentalists."

[26]Jane I. Smith (1975, 205) notes that this book, critical of the regime, made Qutb so dangerous in the eyes of the government that he was executed, along with six other Brothers, in 1966.

Qutb had written it in prison. His sister said to me, "When you finish reading these pages, I will bring you more."

I learned that the general guide had read portions of this book and had given the martyr Sayyid Qutb permission to publish it. When I asked him about it, he said to me, "With God's blessing. This book has fulfilled my hopes in Sayyid, may God preserve him. I read it and reread it. Sayyid Qutb is the great hope for the call now, God willing." The general guide gave me portions of the book, and I read them. He had them so he could give permission for them to be published. I confined myself to a room in the home of the general guide until I had finished reading *Ma'alim fi'l-tariq*.

We recommenced our studies in the form of short pamphlets distributed to the young men for them to study. Then they would be extensively studied in group discussions. Our ideas and goals were in agreement, so the plan of study incorporated the instructions and pages brought to us from the martyred imam, Sayyid Qutb, may God have mercy on him, while he was in prison. Those were good nights and unforgettable days, holy moments with God. Five or ten young men would gather and read ten Qur'anic verses, reviewing their precepts and ordinances and all their implications for the life of the Muslim servant. After we had fully understood them, we would decide to go on to ten other verses, following the example of the Companions of the Prophet, peace and blessing be upon him.

Those days were sweet and good. A blessing from God surrounded us as we studied and studied, training ourselves and preparing men for the cause, with youth who were convinced of the necessity of preparing to establish the call of truth and justice. We believed in the absolute necessity of preparing future generations in the persons of these young men, whom we hope will be the teachers who will guide and prepare the coming generations.

Among the decisions we made, with the instructions of Imam Sayyid Qutb and the permission of Hudaybi, was that the period of training, formation, preparation, and planting belief in the unity of God in hearts would continue. This was accompanied by the conviction that there is no Islam without the implementation of Islamic law and government by the Book of God and the sunna of His Prophet, so that the precepts of the Qur'an would be supreme in the life of the Muslims. We decided that our training program would last thirteen years, the duration of the call in Mecca, with the understanding that the foundation of the Islamic nation now is the Brothers who adhere to the law and precepts of God. We insisted on performing all the commands and prohibitions revealed in the Book and sunna within our Islamic circle, and that obedience to our imam, to whom we had given our oath of loyalty, was necessary, because the establishment of the punishments of Islamic law was not imminent—although we believed in them and defended them—until the

Islamic state was established. We were also convinced that the world today does not have a foundation that would supply the necessary attributes of the Islamic nation in a complete way, as had been the case in the days of the prophethood and the rightly-guided caliphs.[27] Therefore it is incumbent on all Muslims who want to see God's rule and the consolidation of His religion on earth to join in the struggle until all Muslims return to Islam and the true religion is established—not slogans, but an actual, practical reality.

We also studied the condition of the entire Islamic world, searching for examples of what had existed before in the caliphate of the rightly guided caliphs and of what we wanted in God's society now. We decided, after a broad study of the existing painful reality, that there is no single state corresponding to that ideal. We excepted the Kingdom of Saudi Arabia, with some reservations and observations that the kingdom must rectify and correct. All the studies confirmed that the nation of Islam does not exist, although some states have raised slogans claiming they established God's law.

After this broad study, we decided that after thirteen years of Islamic training for young men, old men, women, and girls, we would conduct a comprehensive survey of the country. If we found that the harvest of those who followed the Islamic call, believing that Islam is both religion and state and convinced of the necessity of establishing Islamic rule, reached 75 percent of all the individuals of the nation, men and women, then we would call for the establishment of the Islamic state and demand that the state establish Islamic law. If we found that the harvest was 25 percent, we would renew the teaching and study for thirteen more years, and more if necessary, until we found that the nation was ripe to accept Islamic government.

It does not matter if generations come and go; what matters is that the preparation be continuous, that we keep working until our term of life ends. Then we will give the banner of "There is no god but God, and Muhammad is the Messenger of God" to the noble sons who come after us.

We were in contact with Mr. Muhammad Qutb with the permission of the general guide, Mr. Hudaybi. He used to visit us in my house in Heliopolis to explain to the young men what they could not understand. The young men would ask him many questions, and he would answer them.

[27]The "rightly-guided caliphs" are the first four successors to leadership of the Islamic community after Muhammad's death: Abu Bakr, 'Umar ibn al-Khattab, 'Uthman ibn 'Affan, and 'Ali ibn Abi Talib. Hagga Zaynab's comments reflect a common perception of the pristine condition of early Islamic society, which has suffered a steady disintegration in morality and religious integrity ever since. This view ignores the fact that 'Umar and 'Uthman were both murdered, the latter for corruption, and 'Ali was never universally recognized as caliph. He was even suspected of approving of 'Uthman's murder.

# Chapter 12

# NADIA YASSINE
## 1958–

NADIA YASSINE has arguably joined the ranks of those such as Yusuf al-Qaradawi as the face of so-called moderate Islamism and exemplifies all the promise, pragmatism, and complexity the label suggests. Yassine is the highly visible if unofficial spokeswoman for the most popular Islamist group in Morocco, Jama'at al-'Adl wa'l-Ihsan (the Justice and Spirituality Association, hereafter JSA), as well as the official leader of the JSA's women's division.[1] No ordinary rank-and-file member, Nadia is the eldest daughter of the Association's founder and guide, Abdessalam Yassine.[2] By virtue of this close familial relationship, she has played a crucial role in bringing the JSA's blend of Islamism, Sufism, and nonviolent populism to a new generation of Moroccans, as well as to audiences far beyond North Africa (Dahbi 2004). Yassine is more than a telegenic conduit for her father's ideas, however: erudite, media savvy, and dedicated to women's welfare, she at once articulates and embodies the uneasy union of Islamism and feminism, challenging a host of assumptions about each along the way.

Nadia was born in 1958 in Casablanca and, like her father, is largely an autodidact in the Islamic tradition: her early education was primarily in Francophone "secular" schools, and she graduated from the College of Political Science in Fez in 1980. Her initiation into Islamism occurred, in any case, far beyond classroom walls, when she was just fifteen years old. By her own account, she was transformed from "youthful indifference to a life a responsibility" one night in 1974, when she saw police arrest and drag her father from their family home (N. Yassine 2006b). This was the year of Abdessalam's now famous open letter to King Hasan II of Morocco, an extended epistle notable less for its ideas—many of which had already been advanced by Islamists such as Hasan al-Banna and Sayyid Qutb—than for its blunt and decidedly undeferential tone (Munson 1991, 337). Titled "al-Islam aw al-tufan" (Islam or the Deluge), the letter

---

[1] As the JSA remains illegal but tolerated by the monarchy, the actual number of members is unknown; estimates range from 50,000 to 600,000 (Cavatorta 2006, 213).

[2] Abdessalam was born in 1928, reportedly into an impoverished Berber (Imazighen) family. Although he studied for four years at the Bin Yusuf Institute of Arab and Islamic Studies, he has no formal religious credentials. His training was primarily in language instruction, and his subsequent career as an inspector of primary education prompted one scholar to dub him "Morocco's most famous militant Islamic bureaucrat" (Munson 1986, 277).

addressed the king as a "brother" rather than a superior, admonished Hasan to renounce his greed, accused him of essentially selling Morocco to foreigners and Zionists, and instructed him to abandon his course of corruption and rule in accordance with Islamic prescriptions (A. Yassine 1974). Advised by an influential 'alim (Muslim scholar) that "only a lunatic could attack the king as harshly as Yasin had done" (interview, Munson 1991, 338), Hassan forcibly committed Abdessalam to a psychiatric hospital, where he languished for more than three years.

In the next two decades, Abdessalam spent extended periods of time in jail or under house arrest. It was during one such term of imprisonment that Nadia left her own job as a French-language instructor in private schools to found the JSA's women's division. The move inaugurated her emergence as a particularly adept spokeswoman for the hybrid of Sufi spirituality and Islamist activism her father developed as a result of his years with the Boutchishiyya sufi order.[3] Although Abdessalam had left the order in 1972, the experience transformed his understanding of Islam, engendering a lifelong commitment to a conception of faith dependent less upon ritual performance or adherence to law than on pursuit of spiritual fulfillment and knowledge inaccessible through reason alone. It was this version of Islam that Nadia would make her own. For almost three decades, both Yassines have drawn on this understanding of faith to pioneer a Sufi inflected re-Islamization through da'wa, education, and social welfare projects for the poor, sick, widowed, and unemployed.

The precedent and inspiration for this approach to Islamism was Hasan al-Banna, founder of the Egyptian Muslim Brotherhood, whose work and writing had contributed to Abdessalam's radicalization in the 1970s. Banna's early immersion in the Hasafiyya sufi order had been central to his own experience of Islam, as well as to the model of charismatic leadership he bequeathed to those who came after him. In this as in much else, however, Banna appears to have been the exception rather than the rule. Despite claims to an authority that has sometimes had Sufi overtones, Sunni Islamist thinkers have tended to regard Sufism as suspect at best and, at worst, unacceptable heterodoxy. Many contemporary Sunni Islamists have similarly leaned toward a "Salafi epistemology that exalts exoteric scripturalism and formal instruction [ta'lim] at the expense of mysticism and spiritual guidance [tarbiya]" (Lauzière 2005, 242; also see chapter 1 in this volume).

The Yassines, however, insist that a successful Islamist movement must address both the corporeal and inner aspects of human existence, and thus

---

[3]The social base of the JSA is similar to that of the Boutchishiyya order, which has been characterized as "elite and mass-based," attracting both "upper-middle-class disciples (university professors, engineers, bank executives, etc.) as well as illiterate followers" (Lauzière 2005, 259, n. 15). For a discussion of the overlap in membership between such Sufi orders and Moroccan organizations devoted to "radical Islamic reform," see Hammoudi 1997, esp. 137.

view themselves as completing the Islamist project rather than offering an alternative to it. Such claims have not silenced their Islamist critics.[4] Nevertheless, the JSA's popularity suggests that, in a region characterized as "one of the most important crucibles of Islamic mysticism" (Cornell 1998, xxiv), many Moroccans have a different view of the matter. Unlike Islamists battling secular regimes, Moroccan Islamists must compete for allegiance in a public sphere already suffused with religiously inflected politics and political discourse, ranging from a nationalism indebted to Islamic modernism, to a mosaic of Muslim political parties and Islamist associations, to a constitutional monarchy whose legitimacy is anchored in the religious and political mantle of the "commander of the faithful" (Burgat 1993, 167–73; Munson 1991, 331–44; Ottaway and Riley 2006; Lauzière 2005, 243; Cavatorta 2006, 213, 217, 220). In this context, Abdessalam's Sufi pedigree and the Yassines' integration of spiritual meaning and moral renewal appears to have given the JSA a political edge in a competitive environment.

The Yassines' approach also benefits from the particular imprimatur socially-engaged Sufism enjoys in Morocco. Mysticism is frequently associated with what sociologist Max Weber calls an "other-worldly" orientation in which salvation requires withdrawal from the world in part because engagement with mundane affairs risks alienation from God. In "this-worldly" mysticism, by contrast, salvation in the hereafter (in Arabic, *akhira*) is contingent on good works in this world (*dunya*) or, in Weber's words, "within the institutions of the world, but in opposition to them" (Lauzière 2005, 246–47; Weber 1964, 166). In keeping with this definition, Sufi saints in the Maghrib (Northwest Africa) have been characterized as brokers between the domains of mystical knowledge and this-worldly power:

> The Moroccan saint was above all else an empowered person–empowered to perform miracles, empowered to communicate with God, empowered to help the weak or oppressed, empowered to act on behalf of others, empowered to mediate the course of destiny, and empowered to affect the behavior of other holders of power. (Cornell 1998, 273)

Neither Abdessalam nor Nadia is currently a member of a Sufi order, and both are careful to distance themselves from strands of mysticism condemned by Islamists.[5] At the same time, Abdessalam has successfully positioned himself as a Sufi *murshid* (religious guide, teacher, leader), and

---

[4]The Moroccan Islamist group al-Islah wa'l-Tajdid, for example, published a document in 1983 that attacked the Sufistic elements of Abdessalam's thought (Lauzière 2005, 247).

[5]See Nadia Yassine's interview with *Le Journal Hebdomodaire* (2006c). For an extensive discussion of the Sufistic elements of Abdessalam Yassine's writings, along with a discussion of his distinction between "orthodox Salafi Sufism" and "philosophical Sufism," see Lauzière 2005.

Nadia has stepped seamlessly into the role of his primary disciple.[6] Evidence suggests that some followers have even come to consider Abdessalam a Sufi saint, and the Yassine home a shrine worthy of pilgrimage.[7] This informal religio-political stature has not shielded JSA members from government repression.[8] It has, however, granted the Yassines a measure of religious authority they are unable to claim by virtue of education, given that neither is an 'alim. This has, in turn, given a certain legitimacy to the JSA's role as self-appointed gadfly to the monarchy, particularly to its provocations from outside the formal political process for greater civil freedoms, government accountability, and moral renewal.

A case in point is the 2005 interview Nadia gave to the Moroccan paper *Al-Usbu'iya al-Jadida,* in which she expressed a preference for a republican system of government and suggested that monarchy is not suitable for Morocco. Nadia and the editor of the paper were charged with violating a press code forbidding insult to "national sacred institutions" and faced a fine and up to five years in prison if convicted. In one of many interviews she granted at the time, Nadia argued that the regime's disproportionate reaction to her comments demonstrated the depth of its insecurity rather than the extent of its power. When asked about a possible guilty verdict, she replied that "prison doesn't scare me at all. Aren't we all, in the end, living a suspended sentence in this arbitrary state?" (Yassine 2006d). Capitalizing on the domestic and international media attention sparked by the indictments, Nadia then arrived at court with a red "X" taped over her lips, surrounded by hundreds of supporters, with more than 150 volunteer defense attorneys in tow. The judges postponed the trial indefinitely.[9]

As this instance demonstrates, the Yassines are not only media savvy but occasionally able to draw the support of Moroccans who may be suspicious of Islamism but are dedicated to enlarging the scope of civil liberties. Such skills have also helped them gain a hearing outside the Maghrib, as does an Arabic-English Web site devoted to Abdessalam, and Nadia's own Web site in French, Spanish, English, and Arabic. Both Yassines write with multiple audiences in mind and are as adept at mar-

[6]Nadia has said in an interview that "my father is not only my genitor but my spiritual master as well" (N. Yassine 2006c). Both father and daughter explicitly associate themselves with mystical insight, most recently by references to "true visions" predicting imminent change in Morocco (Brandon 2007).

[7]Munson 1991, 339. A schoolteacher arrested in 1990 reportedly told the police that Abdessalam "is for me a saint. I prefer him to my father and even to my soul. I am devoted to him and his ideas and works body and soul" (ibid., 339, n. 6).

[8]In 2007, Amnesty International reported that more than 3,000 members of the JSA were interrogated by police after the Association began a recruitment campaign in April, and that "over 500 were reportedly charged with offences that included participating in unauthorized meetings or assemblies, and belonging to an unauthorized association" (Amnesty International 2007; Brandon 2007).

[9]The trial has been rescheduled and postponed several times since 2005, and has yet to take place.

shaling references to Plato, Marx, Darwin, and Karl Popper as to the Qur'an. In these respects, the Yassines are distinctive if not entirely original. Other Islamist thinkers pioneered the technique of indicting Western power using arguments from its own critics and contemporary Islamists such as Qaradawi have used the Internet to establish worldwide influence. Even Abdessalam's recuperation of a Salafi-friendly Sufism owes much to the work of the contemporary Syrian 'alim Sa'id Ramadan al-Buti (Lauzière 2005, 249). Indeed, many of the Yassines' political ideas reiterate arguments made by Banna, Qutb, and Mawdudi, and the JSA's popular social welfare projects follow the path of Islamist groups from Hamas to Hizbullah (Simons 1998; al-Wasat 1999).

What does set the Yassines and the JSA apart from other Islamists is an official policy of nonviolence and an explicit if untested commitment to egalitarianism and procedural democracy.[10] In stark contrast to Qutb's argument that modern jahiliyya is a corrosive disease requiring drastic and even brutal remedies, Abdessalam characterizes violence itself as an expression of ancient and modern jahiliyya. For the shaykh, the hadith report stating that Allah grants to *rifq* (kindness, gentleness, leniency) what He does not grant to *'unf* (violence) requires a tolerance for difference and compassion toward all those excluded from power, suffering from injustice, or oppressed by poverty and ignorance (A. Yassine 2000). As in most Islamist work produced after the founding of Israel, such tolerance is notably absent in Abdessalam's rhetoric about "Zionist Jewry" (see, e.g., A. Yassine 2000). In her account of "engaged Sufism," however, Nadia suggests a more inclusive foundation for tolerance, one that evokes the ecumenical Sufi traditions that had flourished early in Muslim history (see, e.g., Rosenthal 1990, 3: 473; Gutas 2000):

> We have a strong conviction that progress towards God and spiritual perfection cannot take place in their most complete and noble form unless affectionate and caring progress is made towards one's neighbor, be he Muslim or non-Muslim. . . . When spirituality embraces the heart of a Muslim (man and woman alike), his horizons will open: he will no longer consider his fellow Muslim brother or sister as heretic or going astray. He will no longer have one exclusive and excluding vision of Islam. He will accept difference of interpretations and abide by the principle of tolerance. He will work for the common good of everyone. He will be vaccinated against the deadly virus of extremism. . . . He will see all human beings, though not being his co-religionists, as brothers and sisters in humanity. (N. Yassine 2003)

[10]As the editor indicted along with Nadia wryly noted, "I would go to jail if I published a picture of a unveiled woman under the rule of Nadia Yassine—on immorality charges" (Faramarzi 2005).

In this respect, Nadia has increasingly taken center stage by building on positions already sanctioned by her father. Central to Nadia's understanding of nonviolence is a definition of jihad as the dedicated struggle against istikbar (arrogance) in all forms, whether in oneself or others. Particularly crucial is the jihad against the most common expression of istikbar: the lust for power and domination equally evident in Moroccan despotism and Western imperialism, Arab patriarchy and Enlightenment rationalism, Usama bin Laden and Jesse Helms (N. Yassine 2003; 2005c). As jihad against istikbar is both a final goal and a prescription for action, Nadia suggests, a true mujahid will never deploy violent instruments or engage in practices that themselves express the urge to dominate others. So understood, when Islamists such as 'Abd al-Salam Faraj and 'Umar 'Abd al-Rahman invoke Islamic sources to legitimize violent revolution (see chapters 13 and 14 in this volume), they simply invert the meaning of jihad to serve their own arrogant ends. Similarly, Bin Laden's decision to "fight evil with evil and barbarity with barbarity" not only violates specific Islamic prohibitions against harming civilians, women, and children but betrays the ethical imperative to embody the message of a merciful God who cautions believers that (Q 88: 22) "You have no power over them" (N. Yassine 2005c; Daily Excelsior 2002).

If jihad against istikbar is in this way both a means and end rolled into one, its primary weapons are not bombs but words, particularly those deployed in the art of persuasion (Faramarzi 2005; N. Yassine 2006a). Nadia's book Full Sails Ahead may be understood in precisely these terms. The book includes what are now de rigueur polemics against Western arrogance, yet at its heart is a plea for Muslims to turn their gaze inward and take up what she characterizes as the urgent task of self-examination and self-criticism. Such a shift in focus, she argues, will not only reveal the extent of Muslims' "devastating ignorance" of their own history (N. Yassine 2006a, 179), but also show that true Islam was betrayed by Muslim despots long before Napoleon ever set foot on Egyptian soil. In Nadia's historical narrative, the original umma established by the Prophet Muhammad was participatory, egalitarian, committed to freedom, expressive of God's mercy, and governed always by shura (literally: consultation). By shura, however, she intends more than either the Qur'anic principle of "mutual consultation" (Q 42:38) or the procedure by which a caliph is elected. Instead, shura signals an entire philosophy of power that places sovereignty in the community rather than in any individual; links virtue to deliberation and continual reflection rather than to reflexive obedience; and defines faith in terms of the tireless effort to adapt Qur'anic principles through ijtihad rather than rote adherence to precedent (N. Yassine 2006a, 182–86).

While the original umma sacralized the principles of contract, consent, and constitutional power, Nadia argues, both the unity of the community and the ideals it embodied were extinguished by the rise of the Umayyad dynasty in the decades after the Prophet's death (N. Yassine 2006a, 191). At this fateful juncture in Muslim history, the proper relationship between politics and ethics was entirely reversed: religion came to serve power, shura was replaced by *fardiyya* (individualism), community was converted to empire, and egalitarianism gave way to nepotism (N. Yassine 2003; 2006a, 179, 189, 192). Most grievously, this "assassination of shura at the very dawn of Islam" has been erased from memory by a "thousand year flow of stupefying jurisprudence," corrupt Muslim regimes, and foreign domination (N. Yassine 2006a, 187–88). All that remains of shura today travels under the name of democracy, a "lovely and brilliant idea" that has too often been reduced to a cosmetic cover for raw domination. Sadly, such hypocrisy is evinced equally in the democratic gestures of a despotic Moroccan king and the cosmopolitan patina of globalization—the newest form of Western profiteering (N. Yassine 2006a, 55–56).

For the younger Yassine, one need look no farther for evidence of this disastrous break in history than the current status of Muslim women. Characterizing the Prophet as no less than a "proto-feminist" (N. Yassine 2003), Nadia argues that the substitution of the "law of the strongest" for shura resurrected the brutal rule of patriarchy under which Muslim women still suffer.[11] So understood, the use and abuse of women have become a "home-grown malady" rooted in a long-standing cultural chauvinism that treats men like gods (Chu and Radwan 2004). As women's oppression is inextricably intertwined with the political subjugation of Muslims, women confront a "double blockade: autocracy and patriarchy" (N. Yassine 2007). In contrast to "Western feminists" who (supposedly) define liberation in opposition to the shackles of religion, Nadia insists that what Muslim women really need is emancipation from "macho interpretations" of Islam upon which men have built their privilege and power (Khalaf 2006). Sounding a call much like that of Muslim feminists Riffat Hassan and Amina Wadud, Nadia exhorts women to recuperate the original intent of the Islamic message by "reappropriating the instruments of classical theology" and engaging the texts directly through ijtihad (N. Yassine 2003; n.d; Hassan 1991; Wadud 1999).

> If Islam is practiced faithfully, fathers, brothers or husbands have to take care of women. According to the hadith, the best man is the one who treats his wife best. A woman cannot be obliged to marry someone against her will. We are not submissive but the family must be solid. The man is the captain of the ship; the woman is the crew. The crew can always go on strike. (Howe 1996)

---

[11] For data and a discussion of gender discrimination in Moroccan law and employment as well as the impact of poverty, illiteracy, and spousal violence on women, see, for example, Laskier 2003; Maghraoui 2001; Fez City 2003; U.S. Bureau of Democracy, Human Rights, and Labor Report 2006.

Just as Nadia locates the degradation of women in the dynamics of political despotism, many skeptics look to Nadia herself for evidence of the claim that Islam, properly understood, restores to women the egalitarian status they once had and again deserve. Perhaps unsurprisingly, the evidence here is ambiguous. Nadia's power and position are entirely dependent upon privileged access to her father and a presumed ability to elaborate his ideas, a fact of which she is clearly aware. When queried about possible successors to the aging shaykh, for example, she ruled herself out, implying that a generalized "chauvinism" would prevent her ascension to the leadership of the JSA rather than, say, the will of her father, to whom she frequently attributes a pioneering commitment to women's equality (N. Yassine 2006c; Cavatorta 2006, 215).

Abdessalam's views, however, tend to hew closely to Islamist gender norms in which women's nature is inextricably tied to the domestic domain and symbolically transformed into an index of cultural and moral virtue. While more attuned to discrimination against women than other Islamists, his writing largely registers "women's suffering" as an abstraction with a specific ideological function: to demonstrate the extent of a moral decay cured only by re-Islamization (A. Yassine 1973; 2000). Like Banna, Qutb, Ghazali, and Mutahhari, the women Abdessalam invokes are less individuals with agency than conduits for corruption or vessels of purity—in his words, "blonde tourist whores" imported along with AIDS, or virtuous Muslim women characterized by "delicate sensitivities and mother love" (A. Yassine 2002, 76; 2000).

In apparent conformity with such a gender ideology, Nadia remains covered in public and writes of herself, a woman married to a JSA member with whom she has had four daughters, as "naturally dispensed to give life and dispense love" (N. Yassine 2006e, 50). Yet she is also a painter and runs her own design business in addition to her work for the Association. She is said to reject the term "feminist" as Western and elitist, and prefers describing herself as a "militant, social neo-Sufi" (Kristianasen 2004). Yet she has also explicitly embraced "Islamic feminism" as necessary to recover "inalienable rights that Muslim societies have underhandedly and systematically confiscated from women more than they have from men" (N. Yassine 2007, 107).

Unlike Zaynab al-Ghazali, Nadia's engagement with "women's issues" is unequivocally more than a platform to secure her own unique status. Her ambivalence about "feminism" ultimately suggests not an uncertain commitment to women's welfare but rather an unwillingness to adopt a label she associates with agendas opposed to her own—the West, the state, Moroccan elites.[12] In this context, she avers, wearing the hijab (Islamic scarf) is actually a subversive expression of women's agency that signals a "triple break" from overlapping constraints: a reconquest of the public space that defies the strictures of domesticity; a declaration of dis-

[12]In this connection, see Bessis's (1999) discussion of how "institutional feminism" helped secure the Moroccan regime ideologically.

sent from the established order; and a public reclamation of faith against all those who view Islam and women's rights as mutually exclusive.

Much of Nadia's writing aims to synchronize Islamism with a commitment to women's agency that she herself seems to embody, although such efforts do not always translate into coherent politics. A case in point is the JSA's opposition to King Muhammad VI's proposed reforms of the *mudawwana,* Moroccan family law, which included raising the age of marriageable girls from fifteen to eighteen, prohibiting marriages arranged without the woman's consent, and changes in polygamy, divorce, and custody laws designed to improve the legal status of women (N. Yassine 2003; 2006f; Abdelhadi 2005). The JSA launched a massive opposition rally in Casablanca in March 2000, and Nadia dismissed the reforms as expressions of foreign values imposed by a despotic regime—despite the fact that many of the proposed changes echoed her own prescriptions for improving the lives of Muslim women.

The JSA reversed its position after the reforms were slightly modified, however, an about-face reportedly spearheaded by Nadia and other female members of the Association.[13] In subsequent interviews, "blogs," and public statements, Nadia claims to have anticipated the necessity of such reforms, while maintaining that they did not go far enough to address the underlying material inequalities that oppress women "in real life" (Gray and Tarvainen 2004; Gupta 2006; Hackensberger 2006; N. Yassine 2006f). Simple political opportunism may go some way toward explaining these events. Yet Nadia's role is also suggestive of an Islamic feminism that Miriam Cooke (2001, 60) characterizes as a "contingent, contextually determined strategic self-positioning . . . [that] invites us to consider what it means to have a difficult double commitment: on the one hand, to a faith position, and on the other hand, to women's rights both inside the home and outside." This is particularly evident in those occasional moments when Nadia contests the script she serves, as in the following rejoinder to the very gender ideology her visibility both ratifies and subverts:

> When spirituality embraces the heart of a Muslim . . . he will consider his fellow Muslim woman not as a baby-making machine, or a lieutenant of Satan, or a commodity or sex target. He will see her as a fully-fledged citizen and full-time partner in the management of societal concerns. (N. Yassine 2003)

[13]Cavatorta 2006, 215–16. Nadia would later refer to the JSA's initial opposition as a "tactical mistake" (Kristianasen 2004).

# MODERNITY, MUSLIM WOMEN, AND POLITICS
# IN THE MEDITERRANEAN

## The Divided Mediterranean

It is quite commonplace to discuss Mediterranean culture as a homogeneous reality encompassing the entire Mediterranean basin. If one wishes to examine the issue seriously, however, it is imperative to define the limits of this view and to recognize that the Mediterranean has two shores and two economic realities. Moreover, it has two social realities that derive from the historical relationship between the northern and southern regions of the Mediterranean, a history that is more the product of dialectic than of an ideal and parallel evolution.

The patriarchy underlying the social structure on both sides of the Mediterranean basin does indeed give the illusion of a historical unity, one that is shared by women in particular. Yet this illusion soon dissipates if we take even a cursory glance at history, at the economic facts, and especially at the political divide that has become more and more pronounced since 9/11, which represents Day Zero in modern international relations. Up until that decisive day, it was just barely adequate to make a distinction between the band of Latin countries, that is, the European Mediterranean, and countries of the Mediterranean Southeast, composed of the Arab world and countries of the East (Turkey, the former Yugoslavia, Albania, Malta, Cyprus, Israel). Today it is clear that such classifications tend to constitute a heuristic method that must be superseded at all costs, because the Arab-Muslim world has become more and more differentiated in this divided Mediterranean.

The reality of the Mediterranean woman is increasingly different according to whether she belongs to the Muslim world or not. One should avoid lapsing into the sort of trivial and simplistic comparison denounced by respected intellectuals such as [French sociologist] Irène Théry, who stated in the eighth "Meeting of Averroes" that one should not engage in a sort of historical evolutionism. It is futile to comprehend the history of Muslim women by adhering to stereotypes whereby the status of the Western woman is a natural—and therefore ideal—end point that Mediterranean women will inevitably reach.

The recent victory of Kuwaiti women fighting for their right to vote may lead us to think that the struggles of women on both sides of the

Mediterranean are similar, separated only by a gap of time. But a survey like the one conducted by the Gallup Institute in 2005 among 8,000 women from eight Muslim countries tells us that "the majority does not think that adopting Western values would help economic or political progress." Expectations may converge, yet the ideological points of reference diverge significantly. It is particularly interesting to know that "an overwhelming majority of the women surveyed think that the most positive aspect of their society is its attachment to moral and spiritual values."

## A New Muslim Female Conscience

Does that mean that the Muslim woman is a resigned individual who has no political claims? The survey categorically contradicts this idea, because in Morocco and Lebanon, 93 percent of the women surveyed said that the women should hold positions of responsibility. The major demands of these women are still voting, the right to work, and active participation in society. What is happening is the birth of a new self-awareness of the Muslim woman, her history, and the world.

The illiteracy that wreaks havoc in most countries of the Arab world and that affects women more than men does not prevent the emergence in civil societies of a real and brand new visibility of the Muslim woman who considers herself, demands her rights, and fulfills her duties as a Muslim woman. This is not just an emotional reaction or an identity in a state of tension; nor is it just the classic tendency toward conservatism that standard political sociology attributes automatically to women. Rather it is a real social phenomenon that is experienced in the Arab-Muslim world and which one might define as revolutionary.

There is certainly no contradiction when the aforementioned survey informs us that most of these women "see the love of religion as the most positive aspect of their country." Nor is it a paradox that in Morocco and in Egypt, which are apparently more modernist than Iran according to the prevailing stereotypes, the percentage of men who favor the participation of women in positions of responsibility is markedly lower. By contrast, 83 percent of Iranian men support the participation of women in society.

It is clear that a dynamic of liberation is being set in motion by way of a return to religious roots. The Muslim world is undergoing a real upheaval that is undoubtedly part of the continual process of reexamination that has recurred throughout its history but also constitutes an especially significant break with these continual attempts at readjustment, however innovative they may have been. The continuity stems from the fact that, in times of crisis, the Muslim world has always been characterized by sudden bursts of awareness and reexamination of its beliefs that derive from a quite natural dialectical process. The break stems from the specific nature of modernity, which is in itself an unprecedented "age of turbulence," as [nineteenth-century German sociologist] Max Weber describes it.

## Muslim Feminism or Female Ijtihad?

New sociopolitical parameters are forcing the Muslim world to generate and manage a new order of things in the process of reexamining its identity, a process that has become inevitable but is above all crucial. Adapting to a global and changing world requires devising new dynamics that enable women to take a central role.

Such adaptation is manifested in the all-encompassing "return to the roots" led by so-called Islamist movements but also in the very specific conception of women within these movements.

Some hasten to accuse this sudden burst of feminism of producing a certain epistemological confusion that appears to support the kind of evolutionism that objective thinking has discredited. As concepts have histories, feminism is a struggle that has proceeded in a secular and agnostic context that is often purely materialistic, which is part of the rationale of liberating women from the last religious strangleholds.

The struggle of Muslim women in the current renascence is a struggle that derives from their religious roots, which were originally a source of liberation, and pits them against a system that has deprived them of the privileges that their religion had granted and guaranteed to them.

This is not a struggle to reclaim the physical body for enjoyment but rather a reclamation of the physical body and soul for greater spirituality, which is constitutive of a woman's dignity and enhances her social status. This reclamation requires that the woman redefine herself within a social structure that is more patriarchal, autocratic, and traditional than Islamic. It also requires that she intrude subversively into the guarded ground of a closed, chauvinistic system that until now has been officially inaccessible to women. What can be called Islamic Feminism is the demand to recover the inalienable rights that Muslim societies have underhandedly and systematically confiscated from women more than they have from men. The right of thinking on behalf of the society to which they belong and in which they produce children is a sacred right for women. In the founding ages of Islam, ijtihad (independent or personal interpretation or judgment) was never the private property of those who supported regimes that radically excluded women.

From now on, the Muslim woman intends to return to the historical source, but not because she is a reactionary. The point of this return is to make use of the legitimacy conferred by the acquisition of theological knowledge in order to better master a world that is rather hostile to her.

The emergence of this awareness and of this effort is part of a trend of thought that is increasingly asserting itself in the Arab-Muslim world but which is still sporadic and scattered. The influence of Wahhabism is a serious constraint on such an emergence.

It would be ideal if this awakening of female conscience became a collective undertaking, one that would become part of a more comprehensive framework of resistance that would protect it from any repressive will. In fact, Rachid Ghannouchi's Islamist movement was the most promising candidate to promote the status of women, but the systematic repression of the movement by Ben Ali's regime has curtailed the expansion of the kind of thinking that would restore to the Muslim woman her right and proper place in our societies.[14]

Are all chances thus lost to see this structure of thought transform itself into a real social movement? The Justice and Spirituality Movement seems to be an original, perhaps unique case in this respect, despite the fact that the Moroccan regime's repression of it grows more intense every day and increasingly targets the women's section because of the way it disrupts all the traditional schemes on which the regime builds its legitimacy.

## An Example of Reclaiming Theological Roots: The Women's Section of the Justice and Spirituality Movement

Contrary to conventional stereotypes, the Justice and Spirituality Movement advocates both nonviolence and the sine qua non participation of women as the best means of reproducing the model of social justice promoted by the original Islam.

For this movement, reviving the Islamic faith consists in denouncing the rerouting of history by regimes that have imposed patriarchy and autocracy upon our societies. Such regimes not only considered these systems to be the only acceptable means of political management but also conferred upon them such a sacred status that they became dogmatic.

In the movement, this denunciation entails the participation of women in a course of study that can only be a militant one—something that is in itself already revolutionary in a deeply conservative society.

Such participation is all the more meritorious and symbolic of a real revolution in relation to both the past and the present Muslim world, as women's participation is sought and practiced at the top levels of the movement's leading bodies. The Majlis Shura, or internal parliament of the movement, is 30 percent women. For every six members elected to

[14]Rachid Ghannouchi (b. 1941), usually considered a "moderate" Islamist thinker, is the leader and principal theoretician of Tunisia's Hizb al-Nahda (Renaissance Party); Ben Ali (b. 1936) has been the president of Tunisia since 1987.

the Secretariat-General, three are women; there has been no need to introduce a quota system. The women's section is very dynamic and influential, as it enjoys total independence in its actions and programs.

In these times of crisis, the movement's basic theory promotes the salvation of our societies by means of a voluntary rehabilitation of the woman in the ijtihad effort. It has made it a sacred duty to promote such participation first and foremost within itself:

"The Muslim woman should become informed of her rights," the founder of the movement [Abdessalam Yassine] writes. "Once she is aware of them and well informed, she should be able to demand their application. No one else will do these things for her. A solid share of material and moral rights will free her from ancestral servitude and will allow her to devote herself to her duties. The good work required to rescue Muslims is arduous; it will take the hard-working goodwill of everyone, women and men side by side, associations in competition with one another in their good works."

So essential is the female element within the movement that the Moroccan regime has deemed it necessary to extend to the women's section the repression that has for decades affected the movement as a whole. Several dozens of women members were arrested during the summer of 2006; some have even been abducted.

My trial occurs within this context, for I have transgressed several taboos by criticizing the regime and for having political opinions that contravene all of the traditions that have been "made sacred." The transgression by a woman of the political code of silence that has been imposed upon us by the autocratic powers is a sort of subversion that is particularly symbolic of—and significant for—our struggle as women who draw from our religious roots.

One of the female members, having been savagely repressed by a Moroccan Intelligence Agency that has fallen back into practices thought to belong to Morocco's past, has courageously transgressed this very code of silence by "speaking" of her abduction in a society where women must not only keep silent but are systematically dishonored if they happen to encounter the police. Indeed, what is required is a revival of Islam's original teachings, which championed women as full-fledged social agents, not as individuals subject to the double obstacle of autocracy and patriarchy.

The educational programs of the women's section promote as models those women who have very strong, positive, and responsible personalities: women who speak out with their opinions, lay claim to their rights, and negotiate their positions within society.

Our reading of the sacred texts is at odds with the ossifying ideology built up over the course of time by a body of exegetes who sapped all dynamic from Islamic Law. The goal for the movement's female members is to unearth this dynamic, to understand its spirit, and to launch a

liberating pedagogy that will destroy all the locks and strangleholds
imposed upon women by the chauvinistic readings accumulated
throughout Muslim history.


## A Cultural Revolution

We must recall and emphasize the fact, however, that this reclamation
of the sacred texts is somewhat specific to women; this is not a matter
of a violent rebellion conducted by a female proletariat against the male
oppressor, of a great march of women against men. The revolution is
certainly cultural, but if reeducation is to begin at all, it must entail
restructuring society from the bottom, with men and women united and
joined together in efforts to reach a new conception of complementarity.

It is not a question of setting up reeducation camps but rather one of
helping our devastated societies achieve a new understanding of their
Muslim identity. The women's section is fully aware that, in order to
garner support for their convictions, they must show some respect for
certain traditional norms. Consequently, it has a clearly established goal
of obtaining official degrees that will not only enable women to master
the tools of theology but also win them widespread social recognition
and acceptance.

In addition to the en masse return of women members to academic
studies in order to achieve a specifically female interpretation of the
movement, the women's section also aims to train fifty female 'ulama
within a short period of time. This project is so appealing to a young
population in search of points of reference within Islam that break
completely away from the archaic schemes of traditional Islam that the
Moroccan regime has simply hijacked it, aiming to train exactly the
same number (fifty) of *murshidats* (spiritual advisers).


## Conclusion

If the Moroccan regime takes these female initiatives seriously, it is
because social dissidence is increasingly spreading throughout the lands
of Islam. The Islamic scarf is a significant symbol of the transformation
of a movement that, in the postcolonial context, originally alienated
women by associating women's liberation with the Western model. The
Islamic scarf, which is a testimony of faith in particular, is also a highly
political act because it expresses a threefold break. When a woman
wears the Islamic scarf, she reclaims her spirituality, reconquers the
public sphere (because the Islamic scarf is a projection of the private
sphere within that public space), and finally makes a political declaration of dissidence against the established order, be it national or interna-

tional. Stereotypes that portray the Islamic scarf as a clear symbol of women's oppression in contemporary Muslim societies are either an expression of obvious bad faith or an admission of ignorance regarding this movement, a movement that it is nevertheless crucial to understand if one does not wish to miss the opportunity to witness history in the making, a history that will certainly no longer occur without its women.

# PART IV

# Violence, Action, and Jihad

# Chapter 13

# MUHAMMAD 'ABD AL-SALAM FARAJ
# 1954–1982

ON OCTOBER 6, 1981, Egyptian president Anwar al-Sadat was gunned down in front of television cameras while watching a military parade. Six months later, five members of Jama'at al-Jihad (the Jihad Group) were executed for the murder, four of the assassins and a twenty-seven-year old electrical engineer from Cairo named Muhammad 'Abd al-Salam Faraj.[1] Faraj had not wielded a machine gun on the parade grounds that day, but evidence of his full participation in the operation was available for all to see: months before the assassination, Faraj penned *al-Farida al-Gha'iba* (The Absent Duty), a pamphlet detailing the Jihad Group's religio-political justifications for armed revolt against infidel rulers. More a revolutionary salvo written by and for ordinary Muslims than a coherent theological doctrine, the booklet has been dismissed in some quarters as an assemblage of quotations and derivative arguments, and Faraj, an autodidact in the Islamic tradition, characterized as no more than a "pubescent thinker" (Kepel 1993, 194, 197, 206). Yet the political purchase of "The Absent Duty" is not so easily dismissed. The remarkable influence exercised by the pamphlet, along with the bloody spectacle with which it is forever associated, have transformed what might have been a footnote in Egyptian history into a classic statement of and catalyst for armed jihad as the preeminent enactment of individual Muslim piety.

The central argument of the pamphlet is deceptively simple: the "absent duty" in question is jihad and, more specifically, the imperative to fight infidels by force of arms. Yet what Faraj represents as clear and self-evident actually reflects a radical reworking of jihad, a redefinition that eliminates all textual ambiguities and interpretive complexities in an effort to delegitimize the multiple meanings jihad has carried for Muslims past and present.

While often translated into English as "holy war," jihad is derived from the verb *jahada* which means "to exert," "to struggle," or "to strive," and is linguistically and conceptually distinct from the Arabic words for fighting and war, *qital* and *harb*.[2] Jihad literally means exerting one's utmost

---

[1] One of the members of the Jihad Group arrested in the wake of the assassination was Ayman al-Zawahiri, a leader of al-Qa'ida second in importance only to Usama bin Laden (see chapter 18, on Bin Laden).

[2] As Bernard Lewis (1988, 71) points out, there is no word corresponding to holy war in classical Arabic usage.

power or ability in striving toward a worthy goal or struggling against what is proscribed, and when qualified by the phrase *fi sabil Allah*, refers to struggle or striving in the path of God. The earliest references to jihad in the Qur'an and hadith refer to a wide range of struggles, from fighting on behalf of the Muslim community to the internal struggle against evil in one's soul. The particular significance of internal jihad is captured in hadith reports in which the Prophet Muhammad is said to have referred to struggling against the baser instincts of the self as "the greater jihad" (cf. Bonner 2006, 51). This has often been interpreted to mean that the internal struggle, the greater jihad, is incumbent upon all individuals, whereas the *jihad bi'l sayf* (jihad of the sword) is the "lesser" of the two and may be performed by some on behalf of others.

For Faraj, these rival understandings of jihad only distract from the paramount struggle against unbelievers and, as such, are both symptom and cause of the humiliations, weaknesses, and internal divisions plaguing Muslims in the contemporary epoch. Faraj sees the crisis at hand in terms articulated by Sayyid Qutb: modernity is a condition of moral bankruptcy that, although Western in origin, has come to corrode the umma from within as a result of so-called Muslim rulers who claim for themselves the sovereignty that belongs exclusively to Allah. The nature of the crisis demonstrates that, in Faraj's now famous words, "to fight an enemy that is near is more important than to fight an enemy that is far," for there can be no victory against foreign enemies until the struggle to put the House of Islam in order is concluded (section 68). Against those who argue that the struggle for Palestinian lands must take precedence over all others, Faraj insists that the liberation of Jerusalem must wait until victory can be at the hands of righteous Muslims rather than apostate Arab regimes. The jihad against Zionists, communists, crusaders, and imperialists must also be deferred until the more immediate challenge of establishing an Islamic state in Muslim lands has been met. In a warning unheeded by those who would launch a "global jihad" twenty years later, he cautions that any fight against imperialists before this goal has been attained is premature, a "waste of time," and a strategic and political mistake.

The imminence and nature of the internal threat dictate not only the focus of jihad but also the proper methods and instruments of its execution. For Faraj, given the immediacy of the danger from Muslim rulers who contravene Islamic law, it is imperative to see jihad against oneself, the devil, and against infidels and hypocrites as three dimensions of a single simultaneous endeavor rather than as successive stages of struggle. As for the means to this righteous end, a true mujahid will take his cue from the only question that matters: does it help to bring about the establishment of the Islamic state (section 48)? Nadia Yassine's (see chapter 12) understanding of jihad as inimical to violence as well as to any practices that express the urge to dominate others has no place here. Just as there is but one overriding question, for Faraj there is only one legitimate answer: the Islamic tradition, history, and the nature of contemporary political power all attest to the primacy of "the jihad of the sword" over any other form of struggle.

The preeminent authority for such claims is the Qur'an, as Faraj understands it. All other evidence and arguments are merely ancillary. Unlike a restaurant menu of items from which customers may pick and choose, for Faraj the Qur'an is an ethical unity expressive of the divine will, and thus demands total obedience rather than selective adherence. Indeed, the sacred book itself asks "Do you, then, believe a part of the Book and reject [another] part?" (Q 2:85). On the matter of armed jihad, Faraj contends, the Qur'an speaks authoritatively and unambiguously, telling believers that "fighting is ordained for you" (Q 2:216); "establish the Truth according to His word and finish off the unbelievers" (Q 8:7); "fight them until there is no more persecution and all worship is devoted to God alone" (Q 8:39); and "wherever you encounter the idolaters, kill them" (Q 9:5). So, too, do the hadith appear to rally believers against the infidels, particularly as Faraj adduces as authoritative only those reports that sustain his claims and summarily dismisses the Tradition suggesting the superiority of internal jihad as a fabrication disseminated to pacify Muslims (section 90).[3]

"The Absent Duty" gives enormous weight to historical precedent, but equally selectively; the past serves only to corroborate what the pamphlet depicts as incontrovertible, timeless commands. For Faraj as for many other Islamist thinkers before and after him, the historical precedent that looms largest—after the formative years of Islam—is the rule of the Mongols, particularly as refracted through the jurisprudence of Ibn Taymiyya (d. 1328). The Mongols had destroyed the 'Abbasid caliphate in 1258, yet, by the turn of the century, many of the invading rulers had converted to Islam. For Ibn Taymiyya, however, these so-called Muslims contravened the shari'a by admixing Islamic prescriptions with Mongol tribal law (the Yasa), thus rendering their rule illegitimate and rebellion justifiable. Eager to drape his arguments in the authority of the illustrious fourteenth-century jurist, Faraj posits a dubious historical parallel between Sadat (whom he does not mention by name) and the most famous Mongol leader, Genghis Khan, while simultaneously insisting that the contemporary crisis is far more dangerous. Mongol rulers incorporated at least some aspects of Islamic law, Faraj complains, but today godless imperialists have put their hands on virtually every corner of the globe, apostates masquerading as Muslim rulers serve as lackeys of foreign will, and the *Dar al-Islam* (the Abode of Islam) is increasingly betrayed from within.

---

[3] As the words of the Prophet rather than of God, hadith reports have a different epistemological standing from that of the Qur'an and have traditionally required careful vetting to distinguish between authentic statements of the Prophet and unreliable accounts attributed to him.

When joined to Qur'an 5:44, which Islamists translate as "those who do not govern by what God has revealed are unbelievers" (see below), historical precedent demonstrates that insurrection against apostate rulers is not only justifiable but imperative.

What history and the Qur'an dictate, the nature of worldly power confirms: only armed struggle is capable of challenging the power of the modern Egyptian regime and its formidable mechanisms of surveillance and control. Indeed, Faraj suggests that the scope of state power is precisely why so many Muslims delude themselves about the true nature of jihad; even devout believers prefer the safety and comfort of devotional acts that put nothing important at risk, such as cultivating their personal piety, establishing Islamic charities, forming political parties, and seeking and propagating Islamic knowledge by study, preaching, and writing. By contrast, Faraj invokes Qutb to argue that all pacific forms of struggle are but poor and cowardly substitutes for the sweat and blood necessary to both enact God's will and combat a regime whose tentacles extend deeply into every dimension of society. As the very foundations of the Egyptian state are rotten to the core, moreover, those who imagine themselves working for Islam "from within" the halls of power are merely complicit in its crimes. Equally delusional are those who claim to emulate the Prophet's *hijra* (his emigration from Mecca to Medina in 622) by searching elsewhere for a place more conducive to establishing an Islamic state.[4] Such arguments are nothing more than misguided claptrap, Faraj avers, the result of "having forsaken the only true and religiously allowed road toward establishing an Islamic state" (section 62).

Following a hadith according to which "the worst of all things are novelties, since every novelty is an innovation [bid'a] and every innovation is a deviation, and all deviation is in hell" (section 2), Faraj depicts his arguments as a simple reflection of the true Islamic essence buried beneath innumerable deviations and misguided innovations. Yet this uncompromising insistence on fidelity to the sacred text is most systematically violated by Faraj himself, particularly in his unacknowledged effort to render the radical traditional and the innovative authentic. A case in point is his claim that the Qur'an unambiguously commands the fighting of unbelievers, and his repeated invocation of the so-called Verse of the Sword (Q 9:5) to substantiate it. In al-Azhar's 1982 rebuttal to "The Absent Duty," however, Shaykh Jadd al-Haqq argues that this use of the verse eviscerates the force of the remaining lines in which believers are told that if idolaters "turn [to God], maintain the prayer, and pay the prescribed alms, let them go on their way, for God is most forgiving and merciful" (Jansen 1986a, 55–56; 1986b).

[4]This is a position associated with Faraj's contemporary, Shukri Mustafa, the leader of an Egyptian Islamist group popularly known as the Society of Excommunication and Emigration.

Faraj thus sees himself as excavating an authentic Islam unsullied by human interpretation at the very moment he is transforming textual fragments into timeless commands stripped of the larger ethical and textual world in which they have been conventionally embedded. This is further evinced in his use of Qur'an 5:44, usually rendered as "He who does not judge by what God has revealed is an unbeliever." As Yvonne Haddad (1983, 27) points out, the radical rereading of this as "those who do not *govern* by what God has revealed are unbelievers" has become central to the "revolutionary ethos" embraced by a range of contemporary Islamist groups.[5] Faraj, as well as 'Umar 'Abd al-Rahman, and, later, Usama bin Laden, invokes this reading to ratify rebellion against apostate "Muslim" rulers. Yet many scholars insist this grossly misuses a Qur'anic fragment whose meaning depends upon the five long verses in which it is embedded, verses that deal specifically with the Torah, Rabbis, Jesus, and the Gospel (Gwynne 2006, 71). Drawing attention to these verses, for example, Shaykh Jadd al-Haqq has argued that Qur'an 5:44 addresses Christians and Jews and hence "the context makes the militant interpretation impossible" (Jansen 1986a, 33, n. 22).

Faraj's claim that the weight of religious scholarship affirms his reading of the "true Islam" is not only challenged by such criticisms from 'ulama, but is also in tension with a thread of deep anticlericalism woven throughout "the Absent Duty." Like Qutb and Banna before him, Faraj evinces a palpable frustration with 'ulama who appear to have a greater stake in stability than justice, and it is as failed custodians of Islam that he calls them to account. For Faraj, the sad state of Muslim affairs attests specifically to the 'ulama's neglect of jihad and misrepresentation of what it necessarily entails. He is particularly aggrieved by the continuing tendency of Muslim jurists to consider jihad a fard kifaya (collective obligation), that is, as something a group of people within the community must perform on behalf of the rest, as distinguished from obligations that must be fulfilled by every single Muslim (e.g., the ritual prayers). This view has largely applied to offensive jihad but, Faraj contends, the conditions that now obtain in Muslim lands are radically different: attacks from enemies both proximate and internal necessitate a defensive jihad that is as much an individual obligation as are daily prayers, requiring no less than "a drop of sweat from every Muslim" (section 86).

Not content to assail the judgment of religious scholars whose views are uncongenial to the "proper" view of jihad, Faraj calls into question their mettle and integrity, accusing them of too often taking refuge in the supposed rigors of rarefied scholarship to avoid the physical hardships and political dangers of armed struggle. Just as the pursuit of knowledge

---

[5]The verbs "to judge" and "to govern" are both derived from the same Arabic root, *ha-kaf-mim*, and it is often unclear in which sense it is intended in the Arabic. Jansen, however, renders it as "govern."

is open to all, he argues, it is incumbent upon scholars as well as non-scholars to participate in the fight against infidels. After all, he writes with a note of contempt, "scholarship is not the decisive weapon that will radically put an end to paganism" (section 64). Moreover, Faraj assures his readers, the very same conditions of crisis that render quiescent religious authority suspect also make formal political authorization unnecessary: when jihad becomes an individual rather than a collective obligation, there is no need for an established caliph deputized to declare war on behalf of the Muslim community.

Many of these arguments will be familiar to readers of Banna, Qutb, and Mawdudi. Yet the significance of "The Absent Duty" derives less from its originality than from the ways in which it captures a collective set of concerns and commitments, synthesizes already existing arguments about jihad, and translates them into "operational terms" (Gerges 2005, 9, 44) that have exercised enormous influence over successive generations of Islamists. Like the Hamas Charter (see chapter 15), the pamphlet is perhaps best understood as a window onto a perspective rather than a particular person: although written by Faraj, it is the culmination of on-going debates at the time among unnamed Islamists in universities, mosques, army barracks, and prisons. As one scholar aptly suggests, reading the pamphlet is much like listening in on a circulating internal document (Jansen 1986a, 6–7; also E. Goldberg 1991, 22)—one collectively authored by the very men "The Absent Duty" depicts as the revolutionary vanguard with the vision and courage necessary to recognize the extent of the crisis and risk everything to bring about its only solution (section 54).[6]

---

[6]The parameters of such discussions reflect, in turn, an emergent interpretive framework forged by thinkers and activists such as 'Umar 'Abd al-Rahman (see chapter 14 in this volume), a formally trained 'alim affiliated with the Jihad Group, as well as those who influenced him, such as Qutb and Mawdudi.

# THE NEGLECTED DUTY

In the Name of God the Most Compassionate

§2. Glory to God. We praise Him, we ask for His help, we ask Him to forgive us, we ask Him to give us guidance. We seek protection with God against the wickedness of our souls and against the evilness of our acts. If God sends someone on the right path, no one can send him astray. If God sends someone astray, no one can guide him. I acknowledge that there is no god but God alone, He has no associate, and I acknowledge that Muhammad is His Servant and His Apostle.

The most reliable Speech is the Book of God, and the best guidance is the guidance of Muhammad, may God's peace be upon him. The worst of all things are novelties, since every novelty is a bid'a (an innovation; plural: *bida'*) and every innovation is a deviation, and all deviation is in Hell.

§3. Jihad for God's cause, in spite of its extreme importance and its great significance for the future of this religion, has been neglected by the 'ulama of this age. They have feigned ignorance of it, but they know that it is the only way to the return and the establishment of the glory of Islam anew. Every Muslim preferred his own favorite ideas and philosophies above the best road, which God—praised and exalted He is—drew Himself (a road that leads back) to (a state of) honor for His servants.

§4. There is no doubt that the idols of this world can be made to disappear only through the power of the sword. It is therefore that (the apostle Muhammad)—God's peace be upon him—said: "I have been sent with the sword at this hour, so that God alone is worshiped, without associate to Him, He put my daily bread under the shadow of my lance, He brings lowness and smallness to those who disagree with what I command. Whosoever resembles a certain group of people will be counted as a member of that group." (This Tradition is) reported by Imam Ahmad (ibn Hanbal) on the authority of Ibn 'Umar.

§31. In his description of the Mongols Ibn Taymiyya says: "Everyone who is with them in the state over which they rule has to be regarded as belonging to the most evil class of men. He either is an atheist (*zindiq*)

and hypocrite who does not believe in the essence of the religion of
Islam—this means that he (only) outwardly pretends to be Muslim—or
he belongs to that worst class of all people who are the people of the
bida' like (the members of sects like) the *Rawafid,* the Jahmiyya, the
Ittihadiyya, etc. These are all groups who commit themselves to bida'.
Or they are from that most criminal and sinful group who although
they are quite able to perform the pilgrimage to the Ka'ba (the Ancient
House) do not perform this pilgrimage, even though there are among
them some who perform the prayers and fast, but the majority (of them)
does not perform the prayers or pay the (Muslim religious) zakat tax."
Is this not (exactly) what is the case (in Egypt today)?

§32. They fight under the banners of Genghis Khan—the name of their
king. Whosoever enters into their obedience becomes their client even if
he is an infidel. Whosoever rebels against their authority is regarded as
their enemy even if he were from among the best of Muslims. They do
not fight under the banners of Islam and they do not impose the head
tax (on Jews and Christians). Many of the Muslim army commanders
and viziers in their camps even have it as their aim that in their (the
Mongols') esteem a Muslim should be equal to the nonmonotheist
(*mushrik*) Jews and Christians to whom they give high positions. (This
is quoted from) *al-Fatawa,* p. 286.

NOTE: Are not these characteristics the same characteristics as those
of the rulers of this age, and their entourage of clients as well? (Do the
members of their entourage not) glorify the ruler more than they glorify
their Creator?

§33. On p. 287 *Shaykh al-Islam* Ibn Taymiyya adds to his description
of the clients of Genghis Khan. He writes on those who outwardly
profess to be Muslims that "they place Muhammad (in a position) equal
to (the position of) Genghis Khan; and if (they do) not (do) this, they—
in spite of their pretension to be Muslims—not only glorify Genghis
Khan but also fight the Muslims. The worst of these infidels even give
him their total and complete obedience; they bring him their properties
and give their decisions in his name. When they disagree with what he
orders them, this is like rebellion against an imam. Above all this, they
fight the Muslims and treat them with the greatest enmity. They ask the
Muslims to obey them, to give them their properties, and to enter (the
obedience of the rules) that were imposed on them by this infidel
polytheist king who so resembles the Pharaoh or Nimrod and their
likes. He is, however, a greater pest than both of these two."

§34. Ibn Taymiyya says in addition: "Whosoever enters into their
obedience (and obeys their) un-Islamic (prescripts) (*ta'atahum al-
jahiliyya*) and their pagan customs is their friend; whosoever disagrees

with them is their enemy even if he were the best of God's Prophets, Apostles or Saints." (This quotation is taken from p. 288.)

## §47. *Ideas and Misunderstandings*

In the Islamic world there are several ideas about the elimination of these rulers and the establishment of the Rule of God—exalted and majestic He is. To what extent are these ideas correct?

## §48. *Benevolent Societies*

There are those who say that we should establish societies that are subject to the state and that urge people to perform their prayers and to pay their zakat tax and to do (other) good works. Prayer, zakat, and good works are (all equally) commands of God—exalted and majestic He is—which we should not at all neglect. However, when we ask ourselves: "Do these works, and acts of devotion, bring about the establishment of an Islamic state?"—then the immediate answer without any further consideration must be "No." Moreover, these societies would in principle be subject to the state, be registered in its files, and they would have to follow (the state's) instructions.

## §49. *Obedience, Education, and Abundance of Acts of Devotion*

There are those who say that we should occupy ourselves with obedience to God, with educating the Muslims, and with exerting ourselves in acts of devotion, because the backwardness in which we live overpowered us on account of our sins and our (own) works. They sometimes prove this with a maxim that says on the authority of Malik ibn Dinar: God—exalted and majestic He is—says: "I am God, the King of Kings; the hearts of the kings are in My hand; When someone obeys Me, I make (the kings) (My instrument of) mercy towards him; When someone disobeys Me, I make (the kings) (My instrument of) revenge towards him. Do not occupy yourselves with kings, but turn in repentance to the most compassionate King you have."

§50. The truth is that someone who thinks that this maxim abrogates the two duties of (1) jihad and (2) ordering to do what is reputable and forbidding to do what is not destroys himself and those who obey him and listen to him. . . .

Whoever really wants to be occupied with the highest degrees of obedience and wants to reach the peak of devotion must commit himself to jihad for the cause of God, without, however, neglecting the other (prescribed) pillars of Islam.

The apostle of God—God's peace be upon him—once described jihad as the best of the summit of Islam, saying: "Someone who does not participate in any way in the raids (against the enemies of Islam), or someone whose soul does not talk to him encouraging him to wage a fight on behalf of his religion, dies as if he had never been a Muslim, or (he dies) like someone who, filled with some form of hypocrisy, only outwardly pretended to be a Muslim."

Therefore (a certain) 'Abdallah ibn Mubarak, someone who waged jihad for God's cause, said (the following lines of poetry) that make the eminent weep:

> O (Ruler,) servant of the two Holy Places (Mecca and Medina)
> If ye looked at us well
> Then you would realize that you only play with what is devotion
> Some people make their cheeks wet with tears
> in great quantities
> but our chests and throats become wet
> by torrents of our blood

§51. Some people say that to occupy oneself with politics hardens the heart and keeps people away from remembering (dhikr) God. The likes of these people do not understand the word of the Prophet—may God's peace be upon him—: "The best form of jihad is a word of truth (spoken to) a tyrannical ruler." The truth is that whoever adheres to such philosophies either is not interested in Islam or is a coward who does not wish to stand up for the Rule of God with firmness.

§52. *The Foundation of a Political Party*

There are those who say: "We must establish an Islamic political party (and add this party) to the list of extant political parties." It is true that this is better than benevolent societies, because a party at least talks about politics. However, the purpose of the foundation (of such a party) is the destruction of the infidel state (and to replace it by an Islamic theocracy). To work through a political party will, however, have the opposite effect, because it means building the pagan state and collaborating with it. . . . (Moreover, such an Islamic political party) will participate in the membership of legislative councils that enact laws without consideration for God's Laws.

§53. *To Exert Oneself in Order to Obtain Important Positions*

There are those who say that the Muslims should do their best in order to obtain (socially) important positions. Only when all important centers are filled with Muslim doctors and Muslim engineers, will the existing pagan order perish automatically and the Muslim ruler (*al-hakim al-Muslim*) establish himself . . . . Someone who hears this argument for the first time will think it is a fantasy or a joke, but there are, as a matter of fact, people in the Muslim world who embrace such philosophies and arguments, although there is nothing in the Book (of God) or the example (of the Prophet) that supports or proves the(se arguments). Moreover, reality prevents (such aspirations) from ever coming true. . . . No matter how many Muslim doctors and Muslim engineers there are, they too will help to build the (pagan) state. Moreover, things will never go so far as to permit a Muslim personality to reach a ministerial post when he is not a 100 percent supporter of the existing order.

§54. *(Nonviolent) Propaganda Only and the Creation of a Broad Base*
Some of them say that the right road to the establishment of an (Islamic) state is (nonviolent) propaganda (da'wa) only and the creation of a broad base. This, however, does not bring about the foundation of an (Islamic) state. Nevertheless, some people make this point the basis for their withdrawal from (true) jihad. The truth is that an (Islamic) state can be founded only by a believing minority. . . . Those who follow the straight path that is in accordance with the Command of God and the example of the Apostle of God—may God's peace be upon him—are always a minority. Scriptural proof of this is found in the Word of God—exalted and majestic He is—: "Few among my servants are thankful" (Q 34:12) and in His Word—He be praised: "If thou obey the majority of those who are in the land they will lead thee astray from the Way of God" (Q 6:116). This is the *Sunnat Allah* (Custom of God) with regard to His world. . . . From where will we get this hoped-for majority? (Did not God) also say: "Most of the people, even though thou shouldst be zealous, are not believers"? (Q 12:103).

§55. Islam does not triumph by (attracting the support of) the majority. Did not God—praised and exalted He is—say: "How many a small band has, by the permission of God, conquered a numerous band?" (Q 2:249)? And also: "(God has already helped you on many fields) and on the Day of Hunayn when ye prided yourselves on your numbers but they did not benefit you at all, and the land, wide as it was, became too narrow for you" (Q 9:25).

§56. (The Apostle)—may God's peace be upon him—says: "God will certainly take away from the hearts of your enemies all awe (which will make them poor fighters), and he will put weakness (and fear) in your hearts (which will make you effective fighters)." This (he said in response to a question) which they asked him—may God's peace be upon him—: "Shall we, on that day, be a minority, O Apostle of God?" He then said: "No, you shall be many on that day, but (looking insignificant) like rubbish swept by a torrent."

§57. But then, how can (nonviolent) propaganda be widely successful when all means of (mass) communication today are under the control of the pagan and wicked (state) and (under the control) of those who are at war with God's religion? The (only) really effective method could be to liberate the media from the control of these people. It is well known that compliance will come about only through a convincing victory. Does not God—praised and exalted He is—say: "When comes the victory of God, and the conquest, thou seest the people entering into the religion of God in crowds" (Q 110:1–2).

§58. In connection with this point we ought to answer those who say that people have to be Muslims in order to have Muslim law applied to them, in order to be obedient to that law, and in order that we should not fail in applying it. Someone who is so foolish as to say this, however, accuses Islam of imperfection and incapability, without realizing (that he implicitly makes this accusation). For this religion is well applicable, in all times and all places, and it is capable of arranging (the affairs) of Muslims and infidels, of sinners and the righteous, of scholars and fools. . . . When people have been able to live under the rules of unbelief, what will their position be when they find themselves under the rule of Islam which is all justice?

§59. Some people have misunderstood what I say and have taken it to mean that we should refrain from (nonviolent) propaganda altogether. "Propaganda" here means "Calling upon people to become Muslims." Here it is basic to take Islam as a whole. This, however, is the refutation of those who see it as their aim to create a broad base and (in doing so) forget about (true) jihad, or even hinder or obstruct (true jihad) in order to realize this (peaceful aim of theirs).

### §60. Hijra *(Emigration)*

There are some who say that the true road to the establishment of an Islamic state is hijra (emigration) to another locality and to establish the (new Islamic) state out there. Then they (want to) return again, as conquerors. These people must, in order to save their efforts (from being wasted on impossible tasks), (first) establish an Islamic state in their (new) *balad* (town, country, or locality) and then they will leave it as conquerors. . . .

Is this (form of) emigration in accordance with God's laws or not? To answer this question we have to study the different forms of "emigration," which are transmitted in the (collections of) Traditions (from Muhammad), that are to be found in the commentary on the Tradition "Someone who emigrates to God and His Apostle really emigrates to God and His Apostle, but someone who emigrates because of worldly possessions or because of a woman he wants to marry, emigrates to whatever he emigrates to (without further religious, or other, merit)." Ibn Hajar says: "To emigrate to something is to move over to it away

from something else." In religion it means: "To refrain from something
which God has forbidden." Hijra occurs in Islam in two ways:

§61. First, by moving over from the House of Unbelief to the House of
Safety, like the two hijras to Ethiopia and the beginning of the hijra
from Mecca to Medina.

§62. Second, the hijra from the House of Unbelief to the House of
Faith. This (variety of hijra) occurred after the Prophet—God's peace be
upon him—had established himself safely in Medina, and those Muslims who could emigrated to him. There is nothing odd in this. There
are, however, those who say that they will emigrate to the desert and
then come back, and have a confrontation with the Pharaoh, as Moses
did, and then God will make the ground swallow the Pharaoh up,
together with his army. . . . All these strange ideas only result from
having forsaken the only true and religiously allowed road towards
establishing an Islamic state. So, what is this true road? God—exalted
He is—says: "Fighting is prescribed for you, though it is distasteful to
you. Possibly ye may dislike a thing, though it is good for you, and
possibly ye may love a thing, though it is bad for you" (Q 2:216).
(God)—praised He is—also says: "Fight them until there is no dissension, and religion becomes God's."

§63. *To Be Occupied with the Quest for Knowledge*
   There are some who say that at present the true road is the quest for
knowledge. "How can we fight when we have no knowledge (of Islam
and its prescripts)? The quest for knowledge is a *farida* (obligation),
too." But we shall not heed the words of someone who permits the
neglect of a religious command or one of the duties of Islam for the
sake of (the quest for religious) knowledge, certainly not if this duty is
the duty of jihad. How could we possibly neglect a personal individual
duty (like jihad) for the sake of a collective duty (like the quest for
knowledge)?
   How can it have come about that we got to know the smallest (details
of the Islamic doctrine of duties like) recommendable and desirable acts,
and call upon people to perform these acts, but at the same time neglect
a duty which the Apostle—may God's peace be upon him—glorified?
   How can someone who has specialized in (Islamic) religious studies
and who really knows all about small and great sins not have noticed
the great importance of jihad, and the punishment for postponing or
neglecting it?
   Someone who says that (the quest for) knowledge (also) is (a form of)
jihad has to understand that the duty (which is indicated by the Arabic

word jihad) entails the obligation of fighting, for God—praised and exalted He is—says: "Prescribed for you is fighting" (Q 2:216).

It is well known that a man (once) pronounced the double Islamic confession of faith in the presence of the Apostle—may God's peace be upon him—and then at once went to the battlefield. He fought (for Islam) till he was killed before he had had the opportunity to occupy himself with anything from either the theory or the practice of Islam. Then the Apostle of God—God's peace be upon him—announced that the works of this man had been few, but that his reward would be great.

§64. An essential characteristic of knowledge is that someone who has knowledge of the obligatory character of the prayer ceremony has the obligation to pray. Similarly, someone who has knowledge of the obligatory character of the Fast must keep the Fast. Whoever has knowledge of the obligatory character of jihad must fight. Whoever frankly admits that he has no knowledge of the way in which Islam regulates jihad must know that the regulations of Islam are simple and easy for someone who sincerely dedicates his intentions to God. Such a person must consciously formulate the inner intention of fighting for God's cause, and from that moment on the regulations of jihad can easily and simply be studied, and in a very, very short time. The matter then has no need for much study.

When someone wants to increase his knowledge above this (elementary) level (he can freely do so), for there is no monopoly on knowledge. Knowledge is available to all, but to postpone jihad for the sake of the quest for knowledge is the line of reasoning of someone who has no case (worth considering).

There have been people who participated in jihad (mujahidin) since the beginning of the call to Islam by the Prophet—God's peace be upon him. In the ages that followed, until recently, they (the participators in jihad) have not been scholars ('ulama). Nevertheless, God conquered many towns at their hands. These people never excused themselves (from participation in jihad) by (saying that they were preoccupied with) the quest for knowledge, or by study of the Traditions, or the science of deriving legal rules from the Qur'an, the Tradition, and other sources (i.e., the 'Ilm Usul al-Fiqh). On the contrary, God—praised and exalted He is—gave at their hands victories to Islam which were not equaled by the scholars of al-Azhar on the day when Napoleon and his soldiers entered al-Azhar on horseback. What did their knowledge help them against this comedy?

Scholarship is not the decisive weapon that will radically put an end to paganism. This can be done only with the weapon that the Lord—exalted and majestic He is—mentioned in His word: "Fight them and God will punish them at your hands, will humiliate them and aid you against them, and will bring healing to the breasts of people who are believers" (Q 9:14). We do not have a low opinion of the importance of scholarship. On the contrary, we emphasize it(s importance). We do, however, not excuse ourselves (by appealing to the need for scholarship) from carrying out the obligations which God prescribed.

### §65. Explanation why the Islamic Community Differs from Other Communities as far as Fighting Is Concerned

God—exalted He is—made it clear that this Community differs from the other (religious) communities as far as fighting is concerned. In the case of earlier communities God—praised and exalted He is—made His punishment come down upon the infidels and the enemies of His religion by means of natural phenomena like eclipses (of the moon), floods, shouts, and storms. . . . With regard to the community of Muhammad—God's peace be upon him—this differs, for God—praised and exalted He is—addressed them saying: "Fight them and God will punish them at your hands, will humiliate them and aid you against them, and will bring healing to the breasts of people who are believers" (Q 9:14).

This means that a Muslim has first of all the duty to execute the command to fight with his hands. (Once he has done so) God—praised and exalted He is—will then intervene (and change) the laws of nature. In this way victory will be achieved through the hands of the believers by means of God's—praised and exalted He is—(intervention).

### §66. Revolt against the Ruler

In (the collection of Traditions entitled) al-Sahih made by Muslim, with the commentary to it by al-Nawawi (we read a Tradition reported) on the authority of Junada ibn Abi Umayya, who said: "Once we visited 'Ubada ibn Samit while he was ill, and we said: 'Tell us—may God give you back your health—a Tradition by which God beneficially gave us guidance which you heard from the Apostle of God—may God's peace be upon him.' He then said: 'The Apostle of God—may God's peace be upon him—once called us and we gave him our oath of allegiance. (In this oath the Apostle) imposed on us to swear that we would listen to him and obey him irrespective of whether we liked (his commands) or not or whether it was difficult or easy for us. He impressed us with this, and (added) that we should not fight for the command (of the community) with his people, saying 'except when you see unbelief publicly displayed—You will have proof from God with you for this." . . .

Al-Nawawi says in his commentary on this Tradition: "The Qadi 'Ayyad says: 'The leading Muslim scholars agree that the (duties of) leadership (of the community) cannot be given to an infidel, and that when (a leader) suddenly becomes an unbeliever, his leadership comes to an end. The same is the case when he neglects to perform the prayer ceremonies, or to urge (others to perform) them. The majority (of the scholars) also holds (this to be true) when (this leader introduces) a bid'a (innovation).

Some of the scholars from Basra say, however, that (the leadership nevertheless) is given to him and continues because he is (only) guilty of allegorizing.

The Qadi says: "When he suddenly becomes an unbeliever, or changes God's Law, or introduces a bid'a, he has no longer the qualifications needed in a leader, to obey him is no longer necessary, and the Muslims have the duty to revolt against him and to depose him, and to put a just imam in his place when they are able to do so. When this occurs to a group of people, they have the duty to revolt and depose the infidel." (This passage is quoted from the collection of Traditions entitled) al-Sahih by Muslim, the chapter on jihad. This chapter is also the refutation of those who say that it is permissible to fight only under a caliph or a commander (taht khalifah aw amir).

§67. Ibn Taymiyya says: "Any group of people that rebels against any single prescript of the clear and reliably transmitted prescripts of Islam has to be fought, according to the leading scholars of Islam, even if the members of this group pronounce the Islamic confession of faith." (This quotation is taken from) al-Fatawa al-Kubra, the chapter on jihad, p. 281.

§68. *The Enemy Who Is Near and the Enemy Who Is Far*
It is said that the battlefield of jihad today is the liberation of Jerusalem because it is (part of) the Holy Land. It is true that the liberation of the Holy Land is a religious command, obligatory for all Muslims, but the Apostle of God—may God's peace be upon him—described the believer as "sagacious and prudent" (kayyis fatin), and this means that a Muslim knows what is useful and what is harmful, and gives priority to radical definitive solutions. This is a point that makes the explanation of the following necessary:

§69. First: To fight an enemy who is near is more important than to fight an enemy who is far.

Second: Muslim blood will be shed in order to realize this victory. Now it must be asked whether this victory will benefit the interests of an Islamic state? Or will this victory benefit the interests of infidel rule? It will mean the strengthening of a state that rebels against the Laws of God. . . . These rulers will take advantage of the nationalist ideas of these Muslims in order to realize their un-Islamic aims, even though at the surface (these aims) look Islamic. Fighting has to be done (only) under the banner of Islam and under Islamic leadership. About this there is no difference of opinion.

§70. Third: The basis of the existence of imperialism in the lands of
Islam are (precisely) these rulers. To begin by putting an end to imperialism is not a laudatory and not a useful act. It is only a waste of time.
We must concentrate on our own Islamic situation: we have to establish
the rule of God's religion in our own country first, and to make the
Word of God supreme. . . . There is no doubt that the first battlefield
for jihad is the extermination of these infidel leaders and to replace
them by a complete Islamic order. From here we should start.

§76. *The Verse of the Sword (Q 9:5)*
   Most Qur'an commentators have said something about a certain
verse from the Qur'an which they have named the Verse of the Sword
(Q 9:5). This verse runs: "Then when the sacred months have slipped
away, slay the polytheists wherever ye find them, seize them, beset them,
lie in ambush for them everywhere."
   The Qur'an scholar Ibn Kathir noted in his commentary on this verse:
"al-Dahhak ibn Muzahim said: 'It canceled every treaty between the
Prophet—God's peace be upon him—and any infidel, and every contract
and every term.' Al-'Ufi said about this verse, on the authority of Ibn
'Abbas: 'No contract nor covenant of protection was left to a single
infidel since (this) dissolution (of treaty obligations) was revealed.'"

§77. The Qur'an scholar Muhammad ibn Ahmad ibn Muhammad ibn
Juzayy al-Kalbi, the author of (a Qur'an commentary entitled) *Tafsir
al-Tashil li-'Ulum al-Tanzil*, says: "The abrogation of the command to
be at peace with the infidels, to forgive them, to be (passively) exposed
to them and to endure their insults preceded here the command to fight
them. This makes it superfluous to repeat the abrogation of the command to live in peace with the infidels at each Qur'anic passage (where
this is relevant). (Such a command to live in peace with them) is found
in 114 verses in 54 surahs. This is all abrogated by His word: "Slay the
polytheists wherever ye find them" (Q 9:5) and "Fighting is prescribed
for you" (Q 2:216).
   Al-Husayn ibn Fadl says: "This is the verse of the sword. It abrogates
every verse in the Qur'an in which suffering the insults of the enemy is
mentioned." It is strange indeed that there are those who want to
conclude from Qur'anic verses that have been abrogated that fighting
and jihad are to be forsworn.

§78. The Imam Abu 'Abdallah Muhammad ibn Hazm, who died in AH
456, says in (his book entitled) *al-Nasikh wa'l-Mansukh* (The Abrogat-
ing and the Abrogated Passages from the Qur'an), in the chapter "On
Not Attacking the Infidels": "In 114 verses in 48 surahs everything is
abrogated by the Word of God—exalted and majestic He is—: 'Slay the
polytheists wherever ye find them' (Q 9:5). We shall discuss this when-

ever we come across it, if God—exalted He is—permits." End of quotation.

§79. The scholar and Imam Abu al-Qasim Hibat Allah ibn Salama says on "Slay the polytheists wherever ye find them": "The third verse is indeed the third verse, and this verse is the verse that abrogates. But it abrogates 114 verses from the Qur'an and then the end of it abrogates the beginning of it, because the verse ends with: 'If they repent and establish the Prayer and pay the zakat, then set them free' (Q 9:5, end of the verse)." (This quotation is taken from) a book (entitled) *Kitab al-Nasikh wa'l-Mansukh.*

§80. *"So When You Meet Those Who Have Disbelieved, Let There Be Slaughter" (Q 47:4)*
Al-Suddi and al-Dahhak say: "The Verse of the Sword was abrogated by: 'So when you meet those who have disbelieved, (let there be) slaughter until ye have made havoc of them, bind them fast, then (liberate them) either freely or by ransom' (Q 47:4). This verse is harsher on the infidels than the Verse of the Sword." Al-Qatada, however, has the opposite opinion, and I do not know anyone who disagrees with the opinion that it is abrogated except al-Suyuti who says in his book (entitled) *al-Ittifaq*: "At the time when the Muslims were weak and few in number, the command was to endure and to suffer. Then this command was abrogated by making fighting obligatory. In reality this is, however, not really abrogation, but it is to be regarded as 'causing to forget.' Did not God—exalted He is—say (in Q 2:106): '. . . or We cause (the Messenger) to forget?'"
The thing that is forgotten is the command to fight, until the time when the Muslims are strong. When, however, the Muslims are weak, the legal ruling is that it is obligatory to endure insults. This weakens a view about which so many are so enthusiastic, namely, that the verse (Q 47:4) on this point is abrogated by the Verse of the Sword (9:5). It is not like that. On the contrary, it is caused to be forgotten.
(Al-Suyuti) also said: "Some mention that verses like (Qur'an 2:109 which runs): 'So overlook and pay no attention until God interveneth with His Command' do not address a specific group of people at a specific time and with a specific aim. Hence, (the command embodied in this verse) is not abrogated but it is postponed until a certain time." Here ends the quotation from al-Suyuti.

§81. In spite of al-Suyuti's disagreement with all the preceding opinions, there is no room for doubt that to adopt the first opinion is correct. Moreover, whoever thinks that the view that nonabrogation of the verses of pardon and forgiveness (like 2:109) means that (1) we are free to neglect the two duties of jihad and (2) urging to what is reputable and prohibiting what is not is mistaken.

It certainly also does not mean that the duty of jihad has come to an end, because the Apostle of God—God's peace be upon him—says: "Jihad continues (*madin*) until the day of Resurrection." Dr. 'Abd al-Wahhab Khallaf says in his book (entitled) '*Ilm Usul al-Fiqh* (The Science of the Roots of the Islamic Legal System) on p. 227: "Because it continues until the Day of Resurrection, this indicates that it will remain (a duty) as long as the world remains."

To do away with jihad with the argument that it was caused to be forgotten puts an end not only to fighting for this religion but also to the intention (*niya*) of fighting for this religion. The danger of that is apparent from the saying of the Apostle of God—God's peace be upon him: "Someone who does not fight for his religion, or someone whose soul does not talk to him encouraging him to fight for his religion, dies as a pagan."

It is, moreover, generally agreed upon that in order to wage jihad the Muslims must have strength. But how can this strength be realized when you abolish the duty of jihad? Does not God—praised and exalted He is—say: "If they intended to go forth, they would make some preparation for it; but God is adverse to their being stirred up and hath made them laggards" (Q 9:46). The fact that you are not willing to go forth has as a consequence your neglecting to prepare (for it). From where now will a Muslim who has abolished the duty of jihad get the means for obtaining strength? Does not the Apostle of God say: "When people yearn for money and wealth, and conclude their bargains upon credit, and neglect the waging of jihad for God's cause, and hold on to the tails of their cows, then God will send a plague upon them from heaven, and He will not remove it from them until they return to their religion?"

### §82. Muslim Positions on Fighting

Muslim armies in the course of the centuries have been small and ill prepared, encountering armies double their size. Some argue that this was a prerogative of the Apostle of God—God's peace be upon him— and his noble companions. The refutation of this view is that God promised victory to the Muslims, lasting as long as the heavens and the earth last. Maybe you know about what happened (centuries after the days of the Apostle) to Zahir al-Din Babur who faced the Hindu King Rana Sanja with an army of 20,000 while the army of the Hindu King was 200,000. The Muslim commander was victorious after he repented from drinking wine. . . . There are many others like him.

### §83. The Meccan and the Medinan Society

There are those who allege that we live in a Meccan society, thereby endeavoring to obtain for themselves the permission to abandon the waging of jihad for God's cause. Whoever puts himself in a Meccan society in order to abandon the religious duty of jihad must also refrain from fasting and prayer (because the Revelations about these duties were given only after the Apostle had emigrated from Mecca to Medina in 622), and he must enrich himself by asking usury because usury was not forbidden until the Medinan period.

The truth of the matter is that (the period in) Mecca is the period of the genesis of the Call (to Islam). The Word of God—praised and exalted He is—(Q 5:3): "Today I have perfected your religion for you, and have completed my goodness toward you, and have approved Islam as your religion," abrogates these defeatist ideas that have to be substantiated by the argument that we are Meccans. We are not at the beginning of something, as the Prophet—God's peace be upon him— was at the beginning (of the establishment of Islam), but we (have to) accept the Revelation in its final form.

### §84. *Fighting Is Now a Duty upon All Muslims*

When God—praised and exalted He is—made fasting obligatory, he said (Q 2:183): "Fasting is prescribed for you." In regard to fighting He said (Q 2:216): "Fighting is prescribed for you." This refutes the view of whoever says that jihad is indeed a duty and then goes on by saying: "When I have fulfilled the duty of engaging in da'wa (missionary activities for Islam), then I have fulfilled the duty (of jihad), because (engagement in missionary activities for Islam) is jihad, too." However, the (real character of this) duty is clearly spelled out in the text of the Qur'an: It is fighting, which means confrontation and blood.

The question now is: When is jihad an individual duty? Jihad becomes an individual duty in three situations:

### §85. First, when two armies meet and their ranks are facing each other, it is forbidden to those who are present to leave, and it becomes an individual duty to remain standing, because God—exalted He is—says: "O ye who have believed, when ye meet a hostile party, stand firm, and call God frequently to mind" (Q 8:45) and also: "O ye who have believed, when ye meet those who have disbelieved moving into battle, turn them not your backs" (Q 8:15).

Second, when the infidels descend upon a country, it becomes an individual duty for its people to fight them and drive them away.

Third, when the imam calls upon a people to fight, they must depart into battle, for God—exalted He is—says (Q 9:38–39): "O ye who have believed, what is the matter with you? When one says to you: 'March out in the way of God,' ye are weighed down to the ground; are you so satisfied with this nearer life as to neglect the Hereafter? The enjoyment of this nearer life is in comparison with the Hereafter only a little thing. If ye do not march out He will inflict upon you a painful punishment, and will substitute (for you) another people; ye will not injure Him at all; God over everything has power." The Apostle—God's peace be upon him— says: "When you are called upon to fight, then hasten."

With regard to the lands of Islam, the enemy lives right in the middle of them. The enemy even has got hold of the reins of power, for this enemy is (none other than) these rulers who have (illegally) seized the leadership of the Muslims. Therefore, waging jihad against them is an individual duty, in addition to the fact that Islamic jihad today requires a drop of sweat from every Muslim.

§87. Know that when jihad is an individual duty, there is no (need to) ask permission of (your) parents to leave to wage jihad, as the jurists have said; it is thus similar to prayer and fasting.

§88. *The Aspects of Jihad Are Not Successive Phases of Jihad*
It is clear that today that jihad is an individual duty of every Muslim. Nevertheless we find that there are those who argue that they need to educate their own souls, and that jihad knows successive phases; and that they are still in the phase of jihad against their own soul. They offer as proof the doctrine of Imam Ibn Qayyim, who distinguished three aspects in jihad:

1. Jihad against one's own soul
2. Jihad against the Devil
3. Jihad against the infidels and the hypocrites

§89. This argument shows either complete ignorance or excessive cowardice, because Ibn Qayyim (only) distinguished *aspects* in jihad; he did not divide it into successive phases. Otherwise, we would have to suspend the waging of jihad against the Devil until we finished the phase of jihad against our own soul. The reality is that the three (aspects) are aspects (only) that follow a straight parallel course. We, in our turn, do not deny that the strongest of us in regard to faith, and the most zealous of us in regard to waging jihad against his own soul is the one (of us) who is the most steadfast.

Whoever studies the biography (of Muhammad) will find that whenever (a state) of jihad was proclaimed, everybody used to rush off for God's cause, even perpetrators of great sins and those who had (only) recently adopted Islam.

It is reported that (once) a man embraced Islam during the fighting and fell in the battle, thus dying a martyr, and the Apostle—God's peace be upon him—said: "A small work, a great reward."

§90. (There is also) the story about Abu Mihjan al-Thaqafi (who was guilty of a great sin because he was) addicted to wine, while his bravery in the war against Persia was famous.

Ibn Qayyim also made mention that the Tradition: "'We returned from the Small Jihad to the Great Jihad—and then someone said: 'What is the Great Jihad, O Apostle of God?'—and then (Muhammad) said:

'The jihad against the soul,'" is a fabricated Tradition, see (the book by Ibn Qayyim entitled *Kitab*) *al-Manar*.

The only reason for inventing this Tradition is to reduce the value of fighting with the sword, so as to distract the Muslims from fighting the infidels and the hypocrites.

### §91. *Fear of Failure*

It is said that we fear to establish the state (because) after one or two days a reaction will occur that will put to an end everything we have accomplished.

The refutation of this (view) is that the establishment of an Islamic state is the execution of a divine command. We are not responsible for its results. Someone who is so stupid as to hold this view—which has no use except to hinder Muslims from the execution of their religious duty by establishing the rule of God—forgets that when the rule of the infidel has fallen everything will be in the hands of the Muslims, whereupon (*bi-ma*) the downfall of the Islamic state will become inconceivable. Furthermore, the laws of Islam are not too weak to be able to subject everyone who spreads corruption in the land and rebels against the command of God. Moreover, the laws of God are all justice and will be welcomed by everyone, even by people who do not know Islam.

In order to clarify the position of the hypocrites in their enmity toward the Muslims and to put at peace the hearts of those who fear (this) failure (we quote) the word of the Lord in surah 59 (verses 11 and 12): "Hast thou not seen those who have played the hypocrite saying to their brethren the People of the Book who have disbelieved: 'Surely, if ye are expelled, we shall go out with you, we shall never obey anyone in regard to you, and if ye are attacked in war, we shall help you?' God testifieth that they are lying. If they are expelled, they will assuredly not go out with them, and if they are attacked in war, they will never help them, and if they do help them, they will certainly turn their backs in flight and then they will not be helped (and gain a victory)."

This is God's promise. When the hypocrites see that the power is in the ranks of Islam they will come back in submission, so we will not be deceived by these voices that will quickly fade away and be extinguished. . . . The position of the hypocrites will be equal to that of the enemies of Islam. God—exalted He is—says: "(O ye who have believed), if ye help God He will help you (and give you victories) and He will set firm your feet" (Q 47:7).

### §92. *The Command*

There are some who excuse themselves (from participating in jihad) because of the lack of a commander who will lead the course of jihad. There are also people who make (the execution of) the divine command to jihad dependent upon the presence of a commander or a caliph. . . .

The people who hold these opinions are the same people who have made (proper) leadership impossible and who have stopped the course of jihad. Yet the Apostle—God's peace be upon him—urges the Muslims, according to the texts of his Traditions, to entrust the (military) leadership to one of them.

Abu Dawud transmits in the chapter on jihad (in his collection of Traditions) that the Apostle—God's peace be upon him—says: "When three (of you) go out on a journey, then make one of them the commander (amir)." From (the text of) this (Tradition) one can conclude that the leadership over the Muslims is (always) in their own hands if only they make this manifest. (The Apostle)—God's peace be upon him—says: "Whosoever is put at the head of a group in which there is someone who is more agreeable to God than him himself, is disloyal to God and His Apostle and the Muslim community." This Tradition is transmitted by al-Hakim. Its reliability is pointed out by al-Suyuti.

§93. (This means that the command) must go to the best Muslim. (The Apostle)—God's peace be upon him—says to Abu Dharr: "You are weak. This is (to our) security!" (The command) must be in the hands of the strongest, which is a relative matter. . . .

Whoever alleges that the (proper) leadership has been lost has no case, because the Muslims can (always) produce leaders from among themselves. If there is something lacking in the leadership, well, there is nothing that cannot be acquired. It is (simply) impossible that the leadership disappears (from among us).

# Chapter 14

## 'UMAR 'ABD AL-RAHMAN
## 1938–

FOR MANY AMERICANS, the events of September 11, 2001, registered as a sharp rupture in historical experience, an assault on United States territory not witnessed before or since the "day of infamy" when the Japanese attacked Pearl Harbor. Yet in February 1993, eight years before al-Qa'ida engineered these events, a bomb exploded beneath the Twin Towers, killing six people and reportedly injuring more than one thousand others. In June of the same year, a plot was uncovered to blow up a series of New York bridges, tunnels, landmarks, and buildings. A Federal indictment cast the 1993 bombing, the foiled plot, and the 1990 assassination of Rabbi Meir Kahane as part of a larger attempt to "levy a war of urban terrorism against the United States" (*U.S. v. 'Abdel Rahman* 1994). The foot soldiers in this "urban war" were the Iraqi, Kuwaiti, Jordanian, Egyptian, Saudi, and Palestinian defendants whose routes to Manhattan were many and varied. Their charismatic maestro, however, was 'Umar 'Abd al-Rahman, a blind Egyptian shaykh with a doctorate in Qur'anic interpretation and a talent for inspiring receptive listeners to transform conviction into action, anger into violence. Convicted of "seditious conspiracy" in 1995, the shaykh is currently serving a life sentence for his crucial—albeit mercurial—participation in what now appears to have been the first sortie on American soil in an ongoing war against Islam's enemies both near and far.

'Abd al-Rahman forged and honed his considerable skills of exhortation, persuasion, and evasion on the rough edge of Egyptian politics. He was born in a village on the Nile Delta and lost his eyesight to diabetes at ten months old. At a disadvantage in many occupations, family members steered him toward religious studies, and he went on to receive both an undergraduate degree and a doctorate from al-Azhar, Egypt's preeminent Islamic university.[1] His first posting was in 1965, to a mosque in a village in al-Fayoum, a province southwest of Cairo, where he served as imam for several years.

Traveling from mosque to mosque, 'Abd al-Rahman became known for his increasingly strident indictments of President Gamal 'Abd al-

---

[1]He reportedly submitted a 2,000-page dissertation for his doctorate, an analysis of the opponents of Islam in *Surat al-Tawba*, chapter 9 of the Qur'an. Part of his dissertation has recently been published in Egypt under the title of *Mawqif al-Qur'an min khusumih* (2006).

Nasser, the Egyptian government, and the Arab defeat in the Six-Day War, as well as agitating ceaselessly for the overthrow of "infidel rule" in favor of an Islamic state. Ever aware of the omnipresent *mukhabarat* (intelligence service), the shaykh became particularly adept at delivering his political polemics by way of metaphor, allegory, and indirection, speaking not of Nasser and his henchmen but only of "pharaoh," "oppressors," and "infidels." In interviews, mosque teaching circles, university classes, religious summer camps, and sermons recorded on cassette tapes, however, 'Abd al-Rahman left little doubt about who the infidels and pharaohs really were. As he writes in the introduction to his 1985 book, *Kalimat haqq* (*A Word of Truth*):

> In my sermons I began to address a few of the transgressions of the state—it was, in fact, transgressive in its entirety—and investigators started to summon me after every sermon. This was in the Nasser era, and so when I took up something about the matter of Pharaoh in the sermon, 'Abd al-Nasser came to mind for all in attendance. ('Abd al-Rahman 1985, 13)

On the occasion of the president's death in 1970, the shaykh abandoned his allegorical code and explicitly urged his fellow Muslims not to pray for Nasser (ibid.). The police promptly arrested him, and 'Abd al-Rahman served eight months in jail.

In 1973, the shaykh joined the Department of Theology at the University of Asyut in Upper Egypt, a move that would prove propitious both for Egyptian Islamism and for 'Abd al-Rahman's future in it. In the 1970s, university campuses in Upper Egypt—in the southern part of the country—were becoming a cauldron of Islamist activism (Fandy 1994; Nedoroscik 2002; Eccel 1988). Nasser's aggressive crackdown on the Muslim Brotherhood in the 1960s had all but decimated the Islamist movement, but his successor, Anwar al-Sadat, initially encouraged the growth of Islamism in the 1970s as a counterweight to leftist forces. Sadat reversed course only when Islamist organizations proliferated exponentially across Egyptian university campuses and became the locus of intense political opposition, but by then it was too late. Islamists had mobilized against, among other things, Sadat's policy of *infitah* (economic liberalization) and the rollback of many social welfare policies it entailed; changes in family law Islamists viewed as a violation of particular provisions of shari'a and the principle of divine authority; and the controversial peace treaty between Egypt and Israel at Camp David.

In Upper Egypt, these policies interacted in complex and combustible ways with regional, ethnic, and class divisions—as well as with local tensions between Muslims and Coptic Christians—to spawn a number of loosely knit and overlapping Islamist student organizations. Although not himself *sa'idi* (a southerner), 'Abd al-Rahman's faculty position at the University of Asyut located him in the heart of an already "vibrant

oral culture in Upper Egypt" that was rapidly becoming the center of renewed Islamist organizing (Gaffney 1997, 258). It also provided an ideal
pulpit from which to showcase his eloquence, religious expertise, and
uncompromising opposition to the regime. It was at this time that the
shaykh assumed the role of religious guide and mentor to al-Jama'a al-
Islamiyya—a fluid consortium of Islamist student associations that would
later evolve into the organization responsible for an escalating series of
violent attacks in Egypt from 1992 to 1997, culminating in the murder of
fifty-eight tourists in Luxor and the attempted assassination of Egyptian
president Hosni Mubarek.[2] The shaykh's affiliation with Jama'at al-Jihad
(often known as the Jihad Group, and later as Tanzim al-Jihad, or Egyptian Islamic Jihad), one of the organizations to emerge from al-Jama'a al-
Islamiyya in the 1970s, was an extension of this tutelary relationship.[3]

Today the Jihad Group is perhaps best known for its recent affiliation
with al-Qa'ida, but the organization first burst onto the international
stage when it engineered the very public assassination of Sadat in 1981
(see chapter 13).[4] 'Abd al-Rahman was arrested along with Sadat's assassins and accused, among other things, of issuing a fatwa (religious opinion) providing religious sanction for the murder at the behest of the young
men who carried it out. At his trial, the shaykh offered a lengthy self-
defense that simultaneously denied his legal culpability and insisted on
the right and obligation to declare the president a *kafir* (unbeliever) who,
if unrepentant, may be considered an apostate (*murtadd*) eligible for
execution. The regime's reluctance to transform the 'alim into a martyr,
coupled with the shaykh's preference for oral over written communication and his tendency to speak in code, ultimately proved the best defense
of all. Absent definitive proof that 'Abd al-Rahman had explicitly legiti-
mized the assassination, the shaykh was ajudged an 'alim (scholar) rather
than an amir (leader) and was acquitted (Zeghal 1995, 392).[5] An un-

[2]The shaykh has explicitly described himself as the "spiritual mentor" of al-Jama'a al-Islamiyya (Weaver 1993, 89) and, in the adulatory opening to *Kalimat haqq*, the group responds
in kind, vowing that 'Abd al-Rahman's words will continue to "live on in our souls and occupy
our minds as if we were hearing them for the first time"('Abd al-Rahman 1985, 7).

[3]Each group's relationship with 'Abd al-Rahman reportedly diverged in 1984, after a debate about the appropriate role of a blind imam in political and military organizations (al-
Zayyat 2004; Zeghal 1999, 393).

[4]Under the leadership of Ayman al-Zawahiri, a faction of Egyptian Islamic Jihad merged
with al-Qa'ida to become Qa'idat al-Jihad. By contrast, al-Jama'a al-Islamiyya has formally
renounced violent tactics as counterproductive. As many of these Islamist groups have
splintered and recombined under a variety of names, the relationship among them is exceedingly complex, as is the relationship between each of these groups and al-Qa'ida (Rashwan 2005; Zeidan 1999; Kepel 1985).

[5]The task of elaborating the assassins' justifications for posterity would fall to a young
electrical engineer named Muhammad 'Abd al-Salam Faraj (see chapter 13 in this volume).
'Abd al-Rahman would, however, include an extensive if one-sided account of the government's charges and his rejoinders in *Kalimat haqq* ('Abd al-Rahman 1985, 81–98).

apologetic 'Abd al-Rahman described the trial in a 1993 interview in the following terms:

> I testified for twelve hours before the judge, and I told him that whoever does not rule as God orders is an infidel. And if you apply that rule to Nasser, Sadat, and Mubarak, they are all infidels. . . . It was Sadat himself who issued the fatwa to be killed, by moving away from his religion and imprisoning people. And it was *his own people* who killed him, and this will be Mubarak's fate as well. (Weaver 1993, 88–89; emphasis in the original)

For much of his life, 'Abd al-Rahman devoted himself to transforming the country of his birth, just as the Islamist groups with whom he has affiliated have targeted Egypt's government institutions, officers, and sources of revenue, such as tourism. His focus would broaden significantly in the late 1980s, however, after a series of trips to Saudi Arabia, Pakistan, Sudan, and Afghanistan.[6] The Afghan mujahidin (see chapter 17 on the Taliban) in particular captured the blind shaykh's imagination, and he took to likening their fight against the Soviet army to the righteous early Muslim followers of Muhammad who secured glorious victories against infidels even when vastly outnumbered. Increasingly committed to a borderless jihad against the enemies of Islam both at home and abroad, he began working tirelessly to recruit new mujahidin wherever they could be found. These endeavors brought him into contact not only with several influential Islamist activists and thinkers but also with what has been described as a CIA-sponsored "pipeline" funneling training, arms, and financial support to the Afghan fighters.

Such connections have come under particularly intense scrutiny since 1990, when the shaykh's recruiting efforts brought him to the United States on a visa he obtained despite the appearance of his name on a State Department "lookout list" of those suspected of dangerous ties to terrorist organizations.[7] 'Abd al-Rahman brought with him an internationalized

---

[6]In a recent book, Montasser al-Zayyat, lawyer for al-Jama'a al-Islamiyya, writes that while 'Abd al-Rahman was under house arrest in Fayoum from 1986 to 1988, he employed a body double to draw off police surveillance, thus enabling him to move more freely (al-Zayyat 2005).

[7]Some have speculated that a long-standing collaboration built on mutual interest had been forged between the CIA and 'Abd al-Rahman in Afghanistan, and that only such a relationship could explain why the shaykh was granted a visa in 1987, a multiple-entry visa in 1990, and a green card in 1991 (Friedman 1993a, 1993b; Weaver 1993, 71–89). According to the State Department's Inspector General, however, 'Abd al-Rahman's visa was a mistake, the result of a "sloppy system" confused by the various transliterations of the shaykh's name into English rather than covert assistance on the part of intelligence agencies (Jehl 1993). Peter Bergen (2001, 66–67) concludes that "at least one of the visas was issued by a CIA officer working undercover in the consular section of the American embassy in Sudan. Whether this was a mistake or something more remains an open question."

understanding of jihad honed by 'Abd Allah 'Azzam in Afghanistan (see chapter 18 on Bin Laden). It was precisely this view of jihad that inspired acolytes in New York and New Jersey to translate their religious and political commitments into violent action, just as students in Upper Egypt had done before them. His incarceration in a federal penitentiary has only added luster to his reputation among Islamists, even if it has curtailed his direct influence. American officials were temporarily recalled from Sudan for their safety immediately following the verdict; Bin Laden has noisily pledged to work for his release; and Egyptian Islamists periodically issue statements in which pledges of devotion to the shaykh are admixed with threats of violence against the United States for imprisoning a "leading light of Islam."

For a generation of Muslim men primed for rebellion, 'Abd al-Rahman's appeal is not difficult to fathom. Rejecting those Sunni jurisprudents who have emphasized unity over fitna (discord), obedience over revolt, jihad against oneself over jihad bi'l sayf (jihad of the sword), the shaykh offers a legitimation for revolt grounded in a highly selective assemblage of Qur'anic verses, hadith, historical precedents, legal scholarship, and creative reinterpretations pioneered by thinkers who preceded him. In *Kalimat haqq*, for example, he draws both explicitly and implicitly on the work of Islamists such as Mawdudi and Qutb (see chapters 3 and 5 in this volume), as well as on earlier thinkers such as Ibn Taymiyya (1263–1328) and Rashid Rida (1865–1935), to advance standard Islamist arguments for divine sovereignty as the realization of God's rule on earth; the establishment of shari'a as the sole source of legitimate law; and, concomitantly, the reduction of government to matters of administration rather than legislation.

Like 'Abd al-Salam Faraj (see chapter 13), the starting premise of the shaykh's argument for revolt is the radical reading of Qur'an 5:44: "He who does not govern by what God has revealed is an unbeliever."[8] Building on this foundation, 'Abd al-Rahman claims that, first, an apostate cannot legitimately rule; second, it is not only a necessity but a duty incumbent upon all committed Muslims to rise up against rulers who have abandoned the prescriptions of Islamic law; and, third, under these circumstances, killing in Allah's cause (*al-qital fi sabil Allah*) must be considered a legitimate and inescapable component of jihad. Such arguments frame the shaykh's effort to portray revolt as an act of restoration rather than destruction. Much as the seventeenth-century English philosopher John Locke sought to legitimize revolution by characterizing a government that violates the purposes for which it was created as an outlaw, 'Abd al-Rahman insists that it is the ruler who violates shari'a that is the source of fitna rather than those who legitimately rise up to depose him (Locke 1689, ch. XIX). In other words, a government that betrays the

---

[8]See discussion of Qur'an 5:44 in chapter 13 on Faraj.

precepts of Islamic law forfeits its claim to obedience and so must bear the blame for any discord that ensues: "The very existence of a threat to the social order is in itself a justification for the overthrow of the regime. This is because the most serious of threats is ultimately that which comes from within the regime; the responsibility to preserve and establish Islam remains with every Muslim" ('Abd al-Rahman 1988; 1990, 18).

Ultimately, 'Abd al-Rahman's influence has far outstripped his originality, and he is more aptly understood as a populist mufti (one who issues legal opinions) rather than a scholar or theologian. He has demonstrated an uncanny ability to adapt others' arguments to particular political circumstances, to transform quotidian indignities into a spur for epic action sanctified by God, and to use his religious training to conjure disciples among disparate audiences. In this he has been greatly assisted by the stature granted to an 'alim from one of the most prestigious educational institutions in the Muslim world. Indeed, his doctorate from al-Azhar in tafsir (Qur'anic interpretation) distinguishes him from many other influential Sunni Islamists, such as Banna and Qutb—who were educated at a series of "secular" institutions and were largely autodidacts when it came to the religious sciences—or Bin Laden, whose education was primarily in management and economics. In this respect, 'Abd al-Rahman may be said to exemplify the political coming of age of what has been called "peripheral 'ulama," those products of al-Azhar whose sympathies and affiliations with Islamists undermine conventional wisdom about a sharp divide between establishment Sunni 'ulama and untrained, anticlerical Islamist upstarts (Zeghal 1999; Zaman 2002, 144–80; see also chapter 1 in this volume).

# THE PRESENT RULERS AND ISLAM:
## ARE THEY MUSLIMS OR NOT?

THE 'ulama are unanimously agreed that the Muslims should, as a general rule, depose their leaders (*khulafa*) for corruption, or indeed for any other justifiable reason. Such justifiable reasons could be deemed to include social disorder and the undermining of religion. This is because one of the fundamental reasons for appointing a khalifa (successor) is to assure the establishment of a social order the foundations of which are firmly planted in religion. The agreement of the 'ulama on this point does not, however, extend to the case of the man whose overthrow may result in fitna (civil discord, dissension) or social and political strife. While some scholars maintain that the khalifa should be replaced whenever there is a justifiable cause, others hold that this may be conditional upon the social and political cost. This latter group says that if a choice is to be made between an undesirable leader and social and political upheaval, then it becomes a matter of the lesser of two evils. Still a third group holds that, in such a situation, the khalifa should remain in place regardless of his actions, so long as his removal threatens to become problematic.

In our view, the strongest case may be made for the first of these three options—that the khalifa should be overthrown whenever there is a justification for doing so even though this may lead to fitna. We would not, in fact, consider any resulting social discord to be fitna at all; rather we would regard it as a struggle for reform because its ultimate aim would be the elevation of Truth, the uprooting of corruption, and the reaffirmation of Islam.

The very existence of a threat to the social order is in itself justification for the overthrow of the regime. This is because the most serious of threats is ultimately that which comes from within the regime, [and because] the responsibility to preserve and establish Islam remains with every Muslim.

Those who place conditions upon the overthrow of an oppressor cite hadith of the Prophet, peace and blessings be upon him, which urge the avoidance of confrontation with the khulafa and the imams and stress the unity of the Islamic community:

Whoever sees in his emir (commander, prince) anything which he dislikes let him be patient. Indeed, whoever differs from the community by but a span, ere he dies, he dies in a state of ignorance.[9]

They also mention the following hadith:

The best of your imams are those whom you love and who love you, those whom you bless and who bless you. The worst of your imams are those whom you despise and who despise you, those whom you curse and who curse you. The people asked him, "Oh Messenger of Allah, should we not resist them?" To which he replied: "Not so long as they establish the prayer. Indeed, whoever takes for himself a protector and then sees him commit an act of disobedience to Allah, let him feel hatred for that act and not diverge from his obedience."

These hadith should not be taken literally but should rather be seen in the light of the Qur'an and the sunna and of the obligations which bind Muslims to the establishment of Islam and to the struggle in its cause, that is, to struggle with one's heart and soul and wealth to reject those who oppose Islam and attempt to undermine it, to encourage the people in virtue and to discourage wrongdoing and impiety, and to fight oppression. This is the Islamic perspective; once this becomes clear, then we can see that the meaning of the hadith is that Muslims are bound to patience with their leaders in whatever is not detrimental to Islam and to the Islamic community, in whatever does not infringe upon the guidelines of what is permitted and what is prohibited, and in whatever can ultimately support the legitimacy and dignity of the leadership by its commitment to truth and its constant reference to it.

Ibn Hazm has considered these hadith and others like them and explains that they do not mean what some jurists have understood them to imply:[10]

If tyranny begins to surface, even though it is small or insignificant, (the Muslims) should approach the leader about it and restrain him. If he accepts their counsel, yields to the guidance of the people and his peers, and establishes the laws of Islam, then there is no means of removing him. But if he refuses to fulfill any of his obligations and is unrepentant, then his removal is imperative. Someone who

[9]In the original English text published by al-Firdous, the hadith and Qur'anic verses appear in Arabic and English (although in a few instances, the English translation was not provided). Due to errors in the Arabic orthography in several of the passages, we have omitted the Arabic script and reproduced—and in some cases inserted—the English translations.

[10]Ibn Hazm (d. 1064), a jurist, historian, theologian, and poet from Muslim Spain, was a leading figure in the now defunct Zahiri school of law. The Zahiris argued that Muslims ought to follow only the apparent and obvious sense (zahir) of the foundational texts and accused other schools of law of reading extraneous, unwarranted ideas into these texts. This medieval Zahiri view, rejected by all major schools of law in medieval Islam, has sometimes been vaguely compared to the literalism of some contemporary Islamists.

will stand by truth should replace him, as Allah has said: "Help one another to do what is right and good; do not help one another towards sin and hostility" (Q 5:2).

[According to 'Abd al-Qadir 'Awda:[11]] "No part of the shari'a may be abrogated. Yet some jurists still adopt the view that we should choose the lesser of two evils if revolt were to lead to strife or fitna. This view should be explained in light of both historical experience and contemporary reality in order to clarify to everyone that if continuing under the regime results in the undermining of Islam or the weakening of its position, then the lesser of the two evils must be revolt and nothing less."

Al-Qurtubi writes that "it is unanimously agreed that an unworthy individual may not be confirmed into the leadership of the community."[12]

How could a Muslim be so bold, after all we have seen, as to replace even one part of the shari'a? How could a ruler claim to follow Islam and still do such a thing? Would he not be aware that by giving preference to his own legislation over that of Allah he would inevitably have excluded himself from the Islamic community? Allah has said: "Do they want judgment according to the time of pagan ignorance? Is there any better judge than God for those of firm faith?" (Q 5:50).

Ahmad Shakir remarks:[13]

Those objectionable people at the margins who associate themselves with Islam, and those who would like to be with them, would be asked: "Do you believe in Allah and that He is the Creator?" To which they will say "Yes." "And do you believe that He knows what was and what is, that He is most knowledgeable about creation, that He knows mankind, what is good for him and what is bad?" "Yes," they will say. "And do you believe that He sent His messenger Muhammad with guidance and the True Faith, and revealed to him this Qur'an in which there is guidance for mankind

---

[11]'Abd al-Qadir 'Awda was a lawyer and one of the Egyptian Muslim Brotherhood's important theoreticians. Along with many other leaders of the Brotherhood, 'Awda was convicted for allegedly participating in a plot to assassinate Egyptian president Gamal 'Abd al-Nasser and was hanged on the gallows in 1954.

[12]Al-Qurtubi (d. 1272), a Spanish scholar and adherent of the Maliki school of Islamic law, is the author of a major commentary concerned specifically with elucidating the legal content of the Qur'an. Qurtubi's commentary is one of the most influential works in this subgenre of the Islamic exegetical tradition.

[13]Ahmad Muhammad Shakir (d. 1958) was an al-Azhar trained jurist and scholar of hadith who served as chief justice of the Shari'a Supreme Court of Egypt. He wrote on topics ranging from poetry to the relationship between Egyptian civil and shari'a courts, and his scholarship evinced a particular interest in figures much revered by the Salafis, including Ibn Taymiyya, Ibn Kathir, and Ibn 'Abd al-Wahhab. Shakir also published an abridged, four-volume edition of Ibn Kathir's influential Qur'an commentary (Shakir 1956–57), which 'Umar 'Abd al-Rahman refers to in his discussion here.

to set right by it both their religion and their worldly affairs?" To which they will reply "Yes."

"Cut off the hands of thieves, whether they are man or woman" (Q 5:38).

[Ahmad Shakir continues:] "And do you believe that this verse is truly from the Qur'an?" To which they will say "Yes." "How much longer, then, will you ignore it? What then is your law?"

Those who claim to be Muslims cannot deny any of these things. It is common knowledge. The common people and their rulers, the educated and the ignorant, the cultured and the illiterate, all agree that these things are fundamental to Islam. Someone who denies any part of this has left Islam and must perish in the mire of apostasy.

How could it be permissible for a Muslim to attempt to rule by secular law, to govern the Muslims with it? Are they not aware of the verse: "How can they believe in others who ordain for them things which God has not sanctioned in the practice of their faith?" (Q 42:21).

Ibn Taymiyya addresses this point when he says: "It is not permitted that anyone should rule over any part of Allah's creation, be it among Muslims or *kuffar* (unbelievers), by agreement or by coercion—not over the army, and not over the poor, nor over anyone else except by the rule of Allah and His messenger. Whoever chooses other than this, the words of Allah would apply to him": "Do they want judgment according to the time of pagan ignorance? Is there any better judge than God for those of firm faith?" (Q 5:50).

Ahmad Shakir asks: "Would it then be permitted to any Muslim to adopt a new religion, or a new legal code, or to follow any judgment derived from outside of Islam, and to implement a thing such as the Yasa[14] and thus reject the clear guidance of the shari'a?"

Mawdudi explains the verse:

"Do you [Prophet] not see those who claim to believe in what has been sent down to you, and in what was sent down before you, yet still want to turn to unjust tyrants for judgment, although they have been ordered to reject them? Satan wants to lead them far astray" (Q 4:60).

This is clearly a denunciation of anyone who governs by laws other than those contained in the shari'a as well as of any system of government that is not in agreement with the supreme authority of Allah and which comes from outside the Revelation of Allah.

[14]Yasa is Mongol tribal law. For 'Abd al-Rahman as for many other Islamists, Mongol rule is one of the most important historical examples of illegitimate Muslim government. Their inspiration here is the fourteenth-century jurist Ibn Taymiyya (d. 1328), who argued that Mongol rulers, while formally Muslim, had contravened the shari'a by admixing Islamic prescriptions with Mongol tribal law, thus rendering their rule illegitimate and rebellion justifiable.

How is it then that Muslims would be allowed to voluntarily adopt
secular laws and base legal judgments upon them? "Satan wants to lead
them far astray" (Q 4:60).

These courts that have been imposed by tyrants in order to judge,
to order our affairs, and to resolve our difficulties in a matter that is
contradictory to our faith in Allah and his revelation, can have no
authority over us. In the view of the Qur'an, denial of the tyrant is as
necessary as having faith in Allah. To submit to Allah and to the tyrant
both is clearly *nifaq* (hypocrisy, dissimulation).

Could it be permissible then for the Muslims to submit to these
*mustabdil* (ersatz) rulers? "But they were commanded to serve only
one God: there is no god but Him" (Q 9:31).

Ibn Taymiyya states:

> Those who take their priests and their monks to be lords; who
> follow them in permitting what Allah has forbidden and in forbid-
> ding what Allah has permitted; who know that they have changed
> the religion of Allah; and who believe that what Allah has forbid-
> den can become permitted and that what Allah has permitted can
> become forbidden, are following human beings at the expense of
> religion. This is kufr (unbelief). Indeed, Allah and his messengers,
> peace and blessings be upon them, have called it shirk (polytheism,
> idolatry). Even though they do not bow down their heads to their
> leaders, nevertheless they follow them and contradict religion in the
> full knowledge that this is a denial of Allah, His messenger and His
> revelation. They are as much mushrik (polytheist) as those they
> follow.

Yet if they firmly believe in the revelation—and that Allah has defined
the prohibited and the lawful—but persist in following their leaders
even though they know it is wrong to do so, then they are disobedient
and should be regarded as such. This approach is confirmed by several
Traditions of the Prophet, upon whom be peace, which state:

> "Obedience is due to praiseworthyness"; and: "The Muslim is bound
> to ready service and obedience in what pleases him and in what dis-
> pleases him so long as he is not ordered to sin"; and: "Creation is not
> bound to disobedience to the Creator"; and finally: "Who orders
> you to disobedience of Allah, do not follow him."

> [Ibn Taymiyya writes:] "Now we come to the prohibition of the
> lawful and the license of the prohibited which results from an effort
> to follow the messenger. Though the effort is sincere, the truth of the
> matter is elusive. Such a case would not be punished by Allah; indeed,
> the people would be rewarded for their effort because by it they had
> sought to obey Allah."

Abu Bakr al-Jaza'iri has mentioned:[15] "One of the manifestations of shirk is submission to non-Muslim rulers and servility toward them. These people make legal what has been prohibited and prohibit what has been made legal. Obedience to them is acceptable only under compulsion, for their rule is unjust and they should be despised and rejected. Surely choosing such rulers, supporting them, being content with them, and maintaining their legitimacy is nothing less than shirk."

How should the Muslims persevere under these laws and under these rulers? How can we divest them of power? Allah has said: "[Believers], fight them until there is no more persecution, and all worship is devoted to God alone" (Q 8:39).

Imam Malik has said: "Whoever prohibits any of the obligations of Muslims before Allah can never be accepted by them; it is their duty to struggle against him until they remove him."[16]

Imam al-Nawawi said: "One of the obligations of Islam is to fight those who prohibit zakat (obligatory alms) or *salat* (prayer) or any other of the obligations of Islam, whether their prohibitions be few or many."[17]

Ibn Taymiyya said: "Any party that abandons any part of the clear and ordered shari'a of Islam is to be the object of struggle. About this the Muslims are agreed, even though such people may pronounce the Profession of Faith. This is the consequence of their abandonment of the shari'a."

[15] Abu Bakr al-Jaza'iri (b.1899) was an Algerian who became an outspoken Salafi during his long career as a professor at the Islamic University of Medina, Saudi Arabia.

[16] Malik ibn Anas (d. 795) was a jurist from Medina, for whom the Maliki school (one of the four Sunni schools) of Islamic law is named.

[17] Al-Nawawi (d. 1277), an influential Syrian scholar, is the author of a major commentary on the *Sahih* of Muslim ibn al-Hajjaj (d. 875), one of the "canonical" collections of hadith in Sunni Islam.

Chapter 15

# HAMAS
## 1987–

THE YEAR 1987 marks both the beginning of the first Palestinian *intifada* (uprising) against Israeli occupation and the establishment of Harakat al-Muqawama al-Islamiyya (Islamic Resistance Movement), known by its abbreviation Hamas, which means "fervor" or "zeal" in Arabic. In the twenty years since it was "born into the storm" of Israeli-Palestinian politics, Hamas has elicited wildly divergent characterizations. It has been described as a terrorist organization and a network of social welfare, an Islamic liberation theology and an ideology of Islamist anti-Semitism, a school for Palestinian violence and an unusually scrupulous political party, a movement either nationalist or religious, dogmatic or pragmatic. It is tempting to attribute these apparently contradictory descriptions to pure partisanship or, alternatively, to the accommodations and compromises produced when systems of ideas inevitably run up against the daily exigencies and messiness of political life. Yet in this instance, these tensions and paradoxes are actually written into the 1988 Charter of Hamas, a foundational declaration of purpose that seeks to recast Palestinian national liberation as both the culmination and epicenter of an Arabo-Islamic resistance to domination dating back to the Crusades.

The Charter opens with a quotation from Hasan al-Banna, a reflection of its origins in the Palestinian branch of the Egyptian Muslim Brotherhood, which established a presence in British Mandate Palestine in the 1930s. The Muslim Brotherhood had been active in the war against the establishment of Israel in 1948, but in the decades that followed, the organization largely eschewed armed resistance and political organizing in favor of what it characterized as the "upbringing of an Islamic generation" (quoted in Abu-Amr 1997, 230). In part, this approach reflected the Brotherhood's commitment to sociomoral transformation as the necessary and necessarily gradual prelude to political or military struggle. But it also derived from old resentments and strategic considerations. Having suffered brutally at the hands of Arab nationalist regimes, the Brotherhood was reluctant to join forces with any nationalist organization, liberationist or otherwise. The perception that the Brotherhood was apolitical, moreover, enabled it to operate relatively freely under Israeli control (Abu-Amr 1993, 9; 1994, 23–52; S. Roy 1995, 7; Budeiri 1995, 92). The result, however, was that Palestinian political and armed resistance came to be dominated by competing nationalist—and largely secular—

political organizations, foremost among them the Palestinian Liberation Organization (PLO), founded in 1964.

The 1970s heralded a sea change in the relative strength and importance of (explicitly) nationalist and Islamist organizations in the Middle East,[1] the culmination of a series of convulsive domestic, regional, and international events. In the first instance, Israel won two wars against neighboring Arab states, the 1967 (or "Six-Day") war and the Yom Kippur war of 1973. Both dealt a severe blow to the stature of secular nationalist and Arab socialist regimes, as well as to the popular appeal of the ideas they claimed to embody. Some Muslims insisted that such defeats mandated a return to Islam, on the grounds that only the greater religious piety of the Jewish state could account for the rout of several large Arab nations by a tiny upstart in their midst. Such claims only gained momentum in the wake of the 1979 Islamic Revolution in Iran, the 1981 assassination of Egyptian president Anwar al-Sadat by Islamists, and the emergence of the Shi'i group Hizbullah (Party of God) as a major force in Lebanon—all of which reflected and in turn accelerated the mobilization of Islam for political transformation.

In the Occupied Territories, the rising tide of Islamism crested later, in part because the framework of national liberation retained a particularly powerful political purchase in the absence of a sovereign and independent state (Legrain 1997, 159; S. Roy 1995, 4–5). In 1970, however, a violent confrontation between armed Palestinian groups and the Jordanian government known as "Black September" ended in the expulsion of guerrilla groups from the country and the loss of a major staging ground for PLO operations against Israel. Following the 1982 Israeli invasion of Lebanon, moreover, the PLO was forced to move its headquarters to Tunis, placing even greater physical distance between the organization and Palestinians contending with the daily frustrations of life under occupation. As Abu-Amr describes it,

> After twenty years the PLO seemed to be going nowhere. It had successfully revived the question of Palestinian national identity and had articulated three objectives for the Palestinian people: self-determination, statehood and the right of return. But the PLO failed to realize any of these objectives. To the contrary, it had been expelled from Jordan in 1970 and from Lebanon in the aftermath of the Israeli invasion of 1982. (Abu-Amr 1997, 232)

At the same time, the late 1970s witnessed the rise of the conservative Likud Party in Israel, along with the ascendance of a settler movement

---

[1] Such distinctions between nationalist and Islamist organizations are often blurred in practice, as is the distinction between "secular" and "religious" politics. Political allegiances often provoke or require what some have characterized as religious devotion, and religious organizations routinely proffer visions of political transformation, as well as engage in the kind of strategic maneuvering for power social scientists see as the essence of politics (cf. Lybarger 2007).

convinced that the territorial gains from the Arab-Israeli wars evinced a divine mandate to reclaim the entire biblical land of Israel. These domestic, regional, and international shifts lent an increasingly religious cast to the Israeli-Palestinian conflict, laying the groundwork for a decisive turn in Palestinian politics toward Islamism by the 1980s (Robinson 2004, 119–23; Abu-Amr 1997, 230–33).

It was in this context that Islamic Jihad first burst into the public arena. Officially founded in 1980, the Islamic Jihad opposed both the gradualism of the Muslim Brotherhood and the PLO's strategy of "occupation management" (Legrain 1997, 160). A geographically diverse and "nebulous circle of small groups organized loosely around and by 'guides' and united by a common ideology," Islamic Jihad did not have the deep roots and organizational structure of its rivals for Palestinian allegiance (Legrain 2004, 416). Nevertheless, its appearance heralded a dramatic shift in the course and tenor of Palestinian politics: wedding Islamism to *wataniyya* (patriotism, derived from *watan*—or homeland), Islamic Jihad insisted that, first, the restoration of Muslim Palestine required no less than the annihilation of Israel and, second, anti-Israeli jihad was therefore a fard 'ayn (individual duty) for all Muslims (Legrain 1997, 160; 2004, 416). Islamic Jihad's high profile and violent attacks against Israeli targets set the stage—symbolically, psychologically, and strategically—for the 1987 intifada, although its prominence was not to last. The group's own organizational weaknesses and the intensity of Israeli reprisals sidelined Islamic Jihad just as the uprising it helped catalyze gathered steam (Legrain 1997, 161; S. Roy 1995, 8; Rashad 1993, 3–5; Abu-Amr 1993, 8–10).

On October 6, 1987, four Islamic Jihad operatives were killed. On December 8 of the same year, several Palestinian workers died when their cars collided with an Israeli truck, sparking widespread riots. Long committed to Islamization without confrontation, the Brotherhood was outpaced by events, forced to reconsider its strategies or risk marginalization. It was at this point that several prominent Muslim Brothers gathered in Gaza to found Hamas—envisioned as the "strong arm" of the Brotherhood—to capitalize on the popularity of Islamic Jihad and the simmering outrage in the streets. Ostensibly new to the public arena, Hamas immediately had at its disposal the web of long-standing and deeply rooted charitable, educational, and social networks built by the Brotherhood over the preceding decades (S. Roy 1995).[2] In addition, Islamic Jihad had cut a clear path for Hamas by welding nationalist aspirations to an Islamist framework, thereby lending a religious imprimatur to every anti-Israeli act, pacific and violent alike.

[2]While Hamas has drawn on the network of Islamic social services built by the Brotherhood, as Roy points out, "in Gaza as elsewhere in the Arab world, the relationship between Islamic institutions in the socio-economic sphere and those in the political-military sphere is not nearly as routine or ineluctable as believed" (S. Roy 1995, 3, 10–11).

Prominent among the group of Hamas founders was Ahmad Yasin, a canny and charismatic shaykh who had helped build the Brotherhood into a formidable political and educational force well before 1987. Born in the 1930s in British Mandate Palestine, Yasin grew up in a Gazan refugee camp and gravitated toward the Muslim Brotherhood at an early age. Much as 'Umar 'Abd al-Rahman's childhood blindness increased the appeal of a religious education, Yasin's involvement in the Brotherhood intensified after an accident in his youth left him almost entirely paralyzed. As part of his work in the Brotherhood, Yasin founded al-Mujtama' al-Islami (Islamic Center) in 1973. With financial assistance from Gulf states awash in oil revenues and the tacit support of Israelis who envisioned Islamists as a useful counterweight to secular opposition, Yasin built the center into a powerful Islamist institution in the years that followed, eventually drawing into its purview the Islamic University and a substantial number of Gazan mosques (Robinson 2004, 119; Budeiri 1995, 92; Legrain 1997, 163; Abu-Amr 1997, 233).

Yasin's move toward increasingly confrontational Islamist mobilization in the 1980s reflects, in part, a savvy assessment of the shifting terrain and mood of Palestinian politics. But it also points to the ways in which the distinctive history of the Gazan Islamist movement primed the narrow strip of land sandwiched between Egypt, Israel, and the Mediterranean Sea to become the launching ground for the 1987 intifada. Egypt had administered the Gaza strip until 1967, and its policies toward the Palestinian branch of the Muslim Brotherhood were quite different from those of Jordan, which ruled the West Bank from 1948 to 1967. While the Brotherhood was the "only continuously legal political organization in the West Bank," for example, Nasser's crackdowns on Egyptian Islamists often extended to the Gaza strip, where the organization was outlawed and many Muslim Brothers were arrested—including Yasin (Robinson 2004, 120). Gazan Brothers thus brought to Hamas the potentially radicalizing experience of incarceration, along with an expertise in "building decentralized and clandestine organizations" (Robinson 2004, 120) and a conviction that, as the charter puts it, "only metal breaks metal."[3]

During the intifada, Hamas quickly became a formidable rival to the PLO, but a series of critical events after 1987 enabled the organization to reposition itself as the only remaining defender of uncompromised Palestinian aspirations. These included the decision of the Palestinian National Council to recognize Israel and accept a two-state solution in 1988, the cooperation of the PLO in the Gulf War peace plan in 1991, and Yasir Arafat's signing of the Oslo Declaration of Principles in 1993. Yet Hamas's fortunes have also fluctuated wildly in a conflict whose twists and turns are too complex and numerous to encapsulate, including the organization's temporary stint as "loyal opposition" to the Palestinian Authority,

[3]The Muslim Brotherhood reorganized in the 1970s to unite its branches in Gaza, the West Bank, and Jordan (S. Roy 1995, 7).

the successor to the PLO established to administer the territories in 1994 (see G. Usher 1997).

Yasin was assassinated in an Israeli missile strike in 2004, so he was not to witness perhaps the most dramatic development in an already turbulent history: Hamas's victory in the 2006 Palestinian Council elections. The adaptation and compromises required of an elected political party brought existing differences within the organization into sharp relief. It made visible the tensions between leaders who live in the territories and those who reside abroad, particularly in Syria, and between the organization's military wing (the 'Izz al-Din al-Qassam Brigades) and what has generally been regarded as its more pragmatic and flexible political wing. It also occasioned a certain shift in the rhetoric and focus of Hamas documents from armed struggle to matters of governance; from fighting Zionists to combating corruption; from an abstract moralism to a preoccupation with accountability and state building (Hroub 2006, 10–11). Such shifts were quickly eclipsed, however, by the fresh cycle of violence that has characterized the postelectoral struggle for control between Hamas and Fatah (the party associated with the PLO and subsequently with the Palestinian Authority) and that continues in the wake of Hamas's takeover of the Gaza Strip in 2007.

The organization's 1988 charter remains, however, unique among all the documents and perspectives that have accompanied the manifold twists and turns of Hamas's brief history. A deliberate echo of the PLO's national charter (al-mithaq), the Charter of Hamas is simultaneously a foundational statement of purpose and a momentary snapshot of an organization in flux. It is less a philosophical treatise than a political manifesto in every sense of the word. In the first instance, the charter is in many ways a collective document: scholars concur that while it bears the clear imprint of Yasin's teachings, it was most likely authored and edited by many people, from Brotherhood shaykhs to radical activists to hardened strategists (Abu-Amr 1997, 248; Rashad 1993, 11). The charter is also collective in the sense that is an argument to and about Palestinians, an attempt to simultaneously capture, exploit, and transform the aspirations of a people by claiming to "make manifest," as it were, truths about themselves and the world they had been unable or unwilling to see.

In this sense, the document is itself an act of political and cultural framing in which "ideological flexibility" and "studied ambiguity" supersede considerations of philosophical coherence or logical consistency (Robinson 2004, 132; Abu-Amr 1997, 248). Indeed, like so many other manifestos, religious and secular alike, the charter seeks not only to persuade but to convert. A case in point is the Qur'anic verses that punctuate the text yet have little substantive connection to what is actually being said. Such invocations serve neither to advance a new Qur'anic interpretation nor to substantiate a particular claim, but rather to swath the charter in the power of the divine word, to give the impression that these (seemingly irrelevant) Qur'anic passages can now be seen in a new light and that, moreover, that they all converge to authenticate the document and the claims therein. As Isaiah Berlin writes in a different context:

> Their essential purpose is to expound an all-embracing conception of the world and man's place and experience within it, they seek not so much to convince as to convert, to transform the vision of those whom they seek to address, so that they see the facts "in a new light," "from a new angle," in terms of a new pattern in which what had earlier seemed to be a casual amalgam of elements is presented as a systematic, interrelated unity. Logical reasoning may help to weaken existing doctrines, or refute specific beliefs, but it is an ancillary weapon, not the principal means of conquest: that is the new model itself, which casts its own emotional or intellectual or spiritual spell upon those who are converted (Berlin 1990, 161–62).

As Hamas emerged into a public arena dominated for decades by the PLO and other secular nationalist organizations, however, such "conversion" was neither easy nor automatic. Hamas faced stiff competition for Palestinians' support and allegiance as well as a discourse of resistance almost entirely framed in nationalist terms. Such nationalism posed a particular challenge to an organization with roots in the Egyptian Muslim Brotherhood, many of whose members have argued that the only legitimate collectivity is the umma, the community of Muslims in which membership derives from belief rather than geography or national citizenship.[4] Indeed, Egyptian Brothers such as Banna and Qutb tended to view secular nationalism as a misguided repudiation of divine sovereignty in favor of human authority and characterized Middle Eastern rulers in particular as corrupt autocrats presiding over nation-states brutally stitched together by colonial fiat, sustained only by foreign money and arms.

The charter attempts to resolve the tension between nationalism and Islamism by casting itself as the embodiment of authentic Palestinian patriotism and, correlatively, recasting the struggle for Palestinian liberation as the historical, religious, and geographic epicenter of a timeless battle against Islam's enemies. The crucial mechanism the charter deploys to graft Islamist purposes onto nationalist liberation is the characterization of all of historical Palestine as a *waqf*. Traditionally understood as an endowment of funds and revenues garnished to support such pious endeavors as maintaining mosques and schools, waqf is here transformed

---

[4] From the root meaning mother, source, origin, foundation, the Islamic *umma* originally described Muhammad's community, but its meaning is so varied in the Qur'an that at a minimum, it "always refers to ethnic, linguistic or religious bodies of people who are the objects of the divine plan of salvation" (*Encyclopaedia of Islam* 1913–36, s.v. "Umma").

from an institution of private property into an argument for divine sovereignty over an indivisible territory, the liberation of which is incumbent on all devout Muslims (Robinson 2004, 130).

The struggle for the Palestinian nation is in this way rendered identical to and the culmination of all previous Muslim struggles to enact God's will on earth. If Palestinians are to fulfill their destiny as the vanguard of this struggle, however, they must first triumph over their internal divisions. Toward this end, the charter engages in an extended discussion of Hamas's relationship with various other Palestinian groups, particularly the PLO, insisting that all are of the same family, united by one plight, one destiny, one enemy. Yet as the charter tends to portray secular nationalists as victims of false consciousness, casualties of the ongoing ideological and cultural crusade to "confuse [Muslims'] thoughts, stain their heritage, and defame their history," it leaves little doubt about who must accommodate whom in the name of unity.

Arrayed against this family is the "Zionist entity" whose evil is, paradoxically, both timeless and historically unique. On the one hand, the charter represents Zionism as just the most recent grab for Muslim Palestine in a long and greedy history peopled by Crusaders and missionaries, Mongol invaders and European imperialists. On the other hand, this portrait traffics in virtually every trope of classic European anti-Semitism, with the added twist of making the terminology of Zionism and Nazism appear interchangeable. While anti-Zionist polemics have characterized much of Islamist discourse since the modern state of Israel was created, arguably none has hewed so closely and fully to the tenets of European anti-Semitism as the charter. Alternatively called Zionists, Jews, and (rarely) Israelis, these enemies are described as rich, vicious, money-grubbing, and all powerful; their plans hatched in secret organizations such as the Freemasons' and Lions' clubs; their interests advanced by international organizations ranging from the United Nations to the Security Council; their propaganda disseminated by every outlet of the mass media; their machinations behind virtually all wars and disasters in the preceding three centuries, from the plague of alcohol and drugs, to the French and Communist revolutions, to both World Wars. As evidence of the power and danger of the Jews—the "businessmen of war"—the charter refers readers to the notorious *Protocols of the Learned Elders of Zion*, nineteenth-century Russian anti-Semitic propaganda purporting to reveal Jewish plans for world domination.

Resting uneasily in the shadow of this uncompromising division of the world into devout Muslims and evil Zionists is a series of disconnected gestures toward tolerance, gender equity, and good deeds. Although the charter states that "death for the sake of Allah is [the Resistance Movement's] most coveted desire," it also insists that struggle under the banner of Islam against such all-powerful enemies must take many forms, including speech, persuasion, and scholarship, along with providing charity, education, and medical care for all who are in need. Islam is depicted as a uniquely "big tent" under whose auspices Muslims, Christians, and Jews can coexist in peace and harmony—in spite of the apparently relentless quest of world Jewry to destroy Islam. Women are central to this jihad, invaluable to the battle of liberation, although this is largely because they are the "factory of men," the caretaker of children, and the foundation of the family which is, in essence, the primary school of Islamic virtue.

Running like an insistent counterrhythm throughout these various paradoxes and jarring juxtapositions is the reassurance that for all these evils and pains, for all this suffering and injustice, there is a solution: Islam, understood as a way of life that provides for all comers a goal, leader, and constitution in Allah, the Prophet Muhammad, and the Qur'an. More than this, the charter does not say, but it is, in fact "Hamas's interpretation of Islam as it pertains to the conflict that becomes the real answer" (Robinson 2004, 131).

# CHARTER OF THE ISLAMIC RESISTANCE MOVEMENT (HAMAS) OF PALESTINE

Ye are the best of Peoples, evolved for humanity,
enjoining what is right, forbidding what is wrong, and
believing in Allah. If only the People of the Book [Jews
and Christians] had faith, it were best for them: among
them are some who have faith, but most of them are
perverted transgressors. They will do you no harm,
barring a trifling annoyance; if they come out to fight
you, they will show you their backs, and no help shall
they get. Shame is pitched over them (like a tent)
wherever they are found, except when under a
covenant (of protection) from Allah and from people;
they draw on themselves wrath from Allah and pitched
over them is (the tent of) destitution. This because they
rejected the signs of Allah, and slew the prophets in
defiance of right; this because they rebelled and
transgressed beyond bounds.
—*Qur'an 3:110–12*

Israel will be established and will stay established until
Islam nullifies it as it nullified what was before it.
—*The martyred Imam Hasan al-Banna (may
Allah have mercy upon him)*

Indeed the Islamic world is burning, therefore it is
obligatory on every one to put a little of it out so he
can extinguish what he is able to do without
waiting for anyone else.
—*Shaykh Amjad al-Zahawee (may
Allah have mercy upon him)*

### INTRODUCTION

All praise is to Allah. We seek His aid, forgiveness, and guidance, and
on Him do we rely. We send peace and blessings on Allah's messenger—
his family, companions, those who follow him, called with his message
and adhered to his way—may the blessing and peace be continued for
as long as the heavens and earth last.

## And After

O people from the center of the affair, from the sea of struggle, from the beat of believing hearts, immaculate arms; upon realization of the duty, responding to the command of Allah, the call, meeting, and gathering the discipline were all based on the system of Allah. The will was persistent to offer its role in life, surpassing all obstacles, surmounting the hazards of the path; the preparation was continuous, as was the willingness to spend the body and soul for the sake of Allah. The seed was formed and began forging its path in the stormy sea of hopes and dreams, desire and wishes, danger and obstacles, and pains and challenges from within and without.

When the idea matured, and the seed grew, and the plant was firmly rooted in reality far away from the momentary emotional outburst and despicable rashness, the Islamic Resistance Movement went forth to perform its role of *mujahada* (struggling) for the sake of its Lord. The movement placed its hands with the hands of all the mujahidin who strive to free Palestine. The souls of its mujahidin gather with all the souls of the mujahidin who strove with their souls on the land of Palestine for all time since it was conquered by the companions of the Messenger of Allah until today.

This is the charter of Harakat al-Muqawama al-Islamiyya (Hamas, the Islamic Resistance Movement) manifesting its form, unveiling its identity, stating its position, clarifying its expectations, discussing its hopes, and calling for aid, support, and members. Our battle with the Jews is long and dangerous, requiring all dedicated efforts. It is a phase which must be followed by succeeding phases, a battalion which must be supported by battalion after battalion of the divided Arab and Islamic world until the enemy is overcome, and the victory of Allah descends.

This is how we perceive them approaching over the horizon.

> And you shall certainly know the truth of it (all)
> after a while.
> —*Qur'an 38:88*

> Allah has decreed: It is I and My Messengers who
> must prevail for Allah is one full of strength able
> to enforce His will.
> —*Qur'an 58:21*

> Say thou: This is my Way: I do invite unto Allah on
> evidence clear as the seeing with one's eyes, I and
> whoever follows me. Glory to Allah and never will I
> join gods with Allah!
> —*Qur'an 12:108*

## CHAPTER ONE

### Introduction to the Movement

- Ideological origin

ARTICLE 1

The Islamic Resistance Movement: Islam is its system. From Islam it reaches for its ideology, fundamental precepts, and worldview of life, the universe, and humanity; and it judges all its actions according to Islam and is inspired by Islam to correct its errors.

- The Islamic Resistance Movement's Connection with the Society of the Muslim Brotherhood

ARTICLE 2

The Islamic Resistance Movement is a branch of the Muslim Brotherhood chapter in Palestine. The Muslim Brotherhood movement is an international organization. It is one of today's largest Islamic movements. It professes a comprehensive understanding and precise conceptualization of the Islamic precepts in all aspects of life: concept and belief, politics and economics, education and social service, jurisdiction and law, exhortation and training, communication and arts, the seen and the unseen, and the rest of life's ways.

- Structure and Formation

ARTICLE 3

The structure of the Islamic Resistance Movement consists of Muslims who gave their loyalty to Allah. They therefore worshiped Him as He truly deserves:

> I have only created jinns and humans that they may
> worship Me.
> —*Qur'an 51:56*

They knew their obligation towards themselves, their people, and their country. They achieved *taqwa* [devoutness, piety] of Allah in all [of their obligations]. They raised the banner of jihad in the face of the transgressors to free country and folk from [the transgressors'] filth, impurity, and evil.

> Nay, We hurl the truth against falsehood, and
> it knocks out its brain, and behold, falsehood
> doth perish!
> —*Qur'an 21:18*

ARTICLE 4

The Islamic Resistance Movement welcomes all Muslims who adopt its doctrines and ideology, enact its program, guard its secrets, and desire to join its ranks to perform the obligation and receive their reward from Allah.

- The Historical and Geographic Dimension of the Islamic Resistance Movement

ARTICLE 5

The historical dimension of the Islamic Resistance Movement originates from its adoption of Islam as a system of life. It reaches far back to the birth of the Islamic Message and to the Pious Predecessors. Therefore, Allah is its goal, the Messenger its leader, and the Qur'an its constitution.

As for its geographic dimension, it is wherever Muslims—those who adopt Islam as a system of life—are found, in any region on the face of the earth. Therefore, it establishes a firm foundation in the depths of the earth and reaching high in the heavens.

> Seest thou not how Allah sets forth a parable? A
> goodly Word like a goodly tree, whose root is firmly
> fixed, and its branches (reach) to the heavens. It brings
> forth its fruit at all times, by the leave of its Lord. So
> Allah sets forth parables for people, in order that they
> may receive admonition.
> —Qur'an 14:24–25

- Differentiation and Independence

ARTICLE 6

The Islamic Resistance Movement is an outstanding type of Palestinian movement. It gives its loyalty to Allah, adopts Islam as a system of life, and works toward raising the banner of Allah on every inch of Palestine. Therefore, in the shadow of Islam, it is possible for all followers of different religions to live in peace and with security over their person, property, and rights. In the absence of Islam, discord takes form, oppression and destruction are rampant, and wars and battles take place.

The Muslim poet Muhammad Iqbal eloquently declares:

> When faith is lost there is no security nor life for he who does not revive religion;

> And whoever is satisfied with life without religion then he would have let annihilation be his partner.

- The Universality of the Islamic Resistance Movement

ARTICLE 7

Muslims throughout the world adopt the system of the Islamic Resistance Movement; they work toward aiding it, accepting its stands, and amplifying its jihad. Therefore, it is an international movement—it is prepared for this [task] because of the clarity of its ideology, its lofty goal, and the sanctity of its objectives. Upon this basis it should be considered, given a fair evaluation and admission of its role. Whoever cheats it of its right, turns away from aiding it, or is blinded to hide its role, is a person who argues with fate. And whoever closes his eyes from seeing reality, unintentionally or intentionally, will one day awake to find that the world has left him behind, and the justification will wear him down trying to defend his position. *The reward is for those who are early.*

> The oppression of the close relations is more painful on
> the soul, than the assault of a sharp sword.

> To thee We sent the scripture in truth, confirming the
> scripture that came before it, and guarding it in safety:
> So judge between them by what Allah hath revealed,
> and follow not their vain desires, diverging from the
> truth that hath come to thee. To each among you have
> we prescribed a law and an open way. If Allah had so
> willed, He would have made you a single people, but
> (His plan is) to test you in what he hath given you; so
> strive as in a race in all virtues. The goal of you all is to
> Allah; it is He that will show you the truth of the
> matters in which ye dispute.
> —Qur'an 5:48

The Islamic Resistance Movement is a link in [a long] chain of the jihad against the Zionist occupation, which is connected and tied with the initiation [of the jihad] of the martyr 'Izz al-Din al-Qassam[5] and his mujahid brothers in 1936. And the chain continues on to connect and tie another episode to add to the jihad of the Palestinians and the jihad of the Muslim Brotherhood in the war of 1948 and the jihad operation of the Muslim Brotherhood in 1968 and thereafter. Even though the episodes were few and far between, and were not continuous in jihad due to the obstacles placed by those in the sphere of [influence of] the Zionist entity in the face of the mujahidin, the Islamic Resistance Movement looks forward to fulfill the promise of Allah no matter how long it takes because the Prophet of Allah (*saas*) says:

> The Last Hour would not come until the Muslims fight against the Jews and the Muslims would kill them, and until the Jews would hide themselves behind a stone or a tree and a stone or a tree would say: Muslim or servant of Allah there is a Jew behind me; come and kill him; but the tree of Gharqad would not say it, for it is the tree of the Jews (Bukhari and Muslim).

• The Motto of the Islamic Resistance Movement:

---

[5]'Izz al-Din al-Qassam (d. 1935) was a religious official from Haifa who led a brief revolt against the British and Zionists. Hamas's militant Qassam brigades are named in his honor.

ARTICLE 8

Allah is its Goal.
The Messenger is its Leader.
The Qur'an is its Constitution.
Jihad is its methodology, and
Death for the sake of Allah is its most coveted desire.

CHAPTER TWO

- Goals

ARTICLE 9

The Islamic Resistance Movement evolved in a time where the lack of the Islamic Spirit has brought about distorted judgment and absurd comprehension. Values have deteriorated, the plague of the evil folk and oppression and darkness have become rampant, cowards have become ferocious. Nations have been occupied, their people expelled and fallen on their faces [in humiliation] everywhere on earth. The nation of truth is absent and the nation of evil has been established; as long as Islam does not take its rightful place in the world arena, everything will continue to change for the worse. The goal of the Islamic Resistance Movement therefore is to conquer evil, break its will, and annihilate it so that truth may prevail, so that the country may return to its rightful place, and so that the call may be broadcast over the minarets [lit. mosques] proclaiming the Islamic state. And aid is sought from Allah.

> And did not Allah check one set of people by means of
> another, the earth would indeed be full of mischief: but
> Allah is full of bounty to all the worlds.
> —Qur'an 2:251

ARTICLE 10

While the Islamic Resistance Movement is forging its path, it will be a support to the weak, a victor to the oppressed; with all its might, using all of its energy, to realize the truth and defeat the falsehood, by words and action, here and everywhere it can reach and effect a change.

CHAPTER THREE

*Strategy and Means*

- The Strategy of the Islamic Resistance Movement: Palestine Is an Islamic Trust

ARTICLE 11

The Islamic Resistance Movement [firmly] believes that the land of
Palestine is an Islamic waqf (trust) upon all Muslim generations till
the day of Resurrection. It is not right to give it up or any part of it.
Neither a single Arab state nor all the Arab states, neither a king nor a
leader, nor all the kings or leaders, nor any organization—Palestinian or
Arab—have such authority because the land of Palestine is an Islamic
trust upon all Muslim generations until the day of Resurrection. And
who has the true spokesmanship for all the Muslim generations till the
day of Resurrection?

This is the legislation in the Islamic shari'a, and the same goes for all
the lands accessed and consecrated by Muslims at the time of conquering for all Muslim generations till the day of Resurrection.

And so it was when the leaders of the Islamic Army, after conquering
Iraq and Sham (Greater Syria), sent [a letter] to the Muslims' Caliph
'Umar ibn al-Khattab [the second caliph, 634–44], asking for his advice
concerning the accessed lands: Shall they divide it up among the army,
or leave it to the original owner, or what? After discussion and consultation between the Caliph of the Muslims, 'Umar ibn al-Khattab, and
the companions of the Messenger, they came to the decision that the
benefits and blessings of the land should stay in the hands of its owner.
As for its real ownership, it should become a trust for the Muslim
generations till the day of Resurrection. Those who are on the land have
the rights to the land's benefits only, and this trust is permanent as long
as the heavens and the earth last. Any action taken in contradiction to
the Islamic shari'a concerning Palestine is unacceptable action, to be
taken back by its claimants.

> Verily, this is the very truth and certainty. So celebrate
> with praises the name of thy Lord, the Supreme.
> —Qur'an 56:95–96

- Nation and Nationalism from the Point of View
  of the Islamic Resistance Movement

ARTICLE 12

Nationalism, from the point of view of the Islamic Resistance Movement, is part and parcel of religious ideology. There is not a higher peak
in nationalism or depth in devotion than jihad when an enemy lands on
the Muslim territories. Fighting the enemy becomes the individual obligation of every Muslim man and woman.

> The woman is allowed to go fight without the permission of her
> husband and the slave without the permission of his master.

Nothing of the sort is found in any other system. This is a reality
about which there is no doubt. If other nationalisms have material,
humanistic, and geographic ties, then the Islamic Resistance Move-

ment's nationalism has all of that and, more important, divine reasons providing it with life and spirit where it is connected with the originator of the spirit and lifegiver, raising in the heavens the divine banner to connect earth and heavens with a strong bond.

> When Musa comes and throws the cane
> Indeed the magic and magician are invalid.
> Truth stands out clear from Error: whoever rejects evil
> and believes in Allah hath grasped the most trustwor-
> thy handhold, which never breaks. And Allah heareth
> and knoweth all things.
> —Qur'an 2:256

- Initiatives, Peace Solutions, and International Conferences

ARTICLE 13

. . . As far as the ideology of the Islamic Resistance Movement is concerned, giving up any part of Palestine is like giving up part of its religion. The nationalism of the Islamic Resistance Movement is part of its religion, in that it educates its members, and they perform jihad to raise the banner of Allah over their nation.

> And Allah hath full power and control over His affairs;
> but most among mankind know it not.
> —Qur'an 12:21

From time to time, the invitation is made for an international confer- ence to look into solving the problem. Some accept and some reject the idea, for one reason or another, asking for some condition or conditions to be fulfilled in order to agree to attend and participate in the conference. Because of the Islamic Resistance Movement's knowledge of the partici- pating parties of the conference, and the participants' past and present opinions and stands on Muslim interests, the Islamic Resistance Movement does not perceive that the conferences are able to deliver the demands, provide the rights, or do justice to the oppressed. Those conferences are nothing but a form of enforcing the rule of the unbelievers in the land of Muslims. And when have the unbelievers justly treated the believers?

> Never will the Jews or the Christians be satisfied with
> thee unless thou follow their form of religion. Say:
> "The guidance of Allah—that is the (only) guidance."
> Wert thou to follow their desires after the knowledge
> which hath reached thee, then wouldst thou find
> neither protector nor helper against Allah.
> —Qur'an 2:120

There is no solution to the Palestinian problem except by jihad. The initiatives, options, and international conferences are a waste of time and a kind of child's play. The Palestinian people are nobler than to be

fiddling with their future, rights, and destiny. It is mentioned in the
honorable tradition:

> The People of Sham (Greater Syria) are God's whip on His earth;
> with them He takes revenge on whom He pleases of His servants. It
> is forbidden for their hypocrites to be ruling over their believers and
> they will not except in worry and darkness. (Ahmad and Tabarani)

• The Three Spheres

ARTICLE 14

The problem of liberating Palestine is related to three spheres: the
Palestinian sphere, the Arab sphere, and the Islamic sphere. Every one
of them has a role to play in the struggle against Zionism. Each has
obligations to fulfill. It is a grave error, and extreme ignorance, to ignore
any of these spheres, because Palestine is an Islamic land accommodating the first qibla, the third Holy Sanctuary,[6] the [place where the]
ascent of the Messenger (saas) took place.

> Glory to Allah who did take His servant for a journey
> by night from the Sacred Mosque to the Farthest
> Mosque, whose precincts We did bless—in order that
> We might show him some of Our signs: for He is the
> One Who heareth and seeth (all things).
> —Qur'an 17:1

Because this is the case, the liberation of Palestine is obligatory for
every Muslim, no matter where he is; it is on this basis that the problem
should be viewed, and every Muslim must know this.

When the problem begins to be solved on this basis, when all the
resources of the three spheres are employed, the current situation will
change and the day of liberation will be near.

> Of a truth ye are stronger (than they) because of the
> terror in their hearts, (sent) by Allah. This is because
> they are people devoid of understanding.
> —Qur'an 59:13

• Jihad for the Liberation of Palestine Is Obligatory

ARTICLE 15

When an enemy occupies some of the Muslim lands, jihad becomes
obligatory for every Muslim. In the struggle against the Jewish occupation of Palestine, the banner of jihad must be raised. That requires that
Islamic education be passed to the masses locally, in the Arab [world]

---

[6]The qibla is the direction Muslims face for prayer. The first qibla established by Muhammad was Jerusalem, but that was later changed. Now worshipers face the Ka'ba, the
most famous sanctuary in Islam, located within the great mosque in Mecca, Saudi Arabia.

and in the Islamic [world], and that the spirit of jihad—fighting and joining the ranks—must be broadcast among the umma (Muslim community). The education process must involve (Islamic and other) scholars, teachers, and educators, communications specialists and journalists, the educated masses, and especially the youth of the Islamic Movement and their scholars. Fundamental changes must be brought about in the education system to liberate it from the effects of the ideological invasion brought about at the hands of the Orientalists and missionaries, whose attack suddenly descended on the area after Salah al-Din al-Ayubi defeated the Crusaders.[7] So the Crusaders then knew it was impossible to defeat the Muslims except by setting the stage with an ideological attack to confuse their (the Muslims') thoughts, stain their heritage, and defame their history, after which a military attack would take place. That was to pave the way for an imperialistic attack where [British] (General Edmund) Allenby claimed when he entered Jerusalem, "Now the Crusades are over," and General Gurud stood by Salah al-Din's (Saladin's) grave saying, "Here we have returned O Saladin." Imperialism has helped and is still helping the ideological invasion to establish its roots firmly. And all that was preparation for the loss of Palestine.

We must instill in the minds of the Muslim generation that the Palestinian cause is a religious cause. It must be solved on this basis because it contains Islamic sanctuaries where Masjid al-Aqsa [al-Aqsa mosque in Jerusalem] is tied firmly to Masjid al-Haram (in Mecca) never to be released, as long as the heavens and the earth last, by way of the night journey (Isra)[8] of Muhammad and ascension (Mi'raj) to the heavens from there (al-Aqsa). "To guard Muslims from infidels in Allah's cause for one day is better than the world and whatever is on its surface, and a place in Paradise as small as that occupied by the whip of one of you is better than the world and whatever is on its surface; and a morning's or an evening's journey by the worshiper in Allah's cause is better than the world and what is on its surface."

"By Him in whose Hand is Muhammad's life, I love to be killed in the way of Allah then to be revived to life again, then to be killed and then to be revived to life and then to be killed." (Agreed upon.)

- Training the Muslim Generation

ARTICLE 16

We must train the Muslim generation in our area, an Islamic training that depends on performing the religious obligations, studying the book of Allah very well, the sunna, the Islamic history and heritage from its

[7]Salah al-Din (1138–93), a Kurd born in what is today Iraq, led a successful jihad against European Crusaders, and is frequently invoked as the paradigmatic Muslim warrior-hero.

[8]The journey Muhammad was said to have made in the company of the angel Gabriel from Mecca to Jerusalem.

authentic sources with the advice of specialists and scholars, and using the curriculum that will provide the Muslim with the correct worldview in ideology and thought. In addition is the necessity of careful study of the enemy's material and human ability, knowing his weaknesses and strengths, knowing the powers that support him and stand by his side, along with the necessity of knowing current events and new trends, studying the analysis and commentaries on it. Also, there is the importance of planning for the present and the future, and studying every trend where the mujahid can live in his time with the full knowledge of his destiny, purpose, path, and the events surrounding him.

> O my son (said Luqman), "if there be (but) the weight
> of a mustard seed and it were (hidden) in a rock, or
> (anywhere) in the heavens or on earth, Allah will bring
> it forth: for Allah understands the finer mysteries, (and)
> is well-acquainted (with them)." "O my son! Establish
> regular prayer, enjoin what is just, and forbid what is
> wrong and bear with patient constancy whate'er betide
> thee; for this is firmness (of purpose) in (the conduct
> of) affairs." "And swell not thy cheek (with pride) at
> men, nor walk in insolence through the earth: for Allah
> loveth not any arrogant boaster."
> —Qur'an 31:16–18

• The Role of the Muslim Woman

ARTICLE 17
The Muslim woman has a role in the battle for liberation, which is no less than the role of the man, for she is the factory of men. Her role in directing generations and training them is a big role. The enemies have realized her role: they think that if they are able to direct her and raise her the way they want, far from Islam, then they have won the battle. You'll find that they use continuous spending through mass media and the motion picture industry. They also use the educational system by way of their teachers who are part of Zionist organizations— which go by different names and forms, such as [Free] Masons, Rotary Clubs, intelligence networks, and other organizations. These are all centers for destruction and destroyers. Those Zionist organizations have great material resources, which allow them to play a significant role in society to realize Zionist goals, and enforce the understanding that serves [the interests of] the enemy. These organizations play their role while Islam is absent from the arena and is estranged from its people. The Islamist should play his role in confronting the plans of those destroyers. When the day comes and Islam has its way in directing life, it shall eliminate those organizations that are opposed to humanity and Islam.

ARTICLE 18

The women in the house of the mujahid (and the striving family), be she a mother or sister, has the most important role in taking care of the home and raising children of ethical character and understanding that comes from Islam, and of training her children to perform the religious obligations to prepare them for the jihadic role that awaits them. From this perspective it is necessary to take care of schools and the curricula that educate the Muslim girl to become a righteous mother aware of her role in the battle of liberation. She must have the necessary awareness and attentiveness in running the home. Being economical and far from carefree spending of the family's income are requirements to continue the struggle in the overwhelmingly arduous situation. She should always keep in mind that money is blood that must not flow except in veins to sustain the life of children and elders equally.

> For Muslim men and women, for believing men and women, for devout men and women, for true men and women, for men and women who are patient and constant, for men and women who humble themselves, for men and women who give in charity, for men and women who fast (and deny themselves), for men and women who guard their chastity, and for men and women who engage in Allah's praise—for them has Allah prepared forgiveness and great reward.
> —*Qur'an 33:35*

- The Role of Islamic Art in the Battle for Liberation

ARTICLE 19

Art has rules and standards with which one can determine whether it is Islamic or ignorant. The Islamic Liberation is in need of Islamic art that raises the spirit and does not emphasize one aspect of the humanity over the others, but raises all aspects equally and harmoniously. The human is of a strange makeup, hand full of clay and breath of spirit. Islamic art communicates to mankind on this basis. Ignorant art communicates to the body and emphasizes the clay aspect.

Books, articles, newsletters, orations, pamphlets, poetry, *nasheed* (songs), plays, and other materials, if the specialties of Islamic art are included in it, are necessary for ideological education and invigorating nourishment to continue the struggle and relax the spirit because the struggle is long and the toil is hard. The souls will be bored, and Islamic art revives the vigor, imparts excitement, and invokes in the soul high spirits and correct deliberation.

Nothing corrects the soul if it is deliberating than change from state to state.

All this is serious and includes no mirth because a nation at jihad does not know merriment.

- Social Welfare

ARTICLE 20

The Muslim society is a cooperative society and the Messenger said "Best of the people are al-Ash'arites. If a difficult situation befell them, in residence or in travel, they would gather what they have (of wealth) and divide it up equally among themselves." And this is the Islamic spirit that must prevail in every Muslim society. The society that opposes a vicious Nazi enemy in its behavior, which does not differentiate between men or women, elder or youth, is foremost in being adorned with this Islamic spirit. Our enemy uses the method of collective punishment, robbing people of their land and property, and chasing them in their migration and places of gathering. They purposely break (bodily) bones; fire (live ammunition directly) at women, children, elders (sometimes) with a reason or without a reason; create concentration camps to place thousands (of people) in inhuman conditions, not to mention the demolition of homes, orphaning of children, and issuance of tyrannical laws on thousands of youth so they spend their best years in the obscurity of prisons.

The Nazism of Jews has included women and children. Terror is for everyone, they frighten people in their livelihood, take their wealth, and threaten their honor. They, with their shocking actions, treat people worse than they treat the worst of war criminals. Deportation from one's land is a form of murder.

In confronting this type of conduct, social cooperation must predominate among all the people and all must oppose the enemy as one body; if a member of it is afflicted the whole of the body is involved both in waking and in fever.

ARTICLE 21

Part of social welfare is providing aid to everyone who is in need of it, be it material or spiritual, or collective cooperation to complete some works. And upon the members of Islamic Resistance Movement falls the responsibility of looking after the needs of the population as they would for their personal needs. And (an obligation) upon them is that they should not spare an effort in realizing it, protecting it and them, and they should avoid, without foul play, what might adversely affect future generations. Because the masses are from them, and to them its power is their power, its future is their future. A duty upon all members of the Islamic Resistance Movement is to take part in people's happiness and grief and they should take as their duty the people's demands and what realizes the people's benefit and theirs. When this spirit (of cooperation) overwhelms, love will deepen and cooperation and mercy will (exist), and ranks will be strengthened in confrontation with the enemies.

• The Powers That Support the Enemy

ARTICLE 22
The enemy planned long ago and perfected their plan so that they can achieve what they want to achieve, taking into account effective steps in running matters. So they worked on gathering huge and effective amounts of wealth to achieve their goal. With wealth they controlled the international mass media—news services, newspapers, printing presses, broadcast stations, and more. With money they ignited revolutions in all parts of the world to realize their benefits and reap the fruits of them. They are behind the French Revolution, the Communist Revolution, and most of the revolutions here and there which we have heard of and are hearing of. With wealth they formed secret organizations throughout the world to destroy societies and promote the Zionist cause; these organizations include the Freemasons, the Rotary and Lions' clubs, and others. These are all destructive intelligence-gathering organizations. With wealth, they controlled imperialistic nations and pushed them to occupy many nations to exhaust their (natural) resources and spread mischief in them.

Concerning the local and international wars, speak without hesitation. They are behind the First World War in which they destroyed the Islamic caliphate and gained material profit, monopolized raw wealth, and got the Balfour Declaration.[9] They created the League of Nations so they could control the world through that organization. They are behind the Second World War, where they grossed huge profits from their trade of war materials, and set down the foundations to establish their nation by forming the United Nations and Security Council, instead of the League of Nations, in order to rule the world through that organization.

There is not a war that goes on here or there in which their fingers are not playing behind it.

> Every time they kindle the fire of war, Allah doth
> extinguish it; but they (ever) strive to do mischief on
> earth. And Allah loveth not those who do mischief.
> —Qur'an 5:64

So the imperialist powers in the capitalist West and communist East support the enemy with all their might—material and human—and they change roles. When Islam is manifest, the unbelievers' powers unite against it because the Nation of the unbelievers is one.

[9]The Balfour Declaration of 1917 was the British government's official statement of support for a Jewish "national home" in Palestine.

> O ye who believe! Take not into your intimacy those
> outside your ranks: they will not fail to corrupt you.
> They only desire your ruin: rank hatred has already
> appeared from their mouths: what their hearts conceal
> is far worse. We have made plain to you the signs,
> if ye have wisdom.
> —Qur'an 3:118

It is not by chance that this verse ends with "if ye have wisdom."

## CHAPTER FOUR

### *Our Positions*

- The Islamic Movements

ARTICLE 23

The Islamic Resistance Movement regards the other Islamic movements
with respect and honor even if it disagrees with them on an issue or
viewpoint. However, it agrees with them on many issues and viewpoints
and sees that those movements—if they have good intentions which
are purely for Allah's sake—fall within the area of ijtihad. As long as
its actions are within Islamic jurisprudence, to every mujtahid there is
a reward.

The Islamic Resistance Movement considers those movements as
beneficial and asks Allah's guidance (about spiritual and worldly
conduct) for everyone, and it raises the banner of unity and continues
striving to realize unity based on the Qur'an and sunna.

> And hold fast all together, by the rope which Allah
> (stretches out for you), and be not divided among
> yourselves
> —Qur'an 3:103

ARTICLE 24

The Islamic Resistance Movement does not allow slander or condemna-
tion of individuals or movements, because the believer is not a slanderer
or curser. However, it is necessary to differentiate between this and
positions and actions of individuals or groups. So, when there is a
mistake in a position or action, the Islamic Resistance Movement has
the right to clarify the mistake and warn against it and work to clarify
the truth and adopt it in current situations with impartiality. So wisdom
is the object of a persevering quest of the believers; he takes it wherever
he finds it.

> Allah does not like bad words to be made public,
> except where injustice hath been done; for Allah is He
> who heareth and knoweth all things. Whether ye

publish a good deed or conceal it or cover evil with
pardon, verily Allah doth blot out (sins) and hath
power (in the judgment of values).
—*Qur'an 4:148–49*

- The Nationalist Movements in the Palestinian Arena

ARTICLE 25
Given due respect, and considering its situation and surrounding factors,
Hamas will lend support to it as long as it does not give its loyalty to the
Communist East or the Crusading West and reassures its (the nationalist
movement's) members and victors that the Islamic Resistance Movement
is a moral and jihadic movement, moral and attentive in its view on life
and in its cooperation with others. It hates opportunism and does not
wish anything except good to people, either individuals or groups. It does
not go after material gain or personal fame, or reward of people. It
utilizes its own resources and what is available to it.

Against them make ready your strength to the utmost
of your power.
—*Qur'an 8:60*

It has no other ambition than to perform the obligation and win Allah's
satisfaction.

All nationalist elements working in the arena for the sake of liberating Palestine should be assured that it is a helper and supporter and will
never be anything but that, by work and action, past and present, by
uniting, not dividing, repairing not destroying, valuing benign advice,
pure effort, and powerful actions, closing the door in the face of petty
disputes, not listening to rumors and defamations while realizing the
right of self-defense. Everything that contradicts these guidelines is
fabricated by the enemy, or those who tread in their footsteps, to
achieve chaos, cleavage of ranks, and entanglement in side issues.

Oh ye who believe! If a wicked person comes to you
with any news, ascertain the truth, lest ye harm people
unwittingly, and afterwards become full of repentance
of what ye have done.
—*Qur'an 49:6*

ARTICLE 26
The Islamic Resistance Movement, while favorably viewing the Palestinian nationalist movements that are not loyal to East or West, is not
forbidden from discussing the options on the local or international
arenas concerning the Palestinian problem. Here an objective discussion
will clarify to what degree the nationalist movement is in the national
interest—from an Islamic perspective.

- Palestine Liberation Organization

ARTICLE 27

The Palestine Liberation Organization is closest of those close to the Islamic Resistance Movement, in that it is the father, the brother, the relative, or friend; and does the Muslim offend his father, brother, relative, or friend? Our nation is one, plight is one, destiny is one, and our enemy is the same. We are all affected by the situation that surrounded the formation of the organization (PLO) and the chaotic ideologies that overwhelm the Arab world because of the ideological invasion that befell the Arab world since the defeat of the Crusades and the ongoing consolidation of orientalism, missionary work, and imperialism. The organization (PLO) adopted the idea of a secular state, and as such we considered it [objectionable].

Secularist ideology is in total contradiction to religious ideologies, and it is from ideology that positions, actions, and decisions are derived. From here, despite our respect for the Palestine Liberation Organization and what it might become, and not underestimating its role in the Arab-Israeli struggle, we cannot exchange the present and future of Islam in Palestine to adopt the secular ideology, because the Islamic nature of the Palestinian issue is part and parcel of our din (religion and way of life) and whosoever neglects part of his din is surely lost.

> And who turns away from the religion of Abraham but
> such as debase their souls with folly?
> —Qur'an 2:130

When the Palestine Liberation Organization adopts Islam as its system of life, we will be its soldiers and the firewood of its fire, which will burn the enemies. Until this happens, and we ask Allah that it be soon, the position of the Islamic Resistance Movement toward the Palestine Liberation Organization is the position of a son toward his father, and the brother toward his brother, and the relative toward his relative. He will be hurt if a thorn pricks him; he supports him in confronting the enemy and wishes guidance for him.

He who has no brother is like one going to battle without weapons.

And know that your cousin is like your wings; and does the falcon fly without wings?

• The Arab Countries and Islamic Governments

ARTICLE 28

The Zionist invasion is a vicious attack that does not have the piety to refrain from using low and despicable methods to fulfill its obligations; it depends enormously on its penetration of and intelligence operations in the secret organizations that were offshoots of it—such as the [Free] Masons, Rotary, and Lions' clubs, and other such networks of spies— and all these secret or public organizations work for the benefit of and with the guidance of the Zionists. Zionists are behind the drug and alcohol trade because of their ability to facilitate the ease of control and expansion. The Arab countries surrounding Israel are requested to open their borders for the mujahidin of the Arab and Islamic countries so they can take their role and join their efforts with their Muslim brothers of Palestine. As for the other Arab and Islamic countries, they are asked to ease the movement of mujahidin from it and to it—that is the least they could do. We should not lose this opportunity to remind every Muslim that when the Jews occupied immaculate Jerusalem in 1967, they stood on the stairs of the blessed Masjid al-Aqsa loudly chanting: "Muhammad has died and left girls behind."

So Israel with its Jewishness and its Jewish population challenges Islam and Muslims.

So the eyes of the cowards do not sleep.

• Nationalist and Religious Organizations, Foundations, Intelligentsia, Arab and Islamic World

ARTICLE 29
The Islamic Resistance Movement would like each and every one of these organizations to stand by its side, supporting it on all levels, taking up its position, pushing forth its activities and movements, and working to gain support for the Islamic Resistance Movement so the Islamic people can be its support and its victors—a strategic dimension on all levels: human, material, media, historical, and geographic. It works through holding supportive conferences, producing clarifying statements, supportive articles, purposeful pamphlets, and keeping the public aware of the Palestinian situation and what is facing it and what is being plotted against it, through educating the Islamic people ideologically, morally, and culturally, in order to play its role in the battle for liberation, just as it played its role in defeating the Crusaders and pushing back the Tartars (Mongols) and saving human civilization, and that is not hard for Allah.

> Allah has decreed: "It is I and my messengers who
> must prevail": for Allah is one full of strength, able to
> enforce His will.
> —Qur'an 58:21

ARTICLE 30
Authors and scholars, people of media and oration, people of training and education, and the rest of the different fields in the Arab and Islamic world: all of you are called upon to adopt your role and perform your obligation, because of the ferocity of the Zionist invasion and its penetration in most countries, its materialistic and media control, and what it has built in most countries of the world.

Jihad is not only carrying weapons and confronting the enemy. The good word, excellent article, beneficial book, aid, and support, if inten-

tions are pure, so that the banner of Allah is the most high, are each a
jihad for the sake of Allah.

> He who provided equipment to a fighter in the way of Allah and he
> who remained behind (to look after the) family of the fighter in the
> way of Allah, in fact fought in the way of Allah. (Abu Dawud and
> Tirmidhi)

- The People of Other Faiths

ARTICLE 31
The Islamic Resistance Movement is a humanistic movement that takes
care of human rights and follows the tolerance of Islam with respect to
people of other faiths. Never does it attack any of them except those
who show enmity toward it or stand in its path to stop the movement
or waste its efforts.

In the shadow of Islam it is possible for the followers of the three
religions—Islam, Christianity, and Judaism—to live in peace and harmony, and this peace and harmony is possible only under Islam. The
history of the past and present is the best written witness for that.

Followers of other religions should stop fighting Islam to rule this
area, because when they rule, there will only be murdering, punishing,
and banishing, because they make life hard for their own people, not to
mention the followers of other religions. The past and present are full of
examples which prove this.

> They will not fight you (even) together, except in
> fortified townships, or from behind walls. Strong is
> their fighting (spirit) amongst themselves: thou wouldst
> think they were united, but their hearts are divided:
> that is because they are a people devoid of wisdom.
> —Qur'an 59:14

Islam gives everyone their rights and forbids enmity toward the rights
of others. The Nazi Zionist efforts will not last as long as their battles.
*The state of oppression is an hour and the state of truth is until the
coming of the hour.*

> Allah does not forbid you to deal kindly and justly
> with anyone who has not fought you for your faith or
> driven you out of your homes: Allah loves the just.
> —Qur'an 60:8

- The Effort to Single Out the Palestinian People

ARTICLE 32
World Zionism and imperialist powers try with audacious maneuvers
and well-formulated plans to extract the Arab nations one by one from
the struggle against Zionism, so that in the end it can deal solely with

the Palestinian people. It already has removed Egypt far away from the circle of struggle with the treason of Camp David,[10] and it is trying to extract other countries by using similar treaties in order to remove them from the circle of struggle. The Islamic Resistance Movement calls upon the Arab and Islamic people to work seriously and constructively in order to not allow that horrible plan to be carried out, and to educate the masses of the dangers of withdrawal from the struggle with Zionism. Today it is Palestine, and tomorrow it will be another country, and then another; the Zionist plan has no bounds, and after Palestine they wish to expand from the Nile River to the Euphrates. When they totally occupy it they will look toward another, and such is their plan in the *Protocols of the Learned Elders of Zion*. Their present is the best witness to what is said.

Withdrawal from the circle of struggle is high treason and a curse on the doer.

> If any one turns his back to them on such a day—
> unless it be a stratagem of war, or to retreat to a troop
> (of his own)—he draws on himself the wrath of Allah,
> and his abode is Hell—an evil refuge (indeed)!
> —*Qur'an 8:16*

It is necessary to gather all forces and abilities to face the Tartarian Nazi invasion, otherwise loss of the homeland, exile of the population, a prompting of evil on the earth and destruction of all religious values [will take place]. Every person should know that he will be held responsible in front of Allah to be questioned.

> Then shall anyone who has done an atom's weight of
> good, see it, and anyone who has done an atom's
> weight of evil, shall see it.
> —*Qur'an 99:7–8*

In the circle of struggle with world Zionism, the Islamic Resistance Movement considers itself the spearhead, or a step on the path; it adds its efforts to the effort of the workers in the Palestinian arena. What is left is that it should be followed step by step by the Arab and Islamic people, and by the Muslim organizations in the Arab and Islamic regions, because they are the people who are prepared for the forthcoming role in the battle with the Jews, the businessmen of war.

> Amongst them we have placed enmity and hatred till
> the day of judgment. Every time they kindle the fire of
> war, Allah doth extinguish it; but they (ever) strive to

---

[10]Camp David here refers to the location of the 1978 Peace Accords between Egypt and Israel signed by Menachem Begin and Anwar al-Sadat and witnessed by U.S. President Jimmy Carter.

do mischief on earth. And Allah loveth not those who
do mischief.
—*Qur'an 5:64*

ARTICLE 33

The Islamic Resistance Movement goes forth with these general understandings, which are equal and in harmony with the patterns of the
universe, like being poured in the river of destiny, to confront the enemy.
And their struggle to defend Muslims, Islamic civilization, and religious
sanctuaries, of which Masjid al-Aqsa is at the forefront, to ignite the Arab
and Islamic people, their governments, and its nationalistic and official
organizations, to fear Allah while considering the Islamic Resistance
Movement—its way of dealing with it, should be, as Allah has wished,
like a supporter and helper spreading its hand to help, with support
followed by support until the will of Allah is manifested. The ranks join
the ranks, and the mujahids join mujahids and other groups that come
forth from everywhere in the Muslim world, answering the call of
obligation, repeating "come to jihad"—a call bursting forth into the
heights of the Heavens, reverberating until the liberation is complete
and the invaders are rolled back and the victory of Allah descends.

> Allah will certainly aid those who aid His (cause)—for
> verily Allah is full of strength, exalted in might (able to
> enforce will).
> —*Qur'an 22:40*

## CHAPTER FIVE

### *Historical Proof*

• Facing the Enemy throughout History

ARTICLE 34

Palestine is the heart of the earth, the meeting of the continents, and the
lure of the avaricious since the dawn of history. The Messenger points
to that in his venerable narration when he says to Mu'adh bin Jabal:

> O Mu'adh, Allah is going to open for you Greater Syria (al-Sham)
> after me. From al-Irish [in the Sinai peninsula] to the Eu-phrates its
> men, women, and children are steadfast till the day of resurrection.
> Whosoever of you chooses a coastal site of Greater Syria or
> Jerusalem (*bayt al-maqdis*), then he is in constant jihad till the Day
> of Resurrection.

The individuals have envied (in taking) Palestine more than once and
they flooded it with armies to fulfill their goals. The hoards of Crusaders carrying their belief and crosses were able to defeat the Muslims for
a specific period of time. The Muslims did not get Palestine back until

they gathered under their religious banner and united together, glorified their lord, and took off as mujahids under the leadership of Salah al-Din al-Ayyubi for nearly two decades, and then it was a clear victory, the Crusaders defeated and Palestine liberated.

> Say to those who reject faith: "Soon will ye be van-
> quished and gathered together to hell—an evil bed
> indeed to lie on."
> —*Qur'an 3:12*

This is the only way to liberation. There is no doubt in the truth of the historical evidence, which is a pattern of the universe and a law of nature—only metal breaks metal—and nothing defeats a corrupt belief except the true belief in Islam, because belief can be defeated only by belief, and in the end the victory is for the truth. Truth is victorious.

> Our word has already been given to Our servants the
> messengers: it is they who will be helped, and the ones
> who support Our cause will be the winners.
> —*Qur'an 37:171–73*

ARTICLE 35
The Islamic Resistance Movement considers the defeat of the Crusaders at the hands of Salah al-Din al-Ayyubi and the liberation of Palestine; the defeat of the Tartars in the (battle) of 'Ayn Jalut, the defeat of their forces at the hands of Qutuz and Zahir Baybars, and the rescue of the world from the destructive onslaught of the Tartars (destroying) all traces of human civilization; and learns from them (valuable) lessons and wisdom. The current Zionist invasion was preceded by many invasions of the Crusading West and others, including Tartars from the east. Just as the Muslims confronted those invasions and prepared for fighting and defeating them, they should be able to confront and defeat the Zionist invasion. And that is not difficult for Allah if intentions are pure, efforts are truthful, and if Muslims have benefited from past experiences, have been freed from the effect of the ideological invasion, and have followed the way of their predecessors.

POSTSCRIPT

*The Islamic Resistance Movement Are Soldiers*

ARTICLE 36
The Islamic Resistance Movement, while forging its way to emphasize time and time again to all our people—the Arab people and Muslim people—that it does not want fame for itself, or materialistic gain, or social status, and is not positioned against any of our people so that it can rival or take their place, will never be against any of the Muslims or

the peacefulness of the non-Muslims, in this place or any place, and it shall only be an aid to all societies and organizations working against the Zionist enemy and those in its orbit. The Islamic Resistance Movement depends on Islam as a way of life, on its belief, its religion, and on whoever adopts Islam as a way of life whether he is here or there, be it an organization, committee, or group. The Islamic Resistance Movement is nothing but its soldiers. Nothing but.

We ask Allah to guide us and guide (others) through us and to decide between us and our people with the truth.

> Our Lord! Decide Thou between us and our people in
> truth, for Thou art the best to decide.
> —*Qur'an* 7:89

And our last prayer is "All praise is due to Allah, Lord of the Universe."

Palestine, 1 Muharam AH 1409      (18 August AD 1988)

# Chapter 16

## MUHAMMAD HUSAYN FADLALLAH
## 1935–

WESTERN OBSERVERS of contemporary Islam have often debated the question of whether Islamist movements arising in one country will be "exported" elsewhere and what might aid or impede their spread to other people and places. The Iranian revolution of 1979 raised this question with great urgency. A seemingly powerful regime had been overthrown by a mass movement led by an exiled religious scholar, Ayatollah Khomeini, putting many an authoritarian Middle Eastern government on notice that it, too, could be successfully challenged in a similar way. Further, large numbers of Shi'i Muslims live in Pakistan, Iraq, Bahrain, Saudi Arabia, and Lebanon, and the example of a Shi'i revolutionary movement could give heart to those among them who were dissatisfied with their political circumstances. There is no doubt that the Iranian revolution did help mobilize the Shi'a in varied contexts, though its impact on Sunni Islamists is harder to measure. Yet among the Shi'a themselves, there has continued to be much debate on Khomeini's conception of Islamic government (see chapter 6 on Khomeini), and whether that sort of government can, or should, be established elsewhere. In a country like Lebanon, with its varied religious communities, the question is not so much if Khomeini's model of Islamic government is acceptable on doctrinal or other grounds but whether *any* Islamic government would be viable. Among the most prominent of those who have been openly skeptical on this account is Muhammad Husayn Fadlallah. Ironically, he is also one of Lebanon's best-known Islamists and its most influential religious scholar.

Fadlallah was born in Najaf, in Iraq, in 1935. Like countless other Shi'is aspiring to a career of religious learning and teaching, his father had come to Najaf from 'Aynata in southern Lebanon. Fadlallah was a contemporary of Muhammad Baqir al-Sadr, who later emerged as one of the most important Shi'i thinkers of the twentieth century (see chapter 7 on Sadr). Like Baqir al-Sadr, Fadlallah received some of his early education at a school that sought to combine modern education with the more traditional emphases of Shi'i religious learning. He completed his advanced religious education in the mid-1960s under the guidance of Muhsin al-Hakim (d. 1970) and Abu'l-Qasim al-Khu'i (d. 1992), two of the most influential religious scholars of their time in the religious establishment of Najaf. Fadlallah would later serve as the representative of al-Khu'i among the Shi'a of Lebanon.

Yet Fadlallah's political orientation was in marked contrast to al-Khu'i's. Whereas al-Khu'i remained staunchly committed to a politically quietist path throughout his long life, Fadlallah, like Baqir al-Sadr, was keen to see the Shi'i 'ulama provide active leadership to the community in all facets of life. In the 1950s, Islamist organizations like the Muslim Brotherhood (founded in Egypt in 1928) and the Hizb al-Tahrir (founded in Jerusalem in 1952) were active in Iraq; and although these were Sunni movements, they had some influence among the Shi'i youth in Iraq. The writings of Sayyid Qutb were also widely read in Iraq, by the Sunnis as well as the Shi'a (Sankari 2005, 65–73). The Shi'a had their own organizations, too, of which the Hizb al-Da'wa, founded in the late 1950s to pursue the establishment of an Islamic state in Iraq, proved to be the most enduring. Both Fadlallah and Baqir al-Sadr were closely, albeit informally, associated with this organization.

For reasons that are not altogether clear, Fadlallah moved from Iraq to Lebanon in the mid-1960s. Now a mujtahid, a religious scholar qualified to issue authoritative legal rulings in his own right, Fadlallah may have wanted to establish himself in an environment other than Najaf, which was always crowded with established and aspiring religious scholars. Even as he acted as the representative of a leading religious scholar based in Najaf, he would have had a freer hand in guiding his own followers. Yet if Fadlallah was seeking to establish himself as a leading figure among the Shi'a of Lebanon, stiff competition awaited him in his ancestral home.

Many Shi'i emigrants from Lebanon had gone on to become distinguished scholars in Iran and Iraq. But apart from well-entrenched families of local notables, the Shi'a of Lebanon were among the poorest of the Shi'a anywhere in the Arab world. It was as part of the effort to ameliorate the social, economic, and political circumstances of the Shi'a—in the country as a whole, but also in opposition to the highhandedness of the Shi'i landed elite—that the enterprising, Iranian-born, religious scholar Musa al-Sadr had been drawn to Lebanon. Like Fadlallah, Musa al-Sadr also had ancestral roots in Lebanon. He had been educated in Qom and Najaf but also, and unusually for the Shi'i 'ulama of the time, at Tehran University's Faculty of Law and Political Economy (Norton 1987, 39). Practically from the moment he had settled in Tyre, in southern Lebanon, in 1959, Musa al-Sadr had devoted himself to establishing charitable institutions for the education, vocational training, and social welfare of the Shi'a. In 1974 this championing of the poor and of all those who saw themselves as the disadvantaged took the form of the *Harakat al-mahrumin* (Movement of the Deprived), with Musa al-Sadr at its head. This movement was to play an important part in the Lebanese civil war

(1975–90), especially through its militant wing, Afwaj al-muqawama al-Lubnaniyya or AMAL (an acronym that translates as "hope"; on this organization, see Norton 1987).

Though Musa al-Sadr and Fadlallah always maintained a seemingly cordial relationship, the differences between them were substantial. Musa al-Sadr was, above all, concerned with the welfare of the Shi'i community in Lebanon. His rhetoric contained anti-Israeli motifs, but he also believed that Palestinian military operations, then waged against Israel from Lebanese soil, exposed the Lebanese Shi'a to the devastating consequences of intense Israeli reprisals (Norton 1987, 43–44; 2005, 200–1). The Shi'a, Musa al-Sadr believed, had their own interests to guard, and he strove to do so on their behalf. To Fadlallah, on the other hand, opposition to Israel has always been a paramount concern, one to which he has sought a continuing Muslim commitment irrespective of sectarian affiliation or national boundaries. Implicit here is a second major difference between the two leaders. Despite his foreign origins, it is the interests of Lebanon, its Shi'a and its disadvantaged, that were foremost among Musa al-Sadr's concerns; and his notoriously shifting alliances may have reflected this commitment (cf. Norton 2005, 197–204). Fadlallah, on the other hand, has long positioned himself on a bigger stage, seeking an audience among all Muslims or, at the very least, the Shi'a around the world. He has also been recognized as a much more serious religious scholar than Musa al-Sadr. Yet, Fadlallah would not have achieved the prominence he has come to enjoy were it not for two crucial though unrelated events: the disappearance of Musa al-Sadr and the Iranian revolution of 1979.

In 1978, in the course of a visit to Libya, Musa al-Sadr mysteriously disappeared. No trace of him was ever found, though it is most likely that he was murdered—for reasons that remain unclear—at the behest of the Libyan leader Mu'ammar al-Qaddafi. Fadlallah's leadership of the Shi'a has scarcely been uncontested since then, though Musa al-Sadr's absence from the scene has contributed much to the growth of his influence. Like Musa al-Sadr, Fadlallah has been actively involved in the establishment of charitable institutions in Lebanon. His Mabarrat Charitable Association, founded in 1978, now controls many orphanages, schools, and hospitals throughout Lebanon (Deeb 2006, 88–89; Norton 2007, 107–12). These institutions have contributed significantly to the steady growth and consolidation of his following.

The Iranian revolution shaped Fadlallah's career in more complex ways. It was, of course, profoundly empowering for the "deprived" among the Shi'a everywhere to see how their coreligionists had brought down a seemingly mighty monarchical regime. As the religious scholars had been among the most prominent leaders of the revolution, the overthrow of the shah further demonstrated that such 'ulama were anything but antiquated figures oblivious to changing social and political conditions—as the stereotypes would have it—but rather that they still had great influence among the people and knew, or could learn, how to use it. For Shi'i religious scholars from Pakistan to Lebanon, Khomeini's path, whether or not one chose to follow it, represented nothing less than a new phase in the history of Shi'ism.

The impact of the Iranian revolution had other dimensions, too. Many among the revolutionaries, as well as their admirers outside Iran, were eager to "export" the revolution. While they sought to do so among Muslims in general, they were especially keen on this in countries where there already were substantial Shi'i populations and a recent history of Shi'i activism—as was clearly the case in Lebanon. To this end, the Iranians helped found Hizbullah in 1982, an organization that has remained closely allied with Iran to the present day (Norton 2007). It has been responsible for numerous kidnappings and bombings, most notably the bombing of the U.S. Marine compound and French military barracks in Beirut in October 1983 that killed more than three hundred people. With Iranian support, the Hizbullah has continued to launch attacks against Israel, both during the Israeli military presence in southern Lebanon (1985–2000) and in subsequent years. In July 2006, Hizbullah's capture of two Israeli soldiers inside Israeli territory and the killing of several other Israeli soldiers led to a month-long war with Israel. Hizbullah survived intense Israeli attacks and the war came to an inconclusive end, but not before it had brought great destruction to Lebanon (Norton 2007, 132–59).

Fadlallah has often been characterized in the Western media as the spiritual leader of the Hizbullah and seen as such by many observers and analysts. He was suspected of involvement in the October 1983 bombings and of blessing many others of Hizbullah's violent acts. Fadlallah, however, has not only disavowed any association with these acts; he has also denied any formal association with Hizbullah (Norton 1987, 103–4). In part, of course, this may have to do with strategy: too close an association with what the United States and many other countries view as a terrorist organization carries serious perils, as it jeopardizes not only his personal safety—Fadlallah has himself been the target of assassination attempts—but also his standing as a religious scholar. But his disavowal also reflects Fadlallah's lifelong unease with being identified with the positions and platform of any party, which would constrain his ability to assume a persona that transcends groups, organizations, and even borders. Nor have Hizbullah's positions been identical with those of Fadlallah; indeed, the relations between Fadlallah and the Hizbullah leadership have sometimes been less than cordial (cf. Norton 2007, 118–19).

While Hizbullah has hewed closely to the official policies pursued by postrevolutionary Iran, Fadlallah, while long maintaining close ties with the Iranian revolutionary leadership, has often charted a more independent path. Two examples of this are worth noting here. First, Fadlallah has come to increasingly resist calls for the establishment of an Islamic state in Lebanon (Sankari 2005, 221–28). As he sees it, the public implementation of Islamic norms is not viable in a country with diverse religious communities (notably, the Shiʻa, the Sunnis, the Druze, and the Christians) that are deeply suspicious of one another. Instead, he has argued that the Muslims of Lebanon ought to forge, and to become part of, a political system that is equally acceptable to members of the country's varied communities. Doing so demands coming to terms with the peculiar conditions of Lebanon—a "Lebanonization of the Islamist movement," as Fadlallah has put it (see the text of the 1995 interview in this chapter). In a similar vein, Fadlallah has argued that Muslims ought to take active part in the electoral process, and to air their views and exert their influence through elective offices. Indeed, for all his efforts to maintain his formal distance from Hizbullah, he is sometimes credited with persuading its leadership to take part in national elections and with thereby helping its integration into the political mainstream (Sankari 2005, 241–47). Fadlallah's endorsement of the Lebanonization of Islam is not quite a vision of a secular state, however. Rather, he sees it as the most effective means available to reshape the country's politics in ways favorable to the Muslims and especially to the Shiʻa, who compose the largest of Lebanon's religious communities.

Second, while Fadlallah embraced Khomeini's view that the authority of the preeminent jurist (Persian: velayat-e faqih; Arabic: wilayat al-faqih) ought to extend to all matters, including the political, he has resisted Iranian efforts to centralize the structure of religious authority for the Shiʻa worldwide. Since the late nineteenth century, the Shiʻa have generally recognized one or more of their most distinguished scholars as their "objects of emulation" (Arabic: marjaʻ al-taqlid; Persian: marjaʻ-i taqlid, or simply marjaʻ), whose opinions they are expected to follow in all matters. Khomeini's doctrinal reformulation had consisted in arguing that the marjaʻ al-taqlid should also exercise *political* authority, a view predicated on the assumption that the person exercising such authority—the *vali-ye faqih*—would already be a widely recognized religious scholar. Some years after Khomeini's death, the Iranian religious establishment headed by his successor, ʻAli Khameneʼi, sought to consolidate his position as the vali-ye faqih in Iran by having Khameneʼi recognized as marjaʻ by the Shiʻa everywhere. This was a dubious move not only because many leading scholars outside Iran had never accepted Khomeini's doctrinal innovations but also because Khameneʼi's scholarly credentials were, at best, modest. While Hizbullah supported the move, Fadlallah did not; instead, he proceeded, in the mid-1990s, to have himself recognized as a marjaʻ, especially among the Shiʻa of Lebanon. For all its self-serving implications, Fadlallah's move reflected his conviction that the position of the marjaʻ need not be limited to a single person at any given time but rather that there ought to be a plurality of such religious authorities. This view strained his relations with both Iran and Hizbullah for a time, though it has also facilitated his emergence as by far the most visible of the Shi'i scholars in contemporary Lebanon (cf. Sankari 2005, 256–58). As the marja', Fadlallah is the recipient of substantial financial contributions from pious Shi'a, both inside and outside Lebanon, and these funds have helped sustain the activities of his Mabarrat Charitable Association, which, in turn, has enhanced his stature and visibility still further.

Fadlallah has sought to walk a fine line between aspirations to global Shi'i leadership—implicit in his differences with Musa al-Sadr and later, on different grounds, with Khamene'i—and one limited primarily to Lebanon. He has walked another fine line between an uncompromisingly militant approach to settling outstanding political grievances and a more nuanced, if ambiguous, course of action. Fadlallah often distances himself from kidnappings, hijackings, and the killing of noncombatants; and, like the Sunni scholar Yusuf al-Qaradawi, he was among those who condemned the terrorist attacks of September 11, 2001. Yet, like Qaradawi, he does not consider Palestinian suicide bombings, or similar actions elsewhere, as impermissible (Sankari 2005, 210, 269–70). As he put it in 1985, "oppression impels the subjugated to discover new weapons and new vigour every day. . . . there is no difference between dying with a pistol in your hand or exploding yourself" (quoted in Sankari 2005, 210). Again like Qaradawi, Fadlallah views such "new weapons" as allowed only if there is any real hope of inflicting harm on the enemy (Sankari 2005, 210). Some of the same "pragmatism" informs his critique of certain long-established practices within the Shi'i community. For example, he has argued that the 'Ashura rituals—which take the form of self-flagellation in commemorating the death of the third Shi'i imam, Husayn (d. 685)—serve no good purpose because participants in these rituals hurt only themselves: "Living Ashura is standing against oppression. Such a stand should fill our hearts and minds each time we face the oppressors and arrogant powers. . . . It is not living in a tragedy of tears and hitting ourselves with swords and chains. . . for swords should be raised against the enemy as we were taught by the Imam" (quoted, from a 2003 sermon, in Deeb 2006, 154).[1]

---

[1] Fadlallah has also critiqued conventional accounts of the suffering of Fatima, a daughter of the Prophet Muhammad and the wife of the first Shi'i imam, 'Ali ibn Abi Talib. Stories of Fatima's tribulations at the hands of some of the Prophet's leading companions in the aftermath of his death have featured prominently in ritual lamentation of Shi'i suffering throughout history; they have also contributed their share to sectarian tensions with the Sunnis, who revere the memory of the very companions the Shi'a hold liable for Fatima's suffering. Fadlallah has argued that Fatima ought to be seen in a different light, not as a mere victim of oppression but as a religious authority and a social and political role model for contemporary Shi'i women. Fadlallah's critique of traditional Shi'i retellings of Fatima's life has generated much controversy in some Shi'i circles (cf. Rosiny 2001). Yet, like his revaluation of the 'Ashura rituals, it serves as an important reminder that Islamism ought to be seen as a political critique, one that seeks to refashion society and polity, though not necessarily—as Fadlallah insists—in the direction of an Islamic state.

Yet even when "swords are raised" in ways that he disapproves of, Fadlallah has opted for an ambivalent juridical appraisal: "One's actions may be wrong in an absolute context but not in view of the circumstances. . . . A negative value may be transformed into a positive value if it serves the public good. . . . if speaking the truth would mean betraying one's nation [umma], then telling the truth would be wrong and lying would be right" (Fadlallah 1995, 64, 65). This remarkable view combines the juristic conception of maslaha—the common good, in light of which established norms are to be rethought—with the Shi'i doctrine of *taqiyya* or precautionary dissimulation, intended to protect one's interests in adverse circumstances. From this perspective, the objection to wanton acts of terrorism, perpetrated even by what he calls "adolescent military commanders," is not so much whether they violate Islamic norms—which, in any case, "do not exist in abstraction"—but whether such actions harm the community's larger interests (cf. Fadlallah 1995, 65; 2002, 81). Whether they do so is a question that requires intimate knowledge of Islam and of the community's interests. And like Khomeini, Fadlallah has long argued that both are crucial prerequisites for the truly authoritative jurist.

# ISLAMIC UNITY AND POLITICAL CHANGE

Interview with Shaykh Muhammad Husayn Fadlallah (1995)

*Mahmoud Soueid*: How would you characterize the state of affairs of Muslims in the world today?

*Fadlallah:* The Muslims are having difficulty bringing forth the kind of Islamic existence to which they aspire. . . . Speaking in general terms, you could say they are seeking what could be termed a concrete expression of Islamic reality—a movement, a way of life, a political position, in particular. There is a visceral Muslim identity, even among secularists who may not be consciously aware of it. This involves a spontaneous identification with other Muslims—in Bosnia, Chechnya, Afghanistan, wherever—irrespective of the merits of the case.

We are still experiencing the deep wounds inflicted on our psyche by Palestine. I would go so far as to say that the average Muslim experiences the Arab-Zionist problem as a Jewish problem. Thus, when Muslims think of Palestine, they are deeply aware of a Jewish challenge. The many political ideologies through which they have responded to this challenge remain superficial and have not penetrated to the depths of the Muslim psyche. Even pan-Arabism had an Islamic content. The Egyptian national anthem adopted by Gamal 'Abd al-Nasser, the father of Arab nationalism, began with the words *Allahu Akbar* (God is Great)]. It was the same cry that motivated the Palestinians who took part in the intifada.[2] Even the Christians living in the Arab world unconsciously think with an Islamic mentality; although they do not have an Islamic affiliation, they take in Islamic civilization as they do the air they breathe, like the fragrance of a rose.

I believe this Islamic identity has grown stronger as a result of the challenges to Islam, particularly the blatant injustice of the United States and to a lesser extent European practices, motivated as they are by economic interests.

Despite this strong identity, the Islamic world is suffering from a lack of a clear and objective understanding of the true situation of Islam and Islamic thought. This is apparent from the proliferation of Islamic

[2]The intifada refers here to the Palestinian uprising against Israel that began in 1987 and continued until the establishment of the Palestinian Authority in Gaza in 1994.

movements, some reactionary, wanting to live as if it were five hundred or six hundred years ago, some anarchic, some resorting to violence in situations where peaceful means can be pursued, some with a sound grasp of reality and whose tactics, whether violent or peaceful, are guided by objective analyses. This disarray in doctrine and tactics makes it impossible to place all the Islamic movements in the same category and to pass the same judgment on them. Muslims sympathetic to Islamist goals are hard pressed to support some of their tactics that are unacceptable to Islam, such as assassinating foreigners or disrupting the school year, and so on, whether the Islamists are in fact guilty of such practices or stand falsely accused.

In addition, it is true at this stage that in most places Islam lacks political clout. We find that the Islamic world, represented by the Islamic Conference, cannot keep its distance from U.S. policy and is always trying to be in harmony with it. Opposition is purely verbal; no firm positions at variance with American policy are adopted. From the political point of view, the Islamic peoples and the Islamic umma are dominated and kept in the wings by their rulers. In our opinion, the forces of international arrogance, with the United States (represented by the Central Intelligence Agency and its sister organizations) at the helm, have pressed Arab rulers into service as watchdogs for their policies and interests in the Islamic world. Consequently, Muslims are repressed by other Muslims. The Egyptians are being beaten by the Egyptian regime, and the Algerians are beaten by the Algerian regime, so the United States does not have to dirty its hands.

Meanwhile, the Islamic countries are beset by internal squabbles. Muslims are fighting more wars among each other than they fought against Israel. A few square meters of land here or there could lead to war between one Islamic country and the other, as between Saudi Arabia and Yemen, for instance. The Afghans are fighting each other more fiercely than they fought the Soviets. The Lebanese could always find justifications for fighting each other, yet many of them speak of the need for realism in politics and say that fighting and resistance are futile when it comes to Israel. . . .

There is also doctrinal intolerance between Sunnis and Shi'ites, which is a sore point in Islamic affairs. International and local intelligence agencies are at work in each Islamic country trying to widen the chasm between Sunnis and Shi'ites and preventing any attempts at dialogue and unity even regarding general Islamic issues.

These political, cultural, and ideological problems culminate in economic problems as well. The Islamic world contains vast mineral resources, but we have seen oil become a curse on Muslims instead of a gift of grace to them. What has happened to our oil revenues? Outsiders, operating through a president they have placed in their service here or a king or a prince there, create wars for us to fight so that we

squander our wealth; what we get from the outsiders with one hand we
give back to them with the other to finance arms purchases.

Still, I believe that an Islamic awakening growing out of the sense of
Islamic unity could provide the impetus for future change. Today, in this
Islamic world tightly controlled by intelligence services and arrogant
[Western] hegemony, there are indications of something deep within
that is trying to come to the surface—a voice can be heard now and
then, a weak movement born here and there. We are not succumbing to
pessimism but are realistically taking a close look at our shortcomings
in order to transform them into advantages. Islam has survived fourteen
centuries and is still going strong—never mind what form that strength
is taking—and I believe it can forge ahead a long time into the future.

*Soueid:* In view of what you have just described, what is your opinion
of what is termed Islamic fundamentalism?

*Fadlallah:* There is no such a thing here as "Islamic fundamentalism" as
the West presents it—in other words, exclusive recourse to violence to
bring about change and negation of "the Other." This description does
not fit the Islamists. Concerning violence, jihad in Islam is a defensive
movement and a deterrent. When God spoke to us about war, He said
we should fight on behalf of the weak, "And fight them on until there is
no more persecution" (Q 2:193). Fight for the helpless, fight those who
fight you. If one undertakes a study of all the verses in the Qur'an on
the subject of warfare, one will not find a single verse that says fight
others to strip them of their humanity or to gain supremacy over them.
On the contrary, God the Majestic and Sublime does not wish one man
to feel superior to another. . . . We therefore consider the call to jihad to
be a call to protect the basic issues affecting human destiny from those
who are committing aggression against us. If someone fires a rocket at
me, I cannot respond by offering him a rose. From an Islamic perspective, we compare violence to surgery: one turns to it only as a last
resort.

As for negating the Other, we read in the Book of God: "Say: 'O
People of the Book! Come to common terms as between us and you:
that we worship none but Allah; that we associate no partners with
Him; that we erect not, from among ourselves, lords and patrons other
than Allah'" (Q 3:64). Christians and Jews differ with Muslims concerning the interpretation of the unity of God and the personality of
God. Despite that, the Qur'an commands: Turn to the principle of
unity—the unity of God and the unity of mankind. We interpret this to
mean that we can meet with Marxists on the common ground of
standing up to the forces of international arrogance; we can meet
nationalists, even secular nationalists, on the common ground of Arab
causes, which are also Islamic causes. Islam recognizes the Other.
During the early days of Islam, the Other took religious form, as the

"People of the Book" [Jews and Christians]. So Islam does not negate the Other; it invites the Other to dialogue. . . .

Therefore we Islamists are not fundamentalists the way the westerners see us. We refuse to be called fundamentalists. We are Islamic activists. As for the etymological sense of *usuliyya* (fundamentalism in Arabic), meaning returning to one's roots and origins (*usul*), our roots are the Qur'an and the true sunna or way of the Prophet, not the historical period in which the Prophet lived or the periods that followed—we are not fundamentalists (*usuliyyin*) in the sense of wanting to live like people at the time of the Prophet or the first caliphs or the time of the Umayyads. . . .

I said earlier that some Islamists are backward in some of their thinking and are deviating from the correct path in some of their practices, but circumstances may overwhelm one and force one into error. One's actions may be wrong in an absolute context but not in view of the circumstances. For example, when we consider the question of hostage taking in Lebanon, the kidnapping of foreigners, we should not consider these actions in abstraction, we must also consider the nature of the pressures the Americans and Europeans were exerting on the Lebanese at the time. I do not wish to claim that hostage taking or other actions emphasized in a propagandistic atmosphere are good or bad in an absolute sense, but that the forces of world arrogance seek to turn our values against us when it serves their interests. We find, for instance, that the Americans try to portray Iran as terrorist because it supports Hizbullah's resistance in south Lebanon and Hamas and Islamic Jihad. They call Palestinian attempts to end the occupation of their country terrorist, as they call Hizbullah's actions to liberate their country terrorist. We cannot silently accept this political lexicon which attempts to transform our liberation movements into terrorist movements. . . . They consider every [social] movement opposed to Western and Zionist policy to be terrorist; whereas if that same movement were operating in a location that suited the interests of international arrogance, they would have considered it an example of "freedom fighting," as was the case with the mujahidin in Afghanistan. . . .

*Soueid:* Whatever this Western lexicon, can one justify hijacking or blowing up a civilian aircraft, or holding a man hostage simply because he is American or European?

*Fadlallah:* What we said was not meant as a justification. We believe in being true to our principles regardless of the negative or positive repercussions on our movement. We are against doing injustice to an unbeliever (kafir) even if the perpetrator of the injustice is a Muslim. Justice is indivisible. Justice for an individual or society or in politics cannot offer scope for discriminating between a Muslim and an unbeliever. That is not what I was trying to say. What I meant was that we need to study individual cases to see if there are extenuating circumstances, and indeed there might not be any.

As to hijacking—be it of an aircraft, ship, or motor vehicle—we have made our position clear at the beginning of all such operations, issuing a fatwa that such actions are forbidden (*muharram*) in all cases involving civilians. We have condemned all hijackings and oppose such tactics categorically. We oppose the killing of foreigners in Algeria and Egypt. It is not permissible to kill an individual who comes trustingly to you just because he belongs to a country you want to fight. Some acts cannot be justified on any grounds.

In other cases, however, there may be extenuating circumstances. Thus, although we are humanitarians, there may be times when the defense of one's humanity or cause may force one to take an innocent person hostage, when the issue may go beyond the individual concerned—if a madman gets you by the neck, you may feel that the only way to save your life is to kill him or cut off his hand. Therefore, some issues have to be viewed in a wider context. Otherwise, how can one justify wars, where there are many innocent casualties? If harming an innocent is categorically wrong, then warfare is categorically wrong.

Islamic values do not exist in abstraction, suspended in midair, as it were; they are human values that apply to real situations in the real world. A negative value may be transformed into a positive value if it serves the public good. Lying is wrong. However, if speaking the truth means betraying one's umma, then telling the truth would be wrong and lying would be right. Speaking ill of someone behind his back is wrong, but when doing so means warning others of his vices so as to help them avoid problems that could arise from contact with him, it could be a duty. When the welfare of mankind is served by a negative value, it is transformed into a positive value. Man was not created to serve religion; on the contrary, religion was created to serve man.

*Soueid:* What can you say about the relationship between Islam and Judaism and Christianity?

*Fadlallah:* Islam, in the most comprehensive sense, means surrender to the Majestic and Sublime God by being in total harmony with His message. In this light, all the monotheistic religions belong under the heading of Islam. The Islam preached by the Prophet Muhammad recognizes the Torah as the Book of God and the New Testament as the Book of God. The Prophet Muhammad did not come to negate or deny these messages, but to endorse and complete them. Abraham, Moses, Jesus were all messengers of God, and it is in their messages that we ultimately believe. A Muslim may not malign the Torah, he may not malign Moses or Aaron, or the New Testament, or Jesus or the Virgin Mary—all these have a sanctity for Muslims. The Qur'an speaks of them with the utmost respect and veneration. This is how Islam came to speak of Christians and Jews as "People of the Book."

Islam's debate with Christianity and Judaism is a debate over what it considers to be deviations from the true message of Moses and of Jesus. Still, Islam calls on Jews and Christians to come together, on the issues of faith, worship, and obedience and the unity of God—and the unity of mankind. One man should not be a lord over another. Thus the Qur'an stresses that the relationship between Muslims and the People of the Book should be based on a dialogue of ideas. . . .

*Soueid:* Does a dialogue between Muslims, Christians, and Jews have a chance for success in view of the intensity of the struggle being waged with Israel and the West?

*Fadlallah:* Naturally, Western arrogance—or American, European, or Zionist arrogance—leaves little room for a tripartite dialogue aimed at reinfusing the hearts of the faithful with a religious message carrying them back to the firm base of a common humanity. A common humanity would require that all men look upon each other in freedom and justice as creatures of God and accept that no human being has the right to expel another from his homeland or gain control over his life through injustice and aggression inspired by covetousness. The true values of Judaism are to be found in its original wellsprings, not in its modern innovations; so too does true Christianity reside in its pure wellsprings, as does Islam in its deep roots. These religions, in their humanitarian depth and in the original purity of their ideas and laws, stand opposed to international arrogance and its practices.

We believe that the Judeo-Christian dialogue was launched by certain circles to create an opening for Islamic-Christian acceptance of the Jewish reality of Israel; in fact, what was needed was to remove the barrier between Judaism (in its Zionist-Israeli manifestation) on the one hand and Muslims and Christians on the other. The call for dialogue was not innocent of this political objective. That is why we had reservations concerning a Judeo-Christian-Islamic dialogue, whereas we were totally open to an Islamic-Christian dialogue because we felt there was a possibility for that dialogue to proceed with pure intentions, unmarred by ulterior motives.

*Soueid:* What should be the state of relations between the Islamic countries and the West?

*Fadlallah:* We have no phobia of westerners: We have nothing akin to the famous saying "West is West and East is East and never the twain shall meet. . . ." The problem arises when the West becomes an arrogant superpower persecuting the weak. The peoples of the third world, foremost among them Islamic peoples, have come to see the West as a power seeking to defeat them and seize their natural resources, deny them self-determination, and undermine their attempts at self-sufficiency and political, security, and economic independence. . . .

But even when we oppose the West, it is the political and economic West with its monopolistic corporations that we oppose. We do not oppose the humanitarian West. We would like to be friends with the humanitarian West. . . . We see the West as a vast area for a drive to convert Western peoples to Islam. . . . The problem between us and the West is not that we are different peoples, but that relations between us are those of oppressor to oppressed. What we want is balanced relations based on mutual interests and mutual respect, respect for human rights, and cooperation in knowledge, the sciences, expertise.

*Soueid:* It is said that you are the leading advocate of the "Lebanonization" of Islam in Lebanon. What does this mean?

*Fadlallah:* First of all, what it does *not* mean is that there should be a Lebanese variety of Islam—or Syrian, Iraqi, Arab, or Persian varieties, for that matter. Islam is the word of God for all mankind.

When I spoke of the Lebanonization of the Islamist movement in Lebanon, what I meant was that the Islamist movement should examine the prevailing circumstances in Lebanon and formulate its strategy within that framework, making allowances for Lebanon's particular circumstances, its confessional sensitivities, its perception of its environment. In other words, in spreading the faith, the Muslims in Lebanon should not follow procedures that would be inappropriate to Lebanon.

*Soueid:* Can you be more specific about Lebanon's special circumstances?

*Fadlallah:* Examining the state of affairs in Lebanon, one finds that the Christian situation is more complicated than it is in other Arab or Islamic countries. Christians in Lebanon have a "complex," or fear of the Islamic reality that leads them to seek control over the presidency of the republic and other key positions and things of that sort. So the Maronite question in Lebanon assumes a large dimension at the political, security, and cultural levels. The Islamists in Lebanon must be sensitive to the problem, taking care not to let it become a bone of contention that could lead to warfare among Lebanese, which would bring Islamic activities to naught, and Christian ones as well.

Another aspect peculiar to Lebanon is its place in the region. As Muhammad Hassanain Haikal[3] remarked, "Lebanon is not a country, it is a role." I myself have likened Lebanon to the lung through which the problems of the area breathe. Thus, Lebanon was not created to be a

---

[3] Muhammad Hassanain Haikal is a prominent Egyptian journalist and the author of many books on Egypt and Middle Eastern politics.

national home for its citizens but as a laboratory for international
political experiments in the region. Lebanon is a listening post for
monitoring all the political trends that exist in the Arab world at least,
perhaps even in the Islamic world. It is this function, rather than
aspirations for democracy, that explains the political freedom enjoyed
by all parties and flags represented in Lebanon. The freedom facilitates
the observation as well as the interference, with the experiment sometimes requiring the heating up of a conflict between groups or trends to
see how such matters can be managed or played out.

Therefore, the way I see it, Lebanon's confessional system has made
of the country a union of confessional governorates instead of a national homeland and symbol of unity of all Lebanese citizens. This is
why the events of the past two decades, which would have brought
down the regime of any other Arab country, did not bring down the
regime here. It is because of Lebanon's role in the international equation
that Lebanon is stronger than any regime in the area in the sense that
no comprehensive change in favor of any side—Marxist, nationalist,
Christian, or Islamic—will be allowed to occur in the country.

Naturally, the Islamists should take these factors into account and
capitalize on this state of affairs in planning their activities in Lebanon;
Lebanon cannot be transformed into an Islamic republic, which is
unrealistic, but the Islamists should give free reign to their ideas in
Lebanon, taking advantage of the fact that Lebanon is not only a
window on the West but also a window for the West on the East. Thus
Lebanon presents the opportunity of interaction with all other arenas
and for conveying our views to the other arenas. Lebanon could thus be
a pulpit from which to spread the word of God, just as it has always
been a theater for political action.

*Soueid:* How do you envisage Hizbullah's future in the Lebanese arena?
And in particular, what about the possibility of participation in the
Lebanese parliament?

*Fadlallah:* In my view, Hizbullah should enter the electoral arena if only
for the sake of Islamic legitimacy in Lebanon, which dictates the formation of a parliamentary party. This is not to say that the Islamists
have embraced the parliamentary system, but parliament does provide
a forum where they can express their views and urge others, if not to
adopt those views, at least to be more accommodating toward them.
Participation in this system may enable Hizbullah to realize some
transitional goals.

I believe that Hizbullah has reached a stage of reasonable political
maturity. It has amassed expertise in military, security, cultural, and
political affairs, which greatly enhances its chances of spreading its
influence in Lebanon, despite the challenge from the international
American-Israeli campaign against it. It would be very difficult to

terminate the role of Hizbullah, because that role has strong grass-roots support and is furthermore well grounded in its structure, methodology, thought, and political activities.

*Soueid:* What about the social services you provide?

*Fadlallah:* We have a number of them. Our orphanages in the Biqa', Hirmel, the South, and Beirut provide refuge for about two thousand orphans. We have a school for the blind and another for the deaf, and a number of model schools in deprived areas in the South, the Hirmel, Riyaq, in the central Biqa' Valley, in Beirut and its suburbs, and elsewhere. We have established several cultural centers and are now in the process of building a large hospital in the suburbs as well as an Islamic cultural center. Our social services office, with an annual budget of eight to ten billion Lebanese pounds, has an outreach program offering financial and material aid and other services to needy families throughout Lebanon. We are also in the process of establishing educational institutions which will offer advanced studies in jurisprudence, shari'a, and related fields.

*Soueid:* Can you elaborate a little concerning the sources of funding for these projects and institutions?

*Fadlallah:* I want first to emphasize that neither Iran nor any other country is a sponsor of any of my projects, which are funded by contributions from philanthropists as well financial obligations prescribed in religious law. One of the realities of Shi'ite life is that people are deeply attached to the active 'ulama who enjoy great authority among the community of the faithful. One of the Shi'ite articles of faith requires that Muslims pay the 'ulama khums (a fifth of their annual profits) after doing their accounts at the end of the year. These sums, along with the donations pledged to God in personal vows and the legally prescribed zakat (alms tax), amount to a revolving fund that frees the 'ulama from dependence on the authorities. It provides continuous funding for these projects. I myself am initiating projects costing millions of dollars and did not need any help from any Arab state, or Iran in particular. The state of Iran has not participated in any of my projects. There are philanthropists in Kuwait and other places, Kuwaitis who believe and trust in me and in what I am doing, who pour vast sums of money into getting these projects off the ground. Each year we issue a statement concerning these projects and the names of the donors. In addition, there is a constant inflow of canonical religious dues from all over the Islamic world to fund these and other projects.

# SEPTEMBER 11TH, TERRORISM, ISLAM, AND THE INTIFADA

INTERVIEW WITH SHAYKH MUHAMMAD HUSAYN FADLALLAH (2001)

*Majallat al-dirasat al-Filastiniyya (MDF):* The United States claims that it launched its "war against terrorism" to eradicate the al-Qa'ida organization and the Taliban government that protects it, whereas the Taliban and Usama bin Laden say that this is a crusade—a religious war, not a political or a security war. What is your opinion about these characterizations, and how do you see the war?

*Fadlallah:* There are two circles for this war. The first is the war on Afghanistan, and the second is what the United States calls the "war on terrorism." As for the war on Afghanistan, my feeling is that it was launched as part of a psychological war to release the pent-up pressure among the American people in response to the events that occurred. These events took Americans by surprise, because until then they had lived in a situation of relaxed security and were the only people on earth who had not been challenged by security issues. In fact, until then it was America that threatened the security of others around the world, and not the reverse, and this on account of its formidable hegemonic power in all domains—politics, economics, and security.

These events also caused the American people to lose faith in the U.S. administration and especially in the intelligence community, particularly the Central Intelligence Agency, which had failed to predict these events although this was their responsibility. Added to all this was the blow to American prestige in the eyes of the world as a result of the disarray of the U.S. government in the hours following the events; whereas America up to then had been seen as the sole superpower on a global scale, suddenly it was just a state like any other that can be targeted by any group with some planning capability, some experience, and some courage and strength.

This is why a scapegoat had to be found. The name of Bin Laden and his al-Qa'ida organization were already on the American media's list as suspects in the blowing up of the U.S. embassies in Kenya and Tanzania, among other acts. As a result, Bin Laden and al-Qa'ida became the scapegoats, and the Taliban were on the list as the regime that harbored them. The Americans knew from their own information that the Taliban would not hand over Bin Laden because of their understanding of the Islamic precept that no Muslim can be handed over to the infidels, as the expression goes, and because of Bin Laden's role in strengthening the Taliban and protecting them from their internal enemies. This is how the Americans knew all along that the Taliban would get mired in the situation, just as they had known during the occupation of Kuwait and their war against Iraq that Saddam would get mired. This is why it sought to give the impression that it had tried to pursue peaceful means in its negotiations with the Taliban, who refused to hand over Bin Laden and his al-Qa'ida. The Taliban said that they were not convinced that Bin Laden was involved and that if America presented evidence to prove its case, they would be willing to hand him over to stand trial in a neutral Islamic court, but of course this would not satisfy American prestige.

As for talk of this war being a religious war, as Bin Laden has claimed, in reality, it is not a religious war, but rather a war of the arrogant against the downtrodden, a war of international interests against those who may threaten these interests. It is indeed a war against Muslims, but it is not necessarily a religious war like the Crusades against Islam. I do not believe that this is the case. I say this despite the fact that after the fall of the Soviet Union, NATO, under American leadership, was looking for an enemy, which it found in Islam. It is true that a war against Muslims, a war that concentrates principally on Muslims as the main terrorists, while adding a few non-Muslim targets (so that the United States can avoid blame without actually using force against these non-Muslim targets), might just as well be a war against Islam in terms of the nature of the outcome. We must therefore take care of ourselves by planning to confront this war. Planning will give us much psychological strength so that we are not defeated psychologically, by psychological warfare, before we are defeated militarily and economically.

*MDF:* You seem to be saying that it is not certain that Bin Laden was behind the bombings, though it is true that Bin Laden blessed the operations. Now, in Arab and Muslim public opinion, in most Arab and Muslim countries, many believe that deliberately hitting civilians and the innocent is a terrorist action that should be unequivocally condemned. On the other hand, there is the religious political discourse of Bin Laden and [his top deputy Ayman] al-Zawahiri and others affirming that this is a religious war against America. There are also those who appear to be issuing fatwas stating, for example, that all American society is responsible for U.S. policy toward the Muslim world. We would like to know what Islam would say about this matter.

*Fadlallah:* First, we are not affirming that Bin Laden is involved because we have no legal evidence, which in any case would need to be evaluated with a cool mind. As for his blessing the attacks, this does not constitute legal proof, as people may bless something that others do because they believe in it, without being responsible for it.

As for considering these acts as possible means to be used against U.S. policy—or any other policy, for that matter—we do not support this from an Islamic point of view. The reason we do not support it is *not* because we do not believe in applying pressure on America, but because it is not right to pressure the American administration by targeting the American people, or others who reside there or who are visitors there, like those people who were passengers on the planes that were blown up or who were working at the World Trade Center or visiting it. The Qur'anic precept states "no bearer of burdens should bear the burden of another." This applies to all those victims who were not connected to the American administration or to any of its policies, not because they were not Americans, but because they were Americans who were not aware of the issues of U.S. foreign policy. For, as is often said, the American people are generally uninterested in their country's foreign policy, concentrating instead on domestic policy.

This is why it is not permissible, on the basis of the shari'a, or jurisprudentially, to commit such acts. This we declared immediately after the events in order to clarify that authentic Islamic values reject this and consider it terrorism, not martyrdom. Regardless of whatever good motives those who committed these acts may have had for doing what they did, these are wrong methods, in disharmony with Islamic thought. This is why it is wrong for anyone to consider this jihad, as jihad is not practiced in this manner.

*MDF:* What about martyrdom operations in Palestine?

*Fadlallah:* There is a difference between martyrdom operations in which civilians are killed, in the Palestinian case, and the case [of the September 11th attacks]. In the Palestinian case, there is a hot war going on in which Israel uses all it can muster of U.S. weapons in its possession— weapons that were designed for use in all-out wars—against Palestinians who have only stones and some light weapons, including mortars, to fight back against F-16 fighter jets, Apache helicopters, missiles, tanks and machine guns, to say nothing of the Israeli blockades, economic closures, and other crimes. This is what forces the Palestinians, given the imbalance between themselves and their enemies in terms of offensive and defensive capabilities, to confront Israeli society with the aim of defeating Israel's security. In other words, the aim is not to kill civilians but rather to kill the Israeli project of "Israeli security," the end-all and be-all of Ariel Sharon's government. The Israelis consider as a matter of course their murder of Palestinian civilians as the regrettable outcome of war. But the regrettable outcome of war also justifies the martyrdom operations of Palestine's mujahidin, even those which occur in civilian areas.

In America, on the other hand, there is no hot war [that can justify] those people's responding the way they did. Some people believe that any means, even those that are not justifiable on principle, can be used to achieve a larger goal whose final outcome would justify small illegitimate actions. We counter this by emphasizing that this act committed by these men was to the benefit of America and did not benefit either Islam or Muslims—assuming that those who committed these acts were Muslims. These acts have negatively affected Muslims worldwide and have given the United States the opportunity, in the name of its war against terrorism, to crush every movement that rejects U.S. policy in the region on all levels, enabling it to brand as "terrorist" all those who oppose the United States and its interests. Indeed, what happened has opened wide the gates of the world to America, making the whole world subject to it (at least this has been the case immediately following these events, regardless of what happens in the future).

This is why I say to those who think that such acts can be justified for the sake of a larger goal, that no larger goal can be achieved using such methods, which can actually bring about the opposite outcome. Which indeed, seems to be what is happening in this case. . . .

*MDF:* Your Excellency, the image of Islam today, at least in the West, is that it creates an environment that fosters terrorism and is a religion incompatible with modernity. The Islam that is offered up in the West as representative is Algerian Islam or the Islam of Egypt's Gama'a al-Islamiyya. Yet you clearly do not see Islam as being unable to integrate itself into the modern world. What, then, is the problem of Islam?

*Fadlallah:* I do not believe that the problem is Islam, but rather the Western media, or to be more precise, Western arrogance in relation to Islam. When we look at the size of the Muslim world, with its 1.1 billion people, and we look at the number of people who commit what the U.S. calls terrorism, we see that the latter are at most 100,000 people. We also have a study, the precision of which I cannot guarantee but which I believe to be precise enough, showing that some 90 percent of the killings in Algeria have been committed by the Algerian army.[4] This is not to say that there are not ignorant and backward Islamists

---

[4]Fadlallah refers here to the massive bloodshed during the civil war in Algeria (1992–97), which was triggered by the government's decision to cancel ongoing general elections in which the Islamists were headed for a major victory. Nearly 100,000 people are estimated to have been killed in the course of the fighting between Islamist militants and government forces.

who know nothing of Islam, such as some of these adolescent military commanders who may have committed some of these acts. It is certain, however, that they did not commit these massacres, at least not on a large scale. Algerian intelligence has infiltrated these organizations and exploited the ignorance of their members.

Why is there terrorism in Egypt? Because Egypt did not allow the Islamists, who constitute a broad social current, any freedom of political action. This was especially the case with the Muslim Brothers, who represent a moderate force. Had the government granted them the right to political action, as it did the Nasserists and the National Party, it would have been possible for them to counter [the radical movements].

This is why we say that the terrorism that has occurred—and we disapprove of much of what is called terrorism—resulted from the political pressures that usurped the rights of the Arab and Muslim peoples, ruling them through emergency laws and the secret police. What exists, then, is not a situation of [Islamic] terrorism, for there is no such thing as an Islamic terrorist spirit. What exists is a situation where you corner people and close off all exits, and these people then have to react in an abnormal way.

Why do we not speak of terrorism in the West itself? It need not only be political terrorism. Clearly, the rate of violent crime in America is higher than anywhere else in the world. We have never had in the Arab world children who carry guns and kill their schoolmates and their teachers, for example. What about the Oklahoma City bombing? What about the bombings in Ireland? What about all the "mafias" of the West? Why do they not focus on them? When Islam was proposed by NATO as the new enemy to replace the Soviet Union [after its collapse], the plan involved amassing all the negative and violent aspects of the Muslim world, which occur on a comparatively small scale, so as to use them against Islam.

Islam calls for kindness and for peaceful and civilized means that transform enemies into friends. We read Almighty God's words which say: "Nor can goodness and evil be equal. Repel (evil) with what is better: Then will he, between whom and thee was hatred, become as it were thy friend and intimate." And we read the words of the Prophet, peace be upon him, who asserts: "Kindness graces what it touches, and disgraces what it touches not. For God is kind and loves kindness and gives to kindness what He gives not to violence." As for the question of jihad, it is a defensive notion and a preventative one: "Fight in the cause of God those who fight you. But do not transgress limits; for God loveth not transgressors"; "And why should ye not fight in the cause of God and of those who, being weak, are ill treated (and oppressed)?"; and, "If thou fearest treachery from any group, throw back (their covenant) to them, (so as to be) on equal terms: for God loveth not the treacherous." Jihad, then, is a defensive notion and a preventative one, just as struggle and war are in all of the world's civilizations. They have tried to use jihad as a justification to use aggression against people and as a justification for brandishing their sword against the entire world. But this is not true. Muslims are oppressed, and the violence that may be committed by some Muslims against their coreligionists or against others is a *reaction* to the absence of freedoms, and not an independent *action*. As for those who are pathologically criminal, well, they exist all over the world and are not a Muslim peculiarity.

# Chapter 17

# THE TALIBAN
## 1994–

In 1996 the movement of the Taliban captured Kabul, the capital of Afghanistan, in an effort to bring peace to a land that had seen extremely brutal and continuous warfare since 1979. Soviet forces had arrived in Afghanistan in 1979, ostensibly at the invitation of the country's newly established Communist regime, but they had been almost immediately challenged by a coalition of Afghan guerrilla groups—the mujahidin—fighting in the name of Islam and of their country's freedom. The Soviet Union eventually withdrew from Afghanistan in 1989. But it was the mujahidin groups that now battled against one another, reducing much of Kabul to rubble and bringing great misery to the inhabitants of the country. It was in this context that the Taliban emerged on the scene.[1] They brought greater peace and security to the large parts of Afghanistan under their control than it had known for the past two decades. Yet, at the same time, they brought to it a version of Islamic law that was harsher than much of the modern Muslim world, let alone Afghanistan, had seen before. In what would become perhaps the greatest source of their international notoriety, the Taliban also played hosts to Usama bin Laden, who was in Afghanistan at the time of the terrorist attacks of September 11, 2001.

At the height of the Afghan struggle against Soviet occupation, there were more than three million Afghans living in the refugee camps of Pakistan . Large numbers of these refugees continued to live in these camps, located near the Afghan-Pakistan border in the Northwest Frontier and Baluchistan provinces of Pakistan, well after the Soviet withdrawal from Afghanistan. Afghans had long studied in Deobandi madrasas of India and Pakistan (cf. Metcalf 1982, 111, 135; Malik 1996, 202–8), and numerous new madrasas were established during the Afghan war, with the support of the Pakistani government, to absorb and educate Afghan refugees. The Taliban (which means "students"—a Persian plural via the Arabic singular *talib*) were the products of these madrasas and of the Afghan refugee camps in Pakistan. During the anti-Soviet struggle, in which Paki-

---

[1] While the term *mujahidin* is often used for those participating in the anti-Soviet Afghan struggle, the Taliban—who took control of much of Afghanistan from the mujahidin in 1996—have often also referred to themselves as mujahidin. They have done so in the generic sense of "those undertaking jihad" (singular: *mujahid*), rather than to claim any affinity with the Afghan groups of the anti-Soviet resistance.

stan, Saudi Arabia, and the United States had played a major role in providing weapons and other resources to the mujahidin, young Afghans studying or staying in Pakistani madrasas would routinely go to Afghanistan to participate in the fighting and then return to these madrasas. They were often joined by many others, including volunteers from Pakistan. As the struggle against the Soviet military presence in Afghanistan wound down in the late 1980s, many observers expected that the mujahidin would cobble together a government of their own and that the refugees living in Pakistan and, in lesser numbers in Iran, would be able to return to their country. The mid-1990s witnessed developments of a quite different sort, however.

Rather than being able to form a new, unified government in Afghanistan, different factions of the mujahidin came to carve out the country into their areas of influence. The war against the Soviet occupation now turned into a deadly civil war. The warring factions often treated each other with great brutality. The warlords also had a reputation for the mistreatment of the local people living in their areas of influence. They "seized homes and farms, threw out their occupants and handed them over to their supporters. The commanders abused the population at will, kidnapping young girls and boys for their sexual pleasure, robbing merchants in the bazaars and fighting and brawling in the streets" (Rashid 2000, 21). International aid agencies and nongovernmental organizations (NGOs) were likewise harassed. The rumored excesses of the Soviet troops against the Afghan populace, especially those suspected of aiding the mujahidin, had contributed their share to strengthening the resolve of the anti-Soviet guerrillas. Similar excesses on the part of the erstwhile mujahidin now began to turn popular sentiment against them.

The civil war in Afghanistan also meant, of course, that plans for the return of the refugees needed to be put on hold. Instead, streams of new refugees had begun heading toward the Pakistani border. For its part, the Pakistani military and government were keen to see a relatively stable and unified Afghanistan not only because it would enable Afghan refugees to return home but also because the potentially lucrative overland trade routes linking Pakistan with the Central Asian states, emerging in the wake of the disintegration of the Soviet Union, were imperiled by the infighting and the extortions of the Afghan warlords. The American oil conglomerate Unocal was also keen to link Turkmenistan, rich in oil and natural gas, via Afghanistan and Pakistan, with the Arabian Sea, but this, too, required greater stability than the existence of the warlords allowed. All this suggests considerable concordance between the interests of the Pakistani ruling elite—and especially the military intelligence, the Interservices Intelligence (ISI)—and those emerging in the mid-1990s from the refugee camps of Pakistan (cf. Rashid 2000). The precise nature and degree of Pakistani involvement in the rise of the Taliban remain rather unclear, however.

Once in power, and irrespective of their provenance, the Taliban quickly proceeded to put their Islamic commitments on full display. Taliban judges began meting out Islamic punishments such as the amputation of a hand for theft and stoning to death for adultery. The playing of music was forbidden, and the sale or ownership of television sets and audio cassettes was made illegal. Men were required to wear beards of a certain length and women were forbidden to go outside their homes unless accompanied by a close male relative. Women were also required to be draped in the burqa, a head to toe covering that, unlike the chador, concealed the face as well. Schools for girls were also closed down. Public morality was regulated by a ministry entrusted with "commanding right and forbidding wrong," and offenders were severely, and often publicly, punished (Dorronsoro 2005, 283–85, 291–301).

In the Taliban's view, all this was what true Islam demanded of them—the Islam as practiced by earlier, and better, Muslims. Mulla Muhammad 'Umar, the leader of the Taliban, had assumed the title of *amir al-mu' minin* (commander of the faithful), which is how the early caliphs had styled themselves; and in 1997 the Taliban had given a new name to the country: the Islamic Emirate of Afghanistan (Dorronsoro 2005, 281). Reflecting their origins in madrasas of Pakistan, Afghan 'ulama were closely involved in all facets of the Taliban administration; and some Deobandi 'ulama of Pakistan also maintained close ties with the Taliban leadership. Many of the laws implemented by the Taliban in Afghanistan are, indeed, sanctioned by the shari'a; and the Qur'an itself instructs Muslims to "command right and forbid wrong." Yet, the precise implications of this imperative have been the subject of vigorous debate among Muslim jurists and theologians throughout Islamic history (Cook 2000), as has the question of how, and in what circumstances, the punishments mandated by Islamic law are to be implemented (see the chapter 8 on Turabi). There is no evidence that the Taliban's understanding of these matters was informed by the historically articulated Islamic discursive tradition; indeed, even some Deobandi 'ulama of Pakistan had expressed public misgivings about some of the Taliban's excesses while they were still in power (cf. Zaman 2002, 139–40).

Although they did not see it this way, what the Taliban had implemented in their Islamic Emirate was a peculiar combination of Islamic legal norms, as they understood them, and some of the tribal norms to which they were most accustomed. Afghanistan is inhabited by people from a wide array of ethnic groups. The Taliban belonged to the Pashtun ethnicity, whose members are found on both sides of the Afghan-Pakistan border. The Pashtuns, and especially those with roots in the countryside, have had some of the most conservative social mores in all of Afghanistan. As rural Pashtuns, the Taliban proceeded to impose these mores *throughout* the territories they controlled. Though many of their decrees, including some of those regarding women, would not have shocked everyone living in Pashtun tribal areas, in either Afghanistan or Pakistan, they were profoundly unsettling for urban Afghans, just as they were for the international community (Dorronsoro 2005, especially 291–301).[2]

Yet, if the Taliban's understanding of Islam was shaped by their tribal customs, they sought also to *repudiate* certain tribal norms for contravening the shariʿa, as they understood it. For example, the custom of making a widow marry her brother-in-law was outlawed, as was the practice of giving away women from the family of the murderer to that of his victim as a way of forestalling tribal vendettas (Dorronsoro 2005, 300; for similar practices in parts of Pakistan, cf. Zaman 2004, 143–44). In such instances, the Taliban offer yet another illustration of Islamist critiques of local customary norms and the desire to abandon and outlaw them in returning to the imagined purity of an "authentic Islam"—an Islam that often continued, paradoxically but inescapably, to be informed by local contexts (cf. Lybarger 2007; and chapter 1 in this volume).

The Taliban were also shaped by their interaction with Islamists from elsewhere in the Muslim world, many of whom had participated in the Afghan jihad and had themselves been radicalized in its course. Not a few among them would later direct their energies against the "godless" regimes of their home countries as well as against the United States—the sole surviving superpower after the disintegration of the Soviet Union. These battle-hardened Islamist militants seem not to have had much to do with the rise of the Taliban (Rashid 2000, 139), though they were clearly among the beneficiaries of the new regime. Among these was Usama bin Laden, who had once participated in the Afghan jihad, and who returned to Afghanistan after being expelled from Sudan in 1996 (see chapter 18 on Bin Laden). Some in the Taliban leadership are reported to have been suspicious of the Arab Islamists, fearing that the latter had their own interests to pursue at the expense of their Afghan hosts,[3] though Mulla ʿUmar came to have cordial relations with Bin Laden and even gave his daughter in marriage to the latter (Dorronsoro 2005, 305, 312). He also continued to resist increasing U.S. pressure to turn over Bin Laden to the United States or to expel him from the country. This ended any prospect of U.S. recognition of the Taliban, increasing their international isolation and, in turn, contributing to actions apparently calculated to provoke an international outcry.[4] Soon after the terrorist attacks of September 11, 2001, Mulla ʿUmar's refusal to extradite Bin Laden to

[2]For a different interpretation of the Taliban's relationship with rural Islam, cf. Edwards 2002, 295–302.

[3]Many Arab Islamists, and especially the Salafis among them, were often highly critical, even contemptuous, of the Taliban, seeing them not only as backward but also as insufficiently committed to "true" Islamic norms. The question of how to view their Taliban hosts was, in fact, a matter of considerable tension within the ranks of the Arab Islamists. Cf. Lia 2008, 229–316.

[4]Perhaps the most striking illustration of this was the destruction, in March 2001, of the Buddhas of Bamyan, a highly treasured ancient monument. See Flood 2002; Dorronsoro 2005, 309–10.

the United States led to the invasion of Afghanistan and the destruction of the Taliban regime.

The movement of the Taliban did not come to an end even after the collapse of their regime, however. While a new government, headed by President Hamid Karzai and backed by the U.S. military and NATO, was established in Kabul, those of the Taliban leaders who had survived the U.S.-led invasion were able to go into hiding. Within a year or so of 9/11, Mulla Muhammad 'Umar had already begun efforts to regroup the Taliban and to recruit new members on both sides of the Afghan-Pakistan border. Since these early initiatives, the Taliban have come to challenge the authority of the government in many provinces of southern Afghanistan (on this, see Giustozzi 2008). They have engaged in numerous suicide bombings and other violence throughout the country, fought Afghan, U.S., and NATO troops, and attacked government buildings and schools. Like those they have targeted, the Taliban, too, have paid a heavy price in terms of casualties within their own ranks. Yet this has not affected their resilience, and their numbers have grown over the years. "In 2004 U.S. estimates were of some 1,000 'hard-core' insurgents inside Afghanistan, a figure which grew to 2–3,000 by 2004 and to 3–4,000 by 2006" (Giustozzi 2008, 33). The Taliban themselves estimated these numbers in late 2006 to be around 15,000 men (see the text of the interview with a Taliban commander, Mulla Sabir, in this chapter).[5] Several factors help account for this resilience.

First, while the U.S.-led forces were able to dislodge the Taliban from power with remarkable swiftness in the aftermath of 9/11, the war in Iraq that began in the spring of 2003 forced a diversion of both the focus and some of the military resources from Afghanistan to Iraq. This provided the remnants of the Taliban with new opportunities to regroup. Second, the Karzai government's lack of effective military and police forces has continued to hamper its ability to effectively meet the Taliban challenge. At the same time, the rampant corruption and inefficiency of this government, its all too visible dependence on a foreign power, and the presence of Western, non-Muslim troops in the country have all contributed to considerable hostility toward the government in some parts of the country. The Taliban have been able to use some of this popular disaffection to recruit new fighters. And, as their "Book of Rules" makes clear,[6] they have been as concerned to maintain some degree of discipline within their own ranks and facilitate the incorporation of new recruits (cf. rules 1–5), as they are with not alienating the local communities among which they operate and whose goodwill they depend on (cf. rules 15–17, 21, 22, 28; also cf. the Afghan proverb, quoted by Mulla Sabir: "You cannot be part of a village if the village doesn't want you").

[5] Antonio Giustozzi, the author of the most detailed study so far of the post-9/11 Taliban, estimates their numbers to have "reached around 17,000 men by 2006, with 6–10,000 active at any given time" (Giustozzi 2008, 34).

[6] "A New Layeha for the Mujahidin," reprinted here. *Layeha* (Arabic: *la'iha*) means a rule or program. *Mujahidin* here refers to the Taliban.

Pakistan, one of only three countries to have once recognized the Taliban (the other two being Saudi Arabia and the United Arab Emirates), has often been accused by President Karzai's government of making only lukewarm efforts to help combat the Taliban or to curtail their movements across the Afghan-Pakistan border. Yet, in the aftermath of the September 11 terrorist attacks, the Taliban have brought much instability to Pakistan as well. For example, the Taliban's implementation of the shari'a in Afghanistan also led to demands for similar measures in Pakistan. Pakistan's reluctant alliance with the United States in helping dislodge the Taliban and in the War on Terror further antagonized many Islamists as well as Pashtun tribesmen in the Northwest Frontier bordering Afghanistan. In certain parts of the province, these Pakistani tribesmen have sometimes also come to style themselves as "Taliban," openly challenging the authority of the central government, implementing the shari'a in the Taliban mode, and closing down schools for girls (Perlez 2007). In response to Pakistani military operations against them—which, as in Afghanistan, have had only limited success—they have also carried out suicide bombings throughout the country, just as the Taliban have in Afghanistan. The Pakistani Taliban were also among the early suspects for the assassination, in December 2007, of former Pakistani prime minister Benazir Bhutto.[7]

Both before and after 9/11, the Taliban reveal a very different facet of Islamism than those represented by many others in this volume. While Islamism is a largely urban phenomenon, the Taliban came from a predominantly rural and tribal background. While many Islamists are well educated, either in westernized colleges and universities or—in case of people like Khomeini, Baqir al-Sadr, Fadlallah, and Qaradawi—in institutions of Islamic learning, the sophomoric nature of the Taliban's often incomplete madrasa education is best captured in their own self-designation as "students." And while Qutb, too, would have seen the government school system, like everything else, as infected by a pervasive jahiliyya, other Islamists have seldom targeted schools and their teachers as have the Taliban. Even so, the Taliban have important affinities with other Islamists, as has been seen in the foregoing. The public implementation of Islamic norms is the most obvious of these, of course, but so, too, is the Taliban's critique of particular local norms in favor of an authentic Islamic piety as well as their pointed rejection of any Western effort to influence their policies (Flood 2002, 653). And, for all their crudeness in the affirmation of patriarchal norms, such affirmations remain at the heart of Islamism in general and, indeed, of fundamentalism across religious traditions (cf. Riesebrodt 1990).

[7]Ironically, it was under the premiership of Benazir Bhutto that the movement of the Taliban had first emerged, though this may have had less to do with her government's policies than with those pursued by the country's quasi-independent military intelligence, the ISI.

# A NEW LAYEHA FOR THE MUJAHIDIN

FROM THE highest leader of the Islamic Emirates of Afghanistan.

Every mujahid must abide by the following rules:

1. A Taliban commander is permitted to extend an invitation to all Afghans who support infidels so that they may convert to the true Islam.

2. We guarantee to any man who turns his back on infidels personal security and the security of his possessions. But if he becomes involved in a dispute, or if someone accuses him of something, he must submit to our judiciary.

3. Mujadidin who protect new Taliban recruits must inform their commander.

4. A convert to the Taliban who does not behave loyally and becomes a traitor forfeits our protection. He will be given no second chance.

5. A mujahid who kills a new Taliban recruit forfeits our protection and will be punished according to Islamic law.

6. If a Taliban fighter wants to move to another district, he is permitted to do so, but he must first acquire the permission of his group leader.

7. A mujahid who takes a foreign infidel as prisoner with the consent of a group leader may not exchange him for other prisoners or money.

8. A provincial, district, or regional commander may not sign a contract to work for a nongovernmental organization or accept money from an NGO. The Shura (the highest Taliban council) alone may determine all dealings with NGOs.

9. Taliban may not use jihad equipment or property for personal ends.

10. Every Talib is accountable to his superiors in matters of money spending and equipment usage.

11. Mujadidin may not sell equipment, unless the provincial commander permits him to do so.

12. A group of mujahidin may not take in mujahidin from another group to increase their own power. This is allowed only when there are good reasons for it, such as a lack of fighters in one particular group. Then written permission must be given and the weapons of the new members must stay with their old group.[8]

---

[8]It is worth noting that several rules in the Taliban's Layeha echo provisions in the so-called Constitution of Medina, a treaty (or set of agreements) between the Prophet Muhammad and those who had emigrated with him from Mecca to Medina, on the one hand, and

13. Weapons and equipment taken from infidels or their allies must be fairly distributed among the mujahidin.

14. If someone who works with infidels wants to cooperate with mujahidin, he should not be killed. If he is killed, his murderer must stand before an Islamic court.

15. A mujahid or leader who torments an innocent person must be warned by his superiors. If he does not change his behavior, he must be thrown out of the Taliban movement.

16. It is strictly forbidden to search houses or confiscate weapons without the permission of a district or provincial commander.

17. Mujahidin have no right to confiscate money or personal possessions of civilians.

18. Mujahidin should refrain from smoking cigarettes.

19. Mujahidin are not allowed to take young boys with no facial hair onto the battlefield or into their private quarters.

20. If members of the opposition or the civil government wish to be loyal to the Taliban, we may take their conditions into consideration. A final decision must be made by the military council.

21. Anyone with a bad reputation or who has killed civilians during the jihad may not be accepted into the Taliban movement. If the highest leader has personally forgiven him, he will remain at home in the future.

22. If a mujahid is found guilty of a crime and his commander has barred him from the group, no other group may take him in. If he wishes to resume contact with the Taliban, he must ask forgiveness from his former group.

23. If a mujahid is faced with a problem that is not described in this book, his commander must find a solution in consultation with the group.

24. It is forbidden to work as a teacher under the current puppet regime, because this strengthens the system of the infidels. True Muslims

---

the inhabitants (including Jewish tribes) of Medina, on the other. The text of this document is preserved in the earliest extant biography of Muhammad, the *Sirat Rasul Allah* of Ibn Ishaq (d. 767). Compare no. 12 in the Taliban Layeha with the following provision of the Constitution of Medina: "No believer shall make an alliance with an ally of another believer to the exclusion of the latter" (Lecker 2004, 33, no.13, with minor modification). Also compare no. 22 in the Taliban Layeha with the following provision of the Constitution of Medina: "It is not permissible to a believer . . . to support a murderer or give him shelter . . ." (Lecker 2004, 35, no. 25, with minor modification). And compare no. 23 in the Layeha with the following in the Constitution of Medina: "Whatever you differ about should be brought before Allah and Muhammad" (Lecker 2004, 35, no. 26). Such parallels might simply reflect the fact that both documents are concerned with stipulating rules and structures of authority in tribal contexts, albeit quite different ones. Alternatively, at least some provisions of the Layeha may well have been self-consciously patterned on the Constitution of Medina as a mark of adherence to the Prophet's normative example.

should apply to study with a religiously trained teacher and study in a mosque or similar institution. Textbooks must come from the period of the jihad or from the Taliban regime.

25. Anyone who works as a teacher for the current puppet regime must receive a warning. If he nevertheless refuses to give up his job, he must be beaten. If the teacher still continues to instruct contrary to the principles of Islam, the district commander or a group leader must kill him.

26. Those NGOs that come to the country under the rule of the infidels must be treated as the government is treated. They have come under the guise of helping people but in fact are part of the regime. Thus we tolerate none of their activities, whether it be building of streets, bridges, clinics, schools, madrasas, or other works. If a school fails to heed a warning to close, it must be burned. But all religious books must be secured beforehand.

27. As long as a person has not been convicted of espionage and punished for it, no one may take up the issue on their own. Only the district commander is in charge. Witnesses who testify in a procedure must be in good psychological condition, possess an untarnished religious reputation, and not have committed any major crime. The punishment may take place only after the conclusion of the trial.

28. No lower-level commander may interfere with contention among the populace. If an argument cannot be resolved, the district or regional commander must step in to handle the matter. The case should be discussed by 'ulama or a jirga (council of elders). If they find no solution, the case must be referred to well-known religious authorities.

29. Every mujahid must post a watch, day and night.

30. These twenty-nine rules are obligatory. Anyone who offends this code must be judged according to the laws of the Islamic Emirates.

This Book of Rules is intended for the Mujahidin who dedicate their lives to Islam and the almighty Allah. This is a complete guidebook for the progress of jihad, and every mujahid must keep these rules; it is the duty of every jihadist and true believer.

Signed by the highest leader of the Islamic Emirates of Afghanistan

# AN INTERVIEW WITH A TALIBAN
## COMMANDER (2006)

*Die Weltwoche*: Mullah Sabir, the top Taliban leadership recently held a conclave at a secret location. What was the mood like?

*Sabir*: Look at the news reports. Half of Afghanistan is again under our control. We have advanced to just outside of Kabul. President Hamid Karzai is a prisoner in his own palace. True, he constantly flies around the world and spends time with the powerful leaders of the West. But in his own country he does not even dare to travel around. You can well imagine that, at our meeting of thirty-three Taliban chiefs, the mood was anything but somber.

*DW*: Until now the Taliban leadership consisted of only ten men.

*Sabir*: That's how it was. Now we have thirty-three. The area under our rule encompasses an ever-increasing number of provinces. This year we have returned to Nimroz, Farah, Mardan, and Logar. This gain in power is reflected in the growth of our governing council.

*DW*: Forty thousand Allied troops are now in Afghanistan, fighting bitterly against the Taliban. Isn't it rather reckless to assemble the entire leadership in one spot?

*Sabir*: A meeting like that is essential to evaluating our position. Normally we meet only once a year. The recent meeting was the second one this year—another sign of our newly regained power.

*DW*: When Western leaders confer, there is generally chaos on the roads and a storm of reporters' flashbulbs. How should we imagine the atmosphere at a summit of the Warriors of God?

*Sabir*: Three members of the Shura (Council) were responsible for organizing the meeting. During two weeks of planning they chose the conference locale. Through informal channels, they then informed us of a point of assembly, from which guides led us to the actual meeting place. The spot was surrounded by mountains, and guards were posted on every summit. The conference took place in a mosque, beneath which there was a bunker where we could have taken refuge in the event of an attack from the air. The meeting lasted for one day and was interrupted only twice, for prayer and to eat.

*DW:* What subjects were discussed?

*Sabir:* The focus was on military strategy and internal behavioral questions.

*DW:* What did you decide that was new?

*Sabir:* The main message was delivered by the Taliban defense minister, Hajji Obaidullah. He presided over the meeting and also issued to us the *Layeha*, our new manual of military rules.

*DW:* How is the discipline in your ranks?

*Sabir:* We had a problem with spies. But their number has shrunk considerably. We've killed hundreds of such traitors, almost all of them Afghans, some even across the border in Pakistan.

*DW:* Who passes judgment on alleged traitors?

*Sabir:* Only district and provincial commanders are permitted to pass such judgment. The trials are subject to precise rules. For example, no one may be punished before a court with proper jurisdiction has confirmed his guilt.

*DW:* What rules are in force regarding civilians?

*Sabir:* We are required to exercise great restraint. The *Layeha* prescribes that we may not enter civilian homes or confiscate civilian property without permission from a provincial or district commander.

*DW:* That doesn't seem to have been the case so far. In recent months the Taliban have burned down dozens of schools. What is the purpose of such actions?

*Sabir:* Our motto is: no official schools. They are merely political tools of the present regime. Whoever permits such schools to operate is also supporting the government of Hamid Karzai and the infidels.

*DW:* What is your attitude toward NGOs that are building roads and digging wells to improve people's lives?

*Sabir:* The organizations that have come here under the new administration only pretend to help the people. In reality they are part of the government. Whatever they may propose to build—bridges, clinics, schools—we will not tolerate their activities.

*DW:* There have been nearly one hundred suicide bombings in Afghanistan since the beginning of this year. Have the Taliban lost their pride and their courage to fight the enemy in open combat?

*Sabir:* With their combat planes and precision bombs, the enemy is far superior to us technologically. The suicide bombings are a tactic with which we drive the enemy to panic. Without this miracle weapon we would never accomplish our goal of reconquering all of Afghanistan.

*DW:* Who wrote the new rule book?

*Sabir:* I don't know exactly. Mullah Abdul Ali, our mufti responsible for religious questions, was certainly consulted. The new *Layeha* was approved by our supreme leader, Mullah Omar.

*DW:* Did Omar participate in the recent conclave?

*Sabir:* No.

*DW:* Rumor has it that he is in poor health.

*Sabir:* There are many rumors. Mullah Omar does not participate in large meetings for security reasons. He remains in a safe place. Only two people have direct access to him: Defense Minister Obaidullah and his brother-in-law Mullah Birader.

*DW:* How strong are the Taliban today?

*Sabir:* We have about 15,000 men. Forty percent are not really Taliban, have not graduated from any religious school; they are youngsters who join our ranks in sympathy [with our cause].

*DW:* How do you explain the increase in the numbers of young fighters?

*Sabir:* People see with increasing clarity how corrupt the Karzai government is. It ignores the problems of ordinary people. Karzai is a puppet, a servant of the Americans.

*DW:* The Afghans chose him in free elections. This was also a vote against the Taliban.

*Sabir:* Let me make one thing clear to you: we would not be here without support from the populace. There is an Afghan proverb which says: "You cannot be part of a village if the village doesn't want you." People do not trust Karzai's corrupt justice. They remember the virtues of our [Taliban] regime. Back then there was absolute security [in the country]. The crime rate dropped to zero. Now, people are once again seeking the advice of our judges. In my province alone we have six shari'a courts.

*DW:* Where do you get your weapons and money?

*Sabir:* During the fasting month of Ramadan, ordinary people donated large sums. They also supply us with food and clothing. Our people take good care of us.

*DW:* Do you get help from al-Qaʿida?

*Sabir:* No. Nor do I have any al-Qaʿida fighters among my troops. The only foreigners in our ranks come from Chechnya and Uzbekistan. But if al-Qaʿida warriors want to join us, they are welcome.

*DW:* Previously, close relations with al-Qaʿida cost the Taliban their governing power. Why don't you keep your distance from such foreign forces?

*Sabir:* Their struggle is against the infidels. Their enemy is our enemy. How could we justify before Allah taking up the sword against them?

# PART V

# Globalizing Jihad

# Chapter 18

## USAMA BIN LADEN
## 1957–

USAMA BIN LADEN would seem to need very little introduction. As the primary founder and financier of al-Qaʿida (Arabic for "the base"), the fluid network of Islamists linked to attacks on military and civilian targets from Africa to Europe, Asia to North America, Bin Laden has the dubious distinction of being the most famous Islamist of the twenty-first-century. Al-Qaʿida has continually reconstituted itself since it was formally founded in the late 1980s, and its recent tendency to function more like a franchise or name brand than an integrated, hierarchical organization has made it an elusive opponent and mercurial object of study.[1] Perhaps the most consistent feature of al-Qaʿida is Bin Laden, who remains the face of its global operations and aspirations, and a catalyst for a wide range of hopes and hatreds.[2] To some, he is the warrior-priest of Muslim resistance to Western domination. To others, he is the terrorist who has twisted Islam into a vehicle for conspiracy theories and a justification for indiscriminate violence. For many, he is just the newest confirmation of the threat to modern politics posed by religious irrationalism in general, and Islamic fanaticism in particular.

Bin Laden has proved to be quite fluent in the visual rhetoric made possible by modern techniques of communication and propaganda, making his dual image of a twenty-first-century Saladin[3] and most-wanted international terrorist a co-production between the religious and historical

---

[1]Devji (2005, 19) argues that the decentralized structure of al-Qaʿida has enabled it to emulate other players in the global marketplace and to operate much as a service provider does: it "does not own or control all its operatives; instead it chooses to link them by providing training, or finances, and certainly information and contacts." Peter Bergen (2001, 30–31) uses a different business metaphor, likening al-Qaʿida to a multinational holding company with Bin Laden as CEO.

[2]Some members of al-Qaʿida are dismayed at what they regard as Bin Laden's undeserved prominence. Indeed, there are several other thinkers and leaders who are regarded as more serious and certainly more central to the global jihad movement than Bin Laden. A Syrian leader within the movement, Abu Musʿab al-Suri, reportedly criticized Bin Laden's love of publicity, arguing that al-Qaʿida is "not an organization, it is not a group, nor do we want it to be; it is a call, a reference, a methodology" and eventually, its leadership will be superfluous (Lia 2008, 7; Wright 2006b).

[3]Saladin is the European name for Salah al-Din (1138–93), a Kurd born in what is today Iraq, who led a successful jihad against European Crusaders, and is frequently invoked as the paradigmatic Muslim warrior-hero.

narrative he proffers and the viewers it repels or with whom it resonates.[4] Yet both images exaggerate Bin Laden's individual power, as well as diminish understanding of his actual arguments and the extent to which they are determined by historical and geopolitical dynamics of which he is neither author nor master (Lesch 2002; Fandy 1999, 178–80). In fact, taken as a whole, Bin Laden's unsystematic body of ideas is at once more illuminating and less original than these images indicate. His arguments are almost entirely derivative of the work of others, but he has put both pen and sword in the service of an unprecedented exhortation to global jihad that, in effect, collapses the distinctions between national and transnational, offensive and defensive war, "near enemy" and "far enemy" that have defined most twentieth-century Islamist thought. In so doing, Bin Laden simultaneously reflects and reinforces the ways in which an Islamist movement increasingly reshaped by globalization is recasting the logic of Islamic renewal in the image of a deterritorialized jihad.

Bin Laden was born in 1957 into a wealthy family close to the Saudi Arabian monarchy, part of the elite in a country immersed in the Wahhabi strand of Islam. Wahhabism is named for Muhammad Ibn 'Abd al-Wahhab (d. 1792), a Hanbali scholar and admirer of Ibn Taymiyya who, in 1745, forged an uneasy alliance with Muhammad Ibn Saud, forefather of the current Saudi ruling family. A crucial force in building the modern Saudi Arabian state, Wahhabism's influence extended well beyond Arabia into Iraq and the Gulf, and would directly and indirectly influence nineteenth-century resistance movements in Afghanistan, India, and North and West Africa (Fandy 1999, 178; Fattah 2003; Rizvi 1982). Its galvanizing power has derived, in part, from Ibn 'Abd al-Wahhab's uncompromising insistence on the moral renewal of Islam by cleansing the umma of unbelief (kufr), any perceived violations of tawhid (belief in the unity of God, monotheism), and all practices thought to corrupt the principles of the pure faith as adumbrated in the scriptures and the example of the salaf, the first generations of Muslims (Lapidus 1988, 673; also see chapter 1 in this volume).

While Bin Laden's opponents frequently characterize him as the unfortunate but inevitable product of Saudi Arabian insularity and "Wahhabi Puritanism," his sympathizers tend to valorize him as the true son of the great Wahhabi mujahidin of yesteryear who fought valiantly in the cause of Islam. Both depictions neglect the extent to which Bin Laden's lineage, education, radicalization, and religio-political commitments reflect an increasingly globalized world—one in which identities are not only shaped by particular places and spaces such as nation and home but also subject

---

[4]Tony Schwartz (1983, 20–21), for example, has argued that the message of an electronic communication is not simply "delivered" but rather is produced by resonances between material and medium (the stimulus) and the "stored information in the minds of those who receive the communication" (O'Shaughnessy 2002).

to the multiple cross-currents and exposures created by rapid economic globalization and cultural hybridization. His father was originally a poor immigrant from Yemen and his mother was reportedly Syrian, making Bin Laden a "double outsider" in a "country that is obsessed with parentage" (interview with family friend, Weaver 2000). He was, moreover, educated in Islamist activism primarily by Muslim Brothers and Brotherhood sympathizers from elsewhere, a reflection of the influx of teachers who had fled government repression in Jordan, Syria, and Egypt and were welcomed into Saudi Arabia by King Faisal in the 1960s (Randal 2004, 62–63; Coll 2005). According to Saudi journalist Jamal Khashoggi, Bin Laden "grew up as a Muslim Brother" (Randal 2004, 63). In high school, he became an avid participant in an after-school Islamic study group under the aegis of a Syrian teacher inspired by the Brotherhood (Coll 2005; Wright 2006a, 75). At King Abdul Aziz University in Jedda, Bin Laden is said to have studied business management, economics, and possibly engineering, but his Islamist education continued under the tutelage of such non-Saudi professors as Muhammad Qutb, Egyptian expatriate and brother of Sayyid Qutb, who had become an influential Islamist in his own right.[5]

Another professor at the university, a Palestinian named 'Abd Allah Yusuf Mustafa 'Azzam (1941–89), would play a particularly crucial role in Bin Laden's life. 'Azzam was born in the West Bank, studied in Damascus, participated in the Palestinian jihad against Israel from Jordan, and obtained his doctorate in Islamic jurisprudence at al-Azhar in 1973, all before briefly joining the faculty at 'Abd al-Aziz University in 1980. He was deeply influenced by Sayyid Qutb and Ibn Taymiyya and, like an increasing number of Islamists from Cairo to Peshawar, had come to regard jihad against unbelievers as an individual obligation second in importance only to faith. When the Soviet Union invaded Afghanistan in 1979, 'Azzam saw an opportunity to put his commitment to jihad into practice; he left his university post to become among the first of the so-called "Arab Afghans" to join the fight against the Soviets (McGregor 2003, 101). 'Azzam went on to play a critical role in internationalizing the Afghan jihad, establishing a recruitment and fund-raising organization, Maktab al-Khidamat (Services Center), with the assistance of the Muslim Brothers

[5]Kepel 1985, 61–64; Lawrence 2005, xii; Bergen 2001, 47. There are different accounts of what Bin Laden studied at the university, with whom and for how long. Lawrence, for example, says he attended the management and business school and took courses in Islamic studies but did not receive a degree, whereas Bergen says Bin Laden received a degree in economics and public administration in 1981, and Kepel claims that he studied engineering (Lawrence 2005, xii; Kepel 2002, 314; Bergen 2001, 47). Scholars and journalists also disagree about whether Bin Laden actually studied with Muhammad Qutb or simply sat in on his lectures. Most identify 'Abd Allah 'Azzam (see below) as one of Bin Laden's professors, although Randal (2004, 63) argues that "only conjecture suggests that 'Azzam actually taught or even knew Osama" when they were both at the university.

(ibid., 101, 105). Equally crucial, 'Azzam articulated the stakes of the Afghan jihad for Arab Muslims with little or no connection to it: in a series of influential writings, he depicted Afghanistan as the front line in a global jihad against jahiliyya that must continue until all formerly Muslim lands are restored to Islam, participation in which is the only sure path to dignity and everlasting glory ('Azzam 1986; 1987a; 1987b; Kepel and Milelli 208; McGregor 2003; Bergen 2006).

Dubbed by Islamists the "imam of jihad," 'Azzam's arguments worked powerfully on the young Bin Laden, who would later describe his mentor as "a man worth a nation" (Lia 2008, 72; Bin Laden 1999). He soon heeded the call to join the Afghan jihad and, with the support of the Saudi ruling family, shuttled back and forth to Pakistan to help recruit mujahidin and raise funds for their effort.[6] Bin Laden would even gain practical experience in the "jihad of the sword" on the hardscrabble terrain of Central Asia, training and fighting alongside Afghans and Muslims from Egypt, Turkey, Yemen, Saudi Arabia, Algeria, Lebanon, and beyond (Fandy 1999, 180). It was here that Bin Laden would found al-Qa'ida as a formalized network of mujahidin, or "army of jihad," that would outlast the Afghan conflict (Bergen 2006, 83, 74–107). Although views vary widely regarding his abilities as a leader or fighter, Bin Laden's reputation for austerity, integrity, generosity, piety, and courage among his fellow Muslims originated in this willingness to abandon the air-conditioned halls of Saudi privilege for the life of a mujahid. Bin Laden has carefully cultivated this image, resorting to mystical language to describe his own fortitude in battle:

> I was never afraid of death. As Muslims we believe that when we die, we go to heaven. Before a battle, God sends us "seqina," tranquility. Once I was only 30 metres from the Russians and they were trying to capture me. I was under bombardment but I was so peaceful in my heart that I fell asleep. This experience has been written about in our earliest books. I saw a 120mm mortar shell land in front of me, but it did not blow up. Four more bombs were dropped from a Russian plane on our headquarters but they did not explode. We beat the Soviet Union. The Russians fled. (Fisk 1996)

The heady experience of the Afghan jihad would prove a watershed not just for Bin Laden but for the contemporary Islamist movement of which he was now an integral part. It captured the imagination of hardened activists, many of whom were already veterans of largely unsuccess-

[6]Saudi Arabia was a major supplier of arms, financing, and intelligence to the Afghan mujahidin. Such support was intended to shore up the religious credentials of the Saudi monarchy, although its efforts to encourage Saudi dissidents and radicals to expend their fervor for jihad elsewhere was as much a matter of political prudence as piety. One such effort entailed having the national airline offer a 75-percent discount to mujahidin on their way to Afghanistan (Bergen 2001, 55).

ful battles against "infidel" regimes back home, and brought them together in one place. For example, Shaykh 'Umar 'Abd al-Rahman, mentor to the Egyptian Islamists who had assassinated Sadat, was frequently seen in Peshawar in the 1980s with 'Azzam, whom he had known at al-Azhar (Bergen 2001, 53). In 1986 Bin Laden met and subsequently forged a particularly strong tie with Ayman al-Zawahiri, a veteran of the Egyptian Islamic Jihad who had been imprisoned along with hundreds of Islamists in the wake of the Sadat assassination (Zayyat 2004). It was Zawahiri who would step smoothly into the role of Bin Laden's closest adviser when 'Azzam was mysteriously assassinated in Peshawar in November 1989, and who eventually led a faction of Egyptian Islamic Jihad to merge with al-Qa'ida (a collaboration announced in the 1998 declaration of war against "Jews and Crusaders"). But perhaps most importantly, once the last of the Soviet troops withdrew in 1989, the Afghan jihad released into the region a new generation of battle-trained and highly mobile mujahidin, convinced they had brought a major superpower to its knees.[7]

Bin Laden was similarly convinced he had been party to a historic victory, one that reversed a long legacy of Muslim defeats and humiliations. In Afghanistan, he told interviewers, "the myth of the super-power was destroyed not only in my mind but also in the minds of all Muslims" (Bin Laden 1997b). When Saddam Hussein invaded Kuwait in 1990, an emboldened Bin Laden offered his services and that of the Afghan Arabs to liberate Kuwait and secure the Saudi Kingdom against Iraqi aggression. The royal family rejected the offer, opting instead to permit thousands of U.S. troops into the Kingdom to launch Operation Desert Storm and pressured several Saudi 'ulama to endorse the decision. Bin Laden, in turn, accused the Saudi regime of relinquishing to infidels the duty of defending the land of Muhammad and of violating Islamic law by entering a pact with non-Muslims to fight other Muslims (i.e., Iraqis). Lacking any formal academic credentials in the Islamic tradition, Bin Laden borrowed arguments from dissident Saudi 'ulama such as Shaykh Salman al-'Awda and Safar al-Hawali to argue that the policy was one among many indications of the replacement of shari'a with man-made law in the Kingdom, "one of the ten voiders that strip a person [of] his Islamic status."[8]

---

[7]The military contribution of the "Afghan Arabs" has been characterized as insignificant compared with the efforts of Afghans shored up by a flood of money, weapons, and tactical support from abroad, particularly from Saudi Arabia and the United States, which had authorized the CIA to funnel aid to the mujahidin through the Pakistani Inter-Services Intelligence Agency (Bergen 2001, 41–75). "In the grand scheme of things," Bergen writes, "the Afghan Arabs were no more than extras in the Afghan holy war" (ibid., 56).

[8]Bin Laden 1996a; Gwynne 2006; Fandy 1999. Al-'Awda and al-Hawali are prominent members of an increasingly vocal group of dissident 'ulama critical of Saudi foreign and domestic policy. Both were imprisoned from 1994 to 1999 as part of a Saudi crackdown on domestic dissent (Fandy 1999; Lawrence 2005).

In an echo of 'Abd al-Salam Faraj's indictment of Egyptian President Anwar al-Sadat (see chapter 13 on Faraj), Bin Laden concludes that, as "those who do not judge/govern by what God has revealed are unbelievers" (Q 5:44), the Saudi rulers are not Muslims at all, but rather apostates unfit to govern.

The Saudi regime responded to Bin Laden's increasingly strident criticisms by restricting his travel within the Kingdom. He used his family connections to leave the country, however, eventually finding a hospitable environment in the Sudan of General 'Umar Hasan al-Bashir and Hasan al-Turabi (see chapter 8 on Turabi). During his five years in the Sudan, Bin Laden built an empire of commercial businesses that simultaneously concealed and subsidized al-Qa'ida's growing membership, arsenal of weapons, military camps, and expanding network of contacts and alliances with Islamists around the world (Bergen 2001, 79–81). These years also witnessed a series of high profile attacks either claimed by or attributed to al-Qa'ida and its affiliates, including the downing of American Black Hawk helicopters in Somalia in 1993; the attempted assassination of Egyptian president Hosni Mubarak in 1995; the bombings of a hotel in Aden, Yemen, in 1992; the National Guard Building in Riyadh in 1995; the Egyptian Embassy in Islamabad in 1995; and the Khobar Towers in Dhahran in 1996. In 1994 the Saudis revoked Bin Laden's citizenship, and the Sudan expelled Bin Laden two years later at the insistence of the Egyptian and American governments (PBS 2001; Bergen 2001).

Bin Laden next settled in Afghanistan, where he was welcomed by Mullah Muhammad 'Umar and the Taliban, the radically conservative regime that had emerged out of the brutal civil war following the withdrawal of Soviet troops in 1989 (see chapter 17 on the Taliban). From its new redoubt in Afghanistan, al-Qa'ida undertook a series of large-scale operations for which it is perhaps best known, including the bombings of the U.S. embassies in Kenya and Tanzania in 1998, the assault on the USS *Cole* in Yemen in 2000, and the hijacking of American jets to attack the World Trade Center and Pentagon in 2001. In the immediate aftermath of the 9/11 attacks, the United States launched a "War on Terror" with the invasion of Afghanistan, quickly terminating the formal rule of the Taliban.[9] Bin Laden, however, eluded capture and is now widely believed

---

[9]There is much evidence suggesting that while the U.S.-led invasion ended the formal rule of the Taliban, the victory may have been Pyrrhic, as many members temporarily relocated to Pakistan and regrouped. In the spring of 2006, for example, the Taliban launched what the *New York Times* called its "largest offensive since 2001, attacking British, Canadian and Dutch troops in southern Afghanistan" (Rohde and Sanger 2007). A Pentagon report issued to Congress on June 27, 2008, stated that the "Taliban regrouped after its fall from power and have coalesced into a resilient insurgency. It now poses a challenge to the Afghan government's authority in some rural areas. . . . The Taliban is likely to maintain or even increase the scope and pace of its terrorist attacks and bombings in 2008" (White 2008). Also see chapter 17 in this volume.

to be living in the border region between Afghanistan and Pakistan. From his hiding place in the Hindu Kush, he has continued to issue sporadic warnings and threats to Arab regimes, Western powers, and any who collaborate with them, as well as encouragement to his fellow "warriors for Islam." The violent operations associated with an increasingly diffuse al-Qa'ida have proceeded apace, expanding geographically to include Indonesia, Turkey, Morocco, Spain, Qatar, the Philippines, Malaysia, Ethiopia, Eritrea, Chechnya, China, Kashmir, England, and, since the 2003 U.S.-led invasion, Iraq.

In this overheated geopolitical climate, the actual content of Bin Laden's many epistles, declarations, fatwas, communiqués, and interviews are often lost, eclipsed by the prism of images with multiple symbolic registers that constitutes his outsized persona. Further complicating matters, virtually every one of his arguments derives from the work of others. His rhetoric about an epic battle between believers and infidels, for example, along with his exhortation to defend Islam against internal corruption and foreign domination everywhere, has been elaborated several times over by thinkers more sophisticated and deeply versed in the exegetical tradition than he is, from Ibn Taymiyya to Ibn 'Abd al-Wahhab, Sayyid Qutb to 'Abd Allah 'Azzam. Years before Bin Laden issued his declaration of global jihad, moreover, a Syrian named Abu Mus'ab al-Suri had developed many of the arguments for deterritorialized warfare that would become central to al-Qa'ida, earning Suri the moniker of "jihadi theoretician" on Islamist Web forums (Lia 2008, 6, 8). Even Bin Laden's critique of the Saudi monarchy borrows from the teachings of dissident 'ulama and shaykhs who have been at the forefront of opposition politics in the Kingdom, critical of what they regard as myriad violations of Islamic law, corruption and nepotism in government and business, and subservience to Western and particularly American power and military might (Fandy 1999, 22, 48–113).

As Bin Laden's thought is as much a product of contemporary political developments as an attempt to remake them, its significance lies less in its originality than in what it represents. Despite his insistence on recuperating an Islamic umma purified of foreign corruption, Bin Laden's arguments reflect the dynamics of a globalized world grown progressively smaller by rapid flows of people, knowledge, and information, one in which "[i]deas, objects, and people from 'outside' are now more—and more obviously—*present* than they have ever been" (Appiah 1998, xi; emphasis in the original). Such hybridization is already evident in Bin Laden's lineage, education, and radicalization, as well as in the emergence of those mobile mujahidin who comprise his transnational army of loyalists. It is also evident in his various messages, the chronology and content of which reveal not a shift in focus from the domestic politics of Saudi Arabia to the dynamics of foreign power but rather the increasingly blurred boundary between the two. In these messages, the internal politics of the Kingdom are central. Foreign perfidy is not only written into the fabric of Saudi society but also deeply implicated in every single site of Muslim struggle, from Saudi Arabia to Iraq, Chechnya to Palestine, Afghanistan to Kashmir. And each seemingly discrete struggle is connected to reveal a larger pattern, an epic war between "global unbelief, with the apostates today under the leadership of America, on one side, and the Islamic umma and its brigades of mujahidin on the other" (Bin Laden 2004a).[10]

This feature of Bin Laden's thought brings into sharp relief several striking continuities and discontinuities with the work of Islamist thinkers from whom he has liberally borrowed. Qutb is frequently cited as a major influence on Bin Laden's thought and is most often characterized as the Islamist who first accorded jihad primacy of place. Yet for Qutb, jihad was in the service of remaking the foundations of an Egyptian state corrupted by jahiliyya from the outside as well as from within. By contrast, for Bin Laden, the ultimate focus is not sovereignty but jihad, which he has characterized as "the acme of this religion" (Bin Laden 1997a). Indeed, aside from a vague call for concerned Muslims to establish temporary consultative councils governed by Islamic law, Bin Laden's discourse is "more episodic than systemic," an ad hoc response to events that, to date, offers little in the way of a political theory, social program, or strategy of moral reform.[11] Describing Bin Laden's thought, one scholar writes that "in place of the social, there is a hypertrophy of the sacrificial" (Lawrence 2005, xxii).

On the other hand, Bin Laden shares with Islamists such as Faraj and 'Azzam the conviction that jihad is now an individual rather than collective obligation second only to faith, one in which violent rather than spiritual struggle is primary. Such a claim is often reduced to irrational blood lust, yet it flows logically from Bin Laden's view of the world as an anti-Islamic minefield in which Muslims are under constant attack. While jihad against a distant enemy is widely understood to be a collective duty (fard kifaya), Bin Laden insists that, under these conditions, it is the responsibility of every Muslim (fard 'ayn) to take up arms and heed Ibn Taymiyya's fatwa regarding the meaning and scope of jihad: "As for the fighting to repulse [an enemy], it is aimed at defending sanctity and religion, and it is a duty as agreed [by the 'ulama]. Nothing is more sacred than belief except repulsing an enemy who is attacking religion and life" (Bin Laden 1998a).

[10]McAuley (2005) adds a third level of analysis, examining the overlap of tribal, national, and transnational group identities in Bin Laden's discourse, as well as analyzing his invocation of a kind of pan-peninsular identity.

[11]Bin Laden 2004b; Fandy 1999, 193; Gwynne 2006, 72. This is not true, however, of all those affiliated with al-Qa'ida. As Roel Meijer points out in reference to Yusuf al-Ayiri, a second-generation al-Qa'ida activist on the Arabian Peninsula, a disproportionate focus on al-Qa'ida's top leaders misses the extent to which such doctrines and ideals have been adapted to specific contexts, often yielding quite thoroughgoing social and political programs (Meijer 2006).

Bin Laden's arguments here are far more widely recognizable than the incantation of Qur'anic and juristic sources immediately suggests. In particular, his justificatory logic recapitulates a series of claims about the legitimacy of violent resistance that have appeared and reappeared in a variety of cultures past and present. Much as Frantz Fanon pointed to the psychic and structural as well as physical violence of colonialism, for instance, Bin Laden presumes that violence against Muslims in the contemporary world is cultural, economic, moral, and symbolic as well as physical (Fanon 2005). It thus includes the killing of Iraqis and the oppression of Palestinians; the coercive globalization of American culture and Western indifference to the fate of Bosnian Muslims; and Danish denigration of the Prophet. It also includes the "occupation" of the Holy Land by (invited) American troops, which Bin Laden characterizes as no less than the culmination of Crusaders' "historic ambitions" to gain "control over the Islamic holy places and the Holy Sanctuaries, and hegemony over the wealth and riches of our umma, turning the Arabian peninsula into the biggest air, land, and sea base in the region" (Bin Laden 1995–96). For Bin Laden, the breadth and nature of this multilevel attack on Islam mean that Muslims who fight it are not *introducing* violence into a heretofore peaceful world but rather engaging in a necessary and legitimate retaliation for a series of *already existing* provocations (Bin Laden 1996c).

In Bin Laden's division of the world into believers and kufr, Islam or atheism, moreover, the embattled umma confronts a largely undifferentiated enemy: a "global Crusader alliance with the Zionist Jews, led by America, Britain and Israel," to whom "the blood of Muslims has no value" (Bin Laden 1998c; 2001b; 2001c). In this narrative, all Muslims by definition become one—the "children of Iraq are our children" (Bin Laden 1996a)—and therefore an attack on a Muslim anywhere becomes an attack on Muslims everywhere. By the same token, all non-Muslims— as well as a great many Muslims unwilling to endorse his views—are implicated in the attack on Islam. For Bin Laden, then, no one is innocent and all are legitimate targets for counterattack. This is reinforced not only by what is included in his call to jihad but also by what is excluded: in the "Declaration of War," for instance, mercy, the special status of Jews and Christians as People of the Book, and instructions on conduct in battle are notably omitted from the scriptural sources and exegetical conventions.[12] Taken together, these premises and claims enable Bin Laden to invoke "self-defense" no matter how spatially removed and contextually specific the threat may be, and to insist, for example, that Islam itself

---

[12] As Rosalind Gwynne points out, the "Declaration" does not begin with the traditional invocation of divine mercy. It invokes Qur'an 3:110 but omits the latter part of the verse that refers to those Jews and Christians who may be considered believers. It ignores the special status granted People of the Book in the Qur'an, instead promising double rewards in Paradise for killing Jews and Christians. And it refers to the Qur'anic instructions to "smite the necks" of the unbelievers (47:4) but dispenses with the remainder of the verse that specifies how to treat prisoners (Gwynne 2006, 66, 68, 71, 74, 79–80).

is at stake in the Afghan jihad; American troops in the Holy Land are an affront to all Muslims; and the fight for Palestinian liberation is as much the responsibility of Muslims in Jeddah as those in Hebron.

These arguments not only erase the heterogeneity of those grouped within the categories of Muslims and unbelievers but, paradoxically, deny the very interpenetration of cultures and regions of which Bin Laden himself is an expression. More important, however, the logic of these claims vitiate distinctions between offensive and defensive war, physical violence and symbolic threat, enemies "near" and "far," civilian and soldier, guilt and innocence. Tensions, resentments, and conflicts are detached from the specific contexts in which they are embedded and are then made to serve a deterritorialized conception of jihad in which Muslims everywhere are exhorted to fight unbelievers anywhere. These very arguments and omissions would find deadly expression in the final note attributed to Muhammad 'Ata, leader of the 9/11 hijackers (see chapter 19), those whom Bin Laden would celebrate as the "nineteen postsecondary students . . . who shook America's throne" (Bin Laden 2001b).

Despite Bin Laden's obvious debts to more learned and formally trained Muslim thinkers, his rhetorical skills and what some have described as his literary lyricism are largely his own.[13] So is his ability to adjust the "polemical register" of his messages to address diverse audiences, Muslim and non-Muslim, American and Iraqi, global elites and Gulf Arabs, frustrated Saudi middle classes and court 'ulama.[14] A case in point is Bin Laden's rhetorical deployment of "humiliation" (in Arabic, *dhull* or *mahana*, meaning to degrade, bring low or debase) to link a series of grievances past and present, distant and proximate, not least of which is the "defilement of her [Islam's] holy places, occupation of her land, and violation and plundering of her sanctuaries" (Bin Laden 1995–96). The repetitive invocation of "humiliation" in this way yields a narrative of unrelieved aggression against ordinary Muslims' lives, lands, and sensibilities that literally cries out for retaliation. Bin Laden then offers participation in jihad as an antidote not only to the historical burden of defeat but also to more immediate experiences of political, economic, and cultural emas-

---

[13]Lawrence 2005, xvi–xviii. Bin Laden may not have composed every line in his messages, but as Lawrence (2005, xvii) argues, they are not "ghostwritten tracts of the kind supplied by professional speechwriters to many politicians in the West" or their Middle Eastern counterparts. Bin Laden's messages "speak in the authentic, compelling voice of a visionary," Lawrence writes, "with what can only be called a powerful lyricism." Bernard Lewis (1998) has characterized some of Bin Laden's prose as "eloquent, at times even poetic."

[14]Lawrence 2005, xvii. McAuley (2005, 281–83) is one of the few who has addressed the ways in which Bin Laden, a member of the elite, has sought to adjust his rhetoric to appeal to Saudi middle-class frustrations with patrimonial rule (see Yamani 2000 for a study of the Saudi middle class). This is particularly evident in the text reproduced here, when Bin Laden addresses the everyday struggles created by inflation and debt for those with limited income—struggles quite distant from his own experience growing up with great wealth.

culation produced by living under authoritarian regimes in thrall to foreign powers. The appeal to Muslim *men* in particular is reinforced by the role of women in his missives, who are invoked either to exhort men to martyrdom or to figure as virginal rewards in Paradise awaiting martyrs "after the first gush of blood" (see also chapter 1 in this volume). The jihad to humiliate the enemies of Islam thus registers symbolically as both a means to recuperate and an enactment of Muslim virility. As Bin Laden crows in the "Declaration of War," just as Americans left Mogadishu in "disappointment, humiliation, and defeat," the enemy now confronts an endless supply of mujahidin whose "love of death" grants them the courage and potency to fight without end and kill without fear.

# DECLARATION OF WAR AGAINST
# THE AMERICANS OCCUPYING THE LAND
# OF THE TWO HOLY PLACES

PRAISE BE to Allah, we seek His help and ask for His pardon, we take refuge in Allah from our wrongs and bad deeds. Whoever has been guided by Allah will not be misled, and whoever has been misled will never be guided. I bear witness that there is no God except Allah—no associates with Him—and I bear witness that Muhammad is His slave and messenger.

"You who believe, be mindful of God, as is His due, and make sure you devote yourselves to Him, to your dying moment" (Q 3:102); "People, be mindful of your Lord, who created you from a single soul, and from it created its mate, and from the pair of them spread countless men and women far and wide; be mindful of God, in whose name you make requests of one another. Beware of severing the ties of kinship: God is always watching over you" (Q 4:1); "Believers, be mindful of God, speak in a direct fashion and to good purpose, and He will put your deeds right for you and forgive you your sins. Whoever obeys God and His messenger will truly achieve a great triumph" (Q 33:70–71).

Praise be to Allah, reporting the saying of the prophet Shu'ayb: "I only want to put things right as far as I can. I cannot succeed without God's help: I trust in Him, and always turn to Him" (Q 11:88).

Praise be to Allah, saying: "Believers, you are the best community singled out for people: You order what is right, forbid what is wrong, and believe in God" (Q 3:110). Allah's blessing and salutations on His slave and messenger who said: "The people are close to an all-encompassing punishment from Allah if they see the oppressor and fail to restrain him."

It is no secret that the people of Islam have suffered from the aggression, iniquity, and injustice imposed on them by the Zionist-Crusader alliance and their collaborators, to the point where Muslim blood has become the cheapest and their wealth as loot in the hands of their enemies. Their blood was spilled in Palestine and Iraq; the horrifying pictures of the massacre of Qana in Lebanon are still fresh in our memory.[15] Massacres have happened in Tajikistan, Burma, Kashmir,

---

[15] On April 18 1996, more than 100 civilians who had taken shelter in a United Nations compound in Qana were killed by Israeli shells aimed at Hizbullah.

Assam, the Philippines, Fatani, Ogaden, Somalia, Eritrea, Chechnya, and Bosnia-Herzegovina—massacres that send shivers through one's body and shake one's conscience. All this happened while the world watched and listened and failed to respond not only to these atrocities but also to a clear conspiracy between the United States and its allies—under the cover of the iniquitous United Nations—that prevented the dispossessed people even from obtaining arms to defend themselves.

The people of Islam have awakened and realize that they are the main target of the aggression of the Zionist-Crusader alliance. All false claims and propaganda about "human rights" have been exposed and discredited by the massacres of Muslims that have taken place in every part of the world.

The latest and the greatest of the aggressions inflicted on Muslims since the death of the Prophet (peace be upon him) is the occupation of the Land of the Two Holy Places [Saudi Arabia][16]—the foundation of the house of Islam, the place of the Revelation, and the place of the noble Ka'ba, the qibla of all Muslims—by the armies of the American Crusaders and their allies.[17] We bemoan this and can only say: "There is no power or strength except through God."

I meet with you today under these circumstances, and under the banner of the blessed awakening which is sweeping the world in general and the Islamic world in particular. This comes after a long absence imposed upon Islamic scholars ('ulama) and preachers by the iniquitous Crusaders' movement under the leadership of America. The Zionist-Crusader alliance has resorted to killing and arresting pious 'ulama and hardworking preachers (may God sanctify who He wishes) out of fear that they will incite the umma against its enemies as did their pious predecessors (may Allah be pleased with them) Ibn Taymiyya and al-'Izz ibn 'Abd al-Salam.[18] They killed the mujahid Shaykh 'Abd Allah 'Azzam, and they arrested the mujahid Shaykh Ahmad Yasin and the mujahid Shaykh 'Umar 'Abd al-Rahman in America.[19]

---

[16]Throughout the declaration, Bin Laden refers to his homeland either as the "Land of the Two Holy Places" (i.e., the land of Mecca and Medina) or simply as "the country," in part to avoid granting the Saud family the legitimacy implied in the name "Saudi Arabia."

[17]Qibla is the direction Muslims must face for prayer. More specifically, worshipers face the Ka'ba, the most famous sanctuary in Islam, which is located within the great mosque in Mecca.

[18]On Ibn Taymiyya, see chapter 1. Ibn 'Abd al-Salam (d. 1262) was an 'alim from Damascus and an adherent of the Shafi'i school of law. Much like Ibn Taymiyya, Ibn 'Abd al-Salam openly criticized the ruling regime under which he lived and was incarcerated for his trouble (Kepel and Milelli 2008, 276, n. 5).

[19]Here Bin Laden accuses the "Zionist-Crusader alliance" of murdering 'Azzam, but the question of who engineered the assassination remains open and will likely remain so. Speculation about who benefited from 'Azzam's death has generated at least five possible theories about who may have killed him and why, along with five corresponding suspects, including Bin Laden himself and/or Ayman al-Zawahiri. Other suspects include the Pakistani

On orders from America, they have also arrested a large number of scholars, preachers, and young people in the Land of the Two Holy Places, among them the prominent Shaykh Salman al-'Awda and Safar al-Hawali [see chapter 1] and their brothers. We bemoan this and can only say: "There is no power or strength except through God." We, myself and my group, have suffered some of this injustice ourselves; we have been prevented from addressing Muslims. We have been pursued in Pakistan, Sudan, and Afghanistan—hence this long absence on my part. But by the Grace of Allah, a safe base is now available in the high peaks of the Hindu Kush mountains in Khurasan. There, by the Grace of Allah, the largest infidel military force of the world was defeated and the myth of the superpower was destroyed amid the cries of the mujahidin, "God is Greatest!" Today we work from the same mountains to lift the iniquity that has been imposed on the umma by the Zionist-Crusader alliance, particularly after its occupation of Jerusalem, route of the journey of the Prophet (peace be upon him) and the Land of the Two Holy Places.[20] We ask Allah to bless us with victory; He is our Protector and He is the most capable.

Here and today we begin the work, talking and discussing ways of correcting what has happened to the Islamic world in general and the Land of the Two Holy Places in particular. We wish to study the means we can follow to restore the situation to its proper course and restore to the people their rights, especially after so much damage and injustice has been inflicted on their lives and religion. Every section and group of people has been affected: civilians, military and security men, government officials and merchants, young and old, university students and unemployed graduates—the largest section of society, now numbering in the hundreds of thousands.

Injustice has affected those in industry and agriculture as well as people of rural and urban areas, and almost everyone has a complaint. The situation in the Land of the Two Holy Places has become like a huge volcano ready to erupt and destroy unbelief and corruption and its sources. The explosions [at the National Guard Building in 1995] in Riyadh and at al-Khobar [the Khobar Towers in Dhahran in 1996] are a warning of this impending volcanic eruption, the consequence of intolerable oppression, suffering, iniquity, humiliation, and poverty.

---

intelligence services, the CIA and Mossad (the Israeli secret service), and rivals among the Afghan mujahidiin (Kepel and Milelli 2008, 96–97; Bergen 2006, 92–93; Wright 2006a, 143–44). Ahmad Yasin (1936–2004) was among the founders of Hamas, the most powerful Islamist movement in the Palestinian territories. At the time this declaration was issued, Yasin was incarcerated in an Israeli prison. 'Umar 'Abd al-Rahman (b. 1938) is the blind Egyptian shaykh currently serving a life sentence in a federal penitentiary for his role in the first attack on the World Trade Center in 1993. He was also religious guide and mentor to the Egyptian Islamist group that engineered the assassination of Egyptian president Anwar al-Sadat in 1981.

[20] The "route of the journey of the Prophet" refers to the night journey Muhammad was said to have made in the company of the angel Gabriel from Mecca to Jerusalem.

People are deeply concerned about their everyday living; everyone talks of the deterioration of the economy, inflation, ever-increasing debts, and jails full of prisoners. Government employees with limited incomes talk about debts of tens and hundreds of thousands of riyals [the Saudi currency]. They complain that the value of the riyal is declining sharply relative to most of the main currencies. Prominent merchants and contractors speak about hundreds and thousands of million riyals owed to them by the government. And the government owes 340 billion riyals to the people in addition to the daily accumulated interest—not to mention the foreign debt. People are wondering: are we really the largest oil-exporting country? They even believe that this situation is a curse Allah has laid upon them for failing to object to the oppressive and illegitimate conduct and measures of the ruling regime, chief of which are: its disregard of Islamic law, its denial of the people's legitimate rights, the permission given to Americans to occupy the Land of the Two Holy Places, and the unjust imprisonment of righteous 'ulama. Pious scholars, merchants, economists, and eminent people of the country are all aware of this disastrous situation.

Each group has attempted to quickly contain and rectify the situation. All agreed that the country is heading toward a great catastrophe, the extent of which only God knows. One prominent merchant commented that "the king is leading the state into a 66-fold disaster." We bemoan this and can only say, "There is no power or strength except through God." Numerous princes have shared their feelings with the people, privately expressing their concerns and objections to the corruption, repression, and intimidation taking place [in Saudi Arabia], but competition among influential princes for personal gain has destroyed the country. The regime has destroyed its own legitimacy through its course of action, which includes:

1. Suspension of Islamic Law, its replacement with man-made civil law, and the regime's bloody confrontation with righteous 'ulama and youths;

2. The inability of the regime to protect the country, and the fact that it permitted the enemy of the umma—the American Crusader forces—to occupy the land for many years. The Crusader forces have become the principal reason for our disastrous situation, particularly in regard to economics, given the regime's unjustified, extensive spending to support these forces. As a result of policies that restrict or expand oil production and fix prices to suit the American economy, our own economy has suffered. The Americans have imposed expensive arms purchases on the country. People are thus asking: what is the justification for the very existence of this regime?

Individuals and different groups throughout society have quickly sought to contain the situation and to prevent the danger. They have advised the government both privately and openly; have sent letters and testimony, reports after reports, reminders after reminders, exploring every avenue and enlisting every influential man in their movement for reform. They wrote with passion, diplomacy, and wisdom, asking for corrective measures and repentance from the "great wrongdoings and corruption" that has engulfed even the basic principles of religion and legitimate rights of the people.

To our deepest regret, the regime refused to listen to the people, calling their demands ridiculous and unwarranted. The situation degenerated as previous wrongdoings were compounded by offenses of even greater magnitude, all of which are occurring in the Land of the Two Holy Places! It is no longer possible to be silent and it is unacceptable to turn a blind eye.

As these transgressions have extended to the highest levels, becoming destructive forces that threaten the very existence of Islamic principles, a group of scholars who could take no more—supported by hundreds of retired officials, merchants, prominent and educated people—wrote to the king asking for implementation of corrective measures. In AH 1411 (May 1991), the time of the Gulf War, the famous petition of Shawwal with more than four hundred signatures was sent to the King demanding that oppression be lifted and corrective measures be implemented. The king humiliated these people by opting to ignore the content of their letter. The situation went from bad to worse.

However, people have tried again and sent more letters and petitions. One particular letter, the glorious Memorandum of Advice, was handed over to the King on Muharram, AH 1413 (July 1992).[21] This memorandum tackled the problem directly by diagnosing the illness and prescribing the medicine in an original, righteous, and scientific style. It identified the gaps and shortcomings of the regime's philosophy and suggested the requisite course of action and remedy. The report detailed:

1. The intimidation and harassment suffered by the leaders of this society, the scholars, heads of tribes, merchants, academic teachers, and other eminent individuals;

2. The state of law within the country and the arbitrary declaration of what is halal (lawful) and haram (forbidden) regardless of the dictates of Islamic law established by God;

3. The state of the press and the media, which has become a tool of propaganda and misinformation in order to carry out the plan of the enemy. The media is used to idolize certain personages and to spread scandals among the believers to push people away from their religion. As Allah, the Exalted said: "A painful punishment waits in this world

[21] Like the Hamas Charter and Faraj's *Absent Duty*, the memorandum was in many ways collectively authored: it was the result of many conversations among Saudi Islamists over time and contains the central components of the Saudi Islamist critique of the monarchy (Fandy 1999, 50–51).

and the next for those who like indecency to spread among the believers" (Q 24:19);

4. The abuse and confiscation of human rights;

5. The frightening financial and economic future of the country given the enormous amount of debts and interest owed by the government. At this time the wealth of the umma is being siphoned off to satisfy the personal desires of certain individuals while the regime is imposing more custom duties and taxes on the nation. As the Prophet said about the woman who committed adultery: "She repented in [a way that was] sufficient to bring forgiveness to a customs collector!!"

6. The miserable condition of our social services and infrastructure and, in particular, the water service and supply, which is a basic requirement for life;

7. The ill-trained and ill-prepared army—despite the enormous amount of money that has been spent on it—and the impotence of its commander-in-chief, which were clearly exposed during the Gulf War;

8. The suspension of Islamic law and its replacement with man-man law;

9. In regard to foreign policy, the report exposed not only how this policy has disregarded Islamic issues and ignored Muslims but also how help and support have been provided to the enemy against Muslims. The cases of Gaza-Ariha [Jericho] and the communists in the south of Yemen are still fresh in memory, and more can be said.

As stated by knowledgeable people, it is no secret that using man-made law instead of Islamic law to support the infidels against Muslims is one of the ten "voiders" that strip a person [of] his Islamic status. The Almighty said: "Those who do not judge/govern according to what God has sent down are unbelievers" (Q 5:44), and "By your Lord, they will not be true believers until they let you decide between them in all matters of dispute, and find no resistance in their souls to your decisions, accepting them totally" (Q 4:65).

Despite the fact that the memorandum was written in a gentle and diplomatic style; despite the fact that it reminded [readers] of Allah and offered truthful and sincere advice; despite the emphasis in Islam on the importance of heeding the advice given to those in charge of the people; and despite the substantial number of people who signed this document as well as their supporters—none of this counted in favor of the memorandum. Instead, its content was rejected and those who signed it and their sympathizers were ridiculed, prevented from traveling, punished, and even jailed.

Thus, it is quite clear that advocates of the reform movement have been intent on using peaceful means to protect the unity of the country and to prevent bloodshed. Why, then, has the regime closed off all peaceful routes [of expression], pushing the people toward armed action as the only remaining choice to implement righteousness and justice?!

Who benefits from Prince Sultan and Prince Nayef pushing the country toward a civil war that will destroy everything? Why are those who ignite internal feuds, playing people off against one another and provoking policemen, the sons of the nation, consulted to abort the reform movement?! And why are traitors who implement the policy of the enemy in order to bleed the financial and the human resources of the umma, as well as the main enemy in the area—the American Zionist alliance—left to enjoy peace and security?!

Zaki Badr—the Egyptian ex-minister of the interior and advisor to Prince Nayef, the minister of interior—was not acceptable even to his own country. He was sacked from his position [in Egypt] on account of his abominable attitude and the aggression he exercised against his own people, yet was warmly welcomed by Prince Nayef to help carry out sins and aggressions [in Saudi Arabia]. He has unjustly filled the prisons with the best sons of the umma and afflicted their mothers with misery. Does the regime want to play civilians off against military personnel and vice versa, as has happened in some neighboring countries?!! No doubt this is the policy of the American-Israeli alliance, because they are the primary beneficiaries of this situation.

But with the grace of Allah, both civilians and military individuals—the majority of the nation—are aware of this wicked plan. They have refused to be played off against one another and to be used by the regime as a tool to carry out the policy of the American-Israeli alliance through their agent in our country: the Saudi regime.

Therefore everyone has agreed that the situation cannot be rectified—when the rod is crooked, its shadow cannot be straightened—unless the root of the problem is tackled. Hence, it is essential to hit the main enemy who has divided the umma into small, fragmented countries and pushed it into a state of confusion over the past few decades. The Zionist-Crusader alliance has moved quickly to contain and abort any reform movement that appears in Islamic countries. Different means and methods have been used to reach its objective. On occasion, the movement is dragged into armed struggle at an unfavorable time and place. At times, officials from the Ministry of Interior—who are also graduates of colleges of Islamic law—are unleashed to mislead and confuse the nation by issuing false fatwas and circulating misinformation about the movement. At other times, righteous people have been tricked into a war of words with the 'ulama and the leaders of the movement, thereby wasting the energy of the nation in discussions of minor issues while ignoring the critical issue, that is, the unification of the people under the divine law of Allah.

These discussions and arguments cast a shadow that hides truthfulness under falsity. Personal feuds and partisanship are created among the people, thereby increasing division and further weakening the umma. The priorities of Islam are lost while the grip of blasphemy and polytheism tightens over the umma. We must be alert to the nefarious plans hatched by the Ministry of Interior and ready to follow what has been decided by the people of knowledge. As Ibn Taymiyya (may Allah's mercy be upon him) said, "People of Islam should join forces and support each other to get rid of the main kufr who is controlling the countries of the Islamic world, even to bear the lesser damage to get rid of the major one, that is, the great kufr."

If there is more than one duty to be carried out, then the most important one should receive priority. Clearly after belief (*iman*), there is no more important duty than expelling the American enemy from the Holy Land. No other priority with the exception of belief should be considered more important. As Ibn Taymiyya stated, "To fight in defense of religion and belief is a collective duty according to consensus; there is no other duty after belief than fighting the enemy who is corrupting life and the religion. There [are] no preconditions for this duty and the enemy should be fought with one's best abilities." If it is not possible to expel the enemy except by the collective movement of the Muslim people, then there is a duty on Muslims to ignore the minor differences among themselves. The ill effect of ignoring such differences at a given period of time is much less than the damage from the occupation of Muslims' land by the kuffar. Ibn Taymiyya explained this issue and emphasized the importance of dealing with the major threat at the expense of the minor one. He described the situation of the Muslims and the mujahidin, stating that even military personnel who do not practice Islam are not exempted from the duty of jihad against the enemy.

After mentioning the Mongols and how they contravened Islamic law, Ibn Taymiyya stated that the ultimate aim of pleasing Allah, raising His word, instituting His religion, and obeying His messenger (peace be upon him) is to fight the enemy fully in every aspect. If the danger to religion from not fighting is greater than that of fighting, then it is a duty to fight even if the intentions of some of the fighters are not pure (i.e., they fight for the sake of personal gain) or they do not observe some of the rules and commandments of Islam. To repel the greater of the two dangers at the expense of the lesser one is an Islamic principle that should be observed. The tradition of the People of the sunna permits Muslims to join with and fight alongside righteous and non-righteous men. Allah may sustain Islam through righteous and non-righteous people, as is told by the Prophet (peace be upon him). If it is not possible to fight except with the help of nonrighteous military personnel and commanders, then there are two possibilities. Either fighting will be ignored and those who are the great danger to this life and religion will take control, or fighting will take place with the help of nonrighteous rulers [with the result that] the greatest of the two dangers will be repelled and most, though not all, of Islamic law will be implemented. In the current circumstances and in many other similar situations, the latter option is the right duty. In fact, many of the fights and conquests that took place after the time of the Rashidun, the rightly guided imams, were of this type.

No one, not even a blind or a deaf person, can deny the pervasive presence of corruption or the prevalence of great sins that have reached the point of grievous iniquity, that is, polytheism sharing with Allah His exclusive right of sovereignty and the authority to make law. The Almighty stated: "Luqman counseled his son, 'My son, do not attribute any partners to God: attributing partners to him is a terrible wrong'" (Q 31:13). Man-made laws were produced that permitted what God had forbidden, such as *riba* (usury) and other matters. Banks dealing in usury are competing within the Land of the Two Holy Places and declare war against Allah by disobeying his order: "God has allowed trade and forbidden usury" (Q 2:276). All this is taking place in the vicinity of the Holy Mosque in the Holy Land! In the Qur'an, Allah made a unique promise to Muslims who deal in usury that had not been offered to any other sinner: "You who believe, beware of God: give up any outstanding dues from usury, if you are true believers. If you do not, then be warned of war from God and His Messenger" (Q 2:278–79). If this is meant for the "Muslim" who deals in usury and believes it is a sin, what is it to a person who makes himself a partner and equal to Allah, legalizing usury and other sins that have been forbidden by Allah? Despite all of the above, the government continues to mislead and divert some of the righteous 'ulama and preachers from the issue of objecting to the greatest sins and kufr. We bemoan this and can only say: "There is no power or strength except through God."

Under such circumstances, to expel the enemy—the greatest kufr—out of the country is a primary duty, and no obligation other than belief is more important. Utmost efforts should be made to prepare and mobilize the umma against the enemy, the American-Israeli alliance, which occupies the Country of the Two Holy Places and the route of the Apostle (may Allah's blessings and salutations be upon him) to the Furthest Mosque (Al-Aqsa Mosque [in Jerusalem]). Muslims must also remember to refrain from engaging in an internal war among themselves, as that will have grievous consequences, namely:

1. Consumption of Muslims' human resources, as most casualties and fatalities will be among the Muslim people

2. Exhaustion of economic and financial resources

3. Destruction of the country's infrastructure

4. Divisions within society

5. Destruction of the oil industries: the presence of American Crusader military forces on land, sea, and air in Islamic Gulf states is the greatest danger threatening the world's largest oil reserve. The presence of these forces in the area is an aggression against Muslims' religion and

feelings of pride and will provoke them to take up arms to struggle against the invaders occupying the land. The spread of such fighting in the region will expose the oil wealth to the danger of being burned up. The economic interests of the Gulf States and the Land of the Two Holy Places will be damaged, and an even greater damage will be inflicted on the world economy. I would like here to alert my brothers, the mujahidin, the sons of the nation, to protect this (oil) wealth and not attack it, as it is a great Islamic asset and a substantial economic resource essential to the soon-to-be established Islamic state, with Allah's permission and grace. We also warn the aggressors, the United States, against burning this Islamic wealth. They may commit this crime in order to prevent the oil from falling in the hands of its legitimate owners at the end of the war and to inflict economic damage on America's European or Far Eastern competitors (especially Japan, the major consumer of the region's oil).

6. Division of the Land of the Two Holy Places, and Israeli annexation of its northern part: dividing the Land of the Two Holy Places has been an essential goal of the Zionist-Crusader alliance. A large country with huge resources under the leadership of the coming Islamic state (by Allah's grace) represents a serious danger to the very existence of the Zionist state in Palestine. The noble Ka'ba—the qibla of all Muslims—makes the Land of the Two Holy Places a symbol of the unity of the Islamic world. In addition, the presence of the world's largest oil reserves makes the Land of the Two Holy Places an important economic power in the Islamic world. The sons of the Two Holy Places are directly related to the conduct of their forefathers, the companions (may Allah be pleased with them). They consider their forefathers' conduct a source and example for reestablishing the greatness of the umma and raising the word of Allah again. Furthermore, the existence of a population of fighters in south Yemen struggling in the cause of Allah is a strategic threat to the Zionist-Crusader alliance in the area. The Prophet (peace be upon him) said: "Around twelve thousand will emerge from Aden/Abian [in Yemen] helping the cause of Allah and His messenger; they are the best in the time between me and them" (narrated by Ahmad with correct and trustworthy references).

7. An internal war is a great mistake, no matter what reasons there may be for it. The occupier, America, will control the outcome of the battle for the benefit of the international kufr.

I address now my brothers in the security and military forces and the national guard—may Allah protect you for Islam and the Muslim people:

O you grandsons of Sa'd ibn Abi Waqqas, al-Muthanna ibn Haritha al-Shaybani, al-Qa'qa ibn 'Amr al-Tamimi, and those pious companions [of the Prophet] who fought jihad alongside them: you competed to join the army and the guards with the intention of carrying out jihad in the path of Allah—raising His word—and defending the faith of Islam and the Land of the Two Holy Places against invaders and occupying forces. That is the ultimate level of belief in this religion. But the regime reversed these principles and their understanding, humiliating the umma and disobeying Allah. Half a century ago, the rulers promised the umma that they would regain the first qibla [Jerusalem], but fifty years later a new generation has arrived and the promises have been changed. Al-Aqsa Mosque [in Jerusalem] was handed over to the Zionists, and the wounds of the umma are still bleeding there.[22]

At this time, when the umma has not regained the first qibla, the route of the journey of the Prophet (Allah's blessings and salutations may be on him), the Saudi regime has betrayed the umma in its remaining sanctuaries, the Holy city of Mecca and the mosque of the Prophet (al-Masjid al-Nabawi), by calling in the Christian army to defend the regime and permitting the Crusaders to be in the Land of the Two Holy Places. Not surprisingly, the king himself wore the cross on his chest. The country was opened wide to the Crusaders from the north to the south, and from the east to the west. The land was filled with the military bases of the United States and its allies. The regime became unable to keep control without the help of these bases. You know more than anyone else the size, intention, and the danger of the presence of American military bases in the area.

The regime betrayed the umma and joined the kufr, assisting and helping them against Muslims. It is well known that this is one of the ten "voiders" of Islam, deeds of de-Islamization. By opening the Arab peninsula to the Crusaders, the regime disobeyed and acted against what has been enjoined by the messenger of Allah (Allah's blessings and salutations may be on him), while he was on his deathbed: "Expel the polytheists out of the Arab Peninsula" (narrated by al-Bukhari) and "If I survive, Allah willing, I will expel the Jews and the Christians out of the Arab Peninsula" (*Sahih al-Jami' al-Saghir*).

It is outdated and no longer acceptable to claim that the presence of the Crusaders is a necessity and only a temporary measure to protect the Land of the Two Holy Places. Especially when the civil and military infrastructures of Iraq were savagely destroyed—showing the depths of the Zionist-Crusader hatred of Muslims and their children—and the idea of replacing the Crusader forces by an Islamic force composed of the sons of the country and other Muslims has been rejected. Moreover, the foundations of the claim and the claim itself have been demolished and wiped out by the sequence of speeches given by the leaders of the kuffar in America. The latest of these speeches was given by William

---

[22]Although the direction Muslims now face for prayer is Mecca, the first qibla established by Muhammad was Jerusalem.

Perry, the secretary of defense, after the explosion in al-Khobar, in which he said that the presence of American solders there is to protect the interests of the United States. The imprisoned Shaykh Safar al-Hawali—may Allah hasten his release—wrote a book of seventy pages in which he presented evidence and proof that the presence of the Americans in the Arab Peninsula is a preplanned military occupation. The regime wants to deceive the Muslim people in the same way that the Palestinian fighters were deceived, resulting in the loss of al-Aqsa Mosque. In AH 1304 (1936), the awakened Muslim nation of Palestine started its great struggle, jihad, against the British occupying forces. Britain was impotent to stop these mujahidin and their jihad, but their devil conspired to stop the armed struggle in Palestine through its agent, King 'Abd al-'Aziz, who managed to deceive the mujahidin. King 'Abd al-'Aziz carried out his duty to his British masters: he sent his two sons to meet the mujahidin leaders and to inform them that King 'Abd al-'Aziz would guarantee the promises made by the British government to leave and respond positively to the demands of the mujahidin if they stopped their jihad. And so King 'Abd 'Aziz caused the loss of the first qibla of the Muslim people. The king joined the Crusaders against Muslims and, rather than supporting the mujahidin in the cause of Allah—the liberation of al-Aqsa Mosque—he disappointed and humiliated them.

Today, his son, King Fahd, is trying to deceive Muslims for the second time to surrender what is left of the sanctuaries. When the Islamic world resented the arrival of Crusader forces to the Land of the Two Holy Places, the king lied to the 'ulama (who issued fatwas about the arrival of the Americans) and to the Islamic leaders gathered at the conference of Rabita held in the holy city of Mecca. The King said that "the issue is simple, the American and alliance forces will leave the area in few months." It is now seven years since their arrival and the regime is not able to move them out of the country. The regime has not admitted this inability and continues to lie to the people, claiming that the Americans will leave. But never—never again. A believer will not be bitten twice from the same hole or snake! Happy is one who takes note of the sad experience of others!!

Instead of motivating the army, the guards, and the security men to oppose the occupiers, the regime used these men to protect the invaders, further deepening the humiliation and the betrayal. We bemoan this and can only say: "There is no power or strength except through God." To those small groups of men within the army, police, and security forces, who have been tricked and pressured by the regime to attack Muslims and spill their blood, we would like to remind them of the Tradition: "I promise war against those who take my friends as their enemy" (narrated by al-Bukhari) and the saying of the Prophet (may Allah's blessings and salutations be upon him): "On the day of judgment a man comes holding another and complaining of being slain by him. Allah, blessed be His Names, asks: Why did you slay him?! The accused replies: I did so that all exaltation may be Yours. Allah, blessed be His Names, says: All exaltation is indeed mine! Another man comes holding a fourth with a similar complaint. Allah, blessed be His Names, asks: Why did you kill him?! The accused replies: I did so that exaltation may be for Mr. X! Allah, blessed be His Names, says: exaltation is mine, not for Mr. X, carry all the slain man's sins and proceed to the hell-fire!" ( In another wording of al-Nasa'i: "The accused says: for strengthening the rule or kingdom of Mr. X.")

Today your brothers and sons, the sons of the Two Holy Places, have started their jihad in the cause of Allah to expel the occupying enemy from the Country of the Two Holy Places. And there is no doubt you would like to carry out this mission too, in order to reestablish the greatness of this umma and to liberate its occupied sanctuaries. Nevertheless, it must be obvious to you that, because of the imbalance of power between our armed forces and the enemy forces, a suitable means of fighting must be adopted, that is, using fast-moving light forces that work in complete secrecy. In other words, initiate guerrilla warfare conducted by the sons of the nation and not the military forces. And, as you know, it is wise, in the present circumstances, for the armed military forces not to be engaged in conventional fighting with the forces of the Crusader enemy unless a great advantage is likely to be achieved, and great losses induced on the enemy side that would shake and destroy its foundations and infrastructures that will help expel the defeated enemy from the country. The exceptions are bold and forceful operations carried out by the members of the armed forces individually, that is, without the movement of the formal forces in their conventional shape, so the responses will not be directed strongly against the army.

The mujahidin, your brothers and sons, request that you support them in every possible way by supplying them with the necessary information, materials, and arms. In particular, security men are asked to protect the mujahidin and to assist them as much as possible against the occupying enemy; and to spread rumors, fear, and discouragement among the members of the enemy forces.

We bring to your attention that the regime, in order to create friction and feuds between the mujahidin and yourselves, might resort to taking deliberate action against personnel of the security, guards, and military forces and blame the mujahidin for these actions. The regime should not be allowed to have such an opportunity.

The regime is fully responsible for what has befallen the country and the nation; however, the occupying American enemy is the principal and main cause of the situation. Therefore, efforts should be concentrated on destroying, fighting, and killing the enemy until, by the grace of

Allah, it is completely defeated. The time will come—by the permission of Allah—when you will perform your decisive role so that the word of Allah will be supreme and the word of the infidels (*kafirun*) will be inferior. You will hit the aggressors with an iron fist. You will reestablish the normal course [of things], give the people their rights and carry out your true Islamic duty. Allah willing, I will talk about these issues separately.

My Muslim Brothers, particularly those of the Arab peninsula: the money you pay to buy American goods will be transformed into bullets and used against our brothers in Palestine and, in the future, against our sons in the Land of the Two Holy Places. By buying these goods, we are strengthening their economy while increasing our own dispossession and poverty.

Muslim Brothers of the Land of the Two Holy Places: it is incredible that our country is the world's largest buyer of arms from the United States and the area's biggest commercial partner with the Americans who assist their Zionist brothers in occupying Palestine and evicting and killing the Muslims there by providing arms, men, and financial support.

To deny these occupiers the enormous revenues from trading with our country is very important in helping our jihad against them. To express our anger and hate to them is a very important moral gesture. By doing so, we take part in the process of cleansing our sanctuaries from the Crusaders and the Zionists and forcing them, by the permission of Allah, to leave disappointed and defeated.

We expect the women of the Land of the Two Holy Places and other countries to carry out their role in boycotting American goods. If economic boycotts are combined with the military operations of the mujahidin, then defeating the enemy will be even nearer, with Allah's permission. However, if Muslims do not cooperate to support their mujahidin brothers, then, in effect, they are supplying the army of the enemy with financial help, extending the war, and increasing the suffering of Muslims.

The security and the intelligence services of the entire world cannot force a single citizen to buy the goods of his or her enemy. Economic boycotts of American goods are very effective weapons to hit and weaken the enemy, and they are not under the control of the security forces of the regime.

Before closing my talk, I have a very important message to the youths of Islam, men of the brilliant future of the umma of Muhammad (peace be upon him). Our talk with the youths is about their duty at this difficult period in the history of our umma, a period in which the youths and no one else have come forward to fulfill variable and different duties. While some well-known individuals have hesitated in their duty to defend Islam to save themselves and their wealth from the injustice, aggression, and terror exercised by the government, the youths (may Allah protect them) came forward and raised the banner of jihad against the American-Zionist alliance occupying the sanctuaries of Islam. Others who have been tricked into loving this materialistic world, and those who have been terrorized by the government, choose to grant legitimacy to the greatest betrayal—the occupation of the Land of the Two Holy Places. We bemoan this and can only say: "There is no power or strength except through God." We are not surprised by the action of our youths: such youths were companions of Muhammad (Allah's blessings and salutations may be on him). And did such youths not kill Abu Jahl, the pharaoh of this umma? Our youths are the best descendants of the best ancestors.

'Abd al-Rahman ibn 'Awf—may Allah be pleased with him—said: "I was at Badr[23] where I noticed two youths, one to my right and the other to my left. One of them asked me quietly (so not to be heard by the other): O uncle, point out Abu Jahl to me. What do you want him for? said 'Abd al-Rahman. The boy answered: I have been informed that he—Abu Jahl—abused the Messenger of Allah. I swear by Allah, who has my soul in His hand, that if I see Abu Jahl I'll not let my shadow depart his shadow until one of us is dead. I was astonished, said 'Abd al-Rahman; then the other youth said the same thing as the first one. Subsequently I saw Abu Jahl among the people; I said to the boys, do you see? This is the man you are asking me about. The two youths hit Abu Jahl with their swords till he was dead." Allah is the greatest, praise be to Him: two young men with great perseverance, enthusiasm, courage, and pride for the religion of Allah, each one asking about the most important act of killing that should be inflicted on the enemy, that is, the killing of Abu Jahl, the pharaoh [despot] of the umma and leader of the unbelievers at the Battle of Badr. The role of 'Abd al-Rahman ibn 'Awf, may Allah be pleased with him, was to direct the two youths toward Abu Jahl. That was the perseverance and enthusiasm of the youth of that time and that was the perseverance and enthusiasm of their fathers. It is this role that is now required from the people who have expertise and knowledge in fighting the enemy. They should guide their brothers and sons in this matter; once that has been done, our youth will repeat what their forefathers said before: "I swear by Allah, if I see him I'll not let my shadow depart from his shadow until one of us is dead."

And the story of 'Abd al-Rahman ibn 'Awf about Umayya ibn Khalaf shows the extent of Bilal's (may Allah be pleased with him)

---

[23]The Battle of Badr (624) was the first major battle of the nascent Muslim community in which Muhammad led his Medinan followers to victory over Meccan nonbelievers.

persistence in killing the head of the Kufr: "The head of Kufr is Umayya ibn Khalaf. . . . I shall live not if he survives," said Bilal.

A few days ago, news agencies reported that the defense secretary of the Crusading Americans had said that "the explosions at Riyadh and al-Khobar had taught him one lesson, and that is not to withdraw when attacked by cowardly terrorists."

We say to the defense secretary: your talk could induce laughter in a grieving mother! It reveals the fears that envelop you all. Where was this false courage of yours when the explosion in Beirut took place on 1983 (AH 1403)? At that time, you were turned into scattered bits and pieces; 241 soldiers—mainly marines—were killed. And where was this courage of yours when two explosions forced you from Aden in less than twenty-four hours?!

But your most disgraceful conduct was in Somalia where, after vigorous propaganda about American power and its post–cold war leadership of the new world order, you moved tens of thousands of international forces into Somalia, including 28,000 American soldiers. But when tens of your soldiers were killed in minor battles and one American pilot was dragged through the streets of Mogadishu, you left the area in disappointment, humiliation, defeat, carrying your dead with you. Clinton appeared in front of the whole world threatening and promising revenge, but such threats were merely a preparation for withdrawal. You have been disgraced by Allah and you withdrew; the extent of your impotence and weaknesses became very clear. It brought pleasure to the heart of every Muslim, and a remedy to the chests of believing nations to see you defeated in three Islamic cities: Beirut, Aden, and Mogadishu.

I say to the secretary of defense: the sons of the Land of the Two Holy Places came out to fight the Russian in Afghanistan, the Serb in Bosnia-Herzegovina, and today are fighting in Chechnya and—by the permission of Allah—they have been victorious over your partner, the Russians. By the command of Allah, they are also fighting in Tajikistan.

I say: because the sons of the Land of the Two Holy Places feel and strongly believe that fighting (jihad) against the kuffar in every part of the world is absolutely essential, they will be even more enthusiastic, more powerful and larger in numbers fighting on their own land—the place of their births—defending the greatest of their sanctuaries, the noble Ka'ba, the qibla of all Muslims. They know that Muslims of the world will assist and help them to victory. To liberate their sanctuaries is the greatest of issues concerning all Muslims; it is the duty of every Muslim in this world.

I say to you William [Perry]: these youths love death as you love life. They inherited dignity, pride, courage, generosity, truthfulness, sacrifice, and steadfastness in war from their ancestors, even from the time of

jahiliyya, before Islam. These values were approved and completed by
the arrival of Islam, as is stated by the messenger of Allah (Allah's
blessings and salutations may be on him): "I have been sent to perfect
the good values" (*Sahih al-Jami' al-Saghir*).

When the pagan King 'Amr ibn Hind tried to humiliate the pagan
'Amr ibn Kulthum, the latter cut off the head of the king with his
sword, rejecting aggression, humiliation, and indignity. If the king
oppresses the people excessively, we refuse to submit to humiliation.

By which legitimacy (or command), O Amru bin Hind, do you want
us to be degraded?!

By which legitimacy (or command), O Amru bin Hind, do you listen
to our foes and disrespect us?!

Our toughness has, O Amru, tired the enemies before you, never
giving in!

Our youths believe in Paradise after death. They believe that taking
part in fighting will not bring their day nearer and staying behind will
not postpone their day either. Exalted be Allah who said: "No soul may
die except with God's permission at a predestined time" (Q 3:145). Our
youths believe in the saying of the messenger of Allah (Allah's blessings
and salutations may be on him): "O boy, I teach a few words. Guard
(guard the cause of, keep the commandments of) Allah, then He guards
you; guard the cause of Allah, then He will be with you; if you ask
(for your need), ask Allah, if you seek assistance, seek Allah's. Know
definitely that if the whole world gathered to (bestow) profit on you
they will not profit you except with what was determined for you by
Allah, and if they gathered to harm you they will not harm you except
with what has been determined for you by Allah. Pen lifted, papers
dried, it is fixed; nothing in these truths can be changed" (*Sahih al-Jami'
al-Saghir*).

Our youths took note of the meaning of the poetic verse: "If death is
a predetermined must, then it is a shame to die cowardly." And the
other poet saying: "Who do not die by the sword will die by other
reasons; many causes are there, but one death."

These youths believe in what has been told by Allah and His messenger (Allah's blessings and salutations be on him) about the greatness
of the reward for mujahidin and martyrs. Allah, the most exalted said:
"He will not let the deeds of those who are killed for His cause come
to nothing; He will guide them and put them into a good state; He
will admit them into the Garden He has already made known to them"
(Q 47:4–6). Allah the exalted also said: "Do not say that those who are
killed in God's cause are dead; they are alive, though you do not realize
it" (Q 2:154). His messenger (Allah's blessings and salutations be upon
him) said: "for those who strive in His cause Allah has prepared a
hundred degrees (levels) in Paradise; the difference between two degrees
is as the distance between heaven and earth" (*Sahih al-Jami' al-Saghir*).

He (Allah's blessings and salutations be upon him) also said: "The best of the martyrs are those who do not turn their faces away from the battle until they are killed. They are in the high level of Jannah (Paradise). Their Lord laughs at them (in pleasure), and when your Lord laughs to a slave of His, He will not hold him to account" (narrated by Ahmad with correct and trustworthy references). And: "A martyr will not feel the pain of death except how you feel when you are pinched" (*Sahih al-Jami' al-Saghir*). He also said: "A martyr's privileges are guaranteed by Allah; forgiveness with the first gush of his blood, he will be shown his seat in Paradise, he will be decorated with the jewels of iman (belief), married off to the beautiful ones, protected from the test in the grave, assured security in the day of judgment, crowned with the crown of dignity, a ruby of which is better than this whole world (dunya) and its entire content, wedded to seventy-two of the pure Houries (beautiful ones of Paradise) and his intercession on behalf of seventy of his relatives will be accepted" (narrated by Ahmad al-Tirmidhi with correct and trustworthy references).

Those youths know that their reward in fighting you, the United States, is double the reward for fighting someone not from the People of the Book [Jews and Christians]. They have no intent other than to enter Paradise by killing you. An infidel and enemy of God like you cannot be in the same hell with his righteous executioner.

Our youths chant and recite the word of Allah, the most exalted: "Fight them: God will punish them at your hands, He will disgrace them, He will help you to conquer them, He will heal the believers' feelings and remove the rage from their hearts" (Q 9:14) and the words of the prophet (peace be upon him): "I swear by Him, who has my soul in His hand, that the man who is killed fighting them today, patiently attacking and not retreating, surely Allah will let him into Paradise." And the Prophet (Allah's blessings and salutations may be on him) said: "Get up to a Paradise as wide as heaven and earth."

The youths also recite the Almighty's words: "When you meet the disbelievers in battle strike them in the neck" (Q 47:4). Those youths will not ask you (William Perry) for explanations, they will tell you, singing, that there is nothing that needs to be explained between us; there is only killing and neck smiting.

And they will say to you what their grandfather, Harun al-Rashid, amir al-mu'minin, replied to your grandfather, Niqfur [Nicephorus I], the Byzantine emperor, when he threatened the Muslims: "From Harun al-Rashid, amir al-mu'minin, to Niqfur, the dog of the Romans—the answer is what you will see, not what you hear." Harun al-Rashid led the armies of Islam to battle and handed a devastating defeat to Niqfur.

The youths you call cowards are competing among themselves to fight and kill you. They recite what one of them has said:

The Crusader army became dust when we detonated al-Khobar.

The courageous youth of Islam fear no danger.
If (they are) threatened: "The tyrants will kill you," they reply:
    "My death is a victory."
I did not betray that king, he betrayed our qibla.
And he permitted in the Holy Country the filthiest kind of humans.
I have made an oath by Allah the Great to fight whoever rejects the
    faith.

For more than a decade, they carried arms on their shoulders in
Afghanistan, and they have made vows to Allah that as long as they are
alive, they will continue to carry arms against you until you are—God
willing—expelled, defeated, and humiliated. They will carry on as long
as they live saying:

O William, tomorrow you will know which young man is con-
    fronting your misguided brethren!
A smiling youth fighting, returning with the spear colored red.
May Allah keep me close to knights, humans in peace, demons in
    war.
Lions in the jungle but their teeth are spears and Indian swords.
The horses witness that I push them forward hard in the fire of
    battle.
The dust of the battle bears witness for me, so also the fighting
    itself, the pens and the books!

So abusing the grandsons of the companions, may Allah be pleased
with them, by calling them cowards and challenging them by refusing
to leave the Land of the Two Holy Places, shows the insanity and
imbalance from which you suffer. Its appropriate remedy, however, is
in the hands of the youths of Islam. As the poet said:

I am willing to sacrifice self and wealth for knights who never
    disappoint me.
Knights who are never fed up or deterred by death, even if the mill
    of war turns.
In the heat of battle they do not care, and cure the insanity of the
    enemy by their "insane" courage.

Terrorizing you, while you are carrying arms on our land, is a legitimate
and moral duty. It is a legitimate right well known to all humans and
other creatures. The example for you and for us is the snake that entered
the house of a man and was killed by him; the coward is someone who
lets you walk, while carrying arms, freely on his land and provides you
with peace and security.
    These youths are different from your soldiers. Your problem will be
how to convince your troops to fight, while our problem will be how to

restrain our youths to wait their turn to fight. These youths are commendable and praiseworthy.

They stood tall to defend the religion at a time when the government misled prominent scholars and tricked them into issuing fatwas that have no basis either in the book of Allah or in the sunna of His prophet, Allah's blessings and salutations be upon him, opening the Land of the Two Holy Places to the Christian armies and handing the al-Aqsa Mosque to the Zionists. Twisting the meanings of the holy text will not change this fact at all. They deserve the praise of the poet:

> I rejected all the critics, who chose the wrong way;
> I rejected those who enjoy fireplaces in clubs discussing eternally;
> I rejected those who, despite being lost, think they are at the goal;
> I respect those who carried on not asking or bothering about the
>    difficulties;
> Never letting up from their goals, despite all hardships of the road;
> Whose blood is the oil for the flame which guides in the darkness
>    of confusion;
> I feel still the pain (the loss) of al-Quds [Jerusalem] in my internal
>    organs;
> That loss is like a burning fire in my intestines;
> I did not betray my covenant with God, even when states did
>    betray it!

As their grandfather 'Asim ibn Thabit said, rejecting an offer of surrender from the pagans:

> What an excuse have I to surrender, while I am still able, having
>    arrows and my bow having a tough string?!
> Death is truth and ultimate destiny, and life will end anyway.
> If I do not fight you, then my mother must be insane!

These youths hold you responsible for all of the killings and evictions of Muslims and the violation of the sanctuaries, carried out by your Zionist brothers in Lebanon; you openly supplied them with arms and financing. More than 600,000 Iraqi children have died because of lack of food and medicine and as a result of the unjustifiable aggression (sanctions) imposed on Iraq and its people. The children of Iraq are our children. You, America, together with the Saudi regime, are responsible for the shedding of the blood of these innocent children. Because of all this, whatever treaty you have with our country is now null and void.

The treaty of Hudaybiyya was canceled by the messenger of Allah (may Allah's blessings and salutations be upon him) once the Quraysh [the tribe of the Prophet] had assisted the Banu Bakr [a Jewish tribe] against Khuza'a, the allies of the prophet (may Allah's blessings and salutations be upon him). The prophet (may Allah's blessings and salutations be upon him) fought the Quraysh and conquered Mecca. He (may Allah's blessings and salutations be upon him) considered the treaty with the Banu Bakr void because one of their Jews publicly hurt a Muslim woman, one single woman, at the market—whereas you have killed hundreds of thousands of Muslims and occupied their sanctuaries.

It is now clear that those who claim that the blood of the American soldiers (the enemy occupying the land of the Muslims) should be protected merely repeat what has been imposed on them by the regime; they fear aggression and are interested in saving themselves. It is now a duty on every tribe in the Arabian Peninsula to fight the jihad in the cause of Allah and cleanse the land of those occupiers. Allah knows that their blood is permitted (to be spilled) and their wealth is booty to those who kill them. The most Exalted said in the "verse of the sword": "When the forbidden months are over, wherever you encounter the idolaters, kill them, seize them, besiege them, wait for them at every lookout post" (Q 9:5). Our youths know that the humiliation suffered by Muslims as a result of the occupation of their sanctuaries cannot be removed except by explosions and jihad. As the poet said:

The walls of oppression and humiliation cannot be demolished
    except in a rain of bullets.
The free man does not surrender leadership to infidels and sinners.
Without shedding blood, no degradation and branding can be
    removed from the forehead.

I remind the youths of the Islamic world who fought in Afghanistan and Bosnia-Herzegovina with their wealth, pens, tongues, and themselves, that the battle is not yet finished. I remind them of the exchange between Jibril [the angel Gabriel] and the messenger of Allah (Allah's blessings and salutations may be on both of them) after the Battle of the Joint Forces, when the messenger of Allah (may Allah's blessings and salutations be upon him) returned to Medina. Before the Prophet had put his sword aside, Jibril (may Allah's blessings and salutations be upon him) descended and said: "Are you putting your sword aside? By Allah, the angels have not yet dropped their arms; march with your companions to Banu Qurayza, I am (going) ahead of you to throw fear into their hearts and shake their fortresses around them." Jibril marched with the angels (Allah's blessings and salutations may be upon them all), followed by the messenger of Allah (may Allah's blessings and salutations be upon him) marching with the *muhajirun* (immigrants) and *ansar* (supporters). (Narrated by al-Bukhari)

These youths know that if one is not killed, one will die (anyway), and the most honorable death is to be killed in the way of Allah. They are even more determined after the martyrdom of the four heroes who bombed the Americans in Riyadh, the youths who raised high the head of the umma and humiliated the Americans—the occupier—by their Riyadh operation. They remember the poetry of Ja'far, the second commander in the battle of Mu'ta, in which three thousand Muslims faced over a hundred thousand Romans:

> How good is Paradise and its nearness, good with cool drink
> But the Romans are promised punishment (in Hell),
> If I meet them, I will fight them.

And the poetry of 'Abd Allah ibn Rawaha, the third commander in the battle of Mu'ta, after the martyrdom of Ja'far, when he felt some hesitation:

> O my soul, if you do not get killed, you are going to die anyway.
> This is the death pool in front of you!

[Youths of Islam], you will get what you have wished for (martyrdom), and if you follow the example of the two previous commanders, you are rightly guided!

As for our daughters, wives, sisters, and mothers: they should take as their primary examples the pious female companions (may Allah be pleased with them) of the prophet (may Allah's blessings and salutations be upon him). They should adopt the conduct of the female companions (may Allah be pleased with them), their courage, sacrifice, and generosity in the cause of the supremacy of Allah's religion. They should remember the courage and character of Fatima, daughter of Khattab, when she accepted Islam and stood up in front of her brother, 'Umar ibn al-Khattab [the second caliph, 634–44] and challenged him (before he became a Muslim) saying: "O 'Umar, what will you do if the truth is not in your religion?!" Remember the stand of Asma, daughter of Abu Bakr, on the day of Hijra, when she attended the Messenger and his companion in the cave and split her belt into two pieces for them. Remember the stand of Nasiba bint Ka'b who, striving to defend the messenger of Allah (may Allah's blessings and salutations be upon him) on the day of Uhud, suffered twelve injuries, one of which was so deep it left a lifelong scar! They should remember the generosity of the early women of Islam, who financed the Muslim army by selling their jewelry.

Our women have set a tremendous example of generosity in the cause of Allah; they motivated and encouraged their sons, brothers and husbands to fight in the cause of Allah in Afghanistan, Bosnia-Herzegovina, Chechnya, and other countries. We ask Allah to accept these deeds from them, and may He help their fathers, brothers, husbands, and sons. May Allah strengthen the belief (iman) of our women in the way of generosity and sacrifice for the supremacy of the word of Allah. Our women weep not, except over men who fight in the cause of Allah. Our women exhort their brothers to fight in the cause of Allah. Our women lament only fighters in the cause of Allah, as is said:

> Do not moan on anyone except a lion in the woods, courageous in the burning wars.
> Let me die dignified in wars, honorable death is better than my current life.

Our women encourage jihad, saying:

> Prepare yourself like a struggler, the matter is bigger than words!
> Are you going to leave us for the wolves of Kufr eating our wings?!
> The wolves of Kufr are mobilizing all evil persons from everywhere!
> Where are the free men defending free women by arms?!
> Death is better than life in humiliation!
> Some scandals and shames will never be otherwise eradicated.

My Muslim brothers of the world: your brothers in Palestine and in the Land of the Two Holy Places are calling for your help, asking you to take part in fighting against your enemy and their enemy: the Americans and the Israelis. They are asking you to do whatever you can, with one's own means and ability, to expel the enemy, humiliated and defeated, out of the sanctuaries of Islam. Exalted be to Allah, Who said in His book: "If they seek help from you against persecution, it is your duty to assist them"! (Q 8:72)

O you horses (soldiers) of Allah, ride and march on. This is the time of hardship, so be tough. And know that your gathering and cooperation to liberate the sanctuaries of Islam is the right step toward unifying the word of the umma under the banner of "No God but Allah."

From our place, we raise our palms humbly to Allah, asking Him to bestow on us His guidance in every aspect of this issue.

> Our Lord, we ask you to secure the release of the truthful scholars of Islam and the pious youth of the umma from their imprisonment. O Allah, strengthen them and help their families.
> Our Lord, the People of the Cross have come with their horses (soldiers) and occupied the Land of the Two Holy Places. And the Zionist Jews fiddle as they wish with the al-Aqsa Mosque, the route of the ascent of the messenger of Allah (peace be upon him).
> Our Lord, shatter their gathering, divide them among themselves, shake the earth under their feet and give us control over them.
> Our Lord, we take refuge in you from their deeds and take you as a shield against them.
> Our Lord, show us a black day for them!

Our Lord, show us the wonder of Your power over them!

Our Lord, You are the Revealer of the book, Director of the clouds, You defeated the joint forces (*ahzab*); defeat them and make us victorious over them.

Our Lord, You are the one who helps us and You are the one who assists us; with Your Power we move and by Your Power we fight. On You we rely and You are our cause.

Our Lord, these youths have gathered together to make Your religion victorious and raise Your banner. Our Lord, send them Your help and strengthen their hearts.

Our Lord, make the youths of Islam steadfast, endow them with patience and guide their shots!

Our Lord, unify the Muslims and bestow love among their hearts!

O Lord pour down upon us patience, make our steps firm and assist us against the unbelieving people!

O Lord, do not lay upon us a burden as Thou didst lay upon those before us;

O Lord, do not impose upon us that which we have no strength to bear; pardon us and grant us protection and have mercy on us, Thou art our patron, so help us against the unbelieving people.

O Lord, guide this umma, and make right the conditions (by which) Your servants will be in dignity, the disobedient people in humiliation, the good deeds will be enjoined and the bad deeds forbidden.

O Lord, bless Muhammad, Your slave and messenger, his family, descendants and companions, and salute him with a (becoming) salutation.

And our last supplication is: all praise is due to Allah.

# Chapter 19

## MUHAMMAD 'ATA AL-SAYYID
## 1968–2001

THE SPECTACULAR destruction inflicted on the United States on September 11, 2001, catapulted the stern visage of Muhammad 'Ata al-Sayed onto virtually every front page, magazine cover, television screen, and Web site in the world. An otherwise undistinguished middle-class Egyptian with a degree in architectural engineering, 'Ata was one of five hijackers on American Airlines flight 11, the airplane that tore into the North Tower of the World Trade Center early that morning. In a videotape shot soon thereafter, no less an authority than Usama bin Laden identifies 'Ata by name as the leader of the nineteen Muslim men who meticulously planned, carried out, and died in the attacks that ultimately felled the Twin Towers, crushed parts of the Pentagon, and killed thousands of people (9/11 Commission Report 2004, ch. 5; Bin Laden 2001a). This event is now written into history as inaugurating an American-led "War on Terror," the scope and scale of which are not only transforming the domestic politics of the United States but also reconfiguring the twenty-first-century geopolitical landscape in unprecedented ways.

There is little in the rather mundane details of 'Ata's life that foreshadow the crucial role he would play in precipitating these large-scale convulsions. Indeed, 'Ata's brief life story is in many ways remarkable for being fairly unremarkable. He was born in Kafr al-Shaikh, Egypt, on September 1, 1968. His immediate family included his parents—a homemaker and an attorney—and two sisters, one of whom would go on to become a zoology professor, the other a medical doctor. After graduating from Cairo University with a degree in architectural engineering, he briefly worked as an urban planner in Cairo. In 1992, 'Ata moved to Germany to continue his education, eventually settling on a program in urban planning at the Technical University of Hamburg-Harburg, where he was registered as a student until 1999.

Although fluent in German, 'Ata's experiences in Hamburg appear to have catalyzed a religious, political, and personal radicalization. The precise nature and extent of this transformation are elusive, obscured by the tendency of hindsight to conjure linear narratives out of the contradictions and lacunae a human life inevitably leaves behind. At one moment, 'Ata is said to be a middling student, overshadowed by his accomplished older sisters; at another, he is described as clever and intellectual, a perfectionist, his master's thesis on urban planning in Aleppo, Syria, as first-rate. Observers have characterized him as abrasive and sullen, but also as polite and shy; his demeanor and appearance were said to be scary, elegant, or delicate (Wright 2006a, 307). Friends in Egypt do not remember 'Ata as particularly political; the one outburst they recall was laced with contempt for violent Islamists. By contrast, those who knew 'Ata in Germany vividly remember his intense focus on politics, as well as his increasingly strident criticisms of Arab regimes, American arrogance, and "global Jewish" power.

'Ata took an extended break from his studies in Hamburg in 1995, and told his thesis adviser that he had taken the hiatus to perform the hajj (pilgrimage) to Mecca. What is known for certain is that 'Ata had become increasingly active in Muslim student organizations in the late 1990s, as well as a crucial member of the so-called Hamburg cell, a fluid group of Islamist students in Germany, many of whom would be crucial to the 9/11 hijacking operation. It is also clear that he traveled to Afghanistan in November 1999 and that he evinced a consistent discomfort with women throughout this period of time ('Ata's faculty adviser recalls him refusing to shake the hand of a female colleague when she attempted to congratulate him upon completing his thesis) (Cloud 2001; 9/11 Commission Report 2004, ch. 5; Tiemann 2005; L. Jackson 2001; Wikan 2001). The extensive details that have emerged about the activities of the al-Qa'ida hijackers in the months, days, and moments leading up to September 11—the ATM machines they used, the flying lessons they took, the last meals they consumed—add little reliable definition to this sketchy portrait.

On the one hand, the scanty facts of 'Ata's life are a poor guide to why he and his compatriots undertook the deadly mission that would end their own lives and the lives of so many others. On the other hand, 'Ata's posthumous notoriety has brought into sharp relief certain patterns in the profiles of those Muslim men consistently willing to heed the call (da'wa) to martyrdom (shahada). Contrary to popular belief, for example, most of the men who organize or carry out martyrdom operations are not impoverished products of parochial madrasas.[1] Rather they are, like 'Ata, middle class, somewhat cosmopolitan, and often quite well educated, predominantly in the natural and applied sciences. Ayman al-

---

[1]Bergen and Pandey 2001, 117–18; Bergen 2001, 27–28. Much has been made of the participation of several women in martyrdom operations, particularly since 2002, when Wafa Idris became the first Palestinian *shahida* (female martyr) to blow herself up. This is neither a new nor unique phenomenon: women have been participants in the violent operations of groups ranging from Germany's Baader-Meinhof gang to the Tamil Tigers, among others. Mia Bloom reports that, of the seventeen groups that currently employ this tactic, "women have been operatives in more than half of them in the Middle East, in Sri Lanka, in Turkey, in Chechnya, and in Columbia" (Bloom 2005, 143–65). Still, the number of occasions in which Muslim women become such "human bombs" remains rare for reasons too complex to enumerate here (Patkin 2004; Copeland 2002).

Zawahiri, widely considered al-Qa'ida's second in command, is a doctor; Mohammed Saddiq Odeh, convicted in connection of the bombing of the American Embassy in Nairobi, studied architecture and engineering in the Philippines; a confederate of 'Ata's, Ziad Jarrahi, was a student at Hamburg's University of Applied Sciences; and Khalid Shaykh Muhammad, said to be crucial to the planning of both 9/11 and the murder of journalist Daniel Pearl, is an engineer (Golden, Moss, and Yardley 2001).[2]

The relative financial stability and education of these men, coupled with the often methodical long-range planning involved in such attacks, further challenge the presumption that those who organize and execute martyrdom operations are by definition insane, irrational, brainwashed, broken by poverty, or otherwise unable to fathom the nature of what they do. The resilience of this assumption in the face of counterveiling evidence has prompted some social scientists to argue that, far from being irrational, such men are strategic rational actors who behave in ways that maximize the chances of obtaining the ends they seek (Bloom 2005; Pape 2005; Gambetta 2005). Yet neither 'Ata nor those like him appear to be engaged in a rational cost-benefit calculus in which martyrdom, for example, buys entry into Paradise. Paradise is promised, but not as payment for services rendered; just as Karl Marx had argued that the triumph of communism is both necessary and contingent on human action, so the inevitable victory of Allah's will requires from His servants deeds that evince great faith, humility, obedience, and discipline. As Sayyid Qutb has argued, divine rewards in this life and the next are far from guaranteed:

> [Allah's wisdom] guarantees that believers will see the signposts along the road clearly and starkly, for [God's wisdom] establishes the course for those who wish to traverse this road to its end, whatever that end may be. Thus, the fate of their mission and of their very lives will be whatever Allah wills. . . . if God intends to actualize His mission and His religion, only He will do so, but not as recompense for human suffering and sacrifices. (Qutb 1991, 184)

The motivations of those who leave deep scars in history are frequently difficult to comprehend in hindsight. This is particularly true of 'Ata, who apparently left behind no diary or memoirs, and whose legacy—unlike that of Qutb, for example—is in the realm of action rather than words, violence rather than reflection. It is perhaps paradoxical, then, that the greatest insight into 'Ata's view of the world is provided by two documents he left behind, a will drawn up in April 1996, and a copy of

---

[2]Weiser and Golden 2001.The apparent affinity of Islamists for advanced education in the sciences has been well documented. Sociological studies have long noted, for example, that Egyptian Islamist groups have drawn much of their membership from universities, disproportionately from among students of engineering, medicine, agricultural science, technical military science, and pharmacy (Ibrahim 1980, 440).

final instructions[3] found in his suitcase by U.S. authorities on September 18.[4] ʿAta's will is little more than a set of highly specific directives for those in charge of conducting his death rites, yet it communicates two things particularly clearly. The first is an investment in the strictest adherence to what he takes to be correct Islamic practice. The second is a palpable discomfort with the opposite sex, a preoccupation with containing women's presence and disciplining their behavior so pronounced that one commentator has characterized the will as "a study in obsessive carnality" (Dickey 2005).[5]

Gender is equally central to the final instructions for hijackers, which might well be described as an exercise in restorative masculinity—an exhortation to what Machiavelli once described as *virtú*, that is, great deeds that are simultaneously a means to recuperate, and an enactment of, virility.[6] The author urges his compatriots to master themselves, purify their carnal impulses, discipline their unruly souls, sharpen their knives for the slaughter or sacrifice (*dhabh*), and heed the call of the hur ʿayn (the black-eyed ones; often rendered as "heavenly brides") awaiting them in Paradise.[7] Such directives seem to be less concerned with strategy and tactics than with rituals conducive to, in essence, "girding the loins" of the men who are to die. Like Bin Laden (see chapter 18), ʿAta's writing tends to represent women as a measure or mirror of masculinity: they figure either as virginal rewards for the courageous martyr in the afterlife or—in the will—as silent symbols of impurity in this one.

As scholars have noted, the language of the "Final Instructions" is often brutally crass or simple-mindedly therapeutic. Moreover, its con-

---

[3]This document is often referred to as the "Suicide Note" (see, e.g., Rubin and Rubin 2002) despite the fact that the word never appears in the document, and that it is clearly written by and for those who regarded themselves as martyrs and adherents of a system of belief in which suicide is prohibited. The admittedly inelegant "Final Instructions" avoids this anachronism.

[4]While the document is routinely attributed to the leader of the mission, ʿAta's name does not appear on it as author, and the copy in ʿAta's suitcase was only one of three discovered by the FBI after the attack. See Kippenberg 2005, for a discussion of various theories about the author and provenance of the document. A facsimile of four of the original Arabic pages released by the FBI (press reports suggest that the full document is five pages), and the three locations where they were found can be viewed at http://www.fbi.gov/press rel/pressrel01/letter.htm.

[5]The original Arabic text of ʿAta's will has not been released, although *Der Spiegel* published a complete German translation of the document in October 2001, an English version of which is available at www.abc.net.au/4corners/atta/resources/documents/will1.htm.

[6]In the context in which Machiavelli uses it, virtú (derived from the Latin "vir," for manliness) is a play on the word "virtue," but it is deliberately meant to evoke images of masculine prowess rather than what was conventionally understood as moral behavior (Machiavelli, *Il Principe*).

[7]Kanan Makiya and Hassan Mneimneh provide a detailed analysis of the hijacker's choice of *dhabh* (with the implication of sacrificing an animal) rather than *qatala* (to kill). Makiya and Mneimneh 2002, reprinted in Silvers and Epstein 2002, 303–27. See also Lincoln 2003, 8–18.

ceptual framework is unyieldingly rigid, and the religious instructions it contains have been stripped of their conventional moral scaffolding. Nevertheless, the document provides a window onto a worldview in which Islam is not simply a repository for reflexive rage or rhetorical camouflage for what are essentially socioeconomic grievances, but rather a particular lens on religion, history, geopolitics, and power. In this worldview, men and women, the heavenly and the earthbound, Muslim and non-Muslim, the righteous and the unjust, figure as players in an epic confrontation in which an aerial assault on Manhattan skyscrapers and a retaliatory raid by the Prophet and his Companions in seventh-century Arabia are part of a single continuous drama.

Toward this end, the document repeatedly invokes the rituals and rules of early Muslim raids (*ghazawat*, sing. *ghazwa*) from practices of filial piety to constraints on plundering fallen enemies. The mujahidin destined to commandeer several high-speed jet airliners are instructed to immerse themselves in two particular chapters of the Qur'an, Surat al-Tawba (Q 9: Repentance) and al-Anfal (Q 8: Battle Gains). These tell of ancient battles and treaties, hypocrites and unbelievers, raids and retribution. They simultaneously exhort Muslims to unity of purpose and recall them to humility with the reminder that there are enemies "unknown to you but known to Allah" (Q 8:60) and "God knows all that is hidden" (Q 9:78). Again and again, the hijackers are explicitly and implicitly reminded of the many occasions when the fledgling Muslim community triumphed over much larger forces arrayed against it and are urged to partake of this glorious legacy by joining the present to the past.

In contrast to these elaborately detailed physical, psychological, and spiritual preparations for engagement, the opponent—the West (*gharb*)— toward which all this effort is directed is specified only once in the document, and almost in passing. The author may have thought it strategically prudent to be vague about his target, a logic in keeping with the decision to use only the first letter for *ta'ira* (airplane) and *matar* (airport) throughout the "Final Instructions," rather than write out the Arabic words. Alternatively, the writer might have assumed that, by the time of the fateful day, the intended readership of the document would know firsthand the equipment and technology, as well as the seductions and moral bankruptcy, of Western civilization.

There may be another reason that the Enemy flickers so briefly in these pages, however. This document is, after all, an attempt to conjure a confrontation among archetypes rather than people; once the designation of "Satan's helpers/allies" has been invoked, all further detail becomes an irrelevant distraction. As long as "the West" is both monolithic and indistinct, all in its purview may be implicated in its transgressions. If all are collectively responsible, no one is innocent, and everyone may be legitimately slaughtered, much as animals are sacrificed at an altar. This is the final twist in these final instructions to religious martyrs: having already released themselves from the regularities of time, the burden of history, and the complexity of politics, 'Ata and his brethren here dispense with the encumbrance of moral distinctions between guilt and innocence, military and civilian, collective and individual responsibility.

# FINAL INSTRUCTIONS

ONE OF THE Companions said the Prophet commanded us to read it before the raid, so we read it and were victorious and safe.

## THE LAST NIGHT

1. Mutual pledge to die and renewal of intent.
   - Shaving of excess hair from the body and the application of perfume.
   - Ritual washing.
2. Thorough knowledge of the plan in all its facets, and the expectation of reaction or resistance from the enemy.
3. Recitation of Surat al-Tawbah [Repentance] and al-Anfal [Battle Gains] with attention to their meanings, and what God has prepared for the believers, a high Paradise for martyrs.
4. Reminding the self to listen and obey that night. You will face decisive situations which require listening and obeying 100 percent. You should therefore tame yourself, make it under-stand, convince it, and incite it to action. God has said: "Obey God and his Messenger, and do not quarrel with one another, or you may lose heart and your spirit may desert you. Be steadfast: God is with the steadfast" (Q 8:46).
5. Staying awake through the night and pleading in prayer for victory, enablement, clear triumph, ease of matters, and discretion upon us.
6. Multiplication of invocation. You should know that the best invocation is the recitation of the Holy Qur'an, by the consen-sus [ijma'] of scholars, as far as I know. It suffices for us that it is word of the Creator of the heavens and the earth, toward whom you are heading.
7. Purify your heart and cleanse it of imperfections. Forget and force yourself to forget that thing which is called the World; the time for amusement is gone and the time of truth is upon us. We have wasted so much time in our life. Should we not

use these hours to offer actions that make us closer [to God] and actions of obedience?

8. Keep a positive attitude. There are between you and your departure but a few moments to start the happy God-pleasing life with the prophets, saints, and martyrs, who are the best of companions (Q 4:69). We ask God for his grace. Be optimistic. The Prophet was optimistic in all of his endeavors.

9. Be prepared if you face adversity; how to behave and how to be steadfast, and to regroup, knowing that what has hit you could not have missed you and what has missed you could not have hit you, this being an affliction from God to raise your status and atone for your misdeeds, and know it is but moments before the adversity dissipates, with God's permission. Blessed is he who has won the great reward from God. God has said: "Did you think that you would enter the Garden without God first proving which of you would struggle for His cause and remain steadfast?"(Q 3:142)

10. Remember God's words: "Before you encountered death, you were hoping for it. Well, now you have seen it with your own eyes" (Q 3:143), and remember how often, by God's will, has a small faction vanquished a large faction. And remember His words: "If God helps you [believers], no one can overcome you; if He forsakes you, who else can help you? Believers should put their trust in God" (Q 3:160).

11. Remind yourself and your brothers of the supplications, and consider what their meanings are (the morning and evening invocations, the invocation for the locality, the invocations for [illegible], the invocations for the confrontation of the enemy).

12. [illegible] (with the self, the suitcase, the clothes, the knives, your tools, your ticket, [illegible], your passport, all your papers).

13. Inspect your weapon before you leave, and well before you leave. "Sharpen your blade and relieve your dhabh."

14. Tighten your clothes well as you wear them. This is the way of the righteous predecessors, may God's blessings be upon them. They tightened their clothes as they wore them prior to battle. And tighten your shoes well, and wear socks that hold in the shoes and do not come out of them. These are all prescriptions that we are commanded to follow. For God suffices us and is the best disposer of affairs (Q 3:173).

15. Perform the morning prayer in group, and consider its rewards. Afterward, [perform] the invocations, and do not leave your apartment except in a state of ritual cleanliness. . . . God's words: "Did you think We had created you in vain, and that you would not be brought back to Us?" (Q 23:115).

### AFTER THAT, THE SECOND PHASE

While the taxicab is taking you to the [airport], recite repeatedly the invocations to God (the boarding invocation, the invocation of the town, the invocation of the place, the other invocations).

When you arrive and see the [airport], and get out of the taxicab, recite the invocation of the place. Wherever you go, recite the invocation of the place.

Smile and feel secure, God is with the believers, and the angels are guarding you without you feeling them.

Then recite the supplication: "God is stronger than all His creation" and say: "God, to You is their end and in You we seek refuge from their evil," and say: "[God had] set barriers before and behind them, blocking their vision: they cannot see" (Q 36:9). And say: "God is enough for us: He is the best protector," recalling God's words: "Those whose faith only increased when people said, 'Fear your enemy: they have amassed a great army against you,' and who replied, 'God is enough for us: He is the best protector'" (Q 3:173).

After reciting, you will find events unfolding beyond your power, for God has promised those who recite this supplication:

1. To return with the grace of God
2. Not to suffer any harm
3. To follow God-pleasing deeds

God said: "[They] returned with grace and bounty from God; no harm befell them. They pursued God's good pleasure. God's favor is great indeed" (Q 3:174).

For all their equipment, and all their gates, and all their technology do not do benefit or harm, except with the permission of God.

The believers do not fear them. Those who fear them are the followers of Satan, those who had feared Satan to begin with, and became his followers [illegible] (Q 3:175). Fear is a great act of worship that can be offered only to God, and He is most worthy of it. God said, following the aforementioned verses, it is Satan who causes fear in his followers. These are the admirers of Western civilization, who have drunk their love for it and their hallowing of it with the cool water, and were afraid for their weak feeble stomachs. "Do not fear them, but fear Me, if you are true believers" (Q 3:175). Fear is indeed a great act of worship offered by the followers of God and by the believers only to the One God who rules over all things, with the utmost certitude that God will annul the treachery of the nonbelievers. For God has said: "God will weaken the disbelievers' designs" (Q 8:18).

You also have to perform in your heart one of the highest invocations. It should not be noticeable that you are repeating: "There is no god but God."[8] If you say it a thousand times, no one should be able to distinguish whether you were silent or you were invoking God. An indication of the greatness of this invocation is the Prophet's saying: "He who said, 'There is no god but God,' with belief in his heart will enter Heaven." Or as the Prophet said in the same meaning: "If the seven Heavens and the seven Worlds are placed on the pan of a scale and 'There is no god but God' is placed on the other, the latter would outbalance the former." You can smile while reciting it, for it is a great invocation.

When meditating on it, one notices that none of its letters are dotted. This is another sign of its greatness, because dotted letters and words are inferior to others.

It is sufficient that it is the invocation of God's oneness that you have come to raise and to fight under its banner, as did the Prophet, and his companions, and as do their righteous followers until the day of judgment.

Also, do not show signs of confusion or tension. Be happy and cheerful, be relaxed and feel secure because you are engaged in an action that God loves and is satisfied by it. You will be soon, with God's permission, with heavenly brides (*hur 'ayn*) in Heaven.

Smile in the face of death, oh young man.

You are heading to the Paradise of Eternity.

Wherever you go and whatever you do, you have to persist in invocation and supplication. For God is with his believing servants, protecting them, facilitating their tasks, granting them success, enabling them, providing them with victory and everything.

### The Third Phase

When you board the [airplane], the moment you step foot in it, before entering it, proceed with the invocations, and consider that this is a raid (*ghazwa*) on a path.

As the Prophet said: "A raid or an attack on the path of God is better than this World and what is in it." The Prophet might have said it differently.

When you step into the [airplane] and take your seat, recite the invocations and known supplications that we previously mentioned and keep busy with the repeated invocation of God. God said: "Believers, when you meet a force in battle, stand firm and keep God firmly in mind, so that you may prosper" (Q 8:45). When the [airplane] starts

---

[8]This is the first part of the Shahada, or profession of faith, "There is no god but God and Muhammad is His Messenger." The Shahada is one of the five pillars of Islam.

moving and heads toward [takeoff], recite the supplication of travel, because you are traveling to God, may you be blessed in this travel.

Then you will find that the [airplane] will stop, then will take off. This is the hour of the encounter between the two camps. Recite supplications to God as He states in his Book: "Our Lord, pour patience on us, make us stand firm, and help us against the disbelievers" (Q 2:250). God also said: "All they said was: 'Oh Lord, forgive us our sins and our excesses. Make our feet firm, and give us help against the disbelievers'" (Q 3:147).

The Prophet said: "Oh God, You who are the source of Revelation, who cause the clouds to pass, who have defeated the factions, defeat [our enemies] and make us victorious. Defeat them and cause them to tremble." Recite supplications that you and all your brothers be granted victory, triumph, and the hitting of the target. Do not be afraid.

Ask God to grant you martyrdom while you are on the attack, not in retreat, with perseverance and awareness.

Each one of you should be prepared to fulfill his role in a God-pleasing manner. Clench your teeth, as did the predecessors, God rest their souls, before engaging in battle.

Upon the confrontation, hit as would hit heroes who desire not to return to the World, and loudly proclaim the name of God, that is because the proclamation of the name of God instills terror in the heart of the nonbelievers. God has said: "Strike above their necks and strike all their fingertips" (Q 8:12).

Know that the Heavens have raised their most beautiful decoration for you, and that your heavenly brides are calling you, "Come on follower of God," while wearing their most beautiful jewelry.

If God grants any one of you a slaughter, you should perform it as an offering on behalf of your father and mother, for they are owed by you. Do not disagree among yourselves, but listen and obey.

If you slaughter, you should plunder those you slaughter, for that is one of the sanctioned customs of the Prophet, on the condition that you do not get occupied with the plunder so you would leave what is more important, such as paying attention to the enemy, his treachery, and attacks. That is because such action is very harmful. If the situation arises, the interest of the action and the group should be placed ahead of [the plunder], that is because this action is an obligation to be fulfilled [by each member of the group], while the plunder is a sanctioned custom, and the obligation precedes the sanctioned custom.

Do not act out of a desire of vengeance for yourself. Let your action instead be for the sake of God. 'Ali ibn Abi Talib, may God be pleased with him, had a duel with one of the nonbelievers. The nonbeliever spit on him. 'Ali paused on his sword and did not strike him. Then he struck him.

At the end of the battle, the Companions asked him about his deed, and about why he had paused before striking the nonbeliever. He said:

"When he spit on me, I feared that if I were to strike him, it would be out of vengeance. So I held my sword." He might have said it differently.

When he became sure of his intention, he struck and killed him. This indicates that the human being can secure himself in a short while that all of his action is for the sake of God.

Afterward, implement the sanctioned custom of prisoners of war. Capture them and kill them as God said: "It is not right for a prophet to take captives before he has conquered the battlefield. You [people] desire the transient good of this world, but God desires the Hereafter [for you]—God is mighty and wise" (Q 8:67).

If everything goes as planned, each of you is to hold the shoulder of his brother from the apartment, in the [airport], the [plane], and the [cabin], reminding him that this action is for the sake of God. Do not confuse or confound your brothers, but announce the good news to them, make them feel secure, remind them [of the purpose], and encourage them. How delightful it would be for one to recite Qur'anic verses, such as God's saying:

"Let those of you who are willing to trade the life of this world for the life to come, fight in God's way" (Q 4:74), and his saying: "Do not think of those who have been killed in God's way" (Q 3:169), or other verses. You may also chant as the Predecessors used to chant in the midst of battle to comfort your brothers and instill tranquillity and happiness in their hearts.

Do not forget to take some of the spoils, even if only a cup of water, to drink from it and offer it to your brothers to drink, if possible. When the moment of truth comes near, and zero hour is upon you, open your chest welcoming death on the path of God. Always remember to conclude with the prayer, if possible, starting it seconds before the target, or let your last words be: "There is no god but God and Muhammad is His messenger."

After that, God willing, the meeting is in the Highest Paradise, in the company of God.

When you see the crowds of nonbelievers, remember the factions [gathered against the Prophet]: they numbered about 10,000 thousand fighters, and remember how God made his believing servants victorious.

God said: "When the believers saw the joint forces, they said, 'This is what God and His Messenger promised us: the promise of God and His Messenger is true,' and this only served to increase their faith and submission to God" (Q 33:22).

May God bless Muhammad.

# GLOSSARY

*'alim*—See *'ulama*

*amir*—Leader of a group or community

*amir al-mu'minin*—"The commander of the believers," a common designation for the caliph in medieval Islam

*ansar*—Supporters

*arda*—Support; supporters; helpers

*'Ashura*—The tenth day of Muharram, the first month of the Islamic calendar; the Shi'a commemorate the martyrdom of their third imam, Husayn ibn 'Ali, on this day

*ayatollah*—"Sign of God"; an honorific title reserved for leading members of the Shi'i religious hierarchy

*al-Azhar*—Egypt's preeminent mosque-university

*baitul mal (bayt al-mal)*—Public treasury

*bid'a*—Reprehensible innovation

*burqa*—A garment that usually covers a woman's body from head to toe as well as her face

*chador*—A sheet of cloth covering a woman's head and body

*caliphate (Arabic: khilafa)*—Institution of Muslim political rule; formally abolished in 1924 by the architect of the Turkish state, Mustafa Kemal

*dar al-harb*—House or Abode of War

*dar al-Islam*—House or Abode of Islam

*dar al-'ulum*—An institution of Islamic learning; the name of a number of such institutions in the Middle East and South Asia

*darura*—"Necessity"; the legal doctrine that juridical norms can be set aside in the face of extreme necessity

*da'iya (feminine plural: da'iyyat*—A person engaging in da'wa (q.v.)

*da'wa*—The act of inviting others to Islam; in cases in which this call is directed toward those who already consider themselves Muslim, it refers to reminding them of their religious obligations

*Deobandi*—The doctrinal orientation associated with the madrasa (q.v.) of Deoband, a town in Uttar Pradesh in northern India; an adherent of this movement

*dhabh*—Slaughter, or sacrifice

*dhikr*—Invocation, remembrance of Allah

*dhull*—Humiliation

*din*—Religion, faith

*dunya*—This world

*fatwa*—A nonbinding legal opinion issued by a jurisconsult (mufti [q.v.])

*faqih (plural: fuqaha)*—A scholar of Islamic law

*fard (also farida)*—Obligation

*fard 'ayn*—An obligation that every single Muslim is expected to fulfill

*fard kifaya*—A "collective obligation," which can be fulfilled by some members of the community on behalf of the community at large

*farida*—See fard

*fardiyya*—Individualism

*fi sabil Allah*—"In the path of God"; a phrase often conjoined with jihad ("jihad in the path of God"

*fiqh*—Islamic law and jurisprudence

*fitna*—Civil strife, temptation, disorder, chaos, sedition, dissension; a common way of referring to the first civil war in Islamic history (656–61), which, broadly speaking, constitutes the point of origin of the division between the Shi'a and the Sunnis

*gharb*—The West

*ghawza*—Raid

*hadith (plural: ahadith)*—A report concerning the words and deeds of the Prophet Muhammad, collected and recorded in the centuries following Muhammad's death

*hakimiyya*—"Sovereignty"; in the Islamist lexicon, this term is used to assert that God alone is the true sovereign and thereby to question all human claims to political authority as well as the legitimacy of "man-made laws"

*Hajj*—The annual pilgrimage to Mecca

*Hanafi*—A school of Sunni law named after Abu Hanifa (d. 767); an adherent of this school

*Hanbali*—A school of Sunni law named after Ahmad ibn Hanbal (d. 855); an adherent of this school

*hanif*—A person of pure faith (cf. Q 30:30)

*haram*—Forbidden; prohibited

*al-Hawza al-'ilmiyya/hawza*—"The enclave of learning"; the collective name of the madrasas in Najaf, Iraq, and Qum, Iran

*hijab*—Some sort of a "covering" used by women as part of their modest dress; cf. Qur'an 33:53. In modern parlance, the hijab is often understood as a headscarf.

*hijra*—The migration of the Prophet and his early followers from Mecca to Medina in 622. This event marks the beginning of the Islamic calendar.

*hudud*—Punishments specifically mentioned in the Qur'an and the sunna (q.v.) and, unlike other "discretionary" punishments, not subject to being mitigated by the ruler or the aggrieved party

*hur 'ayn*—"The black-eyed ones"; a Qur'anic term understood to refer to the women companions of those rewarded with Paradise; cf. Qur'an 52:20 (often translated loosely as "heavenly brides")

*'ibadat (singular: 'ibada)*—Matters of worship; ritual practices

*ijma'*—Consensus of the community or of the leading scholars, recognized in Sunni legal theory as a source of legal norms

*ijtihad*—Systematic reflection on the foundational sources of the law to arrive at new legal rulings. One qualified to do so is called a mujtahid. In modern Muslim discourse, the term ijtihad has come to connote a wide variety of approaches to the Qur'an and to Islamic law, ranging from the effort to address questions not already settled in the legal tradition to radically rethinking Islamic norms in seeking to reform particular institutions and practices.

*'ilm*—Religious knowledge. Those possessing 'ilm are known as 'ulama (q.v.). In modern Arabic, 'ilm (plural: 'ulum) is often used in the sense of "science(s)" or "knowledge."

*imam*—Leader or head of the community; those descendants of 'Ali who are regarded by the Shi'a as their infallible guides; the person leading the ritual prayers

*Imama*—Caliphate; leadership; the Shi'i doctrine of the divinely designated imams (q.v.)

*iman*—Belief, faith

*'irfan*—"Gnosis"; a form of Sufism deeply influenced by medieval Islamic philosophy

*isra*—The night journey Muhammad was said to have made in the company of the angel Gabriel from Mecca to Jerusalem

*istihsan*—A form of legal reasoning guided by a jurist's preference for some rulings over others

*istikbar*—"Arrogance," a cardinal sin in Islam

*jahili*—Adjectival form of jahiliyya (q.v.)

*jahiliyya*—"Ignorance." A common Islamic designation for the "age of pagan ignorance" before the advent of Islam. The term, made popular by the Egyptian Islamist Sayyid Qutb, has been used by many Islamists to assert that a new age of unbelief, apostasy, and pagan materialism has come to envelop the world, including Muslim societies.

*jama'a (Egyptian Arabic: gama'a)*—Group, association, community

*jihad*—"Struggle," including armed struggle against unbelievers; often used synonymously (if inaccurately) with holy war

*jizya*—The tax imposed in early and medieval Islam on non-Muslims living under Muslim rule

*Ka'ba*—The most famous sanctuary in Islam, located within the great mosque in Mecca. It is the direction Muslims face in daily prayer.

*kafir*—"Ungrateful"; a common Islamic term for the unbeliever

*khalifa*—Caliph; deputy; successor. See caliphate

*kharaj*—A tax imposed in early Islam on agricultural lands held by non-Muslims; it later came to be extended to various categories of agricultural lands irrespective of whether they were held by non-Muslims or by Muslims

*Khawarij*—Seceders, outsiders; refers to a breakaway sect in early Muslim history

*khilafa*—see caliphate

*al-khilafa al-rashida*—"The rightly guided caliphate," the common designation in Sunni Islam for the first four caliphs (Abu Bakr, 'Umar ibn al-Khattab, 'Uthman ibn 'Affan, and 'Ali ibn Abi Talib) to rule the community between the death of the Prophet Muhammad in 632 and the death of 'Ali in 661. Of these four, the Shi'a view only 'Ali to have been a legitimate caliph.

*khums*—The "fifth" that all Twelver Shi'a of means are required to pay annually to the leading religious scholars, the latter acting as representatives of the hidden imam

*kufr*—"Ingratitude"; unbelief

*layeha (Arabic: la'iha)*—Rule, program

*madhhab*—School of Islamic law

*madrasa*—"School"; institution of higher Islamic learning

*Maghrib*—"The place of the setting sun"; the west, more specifically the region of Northwest Africa.

*mahana*—Humiliation

*mahdi*—The divinely inspired guide, who, according to Shi'i belief, will arise to lead the community shortly before the Day of Resurrection. The Twelver Shi'a (q.v.) identify this mahdi with their twelfth imam who, they believe, had disappeared in the late ninth century and will remain hidden until his appointed time. Sunnis, too, believe in the mahdi as an eschatological figure, but they do not identify him with the hidden Shi'i imam; nor does the doctrine of the mahdi carry the same religious significance for them as it does for the Shi'a.

*makruh (plural: makruhat)*—Acts that are deemed "reprehensible" by Islamic law without being forbidden outright

*Maliki*—A school of Sunni law named after Malik ibn Anas (d. 795); an adherent of this school

*maqasid al-shari'a*—"The purposes or goals of the shari'a"; the juridical view that the sacred law seeks to protect and promote certain fundamental aspects of human life, among them religion, life, progeny, intellect, and property

*marja' al-taqlid (Persian: marja-e taqlid)*—"The object or source of emulation"; the modern Shi'i doctrine that the most eminent of the Shi'i jurists should be recognized by all other Shi'a as the source of authoritative guidance. Khomeini's doctrine of the velayat-e faqih (q.v.) had built on this nineteenth-century institution of marja' al-taqlid to argue that the preeminent jurist should also hold political power.

*ma'ruf (plural: ma'rufat)*—That which is right and generally recognized as such. The Qur'an enjoins upon Muslims to "command right and forbid wrong" (cf. Q 3:104). See also munkar

*masjid*—Mosque

*maslaha*—Public interest, the common good; the legal doctrine that considerations of public interest ought to guide the enunciation of legal norms and that particular norms can also be set aside in view of considerations of the common good

*millat*—The community as defined in terms of religion

*mi'raj*—"Ascension"; the belief that the Prophet Muhammad had once miraculously traveled from Mecca to Jerusalem and then ascended to heaven before returning back to Mecca, all in the course of one night; cf. Qur'an 17:1

*mithaq*—charter

*mu'amalat*—Those aspects of Islamic law that relate to the relations of human beings with one another, as distinguished from the relationship of the human being with God

*mufti*—Jurisconsult; a jurist giving nonbinding legal opinions

*muhajirun*—Immigrants; see hijra

*mujaddid*—"Renewer"; the term often evokes the belief of many Muslims that, according to a divine plan, reformers periodically arise in the Muslim community to set its affairs in order

*mujahidin (singular: mujahid; feminine: mujahida)*—Those engaging in jihad (q.v.); a common designation of the Afghan guerillas resisting the Soviet occupation of Afghanistan

*mujtahid*—A jurist drawing on the foundational sources of Islamic law to formulate legal rulings; see ijtihad

*mukhabarat*—Intelligence services

*mulla*—A religious scholar

*munkar (plural: munkarat)*—That which is wrong; see ma'ruf

*muqallid*—A person who practices taqlid (q.v.)

*murshid (feminine: murshida)*—"Guide"; a common term for the Sufi master; also the title of the leader of the Egyptian Islamist organization, the Muslim Brotherhood

*murtadd*—Apostate

*mustabdil*—One who (illegitimately) occupies a position that properly belongs to someone else, that is, corrupt worldly rulers taking God's place

*nifaq*—Hypocrisy

*nushuz*—Usually understood in Islamic law as a wife's disobedience of her husband; cf. Qur'an 4:34

*qadi*—A Muslim judge who rules according to the shari'a

*qibla*—The direction Muslims face for prayer; see Ka'ba

*qital*—"Killing," as distinguished from jihad. Depending on usage, jihad may or may not have connotations of violence, but qital does.

*qiyas*—Analogical reasoning

*riba*—Usury

*rifq*—Kindness

*sa'idi*—Upper Egyptian

*salaf*—Pious forbears. See Salafis

*Saladin*—The European name for Salah al-Din (1138–93), a Kurd born in what is today Iraq, who led a successful jihad against European Crusaders, and is frequently invoked as the paradigmatic Muslim warrior-hero

*Salafis*—Those professing to adhere to the practices of the pious forbears, usually understood to refer to the first generations of Islam

*salat*—The Islamic ritual prayers

*Shafi'i*—A school of Sunni law named after Muhammad ibn Idris al-Shafi'i (d. 820); an adherent of this school

*shahada*—To witness, experience firsthand, certify, and confirm; the Islamic profession of faith

*shahid (fem. shahida)*—Martyr

*shaykh (plural: shuyukh)*—Respected elder; learned religious person; a Sufi master

*shari'a*—The totality of Islamic legal and ethical norms; the sacred law of Islam

*Shi'a (sing. Shi'i)*—Community of Muslims who, unlike the Sunnis, believe that after the death of the Prophet infallible religious guidance must continue in the person of the imams (q.v.), who are divinely designated to lead the community in religious and political matters. There are several subdivisions within the Shi'a, of which historically the most important are the Ithna 'ashariyya (q.v.) and the Isma'iliyya.

*shirk*—"Associating partners with God"; contravening the oneness of God (tawhid [q.v.])

*shura*—Consultation

*Sufi*—Muslim mystic

*sunna*—The normative example of the Prophet, usually expressed in the form of reports relating to his teachings and practices (hadith [q.v.])

*Sunnis*—Those professing adherence to the sunna (q.v.) of the Prophet and the agreed upon norms and practices of the Muslim community. The Sunnis constitute the overwhelming majority of Muslims worldwide.

*sura*—A chapter of the Qur'an

*tafsir*—Commentary on the Qur'an

*taghut*—"Idol"; a symbol of godlessness

*taqiyya*—"Precautionary dissimulation"; the Twelver Shi'i view that it is permissible to conceal or misrepresent one's true beliefs in the face of grave danger

*taqlid*—"Investing with authority"; following the legal rulings of earlier scholars, or of the school of law to which one professes adherence; customary norms (plural: taqalid). In Muslim modernist discourse, taqlid carries highly negative connotations and is often understood as "blind imitation."

*tarbiyya*—Upbringing; education

*tariqa (pl. turuq)*—Sufi order, religious brotherhood

*tawhid*—The doctrine of the oneness of God. This central doctrine is typically understood to distinguish Muslim conceptions of God not only from polytheistic beliefs but also from Christian Trinitarian doctrines. Islamists have often taken the implications of this doctrine much further, arguing that tawhid entails not recognizing *any* authority other than God or any law other than the sacred law of Islam (see hakimiyya).

*ta'wil*—Interpretation, usually scriptural interpretation

*Twelvers (Ithna 'ashari)*—A subdivision of the Shi'a (q.v.) whose members regard twelve successive descendants of the Prophet Muhammad through his daughter Fatima and her husband 'Ali to be their infallible religious guides (imams). The twelfth of these imams is the Mahdi (q.v.).

*'ulama (singular: 'alim)*—"People of knowledge." Religious scholars; those with formal training in the religious sciences, especially but not exclusively in those concerned with the Qur'an, hadith (q.v.), and Islamic law

*umma*—Muslim community, derived from the Arabic root meaning mother, source, origin, foundation. Membership is determined not by national citizenship or geography but by religious belief.

*'unf*—Violence

*vali amr (Arabic: wali al-amr)*—The person vested with authority

*vali-ye faqih*—See velayat-e faqih

*velayat-e faqih*—"The guardianship of the jurist." As articulated by Ayatollah Khomeini, this Shi'i doctrine holds that the leading Shi'i jurists deputize the hidden Shi'i imam in all religious and political matters. The doctrine breaks with the earlier and more widely held Shi'i view that the jurist deputizes for the hidden imam only in some respects but cannot lay claim to the fullness of his authority. Khomeini's doctrine of the velayat-e faqih, though still much disputed by many jurists, now serves as the basis of the Iranian constitution. The person recognized as the "guardian jurist" is referred to as "vali-ye faqih."

*Wahhabi*—An adherent of the puritanical teachings of Muhammad ibn 'Abd al-Wahhab (d. 1791). The term Wahhabi is sometimes thought to have pejorative connotations; those characterized by others as Wahhabis prefer to see themselves as Salafis (q.v.).

*wajib*—Obligation, duty

*wali (Persian: vali; plural awliya)*—Ruler, governor, benefactor, saint

*waqf*—Endowment of property for religious endeavors, such as maintenance of mosques, schools, etc.

*watan*—Homeland

*wasatiyya*—"Centrism"; moderation

*zakat*—Islamic alms-tax paid annually on one's accumulated wealth; one of the five "pillars" of the faith

# BIBLIOGRAPHY

'Abd al-Rahman, 'Umar. 1985. *Kalimat haqq: Murafa'at al-Duktur 'Umar 'Abd al-Rahman fi qadiyyat al-jihad.* Cairo: Dar al-I'tisam.

———. 1988. *Al-Maw'iza al-hasana.* Kuwait. N.p.: Dar al-Siyasa.

———. 1990. *The Present Rulers and Islam: Are they Muslims or Not?* Translated by Omar Johnstone. London: al-Firdous.

———. 2006. *Mawqif al-Qur'an min khusumih.* 'Abidin, al-Qahirah: Dar Misr al-Mahrusah.

Abdelhadi, Magdi. 2005. "Accused Morocco Islamist Speaks Out." BBCNews, September 30. http://news.bbc.co.uk/2/hi/africa/4297386.stm.

Abdel Haleem, M.A.S. 2004. *The Qur'an: A New Translation.* Oxford: Oxford University Press.

Abdul Mohsen, Assem. 1981. "Muslim Brothers' Hajja Zeinab: East and West Want to Delay the Return of Islam." *Middle East* 79: 32–34.

Abu-Amr, Ziad. 1993. "Hamas: A Historical and Political Background." *Journal of Palestine Studies* 22 (4): 5–19.

———. 1994. *Islamic Fundamentalism in the West Bank and Gaza: Muslim Brotherhood and Islamic Jihad.* Bloomington: Indiana University Press.

———. 1997. "Shaykh Ahmad Yasin and the Origins of Hamas." In *Spokesmen for the Despised: Fundamentalist Leaders of the Middle East,* edited by R. Scott Appleby, 225–56. Chicago: University of Chicago Press.

Adams, Charles J. 1966. "The Ideology of Mawlana Mawdudi." In *South Asian Politics and Religion,* edited by D. E. Smith, 371–97. Princeton: Princeton University Press.

Ahmad, Aziz. 1967. *Islamic Modernism in India and Pakistan, 1857–1964.* London: Oxford University Press.

Ahmed, Leila. 1992. *Women and Gender in Islam.* New Haven: Yale University Press.

Ahmed, Shahab. 1998. "Ibn Taymiyya and the Satanic Verses." *Studia Islamica* 87: 69–124.

Akhavi, Shahrough. 1996. "Contending Discourses in Shi'i Law on the Doctrine of Wilayat al-Faqih." *Iranian Studies* 29(3–4): 229–68.

———. 1997. "The Dialectic in Contemporary Egyptian Social Thought: The Scripturalist and Modernist Discourses of Sayyid Qutb and Hasan Hanafi." *International Journal of Middle East Studies* 20: 377–401.

Algar, Hamid. 1981. *Islam and Revolution: Writings and Declarations of Imam Khomeini.* Berkeley: Mizan Press.

———. 1985. Introduction to Murtaza Mutahhari, *Fundamentals of Islamic Thought: God, Man and the Universe,* 9–22. Berkeley: Mizan Press, 1985.

———. 1988. "Imam Khomeini, 1902–1962: The Pre-Revolutionary Years." In *Islam, Politics, and Social Movements,* edited by Edmund Burke III and Ira M. Lapidus, 263–88. Berkeley: University of California Press.

Ali, Syed Ameer [Sayyid Amir 'Ali]. 1923. *The Spirit of Islam: A History of the Evolution and Ideals of Islam, with a Life of the Prophet*. New York: G. H. Doran.

*Alserat: Selected Articles (1975–1983)*. N.d. London: Muhammadi Trust of Great Britain.

Altayab, Nadia. 2005. "The Mother of Men." *Islamic Horizons* 34 (6): 62–63.

Amanat, Abbas, and Frank Griffel, eds. 2007. *Shari'a: Islamic Law in the Contemporary Context*. Stanford: Stanford University Press.

Amnesty International. 2007. Report 2007: Morocco/Western Sahara. http://the report.amnesty.org/eng/Regions/Middle-East-and-North-Africa/Morocco-Western-Sahara.

An-Na'im, Abdullahi Ahmed. 1990. *Toward an Islamic Reformation: Civil Liberties, Human Rights, and International Law*. Syracuse: Syracuse University Press.

Appiah, K. Anthony. 1998. Foreword to Saskia Sassen, *Globalization and Its Discontents*, xi–xv. New York: New Press.

Arberry, A. J. 1996. *The Koran Interpreted*. 2 vols. New York: Simon & Schuster.

Arendt, Hannah. 1972. "On Violence." In *Crises of the Republic*, 103–98. New York: Harcourt Brace.

Arjomand, Said Amir. 1986. "Iran's Islamic Revolution in Comparative Perspective." *World Politics* 38 (3): 383–414.

———. 2002. "The Reform Movement and the Debate on Modernity and Tradition in Contemporary Iran." *International Journal of Middle East Studies* 34: 719–31.

Asad, Talal. 2008. "Historical Notes on the Idea of Secular Criticism." http://www.ssrc.org/blogs/immanent_frame/2008/01/25/historical-notes-on-the-idea-of-sec.

Avineri, Shlomo. 1968. *The Social and Political Thought of Karl Marx*. Cambridge: Cambridge University Press.

al-Azmeh, Aziz. 1993. *Islams and Modernities*. London: Verso.

'Azzam, 'Abd Allah. 1986. *Ayat al-Rahman fi jihad al-Afghan*. Amman: Maktabat al-Risala al-Haditha.

———. 1987a. *al-Difa' 'an Aradi al-Muslimin Ahamm Furud al-A'yan* [The Defense of Muslims' Lands—the Most Important of the Individual Duties] Jidda: Dar al-Mujtama'.

———. 1987b. *Ilhaq bi'l-Qafila* [Join the Caravan]. Peshawar: Mu'assasat al-Maswadi.

Badran, Margot, and Miriam Cooke, eds. 2004. *Opening the Gates: A Century of Arab Feminist Writing*. Bloomington: Indiana University Press.

Ball, Terence, and Richard Dagger. 1999. "The Democratic Ideal." In *Political Ideologies and the Democratic Ideal*, 1–43. New York: Addison Wesley Longman.

al-Banna, Hasan. 1974. *Mudhakkirat al-da'wa wa'l-da'iyya*. Cairo: Dar al-Kitab al-'Arabi.

———. 1950. *Risalat al-Mu'tamar al-Khamis*. Cairo: Dar al-Kitab al-'Arabi.

Baron, Beth. 1994. *The Women's Awakening in Egypt: Culture, Society and the Press*. New Haven: Yale University Press.

———. 2005. *Egypt as a Woman: Nationalism, Gender, and Politics*. Berkeley: University of California Press.

Barr, James. 1978. *Fundamentalism*. Philadelphia: Westminster Press.

Bayat, Asef. 2007. *Making Islam Democratic: Social Movements and the Post-Islamist Turn.* Stanford: Stanford University Press.

Behdad, Sohrab. 1994. "A Disputed Utopia: Islamic Economics in Revolutionary Iran." *Comparative Studies in Society and History* 36: 775–813.

Benedict XVI. 2006. "Faith, Reason and the University: Memories and Reflections." Aula Magna of the University of Regensburg, September 12. http://www.vatican.va/holy_father/benedict_xvi/speeches/2006/september/documents/hf_ben-xvi_spe_20060912_university-regensburg_en.html.

Bennoune, Karima. 1994. "Algerian Women Confront Fundamentalism." *Monthly Review* 46 (4, September): 26–39.

Bergen, Peter. 2001. *Holy War, Inc.* New York: Free Press, 2001.

———. 2006. *The Osama bin Laden I Know.* New York: Free Press.

Bergen, Peter, and Swati Pandey. 2001. "The Madrassa Scapegoat." *Washington Quarterly* 29 (2): 117–25.

———. 2005. "The Madrassa Myth." *New York Times*, June 14.

Berlin, Isaiah. 1990. *The Crooked Timber of Humanity: Chapters in the History of Ideas.* Edited by Henry Hardy. London: John Murray.

Berman, Paul. 2003a. "The Philosopher of Islamic Terror" *New York Times Magazine*, March 23.

———. 2003b. *Terror and Liberalism.* New York: W. W. Norton.

Bessis, Sophie. 1999. "Femmes of the Maghreb." *CLIO—Histoire, Femmes et Sociétés* 9. Toulouse: Universitaires du Mirail. http://clio.revues.org/document 286.html.

Binder, Leonard. 1988. *Islamic Liberalism: A Critique of Development Ideologies.* Chicago: University of Chicago Press.

Bin Laden, Usama. 1995–96. "The Invasion of Arabia." In *Messages to the World: Statements of Osama bin Laden*, 15–19. London: Verso.

———. 1996a. "Declaration of War against the Americans Occupying the Land of the Two Holy Places." http://www.pbs.org/newshour/terrorism/international/fatwa_1996.html.

———. 1996b. "I'lan al-Jihad 'ala al-Amrikiyyin al-Muhtallin li-bilad al-Haramayn." *Al-Quds al-Arabi*, August 23.

———. 1996c. "The Saudi Regime." In *Messages to the World: Statements of Osama bin Laden*, 31–43. London: Verso.

———. 1997a. Interview. *al-Huquq*, no. 124 (May 14).

———. 1997b. Interview with Peter Arnett, CNN. http://fl1.findlaw.com/news.findlaw.com/cnn/docs/binladen/binladenintvw-cnn.pdf.

——— (with al-Zawahiri et al.). 1998a. "World Islamist Front For Jihad Against Jews and Crusaders: Declaration of War." http://www.fas.org/irp/world/para/docs/980223-fatwa.htm.

——— (with al-Zawahiri et al.). 1998b. "Bayan al-Jabha al-Islamiyya al-'Alamiyya li-Jihad al-Yahud wa'l-Salibiyyin." *al-Quds al-'Arabi*, February 23, p. 3. http://www.library.cornell.edu/colldev/mideast/fatw2.htm.

———. 1998c. Interview with al-Jazeera, December. "A Muslim Bomb" in *Messages to the World: Statements of Osama bin Laden.* London: Verso.

———. 1999. "The Destruction of the Base." Interview with Usama bin Laden by Jamal Isma'il in Afghanistan. *Al-Jazeera*, air date June 10. Published by the Terrorism Research Center, www.terrorism.com

———. 2001a. Videotape, translated by George Michael and Kassem M. Wahba. English transcript published by the *Pittsburgh Post-Gazette*, December 14.

———. 2001b. "Nineteen Students." In *Messages to the World: Statements of Osama bin Laden*, 145–57. London: Verso.

———. 2001c. Interview with Tayseer Alouni of *al-Jazeera*, October. http://archives .cnn.com/2002/world/asiapcf/south/02/05/binladen.transcript/index.html.

———. 2004a. "Depose the Tyrants." In *Messages to the World: Statements of Osama bin Laden*, 245–75. London: Verso.

———. 2004b. "Resist the New Rome." In *Messages to the World: Statements of Osama bin Laden*, 212–32. London: Verso.

Bloch, Ruth H. 1978. "American Feminine Ideals in Transition: The Rise of the Moral Mother, 1785–1815." *Feminist Studies* 4 (2): 101–26.

Bloom, Mia. 2005. *Dying to Kill: The Allure of Suicide Terror*. New York: Columbia University Press.

Blunt, Wilfrid Scawen. 1882. *The Future of Islam*. London: Kegan Paul, Trench.

Bonner, Michael. 2006. *Jihad in Islamic History: Doctrines and Practice*. Princeton: Princeton University Press.

Booth, Marilyn. 1987. "Women's Prison Memoirs in Egypt and Elsewhere: Prison, Gender, Praxis." *Middle East Report*, November–December, 35–41.

———. 2002. Review of *Women Claim Islam*. *World Literature Today* 76 (2): 249–50.

Brandon, James. 2007. "Arrests Spark Fears of Armed Islamist Takeover." *Washington Times*, June 20.

Brotton, Jeremy. 1998. *Trading Territories: Mapping the Early Modern World*. Ithaca: Cornell University Press.

Brown, Daniel. 1996. *Rethinking Tradition in Modern Islamic Thought*. Cambridge: Cambridge University Press.

Brunner, Rainer. 2004. *Islamic Ecumenism in the 20th Century: The Azhar and Shiism between Rapprochement and Restraint*. Leiden: Brill.

Budeiri, Musa K. 1995. "The Nationalist Dimension of Islamic Movements in Palestinian Politics." *Journal of Palestine Studies* 24 (3): 89–95.

Bunting, Madeleine. 2005. "Friendly Fire: Madeleine Bunting Meets Sheikh Yusuf al-Qaradawi in Qatar." *Guardian*, October 29.

Burgat, François. 1993. *The Islamic Movement in North Africa*. Translated by William Dowell. Austin: University of Texas Press.

Carré, Olivier. 2003. *Mysticism and Politics: A Critical Reading of Fi Zilal al-Qur'an by Sayyid Qutb (1906–1966)*. Translated by Carol Artigues. Leiden: Brill.

Cavatorta, Francesco. 2006. "Civil Society, Islamism and Democratisation: The Case of Morocco." *Journal of Modern African Studies* 44 (2): 203–22.

Chatterjee, Partha. 1990. "The Nationalist Resolution of the Women's Question." In *Recasting Women: Essays in Colonial History*, edited by Kumkum Sangari and Sudesh Vaid, 233–53. New Brunswick, NJ: Rutgers University Press.

Chu, Jeff, and Amany Radwan. 2004. "Raising Their Voices." *Time Magazine*, February 15. http://www.time.com/time/europe/html/040223/story.html.

Cloud, John. 2001. "Atta's Odyssey: How a Shy, Well-Educated Young Egyptian Became a Suspected Ringleader of the Sept. 11 Attacks. The Mystery Begins to Unfold in Germany." *Time Magazine*, October 8, 64–67.

Cockburn, Patrick. 2008. *Muqtada: Muqtada al-Sadr, the Shia Revival, and the Struggle for Iraq.* New York: Scribner.

Cohen, David. 1991. *Sexuality and Society: The Enforcement of Morals in Classical Athens.* Cambridge: Cambridge University Press.

Cole, Juan. 2003. "The United States and Shi'ite Religious Factions in Post-Ba'thist Iraq. *Middle East Journal* 57: 543–66.

Coll, Steve. 2005. "The Young Osama." *New Yorker* 81 (December 12): 48–61.

Commins, David. 1990. *Islamic Reform: Politics and Social Change in Late Ottoman Syria.* New York: Oxford University Press.

———. 1994. "Hasan al-Banna." In *Pioneers of Islamic Revival,* edited by Ali Rahnema, 125–53. London: Zed Press.

Connolly, William. 1995. "Democracy and Territoriality." In *The Ethos of Pluralization,* 135–61. Minneapolis: University of Minnesota Press.

Cook, David. 2005. *Understanding Jihad.* Berkeley: University of California Press.

Cook, Michael. 2000. *Commanding Right and Forbidding Wrong in Islamic Thought.* Cambridge: Cambridge University Press.

Cooke, Miriam. 1994. "Zaynab al-Ghazali: Saint or Subversive?" *Die Welt des Islams* 34 (1): 1–20.

———. 1995. "*Ayyam min Hayati*: The Prison Memoirs of a Muslim Sister." *Journal of Arabic Literature* 26: 147–64.

———. 2001. *Women Claim Islam: Creating Islamic Feminism through Literature.* London: Routledge.

Copeland, Libby. 2002. "Female Suicide Bombers: The New Factor in the Mideast's Deadly Equation." *Washington Post,* April 27, C01, C04.

Cornell, Vincent. 1998. *Realm of the Saint: Power and Authority in Moroccan Sufism.* Austin: University of Texas Press.

Crone, Patricia. 2004. *God's Rule—Government and Islam: Six Centuries of Medieval Islamic Political Thought.* New York: Columbia University Press.

Dabashi, Hamid. 2006. *Theology of Discontent: The Ideological Foundation of the Islamic Revolution in Iran.* 2nd ed. New Brunswick: Transaction Publishers.

Dahbi, Omar. 2004. "Guerre de Succession à Al Adl Wal Ihssane." *Aujourd'hui Le Maroc,* December 1. http://www.aujourdhui.ma/couverture-details24128.html.

*Daily Excelsior.* 2002. "Moroccan Female Fundamentalist Challenges Osama bin Laden." http://www.dailyexcelsior.com/01nov02/inter.htm#5.

Dallal, Ahmad. 2000. "Appropriating the Past: Twentieth-Century Reconstruction of Pre-modern Islamic Thought." *Islamic Law and Society* 7: 325–58.

Davari, Mahmood T. 2005. *The Political Thought of Ayatullah Murtaza Mutahhari: An Iranian Theoretician of the Islamic State.* London: RoutledgeCurzon.

Deeb, Lara. 2006. *An Enchanted Modern: Gender and Public Piety in Shi'i Lebanon.* Princeton: Princeton University Press.

Delong-Bas, Natana J. 2004. *Wahhabi Islam: From Revival and Reform to Global Jihad.* New York: Oxford University Press.

Desai, Meghnad. 2007. *Rethinking Islamism: The Ideology of the New Terror.* London: I. B. Tauris.

Devji, Faisal. 2005. *Landscapes of the Jihad: Militancy, Morality, Modernity.* Ithaca, NY: Cornell University Press.

de Waal, Alex. 2007. "Sudan: The Turbulent State." In *War in Darfur and the Search for Peace*, edited by Alex de Waal, 1–38. Cambridge, MA: Global Equity Initiative, Harvard University.

al-Dhahabi. 1970. *Tajrid asma al-sahaba* (Biographical Dictionary of the Companions of the Prophet). Edited by Saliha 'Abd al-Hakim Sharaf al-Din. Bombay: Sharaf al-Din and Sons.

Dickey, Christopher. 2005. "Women of Al Qaeda." *Newsweek*, December 12, 27–36.

Dorronsoro, Gilles. 2005. *Revolution Unending: Afghanistan, 1979 to the Present*. London: Hurst.

Downing Street Website. 2005. "International Terrorism: Significant Attacks Associated with Al Qaida." http://www.number10/gov.uk/Page7930.

Eccel, Chris. 1988. "'Alim and Mujahid in Egypt: Orthodoxy versus Subculture or Division of Labor?" *Muslim World* 78 (3–4): 189–208.

Edwards, David B. 2002. *Before Taliban: Genealogies of the Afghan Jihad*. Berkeley: University of California Press.

Eickelman, Dale F., and James Piscatori. 1996. *Muslim Politics*. Princeton: Princeton University Press.

El-Affendi, Abdelwahab. 1991. *Turabi's Revolution: Islam and Power in Sudan*. London: Grey Seal.

Enayat, Hamid. 1982. *Modern Islamic Political Thought*. Austin: University of Texas Press.

*The Encyclopaedia of Islam*. 1913–36. Leiden: Brill.

———. 1999. CD-ROM Edition v. 1.0. Leiden: Koninklijke Brill NV.

*The Encyclopaedia of the Qur'an*. 2001–7. Leiden: Brill.

Entelis, John. 2002. "Morocco: Democracy Denied." *Le Monde Diplomatique*, October. http://mondediplo.com/2002/10/13morocco.

Erlanger, Steven. 2007. "A Life of Unrest." *New York Times Magazine*, July 15, 42–48.

Euben, J. Peter. 2003. *Platonic Noise*. Princeton: Princeton University Press.

Euben, Roxanne L. 1999. *Enemy in the Mirror: Islamic Fundamentalism and the Limits of Modern Rationalism*. Princeton: Princeton University Press.

———. 2002a. "The New Manichaeans." *Theory & Event* 5 (4). http://muse.jhu.edu/login?uri=/journals/theory_and_event/v005/5.4euben.html.

———. 2002b. "Killing (for) Politics: Jihad, Martyrdom and Political Action." *Political Theory* 1 (30): 4–35.

———. 2003. "A Counternarrative of Shared Ambivalence: Some Muslim and Western Perspectives on Science and Reason." *Common Knowledge* 9: 50–77.

———. 2007. Review Symposium: Understanding Suicide Terror. *Perspectives on Politics* 5 (1): 129–33.

Fadlallah, Muhammad Husayn. 1995. "Islamic Unity and Political Change: Interview with Shaykh Muhammad Hussayn Fadlallah." *Journal of Palestine Studies* 25(1, Autumn): 61–75.

———. 2002. "11 September, Terrorism, Islam, and the Intifada." *Journal of Palestine Studies* 31(2, Winter): 78–84.

Fandy, Mamoun. 1994. "Egypt's Islamic Group: Regional Revenge?" *Middle East Journal* 48: 607–25.

———. 1999. *Saudi Arabia and the Politics of Dissent*. New York: St. Martin's Press.

Fanon, Frantz. 2005. *The Wretched of the Earth*. New York: Grove Press.

Faramarzi, Scheherezade. 2005. "Trial of the King's Critics Suggest Morocco's New Openness Has Limits." Associated Press, July 3.

Fattah, Hala. 2003. "'Wahhabi' Influences, Salafi Responses: Shaikh Mahmud Shukri and the Iraqi Salafi Movement." *Journal of Islamic Studies* 14 (2): 127–48.

Feldman, Noah. 2007. "Shari'a and Islamic Democracy in the Age of al-Jazeera." In *Shari'a: Islamic Law in the Contemporary Context*, edited by Abbas Amanat and Frank Griffel, 104–19. Stanford: Stanford University Press.

"Fez City: 7 Women out of 10 Victim of Violence." 2003. http://www.arabic news.com/ansub/Daily/Day/030310/2003031022.html.

Fisk, Robert. 1996. Interview with Usama bin Laden. *The Independent*, December 6. http://www.robert-fisk.com.

———. 2001. "What Muslim Would Write: 'The Time of Fun and Waste Is Gone?'" *True Democracy* 1 (4, Fall).

Flood, Finbarr Barry. 2002. "Between Cult and Culture: Bamiyan, Islamic Iconoclasm, and the Museum." *Art Bulletin* 84: 641–59.

Friedman, Robert I. 1993a. "The CIA and the Sheikh." *Village Voice*, March 30: 20–27.

———. 1993b. "Sheikh Abdel Rahman, the World Trade Center Bombing and the CIA." *Open Magazine Pamphlet Series* 27: 1–16.

Gaffney, Patrick D. 1997. "Fundamentalist Preaching and Islamic Militancy in Upper Egypt." In *Spokesmen for the Despised: Fundamentalist Leaders of the Middle East*, edited by R. Scott Appleby, 257–93. Chicago: University of Chicago Press.

Gambetta, Diego, ed. 2005. *Making Sense of Suicide Missions*. Oxford: Oxford University Press.

Geertz, Clifford. 1964. "Ideology as a Cultural System." In *Ideology and Discontent*, edited by David Apter, 47–76. New York: Macmillan.

Gerges, Fawaz. 2005. *The Far Enemy: Why Jihad Went Global*. New York: Cambridge University Press.

al-Ghazali, Zaynab. 1978. *Ayyam min Hayati*. Cairo: Dar al-Shuruq.

———. 1989a. "Ja'ani ma'an." *Liwa al-Islam* 12 (43, March): 48.

———. 1989b. "Radd 'ala Risala." *Liwa al-Islam* 8 (44, November): 50.

———. 1994. *Nazarat fi kitab Allah*. Beirut and Cairo: Dar al-Shuruq.

———. 1996a. *Min khawatir Zaynab al-Ghazali: fi shu'un al-din wa'l-hayat*. Cairo: Dar al-I'tisam.

———. 1996b. *Mushkilat al-shabab wa'l-fatayat fi marhalat al-murahiqa: Rudud 'ala al-rasa'il*. Cairo: Dar al-Tawzi' wa'l-Nashr al-Islamiyya.

Gilbert, Sandra, and Susan Gubar. 1979. *The Madwoman in the Attic: The Woman Writer and the Nineteenth-Century Literary Imagination*. New Haven: Yale University Press.

Gillespie, Michael. 1999. "Liberal Education and the Idea of the West." *America, the West, and Liberal Education*, edited by Ralph C. Hancock, 7–25. Lanham,: Rowman & Littlefield.

Giustozzi, Antonio. 2008. *Koran, Kalashnikov, and Laptop: The Neo-Taliban Insurgency in Afghanistan*. New York: Columbia University Press.

Goldberg, Ellis. 1991. "Smashing Idols and the State: The Protestant Ethic and Egyptian Sunni Radicalism." *Comparative Studies in Society and History* 33 (1): 3–35.

Goldberg, Jeffrey. 2000. "Inside Jihad U: The Education of a Holy Warrior." *New York Times Magazine*, June 25, 32–38.

Golden, Tim, Michael Moss, and Jim Yardley. 2001. "Unpolished Secret Agents Were Able to Hide in Plain Sight." *New York Times*, September 23, B1–2.

Gould, William. 2004. *Hindu Nationalism and the Language of Politics in Late Colonial India*. Cambridge: Cambridge University Press.

Gorky, Maxim. 1920. "The Revolt of the Slaves." *The Call*, March 25. Translated by Richard Clements. *Marxists Internet Archive*. http://marxists.catbull.com/archive/gorky-maxim/1920/03/25.htm.

Graham, William A., and Navid Kermani. 2006. "Recitation and Aesthetic Reception." In *The Cambridge Companion to the Qur'an*, edited by Jane D. McAuliffe, 115–41. Cambridge: Cambridge University Press.

Gramsci, Antonio. 1971. *Selections from the Prison Notebooks of Antonio Gramsci (1948–51)*. Translated by Quintin Hoare and Geoffrey Nowell-Smith. London: Lawrence and Wishart.

Gray, Doris, and Sinikka Tarvainen. 2004. "Moroccan Women Seek Emancipation between Islam and the West." Deutsche Press-Agentur, July 12.

Griffel, Frank. 2007. "The Harmony of Natural Law and Shari'a in Islamist Theology." In *Shari'a: Islamic Law in Contemporary Context*, edited by Abbas Amanat and Frank Griffel, 38–61. Stanford: Stanford University Press.

Grinstein, Joseph. 1996. "Jihad and the Constitution: The First Amendment Implications of Combating Religiously Motivated Terrorism." *Yale Law Journal* 105 (5): 1347–81.

Grunebaum, G. E. von. 1962. *Modern Islam: The Search for Cultural Authenticity*. New York: Vintage Books.

Gupta, Sapan. 2006. "Justice and Spirituality: A Moroccan View." *The Record*, April 20. http://media.www.hlrecord.org/media/storage/paper609/news/2006/04/20/News/Justice.And.Spirituality.A.Moroccan.View-1863637.shtml.

Gutas, Dimitri. 2000. "Sayings by Diogenes Preserved in Arabic." In Gutas, *Greek Philosophers in the Arabic Tradition*, 475–518. Aldershot, Hampshire: Ashgate Variorum.

Gwynne, Rosalind W. 2006. "Usama bin Ladin, the Qur'an and Jihad." *Religion* 36 (2): 61–90.

Hackensberger, Alfred. 2006. "Interview with Nadia Yassine: The System Is Blocked." Translated by John Bergeron. *Qantara.de: Dialogue with the Muslim World*. http://www.qantara.de/webcom/show_article.php/_c-476/_nr-589/i.html.

Haddad, Yvonne. 1983. "The Qur'anic Justification for an Islamic Revolution: The View of Sayyid Qutb." *Middle East Journal* 37 (1):14–29.

Hale, Sondra. 1996. *Gender Politics in Sudan: Islamism, Socialism, and the State*. Boulder: Westview Press.

Hallaq, Wael B. 1997. *A History of Islamic Legal Theories*. Cambridge: Cambridge University Press.

Hamdi, Mohamed Elhachmi. 1988. *The Making of an Islamic Political Leader: Conversations with Hasan al-Turabi*. Boulder: Westview Press.

Hammoudi, Abdellah. 1997. *Master and Disciple: The Cultural Foundations of Moroccan Authoritarianism*. Chicago: University of Chicago Press.

Hanafi, Hasan. 1982. "The Relevance of an Islamic Alternative in Egypt." *Arab Studies Quarterly* 4: 54–74.

Harris, Christina Phelps. 1964. *Nationalism and Revolution in Egypt: The Role of the Muslim Brotherhood*. The Hague: Mouton.

Hartung, Jan-Peter. 2006. "The Nadwat al-'Ulama: Chief Patron of Madrasa Education in India and a Turntable to the Arab World." In *Islamic Education, Diversity, and National Identity: Dini Madaris in India Post 9/11*, edited by Jan-Peter Hartung and Helmut Reifeld, 135–57. New Delhi: Sage Publications.

al-Hashimi, Ibn, ed. 1990. *Humum al-mar'a al-muslima wa'l-da'iya Zaynab al-Ghazali*. Cairo: Dar al-I'tisam.

Hashmi, Sohail. 2003. "The Qur'an and Tolerance: An Interpretive Essay on Verse 5:48." *Journal of Human Rights* 2 (1): 81–103.

Hassan, Riffat. 1991. "The Issue of Woman-Man Equality in the Islamic Tradition." *Women's and Men's Liberation: Testimonies of Spirit*, edited by L. Grob, R. Hassan, and H. Gordon, 65–82. New York: Greenwood Press.

Hatina Meir. 2007. *Identity Politics in the Middle East: Liberal Thought and Islamic Challenge in Egypt*. London: Tauris Academic Studies.

Hawley, John Stratton, ed. 1994. *Fundamentalism and Gender*. Oxford: Oxford University Press.

Haykel, Bernard. 2009 (forthcoming). "On the Nature of Salafi Thought and Action." *In Global Salafism: Islam's New Religious Movement*, ed. Roel Meijer. London: Hurst.

Hefner, Robert W. 2000. *Civil Islam: Muslims and Democratization in Indonesia*. Princeton: Princeton University Press.

———, ed. 2006. *Remaking Muslim Politics: Pluralism, Contestation, Democratization*. Princeton: Princeton University Press.

Hefner, Robert W., and Muhammad Qasim Zaman, eds. 2007. *Schooling Islam: The Culture and Politics of Modern Muslim Education*. Princeton: Princeton University Press.

Hegghammer, Thomas, and Stephane Lacroix. 2007. "Rejectionist Islamism in Saudi Arabia: The Story of Juhayman al-'Utaybi Revisited." *International Journal of Middle East Studies* 39: 103–22.

Helmore, Kristin. 1985. "Islam and Women: An Egyptian Speaks Out." *Christian Science Monitor*, November 26, 11, 14.

Heyworth-Dunne, J. 1950. *Religious and Political Trends in Modern Egypt*. Washington, DC: McGregor & Werner.

Hirschkind, Charles. 2003. "Media and the Qur'an." In *The Encyclopedia of the Qur'an*, 3:341–49. Leiden: Brill.

———. 2006. *The Ethical Soundscape: Cassette Sermons and Islamic Counterpublics*. New York: Columbia University Press.

Hoffman, Valerie J. 1985. "An Islamic Activist: Zaynab al-Ghazali." In *Women and the Family in the Middle East: New Voices of Change*, edited by Elizabeth W. Fernea, 233–54. Austin: University of Texas Press.

———. 1995. "Muslim Fundamentalists: Psychosocial Profiles." *Fundamentalisms Comprehended*, edited by Martin E. Marty and R. Scott Appleby, 209–25. Chicago: University of Chicago Press.

Hourani, Albert. 1983. *Arabic Thought in the Liberal Age, 1798–1939*. Cambridge: Cambridge University Press.

Howe, Marvine. 1996. "Maghreb Mirror: Morocco Is Not Algeria, but Is It Heading in the Same Direction?" *Washington Report on Middle East Affairs* 14 (6): 16.

Hroub, Khaled. 2006. "A 'New Hamas' through Its New Documents." *Journal of Palestine Studies* 35 (4): 6–27.

Huntington, Samuel. 1991. *The Third Wave: Democratization in the Late Twentieth Century.* Norman: University of Oklahoma Press.

———. 1993. "The Clash of Civilizations?" *Foreign Affairs* 72: 22–49.

———. 1996. *The Clash of Civilizations and the Remaking of World Order.* New York: Simon & Schuster.

Ibn Taymiyya. 1988. *al-Fatawa al-kubra.* Edited by 'Ali ibn Muhammad al-Ba'li. Beirut: Dar al-Ma'rifa.

Ibrahim, Saad Eddin. 1980. "Anatomy of Egypt's Militant Islamic Groups." *International Journal of Middle East Studies* 12: 423–53.

Iqbal, Mohammad. 1934. *The Reconstruction of Religious Thought in Islam.* Oxford: Oxford University Press.

Jackson, Liz. 2001. October 18 interview with Professor Dittmar Machule ['Ata's thesis supervisor at the Technical University of Hamburg-Harburg]. *Four Corners,* Australian Broadcasting Corporation, November 12. http://www.abc.net.au/4 corners/atta/interviews/machule.htm.

Jackson, Richard. 2007. "Constructing Enemies: 'Islamic Terrorism' in Political and Academic Discourse." *Government and Opposition* 42 (3): 394–426.

Jameelah, Maryam. 1987. "An Appraisal of Some Aspects of Maulana Sayyid Ala Maudoodi's Life and Thought." *Islamic Quarterly* 31: 116–30.

Jansen, Johannes J. G. 1986a. *The Neglected Duty: The Creed of Sadat's Assassins and Islamic Resurgence in the Middle East.* New York: Macmillan.

———. 1986b. "Tafsir, Ijma' and Modern Muslim Extremism." *Orient* 27 (4): 642–46.

al-Jassas, Abu Bakr. 1971. *Ahkam al-Qur'an.* 3 vols. Beirut: Dar al-Kitab al-'Arabi.

Jehl, Douglas. 1993. "Inspector Doubts C.I.A. Role in Sheikh's U.S. Entry." *New York Times,* April 28, B1–2.

Just, Roger. 1989. *Women in Athenian Law and Life.* New York: Routledge.

Kahhalah, 'Umar Rida. 1977. *A'lam al-nisa' fi 'alamay al-'Arab wa'l-Islam* (Women in the Arab-Islamic World). Beirut: Mu'assassat al-Risala.

Kamal El-Din, Ahmed. 2007. "Islam and Islamism in Darfur." In *War in Darfur and the Search for Peace,* edited by Alex de Waal, 92–112. Cambridge, MA: Global Equity Initiative, Harvard University.

Kamrava, Mehran, ed. 2006. *The New Voices of Islam: Rethinking Politics and Modernity.* Berkeley: University of California Press.

———. 2008. *Iran's Intellectual Revolution.* Cambridge: Cambridge University Press.

Karam, Azza M. 1998. *Women, Islamisms and the State: Contemporary Feminisms in Egypt.* New York: St. Martin's Press.

Kepel, Gilles. 1985. *Muslim Extremism in Egypt: The Prophet and Pharaoh.* Translated by Jon Rothschild. Berkeley: University of California Press.

———. 2002. *Jihad: The Trail of Political Islam.* Cambridge, MA: Harvard University Press.

Kepel, Gilles, and Jean-Pierre Milelli, eds. 2008. *Al Qaeda in Its Own Words.* Translated by Pascale Ghazaleh. Cambridge, MA: Belknap Press of Harvard University Press.

Khalaf, Roula. 2006. "An Islamist Feminist Tackles Moroccan Taboos." *Financial Times*, June 1, 15.

Khalid, Adeeb. 1998. *The Politics of Muslim Cultural Reform: Jadidism in Central Asia*. Berkeley: University of California Press.

Khomeini, Ruhollah Musavi. N.d. *Imam Khomeini's Last Will and Testament*. Washington, DC: Embassy of the Democratic and Popular Republic of Algeria.

———. 1988. *Imam Khomeini's Messages to the Hajj Pilgrims*. New York: Permanent Mission of the Islamic Republic of Iran to the United Nations.

———. 1994. *Da'wa ila'l-tawhid: Risalat al-imam al-Khumayni . . . ila al-za'im al-sovieti Mikhail Gorbachev*. N. p.: Mu'assasat al-Imam Khumayni al-Thaqafiyya. *Also see* Algar, Hamid.

Kippenberg, Hans G. 2005. "'Consider That It Is a Raid in the Path of God': The Spiritual Manual of the Attackers of 9/11." *Numen* 54: 29–58.

Kippenberg, Hans G., and Tilman Seidensticker, eds. 2004. *Terror im Dienste Gottes: Die "Geistliche Anleitung" der Attentäter des 11. September 2001*. Frankfurt: Campus.

Knysh, Alexander. 1992. "Irfan Revisited: Khomeini and the Legacy of Islamic Mystical Philosophy." *Middle East Journal* 46: 631–53.

Krämer, Gudrun. 2006. "Drawing Boundaries: Yusuf al-Qaradawi on Apostasy." In *Speaking for Islam: Religious Authorities in Muslim Societies*, edited by Gudrun Krämer and Sabine Schmidtke, 181–217. Leiden: Brill.

Kramer, Martin. 1993. "Islam vs. Democracy." *Commentary* 95 (1): 35–42.

Kristianasen, Wendy. 2004. "Débats entre femmes en terres d'Islam." *Le Monde Diplomatique*, April, 20–21.

Kurzman, Charles. 1998. *Liberal Islam: A Sourcebook*. New York: Oxford University Press.

———. 2002. *Modernist Islam, 1840–1940: A Sourcebook*. New York: Oxford University Press.

Lapidus, Ira. 1988. *A History of Islamic Societies*. Cambridge: Cambridge University Press.

Laskier, Michael M. 2003. "A Difficult Inheritance: Moroccan Society under King Muhammad VI." *Middle East Review of International Affairs* 7 (3): 1–20.

Lauzière, Henri. 2005. "Post-Islamism and the Religious Discourse of 'Abd al-Salam Yasin." *International Journal of Middle East Studies* 37: 241–61.

Lawrence, Bruce B., ed. 2005. *Messages to the World: The Statements of Osama bin Laden*. New York: Verso.

Laws, Curtis Lee. 1920. "Convention Side Lights." *Watchman-Examiner* 8 (July 1): 834.

Layish, Aharon, and Gabriel R. Warburg. 2002. *The Reinstatement of Islamic Law in Sudan under Numayri*. Leiden: Brill.

Lecker, Michael. 2004. *The "Constitution of Medina": Muhammad's First Legal Document*. Princeton: Darwin Press.

Legrain, Jean-François. 1997. "HAMAS: Legitimate Heir of Palestinian Nationalism?" *Political Islam: Revolution, Radicalism, or Reform?* Edited by John L. Esposito, 159–78. Boulder: Lynne Rienner Publishers.

———. 2004. "Palestinian Islamisms: Patriotism as a Condition of Their Expansion." In *Accounting for Fundamentalisms: The Dynamic Character of Move-*

*ments,* edited by Martin E. Marty and R. Scott Appleby, 413–27. Chicago: University of Chicago Press.

Lesch, Ann M. 2002. "Osama bin Laden: Embedded in the Middle East Crises." *Middle East Policy* 9 (2): 82–91.

Lewis, Bernard. 1988. *The Political Language of Islam.* Chicago: University of Chicago Press.

———. 1998. "License to Kill: Usama bin Ladin's Declaration of Jihad." *Foreign Affairs* 77 (6): 14–19.

Lia, Brynjar. 2008. *Architect of Global Jihad: The Life of al-Qaida Strategist Abu Mus'ab al-Suri.* New York: Columbia University Press.

Lincoln, Bruce. 2003. *Holy Terrors: Thinking about Religion after September 11.* Chicago: University of Chicago Press.

Locke, John. 1689. *Second Treatise on Government.*

Loimeier, Roman. 2005. "Is There Something like 'Protestant Islam'?" *Die Welt des Islams* 45: 216–54.

Lybarger, Loren D. 2007. *Identity and Religion in Palestine: The Struggle between Islamism and Secularism in the Occupied Territories.* Princeton: Princeton University Press.

Machiavelli, Niccolò. 1532. *Il Principe.*

Maghraoui, Abdeslam. 2001. "Political Authority in Crisis: Mohammed VI's Morocco." *Middle East Report* 218 (Spring): 12–17.

Mahbubani, Kishore. 1992. "The West and the Rest." *National Interest* 28: 3–13.

Mahmood, Saba. 2005. *Politics of Piety: The Islamic Revival and the Feminist Subject.* Princeton: Princeton University Press.

———. 2006. "Secularism, Hermeneutics, and Empire: The Politics of Islamic Reformation." *Public Culture* 18: 323–47.

———. 2008. "Is Critique Secular?" http://www.sscr.org/blogs/immanent_frame/ 2008/03/30/is-critique-secular-2/.

Makdisi, George. 1974. "Ibn Taimiya: A Sufi of the Qadiriya Order." *American Journal of Arabic Studies* 1:118–29. Reprinted in George Makdisi, *Religion, Law and Learning in Classical Islam* (Aldershot: Variorum, 1991).

Makiya, Kanan, and Hassan Mneimneh. 2002. "Manual for a 'Raid.'" *New York Review of Books,* January 17, 18–21.

Malik, Jamal. 1996. *Colonialization of Islam: Dissolution of Traditional Institutions in Pakistan.* Delhi: Manohar.

Mallat, Chibli. 1993. *The Renewal of Islamic Law: Muhammad Baqer as-Sadr, Najaf and the Shi'i International.* Cambridge: Cambridge University Press.

Mamdani, Mahmood. 2007. "The Politics of Naming: Genocide, Civil War, Insurgency." *London Review of Books* 29 (5, March 8).

Marsden, George M. 1980. *Fundamentalism and American Culture: The Shaping of Twentieth-Century Evangelicalism, 1870–1925.* Oxford: Oxford University Press, 1980.

Martin, Vanessa. 2000. *Creating an Islamic State: Khomeini and the Making of a New Iran.* London: I. B. Tauris.

Marx, Karl. 1936. *Capital.* New York: Modern Library.

Massee, J. C. 1920. "Opening Address." In *Baptist Fundamentals: Being Addresses Delivered at the Pre-Convention Conference at Buffalo, June 21 & 22, 1920,* 3–11. Philadelphia: Judson Press.

Masud, Muhammad Khalid, ed. 2000. *Travelers in Faith: Studies of the Tablighi Jama'at as a Transnational Islamic Movement of Faith Renewal.* Leiden: Brill.

Mawdudi [Maududi], Sayyid Abu'l-A'la. 1948. *Jihad in Islam.* Translated by Charles J. Adams. Lahore.

———. 1954. *Tahrik-i-islami ki akhlaqi bunyaden.* 5th ed. Karachi and Lahore. Translated by Charles J. Adams as "The Moral Foundations of the Islamic Movement," in Aziz Ahamad and G. E. von Grunebaum, *Muslim Self-Statement in India and Pakistan, 1857–1968.* Wiesbaden: Otto Harrassowitz, 1970.

———.1960. *The Islamic Law and Constitution.* Translated and edited by Khurshid Ahmad. Lahore: Islamic Publications.

———. 1963. *A Short History of the Revivalist Movement in Islam.* Translated by Al-Ash'ari. Lahore: Islamic Publications.

———. 1976. *The Moral Foundations of the Islamic Movement.* Lahore: Islamic Publications.

———. 1983. *Purdah and the Status of Woman in Islam.* Translated by al-Ash'ari. Lahore: Islamic Publications.

———. 1988. *Towards Understanding the Qur'an.* Translated by Z. I. Ansari. Leicester: Islamic Foundation.

McAuley, Denis. 2005. "The Ideology of Osama bin Laden: Nation, Tribe and World Economy." *Journal of Political Ideologies* 10 (3): 269–87.

McGregor, Andrew. 2003. "'Jihad and the Rifle Alone': 'Abdullah 'Azzam and the Islamist Revolution." *Journal of Conflict Studies* 23 (2): 92–113.

Meijer, Roel. 2006. "Re-reading al-Qaeda: Writings of Yusuf al-Ayiri." *International Institute for the Study of Islam in the Modern World* 18: 16–17.

Mernissi, Fatima. 1991. *The Veil and the Male Elite: A Feminist Interpretation of Women's Rights in Islam.* Translated by Mary Jo Lakeland. Reading, MA: Addison-Wesley.

Metcalf, Barbara D. 1982. *Islamic Revival in British India: Deoband, 1860–1900.* Princeton: Princeton University Press.

Miller, Judith. 1997. "Global Islamic Awakening or Sudanese Nightmare? The Curious Case of Hassan Turabi." In *Spokesmen for the Despised: Fundamentalist Leaders of the Middle East*, edited by R. Scott Appleby, 182–224. Chicago: University of Chicago Press.

Mir-Hosseini, Ziba. 1999. *Islam and Gender: The Religious Debate in Contemporary Iran.* Princeton: Princeton University Press.

Mirzoeff, Nicholas. 2002. "The Subject of Visual Culture." In *The Visual Culture Reader*, edited by Nicholas Mirzoeff, 3–23. London: Routledge.

Mitchell, Richard P. 1969, 1993. *The Society of the Muslim Brothers.* New York: Oxford University Press.

Mitchell, Timothy. 1990. "L'expérience de l'emprisonnement dans le discours islamiste: une lecture d'*Ayyam min hayati* de Zaynab al-Ghazzali." In *Intellectuels et militants de l'Islam contemporain*, edited by Gilles Kepel and Yann Richard, 193–212. Paris: Le Seuil.

Moghadam, Valentine M. 1992. "Revolution, Islam and Women: Sexual Politics in Iran and Afghanistan." In *Nationalisms and Sexualities*, edited by Andrew Parker, Mary Russo, Doris Sommer, and Patricia Yaeger, 424–46. New York: Routledge.

Moosa, Ebrahim. 2005. *Ghazali and the Poetics of Imagination*. Chapel Hill: University of North Carolina Press.

Mottahedeh, Roy P. 1985. *The Mantle of the Prophet: Religion and Politics in Iran*. New York: Pantheon Books.

———. 2003. Introduction to Muhammad Baqir as-Sadr, *Lessons in Islamic Jurisprudence*, translated by Roy P. Mottahedeh, 1–34. Oxford: Oneworld Publications.

Moustafa, Tamir. 2000. "Conflict and Cooperation between the State and Religious Institutions in Contemporary Egypt." *International Journal of Middle East Studies* 32: 3–22.

Munson, Henry. 1986. "The Social Base of Islamic Militancy in Morocco." *Middle East Journal* 40 (2): 267–84.

———. 1991. "Morocco's Fundamentalists." *Government and Opposition* 26 (3): 331–44.

Murdock, Deroy. 2002. "The Islamofascist Agenda." *National Review Online*, December 3. http://www.nationalreview.com/murdock/murdock120302.asp.

Mutahhari, Murtaza. N.d. *A Discourse on the Islamic Republic*. Tehran: Islamic Propagation Organization.

———. 1974. *Nizam-i huquq-i zan dar Islam*. Tehran: Daftar-i Nashr-i Farhang-i Islami.

———. 1985. *Fundamentals of Islamic Thought: God, Man and the Universe*. Translated by R. Campbell. Berkeley: Mizan Press.

———. 1986. *Social and Historical Change: An Islamic Perspective*. Translated by R. Campbell. Berkeley: Mizan Press.

———. 1989. *The Islamic Modest Dress*. Translated by Laleh Bakhtiar. 2nd ed. Albuquerque: Abjad.

———. 1991. *Islam va muqtaziyyat-i zaman*. Tehran: Intisharat-i Sadra.

———. 1998. *The Rights of Women in Islam*. Tehran: World Organization for Islamic Services.

———. 2001. "The Fundamental Problem in the Clerical Establishment." Translated by Farhad Arshad. In *The Most Learned of the Shi'a: The Institution of the Marja' Taqlid*, edited by Linda S. Walbridge, 164–82. New York: Oxford University Press.

Nadwi, Sayyid Abu'l-Hasan 'Ali. 1970. *Madha khasira'l-'alam bi'l-inhitat al-muslimin*. 7th ed. Kuwait: Dar al-Qalam.

———. 1978. *Islam and the World*. Lucknow: Academy of Islamic Research and Publications. (Translation of Nadwi 1970.)

———. 1983–94. *Karwan-i zindagi*. 5 vols. Karachi: Majlis-i Nashriyyat-i Islam.

———. 1991. *al-Tafsir al-siyasi li'l-Islam: Fi mira'at kitabat al-ustadh Abi'l-A'la al-Mawdudi wa'l-shahid Sayyid Qutb*. 3rd ed. Sharjah: al-Markaz al-'Arabi.

Nasr, Seyyed Vali Reza. 1994. *The Vanguard of the Islamic Revolution: The Jama'at-i Islami of Pakistan*. Berkeley: University of California Press.

———. 1996. *Mawdudi and the Making of Islamic Revivalism*. New York: Oxford University Press.

———. 2006. *The Shia Revival: How Conflicts within Islam will Shape the Future*. New York: W. W. Norton.

Nedoroscik, Jeffrey A. 2002. "Extremist Groups in Egypt." *Terrorism and Political Violence* 14 (2): 47–76.

Nettler, Ronald. 1994. "A Modern Islamic Confession of Faith and Conception of Religion: Sayyid Qutb's Introduction to the Tafsir, *Fi Zilal al-Qur'an.*" *British Journal of Middle Eastern Studies* 21: 102–14.

9/11 Commission Report. National Commission on Terrorist Attacks upon the United States. 2004. www.9-11commission.gov/report/911Report_Ch5.htm.

Norton, Augustus Richard. 1987. *Amal and the Shi'a: Struggle for the Soul of Lebanon.* Austin: University of Texas Press.

———. 2005. "Musa al-Sadr." In *Pioneers of Islamic Revival,* edited by Ali Rahnema, 184–207. London: Zed Books.

———. 2006. "Thwarted Politics: The Case of Egypt's Hizb al-Wasat." In *Remaking Muslim Politics: Pluralism, Contestation, Democratization,* edited by Robert W. Hefner, 133–60. Princeton: Princeton University Press.

———. 2007. *Hezbollah: A Short History.* Princeton: Princeton University Press.

O'Shaughnessy, Nicholas. 2002. "Selling Terror: The Visual Rhetoric of Osama bin Laden." *Journal of Political Marketing* 1 (4): 83–93.

Ottaway, Marina, and Meredith Riley. 2006. "Morocco: From Top-Down Reform to Democratic Transition?" *Carnegie Papers* 71: 1–24.

PBS (Public Broadcasting Service). 2001. "Osama bin Laden: A Chronology of His Political Life." http://www.pbs.org/wgbh/pages/frontline/shows/binladen/etc/cron.html.

Pape, Robert A. 2005. *Dying to Win: The Strategic Logic of Suicide Terrorism.* New York: Random House.

Papanek, Hanna. 1994. "The Ideal Woman and the Ideal Society: Control and Autonomy in the Construction of Identity." In *Identity Politics and Women: Cultural Reassertions and Feminisms in the International Perspective,* edited by Valentine Moghadam, 45–75. Boulder: Westview Press.

Patkin, Terri Toles. 2004. "Explosive Baggage: Female Palestinian Suicide Bombers and the Rhetoric of Emotion." *Women and Language* 27 (2): 79–89.

Penenberg, Adam, L. 2000. "Companies, People, Ideas—Digital *Jihad.*" *Forbes Magazine,* February 21.

Perlez, Jane. 2007. "Militants Draw New Frontline inside Pakistan." *New York Times,* November 2, A1, A6.

Peteet, Julie. 2000. "Male Gender and the Rituals of Resistance in the Palestinian Intifada: A Cultural Politics of Violence." In *Imagined Masculinities: Male Identity and Culture in the Modern Middle East,* Edited by Mai Ghoussoub and Emma Sinclair-Webb, 103–26. London: Saqi Books.

Peters, Rudolph. 1977. *Jihad in Medieval and Modern Islam.* Leiden: Brill.

———. 1996. *Jihad in Classical and Modern Islam: A Reader.* Princeton: Markus Wiener Publishers.

———. 2005. *Crime and Punishment in Islamic Law.* Cambridge: Cambridge University Press.

Pieterse, Jan Nederveen. 1995. "Globalization as Hybridization." In *Global Modernities,* edited by Mike Featherstone, Scott Lash, and Roland Robertson, 45–68. London: Sage Publications.

Prunier, Gérard. 2007. *Darfur: The Ambiguous Genocide.* Ithaca: Cornell University Press.

al-Qaradawi, Yusuf. 1991. *Nahw wahda fikriyya li-'amilin li'l-Islam.* Cairo: Maktaba Wahba.

————. N.d [1992]. *al-Marja'iyya al-'ulya fi'l-Islam li'l-Qur'an wa'l-sunna.* Cairo: Maktaba Wahba.

————. 1994. *al-Ijtihad al-mu'asir bayn al-indibat wa'l-infirat.* Cairo: Dar al-Tawzi' wa'l-Nashr al-Islamiyya.

————. 1995. *al-Shaykh Muhammad al-Ghazali ka-ma 'araftuhu.* Mansura: Dar al-Wafa li'l-Tiba'a wa'l-Nashr.

————. 1996. *Malamih al-mujtama' al-islami alladhi nunshiduh.* Beirut: Mu'assasat al-Risala.

————. 1997. *Min fiqh al-dawla fi'l-Islam.* Cairo: Dar al-Shuruq.

————. 2000a. *al-Muslimun wa'l-'awlama.* Cairo: Dar al-Tawzi' wa'l-Nashr al-Islamiyya.

————. 2000b. *al-Siyasa al-shar'iyya fi daw nusus al-shari'a wa maqasidiha.* Beirut: Mu'assassat al-Risala.

————. 2001a. *Kayfa nata'amal ma'a'l-turath wa'l-tamadhhub wa'l-ikhtilaf.* Cairo: Maktabat Wahba.

————. 2001b. *al-Shaykh Abu'l-Hasan al-Nadwi kama 'araftuhu.* Damascus: Dar al-Qalam.

————. 2002. "Shar'iyyat al-'amaliyyat al-istishhadiyya." In Yusuf al-Qaradawi et al., *Shubuhat hawla al-'amaliyyat al-istishhadiyya,* 6–22. Miknas: Alwan Maghribiyya.

————. 2002–6. *Ibn al-qarya wa'l-kuttab: Malamih sira wa masira.* 3 vols. to date. Cairo: Dar al-Shuruq.

————. 2003. "Islam al-mar'a duna zawjiha: hal yufarraq baynahuma?" In *al-Majalla al-'ilmiyya li'l-majlis al-urubbi li'l-ifta' wa'l-buhuth,* 2: 421–43. Dublin: n.p.

————. 2005a. *Fusul fi'l-'aqida bayna'l-salaf wa'l-khalaf.* Cairo: Maktabat al-Wahba.

————. 2005b. *Ta'rikhuna al-muftara 'alayna.* Cairo: Dar al-Shuruq.

————. 2006. *Dirasa fi fiqh maqasid al-shari'a.* Cairo: Dar al-Shuruq.

————. 2007. *al-Din wa'l-siyasa: Ta'sil wa radd shubuhat.* Cairo: Dar al-Shuruq.

Qutb, Sayyid. 1949a. *al-'Adala al-ijtima'iyya fi'l-Islam.* Egypt: n.p.

————. 1949b. *al-Taswir al-fanni fi'l-Qur'an.* 2nd ed. Cairo: Dar al-Ma'arif.

————. 1962. *Khasa'is al-tasawwur al-Islami wa muqawwimatihi.* Cairo: Dar Ihya al-Kutub al-'Arabiyya.

————. 1967a. *Fi zilal al-Qur'an.* 5th ed. 30 vols. bound in 6, with independent pagination. N.p.

————. 1967b. *al-Islam wa mushkilat al-hadara.* N.p.

————. 1975. *Ma'arakat al-Islam wa'l-ra'smaliyya.* Beirut: Dar al-Shuruq. Originally published 1950.

————. 1986. *Amrika min al-dakhil bi minzar Sayyid Qutb.* Edited by Salah 'Abd al-Fattah al-Khalid. Jeddah: Dar al-Manara.

————. 1990. *Milestones.* Plainfield, IN: American Trust Publications.

————. 1991. *Ma'alim fi'l-tariq.* Beirut: Dar al-Shuruq. Originally published in 1964.

————. 1996. *Sayyid Qutb and Islamic Activism: A Translation and Critical Analysis of Social Justice in Islam.* Translated by William E. Shepard. Leiden: Brill.

————. 1999–2004. *In the Shade of the Qur'an.* 12 vols. to date. Translated by Adil Salahi and Ashur Shamis. Leicester: Islamic Foundation.

Rahman, Fazlur. 1989. *Major Themes of the Qur'an*. 2nd ed. Minneapolis: Bibliotheca Islamica.

Ramadan, Tariq. 1999. *To Be a European Muslim*. Leicester: Islamic Foundation.

———. 2004. *Western Muslims and the Future of Islam*. New York: Oxford University Press.

———. 2007. *In the Footsteps of the Prophet: Lessons from the Life of Muhammad*. New York: Oxford University Press.

Randal, Jonathan. 2004. *Osama: The Making of a Terrorist*. New York: Knopf.

Rashad, Ahmad. 1993. "Hamas: Palestinian Politics with an Islamic Hue." *The Middle East: Politics and Development Occasional Paper Series*, no. 2: 1–43. United Association for Studies and Research, Annandale, VA.

al-Rasheed, Madawi. 2002. *A History of Saudi Arabia*. Cambridge: Cambridge University Press.

———. 2007. *Contesting the Saudi State: Islamic Voices from a New Generation*. Cambridge: Cambridge University Press.

Rashid, Ahmed. 2000. *Taliban: Militant Islam, Oil and Fundamentalism in Central Asia*. New Haven: Yale University Press.

Rashwan, Diaa. 2005. "Two Targets, One Enemy." *Al-Ahram Weekly*, no. 746 (June): 9–15.

Reichmuth, Stefan. 2006. "The Second Intifada and the 'Day of Wrath': Safar al-Hawali and His Anti-Semitic Reading of Biblical Prophecy." *Die Welt des Islams* 46: 331–51.

Reid, Donald Malcolm. 1990. *Cairo University and the Making of Modern Egypt*. Cambridge: Cambridge University Press.

Renan, Ernest. 1883. *L'Islamisme et la Science: Conférence faite à la Sorbonne le 20 mars 1883*. Edited by Calmann Lévy. Paris: Ancienne Maison Michel Lévy Frères.

Richardson, Louise. 2007. *What Terrorists Want: Understanding the Enemy, Containing the Threat*. New York: Random House.

Rida, Muhammad Rashid. 1947–54. *Tafsir al-Qur'an al-hakim, al-shahir bi-Tafsir al-manar*. 3rd ed. Cairo: Dar al-Manar.

Riesebrodt, Martin. 1993. *Pious Passion: The Emergence of Modern Fundamentalism in the United States and Iran*. Translated by Don Reneau. Berkeley: University of California Press.

Rizvi, Saiyid Athar Abbas. 1982. *Shah 'Abd al-'Aziz: Puritanism, Sectarian Polemics and Jihād*. Canberra: Ma'rifat Publishing House.

Robinson, Glenn E. 2004. "Hamas as a Social Movement." In *Islamic Activism: A Social Movement Theory Approach*, edited by Quintan Wiktorowicz, 112–39. Bloomington: Indiana University Press.

Rohde, David, and David E. Sanger. 2007. "How the 'Good War' in Afghanistan Went Bad." *New York Times*, August 12, A1, A12–13.

Rosenthal, Franz. 1990. *Greek Philosophy in the Arab World: A Collection of Essays*. Brookfield, VT: Variorum.

Rosiny, Stephan. 2001. "'The Tragedy of Fatima al-Zahra' in the Debate of Two Shiite Theologians in Lebanon." In *The Twelver Shia in Modern Times*, edited by Rainer Brunner and Werner Ende, 207–19. Leiden: Brill.

Roy, Olivier. 1994. *The Failure of Political Islam*. Cambridge, MA: Harvard University Press.

———. 2004. *Globalized Islam: The Search for a New Ummah*. New York: Columbian University Press.

Roy, Sara. 1995. "Beyond Hamas: Islamic Activism in the Gaza Strip." *Harvard Middle Eastern and Islamic Review* 2: 1–39.

Rubin, Barry, and Judith Colp Rubin, eds. 2002. *Anti-American Terrorism and the Middle East: A Documentary Reader*. New York: Oxford University Press.

Rubin, Michael. 2005. "Islamists are Intrinsically Anti-democratic." *Middle East Forum*. http://www.meforum.org/article/719.

Runciman, Steven. 1954. *A History of the Crusades*. 3 vols. Cambridge: Cambridge University Press.

Sadiki, Larbi. 2004. *The Search for Arab Democracy: Discourses and Counter-Discourses*. New York: Columbia University Press.

Sadr, Muhammad Baqir. 1980a. *Contemporary Man and the Social Problem*. Translated by Yasin T. al-Jibouri. Tehran: World Organization for Islamic Services.

———. 1980b. *al-Islam yaqud al-hayat*. Beirut: Dar al-Ta'aruf li'l-Matbu'at.

———. 2003. *Lessons in Islamic Jurisprudence*. Translated by Roy P. Mottahedeh. Oxford: Oneworld Publications.

———. 2004. *Iqtisaduna*. Qom: Bustan-i Kitab-i Qom.

Saleh, Walid A. 2004. *The Formation of the Classical Tafsir Tradition: The Qur'an Commentary of al-Tha'labi (d. 427/1035)*. Leiden: Brill.

Salme, Sayyida, and Emily Reute. 1993. *An Arabian Princess between Two Worlds*. Edited by E. Van Donzel. Leiden: Brill.

Sankari, Jamal. 2005. *Fadlallah: The Making of a Radical Shi'ite Leader*. London: Saqi.

al-Sayyid Marsot, Afaf Lufti. 1977. *Egypt's Liberal Experiment*. Berkeley: University of California Press.

———. 1985. *A Short History of Modern Egypt*. Cambridge: Cambridge University Press.

Schimmel, Annemarie. 1975. *Mystical Dimensions of Islam*. Chapel Hill: University of North Carolina.

Schwartz, Tony. 1983. *Media: The Second God*. New York: Doubleday.

Shafi', Mufti Muhammad. 2005–7. *Ma'ariful Qur'an*. Translated by Muhammad Hasan Askari and Muhammad Shamim. 8 vols. Karachi: Maktaba-i Dar al-'Ulum.

Shakir, Ahmad Muhammad. 1956–57. *'Umdat al-tafsir 'an al-Hafiz Ibn Kathir*. Cairo: Dar al-Ma'arif.

Shehadeh, Lamia Rustum. 2003. *The Idea of Women in Fundamentalist Islam*. Gainesville: University Press of Florida.

*Shorter Encyclopaedia of Islam*. 1953. Edited by H.A.R. Gibb and J. H. Kramers. Ithaca, NY: Cornell University Press.

Silvers, Robert B., and Barbara Epstein, eds. 2002. *Striking Terror: America's New War*. New York: New York Review of Books.

Simons, Marlise. 1998. "Morocco Finds Fundamentalism Benign but Scary." *New York Times*, April 9.

Singerman, Diane. 2005. "Rewriting Divorce in Egypt: Reclaiming Islam, Legal Activism, and Coalition Politics." In *Remaking Muslim Politics: Pluralism, Contestation, Democratization*, edited by Robert W. Hefner, 161–88. Princeton: Princeton University Press.

Sivan, Emmanuel. 1983. "Ibn Taymiyya: Father of the Islamic Revolution." *Encounter* 60 (5):41–50.

———. 1985. *Radical Islam: Medieval Theology and Modern Politics.* New Haven: Yale University Press, 1985.

Skovgaard-Petersen, Jakob. 2004. "The Global Mufti." In *Globalization and the Muslim World*, edited by Birgit Schaebler and Leif Stenberg, 153–65. Syracuse: Syracuse University Press.

Smith, Jane I. 1975. *An Historical and Semantic Study of the Term "Islam" as Seen in a Sequence of Qu'an Commentaries.* Missoula, MT: Scholars Press.

Soroush, Abdolkarim. 2000. *Reason, Freedom, and Democracy in Islam.* Translated and edited by Mahmoud Sadri and Ahmad Sadri. New York: Oxford University Press.

Sullivan, Denis J., and Sana Abed-Kotob, eds. 1999. *Islam in Contemporary Egypt: Civil Society vs. the State.* Boulder: Lynne Rienner Publishers.

al-Tabari, Abu Ja'far Muhammad ibn Jarir. 1997. *Tafsir al-Tabari.* Edited by Salah 'Abd al-Fattah al-Khalidi. Damascus: Dar al-Qalam.

Tavakoli-Targhi, Mohamed. 1991. "The Persian Gaze and the Women of the Occident." *South Asia Bulletin* 11, nos. 1–2: 21–31.

Taylor, Charles. 2008. "Secularism and Critique." http://ssrc.org/blogs/immanent _frame/2008/04/24/secularism-and-critique/.

Tiemann, Claus-Peter. 2005. "Neighbor of Lead Sept. 11 hijacker Testifies in Germany That He Seemed 'Psychologically Disturbed.'"Associated Press, February 2. http://www.signonsandiego.com/news/nation/terror/20050202-0737-sept.11trial.html.

Topper, Keith. 2005. *The Disorder of Political Inquiry.* Cambridge, MA: Harvard University Press.

Tripp, Charles. 2006. *Islam and the Moral Economy: The Challenge of Capitalism.* Cambridge: Cambridge University Press.

Troll, Christian W. 1978. *Sayyid Ahmad Khan: A Reinterpretation of Muslim Theology.* Delhi: Vikas Publishing House.

Turabi, Hasan. 1980. *Tajdid usul al-fiqh al-Islami.* Beirut: Dar al-Jil.

———. 1983. "The Islamic State." In *Voices of Resurgent Islam*, edited by John L. Esposito, 241–51. New York: Oxford University Press.

———. 1999. *Qadaya al-tajdid: Nahw manhaj usuli.* Beirut: Mu'assasat al-A'raf li'l-Nashr.

———. 2004. *al-Tafsir al-tawhidi.* Vol. 1. London: Dar al-Saqi.

*United States v. Abdel Rahman.* 1994. U.S. District Court, Southern District of New York, 854 F. Supp. 254, 259 (pretrial order) (quoting Rahman Indictment [paragraph] 9).

U.S. Bureau of Democracy, Human Rights, and Labor. 2006. Country Reports on Human Rights Practices: Morocco 2005. http://www.state.gov/g/drl/rls/hrrpt/2005/61695.htm.

Usher, Graham. 1997. "What Kind of Nation? The Rise of Hamas in the Occupied Territories." In *Political Islam: Essays from "Middle East Report,"* edited by Joel Beinen and Joe Stork, 339–54. Berkeley: University of California Press.

Usher, Sebastian. 2004. "Jihad Magazine for Women on Web." BBCNews, August 24. http://news.bbc.co.uk/1/hi/world/middle_east/3594982.stm.

'Uthmani, Muhammad Taqi. 1998. "Hakim al-ummat ke siyasi afkar." In *Islam awr siyasat*, edited by Muhammad Ishaq Multani, 21–76. Multan: Idara-yi Ta'lifat-i Ashrafiyya.

Vogel, Frank. 2000. *Islamic Law and Legal System: Studies of Saudi Arabia.* Leiden: Brill.

Wadud, Amina. 1999. *Qur'an and Woman: Rereading the Sacred Text from a Woman's Perspective.* New York: Oxford University Press.

Wallis, William. 2006. "Yesterday's Islamist Still Makes Sparks Fly among Muslims." *Financial Times,* April 25, 8.

Warburg, Gabriel. 2003. *Islam, Sectarianism and Politics in Sudan since the Mahdiyya.* Madison: University of Wisconsin Press.

al-Wasat, Talha Jibril. 1999. "Islamist Comeback in Morocco." *Mideast Mirror* 13 (110, June 11).

Watt, W. Montgomery. 1998. *The Faith and Practice of al-Ghazali.* Oxford: Oneworld.

Weaver, Mary Anne. 1993. "The Trail of the Sheikh." *New Yorker,* April 12, 71–89.

———. 2000. "The Real bin Laden." *New Yorker,* January 24, 32–39.

Weber, Max. 1964. *The Sociology of Religion.* Translated by Ephraim Fischoff. Boston: Beacon Press.

Weiser, Benjamin, and Tim Golden. 2001. "Al Qaeda: Sprawling, Hard-to-Spot Web of Terrorists-in-Waiting." *New York Times,* September 30.

Weiss, Bernard G. 1998. *The Spirit of Islamic Law.* Athens: University of Georgia Press.

Welter, Barbara. 1966. "The Cult of True Womanhood: 1820–1860." *American Quarterly* 18 (2): 151–74.

Wendell, Charles. 1978. *Five Tracts of Hasan al-Banna (1906–1949).* Berkeley: University of California Press.

White, Josh. 2008. "Pentagon Report Anticipates Rising Violence in Afghanistan." *Washington Post,* June 28.

Whitlock, Craig. 2006. "Feud with King Tests Freedoms in Morocco." *Washington Post Foreign Service,* February 12, A01, A26.

Wickham, Carrie Rosefsky. 2002. *Mobilizing Islam: Religion, Activism, and Political Change in Egypt.* New York: Columbia University Press.

Wikan, Unni. 2001. "My Son: A Terrorist? (He Was Such a Gentle Boy)." *Anthropological Quarterly* 75 (1): 117–28.

Wittgenstein, Ludwig. 1953. *Philosophical Investigations.* Translated by G.E.M. Anscombe. Oxford: Basil Blackwell.

Wolin, Sheldon S. 2001. *Tocqueville between Two Worlds: The Making of a Political and Theoretical Life.* Princeton: Princeton University Press.

Wood, Ellen Meiksins. 1994. "Democracy: An Idea of Ambiguous Ancestry." In *Athenian Political Thought and the Reconstruction of American Democracy,* edited by J. Peter Euben, John Wallach, and Josiah Ober, 59–80. Ithaca: Cornell University Press.

Wright, Lawrence. 2002. "The Man behind bin Laden." *New Yorker,* September 16, 56.

———. 2006a. *The Looming Tower: Al-Qaeda and the Road to 9/11.* New York: Alfred A. Knopf.

———. 2006b. "The Master Plan." *New Yorker,* September 11, 48–60.

Yamani, Mai. 2000. *Changed Identities: The Challenge of the New Generation in Saudi Arabia.* London: Royal Institute of International Affairs.

Yassine, Abdessalam. 1972. *Al-Islam bayna al-da'wa wa'l-dawla: al-minhaj al-nabawi li-taghyir al-insan.* Casablanca: Matba'at al-Najah.

———. 1973. *Al-Islam ghadan*. Casablanca: Matba'at al-Najah.

———. 1974. *al-Islam aw al-tufan: risala maftuha ila malik al-Maghrib*. Marrakesh: n.p.

———. 1998. *Islamiser la modernité*. Rabat: al-Ofok Impressions.

———. 2000. *Winning the Modern World for Islam*. Translated from *Islamiser la modernité* by Martin Jenni. New Britain, PA, and Iowa City, IA: Justice and Spirituality Publications.

———. 2002. *The Muslim Mind on Trial: Divine Revelation versus Secular Rationalism*. Translated by Muhtar Holland. Iowa City, IA: Justice and Spirituality Publishing.

Yassine, Nadia. N.d. "Justice and Spirituality: Theory and Practice (2/2)." http://nadiayassine.net/en/page/10911.htm.

———. 2003. Interview at the Central European University, Budapest, May 29. http://nadiayassine.net/en/page/10297.htm.

———. 2005a. "Presentation of the Justice and Spirituality Association: A Great Hello to All the Militants!" June 18. http://nadiayassine.net/en/page/10364.htm.

———. 2005b. Interview in *al-Usbou'iya al-Jadida* 33, July 2. http://nadiayassine net./en/page/10513.h6tm.

———. 2005c. "Inside bin Laden's Head." November 8. http://nadiayassine.net/en/page/10135.htm.

———. 2005d. "And the Masks Fall Down!" July 1. http://nadiayassine.net/en/page/10006.htm.

———. 2005e. "Democracy and Islam." Mediterranean Social Forum, Barcelona, June 15–19. http://nadiayassine.net/en/page/10334.htm.

———. 2006a. *Toutes voiles dehors* [*Full Sails Ahead*]. Translated by Farouk Bouasse. New Britain, PA, and Iowa City, IA: Justice and Spirituality Publications.

———. 2006b. Interview with Maati Monjib, January 20. http://nadiayassine.net/en/page/10761.htm.

———. 2006c. "Round the Table with Nadia Yassine. *Le Journal Hebdomadaire* 238, January 7–20. http://nadiayassine.net/en/page/10375.htm.

———. 2006d. "Nadia Yassine Accuses the Moroccan Power of Violating the Law." *Le Journal Hebdomadaire* 244, February 23–March 3. http://nadiayassine.net/en/page/10931.htm.

———. 2006e. "Iraq, or the Last Piece of the Mask: The Repercussions of U.S. Occupation for Iraqi Women Represent the Final Unveiling of Hypocrisy." *Arena Magazine* 83 (June–July): 50.

———. 2006f. "Legal Reforms in Morocco: Views of a Moroccan Feminist Dissident." Lecture at Harvard Law School, April 14. http://nadiayassine.net/en/page/11304.htm.

———. 2007."Modernité, femme Musulmane et politique en Méditerranée." *Quaderns de la Mediterrània* 7: 105–10.

Zaman, Muhammad Qasim. 1998. "Arabic, the Arab Middle East, and the Definition of Muslim Identity in Twentieth Century India." *Journal of the Royal Asiatic Society* ser. 3, 8: 59–81.

———. 2002. *The Ulama in Contemporary Islam: Custodians of Change*. Princeton: Princeton University Press.

———. 2004. "The 'Ulama of Contemporary Islam and Their Conceptions of the Common Good." In *Public Islam and the Common Good*, edited by Armando Salvatore and Dale F. Eickelman, 129–55. Leiden: Brill.

———. 2006. "Consensus and Religious Authority in Modern Islam: The Discourses of the 'Ulama." In *Speaking for Islam: Religious Authorities in Muslim Societies*, edited by Gudrun Krämer and Sabine Schmidtke, 153–80. Leiden: Brill.

———. 2007a. "Epilogue: Competing Conceptions of Religion Education." In *Schooling Islam: The Culture and Politics of Modern Muslim Education*, edited by Robert W. Hefner and Muhammad Qasim Zaman, 242–68. Princeton: Princeton University Press.

———. 2007b. "Tradition and Authority in Deobandi Madrasas of South Asia." In *Schooling Islam: The Culture and Politics of Modern Muslim Education*, edited by Robert W. Hefner and Muhammad Qasim Zaman, 61–86. Princeton: Princeton University Press.

———. 2008. *Ashraf 'Ali Thanawi: Islam in Modern South Asia*. Oxford: Oneworld Publications.

al-Zayyat, Montasser. 2004. *The Road to al-Qaeda: The Story of bin Laden's Right-Hand Man*. Translated by Ahmed Fekry. London: Pluto Press.

———. 2005. *al-Jama'at al-Islamiyya: Ru'ya min al-dakhil*. Cairo: Dar Misr al-Muhrusa.

Zebiri, Kate. 1993. *Mahmud Shaltut and Islamic Modernism*. Oxford: Clarendon Press.

Zeghal, Malika. 1995. *Gardiens de l'islam. Les oulémas d'al-Azhar dans l'Égypte contemporaine*. Paris: Presses de Science Po.

———. 1999. "Religion and Politics in Egypt: The Ulema of al-Azhar, Radical Islam, and the State (1952–94)." *International Journal of Middle East Studies* 31: 371–99.

Zeidan, David. 1999. "Radical Islam in Egypt: A Comparison of Two Groups." *Middle East Review of International Affairs* 3 (3): 1–10.

Zuhur, Sherifa. 1992. *Revealing Reveiling: Islamist Gender Ideology in Contemporary Egypt*. Albany: State University of New York Press.

# INDEX